# Clinical Management in Mental Health Services

Edited by

## Chris Lloyd, Robert King, Frank P. Deane and Kevin Gournay

**WILEY-BLACKWELL**

A John Wiley & Sons, Ltd., Publication

Blackwell Publishing was acquired by John Wiley & Sons in February 2007.
Blackwell's publishing programme has been merged with Wiley's global Scientific,
Technical, and Medical business to form Wiley-Blackwell.

*Registered office*
John Wiley & Sons Ltd, The Atrium, Southern Gate, Chichester, West Sussex, PO19 8SQ,
United Kingdom

*Editorial offices*
9600 Garsington Road, Oxford, OX4 2DQ, United Kingdom
2121 State Avenue, Ames, Iowa 50014-8300, USA

For details of our global editorial offices, for customer services and for information about how to
apply for permission to reuse the copyright material in this book please see our website at
www.wiley.com/wiley-blackwell.

*Library of Congress Cataloging-in-Publication Data*

Clinical management in mental health services / edited by Chris Lloyd . . . [et al.].
      p. ; cm.
   Includes bibliographical references and index.
   ISBN 978-1-4051-6977-6 (pbk. : alk. paper)   1. Mental health services–Management.
I. Lloyd, Chris, 1954–
   [DNLM:   1. Mental Health Services–organization & administration.   2. Leadership.
3. Personnel Management–methods.   4. Psychology, Clinical–methods. WM 30 C64085 2008]
   RA790.5.C546 2008
   362.2068–dc22
                                                                        2008018009

A catalogue record for this book is available from the British Library.

Set in 10/12.5pt Times by Graphicraft Limited, Hong Kong
Printed in Singapore by Markono Print Media Pte Ltd

1   2009

# Contents

iii

# Contributors

**Steve Barnett's** career began as a plastic researcher and development chemist, progressing through corporate business owner/developer, to teacher of organisational change management and developed trans-discipline partnerships at the University of Auckland. Steve's interest in health service organisation sprang from one such partnership. Currently as an organisational communication consultant and business development coach, he applies his expertise in change, production, project, and innovation management to achieving organisational change through changed communication.

**Hazel Bassett** graduated as an occupational therapist from the University of Queensland in 1980. Since graduation, she has worked solely in the field of mental health both in the UK and Australia. Over that time, she has developed interests in the areas of transcultural mental health and parenting with a mental illness. For her masters degree, she developed an observation that can be used in a group setting and observes the parent–child dyad. In 2003 she moved into a management role and has since managed a mental health rehabilitation team and is currently managing a homeless health outreach team. She has also been a strong advocate of clinical supervision and professional development for staff working in the teams she has managed. The Homeless Health Outreach Team that she manages is a multidisciplinary team that includes medical, nursing, allied health, welfare, and administration staffing. She has written a number of articles on a variety of topics and has presented at state, national and international conferences.

**Vicki Biro** has extensive experience in mental health nursing having worked in the area for 29 years. She has worked clinically as a Registered Nurse, a Clinical Nurse Specialist, and as a Clinical Nurse consultant. Vicki has also worked on a variety of research projects including schizophrenia, and genetics research, mental health integration, GP partnerships, and bed management. She is currently employed as a Quality Manager with the South Eastern Sydney Illawarra Mental Health Program (Southern Network), and in this role she has been actively involved in the accreditation process, incident monitoring, and participation in clinical reporting. Vicki is an active member of the Australian College of Mental Health Nurses local branch and is an Honorary Fellow of the Illawarra Institute for Mental Health.

**Susan Brandis** is a registered occupational therapist with additional qualifications in business and health administration. She has many years of management experience having been employed by Queensland Health in roles including as Director of Occupational Therapy, Director of Allied Health, Geriatric and Rehabilitation Services, and Executive Officer Medical Aids Subsidy Scheme. In 2006 she was part of the implementation team responsible for establishing the Quality Monitoring Unit of the Health Quality and Complaints Commission for the Queensland Government. Her career includes leading and publishing a number of state and national quality improvement programmes in areas such as the prevention of falls in older people, improving continence management, consumer engagement and supported discharge initiatives. This has provided her with both theoretical and practical experience and skills in budget and people management. Susan has particular interest in quality improvement, client focused care, cost–benefit analysis, service evaluation and development. She has been an adjunct lecturer at the University of Queensland since 1999.

**Janette Curtis** is an Associate Professor and Director of Mental Health Nursing in the School of Nursing, Midwifery and Indigenous Health at the University of Wollongong. Janette has been instrumental in developing and implementing the undergraduate and postgraduate mental health nursing programmes. Janette's publications and research interests include: p.r.n. medications, empowering nurses, and drugs and alcohol. As Faculty International Advisor, Janette has established and developed off-shore teaching programmes. Janette has held clinical and senior nursing positions in New Zealand and Australia and is actively involved in professional issues with the Nurses and Midwifes Board of New South Wales.

**Frank P. Deane** is a Professor in the School of Psychology and Director of the Illawarra Institute for Mental Health at the University of Wollongong. He has worked in a range of clinical and academic positions in New Zealand, USA, and Australia. He teaches in the Clinical Psychology programmes and has research interests related to the effectiveness of mental health and substance abuse services, the role of therapeutic homework on treatment outcomes and help seeking for mental health and substance abuse problems. He has 110 publications or 'in press' peer reviewed journal articles and has co-authored 12 book chapters.

**Kevin Gournay** is a Chartered Psychologist and a Registered Nurse. Originally he trained in psychiatry, learning disabilities, and general nursing and then in the 1970s as one of the first nurse therapists in cognitive behaviour therapy. After experience as a Charge Nurse, he worked part time to obtain a qualification as a psychologist, obtaining his PhD on the topic of agoraphobia. For the past 30 years, he has combined roles such as: a clinician treating people with post-traumatic stress and anxiety disorders, depression, and psychosis; a researcher; a teacher and a policy advisor to various governments. He has published over 300 papers, chapters and books, and made numerous contributions to TV and radio. He is the President and founding Patron of No Panic, the UK's largest anxiety disorders charity. Among various honours, he is a Fellow of the Royal College of Psychiatrists, a Fellow of the Academy of Medical Science, a Fellow of the Royal College of Nursing, and was elected Nurse of the Year of the American Psychiatric Nursing Association in 2004. He was appointed CBE in the Queen's New Year's Honours in 1999. He has just retired from the Institute of Psychiatry, King's College, London, and in semi-retirement works as a clinician and an expert witness.

**Jennifer Harland's** nursing career spans 25 years and includes mental health, drugs and alcohol, critical care, clinical research, data management, clinical governance, healthcare investigations and teaching. She has held various positions across urban and regional New South Wales including Clinical Nurse Consultant and Nurse Manager roles. She is currently working as a Lecturer at the School of Nursing, Midwifery and Indigenous Health, University of Wollongong. Jennifer's research interests are in alcohol use in people over 65 and brief interventions.

**Robert King** is a Clinical Psychologist and Associate Professor in the School of Medicine at the University of Queensland. As well as a substantial research and teaching career he has had considerable practical experience in leadership and administration of mental health services in Australia. He is currently involved in management of a non-government organisation providing psychosocial rehabilitation services in Brisbane. He also has substantial international experience through consultancy, staff training and research collaboration in the UK, Asia and North America.

**Debra Lampshire's** career in mental health began as a consumer advisor before entering into the field of education. Debra currently works for a private training organisation as well as being the Project Manager for the Auckland District Health Board Psychological Strategies for Enduring Psychotic Symptoms project. She lectures at the School of Nursing, the University of Auckland, and other tertiary non-government organisation providers, and is a well-known advocate and trainer in the recovery approach throughout mental health services. Debra is a dynamic and thought provoking speaker who has presented at a variety of national and international conferences and events.

**Chris Lloyd** is a registered occupational therapist. She received her qualifications in Australia and Canada, and obtained a PhD on the topic of stress and burnout. For the past 30 years she has worked in a variety of mental health settings in England, Canada and Australia. She has worked as a clinician, mostly in psychiatric rehabilitation, a researcher and a university lecturer. She has published over 120 peer-reviewed journal articles, book chapters and books. Among her various awards are the Gold Service Award, Australian and New Zealand Mental Health Service Achievements for developing and implementing a creative, innovative range of rehabilitation services, the Partnerships in Wellbeing Award for the design and implementation of a group programme in mental health, and the OT Australia National Research Award in the Open Category. Her research interests include aspects of vocational rehabilitation for people with a mental illness.

**Victoria Maxwell** since being diagnosed with bipolar disorder and psychosis has become one of North America's top speakers and educators on the lived experience of mental illness and recovery and successful return to work strategies. In addition to being a mental health worker, Victoria has worked for over 20 years as an actress and writer for both film and stage. Her one-person shows, *Crazy for Life* and *Funny . . . You Don't Look Crazy*, tour internationally and have garnered awards in both the USA and Canada. Her company Crazy for Life offers keynote performances and workshops to corporations and conference worldwide.

**Gerry Mullan** is the Nursing Clinical Supervision co-ordinator for the Northside Health Service District in Brisbane, Queensland, Australia. In this role he has developed a model of clinical supervision, with particular emphasis on issues which strengthen and potentially disrupt the nurse–consumer alliance. He co-ordinates a three-day training programme to prepare nurses to act in the role of Clinical Supervision Supervisor. He has worked in clinical, project and management positions during the course of his career.

**Samson Tse** qualified as an occupational therapist with additional qualifications in psychology. He is Associate Professor and Director of the post-graduate mental health programme at the School of Population Health, the University of Auckland. Samson's focus in both teaching and research has been in the areas of mental health, vocational rehabilitation, functional recovery and bipolar disorders, and culturally responsive mental healthcare.

# Foreword

Over the past 50 years, changes in mental healthcare have seen considerable effort and attention paid to the way in which we structure and deliver services. In most countries models of community service provision have evolved as the focus of care shifted from hospital to community. The aim of service reform has generally been to deliver high-quality care, in the least restrictive way, with good outcomes for the consumer at the lowest cost. Often these aims have been in conflict, but we keep tinkering with the service and funding models to try to get the balance right.

Once we have what we think is a good service model, we usually set about developing standards so we can measure whether there is adherence to the preferred model. We often then require services to be accredited against the standards or risk some kind of sanction. Service models and service standards are important. They provide the framework in which care is delivered. However, much less attention is paid to the knowledge and skills, outside the clinical realm, needed by the workforce who will operate within the proposed service model. The management of mental health services requires a knowledge base and a set of skills not readily addressed in discipline-specific undergraduate curricula or post-graduate clinical training programmes.

Reforming service delivery is about much more than service restructuring. Changing how clinicians and managers carry out their tasks is often necessary, much harder, but arguably far more important if we are to achieve desired mental health reform. This text brings together state-of-the-art information in areas about which the modern mental health workforce needs to be cognisant. Some of the areas covered, including information systems, budget management, performance appraisal and quality improvement, are core to running a good service. Others such as managing workload and critical incidents, supervision, and dealing with stress and burnout in staff are less often addressed but critical to being able to sustain high-quality care. And sustaining high-quality service delivery is not easily achieved. Other areas covered, such as leadership, have been given even less attention in the mental health reform literature but are crucial to motivating staff and transforming services. The chapters devoted to these areas provide practical, distilled information.

*Clinical Management in Mental Health Services* responds to one of the most common criticisms of mental health service reform: that the increased investment and expansion of services into the community has not been matched by a commensurate rise in the delivery of quality care. The underinvestment by governments and health providers in the knowledge and skills needed to manage the delivery of modern mental healthcare will potentially undermine decades of structural service reform. We should stop tinkering with service and funding models and start investing more in the people who work in the services. What they do is what matters to consumers. The authors of this text have brought together the evidence base for how to do this.

Harvey Whiteford
Kratzmann Professor of Psychiatry and Population Health
The University of Queensland
March 2008

# Introducing this book

*Chris Lloyd and Kevin Gournay*

Although there is an increasing recognition that mental health problems are highly prevalent in the population, and that there is a need to develop higher-quality services and improved treatments, there is very little guidance on how to manage the services themselves. Indeed to provide effective management requires a wide knowledge base and skills employed at the individual, team, unit and service-wide level. This book sets out to assist and inform all those responsible for mental health service management to make the most of what, in reality, is a case of finite resources targeted at problems of enormous proportion. At the outset we need to say that managing mental health services is not simply for the Chief Executive or Chief Nursing Officer of each local mental health service, all those who work in mental health services have a responsibility for management. This book sets out a range of topics, some or all of which will touch the working lives of clinicians and managers alike.

## Clinical management in mental health services

How do people in management positions prepare for the work that they must carry out? People usually learn the skills they require on the job (Metcalf, 2001). This may include the documentation from the previous manager, attending in-service sessions on aspects of service delivery, reading journals and books relating to what it is they need to know, and undertaking a post-graduate course. How a person learns new skills is very much up to the individual. What may suit one person does not necessarily suit another. This book is designed to provide a manager with the basic knowledge required to manage a mental health team.

Clinical management is a core part of how mental health services are organised. It is often a difficult task since mental health service delivery is complex and many of the people who are in management positions have no specific training in management skills. Many managers and team leaders have been appointed as a promotion from direct clinical work. People in management positions must fulfil a wide variety of roles to make the multidisciplinary team function effectively, for example, they may be involved in such areas as: workload management; clinical information management; budget management; managing critical incidents; communication and public relations; clinical supervision; performance appraisals and staff development; quality improvement; and promotion of evidence-based practice. They may also be involved in changing work practices and professional culture, and dealing with such issues as stress and burnout. Indeed managers have a duty of care for their staff and have to balance service efficiency with ensuring that their staff are provided with appropriate levels of support and supervision. If staff members themselves experience work-related stress or other mental health problems, managers need to act with both speed and the highest level of consideration.

System factors such as buildings, equipment, financing arrangements, referral systems, the work of clinical and non-clinical staff and procedures for recruitment have an impact on whether it is possible to carry out high-quality clinical work. All of these subsystems, such as finance and human resource management, and the supra-systems, such as policy frameworks and regional health system organisation, need to be designed, sustained, and continually improved (Callaly & Minas, 2005). This requires effective management. Much of the pressure experienced by people working in mental health can be attributed to the rapid and frequent changes that have been initiated in recent years (Australian Health Ministers, 2003; Department of Health, 1999, 2001). The proliferation of initiatives put forward as necessary for the improvement of quality, reduction in disparities and improvement of efficiency, all contribute to the sense of overload experienced by practitioners (Callaly & Minas, 2005).

The team can be thought of as a small group of people who come together for a common purpose. Teams in mental health bring specialist assessments and individualised care together in an integrated manner. However, to achieve this requires a carefully considered and systematic approach to case allocation and deciding on a suitable evidence-based approach to the person's needs. This process of course requires a suitable infrastructure of teaching, training and supervision. There is a need for effective application of the necessary skills mix for the best outcomes for the service users. While working in multidisciplinary teams can be efficient, effective and satisfying, it can also involve conflict and inefficient work practices (Rosen & Callaly, 2005). Good teamwork depends on clear structure and accountability, good leadership, delegation of tasks, role delineation and mechanisms to resolve role conflict.

A manager is the person who controls the day-to-day business of the mental health service and organises the team to do what is required by, not only the district mental health services, but also the Department of Health. According to Gilbert (2003) mental health services' greatest assets are the practitioners who provide the care and their managers. Managers come from a variety of disciplinary backgrounds. They may be nurses, occupational therapists, psychologists, psychiatrists or social workers. Often people in management positions have worked through the ranks and applied for the position of manager with no specific training or educational background in management. This may put them at some disadvantage in running a team because they may lack knowledge of all the aspects of mental health service delivery that they are expected to manage. There is also the issue of serving senior managers and simultaneously needing to be the team champion, which may at times result in a conflict of interest. From their own clinical experience, new managers are aware of the practicalities and demands of everyday work, but now they have another set of demands from higher up the system to which they must also respond. In community mental health teams there may be some tension between consultant psychiatrists and other professionals who carry clinical responsibility and managers, who are accountable for the management of a service/team and the allocation of finite resources (Gilbert, 2003).

Mental health service delivery has changed substantially over the past decade with far more accountability being required today. Consumers of mental health services are demanding better quality and more responsive services, increased accountability, and inclusion of consumer views in the planning, delivery of care and evaluation of services (Callaly & Minas, 2005). Managers are also guided by the Department of Health and the corporate values that they expect of everyone. These values concern work practices, appropriate and effective peer and team relationships, and outputs and outcomes that are expected to be achieved. In turn, there is further influence of the health service district and its vision and organisational goals, which are an essential part of what people do in the workplace. Finally, there is the team in which one is employed, which has to meet both the corporate values and the mission and organisational goals of the local district. At the centre of these expectations is the delivery of patient care and the provision of the best care and treatment that is possible. To assist in optimal patient care there are a number of steps that are commonly used. There are routine work requirements such as documentation, outcome measures, and patient reviews that are carried out routinely by staff members. In addition, there are usually requirements for staff development and supervision in order to enhance patient care. Managers are regularly expected to implement, and be accountable for, a vast number of changes (Arnold, 2005). This can occur without the benefit of a comprehensive understanding of the processes involved in initiating, implementing and sustaining change.

In the past few years, in Australia, New Zealand and the UK mental health care has become much more of a priority for governments and as a consequence we have seen an enormous number of policy initiatives ranging from action on youth suicide to improving services for people who suffer social exclusion (Office of the Deputy Prime Minister, 2004). These initiatives are often accompanied by target setting and the unenviable task (for managers) of spending more on priority areas without any real increase in resources. Managers therefore need to keep fully up to date with government thinking. This necessitates not only hours of reading, but also building networks with civil servants and politicians.

In contrast with the situation which prevailed only a decade or so ago, today's managers need to keep abreast of evidence. Services now need to have at their core interventions which are proven. Both service commissioners, as well as the public at large, have such evidence readily available through their computer's search engine. Thus, managerial skills must now include an ability to consider evidence in a discriminating way and to ensure that services adapt accordingly.

Information technology has brought considerable benefits but also major challenges. For example, developments such as electronic patient records and computerised cognitive behaviour therapy require the manager to address the financial dilemma of how much of one's budget should be invested in these innovations at the potential cost to current services.

# How the book is organised

Chapter 1 examines the important issues around leading and managing a multi-disciplinary team. It addresses the key operational components of managing teams. The areas that are addressed include such aspects as operational and strategic planning, managing meetings, style of management, feedback mechanisms, conflict management, building a culture of excellence and team building.

Chapter 2 explores the central issue of workload management and what is required of people to carry out their job efficiently. The topic of caseload management is reviewed and ways in which this can be managed are discussed. This chapter also explores models of case management, time and resource management, and workloads.

An overview of clinical information management is provided in Chapter 3. This chapter sets out the reasons why clinical information is needed and ways in which it can be implemented. Specifically, it covers how to make clinical information work, ways of interpreting the data and how to utilise the data.

Budget management is a core feature of mental health service delivery and is addressed in Chapter 4. Budget terminology, planning a budget, how to understand and operate a budget are the key elements that are described. Consideration is given to understanding budget terminology, how to write up a budget, use of resources and consideration of the stakeholders.

In Chapter 5, the management of critical incidents is explored. It examines the types of critical incident which may occur and management's responsibility in handling the situation. Areas that are covered include critical incidents, risk assessment, managing risk and patient safety.

Communication and public relations are addressed in Chapter 6. This chapter explores the idea of communicating with a range of stakeholders and the importance of public relations. Specifically it addresses having a customer focus, procedure, partnerships, stakeholders and how to include stakeholders.

Chapter 7 explores managing work or professional culture. This chapter looks at how workplace culture is established and the difficulties that can be associated with it. It will focus on adopting a recovery approach and the way in which this can be used in working with people with a mental illness. Stages of change, adopting a recovery approach, difficulties and barriers, and the process that is undertaken in changing workplace culture are considered.

Supervision is an important part of practice in mental health services, and Chapter 8 addresses clinical supervision. It explores how supervision can be implemented and discusses the importance of supervision in assisting people to cope more effectively in the workplace.

Chapter 9 focuses on performance appraisal and personal development and the way it can be used to improve both individual staff performance and the quality of service delivery. The chapter addresses the nature of performance appraisal, why is it useful, how to manage the performance of staff and difficult staff issues, and the benefits for personal development.

The issue of stress and burnout is dealt with in Chapter 10. This chapter explores the causes of stress and burnout in the workplace. It discusses the strategies for handling potentially stressful events and how to minimise or prevent burnout.

In Chapter 11 the topic of quality improvement is addressed. This chapter explores the importance of quality improvement and how to prioritise quality indicators, and strategies for implementing the results into practice.

The final chapter, Chapter 12, addresses evidence-based practice. This chapter looks at what evidence-based practice is and how to integrate results from trials into practice. It also looks at how practitioners can contribute to the evidence themselves by participating in research. Specifically, it covers what is evidence-based practice, the process, creating a culture which is committed to using evidence, and how managers can make it work in the clinical setting.

Each chapter includes some of the following features, which aim to help readers integrate the information into their practice:

- Case studies: these provide practical examples of aspects of clinical management in order to provide managers with guidelines for managing teams.
- Strategies: these are included in diagrammatic form to assist the manager visualise key strategies used to assist in the running of teams.
- Boxes, lists, tables and figures: concise lists and examples of key points discussed in the text are included to assist the manager to quickly and easily identify the context of the chapters.

## Conclusions

Managers face important challenges in mental health services today. To meet these challenges, it is necessary that managers have a sound understanding of many aspects of service delivery. They need to implement strategies and policies to establish and maintain an appropriate culture in the organisation. It is only by doing so that they will be able to have a key role in leading an effective service, which should result in less discrimination and marginalisation of mental health service recipients along with improved mental health outcomes.

## References

Arnold, E. (2005). Managing human resources to improve employee retention. *The Health Care Manager*, 24, 132–140.

Australian Health Ministers (2003). *National Mental Health Plan 2003–2008*. Canberra: Australian Government.

Callally, T., & Minas, H. (2005). Reflections on clinician leadership and management in mental health. *Australasian Psychiatry*, 13, 27–32.

Department of Health (1999). *A National Service Framework for Mental Health – Modern Standards and Service Models.* London: Department of Health.

Department of Health (2001). *The Journey to Recovery – the Government's Vision for Mental Health Care.* London: Department of Health.

Gilbert, J. (2003). Between a rock and a hard place? Training and personal development issues for mental health service managers. *Mental Health Practice*, 6, 31–33.

Metcalf, C. (2001). The importance of performance appraisal and staff development: a graduating nurse's perspective. *International Journal of Nursing Practice*, 7, 54–56.

Office of the Deputy Prime Minister (2004). *Mental Health and Social Exclusion.* London: ODPM Publications.

Rosen, A., & Callaly, T. (2005). Interdisciplinary teamwork and leadership: Issues for psychiatrists. *Australasian Psychiatry*, 13, 234–240.

# Chapter 1
# Leading a multidisciplinary team

*Frank P. Deane and Kevin Gournay*

## Chapter overview

This chapter looks at leadership and management of multidisciplinary teams in the mental health context. It provides an overview of what constitutes a multi-disciplinary team and how policy can change the roles and relationships in teams. The potential conflict inherent in teamwork is outlined. A brief overview of leadership styles is provided, with a more detailed description of the relationship between different leadership styles and team effectiveness and satisfaction in the mental health context. Finally, suggestions about effective leadership styles and practical tips for team building and managing team meetings are provided.

## What is a multidisciplinary team?

Multidisciplinary teams consist of individuals from a range of professional disciplines and backgrounds. The size of the teams can vary considerably with one study indicating that among 54 psychiatric rehabilitation teams, the sizes ranged from nine to 41 members (Garman et al., 2003). However, it has been argued that groups of eight to 10 team members tend to function better than larger groups with small teams of three or four people remaining effective (Diamond, 1996). Generally, teams are relatively stable, retaining the same members over time. Occasionally, some team members act more as 'consultants' who work across teams. These consulting members may not attend all meetings, but may be called in when there is a particular issue for a client for which they have special expertise. Team knowledge and skills usually have overlapping competencies as well as the specific disciplinary skills each team member brings. In the context of psychiatric rehabilitation, Liberman et al. (2001) outlined the expected expertise of team members from different disciplines. Table 1.1 illustrates some of the components of expertise for a selected number of disciplines.

Liberman et al. (2001) included several other 'disciplines' in their table including rehabilitation counsellor, case manager, consumer team member, family advocates, employment specialists and job coaches. In addition, there is a wide range of other areas of expertise in clinical activity, but this example provides some sense of the skill sets that different disciplines bring to mental health. Such summaries are always open to debate and this particular example was criticised for not sufficiently recognising the evidence-based practices and research conducted

**Table 1.1** Percentage expected expertise of selected disciplines in a psychiatric rehabilitation team.

| Area of expertise | Psychiatrist | Psychologist | Social worker | Nurse | Occupational therapist |
|---|---|---|---|---|---|
| Diagnosis | 100 | 75 | 25 | 25 | 0 |
| Monitoring psychopathology | 100 | 75 | 25 | 75 | 25 |
| Crisis intervention | 100 | 100 | 50 | 100 | 0 |
| Engagement in treatment | 50 | 50 | 50 | 50 | 25 |
| Motivational interviewing | 25 | 75 | 50 | 0 | 50 |
| Functional assessment | 25 | 100 | 50 | 0 | 100 |
| Psychopharmacology | 100 | 25 | 0 | 50 | 0 |
| Family psychoeducation | 50 | 75 | 100 | 25 | 0 |
| Patient psychoeducation | 75 | 100 | 25 | 75 | 25 |
| Skills training | 25 | 100 | 25 | 25 | 50 |
| Cognitive behaviour therapy | 50 | 100 | 25 | 0 | 0 |
| Supported employment | 0 | 100 | 50 | 0 | 50 |
| Assertive community treatment | 50 | 25 | 75 | 50 | 50 |
| Team leadership | 50 | 50 | 50 | 50 | 0 |
| Programme development | 50 | 50 | 50 | 25 | 25 |

Adapted from Figure 2, Liberman et al. (2001, p. 1336).

by occupational therapists (Auerbach, 2002; Rebeiro, 2002). Furthermore, concerns were raised that occupational therapists were characterised as 'para-professionals' and there was insufficient recognition of their role in developing employment-related skills for people with serious mental illnesses (Auerbach, 2002).

Although descriptions such as those in Table 1.1 provide broad guidelines, in practice, there are often considerable individual differences within discipline groups as to the skills that a particular practitioner brings. As will be highlighted further, the role of the clinical manager is to be aware of the knowledge and skills that the individuals in the team possess in order to maximise the benefits for a particular service user.

Multidisciplinary teams provide co-ordination of assessment and treatment activities to best meet the complex mental, physical and social needs of service users. A given service user may have the need for medications to manage mental health symptoms and their diabetes. They may need cognitive behaviour therapy (CBT) to help them better manage anxiety in social situations. They may require support to help them access educational or employment opportunities. Or, they may need direct skills training in order to help them become competitive in employment or assistance with accessing affordable housing or community recreational activities. These multiple and often complex needs require a team with broad knowledge and skill sets. The local service demands and models (e.g. focus on acute management versus recovery-oriented care) along with workforce availability (e.g. rural areas typically have poorer access to all professional groups) will also influence the mix of professionals in a given team. Typically, psychiatrists are the most difficult professional group to recruit whereas nurses are usually available in greater numbers and various allied health professionals usually fall somewhere between these two groups.

As noted there are also shared tasks that team members take on, such as engagement with consumers, risk assessments, or a range of general case management activities. At times these 'shared' activities can also produce conflict within teams. For example, in some community mental health teams there is an expectation that all team members will be rostered for on-call acute emergency assessments for a set number of days per week. This often means that ongoing case work needs to be suspended for those days. However, it can also be argued that rostering all team members to such duties may underutilise their specific skill sets. Similar arguments can be made for some case management activities. In an external international review of the Australian second national mental health plan the authors stated:

> '*Psychologists* are, by international standards, relatively few within State and Territory mental health services, and too often work as generic case managers. Therefore, their specialist contributions to the delivery of expert psychological therapies are not sufficiently available to people with mental health problems'
> Thornicroft & Betts (2002, p. 11)

The challenge for clinical managers is to optimise the utilisation of specific expertise while also servicing the generic clinical activities that are required of a service. This requires decisions about how to best utilise various skill sets in the team while also managing the potential of team members to feel that workloads and conditions may not be equitable. However, it needs to be recognised that there are also wide variations in the education of these different groups, which lead to inequities with regard to remuneration. There are historical relationships between professionals that contribute to hierarchies and power differentials (e.g. doctors and nurses). Further to this there can be relatively new challenges to what were considered unique specialist domains (e.g. prescribing of medications by non-physicians). All of these factors may operate to influence the dynamics between various professional groups in a team. Added to this is the increasing emergence of consumer team members or carer advocates. Often the traditional professional groups (and managers) are unsure of the role of these team members and how they are to function within the team.

## Policy and legislative changes affecting team dynamics

There have been several major changes in the skills base of nursing over the past 20 years and these changes will, potentially, affect the boundaries that currently exist between various professions and, arguably, alter the power base. One of the most important changes has been in the legislation, principally in the USA and the UK, which has led to nurses having prescriptive authority. In the USA, the situation is now such that nurses in virtually all states have prescriptive authority and, in many states, can prescribe any psychiatric drug completely independent of a psychiatrist. Having said that, the training provided to such nurses is substantial and their practice is governed by a framework of supervision and continuing professional development. Such changes have benefited many individuals whose healthcare insurance cover (or lack of it) greatly restricted their access to psychiatrists who could prescribe.

In the UK, legislative changes in 2005 have led to very widespread training of nurses to prescribe and, although those nurses will prescribe within pre-set protocols, most of the prescribing that they undertake is, in practice, quite independent of psychiatrists. Arguably, such changes in prescribing have led to the situation where many of the routine prescribing tasks can be undertaken by nurses, thus leaving psychiatrists more time to attend to patients whose needs for medication are much more complex, for example those with co-existing physical health problems or patients who are treatment-resistant. Another argument for nurse prescribing is that nurses have much more time to give to attending to patients' concerns about medication and to carefully monitor side effects. Indeed, there is substantial evidence (e.g. Gray et al., 2004) to suggest that mental health nurse skills in the detection and management of side effects in patients is of considerable benefit, provided that nurses have the relevant training.

While Australia is somewhat behind the USA and the UK in nurse prescribing, there are now, consistent with the international trend, some legislative changes to relevant nurses' acts, and drugs and poisons acts, across the Australian jurisdiction. These grant limited prescribing rights to some nurse practitioners (MacMillan & Bellchambers, 2007). Such changes will, undoubtedly, affect the power balance in multidisciplinary teams, although, as in the USA, it may be several years before the changes become apparent.

Another significant change in the role of nurses is to be found in legislative changes, which have empowered nurses to detain patients. At the time of writing, in late 2007, the UK Parliament is drafting changes that will allow nurses to detain patients for periods of assessment. In Australia, nurses across the various states and territories do not have the same legal powers, or indeed use the same terminologies. However, in some states, nurses are able to detain a patient for assessment for 24 hours, while in another a medical doctor is the only health professional who may detain a patient for assessment. In New Zealand, the Mental Health Act 1992 created a new role – that of Duly Authorised Officer – and this has conferred legal powers on nurses (McKenna et al., 2006). The possession of such legal powers may potentially change the relationship between the nurse and the patient in a community mental health team and, once more, the issue of 'balance of power' will change within the team.

Psychologists are often core members of the multidisciplinary team, although in the USA and Australia this is a variable phenomenon; in some teams psychologists do not carry a caseload, rather they act as consultants to other team members and may only provide specific psychological interventions. Over the past 20 years or so, psychological interventions such as CBT are being used increasingly by professions other than psychologists, and there is now substantial evidence (Turkington et al., 2006) that nurses may be very effective in providing CBT to patients with schizophrenia after a relatively brief course of training. Similarly, family interventions are now provided by a very wide range of professionals and, indeed, some non-professionals. While the dissemination of skills is obviously very welcome, particularly because of the potential to reach more patients in need, such developments serve to 'blur' roles even further.

One of the most notable aspects of working of community mental health teams over the three decades since they were established in the USA and then, fairly soon after, in Australia, has been the increasing development of consumers in mental health services. While this involvement has been largely in areas such as advisory roles and advocacy, consumer involvement has developed across a number of other areas, for example in education and training. Perhaps the most radical development has been the employment of user case managers, i.e. people with a history of mental illness who have become case managers themselves and have adopted paid roles within community teams. While this development still causes some raised eyebrows in professional circles, one needs to be reminded that the development of user case managers can be traced back more than 20 years to the community services in Denver, Colorado. Sherman and Porter (1991) evaluated this initiative and showed quite clearly that, not only do user case managers provide direct benefits to service-user outcomes, but their mental health status is also improved. It is also worth noting that many of the user case managers trained in the innovative Denver scheme suffered serious mental illnesses, such as manic depression, rather than the common mental disorders – which of course may afflict very large proportions of the population and, indeed, therefore affect health professionals. As Sherman and Porter (1991) have demonstrated the presence of such a worker in a community team may be challenging and affect team ethos and functioning.

While consumer empowerment is a feature of Australian and New Zealand mental health policy, the implementation of initiatives such as user case management, where such users are paid workers who are fully functioning team members, is probably variable to say the least and it may be many years before one sees this development spread across all states and territories.

## Boundaries

Renouf and Meadows (2007, p. 231) argue that in effective multidisciplinary services 'there needs to be a certain amount of overlapping (blurring) of roles, and at the same time the specific areas of experience of individual team members will need to be maintained and developed'.

These blurred boundaries can often be viewed by team members as problematic and have the potential to lead to conflict. However, recognition within the team that some degree of role overlap is both necessary and desirable has the potential to further strengthen teams. The role of the team leader is to facilitate this recognition by clarifying common core tasks (e.g. some case management activities) and also specialist areas of expertise. This clarifies the various professional boundaries (e.g. medication review, psychometric testing, etc.).

Another area for potential boundary confusion lies in the distinction between 'upper management', 'middle management' and team leadership. Upper level managers are not usually considered as team members. However, managers 'have considerable influence over team functioning, especially as more sophisticated policies and service frameworks have led to a more interventionist and pervasive managerial role in mental health service delivery' (Renouf & Meadows, 2007, p. 230). The boundary between upper management and team leaders who also have management roles is not often clear. At the same time team leaders are usually team members who also continue to provide direct patient care. The ability to negotiate these various roles can be difficult for managers who are team leaders and also continue to provide clinical services to consumers. It requires flexibility both in the manager and among other team members. In some circumstances, context clarifies the main 'hat' the manager is wearing at a particular time. For example, in a treatment team meeting, where there is discussion of client needs, the manager may contribute as a fellow clinician and team member. However, even within this meeting, there may be a need for allocating cases to already stretched team members, which may require a shift to a more managerial or team leader role. In some circumstances there is a need to be very explicit about which 'hat' a manager is wearing, such as when there is a need to reprimand a team member about some repeated error that has been made.

## Effectiveness of multidisciplinary teams

While the multidisciplinary team is ubiquitous in mental health services there is very little research that has evaluated or challenged the view that such an approach provides more effective care. Burns and Lloyd (2004) reviewed the limited research that assessed whether such teamwork is beneficial. They suggested that historically, the most evidence comes probably from studies in which assertive community treatment that uses a team approach was found to be superior to individual case management approaches. However, this provides only peripheral evidence. The authors could only locate three empirical articles that suggested that aspects of multidisciplinary team functioning produced positive outcomes, but none appeared to have control group comparisons. Given the high cost of running a multidisciplinary team, and that less than 50% of working time may be spent in direct patient contact, Burns and Lloyd (2004) argued that much more research regarding the cost-effectiveness of multidisciplinary teams was warranted.

Although there is little empirical research establishing whether multidisciplinary teamwork leads to better care, a number of authors have outlined their views on what constitutes effective teamwork. The following two examples not only have areas of overlap, but also differences in emphasis around team functioning versus the types of services effective teams should offer.

Renouf and Meadows (2007) highlighted:

- high-quality personal relationships between workers, clients and carers
- clearly defined tasks and care for a well defined client group
- services that target needs beyond just psychiatric symptoms (e.g. housing, employment, family, recreation)
- team ability to flexibly respond to client need (as opposed to sticking with historical staffing patterns)
- clarity about team member roles and responsibilities
- sanctioned team leadership with agreed systems of co-ordination
- collaborative and participative leadership style
- team links with external community services
- team receives regular feedback about its achievement of objectives
- individual members' performance is assessed, with feedback, supervision and professional development.

The attributes of an effective psychiatric rehabilitation team were summarised by Liberman et al. (2001). They suggested:

- high accessibility (preferably 24 hours a day)
- consultation and co-ordination of services with external agencies
- prioritising those with serious and disabling mental disorders
- focus on improving a wide range of areas of need (not just symptoms)
- emphasis on community reintegration
- meeting cultural and linguistic needs of consumers
- maximising clients' natural supports and self-help
- flexible levels of intervention (e.g. crisis to long-term maintenance)
- individualisation of services
- ongoing monitoring of a client's progress
- persistent effort with each client
- accountability and competencies in the team to deliver evidence-based services.

Liberman et al. (2001) particularly emphasise the need to provide services that are individualised and prioritised to meet the personal goals of the client. Such lists of attributes provide ideas about what should be considered as potential goals for a team leader. However, the 'style' by which teams are led is at least as important.

## Management and leadership styles

There is a range of management styles and most people would be familiar with some of these either through their own experiences with a manager or because such terms are now common in the management lexicon. Space does not permit an extensive discussion of all of the various styles, but it is important to realise that these styles occur in combinations and that most of these styles have both advantages and disadvantages.

Authoritarian managers typically make the decisions and then pass these onto the team members and expect that they will then be followed as directed. Such approaches are quite hierarchical with directions being communicated from senior management to middle management and then to team members with little discussion or flexibility in how the directions should be implemented. Such approaches can create problems in teams ranging from resentment due to a lack of autonomy to a loss of motivation due to dependence on all decisions being made for them.

Democratic management styles emphasise a greater degree of equity in decision making and seek extensive discussion and communication between management and the team. Generally, there is an attempt to get some consensus about the way forward on a particular issue. This is often determined by a 'vote' with varying degrees of formality with the majority guiding the decision. The advantage of such an approach is that team members feel more empowered and involved in decisions, but a potential disadvantage is that this process can be very time consuming. Further to this, if there are multiple teams or groups in an organisation they may come to different decisions based on such an approach, which can lead to inconsistency in the way services are delivered. However, more participative management styles have been associated with greater employee satisfaction (Kim, 2002) and most mental health staff want greater involvement in decision making.

Perhaps most problematic for a team are situations where there is a lack of an active and clear leadership or management style. In multidisciplinary teams there are situations where the role of the team leader or clinical manager is somewhat foisted on the more senior member of the team. This may be highlighted in situations where there are very few incentives for taking on the team leader position (e.g. flexible hours, remuneration). These reluctant team leaders may avoid the duties of management, and often what results is confusion about both procedures and directions. The need for active management was highlighted in a study of 96 business school students participating in a group project. It was concluded that active conflict management promoted better performance and that an agreeable conflict management approach promoted group satisfaction (DeChurch & Marks, 2001). Not surprisingly, avoidant conflict management styles do not lead to as effective decision making as with other styles (Kuhn & Poole, 2000). Fortunately, avoidant, passive or laissez-faire styles of management are probably more the exception than the rule and in a study of 77 nurse managers it was found that an avoiding style was least frequently used in managing conflict (Kantek & Kavla, 2007). Experienced directors of psychiatry tend to have a management style that is both high in task orientation where they specify how, when and where to do various tasks and also high in relationship components such that they provide psychological support and opportunities for shared decision making (Marcos & Silver, 1988).

## Transformational Leadership Model

Several studies in mental health contexts have explored the Transformational Leadership Model (TLM) elaborated by Bass (1985). In order to understand the findings from this research, there is a need to briefly describe the components of the TLM. The two factors of transactional leadership and transformational leadership are proposed in this model.

Transactional leadership is more focused on 'the day-to-day tasks which need to be completed to keep a team or a department running smoothly' (Garman et al., 2003, p. 803). Part of this process involves using contingent reward beha viours where team members are rewarded by the leader for achieving established goals or tasks. Transactional leadership is also theorised to involve management-by-exception behaviours. In general, management-by-exception involves identifying 'exceptions' to good practice and thus focuses on correcting problems. Both passive and active management-by-exception strategies can be used. In an active approach a leader would proactively monitor the team's efforts, looking for problems or mistakes, whereas in passive management-by-exception the leader tends to not get involved in the team's work unless more conspicuous problems or mistakes come to his or her attention. Passive management-by-exception has also been closely associated with a 'laissez-faire' leadership style. While the laissez-faire approach has been described as a 'non-leadership' factor (e.g. Garman et al., 2003) together with the passive approach such leaders are characterised as avoidant, resistant to expressing views, delayed in responding to problems (particularly when early or minor), inactive and reactive only to failure or problems (Kanste et al., 2007).

The second major component of TLM is transformational leadership. Transformation leadership goes beyond the day-to-day processes of team activities. It provides a more idealised inspirational form of leadership that includes charisma (the leader's ability to instil respect, loyalty, clear values, mission or vision in the team), intellectual stimulation (ability to support team members' critical thinking, and solve problems in novel ways), individual consideration (ability to treat individual team members with care) and inspirational motivation (the ability to motivate and orient the team toward the future and a common cause). It is thought that this transformational leadership style should lift a team to perform beyond just satisfactory levels and to inspire them to put in extra effort in order to excel. Transformational leadership appears to contribute over and above the effects of transactional leadership in engendering greater perceived effectiveness and satisfaction of leaders among human service workers such as social workers (Gellis, 2001).

## Leadership styles and mental health team functioning

TLM not only provides a good description of different leadership styles but also has a substantial research base supporting both its description and measurement. The various components of the TLM are measured using the Multifactor Leadership Questionnaire (MLQ, Bass & Avolio, 1997). An increasing number of studies are now linking different leadership styles to improved team satisfaction and functioning. Garman et al. (2003) assessed 236 leaders from 54 mental health teams that provided services to people with severe and persistent mental illnesses. They found that the two distinct management-by-exception factors were both supported. Active management-by-exception was associated with both transformational leadership and contingent reward and the passive management-by-exception was associated with laissez-faire leadership (Garman et al., 2003). The authors highlighted previous research showing that passive management-by-exception has been related to lower levels of job satisfaction. They speculated that active management-by-exception may have emerged in this context due to the increasingly strict guidelines being placed by external mental health regulatory bodies in the USA.

This same research group developed the Clinical Team Leader Questionnaire (Corrigan et al., 1998); an analysis of the 346 mental health staff surveys revealed six factors: autocratic leadership, clear roles/goals, reluctant leadership, communicating the vision, diversity issues and supervision. All of these factors were positively correlated with transformational and transactional leadership factors and negatively correlated with the non-leadership scale on the MLQ (Bass & Avolio, 1997). Perceptions of an autocratic leadership style, inability to clarify roles and goals, a reluctant leadership style, inability to communicate a vision and a lack of supervision were all significantly related to the emotional exhaustion factor of burnout (Corrigan et al., 1998). A second study with 305 psychiatric rehabilitation staff members further supported the validity of the Clinical Team Leader Questionnaire measure (Corrigan et al., 1999). In this study again the autocratic leadership, clear roles and goals, reluctant leadership and vision factors clearly emerged. For those team leaders who are interested in getting feedback about the perceptions of team members of their leadership the Clinical Team Leader Questionnaire items are in the public domain and provided in the source article by Corrigan et al. (1998, Table 2, p. 117).

Perhaps the most intriguing work related to mental health team leadership is a study of 143 leaders, 473 team members from 31 clinical teams and 184 consumers served by these teams (Corrigan et al., 2000). This study made a substantial step forward by linking perceptions of team leadership to consumers' ratings of satisfaction with treatment and quality of life. Leaders' and other team members' ratings of leadership were correlated with consumer programme satisfaction ratings. For leaders' ratings there was a significant relationship between inspirational motivation and higher consumer satisfaction ($r = -0.40$). Higher levels of passive management-by-exception and laissez-faire leadership were associated with lower levels of satisfaction ($r = 0.50$ and $r = 0.38$, respectively).

When leaders assume a distant, aloof or hands-off approach to leadership, consumers accessing services from their teams report lower levels of satisfaction. In contrast more inspirational leadership is associated with greater consumer satisfaction. Further to this, leaders' ratings of a more laissez-faire leadership style was associated with lower quality of life ratings by consumers ($r = 0.30$). Team member ratings revealed that almost all components of a transformational leadership style (charisma, inspiration, consideration of individual staff members) were related to higher quality of life ratings by consumers (range $r = -0.30$ to $r = -0.40$). Both leaders' and their subordinate team members' ratings of leadership independently accounted for variance in consumer ratings of quality of life. These data are striking in that they raise the possibility that the style of team leadership can affect patient satisfaction and quality of life. However, further research is needed to confirm the direction of the relationships between leadership and patient outcomes.

## How to use knowledge about leadership styles to improve your team leadership

So what does this theory and research mean for leading multidisciplinary mental health teams? First, it is important to have some self-awareness of your own leadership style. As noted, even self-review with measures such as the Clinical Team Leader Questionnaire (Corrigan et al., 1999) or the commercially available MLQ (Bass & Avolio, 1997) will give you some insight into your style. In addition, getting team members that you lead to rate such a measure provides an important additional perspective. Clearly, an active versus passive management style is preferable. It has consistently been found that passive and laissez-faire styles are associated with lower satisfaction and greater burnout within mental health teams. Further, such styles potentially have negative 'trickle-down' effects on patients (Corrigan et al., 2000). Although active management-by-exception is preferable to passive approaches, the ability to be charismatic, inspirational, visionary and considerate of individual team members is associated with more positive staff and consumer ratings of satisfaction.

However, not all managers view themselves as innately possessing these characteristics. It has been argued that many of these characteristics can be learned (e.g. Corrigan et al., 1998). Fortunately, you do not have to possess all of these characteristics to be a better team leader. Team members want leaders to clarify team goals and a vision. There are already programmes for leaders to enhance these factors. Preliminary research suggests that self-monitoring to provide performance feedback along with setting goals can lead to improved productivity (higher client contact hours) in mental health teams (Calpin et al., 1988). Most mental health organisations provide global 'visions' for their services and strategic plans provide further opportunities to clarify a vision and goals to achieve in order to realise that vision. These processes are highly consistent with the 'recovery' visions that are now enshrined in mental health policy in many countries. For example, the Australian National Mental Health Plan (2003–2008) has a key principle: 'A recovery orientation should drive service delivery' (Australian Health Ministers, 2003, p. 11). Embedded within such an aspirational principle are a number of underlying values that may need to be clarified and reinforced at a team level. For example, there is a shift from a purely symptom reduction and behavioural functioning view of improvement to a focus on living a more hopeful and meaningful life. There is greater valuing and support for autonomy and self-determination in consumers. Such approaches allow consumers to take risks to achieve important goals in this direction.

Initially, the role of a team leader may be to provide opportunities for teams to clarify the meaning of these issues for their day-to-day work and functioning as a team. How different professional training, roles, values and expectations might impact on achieving such a vision can be discussed. Establishment of shared team goals and provision of a structure for monitoring progress toward these goals may be needed. It may be that such structuring includes using a framework during treatment team meetings to review a care plan with specific reference to the 'recovery-oriented' vision (e.g. Does the plan focus on strengths? Was the client involved in collaboratively establishing goals? How does this plan enhance the autonomy and responsibility of a client?).

Some researchers have suggested that management by instructions or by objectives are inadequate in modern, complex and demanding organisations that are constantly changing (Dolan & Garcia, 2002). They highlight the need for a 'new approach, labelled management by values (MBV)' as an emerging strategic leadership tool. Given the push for 'recovery-oriented services' with a strong philosophical and value-based foundation such management and leadership approaches will possibly become increasingly needed.

## Team building

It cannot be assumed that all team members understand the expertise and training of fellow team members or have positive attitudes toward a multidisciplinary team approach. For example, surveys indicate confusion among general medical practitioners regarding the qualifications of professionals such as psychologists (Franklin et al., 1998). Further, there is evidence that medical students do not receive sufficient training in interdisciplinary teamwork and may not see the value in such an approach (e.g. Tanaka & Yokode, 2005). It has been recommended that medical training increases students' understanding of the role and responsibility of different healthcare professionals (Tanaka & Yokode, 2005). It has been argued that there is often role conflict, particularly between the psychiatrist and other members of the multidisciplinary team (Diamond, 1996). This is in part because psychiatrists often tend to view themselves as ultimately having overall responsibility for the patient's entire treatment (Diamond, 1996) or inaccurately perceiving that they are legally liable for the work of other team members (Renouf & Meadows, 2007). Together, these considerations have the potential to

---

**Box 1.1   Examples of team building activities.**

- Recognise unique skills of team members (e.g. perhaps use 'journal club' type activities to highlight specific skills in different occupational groups)
- Model respect by seeking 'consultations' with team members about cases at individual level
- Support strategies to recognise each team member's special skills or training (e.g. make this explicit during team meetings, 'John can do occupational assessment and job skills training')
- Strengthen team identity – especially around shared philosophies, vision, and values
- Try to connect team values to broader organisational values – develop 'team pride' in performance by highlighting both individual and team success
- Make team projects and goals explicit (e.g. start small and build, e.g. data audit – quality activities – individual client successes)
- Clarify the client groups that the team is delivering services to along with the range of services that are to be provided
- Encourage participation by all team members in information sharing and discussions regarding programme development, service planning, through to decision making in treatment team meetings
- Encourage presentation at conferences or professional meetings of team-orientated presentations (e.g. this may be 'parts' of presenters or team data presented by an individual)
- Pursue internal recognition of team within the organisation (e.g. by writing a letter to the Chief Executive Officer praising team achievements)
- Collaboratively establish team goals or targets (that might be matched to service key performance indicators) and be sure to structure regular feedback about the team's progress
- Support team-based learning or professional development activities

---

disempower other team members and cause ambiguity about who is responsible for specific components of treatment. These kinds of considerations reinforce the need for team building. Box 1.1 presents a sample of potential team building activities.

There are also numerous opportunities for informal team-building activities which can revolve around events such as lunches, professional society meetings and holiday season festivities.

## Managing meetings and team communication

To some extent management of team meetings depends on the purpose and goals of a meeting. Typically the most common meetings are 'treatment team' meetings where client progress is reviewed and there is discussion of care plans, goal attainment and the need for additional support or resources to support the client. Team members typically provide suggestions to the key worker about what might be useful and this draws not only on the collective experience, but also the specific disciplinary skills that are available. Often these meetings also discuss caseloads and are part of the caseload allocation procedures. In managing such meetings it is important to have a structure so that they progress in a predictable fashion and are completed in a timely fashion.

In a qualitative exploratory study of professional communication in interdisciplinary team meetings, three main communication practices were identified (Bokhour, 2006). The first, 'giving report', accounted for 27% of all utterances and involved individual team members reporting on problems, status, goals and interventions written in the treatment plan. The second, 'writing report', accounted for 25% of all utterances and involved actively writing and as part of that process discussing the wording of problems, goals and interventions. The third practice was 'collaborative discussion', which accounted for 32% of time. This was most often initiated by a team member raising questions or commenting on a report given by another team member, and overlap of speech was common (Bokhour, 2006). The implications of these findings revolve around understanding the effects of these various communication practices in order to increase levels of collaboration that involve crossing disciplinary boundaries to jointly determine treatment plans and actions. The author highlighted that high levels of 'giving report' reduce opportunities for team collaboration because one person tends to hold the floor. Although 'writing report' allows greater collaboration, it was still somewhat limited to the appropriate manner to document information in the care plan and was constrained by organisational requirements. Thus, informally tracking the time for various activities so as to maximise opportunities for collaborative discussion may be needed in team meetings.

Considerations in managing such meetings revolve around differential levels of participation. This may not be just at an individual level, but may also be influenced by the way different professions interact. For example, one study found that in multidisciplinary team meetings social workers and nurses were reluctant to voice their opinions compared to others (e.g. Atwal & Caldwell, 2005). Thus, some sensitivity to perceived professional hierarchies and power relationships is likely to be needed in managing team meetings (Mohr, 1995).

Although team leaders need to be alert to the processes in team meetings they also need to be clear on the purpose and tasks of the meeting. As Liberman et al. (2001, p. 1335) indicate:

> 'the team leader should focus the meeting on the needs of clients, on how current services are addressing those needs, and on making changes in treatment plans as needed; ensuring that team members keep clients' progress and plan interventions; setting expectations that the reports presented at meetings by team members will be specific and cogent; involving all staff in prioritising the topics and clients for discussion as well as in problem solving, decision making, and treatment planning; and translating the decisions made at the meetings into the written clinical records.'

Short and relatively informal morning briefings can be instituted to catch team members up on the most current information about clients and these have been described as 'the mainstay of communication on assertive community treatment teams' (Liberman et al., 2001, p. 1335). Of course a great deal of informal team work occurs outside formal meetings. Informal communication can occur in the context of simple information sharing, relationship building, one-off special projects or training activities.

# Conclusion

Leading a multidisciplinary team is becoming increasingly complex as policy and legislative changes lead to further blurring of the professional boundaries of team members. However, there is a growing research base that is providing guidance on leadership and management qualities that lead to better team functioning. Active leadership that is clear about the roles and goals of the team and individual team members is associated with better team functioning. Furthermore, leaders who are charismatic, inspirational, and considerate of individual staff members may improve team functioning to the extent that this is a measurable benefit for service user outcomes.

# References

Atwal, A. & Caldwell, K. (2005). Do all health and social care professionals interact equally: a study of interactions in multidisciplinary teams in the United Kingdom. *Scandinavian Journal of Caring Sciences*, 19, 268–273.

Auerbach, E. S. (2002). Occupational therapy and the multidisciplinary team (Letter). *Psychiatric Services*, 53, 767–768.

Australian Health Ministers (2003). *National Mental Health Plan 2003–2008*. Canberra: Australian Government.

Bass, B. M. (1985). *Leadership and Performance Beyond Expectation*. New York: Free Press.

Bass, B. M. & Avolio, B. J. (1997). *Full Range Leadership Development: Manual for the Multifactor Leadership Questionnaire*. Palo Alto, CA: Mindgarden.

Bokhour, B. G. (2006). Communication in interdisciplinary team meetings: What are we talking about? *Journal of Interprofessional Care*, 20, 349–363.

Burns, T. & Lloyd, H. (2004). Is a team approach based on staff meetings cost-effective in the delivery of mental health care? *Current Opinion in Psychiatry*, 17, 311–314.

Calpin, J. P., Edelstein, B., & Redmon, W. K. (1988). Performance feedback and goal setting to improve mental health center staff productivity. *Journal of Organizational Behavior Management*, 9, 35–58.

Corrigan, P. W., Garman, A. N., Lam, C. & Leary, M. (1998). What mental health teams want in their leaders. *Administration and Policy in Mental Health*, 26, 111–123.

Corrigan, P. W., Garman, A. N., Canar, J. & Lam, C. (1999). Characteristics of rehabilitation team leaders: a replication. *Rehabilitation Counselling Bulletin*, 42, 186–195.

Corrigan, P. W., Lickey, S. E., Campion, J. & Rashid, F. (2000). Mental health leadership and consumers' satisfaction and quality of life. *Psychiatric Services*, 51, 781–785.

DeChurch, L. A. & Marks, M. A. (2001). Maximizing the benefits of task conflict: the role of conflict management. *International Journal of Conflict Management*, 12, 4–22.

Diamond, R. J. (1996). Multidisciplinary teamwork. In: Vaccaro, J. & Clark, G. H. Jr. (eds). *Practicing Psychiatry in the Community: A Manual*. Arlington, Virginia: American Psychiatric Press, pp. 343–360.

Dolan, S. L. & Garcia, S. (2002). Managing by values: Cultural redesign of strategic organizational change at the dawn of the twenty-first century. *Journal of Management Development*, 21, 101–107.

Franklin, J., Foreman, M., Kyriakou, A. & Sarnovski, J. (1998). Awareness of psychologists' qualifications, professional associations, and registration amongst general medical practitioners, psychologists and their clients. *Australian Psychologist*, 33, 217–222.

Garman, A. N., Davis-Lenane, D. & Corrigan, P. W. (2003). Factor structure of the transformation leadership model in human service teams. *Journal of Organizational Behavior*, 24, 803–812.

Gellis, Z. D. (2001). Social work perceptions of transformational and transactional leadership in health care. *Social Work Research*, 25, 17–25.

Gray, R., Wykes, T. & Gournay, K. (2004). Randomised controlled trial and medication management in mental health nurses. *British Journal of Psychiatry*, 185, 157–162.

Kanste, O., Miettunen, J. & Kyngas, H. (2007). Psychometric properties of the Mulifactor Leadership Questionnaire among nurses. *Journal of Advanced Nursing*, 57, 201–212.

Kantek, F. & Kavla, I. (2007). Nurse–nurse manager conflict: how do nurse managers manage it? *The Health Care Manager*, 26, 147–151.

Kim, S. (2002). Participative management and job satisfaction: Lessons from management leadership. *Public Administration Review*, 62, 231–241.

Kuhn, T. & Poole, M. S. (2000). Do conflict management styles affect group decision making? Evidence from a longitudinal field study. *Human Communication Research*, 26, 558–590.

Liberman, R. P., Hilty, D. M., Drake, R. E. & Tsang, H. W. H. (2001). Requirements for multidisciplinary teamwork in psychiatric rehabilitation. *Psychiatric Services*, 52, 1331–1342.

MacMillan, M. & Bellchambers, H. (2007). Nurse prescribing: Adding value to the consumer experience. *Australian Prescriber*, 30, 2–3.

Marcos, L. R. & Silver, M. A. (1988). Psychiatrist-executive management styles: nature or nurture? *American Journal of Psychiatry*, 145, 103–106.

McKenna, B., O'Brien, A., Din, T. & Thom, K. (2006). Registered nurses as responsible clinicians under the New Zealand Mental Health Act 1992. *International Journal of Mental Health Nursing*, 15, 128.

Mohr, W. K. (1995). A critical reappraisal of a social form in psychiatric care settings: the multidisciplinary team meeting as a paradigm case. *Archives of Psychiatric Nursing*, 9, 85–91.

Rebeiro, K. L. (2002). Occupational therapy and the multidisciplinary team (letter). *Psychiatric Services*, 53, 767.

Renouf, N. & Meadows, G. (2007). Working collaboratively. In: Meadows, G., Singh, B. & Grigg, M. (eds). *Mental Health in Australia: Collaborative Community Practice*, 2nd edition. New York: Oxford University Press, pp. 227–242.

Sherman, P. & Porter, R. (1991). Mental health consumers as case managers. *Hospital and Community Psychiatry*, 42, 494–498.

Tanaka, M. & Yokode, M. (2005). Attitudes of medical students and residents toward multidisciplinary team approach. *Medical Education*, 39, 1255–1256.

Thornicroft, G. & Betts, V. (2002). *International Mid-Term Review of the Second National Mental Health Plan for Australia*. Canberra: Mental Health and Special Programs Branch, Department of Health and Ageing.

Turkington, D., Kingdon, D., Rathod, S., Hammond, K., Pelton, J. & Mehta, R. (2006). Outcomes of an effectiveness trial of cognitive-behavioural intervention by mental health nurses in schizophrenia. *British Journal of Psychiatry*, 189, 36–40.

# Chapter 2
# Managing workload in mental health services

*Robert King*

## Chapter overview

Workload management is a complex challenge for service managers. Considerations include issues of equity (equivalent workload across the workforce); clinical effectiveness (when does workload adversely impact on work quality?); workplace health and safety (when does workload adversely impact on employee health and well-being?); and service efficiency (how can the most work be achieved with the least burden?). This chapter begins by introducing a framework for conceptualising workload in mental health services so as to enable a constituent analysis of workload. It then surveys the available evidence concerning the relationship between workload and workforce well-being and productivity. Finally, it considers workload standards and discusses ways by which service managers might actively manage the workloads of clinical staff.

## Understanding workload: characteristics and constituents

Determining what constitutes workload is more difficult than might, at first glance, appear to be the case. There are both subjective and objective components to workload and while, necessarily, this chapter will focus on objective components, it is important to acknowledge the subjective dimension. At a personal level, workload is a little like pain. It is apparent to the person experiencing it but not always easy to communicate to another person. Two people may be doing what appears to be a broadly equivalent job, but one person may experience high workload pressure while the other person finds the job quite manageable. The challenge for the manager is to be able to clearly identify the constituents of a workload so as to make decisions regarding allocation of work, or provide guidance as to how a workload might be effectively managed.

At a conceptual level, workload constituents may be broadly equivalent across a range of human services. Morris et al. (2007) developed a model to identify the constituents of a nursing workload after reviewing the substantial published literature dealing with workload and workload-related issues within the nursing profession. Most of this literature concerned nursing activities other than mental health nursing. However, the general model is applicable to a broad range of mental health roles (Figure 2.1).

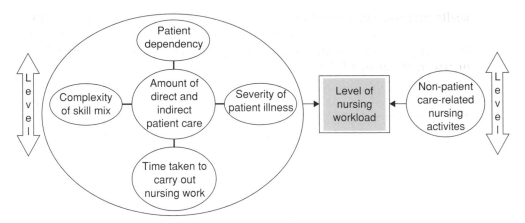

**Figure 2.1**    A model of nursing workload. Reproduced from Morris, R., McNeela, P., Scott, A., Treacy, P., & Hyde, A. Reconsidering the conceptualization of nursing workload: literature review. *Journal of Advanced Nursing*, 57, 463–471, copyright 2007 with permission of Blackwell Publishing Ltd.

In this model, workload is conceptualised as having two broad components. One relates to work with clients (clinical) and the other relates to non-client-related demands (non-clinical). Within the clinical work component, both client characteristics and the requirements of clinical care tasks impact on the workload. Non-clinical demands are not specified in the model. Stuart et al. (2000) in a study of the activities of mental health nurses classified non-clinical activities into three broad groups: clinical communication (e.g. documentation, team meetings, interagency liaison); management activities (e.g. clinical supervision, quality assurance, development of policies and procedures, co-ordination of services, unit level governance, strategic planning); and clerical activities (e.g. house-keeping, purchases, transport arrangements, scheduling appointments). To these we might add various kinds of project work such as community education, staff training, research and evaluation as well as increasingly common clerical activities such as data entry relating to client contact and client outcome measurement.

Objective measurement of workload requires formal evaluation of the time and effort taken to perform the various work activities. The time and motion study is the standard method for measuring the activities that constitute a workload (Finkler et al., 1993). In this method, trained observers use systematic and structured observation procedures to record both the category of activity and the time spent on the activity over a working day. Unfortunately, no recent time and motion studies with mental health practitioners are available. However, time and motion studies of the work of accident and emergency doctors (Brown, 2000) and general hospital nurses (Burke et al., 2000) suggest that even in high clinical demand environments approximately a third of the activity of clinicians is non-clinical.

Early observational studies (Siegel et al., 1983; Foster & Williams, 1989) and more recent self-report studies (Stuart et al., 2000) of the activities of mental health professionals suggest that the proportion of non-clinical work activity in the mental health workforce is likely to be even higher. Stuart et al. (2000) found that nearly two-thirds of the work of 330 inpatient and community mental health nurses employed in a US public mental health service were in non-clinical activities (evenly distributed across clinical communication, management and clerical tasks). They also found that respondents expressed a preference for a higher proportion of clinical and lower proportion of non-clinical activities.

As the model presented in Figure 2.1 suggests, knowledge of work activities alone is insufficient to appreciate workload. For example, performing a mental state examination is a common clinical activity for a mental health practitioner. However, a mental state examination with a co-operative client is a completely different experience from a mental state examination with a hostile or paranoid client. The client profile is therefore an important element of workload. Similarly, the type of intervention will have a major impact on workload. Monitoring medication is relatively less time consuming than intensive psychosocial rehabilitation. Client characteristics and intervention effects may be formally recognised as workload variables in specific models of practice. For example, teams that employ the Assertive Community Treatment model (Allness & Knoedler, 2003; Salyers et al., 2003) specify a low client to staff ratio to ensure that provision of intensive services to a highly disabled client group is feasible. However, in a routine practice environment, evaluation of workload requires consideration of both client profile and interventions provided.

At the level of the individual practitioner, management of workload means addressing the subjective experience of workload in the context of the clearest possible understanding of the objective components. Responding effectively to a grievance about workload requires that the manager is able to recognise that a practitioner feels overburdened while at the same time being able to look objectively at the work activities that are the source of burden. Grievances may be about perceived inequity of workload as distinct from the absolute burden of workload. This means that managers need to be in a position to benchmark the workload of the individual practitioners against the workload of others working within the service and also to benchmark typical workload within a service against workloads in broadly comparable services.

## Workload, work-related stress and work quality

Effective management of practitioner workload is a key role for the team leader or service manager. Workload affects both the well-being of the practitioner (Cushway et al., 1996) and can also impact on the characteristics and quality of services provided to clients (King et al., 2000).

Cushway et al. (1996) identified workload as one of seven key sources of stress for mental health professionals and specified the following components:

- too much work to do
- too many different things to do

- not enough time to complete tasks
- too many clients
- long hours
- not enough time for recreation.

These are clearly inter-related and are also linked with some of the sources that Cushway et al. (1996) linked to home/work conflict:

- taking work home
- not enough family time
- no time for social relationships.

A study of 187 community mental health case managers in Victoria, Australia (King, 2007), found that responses to these items were closely correlated. Respondents were most likely to report that the global item 'too much work' applied to them, followed by 'too many different things to do', 'not enough time to complete tasks' and 'too many clients'. Respondents were least likely to report that 'taking work home' applied to them. This probably reflects the nature of the work in that much of it revolves around client contact and even the paper-work component requires access to secure confidential files that will normally not be taken home. In this study (King, 2007), workload was the single greatest source of stress for participants – although this has not always been the finding when this measure has been applied with samples of mental health professionals (Cushway et al., 1996; Lloyd et al., 2005). Stress associated with lack of resources and conflict has also been prominent in other studies.

It is well established that the mental health workforce experiences moderately high levels of work-related stress as indicated by scores on the workload sub-scale of the Mental Health Professionals Stress Scale (MHPSS, see above) and scores on the emotional exhaustion subscale of the Maslach Burnout Inventory (Lloyd et al., 2002). However, teasing out the sources of high stress and identifying the role of clinical workload has proved to be more difficult (Carson et al., 1996). Walsh and Walsh (2002) found that neither the number of clients nor most of the characteristics of clients reliably predicted stress among professionals (although there was evidence that having a higher proportion of male clients and a higher proportion of psychotic clients increased risk). It is possible that the non-clinical components of workload are a greater source of stress than the clinical components (see Chapter 10 for more detailed discussion of stress in the mental health workforce). Furthermore, when a person is feeling stressed, even though work may not be the primary cause of the stress, work is likely to feel more burdensome.

While high workload does not always result in increased stress, there is evidence it does impact on the quality of work done by mental health professionals. King et al. (2000) surveyed mental health case managers in Australia, using a measure of self-efficacy for a range of standard case management activities. Self-efficacy measures ask people to rate the extent to which they are confident in being able to do a given task. There was evidence of a significant linear relationship between caseload and overall self-efficacy, such that as caseload rose, self-efficacy tended to fall. This relationship was especially clear when caseloads exceeded 28. At higher caseloads, case managers reported they were less able to engage in activities such as visiting clients in hospital and home visiting. Faced with higher caseloads, case managers may attempt to work harder and may work unpaid hours in an attempt to maintain a standard of care but it more likely they will modify the work role and reduce it to the most essential components. This may mean becoming less proactive and less therapeutic, with activities reduced to a minimal monitoring regimen and responding to demands.

It should, however, be noted that, while lower caseloads may enable case managers to undertake a higher range of activities or to provide services more intensively, it cannot be assumed that more services result in better client outcomes. A survey of randomised controlled trials comparing intensive case management, characterised by small caseloads, with higher caseload standard case management (King, 2006), found no evidence of clinical or psychosocial benefits for those receiving higher intensity services.

What this means is that consideration as to what is a reasonable caseload for a community mental health practitioner must take into account a range of considerations. Among these are the well being of the practitioner, the kinds of services that the practitioner is expected to provide and the likely impact on client outcomes. High caseloads are likely to result in limited reactive services while very low caseloads may mean inefficient utilisation of resources.

## Measuring and managing workload: standards, processes and tools

Because of the salience of workload to the well-being of staff and to the quality of services provided to clients, it is important that service managers are able to monitor and adjust workload both to achieve optimal equity and also to make reasonable decisions about resource allocation. As indicated at the beginning of this chapter, workload is complex, being influenced by the volume and characteristics of clients, non-client demands and other considerations such as travel requirements, stage of treatment and the experience of the practitioner.

Inpatient services typically operate with fixed ratios between staff (especially nursing staff) and beds. Ratios vary according to the form of treatment and type of patient with acute intensive care units having higher staff to patient ratios than standard acute units, which have higher ratios than rehabilitation units. However, the presence of standard staffing ratios does not necessarily result in equivalent workload for nursing staff, even when units have nominally equivalent staffing ratios. There are several reasons for this:

- acuity and other patient-related workload factors are quite variable
- workload of more senior or experienced staff is adversely affected by higher proportions of inexperienced or lesser qualified staff
- services often have difficulty recruiting a permanent workforce and rely heavily on casual or agency staff

- workload of the nursing staff may be significantly influenced by the presence or otherwise of allied health staff.

Ryan et al. (2004) in a survey of 93 acute mental health units in England found that although there was a nominal nursing/bed ratio of 1:1 across all units, the actual ratio was 0.51:1 and there was substantial variability from unit to unit. The shortfall reflected an average of 12% vacancy rate among positions for fully trained nurses plus chronic funding shortfalls in many services. Shortfalls were often met through employment of untrained staff, which the authors pointed out increases the work burden on trained staff because of the tasks untrained staff are unable to perform. Because funding is tied to beds and bed occupancy is usually high, there is limited scope for a unit manager to control or adjust the clinical workload of inpatient nursing staff. As a result, units can enter into a 'vicious cycle', in which vacancies and employment of unqualified staff or agency staff increase workload on qualified staff leading to resignations and increased reliance on unqualified or agency staff.

Ryan et al. (2004) suggest that there are few ready solutions to the challenge of inpatient nursing workload because of shortages of trained mental health nurses. These shortages are international and expected to worsen (Roche & Duffield, 2007). As a result, Ryan et al. (2004) suggest that effective management of the clinical workload may ultimately require services to rethink the composition of the inpatient workforce, giving consideration to the use of non-professional staff including consumers and carers. However, in the light of the evidence presented earlier in this chapter, that up to two-thirds of the work activity of an inpatient mental health nurse is non-clinical, one of the most effective means by which a unit manager can reduce workload might be to streamline non-clinical activities.

Community mental health services present different challenges, with workload management being more difficult in some respects but with greater scope for active management in other respects. The major difficulty is that, whereas the number of available beds is a natural work limiting factor in inpatient services there is no equivalent limiter for community services. The closest equivalent to the nurse:bed ratio in inpatient services is the average caseload of community mental health practitioners. The international evidence suggests this is highly variable and dependent on type and location of service. In a review of studies published since 1999 that compared intensive case management with standard case management, King (2006) reported that caseloads for intensive case management ranged from eight to 15 and caseloads for standard case management ranged from 20 to 68.

Within standard case management the high level of variability is probably a function of local norms, staffing (funding) levels and practice models. At the lower end, Hromco et al. (2003) reported that case managers in Oregon had median caseloads of 23 in 1992 and 30 in 2000. This is consistent with an Australian study (King et al., 2000), which found case managers had caseloads of 22 per equivalent full-time case manager. In the mid-range, Hannigan et al. (2000) reported mean caseloads of 37 for community mental health nurses working in Wales. A later study by Nolan et al. (2004) found similar caseloads in two English mental health NHS trusts. At the higher end, McCardle et al. (2007) reported mean caseloads of 61 for community mental health nurses working in Ireland. This is consistent with anecdotal reports provided to the author by services in western Canada.

This suggests that it is difficult for a service manager to use international benchmarking as a means to setting caseload levels. However, we think there is reasonable consensus that the lower end of caseload range is desirable and some empirical evidence to suggest that lower caseloads are likely to result in superior services. More than 25 years ago, Intagliata (1982) suggested that if case management was to be anything other than reactive caseloads in the range 20–30 were desirable so as to enable service planning, support for families and carers and liaison with other services. Subsequent research by Baker and Intagliata (1992), Onyett (1992) and King et al. (2000) have lent support to Intagliata's (1982) proposition.

Although managers of inpatient services have limited capacity to adjust the clinical workload because it is directly linked to the bed ratio, managers of community services can more actively manage the clinical workload by monitoring and adjusting the caseload of team members. Community services usually have a discretionary range for both intake and discharge of clients and can actively manage changes to total caseload. There is then scope to manage the distribution of caseload among team members.

There are two broad approaches to monitoring and adjusting individual caseloads. One might be termed informal and involves the manager or team leader making judgements based on observation of and interaction with team members. This could be supported by very basic quantitative information such as the total number of clients for which each practitioner is responsible or the total number of clinical contacts or contact-hours. The other involves the use of tools or algorithms and attempts to manage complexity by measuring the variables thought to be important and calculating the workload of each team member after taking into account each of the variables.

A variety of workload tools have been used in both general health (Baldwin, 2006) and mental health settings (King et al., 2004). While workload management tools offer the potential benefit of reducing errors associated with human judgement by integrating a complex range of factors to yield a single numerical score, they have been criticised on the grounds that they fail to capture or distort key elements of the practitioner–client relationship (Forchuk, 1996) or that information yielded is unreliable because it is inaccurately or incompletely compiled (Baldwin, 2006). It has also been pointed out that when workload tools substantially rely on practitioner reports of client contact rates, there is risk that practitioners will over-service 'easier' clients to maintain a caseload that appears high but is not well targeted (King et al., 2004). Examples of caseload management tools used effectively in mental health services can be found in Meldrum and Yellowlees (2000) and King et al. (2004).

In an evaluation of the implementation of a caseload management project across Victoria's community mental health services, King (2007) found that most service managers used informal means of monitoring and adjusting the caseloads of team members. They frequently relied on information provided in team meetings or supervision meetings and caseload was often managed more by the practitioner indicating availability to take on new cases than by active intervention on the part of the team leader or manager. King (2008) found that, for the most part, practitioners were satisfied with this approach to caseload management. Even when required under an industrial agreement to introduce a more formal caseload management system that made use of tools or algorithms, services tended to continue to rely substantially on informal approaches. Among those who trialled more formal methods, some abandoned them because of the workload implications of the data collection or because of poor compliance with data collection by key service personnel, while others found them very useful, especially in providing a framework for supervision meetings with team members. One benefit of the use of algorithms or other standardised approaches to caseload management is that it enhances transparency. This means there is reduced risk of actual or perceived unfairness in allocation of cases.

Team leaders and service managers may need to think about workload management at a team level as well as at an individual level. It is not unusual for a team as a whole to feel overburdened and overworked. This may reflect broader morale problems or may be an indicator that the team needs to collectively rethink its approach to the work at hand. The role of the team leader or service manager in such circumstances is to assist the team to identify the source of the problem and to find workable solutions. This may be moderately time consuming but, unless the problem is very simple, is likely to be more effective than a solution based solely on the team leader's assessment and imposed from above.

## Conclusion

Mental health workload is a key issue both in management of the individual practitioner and management of the total service. Mental health workload is made up of both clinical and non-clinical components, with the available evidence suggesting that more than half of the work activity of the average mental health practitioner is devoted to non-clinical activity. Non-clinical activities are often linked to clinical activities so the total workload will be related to clinical demand. However workforce supply factors can also impact on workload when there are high vacancy rates. In inpatient services, clinical demand is associated with the staff to bed ratio, whereas in community services, caseload provides the best general indicator of clinical demand. Clinical demand is not a function of numbers alone and will also be influenced by both client characteristics and clinical interventions utilised. In managing workload, team leaders and unit managers need to identify where there is scope to control clinical demand factors and where there are opportunities to streamline non-clinical activities. The use of standards and tools can assist in decision making.

# References

Allness, D. & Knoedler, W. (2003). National program standards for ACT teams (2003 revision). Arlington, VA, NAMI. Available at: www.nami.org/Content/ContentGroups/Programs/PACT1/National_Program_Standards_for_ACT.pdf (accessed 21 December 2007).

Baker, F. & Intagliata, J. (1992). Case management. In: Liberman, R. (ed.) *Handbook of Psychiatric Rehabilitation.* New York: Macmillan Publishing Co, pp. 213–244.

Baldwin, M. (2006). The Warrington workload tool: determining its use in one trust. *British Journal of Community Nursing*, 11, 391–392, 394–395.

Brown, R. (2000). Activities of accident and emergency consultants – a time and motion study. *Journal of Accident and Emergency Medicine*, 17, 122–125.

Burke, T., McKee, J., Wilson, H., Donahue, R., Batenhorst, A. & Pathak, D. (2000). A comparison of time-and-motion and self-reporting methods of work measurement. *Journal of Nursing Administration*, 30, 118–125.

Carson, J., Brown, D., Fagin, L., Leary, J. & Bartlett, H. (1996). Do larger caseloads cause greater stress in community mental health nurses? *Journal of Clinical Nursing*, 5, 133–134.

Cushway, D., Tyler, P. & Nolan, P. (1996). Development of a stress scale for mental health professionals. *British Journal of Clinical Psychology*, 35, 279–295.

Finkler, S., Knickman, J., Hendrickson, G., Lipkin, M. Jr. & Thompson, W. (1993). A comparison of work-sampling and time-and-motion techniques for studies in health services research. *Health Services Research*, 28, 577–597.

Forchuk, C. (1996). Workload measurement and psychiatric mental health nursing: mathematical and philosophical difficulties. *Canadian Journal of Nursing Administration*, 9, 67–81.

Foster, B. & Williams, R. (1989). Substitution of self-reporting for observing time spent on work activities by mental health professionals. *Psychological Reports*, 64, 945–946.

Hannigan, B., Edwards, D., Coyle, D., Fothergill, A. & Burnard, P. (2000). Burnout in community mental health nurses: findings from the all-Wales stress study. *Journal of Psychiatric and Mental Health Nursing*, 7, 127–134.

Hromco, J., Moore, M. & Nikkel, R. (2003). How managed care has affected mental health case management activities, caseloads and tenure. *Community Mental Health Journal*, 39, 502–509.

Intagliata, J. (1982). Improving the quality of community care for the chronically clinically mentally disabled: the role of case management. *Schizophrenia Bulletin*, 8, 655–674.

King, R. (2006). Intensive case management: a critical re-appraisal of the scientific evidence for effectiveness. *Administration and Policy in Mental Health and Mental Health Services Research*, 33, 529–535.

King, R. (2007). Caseload management practices in Victoria's community mental health services. Report to the Victorian Department of Human Services.

King, R., Le Bas, J. & Spooner, D. (2000). The impact of caseload on mental health case manager personal efficacy. *Psychiatric Services*, 52, 364–368.

King, R., Meadows, G. & Le Bas, J. (2004). Compiling a caseload index for mental health case management. *Australian and New Zealand Journal of Psychiatry*, 38, 455–462.

Lloyd, C., King, R. & Chenoweth, L. (2002). Social work, stress and burnout: a review. *Journal of Mental Health*, 11, 255–265.

Lloyd, C., McKenna, K. & King, R. (2005). Sources of stress experienced by occupational therapists and social workers in mental health settings. *Occupational Therapy International*, 12, 81–94.

McCardle, J., Parahoo, K. & McKenna, H. (2007). A national survey of community psychiatric nurses and their client care activities in Ireland. *Journal of Psychiatric and Mental Health Nursing*, 14, 179–188.

Meldrum, L. & Yellowlees, P. (2000). The measurement of a case manager's workload burden. *Australian and New Zealand Journal of Psychiatry*, 34, 658–663.

Morris, R., McNeela, P., Scott, A., Treacy, P. & Hyde, A. (2007). Reconsidering the conceptualization of nursing workload: literature review. *Journal of Advanced Nursing*, 57, 463–471.

Nolan, P., Haque, M., Bourke, P. & Dyke, R. (2004). A comparison of the work and values of community mental health nurses in two mental health NHS Trusts. *Journal of Psychiatric and Mental Health Nursing*, 11, 525–533.

Onyett, S. (1992). *Case Management in Mental Health*. London: Chapman and Hall.

Roche, M. & Duffield, C. (2007). Issues and challenges in the mental health workforce development. *Contemporary Nurse*, 25, 94–103.

Ryan, T., Hills, B. & Webb, L. (2004). Nurse staffing levels and budgeted expenditure in acute mental health wards: a benchmarking study. *Journal of Psychiatric and Mental Health Nursing*, 11, 73–81.

Salyers, M., Bond, G., Teague, G., Cox, J., Smith, M., Hicks, M. & Koop, J. (2003). Is it ACT yet? Real-world examples of evaluating the degree of implementation for assertive community treatment. *Journal of Behavioral Health Services Research*, 30, 304–320.

Siegel, C., Haugland, G. & Fischer, S. (1983). A comparison of work activities of mental health professionals among disciplines and environments. *Hospital and Community Psychiatry*, 34, 154–157.

Stuart, G., Worley, N., Morris, J. Jr. & Bevilacqua, J. (2000). Role utilization of nurses in public psychiatry. *Administration and Policy in Mental Health*, 27, 423–441.

Walsh, B. & Walsh, S. (2002). Caseload factors and the psychological well-being of community mental health staff. *Journal of Mental Health*, 11, 67–78.

# Chapter 3
# Clinical information management

*Jennifer Harland and Janette Curtis*

## Chapter overview

Clinical information management is increasingly important in healthcare delivery. The probable reason that you have turned to this chapter is because someone has mentioned 'datasets' or 'standardised measures' and although you nodded knowingly at the time, in actual fact you are struggling to understand how and why this information is important to you and your unit. You are not alone. Managers in mental health come from a range of backgrounds, so have a variety of experience with clinical information management. This chapter will give you the theoretical fundamentals you need and, through the use of case studies, highlight how you can integrate this information in practice. It is important to note that this chapter is concerned primarily with the management of data systems, although references are provided for exploring information management systems that will assist clinicians in working individually with consumers of the health service.

## Introduction

Mental health managers and clinicians face similar issues to managers in other areas of care. It is seldom that the words 'clinical information management' sparks joy and excitement. Deliberating over tables and sets of numbers often seems to merely distract from direct patient care. However, health informatics is central to good patient care and provides important links between what could appear abstract and time-wasting managerial activities (Katona, 2002). In fact the rising costs of healthcare is causing great concern, and information technology is viewed as an enabler for introducing efficiencies into the health system (Dogac & Kashyap, 2005).

From both a quality and security perspective, the integrity of clinical information is critical to patient care. Due to changes in politics, government legislation and reforms, managers need to be equipped with the necessary tools and skills to be able to lead and manage effectively (Phillips, 2005). Managers also need to be confident that electronic patient records are secure and information is kept confidential (Osborne, 2006). Understanding the databases that you use is crucial to increase this confidence.

Information technology is capable of transforming healthcare organisations and delivering measurable value (Mahoney, 2002). Practitioners, case managers, consumers and policy makers are increasingly basing their healthcare decisions on timely and relevant clinical data (Connolly, 2002). Increasingly, there is a need to offer 24-hour access to services and towards this end, in the UK, the government granted the National Health Service (NHS) six billion pounds to 'revolutionise its computer systems' (Toofany, 2006). NHS Direct is one such initiative which consist of a sophisticated telephone service staffed by nurses who can give information and advice as well as dealing with emergency calls 24 hours a day (Bloomfield & McLean, 2003).

## Historical perspective

Simpson (2003) outlined a history of clinical information systems that many of us will remember with varying degrees of enthusiasm. Diagnostic Related Groupings (DRG) was a reimbursement-centred strategy in which providers had to justify what they did by proving it produced an outcome worth paying for. However, it soon became apparent that the information system could not collect enough patient data or the type needed to truly analyse and justify care.

As a result of an increasing emphasis on patient-centred care, patient-centred clinical information systems were developed but many professional groups were slow to embrace technology. In addition, such systems were designed with little input from groups such as nurses. As a result nursing interventions went unrecorded and unrecognised (Simpson, 2003). This is gradually being rectified with the emergence of numerous systems aimed at capturing what it is that nurses and other healthcare workers actually do. There is now an awareness of the importance of involving clinicians before and during the installation of data systems and offering ongoing training and support (Venkatesh & Davis, 2000).

## Why is it important to manage clinical information?

Information management is one of five key areas of Quality Improvement or Performance Improvement. The other four areas are: people, infrastructure, work processes and culture (Nash & Goldfarb, 2006). Systematically collected patient information can be analysed and used at local, organisational and national levels and allows information to be available to inform mental health service management (Katona, 2002).

Measuring and quantifying the outcomes of care are essential activities for the ongoing operation of mental health facilities. Centres need a data collection system to collect meaningful data that assist with the development of programmes and services, measure clinical outcomes and promote health policy. Accomplishing these objectives is especially difficult in mental health settings. When tracking the care process over time, it is possible to drown in the data, especially qualitative data. Leonardo et al. (2004) suggested that to be successful, nurse-managed health centres and all providers must systematically evaluate their data and information needs, as well as available systems, and then implement an action plan. Systems are available for accessing medical advice immediately, managing caseloads (Stuttle, 2006), booking appointments, accessing records (Parish, 2006), bringing different datasets together (Lee, 2006), reducing waiting times (Dogac & Kashyap, 2005), prescribing and tracking prescriptions (Kaufman, 2007), conducting clinical trials (Enman, 2006), reducing staffing costs (Tachakra et al., 2006) and telepsychiatry (May et al., 2001) as well as many other functions.

## The key challenges of clinical information management

For the majority of clinicians the term 'information technology' is vague and often met with a look of disdain. Their primary concern is to deliver effective, high-quality care to patients. However, consideration of two aspects of modern mental health services draw attention to the information challenge for clinicians (McClelland, 2002). One challenge is the variability in healthcare practice evident in diagnosis, treatment plans and management strategies. One of the major sources of such variability is a lack of readily accessible information on best practice (McClelland, 2002). A second information challenge is that care within mental health services involves multiple contacts with different professionals across a variety of settings. Effectiveness of clinical care depends on the collection, exchange and transfer of information between clinicians and other services in a flexible form at each and every point of patient contact (McClelland, 2002).

The use of computers in behavioural healthcare has evolved in a steady fashion over the past decade with a veritable explosion in technology in the past few years. Consequently, the behavioural healthcare industry is witnessing an unprecedented capacity to quickly access and process enormous amounts of information (Meredith et al., 2000). Collecting, storing, analysing, interpreting and reporting clinical data promise to dramatically affect the design, delivery and scope of behavioural healthcare services. Computer technology not only facilitates the practice of behavioural healthcare, it also forces change in the delivery systems themselves. Consider the following case study.

Members of a mental health assessment team were informed that a new computer triage system was to be installed. It had been developed by a computer programmer and was based on the Mental Health Outcome and Assessment Tools (MH-OAT; standardised forms used to collect patient information across New South Wales in Australia). This raised a number of questions within the team:

- What training would be provided?
- Had it been tested?
- When and how would it be installed?
- What would happen to the current database?
- How would the information be merged?

One of the clinical staff members who had previously worked as a business analyst raised concerns about the level of testing the new system had been through before the 'go-live' day. After numerous meetings the following plan was implemented:

- The clinical staff member (the tester) with experience both in mental health assessment and system analysis was removed from her current role within the mental health inpatient unit to work in the assessment unit.
- Her role would be to test the new program as part of the assessment team.
- The predicted timeframe was three months.

At the beginning of the testing phase it was found that the system crashed frequently over the first three weeks. Each time this occurred an error report would be generated and the computer programmer would be notified via email and the problem would be fixed. During the testing phase, the triage/assessment information had to be entered twice; once on the old system and once on the new system. This affected workloads as the tester was included in the assessment team numbers, not as supernumerary support. Over time, modifications were made and error reports declined. All staff were trained on the system prior to the official 'go-live' day, six months after the initial testing. The training consisted of one full day training for all intake staff and ongoing support as required. This included the development and distribution of training and user manuals. The staff's level of computer experience varied considerably and extra computer training was offered. Night staff were trained during their shift with the tester providing support.

Measuring the efficacy of the system was important. As part of the audit process the assessment team's clinical nurse consultant (CNC) met with the community team once a month to discuss the quality of the information collected in the assessment form. This included a random audit as well as the opportunity for community staff to bring along examples of completed assessment forms that required further clarification. This information was fed back to the assessment team by the CNC; necessary changes were implemented, thus closing the quality loop. The tester returned to the inpatient unit 12 months later when all staff were confident with the system and her support was no longer required. On reflection, the tester offered the following advice when considering introducing a new clinical information system:

- There is need for user input throughout the development of any clinical information system.
- There is need for 'buy-in' from all levels.
- Be mindful of effects of change on staff. They need to be informed about:
  - why the change is being made
  - how it will affect clinical management
  - what the perceived benefits to client care are
  - what is expected of the staff
  - what is the ultimate goal.

### Making it work for the mental health unit

A crucial set of ingredients for effective information management is the necessary professional skills and understanding in information management, a valuing of information and recognition of the importance of information and information sharing. Learning about clinical information management needs to be embedded in clinical practice and integrated into education and training for all staff. Be aware of your staff's expertise and use all available resources. The best resource when implementing a clinical information system is a data information manager.

### The clinical information/data manager

Most mental health facilities have a clinical information or data manager attached to them in some capacity. The data manager has an intimate knowledge of the unit's data information systems and will be able to advise on how to manage it for the best outcome. The data information manager can explain the meaning and relevance of standard data reports and will be able to advise about generation of unique or specific reports.

The data information manager should be involved in all decisions with regard to the development, purchasing and implementation of any information system. They will be able to advise on which systems 'talk' to each other and whether your investment of time and money is a sound one. Consider the following example.

Staff in a methadone unit were keen to install an automated dispensing device. Following considerable research they purchased one worth Aus$100 000. The machine not only offered automated dispensing but also would store and supply information about the clients and alert staff for key information regarding follow-up, etc. The company offered in-service and ongoing support. The unit did not include the data information manager in the process. Once the automated device was installed the data information manager was contacted to resolve an issue. When the data information manager assessed the issue they realised that the new machine could not 'talk' to their current information system. Although the staff could still use the machine it was not working at its full potential because data had to be entered into both systems separately. If the data manager had been involved in the purchasing process they could have alerted the buyer early and looked at different options.

If you do not have the luxury of a data information manager in your unit, the following ten tips from data information managers are worth considering:

(1) Spend time getting to know your information system. This may mean investing in a course to understand the capabilities of the system.
(2) Remember that the data you extract is only as good as the information you put in. Taking the time to set the data collection fields to the specifics of your needs is essential.
(3) Ensure that all staff are trained in the information system. This may include understanding basic computer technology or finding experienced staff who can support and educate others.

(4) Remember that any field you enter has the capacity to produce a report and this information can be as large or specific as needed.

(5) Look for interesting ways to use the data to guide practice. For example when looking at demographics and drug use there may be a trend of adolescents using cannabis in one particular suburb. This information could be used to look at what current youth and drug and alcohol services you have in that area.

(6) Know and understand the reports generated. They are not just random numbers but can highlight trends, gaps in service and areas for further development.

(7) All new staff members need full orientation to the clinical information system. This may be by either spending one-on-one time with the data manager, using a web-based package or teaching package.

(8) Consider building the use of information systems into staff performance appraisal criteria.

(9) Embrace technology, understand it and customise it for your own purposes.

(10) Identify and support clinical information management 'champions'.

## Confidentiality in clinical information systems

An issue often raised with clinical information systems is confidentiality. While many methods have evolved for ensuring the *actual* security of electronic data, it is often the *perceived* security of information that managers need to address (Caspar, 2004). Staff members may be reluctant to collect and store information for fear that it may end up in the wrong hands or the information may be used for malicious purposes. It should be emphasised to staff that in the case of an electronic medical record, access is password protected and may in fact be more secure than a hard copy file that can potentially be left in a public area. By understanding the security features in the clinical information system, the clinical manager is able to better explain these features and reassure their team members.

## Ethical requirements

Research into the use of technology in mental health settings must adhere to strict ethical requirements. Researchers and healthcare professionals need to adhere to the basic Hippocratic Oath. However, there are guidelines available such as Roberts and Dwyer's (2004) concise guide to ethics in mental health that has provided solutions to specific dilemmas. Coyle et al. (2007) have built on this work and suggest that technologies are:

● based on accepted theoretical models of mental healthcare
● designed in full collaboration with mental health professionals
● designed to integrate with existing working methods
● used by clients under the guidance of a professional therapist.

## Engaging staff

When looking at engaging staff in the use of clinical information management it is important to involve them in the process. This would include ascertaining your team's understanding of the process, the team's existing knowledge and experience with computers, involving the team members in the selection and development of the tools to be used, providing training in the management of the system, investing in staff with a special interest in the area, reporting back on the changes made from data collection and reporting changes in clinical practice.

## The condition of data in a database

Clean data are error free or have very few errors. Dirty data have errors including: incorrect spelling and punctuation of names and addresses, redundant data in several records or simply erroneous data (not the correct amounts, names, etc.). It is vital that all data collected are clean in order to ensure reports are accurate and meaningful. A great amount of time can be wasted if inaccurate data are entered, because this results in the clinicians needing to pull clinical files again to re-enter the data. In such situations staff will become disgruntled with the process and possibly add to staff reluctance to enter data. Staff need to be trained and encouraged to collect and enter accurate data at all times. The consequences of not collecting accurate data should be highlighted.

## Addressing the clinician/system gap

Many clinicians are not impressed with clinical information systems. They feel that the entering of information is another burden on their already stretched time. If this is a recurring theme in your unit it may be time to look at the processes that are in place. In one mental health unit a number of disgruntled clinicians reported that assessments were taking double the time. When these concerns were unpacked, it became apparent that they were writing down the initial assessment and then entering it into the system at a later date and time. Of course this is frustrating and also increases the risk of errors. If the clinician missed important information at the assessment, they have to rely on their memory recall or may have to go through their written notes again. If the clinician can enter the information at the time of assessment, it is more likely that the data will be accurate. To ensure clean data the system can be set up with alerts that block the clinician moving on until all fields have been entered. In some areas clinicians hand over their handwritten information to a data entry person for entering. This is far from ideal. The scope for error is large because misinterpretation of collected information may occur.

A manager must also be aware of the staff's familiarity with resources. Marcy et al. (2005) found that doctors' lack of familiarity with systems impacted on their use of resources and it was recommended that a clinical decision support system may improve knowledge of these resources if the design addresses cost, space and time limitations.

**Key factors that predict clinical information system success**

Much research has been done to identify the key factors that predict clinical information system implementation success. Sittig (2002) claims that over 150 factors have been identified but only two are consistently associated with successful implementation. These are 'top management support' and 'user involvement'. Sittig (2002) identified additional key elements to a successful implementation:

- 'Buy-in' of the organisation is important – all users must see the need for the change if they are to support it (Souther, 2001).
- There must be clear understanding that significant change occurs in multiple stages, and that errors in any of these stages can have devastating consequences (Kotter, 1995).
- Local champions must actively and enthusiastically promote the system, build support, overcome resistance and ensure that the system is actually installed and used (Ash, 1997).
- Senior management must be able to understand and address the challenges ahead and capitalise on opportunities for quality improvement and cost reduction (Pare & Elam, 1998).
- It must be recognised that it can take at least six months of clinical information system usage before any decisions about the success of the technology introduction (particularly in terms of individual worker productivity) can be made (Blignaut et al., 2001).

# How clinical information systems can be used

### Community Health Information Management Enterprise

The Community Health Information Management Enterprise (CHIME) is an operational clinical information system designed to improve service delivery, outcome measures and productivity through improved capture and management of community-based health service information. It is also intended to improve the mechanisms for reporting at the local, area, state and national levels, thereby improving the quality of community health information available and the efficiency with which it is produced.

The CHIME project is a joint venture between New South Wales (NSW) Health, Queensland Health, the South Australian Health Commission and Australian Capital Territory (ACT) Health and Community Care. The joint venture partnership was initiated in 1996 in response to common needs identified by each health authority. CHIME's mandate is to 'facilitate information management for community based health services by developing a client-focused application that delivers and obtains information from other applications'. CHIME allows community-based healthcare staff to:

- accurately document the assessment of clients
- develop individualised management plans based on best practice principles

- monitor outcomes of clinical care
- generate reports for client and management reporting.

The CHIME application benefits service providers because it has been designed to:

- assist with the development of efficient processes for recording client information across the health system. These processes help to eliminate duplicated recording of demographic data for clients.
- track referrals, appointments and service contacts.
- provide real time information, by storage and retrieval of clients' case management information. This enables information to be transferred to other community-based health professionals who are consulting with a client and enables staff to spend more time on case management.
- enable community-based health staff to develop 'clinical practice norms' and case management guidelines and measures in order to assess the effectiveness of their services.
- enable the collection of workload indicators for community-based health staff. This provides measures to assess service efficiency and costs to assist resource allocation and management.
- facilitate the introduction of a 'case mix type' classification system and benchmarking for community-based health services.

Tangible benefits for health authorities include:

- a reduction in clinician time dedicated to clerical work
- rapid responses to changing healthcare needs
- provision of multidisciplinary service delivery (e.g. specific client information is available to mental health staff from different specialties and thereby reducing unnecessary duplication)
- improved service planning and targeting
- improved understanding of the health and needs of the community
- minimising of duplicated effort and functionality
- best practice clinical pathways to provide better client care and reduce unnecessary costs
- improved management of information between (and within) each health authority
- outcome measurement.

## Incident information management

Sadly, the great majority of claims by service users against hospitals and a recurring theme in incident enquiries is that of inadequate or lack of information. The emerging premise is that optimal care and treatment of patients within a modern health environment is highly dependent on the availability, quality and accuracy of information, that is, the ability of professionals to access, use and manage information about individuals and the use of information to enhance the effectiveness of professional practice including information on whether or not actual practice makes a difference (McClelland, 2002).

The NSW Patient Safety and Clinical Quality Program was launched in 2004. The NSW Health Incident Management Policy (2006) identifies seven key issues in effective incident management:

- Identification
- Prioritisation
- Investigation
- Classification
- Analysis
- Action

The Incident Information Management System (IIMS) is a key component of the programme that incorporates both clinical and corporate incidents. All staff are responsible for reporting incidents. This includes entering the information into a reportable incident brief (RIB). The incident is given a severity assessment code (SAC) and action is implemented depending on the severity of the incident. This can range from full root cause analysis (RCA) involving independent expert clinicians for a SAC 1 incident to a local investigation for SAC 3 or SAC 4 incidents.

The analysis of information generated from IIMS can assist clinical practice by helping clinicians and managers understand how and why incidents occur and identify ways of preventing a reoccurrence. Suitable timeframes for the implementation of recommendations is documented in IIMS. Ongoing monitoring is required to ensure recommendations are addressed in a timely manner and to evaluate the success of any actions taken to achieve improvements (NSW Health, 2006).

## Standardised measures

The implementation of standardised measures is part of a broad range of activities that aim to produce greater consistency and a clearer picture of the effectiveness of mental health service provision (NSW Health, 2004). The clinicians and managers need to use the information collected to inform clinical practice and the management of resources.

As outlined by the Centre for Mental Health, NSW Health Department, the use of the information collected by the standard measures and protocols can be categorised into four levels:

(1) Individual client
(2) Service unit
(3) Area health service
(4) State

Each level will have different uses for the information collected. Individual consumer reports are useful for both clinicians and consumers to monitor change and assess the effectiveness of treatments. However, clinicians or case managers will also want information on their individual caseloads or have the ability to compare caseloads.

Most importantly all collectors and users of the information should have an interest in using the information collected responsibly and be committed to assuring the quality and integrity of the data collected. However, clinicians often voice their concern about the amount of time taken filling out forms. Consequently, they need to receive feedback about outcomes and be clear about the meaning of these reports in order to value the process and to continue to collect high-quality data. Consider the following example.

### *A clinician's story*

I sometimes worry about the relevance of all the data we collect. It seems to be time consuming and takes us away from spending time with the clients. I remember a consumer once speaking up at a conference and saying 'this information does not measure what is relevant to a consumer'. This comment has stayed with me. I often wonder where all the collected information goes and does it actually improve patient care or are we just collecting information to justify what we do? I have also had discussions with my colleagues about the possibility that the use of standardised assessment forms can deskill the workforce. A standardised assessment form may be a useful guide for beginning practitioners but it may limit the development of their own assessment skills.

It is often hard for clinicians to complete all the parts of the forms. We are audited and our completion rates are measured. Our unit used to have trouble reaching the 85% completion rate benchmark. I think this was because a lot of staff could not see the relevance. However, our completion rate increased dramatically once a 'champion' was identified. This person was trained in the field and was able to answer all questions. They were motivated and as a result motivated others to complete the forms. This has had a real flow-on effect and we have consistently exceeded the 85% benchmark in recent audits.

I now realise the information collected is useful for providing a snapshot of the client at admission and this is a helpful reference point when measuring progress and planning for discharge. I have found that the information is useful when planning care with the community team as we can measure the progress of the patient.

### Mental Health Outcome and Assessment Tools

MH-OAT is a NSW state-wide initiative to strengthen the mental health assessment skills of clinical staff. The project involves the implementation of uniform assessment protocols and outcome measurement tools across the state. The aim of the MH-OAT initiative is to ensure that:

- clients are accurately assessed and provided with appropriate interventions
- the mental health assessment skills of all direct care clinical mental health staff involved in conducting assessment is strengthened

- all area health services conduct, record and report the mental health assessments and standardised measures in a comprehensive standardised way.

Most health services have implemented a computerised clinical information system to support MH-OAT. Clinicians can enter and view client information directly from the workplace. A clinical information support officer generally co-ordinates the implementation and management of MH-OAT-related protocols throughout the area mental health service. The collection protocols are the rules that guide the standardised collection of outcome measures throughout the state. The protocols serve as guidelines so that clinicians know what measurement tool to use and when to use them.

There are several ways that such information can be used.

## Consumers

- Self-assessment information can be used to inform and empower consumers to monitor their own progress.
- Self-assessment information empowers consumers to become more actively engaged in their own treatment.

## Clinicians

- It supports individual treatment planning.
- It supports case management activities.
- It supports the monitoring of progress by tracking of consumer scores on standard measures over time.
- It supports the revision of treatment plans.
- It identifies consumers who might benefit from additional/alternative approaches.

## Clinical supervisors, team leaders, nursing unit managers

- It supports better understanding of service usage patterns and their relationship to outcomes.
- It involves clinicians in the identification of service gaps and the effectiveness of services.
- It supports clinical supervision by providing a focus for review.
- It supports human resource decisions including continuing education opportunities.
- It supports evidence-based clinical quality improvement.

### Addressing the needs of clinicians

Most clinicians are largely unaware of the information that is collected and held in health information systems (e.g. Greater Metropolitan Transition Taskforce, 2004). Certain specialties have more advanced clinical data systems, but the information is rarely sufficiently detailed to meet clinicians' needs, nor are reports available as needed. Local clinical data on patients' treatment and outcomes have been kept by clinicians, but few have had the necessary resources available to capture all the information on which to base clinical judgements and decisions. Ideally clinicians would like a system which ensures:

- all of the data considered useful for a particular clinical group is defined and captured in accordance with clinical and business processes
- data entry and management are accurate and efficiently maintained
- patients' pre-admission information is captured
- post-discharge information on patient outcomes, readmissions, etc. are captured
- there is a common data format
- all sites have the IT hardware, software and systems infrastructure required and that these are compatible with area health service and state health systems
- all clinicians receive the necessary training to access, analyse and capture information
- hospital systems are changed so that capturing patient data becomes an integral part of the episode of care from admission to discharge
- there is scope to interrogate data gathered over time, i.e. to turn 'data' into 'information'
- timely reports on clinical incidence, prevalence, distribution, treatments, outcomes, etc. are provided through shared information processes.

Most clinical groups have expressed the view that more funded data manager and data entry positions are needed to achieve these objectives. In the case of the information systems in the Greater Metropolitan Transition Taskforce (GMTT), as the programs evolved, it was clear that each clinical programme had significant information management needs. Many of the programs created a position for a data manager. Depending on the scope of the work to be undertaken, appointments varied in term from short projects to permanent positions. Enhancing the clinical information capability within each program was a significant focus.

Improvement in clinical data gathering and promptly relaying back meaningful outcome information to clinicians was slow to achieve. The GMTT found that over time, providing clinicians with support to address their information management needs not only helped to provide clinicians with vital feedback about the outcomes of their patients and about their practice, but also informed patients about their choices. Information on the efficacy of different treatment modalities, the relative risk of procedures undertaken in different hospitals, health outcomes resulting from conservative versus aggressive approaches to care were also thought to be of great interest to the public. As more clinical data became available there was scope for greater transparency in the provision and outcomes of health services.

The manager has a major role to play in these processes. They may need to advocate for additional training and additional data managers to support ongoing development and training of staff as well as working with staff to identify what their data feedback needs are. For example, what continual reporting information is needed, what one-off reports are required. Managers need to take responsibility for accessing information and reporting back to staff during team meetings. They also need to support staff in learning how to access this information so that they can generate their own reports.

As stated earlier in this chapter, managers need to be aware that there are many applications that are suitable and designed for individual client information and therapy. While the following list is not exhaustive, it does touch on some of the individual types of therapies and provides additional references that the manager can follow up as needed.

## Computers in talk-based mental health interventions

The cost to society of mental illness is substantial. Computer-assisted mental health interventions have the potential to assist in improving treatment and offering cost effective interventions. It is outside the scope of this chapter to go into great detail, but it is important that mental health managers are aware of some of the programs that are currently available.

### Electronic contact and online information sources

Email, videoconferencing, text messaging and other information sources are a natural extension of traditional face-to-face therapy. In addition, websites providing psycho-educational information have mushroomed over the past decade (see Heinlen et al. (2003) for examples).

### Computerised questionnaires for assessment, diagnosis and outcome monitoring

Computerised versions of psychological questionnaires have been validated for specific conditions against paper-based interventions. Many of these programs can be used from any internet-enabled device (PCs, laptops, personal digital assistants (PDAs), mobile phones) (e.g. see Butcher, 2004; Percevic et al., 2004).

### Computer-supported treatment

Many DVDs are available which use multimedia and cover the core self-help elements of cognitive behaviour therapy (CBT) (Wright et al., 2002). More recent studies have explored the potential of PDAs in computer-assisted therapy (Przeworski & Newman, 2004).

### Stand-alone treatments

Stand-alone computer therapy systems do not aim to fully remove human intervention, but rather they aim to minimise the required contact time (see Proudfoot et al., 2003a, b).

### Virtual reality treatments

Virtual reality exposure and systematic desensitisation are both widely used in the treatment for many anxiety and panic disorders. Virtual reality is often used in conjunction with CBT (e.g. see Weiderhold & Weiderhold, 2004).

### Therapeutic computer games

There are many therapeutic computer games aimed specifically at adolescents and young people. *Personal Investigator* is a non-biofeedback three-dimensional computer game which incorporates a solutions-focused therapy (Coyle et al., 2005).

## Future directions

Improving technology will continue to change how care is planned, delivered and documented (Peth, 2004). The growing demand for information is juxtaposed with the technological status of today's behavioural healthcare providers (Freeman, 1999). Healthcare facilities will always aspire to improve the quality of care and service while simultaneously reducing costs.

Willmer (2005) recognised that professions such as nursing must deal with increasing use of information technology in day-to-day operations. Patient admissions and discharges have been held on computer databases for decades. Education must therefore reflect this need and encourage student and newly graduated nurses to acquire advanced skills in information and communications technology. Willmer's literature review confirmed that success in this area requires sound change management, an understanding of national health service culture, and effective people leadership skills. One such initiative is the use of a Nightingale Tracker, where nursing students use a computerised clinical communication system to document client care, electronically transfer clinical information to their instructors, and maintain a systematic method for storing clinical data for further use in programme planning, prediction of healthcare trends, and other research endeavours.

French (2005) studied factors influencing research use in nursing and found that wider skills than information management are required. French's research looked at the additional skills required for clinical nurse specialists to put evidence-based research into practice, including being aware of the informal cultural work of organising, facilitating, and maintaining links across professional, team and organisational boundaries.

Slawson and Shaughnessy (2005) discussed the need to teach the applied science of information management along with, or perhaps even instead of, teaching the basic science of evidence-based medicine. All students, residents, and practising physicians need three separate skill sets to practise the best medicine: foraging 'keeping up' tools that filter information for relevance and validity; a hunting 'just in time' information tool that presents pre-filtered, quickly accessible information at the point of care; and the ability to combine the best patient-oriented evidence with patient-centred care, making decisions by placing the evidence in perspective with the needs and desires of the patient. Practising medicine requires life-long learning, so students and residents must be prepared with these information management skills.

## Conclusion

Incorporating best evidence into the real world of busy clinical practice requires the applied science of information management. Clinicians must master the techniques and skills of finding, evaluating and applying information at the point of care. This information must be valid and relevant to both themselves and their patients. Technology marches on. As mental health professionals we need to become familiar with new systems that become available at an amazing rate – systems that will make it easier to collect data and allow the services offered to patients to be better planned and more effective.

## References

Ash, J. (1997). Organizational factors that influence information technology diffusion in academic health sciences centres. *Journal of the American Medical Informatics Association*, 4, 102–111.

Blignaut, P. J., McDonald, T. & Tolmie, C. J. (2001). Predicting the learning and consultation time in a computerized primary healthcare clinic. *Computer Nursing*, 19, 130–132.

Bloomfield, B. P. & McLean, C. (2003). Beyond the walls of the asylum: information and organization in the provision of community mental health services. *Information and Organization*, 13, 53–84.

Butcher, J. (2004). Computers in clinical assessment: historical developments, present status and future challenges. *Journal of Clinical Psychology*, 60, 331–345.

Caspar, F. (2004). Technological developments and applications in clinical psychology: introduction. *Journal of Clinical Psychiatry*, 60, 75–105.

Connolly, P. (2002). Using information technology in community-based psychiatric nursing education: the SJSU/NT project. *Home Health Care Management and Practice*, 14, 344–352.

Coyle, D., Matthews, M., Sharry, J., Nisbet, A. & Doherty, G. (2005). Personal investigator: a therapeutic 3D game for adolescent psychotherapy. *International Journal of Interactive Technology and Smart Education*, 2, 73–88.

Coyle, D., Doherty, G., Matthews, M. & Sharry, J. (2007). Computers in talk-based mental health interventions. *Interacting with Computers*, 19, 545–562.

Dogac, A. & Kashyap, V. (2005). Special issue: semantic web and health care information systems interoperability. *International Journal on Semantic Web and Information Systems* (accessed 3 September 2007).

Enman, K. E. (2006). Deploying mobile devices in clinical trials: practical guidance for effectively integrating PDAs and other handheld devices into CTs [electronic version]. *Applied Clinical Trials*, 52 (accessed 3 September 2007).

French, B. (2005). Contextual factors influencing research use in nursing. *Worldviews on Evidence-Based Nursing*, 2, 172–185.

Freeman, R. K. (1999). Information management in behavioural healthcare. In: O'Donahue, W. & Fisher, J. (eds) *Management and Administration Skills for the Mental Health Professional*. San Diego, CA: Academic Press, pp. 313–339.

Greater Metropolitan Transition Taskforce (2004). *Embracing Change: Report of Greater Metropolitan Transition Taskforce*. Sydney: NSW Department of Health. Available at: www.health.nsw.gov.au/gmct/pdf/embracing_report.pdf (accessed 14 May 2008).

Heinlen, K., Welfel, E., Richmond, E. & O'Donnell, M. (2003). The nature, scope and ethics of psychologists' e-therapy websites: what consumers find when surfing the web. *Psychotherapy: Theory, Research, Practice, Training*, 40, 112–124.

Katona, C. (2002). Informatics in mental health care. *Advances in Psychiatric Treatment*, 8, 163–164.

Kaufman, M. (2007). E-prescribing offers a neat and safe alternative to pad and pen. *Formulary*, 42, 250–251.

Kotter, J. P. (1995). Leading change: why transformation efforts fail. *Harvard Business Review*, March/April, 59.

Lee, C. W. (2006). Development of web-based decision support for business process reengineering in a health-care system [electronic version]. *Academy of Information and Management Sciences Journal*, 33 (accessed 3 September 2007).

Leonardo, M., Resick, L., Kolljeski, A., Bingman, C. & Strotmeyer, S. (2004). The alternatives for wellness centers: drown in data or develop a reasonable electronic documentation system. *Home Health Care Management and Practice*, 16, 177–184.

Mahoney, M. (2002). Transforming health information management through technology. *Journal of Health Information Management*, 23, 52–61.

Marcy, T., Skelly, J., Shiffman, R. & Flynn, B (2005). Facilitating adherence to the tobacco use treatment guideline with computer-mediated decision support systems: physician and clinic office manager perspectives. *Preventive Medicine: An International Journal Devoted to Practice and Theory*, 41, 479–487.

May, C., Gask, L., Atkinson, T., Ellis, N., Mair, F. & Esmail, A. (2001). Resisting and promoting new technologies in clinical practice: the case of telepsychiatry. *Social Science and Medicine*, 52, 1889–1901.

McClelland, R. (2002). Information and communication technology in mental heath – opportunity or threat. *Psychiatric Bulletin*, 26, 362–363.

Meredith, R., Bair, S & Ford, G. (2000). Information management for clinical decision making. In: Stricker, G., Warwick, T. & Shueman, S. (eds) *Handbook of Quality Management in Behavioural Health*. Dordrecht, Netherlands: Kluwer Academic Publishers, pp. 53–93.

Nash, D. B. & Goldfarb, N. I. (2006). *The Quality Solution: The Stakeholder's Guide to Improving Health Care*. Boston, MA: Jones and Bartlett Publishers, pp. xvi, 115–131, 321.

NSW Health (2004). Centre for Mental Health Use of MH-OAT Data. Available at: www.health.nsw.gov.au/policy/cmh/partner.html (accessed 14 May 2008).

NSW Health (2006) Incident Management Policy. Available at: www.health.nsw.gov.au/quality/incidentmgt/onlineguide/analysis.html (accessed 14 May 2008).

Osborne, S. (2006). How IT is shaping up. *Nursing Standard*, 21, 62–64.

Pare, G. & Elam, J. J. (1998). Introducing information technology in the clinical setting. Lessons learned in a trauma centre. *International Journal of Technological Assessment in Health Care Spring*, 14, 331–343.

Parish, C. (2006). Edging towards a brave new IT world: the NHS is due to have a huge centralised computer system, but will it live up to expectations? *Nursing Standard*, 20, 15–17.

Percevic, R., Lambert, M. & Kordy, H. (2004). Computer supported monitoring of patient treatment responses. *Journal of Clinical Psychology*, 60, 285–299.

Peth, T. (2004). The future information technology equation. *Home Health Care Management and Practice*, 16, 302–303.

Phillips, J. (2005). Knowledge is power: using information management and leadership interventions to improve services to patients, clients and users. *Journal of Nursing Management*, 13, 524–536.

Proudfoot, J., Goldberg, D., Mann, A., Everitt, B., Marks, I. & Gray, J. (2003a). Computerised, interactive, multimedia cognitive behavioural therapy reduces anxiety and depression in general practice: a randomised controlled trial. *Psychological Medicine*, 33, 217–227.

Proudfoot, J., Swain, S., Widmer, S., Watkins, E., Goldberg, D. & Marks, I. (2003b). The development and beta-testing of a computer-therapy programme for anxiety and depression: hurdles and preliminary outcomes. *Computers in Human Behaviour*, 19, 277–289.

Przeworski, A. & Newman, M. (2004). Palmtop computer-assisted group therapy for social phobia. *Journal of Clinical Psychology*, 60, 178–188.

Roberts, L. & Dwyer, A. (2004). *Concise Guide to Ethics in Mental Health Care.* Arlington, VA: American Psychiatric Publishing.

Simpson, R. (2003). Got technology? How IT can – and can't – make a difference in nursing practice. *Policy, Politics and Nursing Practice*, 4, 114–119.

Sittig, D. F. (2002). The importance of leadership in the clinical information system implementation process. *Journal of the American Medical Informatics Association*, 19, 1–2.

Slawson, D. & Shaughnessy, A. (2005). Teaching evidenced-based medicine: should we be teaching information management instead? *Journal of the Association of American Medical Colleges*, 8, 685–689.

Souther, E. (2001) Implementation of the electronic medical record: the team approach. *Computer Nursing*, 19, 47–55.

Stuttle, B. (2006). Get connected: National Health Service to put information technology in their agenda. *Nursing Management*, 13, 81.

Tachakra, S., Tachakra, F., Konstantinos, B., Song, Y., Solomon, H. & Corrigan, R. (2006). Using handheld pocket computers in a wireless telemedicine system. *Emergency Nurse*, 14, 20–24.

Toofany, S. (2006). Nursing and information technology. *Nursing Management*, 13, 718–720.

Venkatesh, V. & Davis, F. D. (2000). A theoretical extension of the technology acceptance model: four longitudinal field studies. *Management Science*, 46, 186–204.

Weiderhold, B. & Weiderhold, M. (2004). *Virtual Reality Therapy for Anxiety Disorders: Advances in Education and Treatment.* Washington: APA Books.

Willmer, M. (2005). Promoting practical clinical management learning: the current situation about information and communications technology capability development in student nurses. *Journal of Nursing Management*, 13, 467–476.

Wright, J., Wright, A., Salmon, P., Beck, A., Kuyendall, J. & Goldsmith, J. (2002). Development and initial testing of a multimedia program for computer-assisted cognitive therapy. *Journal of Psychotherapy*, 56, 76–86.

# Chapter 4
# Budget management

*Susan Brandis*

## Chapter overview

Resources are an essential requirement of any service or initiative. This encompasses both financial assets and human assets. A budget is a tool to assist managers in managing resources and achieve the mission and goals of the service. It comprises an estimate of intended expenditure and should balance with the actual amount of resources available.

A budget is defined as

'a systematic means of allocating financial, physical and human resources to monitor progress towards organisational objectives, help control spending and predict cash flow'

The Australian National Audit Office (2000, p. 31)

Budgets do not stand alone and should be closely linked with organisational strategic planning and governance structures. This chapter aims to provide an introduction to the skill of budget management, in the context of managing a mental health service or team.

## Budget management context

### Legislation and financial management standards

Numerous pieces of legislation, standards and accounting practices apply to the management of finances. In Australia, as in many countries, these exist at both a state or local level and at a national or Commonwealth level. The detail of legislation may vary across jurisdictions, but generally include acts to define behaviour in relation to financial administration and audit (Queensland: Financial Administration and Audit Act 1977; Australian Financial Management and Accountability Act 1997), tender and procurement standards (Australian Government Procurement Policy Framework, 2005), and taxation acts. Professional accounting standards and practices ensure that specific financial data collection, analysis and reporting are consistent and comply with public expectations of accountability and transparency. While a detailed understanding of these is not required at the service level, awareness off the existence of these things is appropriate. For example, changes in fringe benefit taxes, superannuation plans and approaches to depreciation need to be considered when the annual budget is being developed. A properly trained and qualified financial accountant can advise on the interpretation and application of these things.

## Funding models

From an international perspective the prevalence rates for the majority of psychiatric disorders are fairly consistent, however, different health systems identify different levels of need for mental health services, allocate different levels of funding and choose different ways to deliver them (McDaid et al., 2005).

Funds for health services come from a variety of sources. In Australia, the main sources of funding for mental health are from the Commonwealth and from the state governments. Insurance providers are a significant player in the private sector. Mental health services are provided through inpatient, hospital-based and community-based services, across all age groups, and a range of funding sources may exist in a manager's area of responsibility. The separation of mental health funding from physical health funding in some countries also poses challenges as to the optimal service delivery model (Druss & Newcomer, 2007).

Funding models for mental health services may include the following:

- Appropriation funds allocate money from treasury to a specific department for a set range of services on an annual recurrent nature. This includes core services such as inpatient beds, outpatient clinics and services (for example). Appropriation funding follows an annual cycle and is driven by the federal and state or area treasury budget process. Behind this are the negotiations which occur in Australia (for example) at a Commonwealth and state level, specifically around the Australian Health Care Agreement 2003–2008, and the National Mental Health Plan 2003–2008 (Australian Health Ministers, 2003), and regulatory requirements (Australian Health Care (Appropriation) Act 1998; Appropriation Act (No. 1) 2005–2006).
- Special grants and initiatives allocate money for a specific range of initiatives to be delivered within a defined time. Special initiatives for rural and remote services are an example of this and the national policy agenda will have a direct bearing on articulating priorities.
- Capital grants include funds targeted at a specific item such as a building, facilities or equipment. These may be by annual appropriation, such as depreciation, or one-off allocations such as funding for a new information management system.

While it may sound elementary, the budget manager does need to understand the nature of the funding to be managed as specific reporting and allocation strategies may be required. An activity-based model may require dollars to be matched with episodes of care and direct client costs such as medications. A specific programme initiative can request information to be collected on a number of clients from a particular demographic, or moneys spent on specific interventions (e.g. counselling services or rehabilitation programmes). Funds for a particular programme can be time limited, with a requirement that unspent funds are returned. In other instances these can be rolled over to the next financial year, or reallocated internally depending on service demand. The service delivery framework, particularly one that has a goal of service integration, might receive financial support from a variety of sources. In these situations, the funding bodies frequently require reporting on their component only. Implicit in this is an accurate understanding of who funds what, their outcome intentions and reporting requirements. A budget analysis is an integral part of any programme evaluation.

### Responsibilities and accountabilities

As a budget manager the responsibilities are large, yet often dismissed. Unless one is running their own business, the funds managed will belong to someone else. This may be the government, the insurance provider or, ultimately, the tax payer. Most organisations will have a defined list of financial and human resource management delegations which state the amount of expenditure, or type of employment agreement that a position can approve. This is one way that agencies manage their financial risk. The authority to approve tenders or purchase external services such as consultants may be restricted to specific positions. So while a manager of a unit might have the money in the budget, he or she may not have the delegated responsibility to purchase particular items.

It is suggested that managers should be clear about what their responsibilities and accountabilities are, including documented delegations. An informed discussion with the direct supervisor and/or financial controller can help clarify and manage expectations, and limit personal risk.

### Ethics

Being a budget manager is not only about managing the budget but also about managing a service and meeting client needs. A particular challenge is the ethical dilemma of managing costs of services in an environment of high demand. In addition to this, people with mental health disorders are disproportionately represented in lower socio-economic groups, are highly vulnerable, and may require care over a longer period time (Amaddeo & Jones, 2007).

The Australian federal government's Charter of Budget Honesty Act 1998 states that 'it is the right of the Australian people to be fully informed about the current state of the Government's finances and the future outlook'. This legislation is one of the drivers and underpinning elements for transparency and accountability in government financial management in Australia and there are similar pieces of legislation in other democratic countries.

### Budget definitions

The two models of accounting are cash accounting and accrual accounting. Accrual accounting is more commonly used in health services (Zelman et al., 1998).

## Cash accounting

Cash accounting is a system of accounting in which revenues are recorded when actually received and outlays are recorded when payment is made.

## Accrual accounting

In accrual accounting revenue and expenses incurred in the same period are matched. The manager places an order for a new photocopier, which takes a month to arrive, and it takes another month for the finance department to process the payment. The cost or liability for the photocopier is recorded on the day the order is placed. Accrual accounting enables the manager to get a day-to-day picture of the current budget status and to plan expenditure accordingly.

## Revenue or allocation

The revenue or allocation is the portion of money assigned to a particular service or unit. This is the bottom line and specifies the resources available to operate a service.

## Expenditure or costs

Expenditure is simply the cost of providing a service, and changes in relation to activity. To understand costs, these can be classified according to the impact they have on output. Costs can be described as fixed, variable, semi-fixed and semi-variable (Cleverley, 1992).

### *Fixed costs*

The costs that do not change for the budget period are called fixed costs. These are easier to predict and are the fundamental items required to run a service. Salaries and wages for permanent staff are fixed costs. The annual salary of the employee is known. Other examples include leasing costs, rent, accommodation expenses, journal subscriptions and software licensing. Fixed costs are just that – 'fixed' – so irrespective of the number of clients who are seen in a month, the cost of the salary, rent, licence or subscription is set. Fixed costs may also be recurrent costs in that they occur on a regular basis, year to year.

### *Variable costs*

Variable costs include things that fluctuate depending on external factors. In a health service setting, this is most commonly influenced by service demand. Some months have high activity, others have less. For example, a service providing a home visiting service will have variable costs that include transport and petrol costs, medications, disposables and clinical supplies. The amount spent on these things will vary with the number of clients accessing the service, the complexity of their individual cases and other factors difficult to contain. Where possible, variable costs are predicted on historical data, and a cost modelling approach is used. In the absence of this they can be projected using a scenario-type approach. They are usually constant and change in a proportional way. For example, if the number of injections doubles, the cost of syringes will double as well.

### Semi-fixed costs

Some costs will change with activity, but their increase or decrease is not proportional. Salaries are an example. An additional full-time staff member, to increase staff from four people to five full-time equivalents, does not necessarily result in a proportional increase in activity of 20%. It may be that a percentage of a position is required, but due to workforce issues a full-time position is a more favourable option in terms of recruitment and retention of staff.

### Semi-variable costs

In the same way that fixed costs may fluctuate, variable costs may also include both fixed and variable components. Electricity and water are good examples of this. The manager knows there will be a core cost for basic utilities, but there is also a direct relationship to the volume of activity in the unit and the utilisation of these.

### Other cost concepts

Accounting is a complex process and there are a myriad of terms that are used. Some additional cost terms include avoidable costs, sunk costs, incremental costs and opportunity costs. Avoidable costs are associated with a decision-making process which provides the manager with the opportunity to 'avoid' the budget impact. There may be an element of risk, in that cost avoidance now may result in an increased cost at a later point in time. An example of this is administrative staffing. A receptionist may add to the efficiencies of the service but not directly to client outcomes. One could increase the number of administrative hours provided to a team, and in doing so, release clinical staff for clinical duties, or current staffing levels could be maintained. The cost is avoidable, but there are some sound reasons why the manager might choose to do this. Sunk costs are unaffected by the decision. Irrespective of whether the service has a receptionist or not, a communication system will be required to manage client enquiries. The unit will still require phones and a reception area for client attendances.

Incremental costs are significant in that they are dependent on a management decision. In some cases the management decision may be made in another unit and the incremental costs reflected elsewhere. From a macro perspective decisions to reduce hospital length of stay may have reduced costs in inpatient units, but there has been an incremental cost increase in other services such as general practice and community health services (Rothbard et al., 1998; Schreter, 2004). A decision in one area to commence a new outpatient treatment programme (e.g. for people with depression) may increase costs for the pharmacy as a different drug regimen is required. The provision of an extended-hours service will not only increase salary and wages but also lead to additional costs such as travel allowance, meal allowance and other industrial entitlements.

The final area of costs to think about are those related to the value missed by using a resource in one particular area, instead of an alternative. This is called opportunity cost. In the situation of multiple service demands this is a frequent dilemma. Imagine the manager has been given an increase of Aus$25 000 in the budget. How will they allocate this? In the reception example, there are two pressing needs:

- The work volume for the clinical staff is high and a waiting list has developed. The staff argue that all clients should be assessed within a 24-hour period of referral and that a particular skill set is missing from the team which would assist in a more comprehensive and efficient assessment process. There is a strong argument for funding some additional clinical sessions with the purpose of recruiting a specific skill set that would assist with the backlog and complement the current team structure. This would also assist in meeting specific service standards.
- An internal review of administrative processes has identified a high number of missed telephone calls, disorganised office systems and frequent loss and misplacement of files and referral letters. The second pressing need is to employ a receptionist/administrative officer. This alternative would provide a person to oversee the office functions so as to support the clinicians to focus on the clinical work. Improving internal processes would assist in the triage process and allow the clinicians to better organise their workloads.

There are benefits and disadvantages of each suggestion, but only enough money to do one of these two things. The opportunity cost is the effect of not investing in the second (the administrative officer) and choosing to employ an additional clinician. Tied in with both of these options are considerations in relation to other cost impacts of the decision. In any situation of choice there will be non-budget impacts as well. Of particular note are legislative requirements and industrial considerations. The receptionist may be argued from a workplace health and safety and efficiency perspective. The clinician may be supported from an industrial workforce perspective.

## Depreciation

Depreciation is a fixed cost which warrants particular attention as it is easily overlooked. All goods owned will depreciate or lose value over time. The term 'depreciation' refers to an estimated or expected view of the decline in value of a tangible asset over a period of time (Zelman et al., 1998). This is particularly relevant where a service may require a large investment in equipment. It is acceptable financial practice to include depreciation in a budget. This may be done at the organisational level, or at the service budget level. The reason this is important is to ensure that the cost of the ageing asset is recorded to enable replacement. This wear and tear on equipment is considered a cost of doing business. For example, the community mental health service owns a van for assisting clients to attend group therapy sessions. In a depreciation model a percentage of the life of the vehicle will be recorded, and the vehicle will have an estimated book life. So the depreciation of the vehicle may be recorded as 20% a year over a five-year period. There are some quite complex mathematical formulas for calculating depreciation. While it is not necessary for the manager to grasp the mathematical detail, an appreciation of the assets within one's area of responsibility and the budget impact of these is useful.

## Budget lifecycle and business planning

To this point, what is apparent is that budgets are unpredictable and that decisions are rarely straightforward. What is predictable is that the budget process of all organisations runs in a 12-month cycle. In an ideal world the budget process will be aligned with the strategic planning process. A strategic plan is developed with a vision for the service. This plan is underpinned by a series of business plans or operational plans at a unit level, and a budget allocated accordingly. In a constrained budget environment, the service vision needs to be contained by the budget reality.

For public sector managers, budget cycles link closely with broader policy debate. An understanding of the budget timeframes and processes, and a degree of business acumen will assist in engaging in the wider debate about government financial priorities and policy implications (Wanna et al., 2000). In this context a manager can take a more strategic and entrepreneurial approach to the management of a specific service. In order to make a submission for additional funding, it is critical to know what the timeframes are, and what the government sees as priorities for funding. A budget submission can have a role to inform the policy agenda (Di Francesco, 1998) and greater input by services into policy development may yield cost-effective gains and assist with prioritisation at a government level (Vos et al., 2005).

Knowing timeframes and government agendas may reveal a growing political interest in a particular subset of clients. Armed with this knowledge, the manager can then be proactive in informing public policy, and in advocating for additional funding. Of importance is the recognition that while the government routinely delivers a budget at a particular time of year, the planning and negotiations and policy formulation will have been in action for several months, and sometimes years prior to any public budget release.

## Steps in the budget process

This section describes the generic stages in budget development, formulated from numerous examples published by a range of public agencies.

### 1. Review the operational context

This stage includes a scan of the environment, identification of themes, trends and policy directions. For example it may be apparent that the government is increasing emphasis on the health and well-being of homeless people. What is also apparent is the trend to treating people in a community setting, and providing culturally appropriate service options. Such a climate may dictate that an initiative for homeless people be viewed more favourably than an expansion of inpatient beds. Demographic data and local knowledge can also be a source of information to assist planning. Shortages of a particular trained specialty may determine the scope of services that are viable, and lead to the development of innovative models of service delivery. The expansion of the multidisciplinary team and generic health worker roles is evidence of this.

### 2. Evaluate prior performance

There has been increasing interest in the area of programme or service evaluation in recent years with varying degrees of success in achieving the goal of cost savings (Di Francesco, 1998). In health, this has been largely driven by concerns in relation to the safety and quality of healthcare, and the significant systems failures where quality care has been compromised by tight fiscal constraint, accompanied by increasing public scrutiny. Approaches to health service evaluation are in some cases a part of the national health agenda resulting in additional demands at a local level. The concepts of scorecards, league tables and quality of life indicators can also guide performance evaluation, and there is a growing body of research into the effective use of measurement indicators to support budget considerations (Kelley et al., 2005; Schmidt et al., 2006). Contemporary approaches to budget review have moved beyond mere bean counting, and frequently include an assessment of performance in a number of areas including consumer satisfaction, workplace performance and innovation, as well as financial success at a service level (Waldersee, 1999; Coop, 2006).

### 3. Set budget parameters

This stage will include a list of givens. There may be very little flexibility regarding number of full-time staff employed, fixed costs and existing commitments such as rents and leases. Many agencies also have caveats on what can be included in a service budget. For example, expenses for information management technology, software licences and internet access may be absorbed at an agency level, or alternatively be allocated to cost centres on a user pays system. A definitive list of what is in the budget and what is not is an important part of the process.

## 4. Prepare the budget action plan

The budget plan for the coming period is often based on the history of the previous period and the learnings from a thorough evaluation of costs and income. It characteristically provides a monthly allocation of costs or resources required. Some costs are a one-off fee, which is charged on an annual basis. Journal subscriptions are an example of this. While the cost is a monthly fee, the actual account is payable annually. Salaries and wages, while being apportioned to the period they have accrued, still vary from month to month. Fluctuations may be the result of staff taking annual leave around peak holiday periods, and the effect of the different time periods of the calendar month. Most financial spreadsheets will factor these variations into the formula. Seasonal variations can also affect service demand as some diagnostic categories are more prevalent at particular times of the year. Accurate information systems can aid in making as good as is possible estimates of expenditure for the budget year.

## 5. Finalise annual planning and implementation/action plans

This stage will require the definition of key performance indicators and identification of risks (Likierman, 1993). Outputs or outcomes expected will also be documented. The literature around outputs and outcomes is large and growing and includes a range of approaches: from case-based payment systems to a more quality-of-life indicator-type approach. In summary, the key components of an action plan are:

- identification or name of the goal
- timeframe for achievement
- the measures or indicators of performance
- resources required
- risks or barriers to goal achievement
- onus of responsibility.

Often this information will be developed at a global or organisational level, with an under-layer of operational or business plans at a service delivery level. Frequently these are presented in table form and may form part of an annual report for a board/community and are open to public scrutiny.

The timing of these five steps may fluctuate according to the nature of the service and the funding model employed.

## Monitoring variance

Budgeting is the phase of accounting that involves preparing a plan or forecast of future operations. One of the primary functions of a budget is to provide a reference point for comparison and to inform management of the activities necessary to achieve its strategic mission.

A budget is a plan, and variance is the ongoing measurement of actual expenditure and activities measured against this plan. Budgets formalise agency outcomes, goals and objectives and monitoring variance is significant as it can guide management decisions. A positive variance means that there are areas of underexpenditure (savings); a negative variance indicates overspending (deficit). The goal is to have the variance balance each other out by the end of the cycle. Vacant positions are one way in which a business unit might have a positive variance show in an end-of-month report. The core budget often is fixed, and the only areas that can be actively managed are where there is a variance. Using an approach of quality review can assist in identifying areas for future improvement. Any budget situation must be sustainable. Targeted campaigns to raise awareness about mental health conditions may result in longer-term increase in demands on mental health services and require effective funding partnerships to be sustained (Hickie, 2004).

## Developing a budget

Individual agencies will have a range of templates and approaches to documenting a budget. The budget development process is often co-ordinated by a business manger or financial controller. The following list provides a basic breakdown of components that should be included:

(1) *Labour costs* include salary and wages, and 'on costs' such as superannuation contributions, annual leave and entitlements loading. A percentage of the salary is used to calculate on costs. Training and development expenses can also be included here.

(2) *Non-labour costs* are items such as leases rent, equipment, consumables/materials transport and travel cost. Licences may be included here as well as clinical supplies such as pharmaceuticals.

(3) *Operational expenses* can be listed to account for items such as stationery, electricity and information technologies.

(4) *Establishment costs* are those identified in the set-up of a new service. These are one-off costs and can include equipment, capital works, telecommunications, furniture, signage, specific training required to provide a service, books or tests. These are vital considerations in a budget proposal for a new or enhanced service.

A basic sample budget for a new service proposal is presented in Table 4.1. The second year budget would omit set-up costs and include depreciation of capital assets.

An example of a monthly budget statement is also provided for the project (Table 4.2). The table shows how the project is tracking financially and identifies budget variance or overspending and underspending. What can be seen is that the project is under budget for the first month. A larger percentage of the capital costs have been apportioned to the first month to cover set-up costs.

**Table 4.1** Basic sample of a new service proposal.

| Labour costs | Comment | Cost (Aus$) | Total (Aus$) |
|---|---|---|---|
| Salaries and wages | 1 FTE level 2 worker | 40 000 | |
| On costs | 25% | 10 000 | |
| Professional development | Two training courses | 1000 | |
| **Total labour** | | | **51 000** |
| Non-labour costs | | | |
| Car lease | For home visits | 5000 | |
| Operating costs | Rent, security, utilities | 4000 | |
| Administrative costs | Stationery, postage | 2000 | |
| Clinical supplies | | 5000 | |
| **Total non-labour** | | | **16 000** |
| Capital set-up | | | |
| Computer and licences | | 2000 | |
| Furniture | Workstation, chairs, files | 3000 | |
| Tests and equipment | | 2000 | |
| **Total establishment costs** | | | **7000** |
| **Total budget** | | | **74 000** |

**Table 4.2** An example of a monthly budget statement.

| Budget summary Month 1 | Month to date | Year to date | Full year |
|---|---|---|---|
| **Budget** | **9010** | **9010** | **74 000** |
| Labour | 4170 | 4170 | 51 000 |
| Non-labour | 1340 | 1340 | 16 000 |
| Capital | 3500 | 3500 | 7000 |
| **Expenditure** | **4470** | **4470** | **4470** |
| Labour | 2170 | 2170 | 2170 |
| Non-labour | 300 | 300 | 300 |
| Capital | 2000 | 2000 | 2000 |
| **Variance (deficit/surplus)** | **+4540** | **+4540** | **+4540** |

# Controllability and risk management

There is much theory, legislation and standard practice surrounding the management of a budget, which leads to the question, 'What then is "controllable" by the manager?'. Controlling activities include meetings, regular budget reports and analysis and local budget policy. These are internal controls with an intention to manage risks. In a mental health service, types of risks to the budget include unfunded activity, unplanned expenditure, waste and corruption.

## Unfunded activity

There are many reasons for unfunded activity, but two common examples are used here to enhance understanding. First, for services operating in geographical areas of high population growth or where there is a changing demographic profile, a situation of unfunded activity can easily develop. Given that the current budget is based on retrospective information, any change in demographics can result in pressures in human services. While a budget may be indexed to account for growth or inflation, this may be insufficient to match the real increase in costs. The ageing of the population or sudden unemployment in a town are examples of social triggers which can (and do) impact on the demand for health services.

The second category of unfunded activity is the result of service delineation models and the inability to fully effect reimbursement for a service provided by a unit that another agency or unit is funded to deliver. This can be a complex situation, and ethically challenging. A case to demonstrate this is funding for chronic diseases such as diabetes, which is often directed to mainstream physical health services. Depending on the funding model employed, it may be difficult for a mental health service to seek reimbursement for the provision of care to a diabetic client with a mental health disorder. Opportunistic health intervention may require that advice on insulin (for example) is provided in an integrated approach with information about other drug therapies. Services that have caseloads with a high percentage of clients with dual diagnosis are often disadvantaged with programme-funded payment systems.

## Unplanned expenditure

In the case of the office used previously, imagine a situation where the premises are robbed, mobile phones and laptop computers stolen and the photocopier vandalised so that it is rendered useless. In such a situation, replacement is an immediate and not negotiable action for the service to maintain its operations. Many events are unplanned. These can include loss of human resources due to sudden illness or resignation, catastrophic events such as cyclones and floods, and from a global perspective changes in the value of the country's currency (which affects drug and medical equipment costs) and stock market values (such as oil). All of these can result in increased costs which were unplanned and leave a hole in a well-managed budget. It is suggested that these events are formalised with an incident report or documentation trail that aligns the increased expenditure with the specific event.

## Waste and corruption

Waste is the inefficient and ineffective use of resources. In a climate of cost control, managing waste is an essential component of managing a budget. This may include considerations of the efficient use of human resources (e.g. nursing hours per patient which can be benchmarked) as well as non-human resources (e.g. utilisation of rooms and equipment). Effectiveness is less concerned with throughput and focuses on the outputs achieved. Both concepts are considered in a cost–benefits approach to service review (Haby et al., 2004). Some areas of waste are quantifiable, as in the nursing hour's example, while others may be more difficult to measure. Further examples include waste of stationery stores, inefficient use of lighting and air-conditioning, and damage or loss of valuable plant and equipment.

Corruption is defined as 'the abuse of public office for private gain' (World Bank, 1997). It may involve fraud, theft, misuse of position or authority or other acts that are unacceptable to an organisation and which may cause loss to the organisation, its clients or the general community. The behaviour need not necessarily be criminal and may also include such elements as breaches of trust and confidentiality.

Fraud is a type of corruption and is a deliberate, intentional and premeditated dishonest act or omission for the purpose of deceiving to gain advantage from a position of trust or authority. It includes acts such as theft, making false statements or representations, evasion, manipulation of information, criminal deception and abuse of property or time (Standards Australia, 2003 – Australian Standard AS 8001 – 2003 'Fraud and Corruption Control').

Internal controls will prevent fraud and corruption. The responsibility of the budget manager is to maintain cost-effective internal control structures within their organisational responsibility. Some examples of managerial strategies at an operational level to protect against waste, corruption and fraud are presented below.

- Understand and regularly monitor the budget so as to identify variance and respond to anomalies. Regular reports of payroll, incident reports and service activity may assist in identifying problem areas and developing a targeted budget management plan.
- Ensure quality review and incident reporting systems are in place to identify areas for improvement and manage risk. This may include formal events such as audits, inspections and accreditation processes, as well as informal local systems such as staff suggestion boxes, client feedback surveys and consumer input.
- Implement local controls and policies for managing smaller expenditures of things such as petty cash, travel bookings, and taxi vouchers.

- Have time sheet procedures in place, and processes to prevent time sheet fraud, sick leave abuse and loss of productivity.
- Maintain asset management registers and security systems to prevent theft and loss.
- Maintain a culture of transparency, honesty and integrity.
- Articulate and document a code of conduct and service values.
- Ensure peer review and articulation of professional standards of practice is in effect.
- Implement performance management and review systems to support and reinforce the above.

While this list is not exhaustive, it aims to provide some guidance in strategies to prevent waste, fraud and corruption.

## Value for money

Having covered a myriad of terms in relation to budgets, the final concept to consider is value for money. Value for money is often determined by the quality of the product or service. Implicit in this is maximising efficiencies and minimising waste. Central to this is the concept that if you cannot decrease the cost of a service, then to increase value you must increase quality. Budgets therefore do not stand alone but are inextricably entwined with all other functions of the management role. Being a good budget manager is much more than counting the beans, including ensuring leadership and governance systems are in place to achieve the clinical and human goals of the service (Druss, 2006). The introduction of new evidence-based approaches may require a realignment of the budget for the service to comply with new standards. There are many clinical practices currently in place which are not cost effective, and many that are evidence-based that are not standard practice (Hermann et al., 2006) and the manager needs the courage to direct the budget to facilitate change.

Workforce management is not only about rostering and skill mix, but requires careful consideration of affordability. An effective budget manager will have a grasp of these issues and be in an informed position to alert the organisation of potential challenges to the integrity of the budget, and balance this against the value to the client.

## Conclusion

Budgets are one component of the accounting process but they are an important tool for managing a service. Consideration of a budget requires a big picture view of the world and an understanding of internal drivers and costs within a service. The area of finance is highly legislated and regulated and the competent manager will have an appreciation of the risks and opportunities in budget management, with the ultimate goal of providing effective and efficient health services.

# References

Amaddeo, F. & Jones, J. (2007). What is the impact of socio-economic inequalities on the use of mental health services? *Epidemiologiae Psichiatria Sociale*, 16, 16–19.

Appropriation Act (No. 1), Act – C2005A00072 (2005–2006). Canberra: Commonwealth of Australia.

Australian Charter of Budget Honesty Act (1998). Canberra: Commonwealth of Australia.

Australian Government Department of Finance and Administration (2005). *Australian Government Procurement Policy Framework*. Canberra: Commonwealth of Australia.

Australian Health Care Agreement (2003–2008). Canberra: Commonwealth of Australia.

Australian Health Ministers (2003). *Mental Health Plan* (2003–2008). Canberra: Commonwealth of Australia.

Australian National Audit Office (2000). *Audit Report No. 25*, 2000–2001, Auditor General. Canberra: Commonwealth of Australia.

Cleverley, W. (1992) *Essentials of Health Care Finance*. Frederick, Maryland: Aspen.

Coop, C. F. (2006). Balancing the balanced scorecard for a New Zealand mental health service. *Australian Health Review*, 30, 174–180.

Di Francesco, M. (1998). The measure of policy? Evaluating the evaluation strategy as an instrument of budgetary control. *Australian Journal of Public Administration*, 57, 33–48.

Druss, B. G. (2006). Rising mental health costs: what are we getting for our money? *Health Affairs*, 25, 614–622.

Druss, B. G. & Newcomer, J. W. (2007). Challenges and solutions to integrating mental and physical health care. *Journal of Clinical Psychiatry*, 68, e09.

Financial Administration and Audit Act (1977). Brisbane: Queensland Government.

Financial Management and Accountability Act (1997). Canberra: Commonwealth of Australia.

Haby, M., Carter, R., Mihalopoulos, C., Magnus, A., Sanderson, K., Andrews, G. & Vos, T. (2004). Assessing cost-effectiveness – mental health: introduction to the study and methods. *Australian and New Zealand Journal of Psychiatry*, 38, 569–578.

Health Care (Appropriation) Act (1998). Canberra: Commonwealth of Australia.

Hermann, R. C., Chan, J. A., Zazzali, J. L. & Lerner, D. (2006). Aligning measurement-based quality improvement with implementation of evidence-based practices. *Administration and Policy in Mental Health and Mental Health Services Research*, 33, 636–645.

Hickie, I. (2004). Can we reduce the burden of depression? The Australian experience with Beyondblue: the national depression initiative. *Australia's Psychiatry*, 12, 38–46.

Kelley, E., McNeill, D., Moy, E., Stryer, D., Burgdorf, J. & Clancy, C. M. (2005). Balancing the nation's health care scorecard: The National Healthcare Quality and Disparities Reports. *Joint Commission Journal on Quality and Patient Safety*, 31, 622–630.

Likierman, A. (1993). Performance indicators: 20 early lessons from managerial use. *Public Money and Management*, Oct–Dec, 15–22.

McDaid, D., Knapp, M. & Curran, C. (2005). *Policy Brief – Mental Health III, Funding Mental Health in Europe*. Geneva: World Health Organization, 2005, on behalf of the European Observatory on Health Systems and Policies.

Rothbard, A. B., Schinnar, A. P., Hadley, T. P., Foley, K. A. & Kuno, E. (1998). Cost comparison of state hospital and community-based care for seriously mentally ill adults. *American Journal of Psychiatry*, 155, 523–529.

Schmidt, S., Bateman, I., Breinlinger-O'Reilly, J. & Smith, P. (2006). A management approach that drives actions strategically: Balanced scorecard in a mental health trust case study. *International Journal of Health Care Quality Assurance Incorporating Leadership in Health Services*, 19, 119–135.

Schreter, R. (2004). Economic grand rounds: making do with less: the latest challenge for psychiatry. *Psychiatric Services*, 55, 761–763.

Standards Australia (2003). *Australian Standard AS* 8001–2003 *Fraud and Corruption Control*. Canberra: Commonwealth of Australia.

Vos, T., Haby, M., Magnus, A., Mihalopoulos, C., Andrews, G. & Carter, R. (2005). Assessing cost-effectiveness in mental health: helping policy-makers prioritize and plan health services. *Australian and New Zealand Journal of Psychiatry*, 39, 701–712.

Waldersee, R. (1999). The art of service v the science of measurement: Measuring and managing service delivery. *Australian Journal of Public Administration*, 58, 38–42.

Wanna, J., Kelly, J. & Forster, J. (2000). *Managing Public Expenditure in Australia*. St. Leonards, Australia: Allen & Unwin, pp. 14–19, 41–47.

World Bank (1997). *World Development Report: The State in a Changing World*. New York: Oxford University Press.

Zelman, E., Mc Cue, M. & Millikan, A. (1998). *Financial Management of Health Care Organisations: An Introduction to Fundamental Tools, Concepts and Applications*. Boston, Massachusetts: Blackwell.

# Chapter 5
# Managing critical incidents in clinical management in mental health services

*Kevin Gournay*

## Chapter overview

This chapter will examine the main serious critical incidents that occur in mental health services and describe approaches to prevention of and using such incidents to learn lessons. The main focus will be on three topics:

- Suicide and self-harm
- Violence
- Homicide

The chapter will refer to several websites which provide detailed information concerning each of these main topics. In addition, the chapter will cover a range of related issues to assist managers in dealing with the wide array of challenges that face them.

## Critical incidents

Managers in mental health services, whether they are based in the community or located in any one of a variety of inpatient care settings, need to be prepared to face the challenge of critical incidents, which, even in the best of services, will occur from time to time. This chapter will not consider critical incidents such as fire or accidents at work, or trips and falls, but rather focus on the main serious critical incidents that occur commonly in the context of direct patient care. That is not to say that other issues, such as worker health and safety and ensuring a safe environment fit for purpose, are not important. However, such issues lie outside of the scope of this book.

What are the common serious critical incidents that occur in patient care?

There are three general areas that should concern mental health services managers, and there is, of course, some overlap between these areas. However, to do justice to the topic, it is best to consider categories which are, in some senses, arbitrary. These categories are:

- Suicide and self-harm
- Violence
- Homicide

It is also important to be clear at this point that this chapter covers clinical critical incidents across the whole range of mental health problems, from people with the very common mental disorders who are managed in primary care to patients with the most serious and enduring problems, who may be cared for in conditions of high security.

# Suicide and self-harm

This is obviously a very broad category and there is certainly no implication, in considering these two topics together, that all cases of self-harm should be treated as failed suicide. It is, of course, clear that in terms of intent, to kill oneself or otherwise, self-harm is a very heterogeneous problem. Nevertheless, the two issues are best considered together because there is a commonality of care approaches, risk assessment and management, and prevention in these two topics.

## Suicide

Suicide is the ultimate tragedy that can occur in mental health services. The latest Australian Bureau of Statistics publication covers suicides in Australia registered in the years 1993 to 2003. To put the issue in context, there was a total of 2213 deaths from suicide registered in Australia in 2003. The data are interesting from the point of view of considering gender differences, methods of suicide and the substantial differences in suicide rates between various states and territories, with the Northern Territory demonstrating figures of 77% above the national rate. Unfortunately, Australia – in common with most other countries – has made no real attempt to consider separately, or in any detail, the issue of suicide in people who have a previous history of mental health problems.

However, in the UK, the government has collected data on suicides through the National Confidential Inquiry into Suicide and Homicide by People with Mental Illness (2006). This Inquiry process was established in 1996 and funded initially by the Department of Health in England. Subsequently, additional funding has been provided by the other three health departments of the UK and now the Confidential Inquiry is truly comprehensive. Its main aims are to:

- collect detailed clinical data on people who die by suicide or commit homicide and who have been in contact with mental health services
- make recommendations on clinical practice and policy that will reduce the risk of suicide and homicide by people under mental healthcare.

This Inquiry, although UK based, has provided an enormous amount of information, which will be of use to managers of clinical services in other countries who need to deal with these tragedies (the section on homicides, below, will also consider data from this Inquiry). The main beneficial outcome of the Inquiry has been the implementation of a number of clinical and managerial initiatives that have resulted in a significant reduction in suicides, particularly in inpatient settings.

From the point of view of managing critical incidents, one of the benefits of knowledge derived from the Inquiry is that it provides a description of the main causes of suicide (and homicide) and, when an individual critical incident occurs, those who are responsible for investigating causation of suicides may be able to use the Inquiry findings as a template for pursuing lines of investigation. Furthermore, once an inquiry into an individual case has been completed, service managers may then be able to look at ways in which the service may respond in order to minimise the possibility that such incidents will occur in the future.

## Overview of the method of the UK Inquiry

In the UK, as in Australia, all deaths are publicly registered and the cause(s) of death are entered on the death certificate. The inquiry process then identifies, from all registered suicides, those people who have been in contact with mental health services in the year prior to the suicide. The process then collects detailed clinical data on these individuals, as well as considering the activities of clinical services where that individual received care and treatment.

The latest Inquiry report (Avoidable Deaths), which was published in December 2006 and covers the period between April 2000 and December 2004, can be found at www.medicine.manchester.ac.uk/suicideprevention/nci/. This report provides information on 6367 cases of suicide by current or recent mental health patients between April 2000 and December 2004 – this being 27% of all suicides occurring nationally. The figure translates into over 1300 suicides per year across the four countries of the UK. The report sets out the main methods of suicide, with hanging being the most common method; hanging and self-poisoning accounting for two-thirds of all deaths. Of all suicides, 49% of patients were in contact with services in the week preceding the event and 19% in the previous 24 hours. The Inquiry also reported on a subset of suicides by patients who were, at the time of their death, inpatients in mental health services. This subset of the population comprised no less than 13.5% of the sample, i.e. 856 cases.

Importantly, the Inquiry highlighted a number of areas relevant to prevention in people with a current or past mental health problem. These are discussed below.

## Absconding from inpatient wards

Approximately a quarter of suicides in inpatients occur after a patient has left the ward without permission. The most common period of time for this to occur is in the first seven days after admission. The Inquiry noted that the trigger factors for absconding often included a disturbed ward environment or a specific incident involving that patient. The Inquiry also noted that mental health services probably need to consider greater use of closed circuit television and more active control of ward entrances and exits. UK psychiatric inpatient wards are in many senses similar to those in Australia. In both countries, wards vary in their 'open door' policy and, given the significant number of suicides that seem to occur in absconding patients, service managers obviously need to look again at whether or not ward exits need to be locked, or at least kept under constant surveillance.

### Dealing with the transition between inpatient care and the community

Of the suicides that occur in the three months following discharge, 15% occur in the first week and nearly a quarter occur before the first appointment in the community. The Inquiry identified several measures that are needed to reduce the problems that occur in the post-discharge period. There is a specific recommendation that risk is regularly assessed during the whole period of discharge planning and trial leave, rather than, as often occurs, carrying out a single pre-discharge review. Furthermore, the risk assessment plan needs to identify any possible stressors that are encountered on leave and discharge and set out methods for dealing with the same. Once the patient has been discharged, they need to have access to services and this should include the patient being provided with telephone numbers to be used 24 hours a day, seven days a week. Staff who work in community mental health services are encouraged to provide early follow-up after discharge and to augment face-to-face contact in the first week with telephone calls, particularly for patients who may be at higher levels of risk.

### Identifying patients at risk, particularly those with severe mental illness and previous acts of self-harm

The report indicates that the risk assessment and risk management plans for patients at the highest levels of risk are often lacking in depth and breadth. The report particularly identifies the need to adopt closer monitoring of high-risk groups of patients and to carry out joint reviews of such patients with other agencies.

### Dealing with the situation arising when a care plan breaks down

According to the Inquiry, a significant number of patients who died by suicide, did so when they dropped out of services or when they stopped taking their medication. This finding is particularly sad, given the fact that we have, for more than 30 years, accepted the need to employ assertive outreach to patients with serious mental illness, who by definition are often unable to comply with their treatment and/or have insufficient levels of motivation to actively pursue a treatment programme. In Australia, such outreach services were established in Sydney nearly 30 years ago (Hoult & Reynolds, 1984).

There are, perhaps, lessons here for those responsible for the education and training of mental health professionals (from those responsible for undergraduate training programmes to post-qualification education and training). It seems clear that the possible serious consequences of non-compliance with treatment and/or dropping out of services need to be reinforced. Some mental health professionals may still hold the belief that people with a mental illness have a right to choose whether they engage with services or not. Arguably, people with a serious mental illness and who lack insight are individuals who do not have full capacity to make such choices and, therefore, in a sense, mental health professionals need to intervene on their behalf. While many mental health professionals will be able to accept this principle without any difficulty, the problem arises when people have, what is deemed to be, a reasonable level of insight and, in the judgement of some members of the team, have capacity. In such cases, there is an obvious need to discuss these issues explicitly and comprehensively and to arrive at an agreed decision.

### Changing attitudes to prevention and dealing with the widespread view that individual deaths are inevitable

In conducting the Inquiry, the investigators gathered information on clinicians' views of suicides. The report stated:

'A feature of these cases we have investigated is the low proportion that clinicians regarded as preventable – only 19% of suicides. To an extent, this reflects the recognition that mental health patients overall are a high risk group – it is therefore unrealistic to expect services to prevent all suicides. However, there is a danger in going on from recognising the risk in patients as a whole to accepting the inevitability of individual deaths.'

The report then goes on to provide a calculation that 41% of inpatients suicides are preventable and concludes this particular section with the comment:

'It is time to change the widespread view that individual deaths are inevitable – such a view is bound to discourage staff from taking steps to improve safety. It may be a reaction to the criticism of services and individuals that can happen when serious incidents occur. Therefore, if mental health staff are to give up the culture of inevitability, it is up to commentators outside clinical practice to give up the culture of blame.'

### Observation of patients on wards

The report highlighted deficiencies in the observation of patients at risk and drew attention to the need to ensure that observation protocols should be strictly followed. Furthermore, the investigators also drew attention to the observation of ward exits and the problems of absconding.

### The ward environment

Suicide by inpatients is a problem throughout the world. In the USA, where inpatient services are more restrictive than in the UK and Australia – for example security staff, high levels of surveillance and mechanical restraint are used – consequently, suicide by inpatients is less common. In the UK and in

Australia, where inpatient care is, in some senses, more liberal and less restrictive, inpatient suicides occur more frequently. In the UK, the most common cause of death by suicide of inpatients is still self-strangulation, although in recent years these rates have reduced because of specific attention paid to ligature points in the ward environment. In both the UK and Australia there have been a number of initiatives, such as removing non-collapsible curtain rails, modifying door handles, ensuring that toughened glass is in place and removing 'barn door' type structures, replacing them, for example, by sliding wardrobe doors.

Service managers need to pay particular attention to regular audits of the environment and to learn lessons from completed and attempted suicides, where patients may often find ingenious ways of harming themselves. A corollary of dealing with ligature points is dealing with ligatures themselves and, when risk assessments are carried out, it is most important to consider whether patients should have access to shoelaces, dressing gown cords and so on. In turn, service managers need to consider the risks attached to certain types of bedsheet, which may be used more readily as a ligature. Such issues also require that considerable thought is given to the development and modification of policies on matters such as searching. Some inpatient suicides relate to fire and service managers need to consider a range of matters relating to items such as aerosols and disposable lighters, which are often implicated. Obviously, the decision to remove various items from patients raises the issue of human rights. Once more, staff on wards need to balance not only the risks and benefits but also their duty of care against the human rights of the patient.

## Dual diagnosis

Many suicides in the community involve patients who have so-called dual diagnosis, i.e. a mixture of mental health problems and substance abuse. Dual diagnosis is now a substantial problem in both inpatient and community services across the world and, because of the higher rates of non-compliance, violence, suicide and self-harm, such patients present a major challenge. Perhaps the biggest issue relating to this problem is that of effective treatment. At present, there is no gold standard approach and the research literature regarding treatment trials is sparse and, largely, confined to patients who have one substance of abuse; this contrasts considerably to the real-life situation, where dual diagnosis patients often use multiple substances, which may vary over time according to availability and cost.

## Suicide in older people

Twelve per cent of all suicides in the UK occur in people over the age of 65 and this population contrasts with people under this age in terms of causative or trigger factors. Older people who commit suicide are characterised by ongoing physical illness and bereavement and loss, and it is these areas that require intervention.

**Learning the lessons**

One approach that has been used increasingly in mental health services is root cause analysis (RCA). RCA is a technique for approaching adverse events in a system-wide way, while at the same time seeking to understand the underlying contributory factors and causes. RCA examines both organisational failure as well as human error, recognising that organisational failure is a commoner cause (Toft & Reynolds, 1994).

Although RCA is now being increasingly used in mental health services across the Western world, the methodologies involved are still in need of improvement. Nevertheless, it does appear that RCA has been very revealing, in terms of identifying causal factors and then providing solutions (Wald & Shojana, 2001). Space does not allow a detailed description of the process of RCA, however, it is worth mentioning some important elements of the process:

- The collection of as much data as possible concerning the individual patient, the care environment and the carers involved.
- The use of independent assessors for different aspects of the event (for example psychiatric nurse, service manager, psychiatrist, social worker).
- The involvement of service users.
- The provision of training for all of those taking part in the RCA exercise.

**Care of significant others following suicide**

It is essential that managers consider the aftermath of suicides in terms of the impact on the family, the health professionals involved and the service in general. Each and every suicide is different and, therefore, the needs of the families, the professionals involved and the service will vary considerably. From the point of view of management, it is essential that every service has a person who is specifically designated, and properly trained, to deal with the emotional aftermath among family members and the healthcare professionals involved. It is essential that this person has the necessary authority to make a referral to the appropriate professional and voluntary agencies. In turn, it is also essential that there are resources available to ensure that, if necessary, people in need of emotional support or treatment can be referred to services outside of the immediate area, if that is more desirable.

# Self-harm

Self-harm, rather than suicide or attempted suicide, is a common event. The vast majority of self-harm never comes to the attention of mental health professionals and is variously dealt with by friends and family members, primary care services and emergency departments in general hospitals. By definition, self-harm which occurs within the context of a patient receiving mental healthcare is a critical incident. However, the response to episodes of self-harm obviously varies considerably. Many mental health professionals will know of patients who may cut themselves many times in a day and that information needs to be recorded. At the other end of the spectrum, self-harm episodes may pose a threat to life and occur within the setting of an exacerbation of a serious mental illness and active suicidal intent.

Service managers need to have clear policies to guide staff in the management of self-harm episodes and also to put in place interventions. In the UK, the National Institute for Health and Clinical Excellence (NICE, 2004) has produced specific clinical guidelines based on evidence and every service in England and Wales (Scotland and Northern Ireland have different processes) is expected to follow these guidelines (see www.nice.org.uk/cg016quickrefguide). The guidance is, perhaps, unique across the world in that not only is it evidence based, but all patients and services users can expect these guidelines to be implemented and, if they do not receive the care outlined, they have proper cause for redress, as these guidelines now carry considerable weight. In summary, the guidance provides advice concerning the physical and psychological management of self-harm and also sets out a number of interventions for prevention in primary and secondary care.

The guidelines provide advice for healthcare professionals working in any setting, whether or not they have a mental health background, and provides detailed advice about the various treatments available for the spectrum of self-harm incidents, including overdose. The guidelines cover advice regarding prescribing to service users/patients at risk of self-poisoning and assessment and management protocols for ambulance personnel. The guidance is particularly focused to treatment in emergency departments and covers that significant population which wish to leave before assessment and treatment. The guidance also includes specific advice for specialist doctors and nurses, including guidance on the collection of samples, interpreting test results and the various information and laboratory services available to clinicians who treat self-harm. There is specific advice about the management of overdose involving paracetamol, benzodiazepines, salicylates and opiates. The guidance covers support and advice for people who repeatedly self-harm, the principles of psychosocial assessment and referral processes. The document also has specific advice on the management of children and young people and older people. Although this guidance is UK based, the vast majority of material published is of considerable relevance to services in Australia and New Zealand, where no such comprehensive guidance exists. The NICE webpage on the guidance document also has links to a comprehensive set of background literature.

# Violence

Violence in healthcare is a major issue across the world and is, unfortunately, increasing in incidence. The growing concern about violence in healthcare in Australia was helpfully set out in an article by Benveniste et al. (2005). The authors point out that many episodes of violence occur in emergency departments and mental health services. Unfortunately, the Australian government has yet to carry out any comprehensive collation of data concerning violence in mental health-care, or to publish guidelines on the management of violence.

While all service managers will be familiar with acts of violence that cause injury, both physical and psychological, to patients, staff and visitors (in the case of inpatient care) there is very little evidence concerning effective interventions at an individual, service or community level. In the UK, NICE (2005) commissioned a three-year work programme, which led to the publication of comprehensive guidance on the short-term management of violence in mental health and emergency department settings (see www.nice.org.uk/cg025quickrefguide). The document is relevant to Australian services, as the conditions of inpatient care are similar to those of the UK and, unlike many European countries, mechanical restraint is rarely used. For ward managers or service managers, any significant violence, which may, of course, include psychological injury, must be treated as a clinically significant event. After an event occurs, there is of course great opportunity for learning. The UK work on managing violence has demonstrated that all staff working in mental health and emergency settings in general departments need to attend to a very wide range of issues. These include:

- prediction of violence
- prevention of violence
- interventions for managing violence, including:
  - o rapid tranquillisation
  - o physical interventions
  - o seclusion
- review of incidents and protocols for carrying out post-incident reviews
- use of interventions in emergency departments in general hospitals
- dealing with patients' needs:
  - o including people with disabilities
  - o including dealing with the risk of human immunodeficiency virus (HIV) infection or other infectious diseases
  - o dealing with women who are pregnant
  - o dealing with mental healthcare environments
- training issues
- implementation issues.

Obviously, the issue of violence in mental healthcare is too large to deal with comprehensively in a chapter such as this and, as with the topic of self-harm identified above, the reader is commended to use the NICE guidance referred to above as a resource that is comprehensive and evidence based. Nevertheless, within the context of this chapter, it is important to address four key issues. Each of these are extremely relevant to running an effective and safe service. These issues are:

- Recording
- Learning lessons
- Policy development
- Training

## Recording

Managers have a particular responsibility for ensuring that all episodes of violence are recorded. This, however, is not as easy as it seems. There is still considerable variation in what staff consider to be violence and, in some services, any verbal abuse directed towards another person is seen as a violent incident, while in other services and at the other extreme, only violent incidents that result in physical injury are so recorded. A further difficulty in whether or not violent incidents are recorded, concerns patients who may be verbally or physically abusive on an almost continuous basis. For instance, there are patients who will subject staff and others to constant verbal abuse and this may, of course, be recorded in the patient's notes. However, if this constant verbal abuse is not recorded on incident forms, an objective audit of violence in a particular service may be compromised. Similarly, there are patients – for example those with dementia – who may continuously flail their arms or slap members of the nursing staff, without causing any significant injury. Just how one records the occurrence of such behaviour on incident forms poses some difficulty.

In many services, episodes of violence are very often under-reported because of the inconvenience of filling what can sometimes be lengthy forms, or in the case of the increasingly prevalent electronic systems, needing to log in and set up the relevant computer program. Managers need to be aware of all of these issues, so that, at the very least, they have knowledge of the extent of under-reporting. Accurate reporting is, of course, essential for the purposes of planning appropriate staffing, but the lack of proper recording may also have legal implications in the case of actions being brought against the services.

## Learning lessons

Staff working in mental health services are only too well aware of the tragedies that sometimes occur in episodes of violence. Unfortunately, in Australia there is little systematic collection of notification of deaths in mental health services, although the Australian Institute of Criminology, a branch of the Australian government, has published a series of reports from the Deaths in Custody Monitoring Programme based on data from 1992 to 1996 (www.aic.gov.au/publications/dic).

In the UK, the Joint Parliamentary Committee on Human Rights (2004) published a report on deaths in custody (www.publications.parliament.uk) which included a systematic account of deaths in mental healthcare. While such incidents provide a considerable amount of food for thought, such deaths are relatively rare. Conversely, most acute mental health services will experience a significant number of violent incidents in any single week and sometimes in any single day. Such violent incidents may include episodes where the patient needs to be physically restrained by a team of nurses, episodes involving seclusion and, increasingly in mental health services, episodes where it is necessary to call the police to contain a violent incident. It is from such incidents that one can learn lessons, and mental health service managers should use auditing as a method of learning lessons. It is important that mental health service managers carry out post-incident reviews of episodes where 'something has gone wrong'. Equally, it is important to audit episodes, for example, involving restraint, where episodes have been brought to a successful conclusion. Post-incident reviews should involve holding discussions with both staff and patients and, where relevant, carers. Such reviews often reveal very important information about how procedures may be improved.

In the NICE guidance referred to above, one of the recommendations is that patients should be able to provide an 'Advance Directive'. Therefore, when a patient with a history of violence during their mental illness is interviewed, that patient may well be able to suggest ways that their violent behaviour may be managed in future episodes. Thus, for example, the patient might be able to say what methods might be successfully used to prevent an episode, for example being given time out or provided with an oral dose of tranquilliser. Such advance directives may then be recorded on a card and in the patient's notes, so that the patient's wishes may be taken into account in planning their care.

## Policy development

It is essential that all services have robust policies for the management of violence and, in particular, that these policies focus on prediction and prevention rather than physical interventions. It is also important that policies also include an emphasis on environmental management, such as the control of noise and the contribution of safe areas and private rooms. That said, policies also need to provide very detailed guidance on the management of specific episodes and, in the UK, policies now provide extensive reference to the NICE guidelines with, for example, the use of laminated summary cards which can be kept in ward offices. Such cards can provide easy access to guidance or to show the algorithms to be used in procedures – for example, rapid tranquillisation.

## Training

Managers need to be aware of a simple principle regarding training. That is that if a violent incident is foreseeable, staff should be appropriately trained to deal with it. A simple template for the training of staff should be as follows:

- For all staff in mental health services, a simple training in conflict resolution, emphasising the need to resolve conflict at an early stage. Such training programmes commonly take one to two days.
- Use of breakaway training. Such training will assist staff in breaking away from assaults and should be made available to all staff working in acute mental health settings and in the community. It should include cleaners, receptionists, and other ancillary staff as well as all nursing staff.
- Comprehensive management of violence training. All staff who come into contact with patients, who are potentially violent, in mental health settings and who may be involved in an intervention, should receive a comprehensive

training, commonly taking a minimum of five days. Such training should cover a very wide range of areas concerning prediction and prevention and also practical training involving the teaching of various physical methods, including control and restraint.

- Training for secure services. Training for secure services will involve a range of management of violence techniques, including control and restraint as outlined above. It should also include much more detailed and practical training on the management of more serious violent incidents and may include interventions involving riot shields and the management of situations that involve hostage taking or sieges. Fortunately, in many forensic services, such training is now essential.

In addition to the above template, the NICE guidelines, referred to above, have also emphasised the need to train nursing staff in the care of patients following rapid tranquillisation and it is essential that all staff involved in such episodes have the relevant training in the use of measures such as pulse oximetry. Finally, it is essential that all training is regularly reviewed and refreshed. Managers should ensure that staff are provided with refresher training at intervals of no more than 18 months.

# Homicide

Despite public perception, homicide involving patients in mental health services is a relatively rare event. However, when it does occur, there is often very significant and indeed disproportionate attention paid in the media to the perpetrator's mental health history. The UK Confidential Inquiry collected data on 249 cases of homicide by current or recent patients, occurring between April 1999 and December 2003 (this being 9% of all homicides occurring in England and Wales during this period). This figure translates into 52 patient homicides per year. The number of homicides by persons with schizophrenia is around 30 per year, this being 5% of all homicides. However, it should be noted that only half of the perpetrators with schizophrenia were current or recent patients and a third had no previous contact with services.

Another issue that needs to be taken into account is that the number of 'stranger' homicides (in which the perpetrator and the victim were not known to each other and the perpetrator was mentally ill) is very small. Therefore, the risks posed to the general public by the proverbial 'madman' are also very small. Because of the rarity of such cases, it is difficult to provide managers with specific advice, particularly as such cases will be subject to wider independent inquiries involving criminal justice and other agencies. The main problems that become evident in cases where homicide may be seen as being preventable generally occur when patients slip through the net and where risk assessment and risk management procedures break down. Such cases emphasise the need for robust methods in community services, including the use of rigorous risk assessment procedures and training for all staff involved. Training is often the Achilles heel in many community services, as risk assessment demands an approach that goes far beyond the ticking of boxes on rating scales and forms.

## Conclusion

Managers in the mental health services are faced with a wide range of challenges from the routine, although very important issues concerning worker health and safety, to the extremes involving violence, self-harm, suicide and homicide. This chapter has provided an overview of the central issues concerning the more serious critical incidents. However, it must be emphasised that for this chapter to be properly effective, managers need to follow up their reading by accessing the important website information provided, particularly relating to suicides, homicides, the management of violence, the management of self-harm and the issues relating to deaths in custody. While the emphasis for managers needs obviously to be on the prediction and prevention of untoward events, managers will inevitably be faced with the management of the aftermath of events that may, in their own way, have a lifelong impact on the patient, the family and/or the staff member. Such responsibilities are obviously very significant and it is important that the managers themselves are provided with an appropriate level of resources, not only in terms of managing critical incidents but also in respect of their own training and support and supervision.

## References

National Confidential Inquiry into Suicides and Homicides by People with a Mental Illness (2006). *Avoidable deaths.* Report of the National Confidential Inquiry into Suicides and Homicides by People with a Mental Illness. Available at: www.medicine.manchester.ac.uk/suicideprevention/nci/ (accessed 20 May 2008).

Benveniste, K., Hibbert, P. & Runciman, W. (2005). Violence in health care: the contribution of the Australian Patient Safety Foundation to incident monitoring and analysis – incident analysis. *Medical Journal of Australia*, 183, 348–351.

Hoult, J. & Reynolds, I. (1984). Schizophrenia: a comparative trial of community oriented and hospital oriented psychiatric care. *Acta Psychiatrica Scandinavica*, 69, 359–372.

Joint Parliamentary Committee on Human Rights (2004). *Deaths in Custody.* A report of the Joint Parliamentary Committee on Human Rights. Available at: www.publications.parliament.uk.

National Institute for Health and Clinical Excellence (2004). Clinical Guidance 16: Self-harm: Quick Reference Guide. Available at: www.nice.org.uk/cg016quickrefguide (accessed 14 May 2008).

National Institute for Health and Clinical Excellence (2005). Clinical Guidance 25: Violence: NICE guideline. Available at: http://guidance.nice.org.uk/CG25/niceguidance/pdf (accessed 14 May 2008).

Toft, B. & Reynolds, S. (1994). *Learning From Disasters: A Management Approach.* Oxford: Heinemann.

Wald, H. & Shojana, K. (2001). *Root Cause Analysis in Making Healthcare Safer: A Critical Analysis of Patient Safety Practices.* AHRQ Publication No.1 – EO 056: Rockville MD: Agency for Healthcare Research and Quality.

# Chapter 6
# Public relations and communication

*Victoria Maxwell, Debra Lampshire and Samson Tse*

## Chapter overview

Recovery is a unique process or journey that resides within the person. However, the external environment created by those who live and interact with that person will hugely impact on their recovery process. That is why management of public relations between mental health services and the families and carers, other relevant social services and the general public is an important topic. Therefore, this chapter switches from focusing on individuals with experience of mental illness, psychotherapeutic techniques or mental health systems to managing public relations or an effective communication with a range of stakeholders. Stakeholders refers to families and carers, relevant social services and the wider general public. It is also argued that consumers or users of mental health services can have pivotal roles in this distinctive management function. Three sections follow the definition of key terms. The first section focuses on why it is important to maintain effective communication with families and carers of members recovering from mental illness and what constitutes meaningful communication with them. In the second section, the public relations network grows to include working with relevant social agencies, so that those agencies are able to provide user-friendly services to individuals with mental health problems. The last section describes how mental health services managers can also use public relations as an overarching framework to reduce stigma and discrimination associated with mental illness among members of the general public (Link et al., 1999).

## Defining public relations and service users

Defining public relations is not as easy as one would think even though it is so commonplace in the twenty-first century. Long-time researchers on public relations Wilcox and colleagues (2003, p. 7) define public relations as:

'a distinctive management function which helps establish and maintain mutual lines of communication, understanding, acceptance and co-operation between an organisation and its publics; involves the management of problems or issues; helps management to keep informed on and responsive to public opinion; defines and emphasises the responsibility of management to serve the public interest; helps management keep abreast of and effectively utilise change, serving as an early warning system to help anticipate trends; and uses research and ethical communication techniques as its principal tools'.

This definition illustrates that public relations not only has a passive role in terms of controlling damage of public image of the organisation or services associated with the establishment but it also serves the purpose of being strategic in promoting positive co-operation and communication between the organisation and the general public. The term 'publics' denotes the multiple stakeholders that are attended to while managing the public relations. There are many different groups, such as service users, healthcare providers, local residents and politicians, all of whom have distinct information needs and performance expectations (Theaker, 2004).

For the purposes of this chapter 'service users' are defined as individuals with psychiatric illness who have used mental health services and who identify themselves as such. There are variations in how these individuals prefer to be addressed (Mueser et al., 1996; Sharma et al., 2000), with literature from the USA favouring the term 'consumer', while the UK and Europe favours 'service user'. In New Zealand, Maori terms *tangata whai ora* (person seeking wellness) or *tangata motuhake* (people with mental illness) are popular alternatives.

## Work with families and carers

The role of families and carers is one of the most significant and challenging relationships for professionals within the mental health sector (Hinshaw, 2005). Families often report being excluded from the rehabilitation process with little or no communication with mental health professionals regarding the treatment being undertaken by their family members.

The definition of families has evolved over the generations and families can now consist of step-parents, same sex parents or birth/adoptive parents; grandparents are also now taking on the role of primary caregiver (Families Commission, 2007). A service user may well identify family as persons who have no blood tie to them but, instead, a profound and well-established connection. This development can prove challenging to processes and procedures which still maintain an adherence to the conventional view of family. It is only correct that clinicians should accept the person nominated by service users as their family regardless of genetics or legal classifications. When a service user is distressed it may well be that they do not wish to have contact with their family members and carers. This does not mean, however, that family members and carers can be excluded altogether. They are still entitled to information regarding the well-being and progress of their family member even if the information is limited.

For clinicians this raises the issue of how to accommodate the needs of the families and carers. Clinicians are highly skilled in engaging service users in conversation and gaining personal and private information. These same skills need to be demonstrated when working with relatives and caregivers. Being honest and open in the communication and being clear about what information may be shared helps develop a trusting, respectful and professional relationship with family and carers.

# Effective elements of working with families and carers

### Therapeutic alliance

Families and carers have an ongoing commitment to, knowledge of and concern for their family member. They are not paid to be there. They are there because they chose to be there and they care. They frequently provide ongoing support long after services have removed themselves from a user's life. Families and carers are especially attuned to their loved ones' early warning signs as they are so familiar with minor and major changes in behaviour and mood. Families and carers often have a long history of frustration with professionals. This may mean clinicians have to learn to listen to families express this frustration without defensiveness or judgement in order to cultivate a working relationship that ultimately assists the families and carers and their loved ones.

Mental health professionals need to discuss with families and carers that the recovery process is not linear and they themselves will cycle through phases of hope and then despair. They need to be reassured that the painful and confusing emotional reactions, even intense episodes, are natural and common responses frequently reported from families and carers. Mental health professionals need to be careful not to imply there is something wrong with families and carers and emphasise that reactions are not pathological but, rather, normal responses to stressful and distressing circumstances.

It is important that families and carers know that they cannot make their loved ones recover. This is a journey that the service users must make for themselves. Service users are required to be proactive in their own recovery, developing lifelong skills that will enable them to live the life they would choose for themselves.

Families and carers and mental health professionals can share knowledge and information about recovery and how best to support the family members. Families and carers also need to know there is support available from organisations in the community and through mental health services to cope with the various levels of uncertainty and personal distress they may experience.

### Legal issues

In New Zealand family members often talk of being denied information based on use of the Privacy Act (1993 and Amendment Act 1994). There appear to be huge inconsistencies in how the Act is interpreted and is perceived by families as a weapon for clinicians to withhold information.

### Needs of families and carers

Families and carers may also need to work through their own recovery process from the shock, denial and disbelief of their and their loved ones' lives being affected by mental illness. Working through the anger, blame and fear, they may also start examining their own contributions, real or imagined, to their family members' situation. This can be followed by a sense of guilt and shame, feeling the need to keep their loved ones' condition secret or experiencing first-hand embarrassing and humiliating situations that expose their family members in very public displays. Families and carers may have occurrences of depression, and experience loneliness and begin to withdraw and isolate themselves from their own friends, relatives and colleagues. If mental health professionals work actively with the experiences of the families and carers, they can address these common responses and assist them to reach a level of acceptance that they are not in this alone and engender hope for their loved one and themselves.

Mental health professionals need to demonstrate good interpersonal skills, especially the ability to listen (Dixon et al., 2001). Families and carers want practical advice for common problems. Teaching them stress management and problem-solving skills may be beneficial. Families and carers wish to maintain a collaborative relationship with their loved ones' clinician and negotiate mutual sharing of information. It is important that mental health professionals validate and point out family strengths, let them know they have talents and skills to contribute, and they are also entitled to live their own lives and pursue their own dreams.

### Including everyone

Siblings of service users see themselves as the forgotten victims of mental illness, taking on role of the 'good child' or the 'pseudo parent' while parents deal with the service users. Resentment often is directed towards the service users as all energies appear to be put into the one sibling. Routines and events are directed or modified to accommodate the service users regardless of the impact it has on the rest of the siblings in the family. The display of 'parentalism' can continue into adulthood when the loved one's well-being remains the parents' primary concern. This can also work to the detriment of the service user as they remain dependent on the parents well past the time when developmentally it would have been expected a child would have begun living independently.

### Empower families and carers by sharing information and knowledge

Families and carers require information about their loved one's specific illness and sometimes they can benefit from a structured psycho-education programme (e.g. Dixon et al., 2001; Pekkala & Merinder, 2001; De Groot et al., 2003). Regardless of whether the information is delivered in group or individual format, written material that can be referred to later on is helpful. Families and carers should be given copies of recovery or wellness plans, if they are included or expected to play a part in those plans. They need to know where they can go to for support and a place that will deal with their issues where their own needs and wants will be validated. They should be informed of their legal rights and the rights of the service users so they can advocate for their loved ones effectively if required. It is useful for families and carers to have the contact detail of those mental health professionals directly involved with the family member and know they are welcome to contact clinicians should they feel the need to.

## Roles of service users in public relations

When the recovery approach was adopted as the preferred way of working within mental health services it necessitated the inclusion of service users to enhance the clinical and scientific knowledge about mental health problems with the wisdom gained from the human experience of distress. Recovery requires clients to be proactive and to take responsibility of the healing process. Clients are no longer passive participants of services and, as such, their role as service users changes. Now, rather than reporting their symptoms *to* clinicians, they work collaboratively *with* clinicians to track factors that contribute to their wellness. This results in service users functioning at a level where they also reclaim the life they envisage for themselves prior to an episode. These skills of self-reflection and articulation prove transferable so clients are now in a stronger position to inform mental health services of the processes and practices that assist them in their recovery and also those practices that impede. There are those who, guided by their experiences both positive and negative within the services, have chosen to share these insights to facilitate better outcomes and advocate for independence and quality-of-life issues for clients through their involvement with mental health service providers (Marsh, 2000; Rigby, 2007). So the development of professional roles played by service users was born. Potential professional roles include case manager, peer-support specialist, patient advocate, or adviser in public policy and public relations.

## Work with key social agencies: a case study to achieve common goals

Mental health services need to be proactive in cultivating relationships with social agencies that have associations with mental health service users. It should be seen as core business for a mental health provider to assertively challenge the difficulties faced by clients from social services. One way in which this is being addressed is by providing training to closely related services.

Work and Income New Zealand (WINZ) is a service of the Ministry of Social Development that helps job seekers and pays income support on behalf of the government and includes residential care, support subsidies, superannuation payments to retired people, along with the administration of war pensions. It is also an agency in which a number of service users have consistently experienced prejudice and discrimination. When WINZ was approached, it welcomed the opportunity for its staff to be informed and educated in the area of mental health.

WINZ recognised that mental health service users were a client group that regularly used their services and staff had expressed their anxiety and discomfort in dealing with this group of service users.

WINZ arranged for monthly seminars to be presented by a service user who provided information about the various diagnoses. An environment of safety was created by making all sessions exclusive of senior management and confidentiality (with some limits in regard to safety issues) was guaranteed. At the beginning of the workshop, guidelines were established around how the workshop would be run and then people were given a fun activity to help disarm those who may have felt suspicious of the intent of the workshop. It was important to assure staff the workshop was not meant to imply their professional practices were lacking and it was taken as a given that all staff were endeavouring to provide the most effective service while demonstrating respect and regard to all clients. The workshop was divided into two distinct sections. The first section explained the diagnostic categories from a clinical perspective and the second section explained the diagnoses from the experiential aspects.

The participants needed to be assured that the presenter did have some expertise in the area of mental illness but it was not made explicit that the presenter was a service user. Then they were invited to be as open and honest in their discussions with no fear of repercussions from managers for their comments. They were also asked to give examples of situations in which they had felt uncomfortable, threatened or were beyond their scope of practice. From these examples people discussed ways to alleviate their anxiety and how they could achieve better outcomes. Generally people wished to be better equipped to handle 'challenging situations'. Frank discussions suggested in some cases how staff may have contributed to incidents where clients became irate and possibly became verbally abusive and finally would be required to leave the premises. When explored, staff conceded this occurred due to employees feeling they had no skills to deal with any possible tense situations or simply because they did not want to deal with 'those people'.

## Effective elements of working with social agencies

### *Aim at changing attitudes*

Teaching people skills can produce confidence in the area of possible conflict and is a simple solution for management to adopt. What is more complex is dealing with the negative and hostile attitudes people hold for those with mental illness which can often only surface when a person is faced directly with a situation in which they feel unable to cope. These negative attitudes can also be fed if other members of the team also hold such views. Later on the senior staff or those whom the organisation identified as influential in establishing staff culture were also requested to go through the training programme. It was hoped that these individuals would not only act as role models but also champion and advocate conscientiously for service users.

### *Reframe mental symptoms*

During the workshop, participants were able to identify a number of 'symptoms' or traits that either they or family members demonstrated and began to make the connection to human responses to stress and distress. Therefore what was required was a more empathic and common sense approach to service users. By reframing the presentations of service users, participants discovered that the way to work with them was no different than dealing with any other clients. The staff began to feel more comfortable with dealing with service users as they came to the conclusion that the same principles applied when dealing with all clients. If one acknowledged and validated people's responses to stressful situations this approach goes a long way to enabling effective dialogue while also alleviating possible tensions. It was also discussed how staff would respond or feel when they were not listened to, not feeling valued and their concerns were ignored. This gave them an understanding of what service users were exposed to frequently from society, health and social service professionals and even families. Given the opportunity to explore what staff and service users had in common as well as examining differences, staff attitudes changed and they began viewing service users as people first and not as 'dangerous lunatics'.

### *Service users make significant contribution*

The workshop provided an ideal and safe opportunity for a service user to relay to workers their concerns. It proved useful for employees to see that service users are able to participate in the community, the workforce and can cultivate successful relationships and have meaningful lives, filled with family and friends. Staff commented they had no idea that someone with mental health problems got well. They always believed service users would live a life of dependency and illness. Staff members were made aware of the prevalence of mental illness and shown statistics which demonstrate the large number of people who cope with mental health problems on a daily basis but manage to live a flourishing life, supported by family and friends without the intervention of mental health services. The presenter constantly referred to the human desires that drive us all: to have a life worth living, to form significant relationships and to be a valued member of our family and society. This helped employees grasp the concepts of our humanness and the threads that bind us all as human beings regardless of the labels placed on us by others.

## Work with general public: a case study of contact, personal narrative and disclosure

Not only can it be effective for service users to provide training to the agencies and individuals who help them, but additionally service users play an essential role in reducing the overriding stigma in the general public. Numerous studies cite consumer contact produces the highest improvement in attitudes, better than protest, education and control conditions (Corrigan et al., 2001, 2002; Watson & Corrigan, 2006).

Effectively reducing stigma is not unlike advertising or, to coin a phrase, 'mad-vertising'. Like commercials aiming to pocket part of our coveted 'psychic real estate', that is, monopolise our thoughts about one particular product or issue, so too can the best anti-stigma vehicles change our feelings and minds about mental illnesses and the people who live with them. It is logical and, in fact, vital to have persons with mental illness participate in anti-stigma activities. It is not new to have service users actively participate in these initiatives, but the forms to which they contribute have evolved and certain types are emerging as more effective than others.

The more public stigma is reduced the better the chances for improved social inclusion for those with mental health problems. The effectiveness of treatment and the maintenance of positive results cannot happen without considering the wider ecology of the society in which service users are living. Therefore it is imperative public prejudice be reduced as much as possible because recovery from mental illness is enormously difficult without community support and understanding.

Dr. Patrick Corrigan, well-known researcher on stigma and mental illness and principal investigator of the Chicago Consortium for Stigma Research (CCSR), defines 'contact' as 'introducing people with mental illness to the rest of the population'. And face-to-face interaction appears to have the most impact (Pettigrew & Tropp, 2000). Contact can range from discovering a friend or co-worker has a mental illness, collaborating on a community project with a neighbour who happens to have a disorder, to seeing a public service announcement with people disclosing they have a mental illness. Yet another powerful mode is that of personal narrative, the sharing of the 'lived' experience of mental illness.

Personal narrative at its most basic is sharing one's own experience of a particular event or time. When done well, personal narratives allow others to vicariously experience the events that happened to the 'storyteller'. It places the listener in the midst of the action, letting him or her live through that experience. One of the most powerful methods of changing attitudes and dismantling stigma occurs when services users describe their experiences of what it is like to have mental illness, allowing an entry into that particular, very often hidden world of psychiatric disorder (Corrigan & O'Shaughnessy, 2007).

Although accounts revealed by families and mental health professionals of those who face mental illness can prove helpful, their stories are still once removed from the actual insider's experience. Theirs is not the voice of one who actually lived through and coped with psychosis, for example. It is when an individual who has 'been-there-done-that' discloses their story that it has the greatest impact (Corrigan & O'Shaughnessy, 2007).

Memoirs such as *Electro Boy* (Berhman, 2003), *An Unquiet Mind* (Redfield, 1995) and *Brilliant Madness* (Duke & Hochman, 1992) are examples of insightful personal narratives in the tradition of disclosing mental illness, as is when a person publicly tells of their experience, such as Margot Kidder's disclosure of bipolar disorder, or the recent public admission of Margaret Trudeau's, wife of the former Canadian Prime Minister Pierre Trudeau, having bipolar disorder. Both these varieties of personal narratives can be influential. But there remains another form gaining popularity in recent years that is unique in the approach it takes in comparison to the ones stated above: stand-up comedy centring on the lived experience of mental illness.

Since its inception in 2004, David Granirer has been teaching individuals with mental illness to be comics in his innovative programme *Stand Up For Mental Health* (SUFMH). Over a 12-week period students learn to write, edit and perform stand-up comedy about their mental illnesses and the experiences surrounding them. At the close of the three months, participants perform for the public in a gala show usually followed by a question and answer period. In most cases, the course continues for an additional nine months where students hone their skills and perform up to 20 more shows.

Granirer, a comic and registered professional counsellor who lives with depression himself, founded the programme to teach the art of stand-up to people with mental illness as a way of building self-esteem and fighting public stigma. Classes are held across Canada, with plans to take it to the USA. The SUFMH programme demonstrates key elements of a successful 'stigma-busting' vehicle. Some of these crucial components are: context, face-to-face interaction, credibility, candidness and irreverent humour.

## Effective elements of 'stand up for mental health'

### Context

The very context within which SUFMH happens, stand-up comedy, works to fight surrounding stigmas on two levels. First, when service users use stand-up to tell their stories, they become the medium that triggers change, not just because of content but because the audience sees people with mental illness doing something they thought they could not – an activity, in fact, most of the general public would find daunting. Granirer explains: 'We reverse the positions of status. Most people would never want to do stand-up comedy. Seeing people with mental illness do it forces audiences to re-evaluate their perceptions and biases against people who are mentally ill' (personal communication, 2007). The individuals on stage become admired for bravery, for talent, directly challenging the myths that people with mental illness are weak, less intelligent and less capable. Attitudes shift because there is dissonance with the status quo of what it means to be mentally ill. In the words of the eminent educator and philosopher Marshall McLuhan: 'the medium is the message'. Here the comedians become both the medium and the message.

Second, identities of those on stage become that of a comic first rather than a 'schizophrenic'. Audience members see a comic who happens to have major depression, further challenging the typical stereotypes of the 'mentally ill'.

## Face-to-face contact and interaction

On stage comedy routines provide audiences pivotal 'face-to-face' contact and interaction with service users that engenders reduction in stigmatising attitudes. 'Face-to-face' contact leads to the most significant kinds of changes in attitudes and beliefs (Pettigrew & Tropp, 2000).

Question and answer periods after the shows provide opportunities for the public to challenge their ideas of mental illness through conversation and dialogue. Attitudinal shifts through direct contact are enhanced even more when coupled with discussion and interaction (Gaertner et al., 1996; Corrigan & O'Shaughnessy, 2007).

## Credibility and 'relate-ability'

For any impact to be made, comics must identify themselves as service users through disclosure of their experience and illness. That is, they must establish their 'credibility' as individuals who live with mental illness. This authenticates them as the experts they are in the 'lived' experience of mental illness.

Contact with individuals who 'moderately disconfirm stereotypes' (Johnston & Hewstone, 1992; Corrigan & Watson, 2006; Watson & Corrigan, 2006; Corrigan & O'Shaughnessy, 2007) challenge stigma more than contact with celebrities who disclose their experience of mental illness or individuals who highly conform to prevailing public typecasting (for example meeting someone who has a mental illness and is homeless) (Corrigan & White, 2004). This 'middle contact' group is the kind represented by Granirer's students. SUFMH comics can be seen at www.standupformentalhealth.com. And it is this 'relate-ability' that is the linchpin for helping audiences change their beliefs about people who have mental illness. Meeting someone who is similar to oneself can exact a greater anti-stigma influence than any other kind of individual.

> 'My psychiatrist said I'm a paranoid bipolar. So I said: "Where'd you hear that?"'
>
> Joan Stone (SUFMH comic, 2005/2006)

## Candidness and honesty

Disclosure is at the core of personal narrative and is the very foundation upon which SUFMH is built. Disclosure has proven to 'massively increase the power of contact on stigma' (Corrigan & O'Shaughnessy, 2007).

All comedy gives expression to the personal and universal, but this 'stigma-busting' stand-up comedy also illuminates the forbidden, the outlawed and the unspoken.

> 'I have to be honest, I have attempted suicide. Obviously I didn't succeed. But I wasn't a complete failure because I learned I *can* tie a knot to save my life.'
>
> Roxanne Teale (SUFMH comic, 2005/2006)

It is this candid and revealing approach that makes the programme so compelling. As comics divulge their personal stories of mental illness diagnosis, medication trials and hospitalisations (to name a few), they also indirectly unearth prejudices, offer information and challenge deeply entrenched perceptions. Audiences are forced back on themselves and their own ideas of what mental illness is all about. This is where the power of personal narrative and comedy lie.

### Irreverent humour

'Laughter is breaking through the intellectual barrier; at the moment of laughing something is understood.'

Anonymous

Humour, and in particular irreverent humour, is the primary ingredient in the work of Granirer's students. Research shows protest, which uses a 'shame on you for thinking that' approach, is not effective in changing public stigma and in fact can often result in backlash (Macrae et al., 1994; Corrigan et al., 2001).

Humour, however, puts people at ease, giving people permission to laugh at what is usually a serious subject. Humour inspires conversations to begin and allows awkward dialogues to become comfortable. Irreverent humour works in two ways. It guides the audience into sacred and taboo territory to illuminate collective, long-held and erroneous beliefs and then lets us laugh at the ignorance of those beliefs.

'I wanted to go to Paranoids Anonymous. But nobody would tell me where the meetings were.'

Paul Decarie (SUFMH comic, 2005/2006)

The comedy works through exaggeration, absurdity and compassion rather than judgement and shame. The audience giggles despite the forbidden nature of the material, and in fact is giggling *because* of the material. That is the gift of irreverent humour. It gives consent to laugh at what is seen as too sombre to joke about. But that very laughter is what allows people to reflect more easily on what they are responding to. It offers a compassionate light in which to see their misconceptions.

---

**Box 6.1   Suggestions for creating 'personal narrative' initiatives to combat stigma.**

- Put a call out for service users willing to share their story and participate in panel discussions
- Meet to provide guidance and time to write a five-minute 'my story' talk
- Practise the talks in front of the group first
- Have an invited audience of friends and family followed by a discussion
- Then hold small public event(s); include a question and answer period

Using comedy and disclosure in the way SUFMH does, entices a public, who might otherwise turn away, to look more closely and respectfully at those who live with mental illness. And it is this open-mindedness on the part of the service user, public and mental health providers that will create the transformation that is sought.

## Final thoughts

Research strongly suggests that contact with individuals with whom the public can relate to and who disclose their experiences living with mental illness may in fact be the leading method for eliminating stigma and prejudice surrounding mental disorders. It follows that service users must be key players in public relations initiatives if those initiatives are to be successful. In addition, creating opportunities for service user participation in public relations must be a priority.

Through performing stand-up comedy about their illnesses, service users in David Granirer's course SUFMH provide an ideal vehicle for transforming current views of what it means to 'be mentally ill'. Context, contact, credibility, candidness and irreverent comedy prove to be essential ingredients in making his programme flourish and his 'service-users-turned-students-turned-comics' successful.

Stigma is cited as one of the main reasons why people refuse to seek treatment. As more service users become involved in public relations building and the attitudes about mental illness changes, people who suffer from mental illness in secrecy will reach out for help sooner. It is therefore imperative that not only public stigma be reduced, but to have individuals with mental illness be involved in reducing the very stigma they often experience by creating the true and accurate picture of what it means to have a mental illness. Positive results that individuals gain in mental healthcare settings are easier to maintain within a community ecology in which basic knowledge and skills about mental health and mental illness are widely distributed and a community which is less fearful and perhaps even welcoming to individuals affected by mental health problems (Jorm, 2000).

# Conclusion

The recovery model adopted within mental health services changed the role of service users from passive to proactive. As a result, for service users who wish, there are now opportunities for them to share their 'lived experience' wisdom to advance better outcomes, act as mental health advocates and enhance public relations. The external environment in which a person recovers plays a pivotal function in that individual's road to wellness. Therefore, management of public relations between mental health services and family and carers, related social agencies and the public is a significant issue.

It is critical, yet often challenging, for mental health professionals to create and preserve clear and successful communication with loved ones and carers of individuals recovering from mental illness. Accommodating the needs of family members and carers, while respecting the wishes of the person with mental illness, is a delicate task requiring diplomacy, clarity and excellent listening and interpersonal skills. A salient element in upholding a helpful relationship with family and carers is offering practical advice and resources about their loved one's illness and what they may face as he or she recovers.

When service users have a central role in anti-stigma initiatives, the greatest impact is seen. Contact with chances for exchange of ideas produces the most significant improvement in attitudes. Community integration and social inclusion for service users can be less difficult when public stigma and prejudice is diminished. When disclosure of one's own mental illness story or personal narrative occurs within the context of this kind of contact, attitudes shift most significantly, more than with anti-stigma protests and education tactics.

It is through the engagement of the wisdom of service users, their insights from living with and recovering from mental illness that will best help public relations prosper. Communities, families, service agencies and other stakeholders learn the most when mental health information is provided by those who know the illnesses from the inside out. The more programmes that are developed with services users as the driving force and at the forefront, the better the outcomes will be.

# References

Berhman, A. (2003). *Electro Boy: A Memoir of Mania.* New York: Random House Trade Paperbacks.

Corrigan, P. W. & O'Shaughnessy, J. R. (2007). Changing mental illness stigma as it exists in the real world. *Australian Psychologist*, 42, 90–97.

Corrigan, P. W. & Watson, A. C. (2006). Challenging public stigma: a targeted approach. In: Corrigan, P. (ed.) *On the Stigma of Mental Illness*. Washington, DC: American Psychological Association, pp. 281–295.

Corrigan, P. W. & White, R. F. (2004). How stigma interferes with mental healthcare: an expert interview with Patrick W. Corrigan. *Medscape Psychiatry and Mental Health* 9. Available at: www.medscape.com/viewarticle/494548 (accessed 23 July 2007).

Corrigan, P. W., River, L., Lundin, R. K., Penn, D. L., Uphoff-Wasowski, K., Campion, J., Mathisen, J., Gagnon, C., Bergman, M., Goldstein, H. & Kubiak, M. A. (2001). Three strategies for changing attributions about mental illness. *Schizophrenia Bulletin*, 27, 187–195.

Corrigan, P. W., Rowan, D., Green, A., Lundin, R., River, L., Uphoff-Wasowski, K., White, K. & Kubiak, M. A. (2002). Challenging two mental illness stigmas: personal responsibility and dangerousness. *Schizophrenia Bulletin*, 28, 293–310.

De Groot, L., Lloyd, C. & King, R. (2003). An evaluation of a family psychoeducation program in community mental health. *Psychiatric Rehabilitation Journal*, 27, 18–23.

Dixon, L., McFarlane, W. R., Lefley, H., Lucksted, A., Cohen, M., Falloon, I., Mueser, K., Miklowitz, D., Solomon, P. & Sondheimer, D. (2001). Evidence-based practices for services to families of people with psychiatric disabilities. *Psychiatric Services*, 52, 903–910.

Duke, P. & Hochman, G. (1992). *Brilliant Madness: Living with Manic Depressive Illness.* New York: Bantam Books.

Families Commission (2007). *Moving On: Changes in a Year in Family Living Arrangements.* Wellington: Families Commission. Available at: www.familiescommission. govt.nz/download/moving-on.pdf (accessed 27 July, 2007).

Gaertner, S. L., Dovidio, J. F. & Bachman, B. A. (1996). Revisiting the contact hypothesis: the induction of a common ingroup identity. *International Journal of Intercultural Relations*, 20, 271–290.

Hinshaw, S. P. (2005). The stigmatization of mental illness in children and parents: Developmental issues, family concerns, and research needs. *Journal of Child Psychology and Psychiatry*, 46, 714–734.

Johnston, L. & Hewstone, M. (1992). Cognitive models of stereotype change: III. Subtyping and the perceived typicality of disconfirming group members. *Journal of Experimental Social Psychology*, 28, 360–386.

Jorm, A. F. (2000). Mental health literacy: public knowledge and beliefs about mental disorders. *British Journal of Psychiatry*, 177, 396–401.

Link, B. G., Phelan, J. C., Bresnahan, M., Stueve, A. & Pescosolido, B. A. (1999). Public conceptions of mental illness: labels, causes, dangerousness, and social distance. *American Journal of Public Health*, 89, 1328–1333.

Macrae, C., Bodenhausen, G. V., Milne, A. B. & Jetten, J. (1994). Out of mind but back in sight: stereotypes on the rebound. *Journal of Personality and Social Psychology*, 67, 808–817.

Marsh, D. T. (2000). Personal accounts of consumer/survivors: insights and implications. *Psychotherapy in Practice*, 56, 1447–1457.

Mueser, K., Glynn, S., Corrigan, P. & Baber, W. (1996). A survey of preferred terms for users of mental health services. *Psychiatric Services*, 47, 760–761.

Pekkala, E. & Merinder, L. (2001). Psychoeducation for schizophrenia. *The Cochrane Library.* Oxford: Update Software. Available at: www.mrw.interscience.wiley.com (accessed 28 July 2007).

Pettigrew, T. F. & Tropp, L. R. (2000). Does intergroup contact reduce prejudice: recent meta-analytic findings. In: Oskamp, S. (ed.) *Reducing Prejudice and Discrimination.* Mahwah, NJ: Erlbaum, pp. 93–114.

Redfield, J. K. (1995). *An Unquiet Mind: A Memoir of Moods and Madness.* New York: Alfred A. Knopf Inc.

Rigby, C. (2007). *What It's Like: How Consumer Staff Members Experience Working in Mental Health.* Unpublished Master's thesis, Auckland University of Technology, Auckland, New Zealand.

Sharma, V., Whitney, D., Kazarian, S, S, & Manchanda, R. (2000). Preferred terms for users of mental health services among service providers and recipients. *Psychiatric Services*, 51, 203–209.

Theaker, A. (2004). *The Public Relations Handbook.* London: Routledge.

Watson, A. C. & Corrigan, P. W (2006). Challenging public stigma: a targeted approach. In: Corrigan, P. (ed.) *On the Stigma of Mental Illness.* Washington, DC: American Psychological Association, pp. 281–295.

Wilcox, D. L., Cameron, G. T., Ault, P. H. & Agee, W. K. (2003). *Public Relations Strategies and Tactics,* 7th edition. New York: Allyn & Bacon.

# Chapter 7
# Organisational changes towards recovery-oriented services

*Samson Tse and Steve Barnett*

## Chapter overview

This chapter covers the organisational implications of several decades of changes in the concepts, espoused values and intended design of mental health services. Practical strategies are offered for mental health practitioners who are frustrated that their arguments for change seem to fail. Solutions focus on changed communication and relational behaviour.

The recovery approach is used as a metaphor to interpret presenting organisational problems, reach a diagnosis and outline the indications for intervention to aid recovery. The chapter first describes the organisational setting from the mental health practitioner's perspective with a synopsis of the three main drivers for change in mental health services over the past decade:

- deinstitutionalisation of care
- the rise of the population perspective on mental health
- adoption of the recovery approach as the guiding principle of mental health service.

The organisational perspective is further developed by presenting the issues in organisational change as they likely apply to the mental health settings. In this analysis it is suggested that the issues be regarded as symptoms of organisational illness, then show how the recovery approach, originally devised for intervention of individuals with mental health problems, is applied to organisational illness to regain organisational health. Rejecting conventional management of the transformation process, a change-project management case example is developed along with tools and strategies to manage the transformation.

## The changing faces of mental health services

The major shaping forces and locations of the considerable changes in mental health services over the past several decades can be broadly classified into three main themes.

## Deinstitutionalisation

Patients are relocated from large-scale psychiatric facilities into the community where care and support are presumably being provided by alternative psychiatric services together within their social network. In the mid-1970s, a series of meetings at the National Institute of Mental Health in the USA resulted in the concept of community support systems (CSS). The CSS was defined as 'a network of caring and responsible people committed to assisting a vulnerable population meet their needs and develop their potentials without being unnecessarily isolated or excluded from the community' (Anthony, 1993, p. 523). The intention was for community mental health centres to provide the link in helping individuals with mental illness in their transition from institutionalisation to the community. They were to provide for the differing needs of all peoples and support the goal of humane care delivered in the least restrictive way (Morrison, 1997).

Community mental healthcare is considered a different approach from more conventional forms of psychiatric services such as hospital-based acute treatment and rehabilitation services (Sayce et al., 1991). Between 1998 and 2001 a major research project to investigate the concept of good community mental healtcare concluded that good care is associated with (Liegeois & Van Audenhove, 2005):

- a trusting and stimulating relationship between individual clients and their professional helpers
- interventions tailored to meet individual needs
- comprehensive and locally available services which are accessible to those who need them
- support and care provided by the client's family or other informal carers, whose needs for information and backing should also be addressed.

To effectively achieve all these individualised, decentralised, relationship-oriented outcomes for clients, their families and other carers, will require a fairly radical change in professional practice of individual workers and their workplace organisation and culture.

## Population perspective on mental health

There is an emergent and rapidly growing concern to address issues of population mental health. In 2003, the World Health Organization (WHO) estimated as many as 450 million people have a mental or behavioural disorder. Nearly one million people commit suicide every year. WHO (2003) also projects that the number of individuals with mental disorders is likely to increase further in view of the ageing of the population, worsening social problems (e.g. family violence, illegal drug use) and civil unrest.

In Australia, depression is the leading cause of non-fatal disease burden in the total population, causing 8% of the total years lived in disability (YLD) in 1996 (Mathers et al., 1999). The latest New Zealand mental health survey, Te Rau Hinengaro, estimates that 46.6% of the population meet criteria for a mental disorder at some time in their life (Oakley Brown et al., 2006). Such population statistics signal that mental health professionals have to work closely with primary healthcare services, address problems of stigma and discrimination associated with mental health problems, engage in health promotion activities and raise the level of mental health literacy of the general population (Barry, 2001; European Commission, 2005).

## Recovery-oriented services

The recovery approach to mental health services has been adopted as a fundamental value and guiding principle in most mental health services. It spans and penetrates funding, policy planning, services development and delivery, legislative support, advocacy and workforce training.

Recovery can be defined as a 'process of learning to approach each day's challenges, overcome our disabilities, learn skills, live independently and contribute to society; this process is supported by those who believe in us and give us hope' (Ralph, 2000, p. 27). In the early 1980s, the term recovery seldom appeared in articles. In the late 1980s and early 1990s, the word recovery was introduced in consumer writing by Deegan (1988) in the paper 'Recovery: the lived experience of rehabilitation' and in a non-consumer paper by Anthony (1993) in 'Recovery from mental illness: the guiding vision of the mental health service system in the 1990s'. Since then there has been a surge of research studies and concept papers on recovery. For example: how recovery is defined; the theoretical underpinnings and the psychological construct; the barriers and facilitators during the recovery process; evidence on whether the recovery approach works; how recovery is described by individuals with various backgrounds such as someone with personal experiences of mental illness; and family/other carers and mental health professionals (e.g. Spaniol & Koehler, 1994; Corrigan et al., 1999; Marsh, 2000; Smith, 2000; Carpenter, 2002; Lapsley et al., 2002; Anthony et al., 2003).

Since the beginning of the twentieth century, recovery research has focused very much on how to create a 'recovery enhancing environment' or a 'recovery-transformed system'; and how to measure recovery-based mental health services (e.g. Ridgway, 2003; Zahniser et al., 2005; Andresen, et al., 2006; Crowe et al., 2006).

Essentially the latest focus to advance the understanding and application of recovery approach is on how to reorientate existing services to put recovery into practice and gather evidence about its effectiveness or otherwise. Together, these three main themes highlight change issues:

- individualisation, decentralisation, relationship orientation of practice that is directed not only at patients but also at their families and other carers
- working closely with primary healthcare services and engaging in general health promotion and education
- reorientating existing services to enable the recovery approach to be put into practice and to gather evidence of its effectiveness or otherwise.

They each spell major transformative change: transformation in behaviour, orientation and organisation; a transformation in administrative practice and culture; and transformation of client–practitioner (therapeutic), practitioner–practitioner (professional) and organisational relationships.

## Changing workplace culture

Perhaps the most difficult aspect of the transformation is to change the organisational culture within which mental health workers operate. This is because the organisational context is typically not practitioners' primary professional concern, though it may be their primary frustration. It is also because organisational culture is underpinned by a set of assumptions about the form, content and conduct of interpersonal relationships within an organisation. For example, some community mental health centres, which are presumably sources of mental health knowledge and expertise, are criticised by their own colleagues and users for inability to make changes and for lack of recovery vision. This apparent failure might be due to the fact that the service and the set-up is not organised for change but to generate and dispense clinical expertise.

Using the community mental health centre as an example, it is argued that change in practice is precluded by the extant organisational culture and climate rather than lack of expert knowledge. Thus it is proposed that to transform practice, practitioners, administrators and managers must transform their assumptions about their individual and collective identity and the conduct of their organisational relationships.

Mental health practitioners can achieve that provided they learn to apply their knowledge and expertise, normally applied to their clients and client relationships, to themselves and their organisational relationships. In particular they apply the recovery approach to their professional and organisational behaviour.

In developing this organisational recovery scenario it is important to first take a closer look at the likely roots and drivers of the tacit organisational culture. This analysis is extended to indicate how dysfunction between organisation and practice might be characterised as an organisational illness and therefore 'treatable' by using a recovery approach.

## Cultural dysfunction and organisational illness

Tacit organisational context lies, iceberg-like, beneath the surface. For instance, the triangular-shaped organisational diagrams consisting of interconnected boxes representing hierarchical positions with subgroups representing departments or divisions are an abstract, partial representation of the actual organisational and interpersonal relationships and processes. These triangular representations are strongly associated with bureaucratic models and the machine metaphor of organisation. This model/metaphor was, and still is, a productive way of

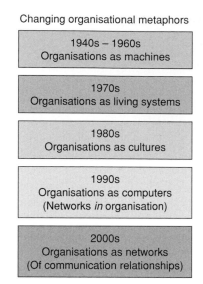

Changing organisational metaphors

**Figure 7.1**    Change of organisational metaphors (adapted from Contractor, 2002).

conceptualising and understanding large organisations operating in stable, unchanging environments. However, with increasing rates of change new metaphors have emerged (Figure 7.1) in response to a general need to conceptualise organisations in more productive ways.

The living system metaphor of the 1970s replaced the rigidity of the dispassionate bureaucratic machine metaphor in the 1940–1960s. The culture metaphor of the 1980s highlighted the concept of organisation as consisting of people, the social beings. Organisational change was synonymous with culture change. The computer metaphor of the 1990s seemed to conveniently simplify and objectify the complexity of culture by attending to information, information systems, information management. Knowledge was synonymous with information.

The phenomenon of the worldwide web (www) has given rise to the notion of organisations as networks – blurring organisational boundaries and informational pathways. Furthermore the www phenomena has produced the possibility of organisations as virtual communities that only exist as the intercommunication between members. So the concept of organisation simply as communication relationships has emerged.

These metaphors, viewed together, comprise a colourful and rich description of the various facets of organisation and practice, suggesting possibilities and meaningful models for change and innovation. However, that possibility has been dominated, especially during the past two decades, by managerial ideology (Freidson, 2001; Parker, 2002) focusing on organisational structures, the centrality of managers and their supposedly value-neutral managerial logic. Managerial assumptions, practices and expectations may be productive in some business settings. But when complexity and diversity cannot be avoided, and expectations are not readily manageable, such as in mental health services, then pervasive

**Table 7.1**  Characteristics of two communication climates (Gibb, 1961, p. 412).

| Characteristics of a defensive communication climate | Characteristics of a supportive communication climate |
| --- | --- |
| Evaluation | Description |
| Control | Problem orientation |
| Strategy | Spontaneity |
| Neutrality | Empathy |
| Superiority | Equality |
| Certainty | Provisionalism |

managerial assumptions and practices may produce organisational dysfunction. This dysfunction may be evident in interpersonal conflict between practitioners, between managers, and between practitioners and managers; in passive/aggressive communication behaviours associated with defensive rather than supportive communication climates (Table 7.1; Gibb, 1961).

Under such conditions it is little wonder therefore that: mental health professionals would struggle to maintain and improve service quality within shrinking resources and increasing expectations; in some cases they would appear to become increasingly cynical in their dealings with their employing organisations; mental health programmes would be conceived with little understanding of recovery values and principles; and in the extreme, the dysfunctional organisation would become incapable of delivering recovery-oriented mental health services.

## Recovery in practice

Though it describes process and outcome for an individual with mental health problems, the 'guideline to the recovery approach' illustrated in Figure 7.2 can also apply to enable practitioners to better collaborate to develop new individual and organisational identity and support new recovery-centred practice. For instance 'recovery as outcomes' for mental health services might involve: confidence, productivity, (functional) wellness, new knowledge and skills, quality (internal and external) relationships, and mobilisation of external collaboration to develop new opportunities to deliver improved services.

The implications, for professional and organisational culture, of recovery practice have received recent close attention. For example, key ingredients of a Recovery Oriented Mental Health Program (ROMHP) have been characterised by explicit statements about the programme structures such as mission, policies, procedures, record keeping and quality assurance. It has been argued that these factors are consistent with fundamental recovery values regardless of the specific mental health service delivered (Table 7.2; Farkas et al., 2005).

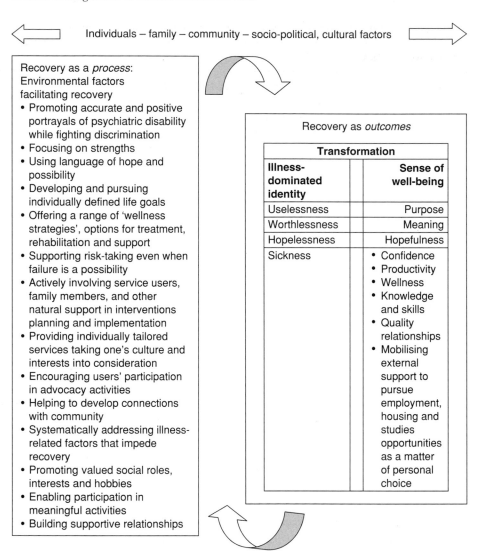

Recovery as a *process*:
Environmental factors
facilitating recovery
• Promoting accurate and positive portrayals of psychiatric disability while fighting discrimination
• Focusing on strengths
• Using language of hope and possibility
• Developing and pursuing individually defined life goals
• Offering a range of 'wellness strategies', options for treatment, rehabilitation and support
• Supporting risk-taking even when failure is a possibility
• Actively involving service users, family members, and other natural support in interventions planning and implementation
• Providing individually tailored services taking one's culture and interests into consideration
• Encouraging users' participation in advocacy activities
• Helping to develop connections with community
• Systematically addressing illness-related factors that impede recovery
• Promoting valued social roles, interests and hobbies
• Enabling participation in meaningful activities
• Building supportive relationships

Recovery as *outcomes*

| Transformation | | |
|---|---|---|
| Illness-dominated identity | | Sense of well-being |
| Uselessness | | Purpose |
| Worthlessness | | Meaning |
| Hopelessness | | Hopefulness |
| Sickness | | • Confidence<br>• Productivity<br>• Wellness<br>• Knowledge and skills<br>• Quality relationships<br>• Mobilising external support to pursue employment, housing and studies opportunities as a matter of personal choice |

Individuals – family – community – socio-political, cultural factors

**Figure 7.2** Recovery as a process and outcomes (adapted from: Mancini et al., 2005; O'Connell et al., 2005; Roe et al., 2007).

In another example, Crowe and colleagues (2006) provided a two-day training session titled 'Collaborative Recovery Training Program' to increase mental health professionals' knowledge, attitudes and hopefulness regarding the possibility of recovery. The preliminary findings showed that over the course of the session, desired changes were found in trainees' recovery-related knowledge, beliefs and attitudes. This seems to indicate that through intensive collaborative learning processes, mental health professionals can change. However, researchers

**Table 7.2** Critical dimensions of recovery-oriented mental health programme.

| Key recovery values | |
| --- | --- |
| Person orientation | The service focuses on the individual first and foremost as an individual with strengths, talents, interests as well as limitations rather than treating the person as a 'case' |
| Person involvement | The service focuses on people's right to full partnership in all aspects of their recovery including planning, implementing and evaluating the services that is meant to support their recovery |
| Self-determination/choice | The service focuses on people's rights to make individual decisions about *all aspects* of their recovery process |
| Growth potential | The service focuses on the inherent capacity of any individual to recover, regardless of whether, at the moment, he or she is overwhelmed by the disability, living with or living beyond the disability |

Examples of values-based recovery standards by programme dimensions

*Organisation and administration*

| Programme dimensions | Examples of recovery standard |
| --- | --- |
| Mission | Help people improve their functioning so that they can be successful and satisfied in the environment of their choice |
| Policies | People will have the opportunities and assistance to choose and plan for whatever services they want to promote their own recovery |
| Procedures | Provide orientation steps in different communication modalities to ensure clients receive sufficient information about the programme (e.g. what the programme offers, cannot offer, what it expects and how clients can give feedback) |
| Record keeping | Records are designed to include process and outcome measures related directly to the programme's mission |
| Quality assurance | Monitor programme outcomes include measures selected by clients |
| Physical setting | Programme facilities are for everyone's use |
| Network | Programme links to services in both community and professional settings |

*Staffing*

| Programme dimensions | Examples of recovery standard |
| --- | --- |
| Selection | Staff members are hired based on their knowledge, attitudes and skills in recovery |
| Training | Staff training includes interaction and interview with individuals who have recovered or are living beyond their disability |
| Supervision | Promotions, rewards and supervisors' reinforcement reflects staff's ability to demonstrate the knowledge, attitudes and skills necessary for recovery and recovery outcomes |

Adapted from Farkas et al. (2005).

acknowledge (e.g. Farkas et al., 2005; Deane et al., 2006; Crowe et al., 2006, 2007) the challenge of translating the prescribed process and isolated professional awareness into widespread cultural change within an organisation necessary to actually incorporate the complex and multidimensional recovery process in a mental health service.

In many cases the challenge may be to manage the recovery treatment of a dysfunctional organisation. Clearly the organisational and management model that produced the dysfunction is unlikely to provide the solution. A communication-based, relational alternative to conventional organisation and management is proposed.

## Fostering organisational recovery: a relational approach

The strength of conventional bureaucratic management is its comparative efficiency at operating standardised routines and procedures in stable environments where incremental change is sufficient to maintain a balance between operational capability and stakeholders' expectations (Mintzberg, 1983). When this comparative organisational stasis is disturbed, or pushed beyond equilibrium by the changing organisational environment, the conventional management assumptions and processes may no longer suffice.

The usual reactions will likely be to tighten and heighten conventional managerial controls. This may be evident in increased demand for detailed analyses, and demand for new policies, typically prescriptive procedures and related compliance audits. This reaction is problematic because a loosening rather than a tightening of conventional control is needed so that new knowledge, new ways of responding can be collaboratively discovered, experimented and communicated (Argyris, 1998). The question is, can such loosening be achieved without compromising the quality of current service? In other words, can organisational looseness and tightness be achieved simultaneously?

Mintzberg (1983) suggested this apparent contradiction can be achieved through professional autonomy (looseness) operating within an administrative bureaucracy (tightness). Such organisation was, and often still is, a characteristic of institutions such as universities and teaching hospitals. However, these institutions were designed or evolved for relatively stable environments, not for collaborative change in dynamic and complex environments.

It seems fairly clear that new organisational knowledge is needed and that generating it will require at least an augmented set of organisational processes. The augmentation must not diminish the functional capability to continue standard operations but at the same time must enable experimentation and accommodate ambiguity and not-knowing. It must support new shared understanding and successful collaborative action without compromising conventional bureaucratic action. In other words, the augmented processes must generate a culture that values socially situated knowledge, as contained in and enacted through relationships in addition to what is conventionally available in individuals or in manuals

(Argyris & Schon, 1978; Araujo, 1998; Brown & Duguid, 1991, 2001; Gherardi, 2001).

Such organisational augmentation would typically be attempted as a project managed by a multidisciplinary team to devise, plan and implement the changes. The inter-relationships among various team members and responsibilities allocated would typically be in addition to members' normal functional connections. Such a minor structural modification or a 'rewiring' of the conventional organisational structure is unlikely to generate new culture for transformation. That requires reconceptualisation of the project as a relationally focused rather than a task-focused enterprise. This begins with transformation of project team members' interpersonal communication and then extends to the wider organisation. A communication-based relational strategy is proposed in which mental health workers and managers reflectively adapt and apply recovery values (Farkas et al., 2005) and the contextual factors (see Figure 7.2) to themselves, their inter-relationships and their organisation.

## Communication-based relational strategy

Conventional project management is typically task focused. Success depends on the accuracy of the planning and controlled completion of the sequence of tasks.

In a project to achieve transformational change, the exact, objective outputs cannot be known at the outset. They emerge from the project process. The sequence of tasks and events is similarly not known. Success centres not on conventional objective knowing but on knowing the processes that have the highest probability of producing success. It is about processes of continual learning and adjustment to first discern the target and then to reach it. Clearly in such emergence, change will be endemic, necessary, desired, even welcomed in contrast to being dreaded in conventional project management.

The authors suggest that the fundamental knowledge and skills for emergence are in the area of interpersonal relationships and a related set of concepts of organisation and leadership for change:

- organisation as a web of communication relationships rather than structures (Weick & Ashford, 2001)
- organisational knowledge, learning and hence change, being socially situated in relationships (Lave, 1996; Wenger, 2000)
- leadership through cohering frameworks of a widely and deeply shared sense of vision and purpose (Senge, 1990; Senge et al., 1994; Collins, 2001).

A project-based strategy for achieving organisational change in mental health services is proposed. In particular a relationally focused approach is suggested in contrast to a typical task-focused approach to project leadership. A web of purposeful communication relationships should be built rather than conventional reporting structures, mechanisms and task sequences. Collaborative organisational experimentation and learning is encouraged rather than managerially determined tasks and accountabilities. Furthermore, this should be operated within a widely and deeply shared sense of purpose and vision.

Such approaches have a higher chance of success because mental health professionals typically have strong sense of vocational vision and purpose, understand the central therapeutic value of interpersonal relationships, and generally have skills to achieve therapeutic change. Because task-focused managerial assumptions are endemic in the general organisational environment, especially of large bureaucratic organisations, the project leaders and members will need continual coaching and support to maintain their relational, process focus.

Coaching support is primarily for the project leaders who will likely experience pressure from internal and external stakeholders to abandon the relationally focused strategy in order to achieve early progress on tasks. Task progress is managerially attractive because it is generally tangible, objectively measurable and time saved by early task completion is typically regarded as the best hedge against later unplanned change.

The conventional ideal path to project completion is represented by the straight line in Figure 7.3. The curved upper line represents early attention to tasks, minimising the possibility of unexpected change and accumulating slack time in the knowledge that change unfortunately will probably occur. However, in a transformational change project, the strategy is to enable new ideas, new perspectives and new leaders to emerge. This emergence is enabled and supported through a web of interpersonal relationships and collaborative behaviours that are expressed in the agreed framework of high-level goals and objectives for the project. The best time to build these relationships and behaviours is in the early phases of the project. It is too late in the advanced planning and execution phases when the behavioural climate and trajectory is already 'locked in' by the resources spent.

It is hypothesised that a project with a strongly developed relational network and open, supportive communication climate (the lower curved line in Figure 7.3)

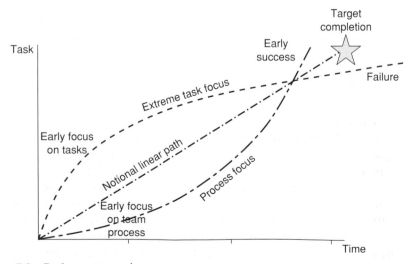

**Figure 7.3**   Pathways to project success.

is more likely to succeed than a task-focused project with weak relational development because it is more likely to produce and effectively respond to transformative
change.

## Patterns of change and the role of the project manager

The fruits of transformative organisational change are unlikely to emerge within
one, or even two years. Some indicative benefits may appear during the first
year but clear results typically take two to five years (Edwards Deming, 1994).
Significant progress can be achieved in as little as 12 weeks within particular teams
and clusters. These pockets of changed behaviour, though fragile in the midst
of unchanged assumptions, practices and behaviours that pervade the wider organisation, are the nuclei around which change grows – a 'strategic termite' model
of change (Morgan, 1993).

Given the comparative slowness of the change process, conventional expectations for early outcomes are therefore another pressure on project leaders to
truncate the typically messy, complex early project phases. These early phases
are where shared understanding is achieved to reduce the chances of persistent
misunderstanding and expensive later repair. The early phases are also the critical
time where the foundations and relational infrastructure of distributed leadership and responsibility are established.

Project leaders must resist pressure, stemming from others' or their own sense
of uncertainty, for early detailed specification, analysis and planning. This pressure will be evident from expectations of superiors and subordinates alike for
answers, managerial direction, detail and objective progress. The pressure and
expectation is for early resolution of ambiguity. Yet that ambiguity and the related
anxiety and uncertainty are key factors in achieving the transformation. The ambiguity is strategically desirable in the change process (Eisenberg et al., 2001), especially the early phases, and the associated anxiety a key indicator of progress.

Rising anxiety indicates progress towards the 'tipping point' (Gladwell, 2000;
Kim & Mauborgne, 2006) in a particular transformational change process. The
anxiety is both the trigger and the motivation for change in communication and
relational behaviour from conventional, largely individualistic behaviours to
collaborative behaviours that enable new, experiential organisational learning
(Lichtenstein, 1997).

The key to achieving the transformation, to successfully moving through the
crisis of the tipping point rather than slipping backwards to conventional status
quo, lies in anticipating and recognising the tipping point and seizing the opportunities it presents. The early signs of successful transformation include: previously
unspoken ideas are shared; uninterested people show signs of engagement; new
leaders and new followers emerge; individuals risk new openness in relationships
with colleagues, managers and subordinates; previously hidden talent, skill
and aptitude surfaces. In other words the organisation, team by team, cluster
by cluster, pocket by pocket, begins to transform with a new widely and deeply
shared purpose.

The project is not a managerially engineered, company-wide change pro-gramme, the likes of which are evidently one of the greatest obstacles to effect-ing real change (Beer et al., 1990; Clarke, 1999). It is a raft of collaborative, interpersonal relationships. It consists of a series of mini-projects centred on the relationships and communication that makes up actual organisational life and practice. The overall two-to-five-year change-project can usefully be regarded as cumulative learning through a web of 12-week mini-change-projects. Each has its own particular cycle of anxiety, tipping point and transformation, with the tipping point occurring between the eighth and twelfth weeks. This cycle is driven by the generally acknowledged need to change and is supported by the reflective practice and performance appraisal tools that are described and discussed later in this chapter.

Thus the general purpose of the transformation project, whatever the presenting technical issue, is to achieve change in communication relational behaviour in the belief that dysfunction is healed through collaboratively changed relationships and communication behaviour. Broadly speaking the desired change is from closed, manipulative aggressive/defensive communication (Gibb, 1961) characterised by blaming, shaming and justifying, to assertive/supportive communication. Assert-ive communication is characterised by open agendas and individuals confidently, openly voicing their perspectives in the robust interaction for consensus-based prioritisation and decision-making; here consensus means unity not unanimity or uniformity.

For instance, assertive communicators typically begin by describing, without blame, the situation as they perceive it. They disclose the observations or data that form the basis of their perception; they then describe their feelings about the situation; then, based on that perception and the data, they say what they want to happen; and finally they ask for others' perceptions, as the following exemplar illustrates.

'The proposed key performance indicators (KPIs) *seem to me* to measure com-pliance with an administrative process that *as far as I know* has no established correlation with successful clinical intervention. For instance *I appreciate* that we need guidelines for [interviewing children] but gauging our professional performance from simple procedural compliance data, to be collected by a junior clerk, *seems to me* to be an unhelpful, unreliable measure of complex professional service.

*I feel* confused and annoyed about this: confused because *I don't know* whether to pay attention to the KPIs or to the quality of my professional prac-tice; annoyed because *it seems to me* that these KPIs have been developed and will now be implemented without adequate thought and design.

*I want us* to collaborate to devise some KPIs that more reliably indicate the quality of our service. What do you think?'

(Notice that this exemplar has the characteristics of Gibb's Supportive Communication Climate, see Table 7.1.)

The project leader's role is to not be the technically expert manager and task master. It is to model, mirror and mentor collaborative relational behaviour. In other words to 'talk the walk' and 'walk the talk'; to model the process of exposing untested assumptions about communication and organisation so that they can be checked, modified and change can begin; to model constructive giving, receiving, and learning from feedback and openly enacting that learning; and to commend, encourage and respond collaboratively to collaborative behaviour.

It requires a project leader with a different set of skills to thus reflect the rising, projected anxiety back to the project team and mentor them in communication and relational behaviour for collaboration. In that sense the project leader's job is to not meet conventional managerial expectations but to operate the recovery approach (Tables 7.1 and 7.2) at the professional and organisational levels. In a managerial sense this is risky territory. Risk-averse, individualistic managers and subordinates will tend to 'cut and run' or disengage when they feel they are losing control or 'getting out of their depth'. Hence the need for experienced external coaching support for the leaders.

Coaching support is probably best initiated by the coach facilitating a one-day intensive interactive workshop to lay the foundations of the developing and growing web of relationships. The intended outputs are shared vision, purpose and high-level goals. This initial understanding will change and develop as the project unfolds. The workshop is more about process than outputs though outputs are important too. Managers are typically surprised at the high levels of congruence and the energy and excitement that a well facilitated workshop produces.

The workshop would probably consist of a sequence of around nine segments.

(1)  Revisit core values – an important process for relationship building and for building a sense of shared purpose is to workshop the shared core values of the organisation and its members. This is essentially a brainstorming exercise that includes all members of the immediate organisation. The aim is to achieve a distillate of four or five core values. It is important at this point to identify champions from among the participants, for each of the core values. Their role is to be accountable for maintaining the ongoing visibility of these values in strategic decision making. In a political sense the champions lead the lobbying to ensure the visibility of the values in meetings and conversations, performance measures and recruitment. The champions are accountable for that visibility.

(2)  Identify three or four cornerstones of the organisation's purpose – its promise to the people it serves. This brainstorming and distilling process is also important for building a sense of shared purpose. These cornerstones will be congruent with the core values. For instance they might be 'recovery-oriented', 'reliable' and 'accessible'. Try to qualify these terms as a way to discover the various meanings that underpin them. These cornerstones serve as durable reference criteria for organisational decisions (as do the core values).

(3)  Generate a shared vision and a challenging long-term (say 10-year) goal on the path to achieving the higher vision. Imagine what could be if all the

perceived barriers and constraints could be overcome. This is an opportunity to visualise beyond the current limitations: a way 'out of the square'. Again, in this process, organisation members are encouraged to learn about themselves and their colleagues and build an awareness and clarity about the natural alignment of purposes within the variety of perspectives.

(4) Break that long-term goal down successively into a medium-term (three-to-five-year) goal and then a one-year goal. Later (below) break that one-year goal into 12-week goals. That's when detail is considered.

(5) Identify the main strengths, weaknesses, opportunities and threats to the group achieving its one-year goal. In brainstorming the possibilities pay special attention not only to their effect on achieving the goal, but also on the *communication and relational behaviours and processes* within and external to the group.

(6) Classify the possibilities into four categories (Figure 7.4) according to their effort and effect required to achieve increased benefit.

(7) Agree on a selection of up to five preferably high value/easy-to-achieve possibilities for attention during the next 12 weeks. Take care not to overlook possibilities in the high value, hard-to-achieve category. Identify a champion for each and determine generally how progress will be apparent and measured.

(8) Establish a schedule for both regular short and long meetings and other information gathering and feedback opportunities. The simplest, shortest, most frequent meetings may simply be each team member in turn briefly telling the others what they are doing that day, what their immediate issues are, and how they feel about the prospects. The core values should be visible and enacted in these regular meetings. One way to explicitly achieve that is to ask members to bring stories about enacting (or not enacting) the core values in their organisational relationships and activities. In mental health services the values that underpin the recovery approach would probably figure prominently.

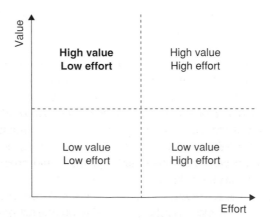

**Figure 7.4**    Four categories of effort and effect.

(9)  Celebrate having completed these initial steps. The key is to maintain the momentum achieved in the workshop through ongoing communication where emergent issues and the change progress can be tracked.

# Management tools and systems for change

Two systems are outlined in this section: shared reflection and peer performance appraisal. These are designed to support the project leaders as coaches or mentors of intrapersonal, interpersonal and organisational communication and interrelationship. The aim is to change the way mental health service is organised: to change the mental health practitioners', managers' and administrators' formal and informal communication pathways; their interpersonal behaviours and roles; their assumptions about the way to behave and interact with each other; and other facets of tacit and explicit organisational knowledge. The focus is on changed communication behaviour.

Crucially, communication behaviour and behaviour change are best monitored and managed by peers within individual and group reflective process. These two systems are based on three fundamental values:

- the concept of organisation as communication relationships (Senge, 1990; Senge et al., 1994; Weick & Ashford, 2001);
- the principles of reflective practice (Argyris, 1991);
- the values and attitudes embedded in the recovery approach (see Figure 7.2 and Table 7.2).

## Shared reflection

Shared reflection on shared experience of organisational (as distinct from clinical: practitioner–patient) practice and change is the core activity. It is used to reveal assumptions about self, group and organisation; and to discover and utilise valid data (Argyris & Schon, 1978). The performance appraisal system outlined below assists this evidence-informed change process. The quality of reflection is indicated not so much by the scholarly or intellectual content as it is by the depth of interpretation of specific intra- and interpersonal communication behaviour in actual, shared communication events and episodes within the organisational change project.

To encourage personal disclosure within small mentored groups of practitioners, access to shared reflection is restricted to the group members and their mentor. The mentor models and encourages reflection that is personal, specific to particular communication acts (dialogue), insightful, and proposes and monitors plans for personal behaviour change.

For best effect, reflection should be frequent. For example, each team member of practitioners completes a reflection weekly on at least one communication event. A communication event occurs in a particular context and is typically around an issue, problem, conflict, or a segment of a routine process. The mentor leads discussion on the quality and usefulness of each reflection. The quality standards are indicated by the list 'Environmental factors facilitating recovery' in Figure 7.2.

Virtual, asynchronous communication channels such as electronic discussion boards and blogs can be used to overcome difficulty of sharing reflections and feedback. This is especially because computer-based information and communication technology (ICT) is increasingly accessed by members of mental health service organisations in their work and private lives. Textual, asynchronous communication has the added advantage of providing continuity of narrative plus requiring more thought and explicit care than verbal communication.

Depending on the assumptions that they bring to this medium members will respond differently. Some may be more reluctant to disclose than by face-to-face, preferring more immediate, dynamic interactions or perhaps because they are wary of written records. Conversely, others may feel freer to disclose and experiment because they prefer to have time to consider their interactions or because shyness, perceived power dynamics or language difficulties constrain them in more immediate, dynamic media. Whatever medium is used, the aim is to provide a variety of avenues to build trust and openness for shared reflection amongst the group.

### Peer performance appraisal

Appraisal of communication behaviour is the job of team peers. Appraisal against a suitable set of standard behaviour-based criteria can enable tracking of change and development over time. Such appraisal is a normal part of many comprehensive commercial performance management systems. In such systems, behaviour-based, process-focused performance appraisal by an individual's peers, supervisors and subordinates (360-degree appraisal) balances the typically output-based goal-focused measures used as KPIs. Peer appraisal in commercial systems is usually anonymous whereas an open appraisal within the project team is mentored by project team members.

A set of criteria specifically applicable to the mental health service context could be developed from the list of facilitating environmental factors in Figure 7.2. Each factor can be expanded into a range of specific observable behaviours that indicate different levels of performance. For example the set of four criteria in Figure 7.5 have been derived from the factor 'Enabling participation in meaningful activities'. The objective in designing the appraisal questionnaire is to cover the diverse contributions and levels of competency that individuals contribute to collaborative activity. Figure 7.5 shows a typical appraisal pattern and score, out of 50.

Peer performance appraisals can be consolidated for each appraisee and the individual and consolidated results can be openly shared to further inform the reflective process. Change can be tracked by subscale and total scores. After allowing time for the peers to pilot the system to familiarise themselves with the way the scoring works and building trust and openness, the appraisal system can be

| Enabling participation in meaningful activities | Always (5) | Mostly (4) | Often (3) | Sometimes (2) | Rarely (1) | Unknown (0) | Score |
|---|---|---|---|---|---|---|---|
| **Novice: keeps learning**<br>Shares new information with the team?<br>(1 ×) | ● | | | | | | 5 |
| **Intermediate: acts as a coach**<br>Offers practical advice, demonstrations and the insight of experience?<br>(2 ×) | | ● | | | | | 8 |
| **Experienced: increases the team skill base**<br>Encourages and supports others take the lead and practice leadership?<br>(3 ×) | | | ● | | | | 9 |
| **Sophisticated: pushes the team**<br>Challenges the team to go beyond the accepted barriers?<br>(4 ×) | | | | | ● | | 4 |
| | | | | | | | 25 |

**Figure 7.5** Example of items and scores for 'enabling participation in meaningful activities'.

given 'bite' (Collins, 1999) by linking the consolidated results to apportionment of group reward and recognition.

For instance, a team that has achieved a recognised high level of success in, or as a result of, collaborative professional practice, can use the peer appraisal data to identify and acknowledge particular team members for their contribution to building the underpinning relationships. The power in this is that the team, not the manager, decides by systematic process which members to especially recognise or reward. This contrasts and balances conventional processes that are decided by managers and tend to focus on individual performance. It helps stimulate, encourage and reward behaviours that support and enable organisational learning to collaborate more effectively.

# Conclusion

The massive pressure and scope for change in mental health services indicates a transformation in practice and organisation. Though the requirements seem well, even widely understood, effective implementation of the espoused change has proved difficult and frustrating.

The roots to this difficulty and frustration lie in the tacit assumptions about organisation that we call culture. For transformation to occur, this tacit culture must be identified, acknowledged, examined and purposefully modified. This is a communication-intensive process where normally acceptable communication behaviours and processes are not effective. A fundamental or driving element of the transformation process is to develop more effective interpersonal and organisational communication behaviours and processes.

A diagnosis of the persistent organisational dysfunction as 'mental illness' suggests that organisational wellness might well be achieved by adaptation of the recovery approach to the professional and organisational levels of change in health services. Transforming the culture of the organisation is thus similar to transforming the health and well-being of the individual.

While such a novel application of mental health knowledge may make intellectual sense, it is expected that this intellectual understanding will not readily translate into behaviour change. Major barriers are organisational and management assumptions, behaviours and processes that produced the dysfunction. They are unlikely to enable and support effective treatment. The transformation project therefore requires a new approach to management, that is, a recovery approach.

Thus we advocate a carefully designed and managed project to transform mental health service organisation from managerial to recovery-based culture to enable the delivery of quality mental health services to clients with mental health problems and the population in general. Two main tools for design and management were proposed: (i) shared reflection on inter-relational communication behaviour and (ii) shared peer performance appraisal to drive, inform and measure the behaviour change. These tools are operated within the overarching values and programme of the recovery approach to achieve the necessary communication and relationship climate for recovery.

# References

Andresen, R., Caputi, P. & Oades, L. (2006). Stages of recovery instrument: Development of a measure of recovery from serious mental illness. *Australian and New Zealand Journal of Psychiatry*, 40, 972–980.

Anthony, W. A. (1993). Recovery from mental illness: the guiding vision of the mental health service system in the 1990s. *Psychosocial Rehabilitation Journal*, 16, 11–23.

Anthony, W. A., Rogers, E. S. & Farkas, M. (2003). Research on evidence-based practices: future directions in an era of recovery. *Community Mental Health Journal*, 39, 101–114.

Araujo, L. (1998). Knowing and learning as networking. *Management Learning*, 29, 317–336.

Argyris, C. (1991). Teaching smart people how to learn. *Harvard Business Review*, 69, 99–110.

Argyris, C. (1998). Empowerment: the emperor's new clothes. *Harvard Business Review*, 76, 98–106.

Argyris, C. & Schon, D. A. (1978). *Organization Learning: A Theory of Action Perspective*. Reading: Addison Wesley.

Barry, M. M. (2001). Promoting positive mental health: theoretical frameworks for practice. *International Journal of Mental Health Promotion*, 3, 25–34.

Beer, M., Eisenstat, R. & Spector, B. (1990). Why change programmes don't produce change. *Harvard Business Review*, 68, 158–166.

Brown, J. S. & Duguid, P. (1991). Organization learning and communities-of-practice: toward a unified view of working, learning and innovation. *Organization Science*, 2, 58–82.

Brown, J. S. & Duguid, P. (2001). Knowledge and organisation: a social practice perspective. *Organization Science*, 12, 198–213.

Carpenter, J. (2002). Mental health recovery paradigm: implications for social work. *Health and Social Work*, 27, 86–94.

Clarke, M. (1999). Management development: a new role in social change? *Management Decision*, 37, 767–777.

Collins, J. (1999). Turning goals into results: the power of catalytic mechanisms. *Harvard Business Review*, 77, 70–82.

Collins, J. (2001). Level 5 leadership: the triumph of humility and fierce resolve. *Harvard Business Review*, 79, 66–76.

Contractor, N. S. (2002). New media and organising. In: Lievrow, L. & Livingstone, S. (eds) *The Handbook of New Media.* London: Sage, pp. 203–205.

Corrigan, P. W., Giffort, D., Rashid, F., Leary, M. & Okeke, I. (1999). Recovery as a psychological construct. *Community Mental Health Journal*, 35, 231–239.

Crowe, T. P., Deane, F. P., Oades, L. G., Caputi, P. & Morland, K. G. (2006). Effectiveness of a collaborative recovery training program in Australia in promoting positive views about recovery. *Psychiatric Services*, 57, 1497–1500.

Crowe, T. P., Couley, A., Diaz, P. & Humphries, S. (2007) The adoption of recovery-based practice: the organisation's journey. *New Paradigm: Australian Journal on Psychosocial Rehabilitation*, June, 51–57.

Deane, F. P., Crowe, T. P., King, R., Kavanagh, D. J. & Oades, L. G. (2006). Challenges in implementing evidence-based practice into mental health services. *Australian Health Review*, 30, 305–309.

Deegan, P. E. (1988). Recovery: the lived experience of rehabilitation. *Psychosocial Rehabilitation Journal*, 11, 11–19.

Edwards Deming, W. (1994). *The New Economics for Industry, Government, Education*, 2nd edition. Cambridge, Massachusetts: MIT, Centre for Advanced Education Services.

Eisenberg, E. M., Goodal, H. L. Jr. & Goodal, H. L. (2001) *Organizational Communication. Balancing Creativity and Constraint*, 3rd edition. New York: Bedford.

European Commission (2005). *Green paper. Improving the mental health of the population: towards a strategy on mental health for the European Union.* Brussels: European Commission.

Farkas, M., Gagne, C., Anthony, W. & Chamberlin, J. (2005). Implementing recovery oriented evidence based programs: identifying the critical dimensions. *Community Mental Health Journal*, 41, 145–153.

Freidson, E. (2001). *Professionalism: The Third Logic.* Chicago: University of Chicago Press.

Gherardi, S. (2001). From organizational learning to practice-based knowing. *Human Relations*, 54, 131–139.

Gibb, J. (1961). Defensive communication. *Journal of Communication*, 11, 141–148.

Gladwell, M. (2000). *The Tipping Point: How Little Things can Make a Big Difference.* London: Little, Brown.

Kim, W. C. & Mauborgne, R. (2006). *Tipping point leadership. Harvard Business Review on Leading Through Change*. Boston: Harvard Business School Press.

Lapsley, H., Nikora, L. W. & Black, R. (2002). *Kia Mauri Tau! Narratives of recovery from disabling mental health problems.* Wellington: Mental Health Commission.

Lave, J. (1996). The practice of learning. In: Chaiklin, S. & Lave, J. (eds) *Understanding Practice: Perspectives on Activity and Context.* New York: Cambridge University Press, pp. 35–64.

Lichtenstein, B. M. (1997). Grace, magic and miracles: a 'chaotic logic' of organizational transformation. *Journal of Organizational Change Management*, 10, 393–411.

Liegeois, A. & Van Audenhove, C. (2005). Ethical dilemmas in community mental health care. *Journal of Medical Ethics*, 31, 452–456.

Mancini, M. A., Hardiman, E. R. & Lawson, H. A. (2005). Making sense of it all: consuming providers' theories about factors facilitating and impeding recovery from psychiatric disabilities. *Psychiatric Rehabilitation Journal*, 29, 48–55.

Marsh, D. (2000). Personal accounts of consumers/survivors: insight and implications. *Journal of Clinical Psychology*, 56, 1447–1457.

Mathers, C., Vos, T. & Stevenson, C. (1999). *The Burden of Disease and Injury in Australia.* The Australian Institute of Health and Welfare cat. no. PHE 17. Canberra: AIHW.

Mintzberg, H. (1983). *Structures in Fives.* Englewood Cliffs, New Jersey: Prentice-Hall.

Morgan, G. (1993). *Imaginization, the Art of Creative Management.* Newbury Park, CA: Sage.

Morrison, P. (1997). *Caring and Communication: Essential Nursing Treatment.* London: Macmillan.

Oakley Brown, M. A., Wells, J. E. & Scott, K. M. (eds) (2006). *Te Rau Hinengaro: The New Zealand Mental Health Survey.* Wellington: Ministry of Health.

O'Connell, M., Tondora, J., Croog, G., Evans, A. & Davidson, L. (2005). From rhetoric to routine: assessing perceptions of recovery-oriented practices in a state mental health and addiction system. *Psychiatric Rehabilitation Journal*, 28, 378–386.

Parker, M. (2002). *Against Management.* Cambridge: Polity Press.

Ralph, R. (2000). *Review of Recovery Literature: a Synthesis of a Sample of Recovery Literature* 2000. Alexandria, Virginia: National Association of State Mental Health Program Directors, National Technical Assistance Center for State Mental Health Planning.

Ridgway, P. (2003). *The Recovery Enhancing Environment Measure (REE): Using Measurement Tools to Understand and Shape Recovery-oriented Practice.* Available at: www.mhsip.org/2003%20presentations/Plenary/RidgewayPlenary.pdf (accessed 28 March 2007).

Roe, D., Rudnick, A. & Gill, K. (2007). Commentary: The concept of 'being in recovery'. *Psychiatric Rehabilitation Journal*, 30, 171–173.

Sayce, L., Craig, T. K. J. & Boardman, A. P. (1991). The development of community mental health centres in the UK. *Social Psychiatry and Psychiatric Epidemiology*, 26, 14–20.

Senge, P., Roberts, C., Ross, R., Smith, B. & Kleiner, A. (eds) (1994). *The Fifth Discipline Fieldbook.* New York: Currency/Doubleday.

Senge, P. M. (1990). *The Fifth Discipline: The Art and Practice of the Learning Organization.* New York: Doubleday/Currency.

Smith, M. K. (2000). Recovery from a severe psychiatric disability: findings of a qualitative study. *Psychiatric Rehabilitation Journal*, 24, 149–158.

Spaniol, L. & Koehler, M. (1994). *The Experience of Recovery.* Boston: Center for Psychiatric Rehabilitation, Boston University.

Weick, K. E. & Ashford, S. J. (2001). Learning in organizations. In: Jablin, F. & Putnam, L. (eds) *The New Handbook of Organizational Communication.* Thousand Oaks: Sage, pp. 704–731.

Wenger, E. C. (2000). Communities of practice and social learning systems. *Organization*, 7, 225–246.

World Health Organization (2003). *The World Health Report* 2003. Geneva: World Health Organization.

Zahniser, J. H., Ahern, L. & Fisher, D. (2005). How the PACE program builds a recovery-transformed system: results from a national survey. *Psychiatric Rehabilitation Journal*, 29, 142–145.

# Chapter 8
# Clinical supervision

*Robert King and Gerry Mullan*[1]

## Chapter overview

Clinical supervision has attracted substantial interest in recent years as a core process in the operation of mental health services (White & Winstanley, 2006; Butterworth et al., 2008). Advocacy for introduction of clinical supervision has been especially strong within the nursing profession (for which it is relatively new) and in the UK, where it has become mandatory in some services (Abbott et al., 2006). This chapter discusses the role of clinical supervision in mental health services. It argues that there is sufficient evidence regarding the benefits of clinical supervision to warrant its utilisation as part of standard operational practice within mental health services. Recommendations are made concerning ways by which service managers can promote, support and monitor clinical supervision. The chapter begins by differentiating clinical supervision from related processes, especially line management and clinical review. The existing evidence base concerning the effectiveness of clinical supervision is then considered, having reference to each of the three domains (formative, normative and restorative) set out in Proctor's (1986) model. An overview is provided of ethical and legal issues that may arise in the context of clinical supervision. The chapter concludes with recommendations regarding processes by which clinical supervision can best be introduced and sustained within a service.

## What is clinical supervision and how does it differ from line management and clinical review?

There have been a number of attempts to provide a definitive statement that captures the core characteristics of clinical supervision (Milne, 2007). In this section, rather than providing a single definition, we attempt to differentiate clinical supervision from related processes such as line management and clinical review.

Clinical supervision is a process by which a trainee or professional discusses clinical work with a colleague. Clinical supervision usually involves the sharing of considerable detail regarding assessment and/or treatment of a client but can also involve exploration of the emotional impact of the client on the clinician

[1] The authors would like to thank John Devereux who kindly reviewed the section on legal and ethical issues and made a number of helpful suggestions.

and aspects of the supervisee's work life that are impinging on clinical work. The clinical supervisor will not usually provide direction (except in some circumstances to trainees and junior practitioners, which are considered in more detail below) and may or may not provide advice or recommendations. The role of the supervisor may be simply to assist the supervisee to explore and better understand her or his experience of a client.

Line management is concerned with the allocation of work, review of work performance and provision of general work role support, including assistance with planning for professional development. The line manager is in a position of authority and is accountable (within broad parameters) for the work performance of those for whom they have responsibility. Line managers are often able to provide directions that subordinates must follow. In a clinical setting, line managers will not usually become involved with the detail of the clinical work undertaken by professional staff but rather will monitor broad performance indicators such as caseload, client throughput, complaints and compliments, and compliance with record keeping obligations.

Whereas the line manager is required to make judgements about the quality of a subordinate's work, the clinical supervisor will usually adopt a non-judgemental position. The line manager is likely to have a critical role in professional progress matters such as promotion and will often approve leave and make decisions concerning work rosters or other matters that impact on the work environment of the clinician. This means that the line manager is in a position of power by virtue of authority whereas the clinical supervisor may be in a position of influence but has no formal authority.

Notwithstanding these conceptual and role distinctions, line management and clinical supervision are sometimes performed by the same person. There are different views as to whether or not this is a desirable arrangement and the parameters of this debate are considered later in this chapter.

Clinical review processes also share some common ground with clinical supervision processes. Most mental health services have routine clinical review processes in which client progress is considered in some depth and recommendations are made concerning the direction of the treatment plan. These may occur within the framework of ward rounds or community team meetings. Sometimes they occur in one-on-one meetings between a senior practitioner and the clinician with primary care responsibility. Typically a psychiatrist or other senior clinical professional presides over these clinical review processes.

While clinical review processes are similar to clinical supervision in that they involve detailed consideration of an episode of clinical work, there are important differences. The first is that clinical review processes form part of clinical quality assurance. The primary purpose is to ensure that assessments and treatment plans are appropriate. The second difference follows from this: clinical reviews are a form of clinical governance and have the capacity to override the clinical judgement and decisions of the primary clinician. A third difference is that clinical review processes are often conducted as a forum that enables a spectrum of professional perspectives (the multidisciplinary team) to contribute to clinical planning and decision making. Clinical supervision may, but often does not, include a contribution from a different professional perspective. Finally, the primary and often entire focus of clinical review is on the client, whereas in clinical supervision the focus may be equally on experience of clinician. While it is expected that clients may be beneficiaries of clinical supervision the value of the process is not contingent on specific client benefits.

In summary, while clinical supervision shares some characteristics in common with line management and clinical review, it can be readily differentiated from these processes. It cannot be assumed that the existence of satisfactory line management and clinical review processes obviates the need for clinical supervision.

## What can clinical supervision achieve?

Proctor (1986) usefully classified the potential benefits of clinical supervision as being formative, normative and restorative. *Formative* benefits occur when the supervisee develops new clinical knowledge and skills and forms more constructive attitudes as a result of clinical supervision. This may occur because of direct transmission of ideas, information or techniques from the supervisor to the supervisee or it may occur because the process of discussing a client enables the supervisee to take a fresh perspective and develop new ideas about how to conduct a treatment. *Normative* benefits occur when, as a result of supervision, clinicians practise in a manner which is more consistent with expectations of the service. This may be through practice which is more consistent with service priorities, which is more evidence based or which is more cost effective as just a few examples. By its nature normative practice will depend on the standards, policies and expectations of the service in question. *Restorative* benefits occur when, as a result of clinical supervision, clinicians are better able to manage the stresses and strains associated with mental health practice. This may be evident in a more positive attitude to work and indicated by fewer sick days, reduced staff turnover and greater willingness to take on responsibilities and challenges.

The formative benefits of supervision are those with the greatest potential to flow through to clients through improved assessment and/or treatment by the supervisee. However, a 2002 review of research into the impact of clinical supervision on client outcomes found the field surprisingly sparse (Freitas, 2002). Since then, a randomised controlled trial by Bambling et al. (2006) found that clients being treated with psychotherapy for depression had better outcomes if their therapists were supervised than did those whose therapists were unsupervised. This study also found better therapeutic alliance with supervised therapists. Bradshaw et al. (2007) found that nurses receiving clinical supervision showed an increase in knowledge of psychological interventions compared with peers who were not receiving supervision. They also found that the clients of the nurses receiving supervision showed greater reduction in symptoms. Thus, while the literature is still modest, there is preliminary evidence to support the proposition that clinical supervision has a formative function that can benefit clients.

It is likely the normative effects of clinical supervision occur overtly and indirectly. Overt effects occur through advice or instruction provided by the supervisor. Indirect effects arise through the responses of the supervisor to a case presentation or clinical situation. Some have suggested that clinical supervision should not venture too far into the normative, which is more properly the function of line management functions (Yegdich, 1999; Schulz et al., 2002). However, it is likely that, even when supervision is provided independently of line management, normative dimensions of professional practice will be transmitted through the supervision process. As far as we are aware there has been little if any empirical research into the extent to which supervision has a normative impact.

The restorative benefits of supervision are those associated with the emotional well-being of the supervisee. Mental health practice is widely regarded as stressful because of high levels of responsibility (especially in relation to risk factors such as suicide and aggression) associated with the client population and because of the complex interpersonal issues (such as transference and countertransference) that characterise at least some treatments. Clinical supervision enables some diffusion of responsibility as well as an environment in which interpersonal challenges can be examined with some objectivity. Proctor (1986) argues that the restorative capacity of clinical supervision is its single most important function. It is our view that, when morale is low and there is evidence of negativity or burnout, the priority in supervision is to address these issues. Only then can there be a meaningful focus on normative and formative functions. There is both quantitative (Hyrkas, 2005) and qualitative (Bégat & Severinsson, 2006) evidence to support the restorative value of clinical supervision. However, it should also be noted that some other studies have found benefits to be modest or non-existent (Palsson et al., 1996; Teasdale et al., 2001; Meldrum et al., 2002; Bégat et al., 2005). It would be unrealistic to expect supervision to solve major systemic problems affecting the morale of clinicians.

## Ethical and legal issues in clinical supervision

It is beyond the scope of this chapter to provide a comprehensive guide to the various ethical and legal issues that arise in the context of clinical supervision. However, it is important for managers to be alert to the key considerations. Failure to be mindful of ethical and legal issues not only increases the risk of exposing the service to complaint or even litigation, in the event of problems arising in one or both of these areas, but also may inhibit supervisors from becoming involved in providing clinical supervision. Without guidelines to advise on best practice, senior clinicians may shun the responsibility of supervising juniors (Cutcliffe et al., 1998a, b).

### Duty of care

In general we think that all supervisors must accept responsibility for the quality of advice or information they provide to supervisees. In this respect supervision is no different from the discharge of any other professional responsibility. Negligence occurs when:

- a duty of care is owed
- a duty of care is breached
- harm resulted, and
- the situation was reasonably foreseeable.

In the case of clinical supervision the duty of care is primarily to the supervisee. This means there is a legal obligation to provide the supervisory service in a competent manner. The broad test of competence is whether or not a competent professional in the same role would act in a similar fashion. Ultimately this is normative and there would likely be a range of opinions as to whether or not a particular piece of advice or recommendation (or omission to provide advice or recommendation) is competent. A supervisor would not be likely to be considered incompetent unless the advice (or omission) was clearly out of line with prevailing standards within the profession.

Supervisors will often want to know to what extent the act of supervision implies assuming a degree of responsibility for the conduct of the treatment provided by the supervisee. In other words, does the supervisor have a duty of care to the person the supervisee is treating? We think there is an important distinction between supervision provided to a person whose competence to practise is contingent on a supervisory arrangement and supervision provided to a colleague who is a fully qualified practitioner. Supervisees in the first category include students, practitioners whose registration requires a period of supervision and practitioners who have been required following some form of performance or professional review to practise under supervision. For this group it is implicit in the supervision contract that the practitioner is unable to make sound autonomous clinical decisions and requires the assistance of a more experienced or better qualified practitioner to assist in decision making. In such circumstances, the supervisor is not only responsible for providing sound advice but also for monitoring the implementation of this advice. It is only in this way that the duty of care to the ultimate recipient of the services can be discharged.

However, the focus in this chapter is peer-to-peer clinical supervision. Under this kind of arrangement, the supervisee must be regarded as having capacity to make autonomous clinical decisions, including capacity to make use of or disregard advice provided by a clinical supervisor. The supervisor is in possession only of clinical information provided by the supervisee and any perspective or advice provided by the supervisor is necessarily limited by the quality of information available. Whereas the supervisor of a student will often 'sit in' on clinical interviews conducted by the student so as to both directly observe student conduct and to be in a position to provide informed clinical advice, this is unlikely to occur in peer-to-peer clinical supervision. Finally the focus of the supervision may not be on the implementation of a clinical treatment plan but rather on aspects of the supervisee's emotional experience of the treatment. In this respect clinical supervision is quite different from the clinical review processes discussed above. For these reasons we think it is relatively unlikely that the supervisor will assume any form of clinical responsibility for the treatment. There are, however, some exceptions that supervisors need to be alert to.

- If the supervisor forms the reasonable view that a supervisee is impaired or, for some other reason, incompetent there is a responsibility to take effective action to protect the interests of clients.
- The supervisor may have legal reporting obligations in circumstances where, for example, there are reasonable suspicions that a client is experiencing sexual abuse (as a child).
- Reasonable concern that a client is at imminent risk of self-harm or a client is likely to harm a third party may impose a secondary duty of care that requires the supervisor to ensure that supervisee is taking appropriate steps to minimise the risk.
- When a supervisor holds herself or himself out as an authority providing direction for the treatment provided by the supervisee, a duty of care may extend to the person or persons receiving treatment from the supervisee.

### Dual relationships

Among ethical issues in clinical supervision, the most contentious is that of the dual relationship arising when the clinical supervisor is also a line manager. There has been considerable debate in the literature as to the merits of line managers providing clinical supervision to those for whom they have line management responsibility. For those who oppose such arrangements, the major concern is that supervisees will be unwilling to openly discuss difficulties or situations they handled poorly when the person supervising is also required to conduct performance appraisals and make decisions that impact on career progression (Feltham & Dryden, 1994; Scanlon & Weir, 1997; Consedine, 2000; Kelly et al., 2001; Sloan & Watson, 2001; Cole, 2002; Cottrell, 2002). In other words, the line management relationship is not conducive to the development of a relationship of trust that is essential for open communication about complex clinical issues, especially when such communication may cause a supervisee to be judged negatively.

However, others have taken the view that it is possible to achieve both quality improvement that meets administration goals and lifelong learning within a single supervisory process (McSherry et al., 2002; Howartson-Jones, 2003; Clouder & Sellers, 2004). While the debate has been characterised more by opinion than by evidence, one study (Tromski-Klingshirn & Davis, 2007) found that counsellors were equally satisfied regardless of whether or not supervision was provided by line managers. Furthermore, a majority whose supervision was provided by line managers reported specific benefits or advantages associated with receiving supervision from a line manager.

We think that the evidence suggests that the organisational and even professional context may be important in determining whether or not line supervisors make appropriate clinical supervisors. Much of the argument favouring separation has been from the nursing literature. There is evidence that nurses are more wary about clinical supervision than some other professionals and supervision through line management may be more problematic for this reason (Wolsey & Leach, 1997; Yegdich, 1999; Kelly et al., 2001). Scanlon and Weir (1997) found that unless the line manager had psychotherapy training, clinical supervision tended to operate as line management.

It is our view that neither broad ethical principles, nor the empirical literature, suggest that the dual relationship involved in line management and clinical supervision is so vexed that it *must* be proscribed. However, we do think that both service managers and clinical supervisors who are line managers must appreciate that it is a dual relationship and that there are significant risks as well as possible benefits that arise as a result. Whether this creates difficulties that are insurmountable will depend on both the culture within the organisation and the specific characteristics of the relationship between line manager/supervisor and supervisee. We can envisage circumstances, especially in implementation of clinical supervision of nurses, where it might be wise to proscribe provision of clinical supervision by line managers in order to build confidence on the safety of the supervision framework. We think that, even when the line manager is not excluded as a supervisor, it is very important that all supervisees have access to a supervisor outside of line management.

Another dual relationship risk arises because discussion of the emotional impact of clinical work on the practitioner is a common and perhaps necessary element of clinical supervision. The risk is that the supervisor may unwittingly assume the position of a personal therapist in this context. The risk is especially great when the impact of clinical work is in some way linked with personal stresses or issues the practitioner is struggling with. Supervisors are often themselves therapists and are required to consciously inhibit an almost automatic tendency to explore emotional issues from a therapeutic perspective.

Straying into personal therapy is problematic for multiple reasons. A clinical supervisor does not have sufficient objectivity and independence to provide competent therapy. Furthermore, engagement in the complex interpersonal relationship that characterises therapy will almost certainly compromise capacity to provide effective clinical supervision. When a clinical supervisor and supervisee work in the same service, a therapeutic relationship is likely to complicate if not damage a work relationship. For these reasons both supervisors and supervisees must be alert to when the clinical supervision is developing a focus beyond the professional activity of the supervisee. The supervisor might reasonably alert the supervisee to issues better addressed in a personal therapy arrangement but should not be tempted to even explore in depth the need for personal therapy. Managers must ensure that all staff involved in clinical supervision have a clear understanding of the boundary between clinical supervision and personal therapy.

## Confidentiality

Confidentiality is another ethical issue that arises in clinical supervision. A sound understanding of issues relating to confidentiality is vital at the commencement of the clinical supervisory process (White et al., 1998). In general, the supervisory relationship requires that privacy and confidentiality are to be respected at nearly all times. However, as discussed above there are circumstances such as concerns about supervisee competence, imminent risk to clients or the public, and mandatory reporting requirements, when confidentiality must be broken (Nicklin, 1995). One such scenario that invariably results in the disclosure of confidential material relates to dangerous practice that may jeopardise patient safety (Dimond, 1998). Cutcliffe et al. (1998a) suggest that, where possible, the supervisor obtain the consent of the supervisee, be guided by statutory requirements and act in the public interest. When issues of supervisee impairment arise, such as evidence that the clinician is depressed, affected by alcohol or other substances, the supervisor may need to alert the line manager. Ideally, this is negotiated with the supervisee prior to the supervisor taking any action. When the matter has been tested in the courts, breaching confidentiality has been upheld where there is a serious and imminent risk of harm to a third party (*W* v *Egdell* [1989] 1 All ER 1089).

# Implementing clinical supervision in a mental health service

Attempts to implement clinical supervision frequently fail (Cottrell, 2002). One of the factors identified as contributing to this is the lack of involvement of all relevant parties, including managers, supervisors and supervisees. Without this, the needs of all stakeholders will not be considered and included in the implementation plan. Clear documentation of the implementation process as it evolves is essential to facilitate a clear understanding of clinical supervision and its implementation (Hawkins & Shohet, 2000).

It is essential that all parties reach agreement in relation to three principles which are crucial to the ultimate success of the process.

- The process of clinical supervision must be given the same priority as other essential quality assurance activities such as regular client review (Arvidsson et al., 2001).
- Health professionals must be provided with the time to devote to clinical supervision sessions and the sessions must be located in an environment free from distraction and well away from work pressures (White et al., 1998).
- Each supervisory service requires supervisors with appropriate skill level and a high level of commitment (Bishop, 1998).

To maximise the chance of a positive response when introducing a clinical supervision programme, a modest size project is initially recommended, as it involves a far lesser financial outlay by administrators working within a confined budget (White et al., 1998). Given that emotional exhaustion and a perception of not being supported are reliable predictors of sickness and absence from the workplace, managers who can establish better support mechanisms for their staff can expect to reduce non-attendance at work (Firth & Britton, 1989).

We recommend that services appoint a clinical supervision co-ordinator (CSC) whose singular role is to establish and implement the clinical supervision service. This role ensures momentum is maintained and links all involved parties. The CSC role is especially important in generating interest and enthusiasm within the clinical team. Approaches by the CSC to staff individually or in small groups provides general information on the plan, establishes levels of interest, and clarifies any misconceptions regarding the process. An active and engaged CSC counteracts the risk that those who require it most are the least likely to attend (Dimond, 1998). While we recognise that some professional associations may mandate supervision we do not recommend that services mandate clinical supervision because of the adverse impact on formation of a trusting relationship (Faugier, 1994). Prescribing supervision as part of a disciplinary process is to be avoided at all costs. This gives the message that supervision is only for those with identified deficits and not for the purposes of professional development (Dimond, 1998).

We think that Proctor's (1986) tripartite model can inform planning and development of clinical supervision within a mental health service. Different stakeholders within a service will attach different degrees of importance to the normative, formative and restorative aspects of supervision. One of the key roles of the CSC is to identify the stakeholders and ascertain which aspect is most salient for them. Engagement is most likely to be successful when discussions concerning supervision focus on the most salient aspect. We think there are three core groups of stakeholders that need to be considered in implementation of clinical supervision: senior management, middle management and clinical staff.

Implementation of supervision depends on management sanction (Yegdich, 1999) and, without active management support, is unlikely to succeed (Butterworth et al., 1996). Discussions with senior administrators are likely to be most productive when the *normative* functions of the clinical supervisory process are identified. Such functions include the role of clinical supervision in enhancing ethical practice, evidence-based practice and effective risk assessment/ management. In general, managers are likely to support clinical supervision if it is seen as leading to improvements in service delivery (Wolsey & Leach, 1997). The support of middle managers (team leaders, unit managers) is equally important to ensure clinicians are allowed time and encouraged to attend clinical supervision (Butterworth & Faugier, 1992). While this necessitates a potentially disruptive removal of staff from the available clinical pool, the *restorative* benefits such as improved staff morale and increased professional satisfaction have obvious ramifications for the service through better staff retention, a positive attitude to work (reduced sick leave) and a work environment that favours recruitment of new staff (Darley, 1995).

The most salient aspect of supervision for clinical staff are the *formative* and the *restorative*. We think that focus on the *formative* aspect is likely to be most effective because it appeals to core values and aspirations to be the best possible clinician. Focus on the restorative aspect can be somewhat negative because it carries the implication that clinicians are stressed or burnt out. Even where this is the case, clinicians may not want to acknowledge it and may not be comfortable in a process which is seen as having a 'therapeutic' dimension. The restorative value of supervision is best promoted when staff have either individually or collectively identified that there is a problem with morale or stress in the workplace.

## Promoting ownership of supervision among clinical staff

While the role of the CSC is vitally important, it is equally important that clinical supervision is owned by the people who will be using it. In our experience this can be achieved through group processes facilitated by the CSC. The CSC invites interested clinicians to participate in a group consultation that focuses on the concept of supervision, its process and its potential benefits. An important early objective is to ensure that potential participants understand the distinction between clinical supervision and supervisory activities concerned with quality control or line management and the distinction between clinical supervision and personal therapy (Kelly et al., 2001). The group is encouraged to think about ways by which supervision could assist them personally, with a focus on *formative* aspects unless there is clear evidence of stress or burnout, in which case *restorative* aspects should be equally emphasised.

The group formulates its own definition of supervision, reflecting their collective viewpoint having previously become familiar with other definitions from the literature, and arrives at a consensus of 'What clinical supervision will be' in that given service (Hawkins & Shohet, 2000). A working agreement is drawn up by the group, outlining the rights and responsibilities of both the supervisee and supervisor within clinical supervision (Bond & Holland, 1998). Issues such as punctuality, openness, honesty, boundaries, lines of communication and confidentiality are included. In short, a clear outline of the expectation of all involved is generated from a service user perspective.

This process ensures that clinical staff commence their experience of supervision with a clear framework, reasonable expectations and free of unnecessary fears of being judged or criticised or 'therapised'. Because it is a framework they have actively contributed to, it is less likely to feel like something imposed.

Finally, Cleary and Freeman (2006) argue that successful implementation of clinical supervision can only occur when there is a 'learning culture' within the service. This means that there must be a service-wide commitment to staff development and to supportive and restorative processes that will foster staff development. This takes us beyond the scope of this chapter but is an important reminder that clinical supervision cannot be considered in isolation from the wider system within which it occurs.

## Conclusion

There is growing recognition of the role of clinical supervision in mental health services. Clinical supervision provides potential benefits to individual clinicians and to the service as a whole that are over and above those produced by related but different processes of line management and clinical review. While the empirical literature is limited, there is evidence to support the proposition that it has formative, normative and restorative attributes. Service managers can reasonably expect that clinical staff will seek opportunities for clinical supervision. Successful implementation of clinical supervision requires an understanding of ethical and legal implications as well as appreciation of cultural and systemic factors within the service. A commitment to the process is required at every level within the system if clinical supervision is to flourish and endure as a successful component of a mental health service.

# References

Abbott, S., Dawson, L., Hutt, J., Johnson, B. & Sealy, A. (2006). Introducing clinical supervision for community-based nurses. *British Journal of Community Nursing*, 11, 346–348.

Arvidsson, B., Lofgren, H. & Fridlund, B. (2001). Psychiatric nurses' conceptions of how a group supervision programme in nursing care influences their professional competence: a 4-year follow-up study. *Journal of Nursing Management*, 9, 161–171.

Bambling, M., King, R., Schweitzer, R. & Raue, P. (2006). Clinical supervision: its influence on client-rated working alliance and client symptom reduction in brief treatment of major depression. *Psychotherapy Research*, 16, 317–331.

Bégat, I. & Severinsson, E. (2006). Reflection on how clinical nursing supervision enhances nurses' experiences of well-being related to their psychosocial work environment. *Journal of Nursing Management*, 14, 610–616.

Bégat, I., Ellefsen, B. & Severinsson, E. (2005). Nurses' satisfaction with their work environment and the outcomes of clinical nursing supervision on nurses' experiences of well-being – a Norwegian study. *Journal of Nursing Management*, 13, 221–230.

Bishop, V. (1998). Clinical supervision: what is going on? Results of a questionnaire. *NT Research*, 3, 141–151.

Bond, M. & Holland, S. (1998). *Skills of Clinical Supervision for Nurses*. Buckingham, Philadelphia: Open University Press.

Bradshaw, T., Butterworth, A. & Mairs, H. (2007). Does structured clinical supervision during psychosocial intervention education enhance outcome for mental health nurses and the service users they work with? *Journal of Psychiatric and Mental Health Nursing*, 14, 4–12.

Butterworth, T. & Faugier, J. (1992). Supervision for life. In: Butterworth, T. & Faugier, J. (eds) *Clinical Supervision and Mentorship in Nursing*. London: Chapman & Hall, pp. 230–239.

Butterworth, T., Bishop, V. & Carson, J. (1996). First steps towards evaluating clinical supervision in nursing and health visiting, I. Theory, policy and practice development. A review. *Journal of Clinical Nursing*, 5, 127–132.

Butterworth, T., Bell, L., Jackson, C. & Pajnkihar, M. (2008). Wicked spell or magic bullet? A review of the clinical supervision literature 2001–2007. *Nurse Education Today*, 28, 264–272.

Cleary, M. & Freeman, A. (2006). Fostering a culture of support in mental health settings: alternatives to traditional models of clinical supervision. *Issues in Mental Health Nursing*, 27, 985–1000.

Clouder, L. & Sellers, J. (2004). Reflective practice and clinical supervision: an interprofessional perspective. *Journal of Advanced Nursing*, 46, 262–269.

Cole, A. (2002). Someone to watch over you: clinical supervision. *Nursing Times*, 98, 22–25.

Consedine, M. (2000). Developing abilities: the future of clinical supervision? *Journal of Psychiatric and Mental Health Nursing*, 7, 471–474.

Cottrell, S. (2002). Suspicion, resistance, tokenism and mutiny: problematic dynamics relevant to the implementation of clinical supervision in nursing. *Journal of Psychiatric and Mental Health Nursing*, 9, 667–671.

Cutcliffe, J., Epling, M., Cassedy, P., McGregor, J., Plant, N. & Butterworth, T. (1998a). Clinical supervision. Ethical dilemmas in clinical supervision 1: need for guidelines. *British Journal of Nursing*, 7, 920–923.

Cutcliffe, J., Epling, M., Cassedy, P., McGregor, J., Plant, N. & Butterworth, T. (1998b). Ethical dilemmas in clinical supervision 2: need for guidelines. *British Journal of Nursing*, 7, 978–982.

Darley, M. (1995). Clinical supervision: the view from the top. *Nursing Management (London)*, 2, 14–15.

Dimond, B. (1998). Clinical supervision. Legal aspects of clinical supervision 1: employer vs employee. *British Journal of Nursing*, 7, 393–395.

Faugier, J. (1994). Mental health thin on the ground. *Nursing Times*, 90, 64–65.

Feltham, C. & Dryden, W. (1994). *Developing Counsellor Supervision*. London: Sage.

Firth, H. & Britton, P. (1989). Burnout, absence and turnover amongst British nursing staff. *Journal of Occupational Psychology*, 62, 55–59.

Freitas, G. (2002). The impact of psychotherapy supervision on client outcome: a critical examination of 2 decades of research. *Psychotherapy: Theory, Research, Practice, Training*, 39, 354–367.

Hawkins, P. & Shohet, R. (2000). *Supervision in the Helping Professions*. Buckingham, Philadelphia: Open University Press.

Howartson-Jones, I. (2003). Difficulties in clinical supervision and lifelong learning. *Nursing Standard*, 17, 37–41.

Hyrkas, K. (2005). Clinical supervision, burnout and job satisfaction among mental health and psychiatric nurses in Finland. *Issues in Mental Health Nursing*, 26, 531–556.

Kelly, B., Long, A. & McKenna, H. (2001). A survey of community mental health nurses' perceptions of clinical supervision in Northern Ireland. *Journal of Psychiatric and Mental Health Nursing*, 8, 33–44.

McSherry, R., Kell, J. & Pearce, P. (2002). Clinical supervision and clinical governance. *Nursing Times*, 98, 30–32.

Meldrum, L., King, R. & Spooner, D. (2002). Secondary traumatic stress among mental health case managers. In: Figley, C. (ed.) *Treating Compassion Fatigue*. New York: Brunner-Routledge, pp. 85–106.

Milne, D. (2007). An empirical definition of clinical supervision. *British Journal of Clinical Psychology*, 46, 437–447.

Nicklin, P. (1995). Super supervision. *Nursing Management (Harrow)*, 2, 24–25.

Palsson, M., Hallberg, I., Norberg, A. & Bjorvell, H. (1996). Burnout, empathy and sense of coherence among Swedish district nurses before and after systematic clinical supervision. *Scandinavian Journal of Caring Sciences*, 10, 19–26.

Proctor, B. (1986). Supervision: a co-operative exercise in accountability. In: Marken, M. & Payne, M. (eds) *Enabling and Ensuring. Supervision in Practice*. Leicester: National Youth Bureau, pp. 21–34.

Scanlon, C. & Weir, W. (1997). Learning from practice? Mental health nurses' perceptions and experiences of clinical supervision. *Journal of Advanced Nursing*, 26, 295–303.

Schulz, J., Ososkie, J., Fried, J., Nelson, R. & Bardos, A. (2002). Clinical supervision in public rehabilitation counseling settings. *Rehabilitation Counseling Bulletin*, 45, 213–222.

Sloan, G. & Watson, H. (2001). Illuminative evaluation: evaluating clinical supervision on its performance rather than the applause. *Journal of Advanced Nursing*, 35, 664–673.

Teasdale, K., Brocklehurst, N. & Thom, N. (2001). Clinical supervision and support for nurses: an evaluation study. *Journal of Advanced Nursing*, 33, 216–224.

Tromski-Klingshirn, D. & Davis, T. (2007). Supervisees' perceptions of their clinical supervision: a study of the dual role of clinical and administrative supervisor. *Counselor Education and Supervision*, 46, 294–304.

White, E. & Winstanley, J. (2006). Cost and resource implications of clinical supervision in nursing: an Australian perspective. *Journal of Nursing Management*, 14, 628–636.

White, E., Butterworth, T., Bishop, V., Carson, J., Jeacock, J. & Clements, A. (1998). Clinical supervision: insider reports of a private world. *Journal of Advanced Nursing*, 28, 185–192.

Wolsey, P. & Leach, L. (1997). Clinical supervision: a hornet's nest? *Nursing Times*, 93, 24–27.

Yegdich, T. (1999). Clinical supervision and managerial supervision: some historical and conceptual considerations. *Journal of Advanced Nursing*, 30, 1195–1204.

# Chapter 9
# Performance appraisal and personal development

*Hazel Bassett*

## Chapter overview

When I recently spoke with my new team members about their upcoming performance appraisal and development plan, great sighs and groans were heard. This is a common experience for managers who are responsible for the performance appraisal and development plan of staff, and its review. Staff are often sceptical of the process and see it a 'paper exercise', while managers see it as one of the most difficult aspects of their work (Chandra & Frank, 2004). Yet when the performance appraisal and development planning process is performed effectively, both staff and managers see it as beneficial and valuable (Spence & Wood, 2007).

The aim of this chapter is to define performance appraisal and development and consider how it fits into performance management in the mental healthcare setting. We will then examine the main ingredients of performance appraisal and how to formulate a development plan that is supported by and supports the performance appraisal process. Strategies for conducting performance appraisal and the accompanying development plan will then be explored. Managing some of the more difficult staff issues that arise or are identified in the performance appraisal process will be discussed. Finally, benefits of the process for all stakeholders will be identified.

## What is performance appraisal?

Performance appraisal is defined as the process undertaken by managers to analyse and assess a staff member's range of professional knowledge, skills and attitudes which impact on that staff member's performance in fulfilling his or her duties within the work environment (Bromwich, 1993). It also can provide an avenue for identifying strengths and correcting performance imperfections as well as promoting career planning (Chandra & Frank, 2004; Fulmano, 2004). It has been noted that individual performance is a joint function of ability and motivation thus dictating that performance appraisal has as its goal motivating a staff member to improve his or her performance (Roberson & Stewart, 2006). For successful performance appraisal, however, a number of things must be clear including (Arnold & Pulich, 2003):

- which performance standards the staff member's performance is being assessed against
- how these standards are defined
- what are the requirements of the standards
- how feedback on the staff member's performance will be given
- the exploration of how to improve performance.

When staff members are motivated to improve their performance, the organisation as a whole benefits (Chandra & Frank, 2004). For the manager, it is important to remember that performance appraisal is about motivating staff to improve performance and to perform at the optimal level (Hoban, 2003) rather than it being seen as a disciplinary process. Budgetary matters while important should not be the main focus of performance appraisal, even when performance may be related to monetary rewards (De la Cour, 1992). Relating the review process to the reward process can be detrimental to staff morale (Curran, 2004). Performance appraisal has at its essence the desire for staff to maximise their potential in their chosen field of employment. In doing this, the manager, through performance appraisal as well as other performance management strategies, will develop an effective workforce (Chandra & Frank, 2004).

If the performance appraisal process identifies areas of improvement and also identifies areas for career development, then a development plan can be devised. This plan can focus on the provision of education, training and experiences that will improve performance as well as assist the staff member to develop skills that will provide further career options. When the development plan relates to the performance appraisal, opportunities for further education and skill development can be supported by management. This in turn empowers the staff member to see value in and, therefore, participate in the performance appraisal process. He or she will no longer see it as a 'paper exercise' but rather see it as a way to improve his or her career options (Chandra & Frank, 2004)

## How does performance appraisal fit into performance management?

McConnell (2004, pp. 273–274) defines performance management as:

> 'The art and science of dealing with employees in a manner intended to positively influence their thinking and behaviour to achieve a desired level of performance.'

In other words, performance management is the primary responsibility of the manager. At all times, the manager should be managing staff so that what needs to be done gets done and at an appropriate standard (McConnell, 2004). Part of the performance management process is the performance appraisal, but performance management is more than just the appraisal. Performance management requires the manager to be aware of what extrinsic obstacles might be impeding staff performance. Sometimes these can be an organisational process (the duplication of paperwork); the process may be resource based (a lack of resources such as equipment, computers, etc.) or personnel based (personality conflict in the workplace). As McConnell (2004) has noted, the manager has the role of addressing obstacles to staff performance so that staff can perform at their best. Therefore, it can be seen that the role of the manager can be a complex one.

Organisations are now beginning to recognise that star performance in the technical field does not equate to star performance in the management field (Martin, 2004). The manager needs to have 'people expertise' which includes knowing how to motivate others and how to provide an environment that encourages optimal performance. Chandra and Frank (2004) have identified an effective manager as one who creates an environment that motivates others. The manager, they believe, needs to be a coach, a teacher, a guide and a supporter if the best environment for staff performance is to be created. Staff members want a manager who sets clear expectations, yet can teach them how to achieve what is required including competencies that will improve their career prospects (Martin, 2004). When that kind of environment exists, then people will want to work in that environment and substandard performance will not be tolerated (Simmons, 2005). In fact, having a culture of excellence where high performance is a non-negotiable condition will assist in retention of staff (Martin, 2004). In this kind of environment, performance appraisal is seen as one tool of managing performance rather than being the only tool of performance management.

When an issue surfaces in this environment, the manager is able to address it in a positive way providing whatever coaching, counselling and training is necessary to assist the staff member to improve his or her performance (McConnell, 2004). Umiker (1994) notes that feedback, which is an integral part of this process, is more effective when given frequently rather than when it is only given at the yearly or semi-yearly performance appraisals. Managers need to have frequent contact with their staff. Performance appraisal is not enough for managing performance in the complex field of mental health. Managers need to be seen by staff as being involved in the work area and having an intimate knowledge of staffing issues. Such managers are then seen as having the kudos for overseeing a fair and equitable performance appraisal process (Roberson & Stewart, 2006).

## What are the main ingredients for performance appraisal?

In considering what goes into making a performance appraisal process successful, one needs to consider the manager and the organisation, the staff member being appraised, the appraisal process and the outcome of the appraisal.

### The manager and the organisation

The most important ingredient of the appraisal process is the setting of clear goals for the staff member to achieve. Curran (2004) noted that the most successful organisations have designed staff positions (or job descriptions) that clearly state the responsibility and desired outcomes of the position while allowing the staff member flexibility and creativity in how those responsibilities are fulfilled and outcomes achieved. Therefore, it is the responsibility of the organisation to have job descriptions that outline exactly the expectations and the required outcomes of the role. This is essential if optimal performance is to be achieved. Without this, it is difficult for the staff member to know what is required of him or her.

The organisation also needs to have clearly defined criteria regarding the performance appraisal process in the workplace (Hayworth, 2006). The criteria should be set out in the orientation or employee manual. It should include the aim of the process, how the process should occur and what to do if the staff member is unhappy with the process or feels he or she has not had a fair and equitable appraisal. The organisation should also be prepared to evaluate the process and receive feedback on the process from the staff member (Chandra & Frank, 2004; Roberson & Stewart, 2006). This feedback can then be used by the organisation to improve the appraisal process and make it more 'user friendly'.

Another issue for the organisation is the use of rewards. The organisation must decide how it will reward appropriate performance. These rewards need to be in line with the values of the organisation and can include monetary rewards (Curran, 2004). However, rewards can come in many different forms and the creative organisation will set up a variety of reward systems with which to reward staff members who are achieving acceptable levels of performance or who are performing at a higher level than required.

Another important aspect in the process of performance appraisal is the way the manager views the process. Too often the process can be undervalued by the manager as the need to complete 'the paperwork' becomes all consuming (Bromwich, 1993). For the process to be successful and to achieve the best outcome for both the manager and the staff member, both need to be committed to the process and need to have an understanding of what the process can offer in the way of guidance in the workplace. Paperwork is important in the sense that it guides the process, but the value of the performance appraisal is the direction and clear understanding it gives the staff member of what is expected in his or her role and the guidance it gives the manager in knowing how to measure the staff member's performance (Bromwich, 1993). If the manager does view the process as 'a paper exercise', then that is all it will be.

Another important element of the appraisal process for the manager is that confidentiality needs to be maintained (Bromwich, 1993). If corrective action is required, and it will necessitate involving someone other than the manager and the staff member, then the staff member should be made aware of the person's involvement and what will be made known to the third party. Staff members' performance appraisal should not be the topic of discussion around the managerial lunch table. The most likely person who will be involved in this process would be the professional senior of the staff member. Ideally, the professional senior would not be the line manager. This person would also be the person who provides clinical or practice supervision for the staff member, thus having some understanding of the workplace and the performance required of the staff member. It is beneficial to involve the professional senior in the appraisal process in case professional practice issues are identified. Again, all people involved in the process need to maintain confidentiality.

This leads to a discussion of the qualities required in a manager who is engaged in staff performance appraisal. McConnell (2004) makes it clear that the manager who models the behaviour he or she expects in the workplace will gain respect, agreement and compliance from staff. The manager needs to lead the way in the behaviours required (Fulmano, 2004). By doing this, the manager then earns the right to speak to staff about behaviour. The successful manager will also recognise that the good parts of the staff member's performance needs to be acknowledged (Curran, 2004). The manager who is prepared to verbally reward good performance by the staff member is more likely to see that behaviour occur again. Spence and Wood (2007) have noted that praise, feedback and direction given in a respectful way will not only assist in the professional growth of the staff member but will also improve job satisfaction and retention of staff.

Also, a successful manager builds one-to-one relationships with each staff member and takes an interest in each member's contribution. The wise manager has learnt that there are times when their mind needs to open and their mouth to be closed (McConnell, 2004). Some of the best ideas for improvement come from those who have to work within the system.

Finally, to successfully lead a productive performance appraisal, the manager needs to be appropriately trained in performance appraisals (Bromwich, 1993). While this may seem obvious, a number of managers receive little or no training in how to conduct a successful performance appraisal. One of the goals in the manager's own performance appraisal needs to be training in performance appraisal and then attendance at regular refresher training. Training will assist the manager in keeping a clear focus on the purpose and usefulness of the performance appraisal. If the manager values the process and sees it as important, it will impact on staff's view of the process. Instead of being a chore that is to be endured, the process will be viewed as a useful and valuable tool in the workplace.

### The staff member

The attitude the staff member has towards the performance appraisal process will also impact on its success or otherwise. Some staff members can be quite defensive about the process. This is usually linked to an experience where the appraisal was used only as a performance correcting tool. One way to overcome this defensiveness is to encourage the staff member to take an active role in the appraisal process. This is because appraisals are much more effective and achieve better outcomes when the staff member takes an active role (Lawler et al., 1984). One way to do this is to have the staff member do a self-appraisal (Chandra & Frank, 2004). Involving staff in the process enables the staff to identify strengths and weakness and to brainstorm ways of improving performance in light of these (Arnold & Pulich, 2003). By allowing a staff member to have a voice in the process, they are more likely to own the appraisal and any suggested improvement thus increasing the likelihood of positive changes occurring. This then becomes a win-win situation for the manager and the staff member.

## The appraisal process

As stated earlier, the appraisal process needs to be clearly set out so that both the manager and staff member are clear about what to expect. Processes that are unclear can lead to inequitable appraisals (Roberson & Stewart, 2006). The aim of the process needs to be clearly defined and mechanisms for challenging the process need to be readily accessed by all.

Another important aspect of the process is that there should be no 'hidden' surprises or agendas for the staff member (Hoban, 2003). Rather the process should consolidate any action plan for dealing with issues or problems that should have already been raised with the staff member. This is essential if the process is to be seen as transparent and equitable. The process should be characterised by three features (Erdogan et al., 2001):

- adequate notice that it is happening
- a fair hearing that identifies how the assessment was made
- judgement based on evidence and without bias.

When the appraisal is seen to be based on feedback that is considered to be coming from an accurate source, then acceptance of the feedback is more likely and improvement of performance will have more chance of occurring than if the source is seen as inaccurate or biased (Roberson & Stewart, 2006).

One possible source of information is peer review. One benefit of peer review is that it allows the input of those who work closely with the staff member, particularly if the manager is not always present in the workplace (Arnold & Pulich, 2003). For those working in community mental health, peer review might provide a good source of information for the manager about a staff member's performance. However, this kind of process needs to be used wisely. There is scope for personality differences to influence such a review. Therefore, the peer review should not be the only source of information used in evaluating a staff member's performance (Chandra & Frank, 2004).

Another possible source of input is consumer satisfaction with the service provided. Again this source of information needs to be used wisely in the mental health workplace as certain factors (such as the Queensland Mental Health Act 2000 conditions, personality differences, etc.) may impact on the perception of the service received. Nevertheless, it can be a valuable source of feedback for the staff member and is one that is rarely considered in the performance appraisal process.

## Outcome and follow-up of performance appraisal

The outcome of the appraisal process should be twofold: it should guide future performance by clarifying areas for improvement; and it should acknowledge achievements made over the appraisal period (Taylor, 2005). Acknowledging achievements is the easier of the two outcomes. Giving positive feedback is a pleasant experience for all involved. However, giving feedback on how to improve performance requires that deficits in performance are identified and acknowledged. It also requires a plan to be put in place to address performance improvement (McConnell, 2004). In these cases, the plan should contain all possible approaches to positively elicit the improvement required. This might include refresher training, modelling and/or work shadowing. The staff member needs to be involved in the process of deciding the methods to be taken for facilitating improvement (McConnell, 2004). The wise manager will only use criticism when absolutely necessary and will always use it constructively by giving the staff member suggestions for correcting his or her performance (McConnell, 2004).

Only after all positive responses to the issue have been exhausted should the manager engage in corrective processes (McConnell, 2004). Such processes include: diminished work performance (including monetary implications such as decreased pay), written performance expectations that are quantifiable and assessed on a weekly basis, transfer, or in the worst case scenario, termination. The organisation will determine the process and the corrective measures to be used. The staff member needs to understand why the process is being enacted, what the process is and what is required from him or her (Roberson & Stewart, 2006). At this point the manager would be wise to engage the human resource management of his or her organisation to be sure that proper process is followed in case the staff member starts litigation proceedings against the organisation and/or manager.

## The development plan

The performance appraisal has as its goal the identification of areas requiring improvement as well as identifying possible career directions for the staff member. Therefore, no appraisal is complete without a development plan. The appraisal helps the manager to identify the development needs of the team as a whole and of individuals within the team (Hoban, 2003). Armed with this information, the manager can devise development plans for both the team and the individuals which will enable them to achieve the goals set out in the performance appraisal. In this sense, the development plan needs to be tied to and support the performance appraisal. Staff members need to be given the opportunity to access whatever developmental programme will assist them in improving their performance and being able to develop skills that will assist with their career development (Bromwich, 1993). The development plan should aim for improved functioning within the workplace (Simmons, 2005). The development plan should contain both short-term and long-term goals and the creative manager will include a wide range of activities rather than just educational activities.

Staff development needs to be based on planned activities with a definitive aim rather than sending staff haphazardly to a variety of study days (Bromwich, 1993). The development activities need to be focused, anchored to and justified by the appraisal process. As stated earlier, development activities are not just exclusively education sessions. There are a variety of ways that staff can be helped to develop skills. The creative manager will consider educational and training activities as well as activities such as work shadowing, opportunities for acting in higher positions, taking on some simple managerial activities, leading in-services and journal clubs, and opportunities for secondment to other areas within the organisation. For those attending educational or training activities there should be an expectation staff will share with other staff (usually through in-service opportunities) the information learnt (Bromwich, 1993).

Staff development plans, when designed properly, will assist in retention of staff by anchoring them through the ups and downs of the everyday work life (Rollins, 2006). Staff feel valued by the organisation when time is allocated and is quarantined regardless of the everyday needs of the workplace (Chandra & Frank, 2004). This leads to greater job satisfaction and better staff retention rates (Martin, 2004).

## Practical steps for conducting a performance appraisal and developing a development plan

Having considered the theory of the performance appraisal and development plan process, we now should examine the practical 'nuts and bolts' of how to actually make one happen.

### Beginning the process

The appraisal process should be a cycle that is continually occurring within the workplace. Therefore, staff members need to be aware of the process and where they are in the process. When a staff member is recruited, the performance appraisal process should begin as part of the orientation process. Within a month of starting employment, a staff member should have met with the manager to set out performance goals for the year ahead and identify any developmental needs. Then at least every six months – if not every three months – the manager and staff member should meet to review the goals and development needs and check if these are being addressed.

To begin the appraisal process and any subsequent review, it is important that the staff member is given plenty of notice that a review meeting or formal performance appraisal is occurring (Hoban, 2003). The organisation should clearly set out a timeframe for this. A possible timeframe is one week's notice, with the staff member being given relevant paperwork for the appraisal (Hayworth, 2006). Paperwork might include the job description, a copy of the previous review with performance goals identified and the development plan. The manager might want to include a list of questions designed to prompt thought and discussion about 'where to now', for example:

- What have you achieved since we last met?
- In what ways do you think your performance has improved since the last review?
- What do you enjoy about your position?

- What things do you not enjoy?
- What skills have you developed since we last met?
- What are your future goals (are they still the same as in the last review)?
- What can the organisation do to assist you to achieve those goals?

As a manager, you might wish to use a routine list of questions or you might wish to develop individual questions for each staff member. A routine list means that you cannot be accused of targeting a staff member on performance issues. An individual list, however, allows you and the staff member to focus specifically on his or her performance and development.

Once the time for the appraisal has been set and the appropriate paperwork given to the staff member, the manager can then prepare for the appraisal. Firstly, the manager needs to familiarise him or herself with previous reviews and identified performance goals of the staff member. The manager should then identify: any extra responsibilities taken on by the staff member; any achievements by the staff member since the last review; and any specific issues that have arisen since the last review (Bromwich, 1993). The manager needs to prepare feedback on performance. Feedback needs to be accurate, thoughtful, balanced and true with regards to the performance goals set previously and not just a knee-jerk reaction (Martin, 2004). When feedback is accurate and able to be backed up with specific examples, staff members are more likely to trust and value the feedback and the manager giving it. This feedback also needs to be in line with feedback given between appraisals and reviews. As stated earlier, there should be no surprises for the staff members. Any performance issues should have already been raised and processes put in place to address these. The manager, who prepares for the performance appraisal process, will be able to stay on track and will not be waylaid by side issues.

At the time of the appraisal or review, the manager needs to create a welcoming environment. Several researchers have commented on the need for the appraisal to occur in a relaxed setting (Bromwich, 1993; Hoban, 2003; Taylor, 2005). Taylor (2005) even suggests that the appraisal meeting should not be conducted in the manager's office – a neutral relaxed interview room away from the actual workplace is the best option. He also suggest that the furniture needs to be arranged in a way that underlines a lack of status differentiation (i.e. do not sit behind a desk) and minimises confrontation.

The manager and the staff member also need to set aside the appropriate amount of time for the appraisal to be carried out without interruption. Taylor (2005) suggests that a period of two hours allows time for the appraisal, for development plans to be put in place and evaluation of the process, and for the manager to make notes about the session.

## The process

To begin the process, the manager will need to employ all the skills he or she has developed in building rapport with people. Taylor (2005) suggests starting with small talk and checking out the expectations of the staff member. Remember to ask open questions that allow the staff member to reflect on his or her own practice enabling him or her to then identify strengths and weaknesses openly and honestly. Remember McConnell's (2004) sage advice and keep your ears and mind open and your mouth closed as much as is possible. People are more likely to own and try solutions that they have formulated themselves than pat responses from their supervisors. Use reflecting and summarising skills to their best advantage (Taylor, 2005).

Remember to balance praise and criticism – do not lose sight of the positive contributions that the staff member has made over the review period. While performance in one area may be an issue, Martin (2004) challenges managers to not allow the need for performance improvement to overshadow the person's value. Always focus on the behaviour not the person, and when focusing on deficits also explore possible solutions for dealing with the deficits. Staff members should walk away from the process encouraged and with an action plan for improvement.

The staff member needs to be encouraged to take an active role in the process. Self-appraisal is not an easy task but is more likely to bring about change behaviour if deficits in behaviour are identified (Bromwich, 1993). Positive achievements also need to be identified and acknowledged in an appropriate way. Overall the staff member should emerge from the process feeling encouraged and acknowledged for his or her strengths and achievements, while feeling motivated to lift performance to improve areas identified as needing improvement.

Areas that the performance review should focus on should have been defined by the organisation and should be clearly set out in the performance appraisal guidelines. Possible areas for discussion include: clinical performance and skills; approach to work; team skills; management skills (Bromwich, 1993). The staff member's level of experience and role within the workplace will define the focus on the above areas. It is also important to spend time identifying likes, dislikes and frustrations experienced. This can help guide the manager and the staff member in considering future career development. Martin (2004) points out that when managers identify people's likes and encourage engagement in tasks that encompass those likes, they are creating ideal positions for staff.

It is also worthwhile discussing with the staff member if there are any skills that he or she has that are being underutilised in the workplace (Bromwich, 1993). Identifying these and ensuring ways that skills or expertise can be used within the workplace will not only empower the staff member but will also benefit the workplace and the organisation. Discussion should also include career direction and any learning or workplace experience that would aid the staff member's development in that direction.

Time is also needed to define performance goals for the next appraisal period. The goals need to be clearly defined with appropriate development plans in place to maximise the potential for the staff member to succeed.

Thus by the end of the process, the staff member should have a clear understanding of how he or she is performing against the set criteria for his or her

**Table 9.1** Performance appraisal and development plan.

| Job description descriptor | Target behaviour | Performance indicator | Development plan |
|---|---|---|---|
| Provides appropriate occupational therapy (OT) assessments for mental health consumers | Competent in the area of functional assessments | Presents three different OT functional assessments reports e.g. Domestic and Community Skills Assessment (DACSA), Allen Cognitive Levels (ACL) and Brookvale Living Skills Assessment | Attends workshop on the use of and report writing for the ACL assessment |

position. He or she should know against what performance criteria he or she will be reviewed for the next appraisal. The staff member should also have a clear understanding of performance goals and also any development plans that are in place to assist with achieving those goals. In other words, the staff member knows how he or she is performing so far, what is expected in the future and how the organisation will support the person in achieving those expectations. Table 9.1 outlines a possible way of setting out the performance appraisal and development plan.

### Continuing the process

Having engaged in the formal appraisal process, it is now the manager's responsibility to see that recommendations from the process are not placed aside and forgotten. The manager needs to follow up with development opportunities and encourage staff members to make the most of these opportunities. The manager also needs to encourage performance improvement. The skilful manager will do this in the least threatening and most collegial way. The wise manager will role model the behaviours required while spending time in the workplace. Use of praise and constructive criticism will be a part of the manager's repertoire. The staff member will receive feedback that is fair and true throughout the review process. By the manager investing time into staff, workplace performance will improve and the work environment will be seen as positive and supportive. Not only does this have excellent outcomes for the staff and manager and the organisation as a whole, but this will also have benefits for the consumers who access the service.

## Difficult issues

When staff are performing well in the workplace, everyone is happy. However, there is usually at least one staff member who is not. This person needs to be managed or he or she can have a negative influence within the workplace. To begin the management process, the manager needs to clarify what the issue is. The manager needs to consider if the issue actually sits with him or herself. Arnold and Pulich (2003) identified four possible influences the manager may be under.

- *'Similar to Me' effect*: the manager rates the performance as higher or lower depending on how much the person is perceived to be like the manager, i.e. same characteristics and beliefs.
- *Halo effect*: the manager generalises one positive characteristic of performance to all areas therefore resulting in an overall high rating.
- *Horn effect*: the manager generalises one negative characteristic of performance to all areas therefore resulting in a low overall rating.
- *Recent behaviour bias*: the manager remembers a recent behaviour, recalling it clearly and rating overall performance based on that behaviour rather than on the behaviours evident throughout the performance period.

If these are evident, it is the manager who needs to improve his or her performance. Hopefully, the manager can explore these and the solutions to the problems that arise in his or her own supervision sessions and performance appraisal with his or her manager.

If, however, the issue lies with the staff member, the manager needs to use the performance appraisal mechanisms to give the person every opportunity to improve his or her performance. This might including breaking down the target behaviours into specific tasks with clear behavioural components that the staff member will be expected to meet. This removes the possibility that the staff member does not understand what is required (McConnell, 2004). It may also be necessary to increase the number of reviews, either three monthly or even monthly instead of six monthly. The development plan also needs to be specific, with specific activities in which the person is expected to engage. If all else fails to bring about the behaviour changes required to lift the person's performance into the realm of acceptable, then it will be necessary to engage performance management strategies that are more corrective in nature such as diminished work performance (where salary is impacted by poor performance and remains so until performance improves). Whenever it gets to this point, it is important for the manager to engage his or her operational manager in the process and to also engage someone from human resource management of the organisation in the process. This can be a difficult time for both the manager and the staff member and it is important that both have support through the process.

## Benefits of performance appraisal and development

The benefits of effective performance appraisal and development can be enjoyed by the staff member, the manager, the organisation and the consumer. For the staff member, effective performance appraisal motivates improved practice, provides job satisfaction and assists with career development (Spence & Wood,

2007). For the manager, there are many benefits including (Alban-Metcalfe et al., 1989):

- being aware of the staff member's job satisfaction, frustrations, needs, strengths and weaknesses
- setting objectives for the workplace
- improving communication and working relationships
- documenting processes.

For the organisation, having staff members who are performing to an acceptable level and are in fact improving and developing means that the organisation can function and provide the service that is required of it. Also, when staff feel valued and are encouraged to grow and develop their skills, they are more likely to stay in that employment. This means that recruitment and retention is more effective and less time and resources are used continually recruiting. Finally, there are benefits for the consumer, including improved and appropriate service, and better outcomes of the service provided by the staff.

## Conclusion

Performance appraisal and development is an important aspect of performance management. When performed effectively, all stakeholders in the process benefit. When it is poorly carried out, it builds frustration and resentment and becomes nothing more than a paper exercise. The wise manager will engage the process as a way to develop his or her staff and to improve the service that is provided to the consumer. In doing this the manager will build a workplace culture that is built on respect, problem solving, mutual support and team performance (Curran, 2004). Staff will be attracted to the workplace and excellence will be the order of the day. Therefore, it can be seen that performance appraisal and development when carried out properly can be an effective staff management tool.

## References

Alban-Metcalfe, B., Hurst, K. & Jones, R. (1989). Honest, open and frank. *Health Services Journal*, 99, 952–953.

Arnold, E. & Pulich, M. (2003). Personality conflicts and objectivity in appraising performance. *The Health Care Manager*, 22, 227–232.

Bromwich, N. (1993). Implementing individual performance review. *British Journal of Nursing*, 2, 929–933.

Chandra, A. & Frank, Z. D. (2004). Utilization of performance appraisal systems in health care organizations and improvement strategies for supervisors. *The Health Care Manager*, 23, 25–30.

Curran, C. R. (2004). Rewards, respect, responsibility, relationship and recognition. *Nursing Economics*, 22, 57 & 63.

De la Cour, J. (1992). Assessments of staff appraisal systems. *British Journal of Nursing*, 1, 99–102.

Erdogan, B., Kramer, M. L. & Liden, R. C. (2001). Procedural justice as a two-dimensional construct: An examination in the performance appraisal context. *Journal of Applied Behavioural Science*, 37, 205–222.

Fulmano, J. (2004). Let's target and achieve standards of excellence. *Nursing Management*, March, 10–11.

Hayworth, S. D. (2006). Practice management 'in the trenches' part 3: managing people. *Contemporary Obstetrics and Gynaecology*, July, 56–63.

Hoban, V. (2003). How to give effective appraisals. *Nursing Times*, 99, 64–65.

Lawler, E., Mohrman, A. & Rosnick, S. (1984). Performance appraisal revisited. *Organisational Dynamics*, Summer, 20–35.

Martin, C. A. (2004). Turn on the staying power. *Nursing Management*, March, 21–26.

McConnell, C. R. (2004). Managing employee performance. *The Health Care Manager*, 23, 273–283.

Roberson, Q. M. & Stewart, M. M. (2006). Understanding the motivational effects of procedural and informational justice in feedback processes. *British Journal of Psychology*, 97, 281–298.

Rollins, G. (2006). Professional development plans in action. *Journal of AHIMA*, September, 42, 44.

Simmons, S. L. (2005). Getting high on performance. *Neonatal Network*, 24, 67–68.

Spence, D. G. & Wood, E. E. (2007). Registered nurse participation in performance appraisal interviews *Journal of Professional Nursing*, 23, 55–59.

Taylor, C. (2005). How to excel at giving appraisals. *Nursing Times*, 101, 38–39.

Umiker, W. (1994). *Managing Skills for the New Health Care Supervisor*, 2nd edition. Gaithersberg, Maryland: Aspen Publishers.

# Chapter 10
# Dealing with stress and burnout

*Chris Lloyd and Robert King*

## Chapter overview

Since the mid-1980s, there has been increasing interest in the issues of stress and burnout in the human service professions. Job stress can have a detrimental effect on the person, the workplace, and society. The construct of burnout has been linked to job stress and is thought to be a unique response to frequent and intense client interactions. This chapter explores stress and burnout and offers some strategies for minimising the effects that stress and burnout have on the individual and his or her workplace.

## Stress

Occupational stress has been identified as affecting 28% of all European Union workers and being responsible for 50–60% of all lost working days (Ryan et al., 2005). Minimising stress and responding effectively when it is identified is therefore a key component of effective workforce management.

Stress has been defined as (Sutherland & Cooper, 1990, pp. 23–24):

'the interactions between, or misfit of, environmental opportunities and demands, the individual needs and abilities, and expectations, elicit reactions. When the fit is bad, when needs are not being met, or when abilities are over or undertaxed, the organism reacts with various pathogenic mechanisms. These are cognitive, emotional, behavioural, and/or psychological and under some conditions of intensity, frequency or duration, and in the presence or absence of certain variables, they may lead to precursors of disease.'

Potential sources of stress include stress from the job itself, work roles, relationships with others, career development, and the organisational structure and climate (Sutherland & Cooper, 1990; Dunn & Ritter, 1995; Moore & Cooper, 1996). Two stressors specific to a health environment include financial cutbacks and the rationalisation of services and the shift from hospital-based services to the community (Fagin et al., 1996). Response to stress is the product of the situation and the person, taking into account the factors that influence a person's resistance to stress or increase his or her vulnerability. Potential moderators and mediators to the response to stress can include personality traits and behavioural characteristics, physical conditions, and life-stage characteristics of the individual

(Tyler & Cushway, 1995; Moore & Cooper, 1996). Individual vulnerability to stress is dependent on a large number of complex factors, including personality, personal history, needs, wants and coping strategies adopted. Supervision, training and relationships at work (support from colleagues and supervisors) are considered buffers to stress.

## Definition and characteristics of burnout

Breaking down the three components of burnout as described by Maslach and Florian (1988), emotional exhaustion refers to a depletion of one's emotional resources and the feeling that one has nothing left to give to others at a psychological level. Depersonalisation refers to the development of negative and callous attitudes about the people with whom one works. The last aspect of burnout is a negative evaluation of one's accomplishments in working with people. Specifically, workers may feel unhappy about themselves and dissatisfied with their accomplishments on the job. Healthcare professionals' work often involves close contact with people who can be emotionally difficult to manage on a continuing basis. For health professionals who experience burnout, there may be a gradual loss of caring about the people with whom they work, as over time they find they cannot sustain the level of personal care and commitment required of them (Maslach et al., 1996).

According to Maslach et al. (1996), burnout differs from occupational stress in that it is specific to work that requires intense involvement. The defining feature of occupational stress is an imbalance between occupational demands and available coping resources. The burnout concept integrates a feeling of exhaustion with staff members' involvement in their work, especially the people with whom they work, and their sense of efficacy or accomplishment. Burnout is usually thought of as the outcome of chronic stress (Cushway et al., 1996).

Unmet job expectations in general and specific aspects of job experiences are associated with burnout. It has been suggested that there is a prevalence of unrealistic job expectations among human service professionals and that this mismatch between expectations and reality is a major contributor to the stress that they experience (Jackson et al., 1986). It has been suggested that two types of employee expectations are implicated as possible causes of burnout. These are achievement expectations about what one will achieve with clients, and organisational expectations about the nature of the job and the systems within which one operates as an employee and a professional (Jackson et al., 1986).

The person who burns out is unable to successfully deal with the emotional stress of the job, and this failure to cope can be manifested in a number of ways, including low morale, impaired performance, absenteeism and high turnover. A common response to burnout is to change jobs, move into administrative work or leave the profession entirely. In addition, burnout is correlated with various indices of personal dysfunction. Emotional exhaustion is often accompanied by physical exhaustion, illness, psychosomatic symptoms, increased use of alcohol and drugs, and increased marital and family conflict. As a result of these factors, the quality of care that service recipients receive may deteriorate.

## Client-related factors

In human service occupations the worker must deal directly with people about issues that may be problematic. Maslach et al. (1996) suggested that as a consequence of this, strong emotional feelings are likely to be present in the workplace and that this chronic emotional stress can induce burnout. Client characteristics and contact are a defining factor in burnout among human service providers.

### Caseload

Higher rates of emotional exhaustion and depersonalisation and lower rates of personal accomplishment are related to having a larger caseload (Maslach et al., 1996). The larger the ratio of clients to staff, the less liked their job and the more they said they would change their jobs if given an opportunity. McLeod (1997) found that 80% of community nurses working with severely mentally ill people had a caseload higher than the national average, with some staff having as many as 60 clients in their caseload. Seventy-five per cent of the community nurses reported that having too many referrals and a large caseload were the most significant stressors.

### Case type

The higher the percentage of people with schizophrenia in the client population, the less job satisfaction staff members expressed. The findings from McLeod's (1997) study of 60 community psychiatric nurses in the UK revealed that higher levels of stress were experienced by community mental health nurses working with severely mentally ill people than those working with people with a range of diagnoses (affective, anxiety and adjustment disorders). Potentially threatening clients were found to be a major source of stress for mental health nurses, with staffing shortages putting them at physical risk because of the nature of their client group (Schafer, 1992). Violent or aggressive clients have been found to be a source of stress for social workers.

The type of client problem has an effect on staff stress and burnout. Some clients may have problems that are far more emotionally stressful for staff than others. If the interaction with clients is particularly upsetting, depressing or difficult in some way, then staff burnout may be more severe and/or occur more quickly. Related to the stressfulness of the client's problems is the probability of successful change. It may be more difficult for staff to work with people and see few changes over time. Another stressor has been found to be the client's reaction to staff. It is common to receive more negative than positive feedback from clients.

## Contact level

Savicki and Cooley (1987) found that high work pressure related to high levels of emotional exhaustion and that high contact workers showed higher levels of depersonalisation than low contact workers. Maslach et al. (1996) reported that doctors who spent most of their working time in direct contact with clients scored high on emotional exhaustion. Rogers and Dodson (1988) found that the number of direct client contact hours was positively correlated with the intensity dimension of emotional exhaustion and the frequency dimension of depersonalisation for occupational therapists. The frequency and intensity of these feelings may be exaggerated by increased client contact.

# Work-related factors

### Work environment

Work environments associated with high burnout are those that demand high personal adherence to work through restriction of worker freedom or flexibility and that de-emphasise planning and efficiency for the task at hand. Other work environments related to higher levels of burnout are those in which job expectations are vague or ambiguous, in which management imposes extensive rules and regulations, and in which support and encouragement of new ideas and procedures are low.

Key stressors for ward-based mental health nurses were found to be staff shortages, health service changes, poor morale, lack of consultation from management, and not being notified of changes before they occurred (Fagin et al., 1996). Schafer (1992) identified that, for community mental health nurses, the principal stressors related to the perceived inadequacies in management and perceived need for supervision. Some of the stressors for British psychologists working in the National Health Service (NHS) included pressure of workload, lack of resources, conflict in relationships with other professionals, and poor organisational communication and management (Cushway & Tyler, 1994).

A possible explanation for the high stress levels may be the impact of enforced reorganisation involving major changes in service delivery and supporting systems with deadlines for implementation. Jones and Novak (1993) suggested that social work practitioners seemed demoralised, exhausted, and overwhelmed by constant change. The way the department is managed was a significant source of dissatisfaction among social work staff and managers. Job dissatisfaction in relation to organisational structures and processes has been related to high turnover of social workers (Bradley & Sutherland, 1995). Issues relating to how clinicians spend their time are also associated with stress. For example, it was found that being unable to reach planned work targets, and other caseload factors such as having too much administrative and paper work appears to be strongly associated with high measured stress for social workers (Collins & Murray, 1996) and occupational therapists (Leonard & Corr, 1998).

## Work location

With the downsizing of psychiatric hospitals and an increase in community-based services, the nature of mental health service delivery has changed greatly. There has been ongoing concern about whether community mental health teams have adequate resources, including staff, to provide a service for all people with severe mental illness living in the community (Prosser et al., 1996). Concerns have also been raised about the lack of day facilities, supported housing and appropriate hostels with skilled staff (Reid et al., 1999). Reid et al. (1999) found that lack of resources was the third most frequently mentioned source of pressure at work. Another cause of stress appeared to be the lack of inpatient care for those clients in acute distress (McLeod, 1997). Mental health nurses indicated that the stress of working with difficult clients was associated with a lack of resources (Cushway et al., 1996). Insufficient resources and a lack of alternative facilities to which to refer clients have been identified as two of the top stressors for a number of professional disciplines, including community mental health nurses (McLeod, 1997), occupational therapists (Leonard & Corr, 1998), psychologists (Cushway & Tyler, 1994) and social workers (Bradley & Sutherland, 1995).

## Role-based stress

These organisational stressors include role conflict, role ambiguity, role over-load, and the responsibility associated with the role of the individual (Moore & Cooper, 1996). Reid et al. (1999) found that community mental health social workers expressed more concerns about role conflict and role ambiguity than any other professional. This study also found that 75% of doctors, all team leaders and 33% of the social workers had difficulties managing multiple demands on their limited time. An increased level of responsibility following the introduction of new legislation was found to create additional pressure at work for community nurses and occupational therapists (Reid et al., 1999).

Table 10.1 presents a summary of workplace stressors.

Stress can be very costly in both human and economic terms for individuals and for society. Health professionals may have a profound effect on peoples' lives. Stress in health professionals may have far-reaching effects on the clients with whom they work (Cushway, 1995). It is clear that a critical first step in managing stress is acknowledging the problem. What can be done about it?

# Dealing with stress and burnout

Given the range of sources of stress and the complex demands of mental health work, it can be expected that team leaders, professional seniors and unit managers will frequently have to assist colleagues who are affected by stress. It can also be expected that they will themselves be affected by stress. The following sections aim to assist with responding effectively to others' stress as well as appropriate self-help.

**Table 10.1** Workplace stressors.

| Factors contributing to workplace stress | Type of stressor |
| --- | --- |
| Client-related factors | Caseload |
| | Cast type |
| | Contact level |
| Work-related factors | Work environment |
| | Staff shortages |
| | Health service change |
| | Poor morale |
| | Lack of consultation from management |
| | Lack of supervision |
| | Time management |
| | Work location |
| | Role-based stress |

## The obligations of the supervisor

Supervisors have a duty of care in respect of those staff members for whom they are responsible. Stress is a workplace health and safety issue and supervisors must identify and minimise risks and assist anyone affected by stress. This means both being aware of potential sources of stress and also being receptive to staff at an interpersonal level. If the first time a supervisor learns about stress is when a team member takes sick leave, it usually means that something has been overlooked. However, the duty of care does not provide a licence to intrude into the personal life of team members. Unless there are clear indications of impaired work performance the correct position of the supervisor is clear communication of availability and willingness to assist. Stress often results from a complex mixture of personal and work factors and the team member may prefer to address sources of stress outside the workplace. In these circumstances the role of the supervisor is to assist with referral where required and monitor, in a general way, the effectiveness of any external support provided.

## Levels of intervention

Management and supervisory response to risk or actuality of workplace stress has been conceptualised (Cottrell, 2001) as operating at three levels: primary, secondary and tertiary (see Table 10.2). Another way of conceptualising this is prevention (introducing measures to reduce risk of stress), intervention (providing active assistance during a stressful event or experience) and postvention

**Table 10.2** Matrix of organisational stress management interventions.

| | Prevention | Intervention | Postvention |
|---|---|---|---|
| Community Mental Health (Individual perspective) | Caseload monitoring and management | Healthy lifestyle | Counselling |
| | Caseload characteristics monitoring and management | Reflection | Psychotherapy |
| | | Clinical supervision | Occupational health interventions |
| | Assertiveness | Mentorship | Physical wellness: diet, exercise, addictions |
| | Communication skills | 'Buddy' systems | Lifestyle work |
| Inpatient Services | Psycho-education | Relaxation | |
| | | Home/work interface | |
| | | Support mapping | |
| | | Biofeedback Imagery | |
| Both Inpatient and Community Services | Effective team functioning | Group development, diagnosis and intervention | Availability of critical incident debriefing |
| | Thoughtful and consultative rostering | | Access to counselling/ psychotherapy |
| | Clinical supervision | Clinical team supervision | Access to career planning |
| | | Dependency/skill mix | |
| | | Workload analysis and review | |
| Organisation (Systems perspective) | IPR | Workload management | Therapeutic consultancy |
| | PDR | Mission clarification | Reorganisation |
| | Job descriptions and Role | Risk analysis and management | Organisational transformation programmes |
| | Clarification | Employee participation | Employee Assistance Programmes (EAP) |
| | Participation and empowerment | | Process redesign |
| | Schemes | | Cultural change work, e.g. combating 'presenteeism' |

Reproduced with permission from Cottrell, S. (2001). Occupational stress and job satisfaction in mental health nursing: focused interventions through evidence-based assessment. *Journal of Psychiatric and Mental Health Nursing*, 8, 157–164, copyright 2001 with permission of Blackwell Publishing Ltd.

(providing assistance in the aftermath of stress). Managers must have effective strategies in place at each level and also need means of monitoring the effectiveness of these strategies.

## Workload and work quality

Supervisors can and should monitor workload and work quality (Meldrum & Yellowlees, 2000; King et al., 2004). Workload factors may include hours of work, travel time and non-clinical duties in addition to caseload size and characteristics. While there may be no clearly defined benchmarks as to what is an acceptable workload, it is not difficult to gauge whether a practitioner has workload that is higher than normative. Client factors are especially relevant to work quality. Acute, suicidal, violent and unresponsive clients increase the stress associated with clinical work, and a disproportionate number of such clients can significantly increase risk of stress or burnout (Meldrum & Yellowlees, 2000). Clinicians who work with victims of abuse are at increased risk of vicarious trauma, which is a form of stress (Thomas & Wilson, 2004). It is not uncommon for clinicians to develop a specialist interest in groups of clients who have such risk factors. While this has potential benefits (see below) because it capitalises on the development of specialist clinical skills, it is important that such clinicians are monitored to ensure that there are no unintended effects, such as vicarious trauma.

## Burden of responsibility

The evidence that clinicians working in community settings are probably under greater stress than clinicians working in inpatient settings presents a challenge for the team leader or service manager in these settings. As discussed above, workers in such environments often attribute stress to inadequate resources such as access to inpatient beds, emergency housing or after-hours support. While these may be legitimate concerns, they are often not under the control of the team leader. This raises the question of what can the team leader do to minimise stress associated with these kinds of environmental deficiencies?

One reason that the absence of resources is so stressful for community-based clinicians is because of feelings of responsibility resulting in a burden of care. When clients are unstable or acutely unwell, clinicians look to inpatient services, respite services and other community supports to relieve their burden of care. In the absence of such services, they feel overwhelmed by responsibility for the well-being of the client. In this respect, clinicians may be in an analogous position to that of family and carers. It is important that community-based workers are not left to deal with this burden on their own.

The most important resource for a community-based mental health clinician is a supportive team. A team can share responsibility for decision making and also allocate additional resource to ensure that a single case manager does not have to provide all the care in a crisis situation – or at least knows that help can be provided if needed. The team leader has the responsibility of managing the team and ensuring that the team processes are supportive – that individuals have the opportunity and are encouraged to present challenging cases, that the team deals with the issues respectfully and thoughtfully and that the team mobilises its collective resources to develop a plan for which it will assume responsibility. When a team has a consultant psychiatrist or other senior clinician, that person will usually provide ultimate clinical accountability for team plans.

Sometimes community services comprise single individuals or just a couple of individuals. In these circumstances, clinical supervision is a key component of prevention of stress associated with burden of care (Edwards et al., 2006). The responsibility of the service manager is not necessarily to provide the supervision but to ensure that each practitioner has access to appropriate support.

## Work–life balance

The evidence suggests that problems outside the work environment and difficulties achieving a satisfactory balance between work and non-work life demands cause stress as much as experiences within the workplace (Bolger et al., 1989). Most members of the contemporary workforce struggle to balance workplace responsibilities with responsibilities to partners, children, parents or others and with recreational activities or community services. The team leader or service manager can be a positive or negative force in respect of these challenges.

Rostering of after-hours duties is an example of an administrative responsibility with high potential to impinge on work–life balance. Inpatient services and many community services require 24/7 or extended hours staffing. This means that many clinicians will be required to work evenings and/or weekends, imposing limitations on time available for shared activities with family and friends. Rostering is a sensitive issue, partly because it impinges directly on the work–home balance issue (Clissold et al., 2002) and partly because it can easily be perceived to be a means by which management exercises control and provides benefits for those who have the 'ear' of management and disadvantages for those who do not. Rostering can be a source of chronic discontent.

While management may not have capacity to eliminate extended hours work, there are some general principles which, if consistently used, reduce the risk of roster-induced stress and discontent:

- Ensure there is a need for extended hours services. Demand should be monitored and alternative ways of providing services investigated. Rostering staff to provide after-hours services that are not really necessary is not only expensive but may unnecessarily promote grievances.
- Use rostering systems that maximise staff autonomy and decision making and adhere to principles of transparency and fairness. Self-rostering is an example of an established approach with a track record of increasing staff satisfaction (Wortley & Grierson-Hill, 2003; Jennings, 2005; Pryce et al., 2006).
- Regularly monitor rostering systems using confidential satisfaction surveys. Anonymous surveys are more likely to elicit meaningful information than

informal face-to-face feedback. When staff feel vulnerable, they are reluctant to provide honest feedback that may be unwelcome.

## Stress antidotes

While mental health professionals report moderately high levels of emotional exhaustion, they do not typically report lack of satisfaction with their work with clients (Hannigan et al., 2000). Clinical work is often experienced as highly satisfying and there is evidence that clinicians want more opportunities to deploy their professional skills in work with clients (Lloyd et al., 2004). Service managers and team leaders can actively contribute to employee work satisfaction by maximising their opportunities to deploy their clinical skills and capacities. This means maintaining a strong awareness of the clinical interest and expertise of team members and ensuring that, wherever possible, they have opportunities to work with clients in a way that will utilise these capacities. This does not mean that clinicians should be supported to provide any form of intervention that interests them. Considerations such as efficacy and cost-effectiveness remain relevant. However, clinicians should be granted as much autonomy as is consistent with operation within an evidence based practice paradigm (see Chapter 12) and within the resource limitations of the service. Transparency concerning these issues will encourage clinicians to develop and utilise interventions that are personally satisfying as well as beneficial to clients.

Supporting clinician autonomy as a strategy for stress prevention is consistent with research that suggests that enhancing the degree to which a worker has control in the job, including discretion and choice, reduces work-related stress and associated phenomena such as absenteeism (Bond & Bunce, 2001).

## Staff training for stress reduction

While there is evidence that stress reduction courses, whether provided one-on-one or in group settings, can be effective (Edwards & Burnard, 2003; Marine et al., 2006), it is less clear as to whether there are benefits in providing staff training designed to prevent or reduce stress. Kagan et al. (1995) reported positive results of psychoeducational interventions for emergency medical staff. However, the multisite OSCAR project (Ryan et al., 2005) found otherwise. This group provided a four-day staff training programme for mental health staff that focused both on recognising and managing stress at individual, team and organisational level and on responding to client crisis and violence. Unexpectedly, stress increased rather than reduced following the training. The authors concluded that these paradoxical results may have been due in part to increased staff expectations that were not fulfilled because organisations were unwilling or unable to respond to identified needs. Both Edwards et al. (2003) and Marine et al. (2006) concluded that methodological problems made it difficult to evaluate the findings of the identified studies that had evaluated stress management interventions in mental health staff and healthcare workers, respectively.

**Post-incident stress debriefing**

Considerable controversy surrounds the role of debriefing following a work incident or other trauma likely to be stressful, such as an assault or accident causing or threatening significant harm or death (Everly & Mitchell, 2000). Critical Incident Stress Debriefing (Mitchell, 1983; Mitchell & Everly, 1997) is a process designed to assist people affected by trauma to psychologically process the experience and to recognise and respond effectively to trauma-related stress symptoms.

A Cochrane review (Rose et al., 2002) identified nine studies using an experimental or quasi-experimental design with broadly similar interventions and study populations. The review concluded that there was no evidence that debriefing was superior to no intervention and that there was some evidence that it may increase risk of depression or trauma. Likewise, van Emmerik et al. (2002) concluded from a meta-analysis that natural recovery was as effective as any kind of debriefing after trauma. Proponents of debriefing have, however, continued to argue that it is effective when applied in an appropriate fashion to the populations for whom it was intended (Everly & Mitchell, 2000; Jacobs et al., 2004).

There is little basis, given the current state of knowledge, for the use of mandatory debriefing procedures when staff are exposed to traumatic events. Voluntary debriefing may or may not be helpful as a preventive measure. While it is important to provide psychological support for staff who are distressed following exposure to a traumatic event, it may be more important to ensure that targeted interventions are available to people who are showing signs of a stress reaction (Rose et al., 2002).

# Conclusion

Stress is connected to the job itself, work roles, clients, relationships with others, career opportunities and organisational structure and climate. The person who burns out is unable to successfully deal with the emotional stress of the job. Stress is very costly in both human and economic terms. Team leaders and other people in a management role will frequently have to deal with people affected by stress. Some strategies for assisting managers to identify and deal with stressful situations have been outlined in the chapter.

# References

Bolger, N., DeLongis, A., Kessler, R. & Wethington, E. (1989). The contagion of stress across multiple roles. *Journal of Marriage and the Family*, 51, 175–183.

Bond, F. & Bunce, D. (2001). Job control mediates change in a work reorganization intervention for stress reduction. *Journal of Occupational Health Psychology*, 6, 290–302.

Bradley, J. & Sutherland, V. (1995). Occupational stress in social services: a comparison of social workers and home help staff. *British Journal of Social Work*, 25, 313–331.

Clissold, G., Smith, P., Accutt, B. & Di Milia, L. (2002). A study of female nurses combining partner and parent roles with working a continuous three-shift roster: the impact on sleep, fatigue and stress. *Contemporary Nurse: A Journal for the Australian Nursing Profession*, 12, 294–302.

Collins, J. & Murray, P. (1996). Predictors of stress amongst social workers: an empirical study. *British Journal of Social Work*, 26, 375–387.

Cottrell, S. (2001). Occupational stress and job satisfaction in mental health nursing: focused interventions through evidence-based assessment. *Journal of Psychiatric and Mental Health Nursing*, 8, 157–164.

Cushway, D. (1995). Stress management and the health professional. *British Journal of Therapy and Rehabilitation*, 2, 260–264.

Cushway, D. & Tyler, P. (1994). Stress and coping in clinical psychologists. *Stress Medicine*, 10, 35–42.

Cushway, D., Tyler, P. & Nolan, P. (1996). Development of a stress scale for mental health professionals. *British Journal of Clinical Psychology*, 35, 279–295.

Dunn, L. & Ritter, S. (1995). Stress in mental health nursing: a review of the literature. In: Carson, J., Fagin, L. & Ritter, S. (eds) *Stress and Coping in Mental Health Nursing*. London: Chapman and Hall, pp. 29–45.

Edwards, D. & Burnard, P. (2003). A systematic review of stress and stress management interventions for mental health nurses. *Journal of Advanced Nursing*, 42, 169–200.

Edwards, D., Burnard, P., Owen, M., Hannigan, B., Fothergill, A. & Coyle, D. (2003). A systematic review of stress management interventions for mental health professionals. *Journal of Psychiatric and Mental Health Nursing*, 10, 370–371.

Edwards, D., Burnard, P., Hannigan, B., Cooper, L., Adams, J., Juggessur, T., Fothergil, A. & Coyle, D. (2006). Clinical supervision and burnout: the influence of clinical supervision for community mental health nurses. *Journal of Clinical Nursing*, 15, 1007–1015.

Everly, G. & Mitchell, J. (2000). The debriefing 'controversy' and crisis intervention: a review of lexical and substantive issues. *International Journal of Emergency Mental Health*, 2, 211–225.

Fagin, L., Carson, J., Leary, J., de Villiers, N., Bartlett, H., O'Malley, P., West, M., Mcelfatrick, S. & Brown, D. (1996). Stress, coping and burnout in mental health nurses: findings from three research studies. *International Journal of Social Psychiatry*, 42, 102–111

Hannigan, B., Edwards, D., Coyle, D., Fothergill, A. & Burnard, P. (2000). Burnout in community mental health nurses: findings from the all-Wales stress study. *Journal of Psychiatric and Mental Health Nursing*, 7, 127–134.

Jackson, S., Schuler. R. & Schwab, R. (1986). Towards an understanding of the burnout phenomenon. *Journal of Applied Psychology*, 71, 630–640.

Jacobs, J., Horne-Moyer, H. & Jones, R. (2004). The effectiveness of critical incident stress debriefing with primary and secondary trauma victims. *International Journal of Emergency Mental Health*, 6, 5–14.

Jennings, C. A. (2005). Self-rostering system gives nurses choice. *British Journal of Healthcare Computing and Information Management*, 22, 33–34.

Jones, C. & Novak, T. (1993). Social work today. *British Journal of Social Work*, 23, 195–212.

Kagan, N., Kagan, H. & Watson, M. (1995). Stress reduction in the workplace: the effectiveness of psychoeducational programs. *Journal of Counseling Psychology*, 42, 71–78.

King, R., Meadows, G. A. & Le Bas, J. (2004). Compiling a caseload index for mental health case management. *Australian and New Zealand Journal of Psychiatry*, 38, 455–462.

Leonard, C. & Corr, S. (1998). Sources of stress and coping strategies in basic grade occupational therapists. *British Journal of Occupational Therapy*, 61, 257–262.

Lloyd, C., King, R. & McKenna, K. (2004). Actual and preferred work activities of mental health occupational therapists: congruence or discrepancy? *British Journal of Occupational Therapy*, 67, 167–175.

Marine, A., Ruotsalainen, J., Serra, C. & Verbeek, J. (2006). Preventing occupational stress in healthcare workers. *Cochrane Database of Systematic Reviews*, Issue 4. Art. No.: CD002892.

Maslach, C. & Florian, V. (1988). Burnout, job setting, and self-evaluation among rehabilitation counselors. *Rehabilitation Psychology*, 33, 85–93.

Maslach, C., Jackson, S. & Leiter, M. (1996). *Maslach Burnout Inventory.* Palo Alto, California: Consulting Psychologists Press, Inc.

McLeod, T. (1997). Work stress among community psychiatric nurses. *British Journal of Nursing*, 6, 569–574.

Meldrum, L. & Yellowlees, P. (2000). The measurement of a case manager's workload burden. *Australian and New Zealand Journal of Psychiatry*, 34, 658–663.

Mitchell, J. (1983). When disaster strikes . . . the critical incident stress debriefing procedure. *Journal of Emergency Medical Services*, 8, 36–39.

Mitchell, J. & Everly, G. (1997). The scientific evidence for Critical Incident Stress Management. *Journal of Emergency Medical Service*, 22, 86–93.

Moore, K. & Cooper, C. (1996). Stress in mental health professionals: a theoretical overview. *International Journal of Social Psychiatry*, 42, 82–89.

Prosser, D., Johnson, S., Kuipers, E., Szmukler, G., Bebbington, P. & Thornicroft, G. (1996). Mental health, 'burnout' and job satisfaction among hospital and community-based mental health staff. *British Journal of Psychiatry*, 169, 334–337.

Pryce, J., Albertsen, K. & Nielsen, K. (2006). Evaluation of an open-rota system in a Danish psychiatric hospital: a mechanism for improving job satisfaction and work–life balance. *Journal of Nursing Management*, 14, 282–288.

Reid, Y., Johnson, S., Morant, N., Kuipers, E., Szmukler, G., Thornicroft, G., Bebbingotn, P. & Prosser, D. (1999). Explanations for stress and satisfaction in mental health professionals: a qualitative study. *Social Psychiatry and Psychiatric Epidemiology*, 34, 301–308.

Rogers, J. & Dodson, S. (1988). Burnout in occupational therapists. *American Journal of Occupational Therapy*, 42, 787–792.

Rose, S., Bisson, J., Churchill, R. & Wessely, S. (2002). Psychological debriefing for preventing post traumatic stress disorder (PTSD). *Cochrane Database of Systematic Reviews*, Issue 2. Art. No.: CD000560.

Ryan, P., Hill, R., Anczewska, M., Hardy, P., Kurek, A., Nielson, K. & Turner, C. (2005). Team-based occupational stress reduction: a European overview from the perspective of the OSCAR project. *International Review of Psychiatry*, 17, 401–408.

Savicki, V. & Cooley, E. (1987). The relationship of work environment and client contact to burnout in mental health professionals. *Journal of Counselling and Development*, 65, 249–252.

Schafer, T. (1992). CPN stress and organisational change: a study. *Community Psychiatric Nursing Journal*, February, 16–24.

Sutherland, V. & Cooper, C. (1990). *Understanding Stress.* London: Chapman and Hall.

Thomas, R. & Wilson, J. (2004). Issues and controversies in the understanding and diagnosis of compassion fatigue, vicarious traumatization, and secondary traumatic stress disorder. *International Journal of Emergency Mental Health*, 6, 81–92.

Tyler, P. & Cushway, D. (1995). Stress in nurses: the effects of coping and social support. *Stress Medicine*, 11, 243–251.

van Emmerik, A., Kamphuis, J., Hulsbosch, A. & Emmelkamp, P. (2002). Single session debriefing after psychological trauma: a meta-analysis. *Lancet*, 360, 766–771.

Wortley, V. & Grierson-Hill, L. (2003). Developing a successful self-rostering shift system. *Nursing Standard*, 17, 40–42.

# Chapter 11
# Quality improvement

*Frank P. Deane and Vicki Biro*

## Chapter overview

'Performance monitoring and readjustment . . . does not in and of itself create a commitment to quality; it only serves that commitment. A genuine, persistent, unshakable resolve to advance quality must come first. If that is present, almost any reasonable method for advancing quality will succeed. If the commitment to quality is absent, even the most sophisticated methods will fail.'

Donabedian (2003, p. 137)

In this quote and in his writings Donabedian highlights one of the most important foundations of quality improvement, the need to have genuine commitment to quality that is internally motivated and not just a response to external pressures or demands. Furthermore, he argues that the commitment needs to be by everyone at all levels of an organisation (Donabedian, 2003). Herein lies one of the first challenges to managers in mental health – the capacity to develop and nurture an environment in which others in a service value quality and the ability to demonstrate it.

## Defining quality improvement

Quality improvement and quality assurance have been used somewhat interchangeably in the past. Quality assurance has been defined as 'all actions taken to establish, protect, promote, and improve the quality of health care' (Donabedian, 2003, p. xxiii). However, the term assurance has been criticised because of the sense of guarantee that is implied. Instead, quality improvement or continuous improvement has been suggested as better alternatives because they imply an ongoing process of quality enhancement activities (Donabedian, 2003).

Goh (2007) further elaborates that quality assurance involves the consistent delivery of standards of care. One of the difficult aspects of this definition is that specifying appropriate standards is not always straightforward. A standard has been defined as 'a specified quantitative measure of magnitude or frequency that specified what is good or less so' (Donabedian, 2003, p. 60). Many stakeholders are involved in deciding standards, and the notion of appropriate or good standards from the perspective of clinicians, hospital managers, politicians and consumers is likely to vary considerably. Despite this, there is some consensus that meeting the needs of consumers is an important consideration in setting standards. The point is that there are many drivers of what is considered to be an appropriate standard of care. For many clinical managers the most frequent formal demands for quality improvement activities often occur in the context of accreditation or quality reviews.

## Determining priorities

In most Western countries, national mental health plans and national standards for mental health services have been developed and probably drive decisions about which standards are important at any particular point in time (e.g. Australian Health Ministers, 1996, 2003). Where there is mental health reform there are likely to be a set of performance indicators that reflect progress toward achieving reform goals (e.g. McEwan & Goldern, 2002). For example, the Department of Health (2006) in the UK has specified increased access to computerised cognitive behaviour therapy as part of its goal to provide better support for mental health and emotional well-being. The Australian National Mental Health Plan (Australian Health Ministers, 2003) highlights the need for services to become 'recovery-oriented' and provides definitions of what that means. Similarly, New Zealand has a blueprint for mental health services that also highlights a recovery approach (Mental Health Commission, 1998), a set of national standards for providing care (Ministry of Health, 1997) and a set of recovery competencies for New Zealand mental health workers (Mental Health Commission, 2001). While such documents may provide some direction for prioritising quality improvement activities, typically there are many more potential targets (goals, standards, competencies) than can be measured in most services.

At a more local level such as a community mental health service, changes in service delivery, specific problems or complaints may drive which set of standards will be targeted or prioritised. For example, a project integrating psychiatric rehabilitation into a managed healthcare structure, identified desirable consumer outcomes as 'personally satisfying role functioning in the client's social, residential, educational or occupational status' along with increased ability to function independently as key quality assurance targets (Ellison et al., 2002, p. 387). Other factors may be problem related such as an increase in rates of suicide attempts or injuries to staff that require quality reviews that have a more occupational health and safety focus.

Different professional organisations also specify competencies and professional standards for their clinicians (e.g. Coursey et al., 2000; Scheiber et al., 2003). Such competencies are also likely to have bearing on standards of care. There are many standards to strive for and we will provide a case example and other suggestions about considerations in determining which standards to assess. However, there are also usually multiple ways of determining whether such standards have been achieved. A variety of measurement tools may be used to gain information about standards and practices of the healthcare service and include both quantitative and qualitative measures. The measurement of whether particular goals or standards are being met is an important part of quality improvement activities. The use of performance indicators and monitoring techniques are common elements of measurement. But, as with establishment of standards, what, how, when and why particular measures are taken varies widely depending on context and the issues driving particular quality goals.

## Quality measurement

Quantitative measures provide a form of information that can be compared across different studies, populations and over time such as the frequency or duration of an event. Quantitative measures include things such as the number of treatment contacts or hospitalisations, duration of direct treatment contacts or length of stay in hospital. Other quantitative measures might be scores on particular questionnaires or rating scales. Qualitative measures tend to provide a context for quantitative measures and may highlight an issue or area of concern not directly measured by a specific quantitative measure. Qualitative data may be derived from case studies, interviews, focus groups or review of notes from files. Both measures may be used effectively in combination or separately, and are valid tools for monitoring and evaluating service activities and projects (Goff et al., 2001). The use of performance indicators and performance measures are helpful tools in quality improvement systems. In addition, activities that can provide information about the provision of quality of care and services may include incident review and monitoring, complaint monitoring, use of clinical indicators, review meetings, audits and surveys.

A study of quality measurement in substance abuse and mental health services across 434 managed care organisations found 70% used patient satisfaction surveys, 73% used performance indicators, 74% used practice guidelines for behavioural health and 49% assessed clinical outcomes (Merrick et al., 2002). Although consumer satisfaction surveys are relatively frequently used, there is not always a clear association between satisfaction and clinical outcomes. This requires the need to consider a range of quality measures. Increasingly, mental health services are introducing minimum mental health datasets to assist in quality measurement (Clarkson & Challis, 2002). For example, routine outcome assessment in Australian mental health services using the Health of the Nation Outcome Scales (HoNOS) and Life Skills Profile (LSP) is now well established (Eagar et al., 2005), and these scales have the potential to be used in quality improvement activities.

### Key performance indicators

Key performance indicators (KPIs) are variables (e.g. number of staff contact hours) that are assumed to reflect how well a service is performing in important areas related to quality of services. They are termed 'indicators' because they do not guarantee quality, but *probably* reflect quality; they are used to screen or flag processes or outcomes for review. For example, clinical indicators are usually rate based and demonstrate trends or variations within results thus highlighting areas that may need addressing (Australian Council on Healthcare Standards, 2006a). As a clinical manager, you may not always have a lot of choice about which KPIs are requested. However, wherever possible you should try to be involved in decisions about the selection of KPIs and the discussions leading to their selection.

Goff et al. (2001) recommend that when developing performance indicators, managers and evaluation teams should ensure that they relate directly to the goals, outcomes and objectives of the activity or initiative. They go on to recommend that consideration be given to the performance indicator in terms of whether it provides a logical link between the available evidence and whether it has demonstrated the capacity to measure change within a given timeframe. Other considerations are: whether the performance indicator is achievable, measurable and affordable (cost–benefit); whether it is clear, concise and understandable for relevant stakeholders; and whether it measures a specific aspect of behaviour, attitude, condition or status that relates directly to the objectives, outcomes and goals of the initiative/activity.

By way of example, Sorensen et al. (1987) described 25 KPIs to support managers and policy makers in assessing the performance of their programme relative to others. The focus was on community mental health organisations. The initial set of indicators had an efficiency orientation (use of resources) while the later ones had a focus on effectiveness (attainment of goals). In addition, KPIs were blocked into the four groups of revenue, clients, staff and service. Sorensen et al. suggest that before comparing with external sources, the organisation's own trends should be considered and this involves calculation of percentage change from previous year to current year. Use of medians was suggested to avoid effects of extreme mean values. These median values can then be compared to appropriate comparison groups (specific to organisational needs, national or state). For example, an area health service may choose to benchmark against other area health services with similar population or geographical characteristics. The authors suggested locating organisational data in quartiles compared with comparison groups. For example, those organisations in the first quarter would be among the lowest 25% of organisations on a particular measure (Sorensen et al., 1987). It is recommended that at a minimum, cautions should be made for special circumstances that may lead to accurate but potentially misleading conclusions (for example, special projects occurring within a service that may influence results). Examples of managerial applications of the data are provided with the suggestion that KPI measures that fall in the first or fourth quartiles are 'potential areas of managerial inquiry' (p. 242) (i.e. we may have a problem).

Of the 25 KPIs in Sorensen's list many were heavily weighted toward revenue or financial consideration. For each KPI an operational definition is provided along with uses, limitations, potential problems in data collection and advantages. Although this was an attempt to suggest a set of KPIs given the emphasis on revenue and efficiency indicators (the ability to lower the cost of care without reducing health outcomes) these appeared more relevant to managers with strong fiscal responsibilities. However, clinical managers may be more concerned with acceptability of care such as the extent to which patients' preferences and expectations of treatment are met (Donabedian, 2003). Thus, there is usually some need to make decisions about what to monitor and this can be influenced by external factors (e.g. required by government) or internally (e.g. routine problem identification within a team or by consumers of a service). The following case example illustrates how one mental health service approached prioritising and selecting KPIs to be monitored.

### Selecting KPI priorities

In a local area mental health service project 87 KPIs had been identified by service management as relevant for monitoring progress toward achieving the goals of the service strategic plan. Achievement of these KPIs was then passed to clinical managers with the view that they would monitor and report these on a regular basis. However, the large number of KPIs necessitated some way of prioritising and organising them so as not to overwhelm both the clinical managers and the administrative and other frontline staff.

Initially, these KPIs were organised into six target goal groups: safety of service (20), effectiveness (19), efficiency (8), access (29), appropriateness (4) and participation (7). This process allowed decisions about which domains appeared to have more indicators which might suggest some redundancy. As recommended by Sorensen et al (1987), there was a need to provide an operational definition for each KPI, the system source of data and its uses. As part of this process and in order to make decisions about which KPIs should be prioritised, limitations of the KPI, potential problems in data collection and advantages were considered and listed.

In prioritising the KPIs to be collected and reported, several criteria were used. The first block, listed below, relate to 'ease of collection' while others focused on the ability of the KPI to provide meaningful data in relation to goal achievement.

- Are the data already being collected and reported?
- Are the data already being collected but not collated and reported?
- Ease and cost of collection and reporting.
- Capacity of one KPI to address more than one strategic goal or standard.
- What are evaluation priorities of key stakeholders (especially consumers, carers, general practitioners (GPs), etc.)?
  - What are meaningful indicators to stakeholders?
  - What are their strategic goal priorities?
- Which KPIs will tell us whether a strategy has been achieved (i.e. how close do the KPIs link with achievement of strategic goals)?

- Is a KPI amenable to implementing change in the organisational system (i.e. will measuring the KPI lead to change, or can it be interpreted in a way that allows change to occur to achieve a specific strategic goal)?
- Do KPIs overlap such that they provide redundant information?

For the 87 KPIs in our case study, 17% were already being collected, aggregated and reported usually for the local clinical governance executive committees, quality council, state, or accreditation organisation. Twenty-eight per cent had data that were available in various forms (e.g. medical records, accounting, human resources, etc.), but would require additional systems and resources in order to be collected, aggregated and reported.

Thus, 45% of the KPIs did not require data generation procedures in addition to data collection. However, many of these KPIs were generated as a function of standard state-wide data collection and reporting requirements. As a result they largely reflected the priorities of the state centre for mental health or management. Without elaborating the process fully, it can already be seen that several of the KPIs could be selected based on relative ease of data collection. Clearly, there is a need to continue the process to be sure that the KPIs are also relevant and meaningful in terms of the targeted goals. However, while these issues are important considerations in selecting KPIs there is also a need for input from other stakeholders about preferences or meaningfulness of different KPIs.

### Stakeholder considerations in prioritisation and selection of measures

Wilkerson et al. (2000) described an accreditation system and its performance indicators project. Performance indicators were identified using a consultative approach to the accreditation survey process and gave service providers and stakeholders guidance in gathering and interpreting data on outcomes so that these were completed in a uniform way.

Consideration of consumer or other stakeholder preferences can be achieved in many ways. There may already be consumer representation within the organisation (e.g. consumer review groups). Alternatively, there is the possibility of contracting external consumer review. The goal is not to generate strategic direction since this has presumably already been accomplished through an extensive process of consultation. Instead the goal is for a consumer group to review the existing strategic goals and provide recommendations about what would be meaningful indicators (measures) of the achievement of these goals. In addition, it might be possible for this consumer group to review any existing list of indicators (e.g. the list of 87 indicators) to provide feedback about which in their view have the potential to reflect or inform achievement of strategic goals. It is important to have a set of consumers with some evaluation sophistication for these purposes because there is often a gap between goals and 'indicators' that are not always readily apparent. For example, understanding how and by whom indicators are reported may be important to determine the extent to which they capture goals. Often strategic documents are written in general terms with varying degrees of specificity with regard to criteria of goal achievement. Similarly, there are often multiple KPIs that will provide data regarding the achievement of a single goal. Often 'indicators' are not direct measures. For example, the KPI 'percentage of active consumers with a current care plan' does not indicate the quality of the care plan, how meaningful the plan is to the consumer, nor how actively or collaboratively the consumer and clinicians are working together using the plan. Where relevant to the strategic goals being addressed other stakeholders may need to be consulted (e.g. access to services by referrers may involve carers, GPs or the police).

Other criteria for considering priorities for monitoring include: patient welfare; meeting externally imposed requirements; risk reduction; institutional enhancement; attempts to get a representative sample (statistically); fairness and feasibility (e.g. organisational readiness) (Donabedian, 2003).

## Selecting an approach for measuring performance

From some of the examples above it can be seen that there are multiple methods for collecting data. Donabedian (2003) provides a three-part structure in selecting an approach to assessing performance.

(1) *Structure*, which includes material and human resources (e.g. equipment and number, variety or qualifications of staff) and organisational structures (e.g. supervision, training, funding mechanisms).
(2) *Process* relates to the activities that make up mental healthcare (e.g. diagnosis, treatment, etc.).
(3) *Outcomes*, such as changes in mental health status or satisfaction of consumers and carers about care received.

All three components can provide information from which quality can be inferred. However, Donabedian argued that quality can only be inferred when there is a predetermined relationship among the three components and suggests a simplified linear relationship as:

Structure → Process → Outcome

Between each of the components the arrows represent causal probabilities rather than certainties. Often KPIs are provided that can potentially fall under Structure, Process or Outcome. It is useful to locate where KPIs fall in this system in order to better understand what parts of performance they are mostly capturing but as we will see this process also helps clarify what might be done to improve performance.

You can also see from Table 11.1 that in this service more than one KPI may relate to the same sequence of Structure–Process–Outcome (example 1 in Table 11.1). Thus, the process of organising KPIs (or other measures) may also allow integration and remove redundancy. In addition, the examples highlight

**Table 11.1**  Examples of KPIs located in Structure–Process–Outcome categories.

|  | Structure | Process | Outcome |
|---|---|---|---|
| Example 1 | **KPI** 'Number of clinical full time equivalent vacancies' | Sufficient staff are available to deliver care | More clients have access to appropriate care **KPI** 'Number of complaints from *consumers and carers* relating to poor access to services' |
| Example 2 | **KPI** 'Number of full time equivalent staff who completed child protection training in the past 12 months' | Appropriate screening and identification of children at risk of abuse | Prevention of abuse and negative mental health outcomes for children |
| Example 3 | Staff receive training in how to engage consumers in collaborative care planning | **KPI** 'Percentage of active consumers who signed their own care plan' | Consumers will have greater satisfaction with care. Specifically, collaborative approach |
| Example 4 | Computers and information system to streamline referral procedures | Referral information received and entered by administrative intake worker within four hours | **KPI** 'Number of complaints from *referrers* relating to poor access to services' |

the probabilities that are implicit between each of the components and how these vary.

If we take example 4 in Table 11.1, the probability that provision of computers and an information system (structure) leads to referral information being entered (process) could be viewed as fairly moderate to high. However, the probability that referral information being entered leads to fewer complaints (outcome) from referrers may be lower because there is probably a range of other uncontrolled factors that lead to complaints being made and variances that impact on efficient referral processes and outcomes. In addition, there are methodological issues associated with the measurement of this outcome. It is possible that the frequency of complaints is coming from a relatively low baseline and it may be that this measure is not sufficiently sensitive to detect any changes as a result of the structural changes made to address the problem.

Donabedian (2003) also offers guidelines for how to choose outcomes as an indicator of quality. The outcome should:

- be relevant to the objectives of care
- be achievable with good care (i.e. methods are available to mental health system)
- be attributable to healthcare or the practitioner delivering care

- consider duration and magnitude
- have information about the outcome available (i.e. it must be obtainable)
- consider consequences of taking an action and also not taking an action (i.e. is the outcome able to detect effects of inaction?)
- consider the means used to achieve the outcome.

It is likely that for most quality assurance projects a combination of Structure–Process–Outcome approaches will be used. One advantage of this is that where inferences about quality differ between the approaches, this may indicate problems with either measurement accuracy, timing or faulty assumptions about the sequencing (Donabedian, 2003).

## Identifying standards

Table 11.1 also highlights how the role of 'standards' operates in quality assurance. For example 2, the standard for training in child protection (Structure) may be 100% of staff within 12 months of commencing employment. The standard for appropriate screening and identification of children at risk of abuse (Process) might be not less than 90% use of specific oral screening question and use of structured questionnaire following positive screen. The standard for prevention of abuse (Outcome) may be no more than 5% of children who screen positive go on to have documented abuse.

As noted, earlier standards are often defined by government policy, professional organisations and other stakeholders. Wherever possible, good practice and standards should be based on empirical research. In practice this can at times be a complicated process (see Chapter 12). However, there are many accessible sources of information to help establish standards if these have not already been provided. For example, practice guidelines for the treatment of anorexia nervosa reveal that 50% of patients get better (Haliburn, 2005). These data have the potential to serve as a standard for outcomes. Similarly, there is a range of practice guidelines for disorders such as depression (Ellis, 2004) and schizophrenia (Lehman et al., 2004; McGorry, 2005). These guidelines offer further opportunities to identify standards for use in quality assurance activities (e.g. for schizophrenia, 'Clozapine should be used early in the course, as soon as treatment resistance to at least two antipsychotics has been demonstrated', McGorry, 2005). Zaenger and Al-Assaf (1998) specified other methods for setting standards such as identifying and conferring with experts, literature reviews, benchmarking (normative comparisons), and reviewing past experiences within an organisation.

## Obtaining information

There are many sources of information that can be used in quality assurance and improvement activities. As noted, in the review of KPIs, consideration should be given to how accurately the information reflects the target behaviour or performance being assessed (validity). In addition, consideration should be given to how well the sample of information represents most or all occurrences of the behaviour or performance (generalisability). The third major consideration is whether the information can be collected reliably. This can have several implications. For example, if data are being extracted from clients' medical records in some form of audit, reliability might refer to whether the specific data extracted by one person is the same as it would be if a second person were to complete the same review. It may also refer to how complete the data are, it is possible that 90% of data is collected from one community mental health centre, but only 50% is able to be located from a second. Such variation may be a function of incomplete data recording by clinicians or administrative support staff at the different settings.

### Records and electronic databases

There are several potential sources of data and the practical difficulties and effort in actually obtaining it will also vary considerably. Medical records are increasingly becoming electronic and while in theory this offers potential for relatively easy access, this will depend on how 'user friendly' the system is or the availability of technical support. Concerns about completeness, reliability and validity of medical record information have been voiced by others and as a consequence there may be occasions where there is first a need to improve the quality of information in records. Improving the completeness and quality of information in records may involve simply insisting that existing requirements be completed (e.g. through team meetings) or may require the provision of additional training of clinical or administrative staff.

There is potential to supplement medical records in order to obtain quality data but there is a need to be sensitive to the extra burden this may place on staff. A compromise to this is to identify selected clinicians who agree to participate in the quality activities and to obtain the extra information. Such a strategy needs to balance the loss of representativeness with improved completeness and accuracy of information.

Many healthcare organisations have electronic information systems that have the capacity to collect and report activity within the organisation (e.g. length of stay, bed occupancy, occasions of service). Strategic development and resource allocation is required by the organisation to ensure reliability of the data entered into the system, ease of accessibility to the information stored in the system, efficient management of data storage and timely reporting of statistical data and trends to relevant managers and service providers.

Another form of record that is frequently used in quality activities are financial records. Financial records are used particularly when assessing the efficiency of care. Efficiency is 'defined either as the amount of medical care for a given cost (where more is better care) or similarly as the lowest costs incurred to provide a given level of medical care (where less is better)' (Benneyan & Valdmanis,

1998, p. 186). The structure and detail of financial management systems will vary in their ability to support resource allocation decisions. From our case example, KPIs that might access financial records to determine costs are: 'Hours per month per employee spent in supervision', 'Average days per annum spent by staff on study leave', 'Number of shifts covered by overtime'.

It should be noted that fiscal or economic information can also be assessed using surveys and this is particularly useful when collecting patient information (e.g. resource usage, work absences, etc., see Gournay & Brooking, 1995).

## Surveys

Surveys or questionnaires are a commonly used form of data collection. There is a whole set of specialty skills associated with the development of surveys and it may be helpful to consult with colleagues, consultants or academics who have experience in the design of such measures. If you do not have access to this support then try to identify an existing measure with established reliability and validity. For example, there are many consumer satisfaction questionnaires ranging from a few items to many that cover a wide range of service elements. These can usually be located through library database searches such as Psychinfo or Medline. If you need additional help with this you should contact your institute's librarian. Other sources of information about potential questionnaires can be found on government health department websites and publications (e.g. Stedman et al., 1997).

Surveys can be administered to patients, families, populations or practitioners. Practitioners may include those within the organisation or those external to the organisation who have a collaborative working relationship (e.g. GPs who are a major referral source). Population or community surveys need particular care and planning with regard to representativeness. Usually, clear specification of the target subset within the community is needed (e.g. youth 16–24 years, older people, poor, etc.).

As noted earlier, many countries now have mandated routine outcome measures in mental health services that are completed by clinicians and consumers (e.g. Eagar et al., 2005). These are typically entered into databases, and there is the potential to access this information to reflect amount and rates of improvement for particular client groups or service types.

## Observation

Direct observation is another method of gathering information although this can often be a relatively expensive approach. Using the Structure–Process–Outcome structure various approaches to observation can be used. For example, there may be a desire to improve the intake procedures and experience of consumers attending community mental health services. It may be useful to observe first the physical *Structure* of the various waiting areas across several centres. Other structural elements might include the number of administrative staff available, availability of medical records and forms used in the intake procedure. *Process* observations might involve watching as patients arrive at the centre, how they are greeted by staff, recording their wait times and also time in the initial intake interview with clinical staff. Process observations could be made of the actual intake interviews by having clinical supervisors or colleagues sit in on intake interviews and rating specific behaviours. It may be possible to audiotape or video-tape the intake interviews for rating at a later date. Clearly these strategies require the consent of consumers. *Outcome* related observations in this context might involve recording whether patients return for a second visit. The assumption being that having a positive initial intake experience increases the probability they will return for future visits. This could be supplemented by a brief questionnaire asking them how satisfied they were with their initial appointment experience.

### Clinical review activities

Service providers can gather information about the quality of care provided to consumers through a range of clinical review activities. These activities may include incident monitoring and sentinel event management. An incident monitoring system facilitates the identification, processing, analysis and reporting of incidents with the purpose of minimising or preventing their recurrence. Effective incident monitoring is dependent on a commitment by the organisation to act on the information that arises from the review process and to facilitate improvements to care and services. Sentinel events are occurrences that have a serious adverse outcome such that an individual investigation is warranted. Circumstances surrounding the event are investigated by the healthcare organisation in order to understand the underlying causes and system vulnerabilities contributing to the event. The product of the sentinel event review and analysis is an action plan that identifies strategies for the implementation of system changes to reduce the probability of the event occurring in the future and to measure the effectiveness of these actions (New South Wales (NSW) Health, 2001).

## Reviewing data, feedback and change

Once information has been collected there is a need to make sense of it. As a frontline manager responsible for quality improvement activities, you may not have extensive experience with data analysis. Analysis will be dependent on the type of questions asked and data collected. However, at a minimum, frequencies, percentages, means and medians provide important descriptive data. When attempting to determine whether improvements occurred following some kind of service change, it is likely that statistical analysis will be needed in addition to descriptive data in order to determine whether the change is of sufficient magnitude to be considered reliable and replicable. This provides some reassurance that improvements are not entirely due to chance. For most quality improvement activities basic descriptive data are often sufficient.

There is a need to feed back these results to those in the system who are responsible for implementing any change that may be required or to sustain improvement. Feedback of quality information serves several purposes. It offers staff the opportunity to provide some comments on interpretation of results. It often helps those who are sceptical of information gathering activities to see how their efforts are put to work. Feedback is the initial part of the process that starts to bring staff on board in preparation for making change. It is often preferable to provide frontline staff with opportunities to problem solve around how improvements might be made in relation to specific areas of performance and in relation to the data provided. Where possible a negotiated and agreed strategy for behaviour change should be developed since this is more likely to lead to commitment to change. The preparation for change and attitudes that support this commitment to quality starts at the beginning of the quality improvement process when decisions about which aspects of performance are being determined.

Again, the Structure–Process–Outcome strategy is helpful in determining what behaviour changes might be needed to improve quality. This strategy proposes causal linkages between each of the components and these offer insights into where, when and how change might be made. For example, it may be that there are insufficient human resources (structure) leading to poor performance. It may be that the resources are sufficient, but the skills of staff need to be improved (process) in order to improve quality. The capacity to address particular problems with these components will also vary. It may be that there is no more immediate funding available to increase staffing (structure), so this may become a longer-term target for change whereas improving staff skills may be able to be addressed more immediately through educational and motivational strategies. It is possible that other structural changes, such as provision of better information systems, may clear staff time such that they are able to reallocate human resources to more direct patient care.

An essential part of the quality improvement cycle requires that any changes and actions implemented should in turn have their effects monitored in order to determine whether the changes lead to improvement. Continuous quality improvement is contingent on the organisation ensuring mechanisms are in place to sustain improvement. Sustaining improvement may involve (NSW Health, 2002):

- standardisation of systems and processes for performing work activities
- documentation of associated policies, procedures and guidelines
- ongoing measurement and review to ensure changes become part of routine practice
- training and education of staff to support changes to practice and service delivery.

## Quality improvement and accreditation

A number of organisations are involved in both quality improvement monitoring and accreditation. For example, the Australian Council on Healthcare Standards has a major role in promoting quality and safety in healthcare through the continual review of performance, assessment and accreditation using the Evaluation and Quality Improvement Program: EQuIP (Australian Council on Healthcare Standards, 2006b). The Australian Council on Healthcare Standards uses a set of national standards for health services and also includes an in-depth review of mental health services using the National Standards for Mental Health, 1996. The Australian standards for mental health services pertain to: access, continuity, appropriateness and effectiveness of care, patient safety and the extent to which the service is consumer focused (Goh, 2007).

EQuIP is a four-year quality assessment and improvement programme for organisations that focuses on patient care and service provision. Organisations undertake yearly self-assessments to review and evaluate their performance against national standards and participate in biennial on-site surveys by an external team of accreditation surveyors. Surveyors provide independent assessment of the organisation's performance against the recognised standards. Recommendations from on-site surveys enable the health service to undertake an improvement process that meets professional and practice standards through ongoing monitoring and review (Australian Council on Healthcare Standards, 2006b).

The EQuIP standards focus on issues considered important in providing quality and safe healthcare and are grouped into related areas such as clinical, corporate and support functions. Within each standard there are mandatory and non-mandatory criteria that describe key components of meeting the standard and elements that identify what should be in place within the organisation to meet each criterion. Accreditation of an organisation requires a minimum level of attainment of all the mandatory criteria. This level of attainment demonstrates the health service is evaluating and monitoring key components of each standard.

The clinical function focuses on care delivery processes and systems, access to services and provision of appropriate and safe care and services that include consumer participation. The support function concentrates on performance in areas such as clinical and corporate risk management, information systems, human resource and workforce management and research. The corporate function focuses on leadership and governance of the organisation including its strategic direction and safe environment.

While not required for accreditation, reporting of standardised clinical indicators to the Australian Council on Healthcare Standards and participation in a national comparative report may be used by healthcare organisations for internal and external benchmarking using trended analysis and comparative reports. Through this process they can also demonstrate how they are monitoring and evaluating services for the accreditation process.

Preparing for accreditation in mental healthcare, as with any health service, requires commitment from the organisation to quality improvement and the processes that support performance monitoring. Structures, systems and resources should be in place that support the organisation's self-assessment using the EQuIP standards, criteria and elements and thereby enable services to identify what they are doing, how well they are doing it, what evidence they have to

**Table 11.2**   Example of addressing an EQuIP standard and related criteria.

**EQuIP Function – Clinical**

| | |
|---|---|
| EQuIP standard | *Consumers/patients are provided with high quality care throughout the care delivery process* |
| Mandatory criterion | The assessment system ensures current and ongoing needs of the consumer/patient are identified |

**Levels of attainment**

| | |
|---|---|
| Awareness level (LA) | Assessment guidelines, policies and referral systems are in place within the mental health service |
| Implementation level (SA) | Mental health presentations are assessed in timely manner; assessment processes and outcomes are documented in the medical record; at-risk patients are identified, managed and referred to appropriate services; multidisciplinary team approaches are co-ordinated within the mental health service |
| Evaluation level (MA) | Assessment, referral, care management and discharge processes are evaluated and improved, using, for example, waiting times in emergency departments, audit of medical record documentation, and incident and complaint monitoring and review, and initiatives to improve problems identified in the evaluation of services and systems are undertaken |
| Excellence level (EA) | Internal and external benchmarking and comparison of systems of care and assessment practices that facilitate practice improvement can be demonstrated |
| Leadership level (OA) | The mental health service can demonstrate they are a leader in assessment of mental health service provision |

demonstrate it and to provide a gap analysis to use for ongoing planning and quality improvement activities. In doing this, the organisation also provides the external survey team with information that facilitates a good understanding of service systems and allows a more efficient verification process. By way of illustration Table 11.2 shows an example using an EQuIP standard and mandatory criteria to highlight the accreditation and quality assurance requirements.

The challenge for mental health programmes and services through the accreditation cycle is to:

- identify what services, processes and systems are in place to address both EQuIP and National Standards for Mental Health through the self-assessment process
- ensure there is evidence to support statements pertaining to service delivery and performance

● demonstrate implementation of quality improvement activities and the use of performance monitoring information to evaluate service activities and implement change.

### Steps in quality improvement processes

A number of authors have provided steps in the quality improvement process but these tend to be very broad overviews of the process. We briefly summarise two, since most overlap considerably.

Lavender et al. (1994) described several stages in their approach:

● commitment to service principles and a quality review strategy by service management
● selection and training of quality reviewers
● quality review by consultant in collaboration with staff
● goal setting and action plan by staff and submission of quality report
● monitoring of achievement and further review in a cycle.

Furthermore, they identified a schedule for their quality review that covered environment resources, external links, working practices and service provision.

Goh (2007) provides a practical outline of the quality improvement process that involves five steps. The first involves *preparing the team* by identifying a project, choosing a leader and facilitator, orienting the team, defining roles, and stating a problem and objectives. Step two, *problem investigation*, is similar to Donabedian's (2003) Structure–Process–Outcome framework and involves analysing the effects of the problem on consumers, describing the processes and theorising the causes. This step also gathers data and considers alternative solutions to the problem. Step 3 focuses on *process improvement* by implementing change and a trial of new procedures while measuring the results of this trial. Step 4, *return or rest*, reflects the cyclic nature of the process and refers back to steps 2 and 1. The final step, *close*, involves documentation of the project, recognition and disbanding the team.

## Conclusion

A major practical issue for most organisations and managers is that quality improvement activities require commitment and time. As outlined in this chapter, there are a number of steps to be considered in determining appropriate targets and indicators of quality (e.g. KPIs). It takes time to review and consult around these issues. It also takes time to establish systems to collect data and time to maintain and support these systems. Engaging and maintaining staff involvement in this process also requires considerable skill. Further to this, after data has been collected, analysed and conclusions and suggestions for change have been made, the quality review cycle 'begins' again. For very specific problems that become the focus of quality concerns, it is sometimes possible to draw in other resources or support. For example, specific funding to address service issues may be available to support quality activities. It may be possible to link with local universities. The challenge of providing effective, efficient and sustainable quality healthcare is of great interest to many academics. There is usually overlap between quality improvement, programme evaluation and research activities. While research often requires higher levels of specificity and control in their methods, these demands vary a great deal from project to project and it may be possible for formal research projects to support and contribute substantially to quality improvement activities. The role of a clinical manager in such situations might be to focus on providing feedback in order to improve services since this is not always a primary consideration in research projects (Lavender et al., 1994). However, as noted at the beginning of this chapter, no matter whether quality improvement is driven as a function of formal research projects, complaints by consumers, or accreditation process, the key to success is a genuine and persistent commitment to quality.

# References

Australian Council on Healthcare Standards (2006a). *ACHS Clinical Indicator Report to ANZ 1998–2005: Determining the Potential to Improve Quality of Care*, 7th edition. Sydney: Australian Council on Healthcare Standards.

Australian Council on Healthcare Standards (2006b). *The ACHS EQuIP 4 Guide: Part 1 – Accreditation, Standards, Guidelines.* Sydney: Australian Council on Healthcare Standards.

Australian Health Ministers (1996). *National Standards for Mental Health Services.* Canberra: Commonwealth of Australia.

Australian Health Ministers (2003). *National Mental Health Plan 2003 2008.* Canberra: Australian Government.

Benneyan, J. C. & Valdmanis, V. (1998). Balancing quality with costs in managed care settings. In: Al-Assaf, A. F. (ed.) *Managed Care Quality: A Practical Guide.* New York: CRC Press, pp. 181–206.

Clarkson, P. & Challis, D. (2002). Developing performance indicators for mental health care. *Journal of Mental Health*, 11, 281–294.

Coursey, R. D., Curtis, L., Marsh, D. T., Campbell, J., Harding, C., Spaniol, L., Lucksted, A., McKenna, J., Kelly, M., Paulson, R. & Zahniser, J. (2000). Competencies for direct service staff members who work with adults with severe mental illnesses: specific knowledge, attitudes, skills, and bibliography. *Psychiatric Rehabilitation Journal*, 23, 378–392.

Department of Health (2006). *Our Health, Our Care, Our Say: A New Direction for Community Services.* London: Department of Health. Available at: www.dh.gov.uk/assetRoot/04/12/74/72/04127472.pdf (accessed 17 February 2007).

Donabedian, A. (2003). *An Introduction to Quality Assurance in Health Care.* New York: Oxford University Press.

Eagar, K., Trauer, T. & Mellsop, G. (2005). Performance of routine outcome measures in adult mental health care. *Australian and New Zealand Journal of Psychiatry*, 39, 713–718.

Ellis, P. (2004). Australian and New Zealand clinical practice guidelines for the treatment of depression. *Australian and New Zealand Journal of Psychiatry*, 38, 389–407.

Ellison, M. L., Anthony, W. A., Sheets, J. L., Dodds, W., Barker, W. J., Massaro, J. & Wewiorski, N. J. (2002). The integration of psychiatric rehabilitation services in behavioral health care structures: a state example. *Journal of Behavioral Health Services and Research*, 29, 381–393.

Goff, S., Pryor, K. & van Ewyk, V. (2001). *Evaluation: A Guide to Good Practice.* Canberra: Commonwealth of Australia National Mental Health Strategy.

Goh, J. (2007). Evaluation as a management tool in the pursuit of quality. In: Meadows, G., Singh, B. & Grigg, M. (eds) *Mental Health in Australia: Collaborative Community Practice*, 2nd edition. Oxford: Oxford University Press, pp. 254–269.

Gournay, K. & Brooking, J. (1995). The community psychiatric nurse in primary care: an economic analysis. *Journal of Advanced Nursing*, 22, 769–778.

Haliburn, J. (2005). Australian and New Zealand clinical practice guidelines for the treatment of anorexia nervosa. *Australian and New Zealand Journal of Psychiatry*, 3, 639–640.

Lavender, A., Leiper, R., Pilling, S. & Clifford, P. (1994). Quality assurance in mental health: the QUARTZ system. *British Journal of Clinical Psychology*, 33, 451–467.

Lehman, A. F., Kreyenbuhl, J., Buchanan, R. W., Dickerson, F. B., Dixon, L. B., Goldberg, R., Green-Paden, L. D., Tenhula, W. N., Boerescu, D., Tek, C., Sandson, N. & Steinwachs, D. M. (2004). The schizophrenia Patient Outcomes Research Team (PORT): updated treatment recommendations 2003. *Schizophrenia Bulletin*, 30, 193–217.

McEwan, K. L. & Goldern, E. M. (2002). Keeping mental health reform on course: selecting indicators of mental health system performance. *Canadian Journal of Community Mental Health*, 21, 5–16.

McGorry, P. (2005). Royal Australian and New Zealand College of Psychiatrists clinical practice guidelines for the treatment of schizophrenia and related disorders. *Australian and New Zealand Journal of Psychiatry*, 39, 1–30.

Mental Health Commission (1998). *Blue Print for Mental Health.* Wellington: New Zealand Government.

Mental Health Commission (2001). *New Zealand Recovery Competencies.* Wellington: New Zealand Government.

Merrick, E. L., Garnick, D. W., Horgan, C. M. & Hodgkin, D. (2002). Quality measurement and accountability for substance abuse and mental health services in managed care organisations. *Medical Care*, 40, 1238–1248.

Ministry of Health (1997). *New Zealand Standards.* Wellington: New Zealand Government.

NSW Health (2001). The clinician's toolkit for improving patient care. Sydney: NSW Department of Health.

NSW Health (2002). *Easy Guide to Clinical Practice Improvement: A Guide for Healthcare Professionals.* Sydney: NSW Department of Health.

Scheiber, S. C., Kramer, T. A. M. & Adamowski, S. E. (2003). The implications of core competencies for psychiatric education and practice in the US. *Canadian Journal of Psychiatry*, 48, 215–221.

Sorensen, J. E., Zelman, W., Hanbery, G. W. & Kucic, A. R. (1987). Managing mental health organizations with 25 key performance indicators. *Evaluation and Program Planning*, 10, 239–247.

Stedman, T., Yellowlees, P., Mellsop, G., Clarke, R. & Drake, S. (1997). *Measuring Consumer Outcomes in Mental Health.* Canberra, ACT: Department of Health and Family Services.

Wilkerson, D., Migas, N. & Slaven, T. (2000). Outcome-oriented standards and performance indicators for substance dependency rehabilitation programs. *Substance Use and Misuse*, 35, 1679–1703.

Zaenger, D. & Al-Assaf, A. F. (1998). Quality assurance activities. In: Al-Assaf, A. F. (ed.) *Managed Care Quality: A Practical Guide.* New York: CRC Press, pp. 69–90.

# Chapter 12
# Evidence-based practice in mental health services: understanding the issues and supporting and sustaining implementation

*Robert King and Frank P. Deane*

## Chapter overview

The purpose of this chapter is to assist service managers to support and promote evidence-based practice (EBP) in mental health services. EBP is, from a service management perspective, a key service quality issue. When a service is operating within an EBP culture both service users and the wider public can be confident that the highest quality and most appropriate clinical services are being provided. When a service operates outside an EBP culture there is risk that clinical services are outdated, idiosyncratic or simply ineffective. The chapter begins by clarifying what is meant by EBP and then considers practical means by which service managers can monitor the extent to which EBP provides the framework for service delivery and can advance EBP within the service. The focus is on psychosocial interventions but the general principles apply equally to biological interventions – although, determination as to whether or not a psychosocial intervention is evidence based may sometimes be more complex and challenging.

## Understanding the issues

### Defining evidence-based practice

The American Psychological Association (APA), in August 2005, adopted as policy the statement:

> 'Evidence-based practice in psychology (EBPP) is the integration of the best available research with clinical expertise in the context of patient characteristics, culture, and preferences.'

This is broadly consistent with a widely quoted earlier definition applied by Sackett et al. (1997, p. 2) to evidence-based medicine: 'the conscientious, explicit, and judicious use of current best evidence in making decisions about the care of individual patients'.

The APA definition arose out of a period of highly contentious debate within the profession (APA Presidential Task Force on Evidence-Based Practice, 2006).

One way of understanding this debate is to view it as a debate between researchers and practitioners. Researchers attach high levels of importance to the results of clinical trials and tend to the view that clinical outcomes will be best when practitioners conduct their treatments in the manner of a clinical trial. By contrast, practitioners are suspicious of clinical trials and fear that clinical judgement will be replaced by a straitjacket of highly standardised treatment protocols. The consensus definition, like the Sackett et al. (1997) definition, is an attempt to accommodate the values and concerns of both groups.

Both definitions suggest that practitioners and service administrators must consider three questions when determining whether or not EBP is in operation:

- Are clinical decisions and interventions informed by the best available research evidence?
- Is the application of research evidence tempered by thoughtful and conscientious clinical assessments and judgements?
- Have the characteristics of clients (including preferences and culture) been taken into consideration in clinical decision making and implementation of clinical interventions?

If the answer to each of these questions is yes, then EBP is being used. If the answer to any of the questions is no, then something other than EBP is in operation. This means that there is much more to EBP than the application of 'empirically supported treatments' (ESTs). An intervention might have strong empirical support but be either inappropriate for application in the specific clinical circumstances of a client or it may have both empirical support and application to the client but may be culturally unacceptable or in some other respect unpalatable to the client.

### What is the 'best available evidence'?

The term 'best available evidence' accepts that the quality of evidence underlying a practice is not always exemplary. Sometimes there will be no evidence at all and the APA Presidential Task Force (2006) points out that lack of evidence does not mean that an intervention is ineffective. However, when there is a choice between using an intervention for which there is higher-quality evidence and an intervention for which there is lower-quality evidence or no evidence, the former would usually prevail, unless inconsistent with clinical judgement or client preferences. Furthermore, the burden would be on the service or clinician to make the case that clinical judgement and/or client preference factors outweigh evidentiary factors.

Evidence for the effectiveness of an intervention may come from one or both of two sources:

- published evidence of effectiveness with analogous populations
- evidence of effectiveness in this specific treatment.

The literature on EBP is dominated by the former category – interventions that are sometimes described as 'empirically supported treatments' (ESTs). However, there is growing interest in the second category of evidence and there is evidence that feedback to practitioners regarding the effectiveness of a specific treatment with a specific client can improve the effectiveness of the intervention. Both sources of evidence are considered here. We discuss them under two broad headings: ESTs and Emergent evidence.

### Published evidence: empirically supported treatments

There is a very substantial (and constantly growing) literature reporting on the effectiveness of psychosocial interventions for people with severe mental illness. The challenge both for practitioners and for service managers is to determine when evidence of effectiveness is sufficient for an intervention to be considered as being 'evidence based' or 'empirically supported' for application in a mental health service.

Flay et al. (2005) suggested that for evidence to be sufficient to warrant dissemination of an intervention, there should have been reported at least two trials that meet five requirements: defined samples from defined populations; psychometrically sound measures and data collection; rigorous data analysis; consistent positive effects; and at least one long-term follow-up showing sustained effects.

Dissemination is a highly relevant concept for service managers. Whenever managers advocate use of an intervention, introduce training in an intervention or introduce a programme based around an intervention, they are engaged in dissemination. They are also potentially overriding the judgement of specific practitioners. This is good practice when the effect is to improve services to clients, especially when services result in improved outcomes or more cost-effective service delivery. However, dissemination requires confidence that the mandated intervention is in fact at least as effective as (and preferably more effective than) standard care.

The requirements specified by Flay et al. (2005) ensure that idiosyncratic, 'one-off' findings do not provide a basis for dissemination of an intervention and that the reported findings are from studies that meet minimum scientific standards. They also protect against the risk that an intervention has only transient effectiveness.

We think that there is reason to add three further requirements: there is no reason to suspect that the evidence no longer has validity; it is reasonable to assume treatment effects derive from treatment-specific factors, and the intervention is robust in the face of fidelity violations (Box 12.1).

The reason for the sixth requirement ('no reason to suspect that the evidence no longer has validity') is that the effectiveness of some psychosocial interventions may be contingent on specific contextual requirements. An example is intensive case management (ICM). King (2006) showed that, whereas studies published prior to 1999 typically showed positive ICM impact compared with usual care, more recent studies showed little or no advantage for ICM. He concluded

---

**Box 12.1  Eight requirements for a treatment to be regarded as empirically supported for purposes of implementation in a mental health setting (assuming at least two published studies).**

- Defined samples from defined populations
- Psychometrically sound measures and data collection
- Rigorous data analysis
- Consistent positive effects
- At least one long-term follow-up showing sustained effects
- No reason to suspect that the evidence no longer has validity
- It is reasonable to assume treatment effects derive from treatment-specific factors
- The intervention is robust in the face of fidelity violations

---

that the most likely reason for this was that the clearest ICM effect in earlier research was on inpatient admission days and a trend towards briefer admissions meant that there was much less scope now to achieve relative reductions. One of the strongest arguments for ICM was that it was cost-effective because of admission offsets and this argument was seriously weakened by the results of more recent studies. The evidence that ICM caused symptomatic and/or functional improvements relative to standard care was always weaker and more recent studies suggest that such benefits are unlikely.

The reason for the seventh requirement ('it is reasonable to assume treatment effects derive from treatment-specific factors') is that the effectiveness of psychosocial interventions can be attributed to some combination of treatment-specific factors and what are usually termed 'common' factors. This is analogous to 'active agent' and 'placebo' effects in drug treatments. Psychosocial interventions are often evaluated against 'no treatment' comparisons. When this is the case, it is not possible to determine what treatment effects can be attributed to treatment-specific factors and what treatment effects are the result of common factors such as positive expectation, alliance with the therapist and active participation in recovery-oriented activity. A good example is the psychological treatment of depression. It was once thought that treatment-specific factors in the cognitive behaviour therapies were critical to positive outcome but it is increasingly clear that a wide spectrum of treatments are equally effective, probably as a result of the overwhelming importance of common factors (King, 1998; Wampold et al., 2002; Parker, 2007). There is a strong likelihood that any purposeful psychological intervention designed to alleviate depression will be effective so long as it activates the common factors. It is therefore difficult to argue that any specific treatment has a stronger evidence base than any other, even though intervention in general is clearly superior to no intervention.

The reason for the eighth requirement ('the intervention is robust in the face of fidelity violations') is that real-world services often make modifications to standardised treatments to tailor them to the specific requirements and resources of the service. Researchers, and especially those who develop interventions, do not like this, and refer to such changes as loss of fidelity. Poor performance of intervention is often attributed to low fidelity implementation (Clarke et al., 2000; Duan et al., 2001). However, loss of fidelity is a fact of life in actual service delivery, even when the aim is to maintain fidelity as best as possible (McGrew et al., 1994). Interventions worthy of dissemination into practice environments are those that retain their effectiveness despite compromises with fidelity (Burgess & Pirkis, 1999; Duan et al., 2001; King, 2006).

What this means in practice is that management would be on shaky ground when advocating implementation of an intervention that failed to meet these eight standards (see also, Messer (2004) and Westen et al. (2004) for additional discussion of problems and limitations associated with the EST approach). Managers could, however, reasonably recommend use of interventions that do meet these standards and the burden would be on the clinician to justify an alternative intervention, having reference to sound clinical judgement and/or client preferences (culture).

### Effectiveness of a specific treatment: emergent evidence

It may be that the 'best available evidence' is not evidence pertaining to ESTs but rather evidence about the effectiveness of the treatment that is actually being provided to a specific client. In this section we consider the means by which evidence concerning the effectiveness of current treatment can be obtained and utilised in EBP. We also examine research that suggests that routine use of such evidence might in fact enhance treatment effectiveness in itself.

The Outcomes Measurement Project in Australia's mental health services (Pirkis et al., 2005) provides an example of a national initiative designed to ensure that some emergent evidence of clinical effectiveness is available to practitioners and service managers. Under this initiative, services are required to routinely administer standardised measurements of client symptoms and disability at fixed intervals (three-monthly) or when there are major events such as inpatient admissions. Comparing scores from interval to interval shows whether the client is improving, deteriorating or maintaining a steady course. Services and individual practitioners can use these data to track progress and modify interventions when progress is unsatisfactory.

There are, however, several limitations associated with use of routine outcome measures as a tool in achieving EBP. One is the challenge of compliance (ensuring practitioners actually implement the measures in a timely fashion). This issue will be considered below, when we discuss challenges and solutions in implementing and sustaining EBP. Aside from compliance, there are two more fundamental problems. The first is that outcome measurement scores, and especially changes in outcome measurement scores, have to be interpreted. The practitioner or service manager needs a means of determining when a deteriorating score is significant and requires reconsideration of current treatment or when an improvement is sufficient to warrant consideration of discharge. In other words, someone has to make a decision as to whether or not a score is within normal limits given measurement error and the expected recovery trajectory for the client. The scores do not in themselves ensure correct interpretation and without correct interpretation it is hard to be confident that any clinical response arising will be superior to clinical judgement alone. The second is frequency of measurement. When administered at three-monthly intervals, outcomes measures are not sensitive to week-by-week changes and, by the time practitioners or service managers become aware of a problem, the optimal time for change of intervention may well have passed.

These two problems were addressed by Lambert et al. (2005) in research designed to improve psychotherapy and counselling outcomes that has potential application in the broader spectrum of clinical services. Lambert's approach is based on high-frequency application of a single standardised measure with scores interpreted automatically having reference both to measurement error and to empirically based trajectory of client recovery. The practitioner receives an alert whenever scores hit a threshold that indicates client progress is poorer than expected. The practitioner is also alerted when recovery targets are attained. The evidence accumulated by Lambert's team (Lambert et al., 2005) suggests that this kind of feedback does enhance clinical outcomes independently of the kind of treatment deployed.

There are a number of obstacles to implementing this approach in mental health services. First it is important to have measures that are in fact sensitive to the kinds of client changes that should trigger review of treatment. It is not clear that the measures used in the Australian Outcomes project meet this requirement. The second is that it is necessary to have accurate information about client recovery trajectories so as to enable meaningful alerts about progress. The diversity of recovery trajectories in severe mental illness and the uneven progress of recovery makes this more difficult than in the kind of population that Lambert's work is based on. However, the process of systematically assessing and measuring outcomes is part of EBP in the sense that it attends to fundamental criteria of trying to using psychometrically sound measures and data collection along with rigorous data analysis.

### So, how does a manager decide whether clinicians are using the best available evidence in routine practice?

Whether a service relies on use of ESTs or emergent evidence or some combination of both, it is clear that there is no simple pathway to determining the best available evidence. It is incumbent on a service manager seeking to operate within an EBP framework to grapple with these issues and to monitor use of ESTs and use of emergent evidence in the service. We provide some recommendations and guidelines for managers later in this chapter when we look at implementing and sustaining EBP. However, an essential starting point is that the manager has a framework for a sophisticated and constructive dialogue with clinicians about the use of the best available evidence. An understanding of the issues discussed so far should assist in the development of such a framework.

### Clinical judgement and client preferences in EBP

In relation to the related concept of 'clinical expertise' the APA Task Force (2006, p. 2) stated:

'Clinical expertise is used to integrate the best research evidence with clinical data (e.g., information about the patient obtained over the course of treatment) in the context of the patient's characteristics and preferences to deliver services that have a high probability of achieving the goals of treatment.'

The Task Force further stated that:

'Many patient characteristics, such as functional status, readiness to change, and level of social support, are known to be related to therapeutic outcomes.'

Among other patient characteristics pertinent to the application of clinical expertise are (APA Task Force, 2006, p. 2):

'personal preferences, values, and preferences related to treatment (e.g., goals, beliefs, worldviews, and treatment expectations).'

Finally, the Task Force (2006, p. 2) stated that:

'A central goal of EBP is to maximize patient choice among effective alternative interventions.'

What this means is that EBP is not a 'one size fits all' approach to treatment. Nor is it a paternalistic application of the principle that the practitioner knows what is best for the client. Rather it implies careful assessment of client goals and priorities and sensitivity to cultural background and values as they relate to treatment. This provides the basis for a collaborative process by which the practitioner and client make decisions about treatment in the light of goals and preferences.

The implication for the manager is that EBP is not occurring unless treatment planning and implementation of treatment is consistent with these principles. It is not enough to take an interest in the extent to which practitioners are having reference to evidence in planning and implementing clinical interventions. The manager must also ensure that sound processes are in place to ensure the proper place of clinical judgement and client preferences.

## Implementing and sustaining EBP in mental health services

### Establishing a positive climate for EBP

Any attempt to implement EBP in clinical settings and services needs to consider individual attitudes and organisational culture and climate. We have many examples of attempts to introduce EB practices that have failed, even though practitioners accept that recommended approaches are effective and even that they have the skills to implement that but nonetheless state, 'I just don't work that way'. Statements such as these reflect underlying beliefs or attitudes regarding how one practises. For some individuals, these beliefs can be difficult to shift. Service managers need to anticipate difficulties and objections that practitioners are likely to raise and be able to respond to them in a reasonable and balanced fashion. More than 10 years of EBP debate plus research into the attitudes of practitioners means that anticipating the objections will be the easy part. Managers are likely to encounter a mixture of 'in principle' objections and concerns about practical issues.

A focus group study involving 19 clinicians working in community mental health centres in the mid-west in USA identified themes around challenges to implementing EBP (Nelson et al., 2006). The main challenges identified were that most evidence-based treatments were too long to be effectively implemented in community practice. They required substantial training to become competent and the practitioners believed that the research supporting most EBP was not applicable to their settings (i.e. highly controlled trials with restrictive sample characteristics). Further to this highly controlled studies were described by some as 'irrelevant'.

The practitioners repeatedly indicated that their heavy caseloads did not allow them the time to learn new approaches and that they did not have the training or supervision needed to implement EBP. Client characteristics added to these barriers including complex client presentations with multiple diagnoses, client resistance to some procedures, and poor attendance at sessions. The practitioners also identified the characteristics of EBP that would make it more desirable – specifically, flexible approaches which are easy to implement. Hearing about or seeing positive experiences using the new approach were also considered important to uptake. Not surprisingly, many participants highlighted their preference for treatments that emphasise the importance of the therapeutic relationship (Nelson et al., 2006).

These concerns reflect many of the concerns unleashed when the APA Task Force provided criteria for empirically validated treatments and a listing of those treatments with documented efficacy (APA, 1995). It was argued that the research on the basis of which these decisions were made was not relevant to practitioners because the samples excluded patients with multiple problems and tended to focus on narrowly circumscribed disorders. Practitioners argued that in clinical practice most of their clients had multiple co-occurring problems. Much was made of the 'politics' of science and its influence on what was considered EBP. For example, it was argued that a large number of research studies were discounted because they did not meet strict 'gold standard' design criteria (Henry, 1998). There were concerns that the treatments that were identified as empirically validated over-emphasised technique whereas a great deal of psychotherapy research confirmed the importance of common factors such as therapeutic alliance.

Some commentators in the USA worried that the managed care organisations' desire for highly specified and quantifiable approaches to treating specific disorders would overly influence which treatments were 'accepted'. It was argued that the requirement of manualised treatment protocols excluded some treatment approaches where it was more difficult to clearly specify the approach in manualised form (Henry, 1998). Further, for some psychotherapies such as humanistic approaches the assumptions of the criteria for establishing evidence were considered inappropriate. Many humanistic therapists argue that the goal of humanistic approaches is not to cure disorder but to create a therapeutic relationship and environment that facilitates self-reflection and promotes personal growth. The emphasis is on making new meaning, focusing on future goals and personal development rather than reducing symptoms (Bohart et al., 1998). As such, there may be something of a philosophical objection to EBP whose evidence is based on assumptions that symptoms will be eliminated and disorders will be cured. There are many other elements of debate about EBP that are beyond the scope of this chapter, but these are critically and thoroughly elaborated in Norcross and colleagues' (2006) excellent book.

The ultimate achievement of the APA Presidential Task Force (2006) has been to steer a path through these complex and difficult issues and adopt a position that creates an imperative for practitioners to have regard to evidence without creating inappropriate constraints on practice. We think that managers who develop a clear understanding of the APA position will find that it readily translates into multidisciplinary mental health practice and addresses the 'in principle' concerns that they are likely to find practitioners expressing.

Managers who want to take a more formal reading of the readiness of the workforce to practise within an EBP framework might consider the use of the Evidence Based Practice Attitude Scale (EBPAS), developed by Aarons (2004). This assesses four dimensions of attitudes toward adopting EBP: appeal, requirements, openness and divergence. In a sample of 322 clinical and case management mental health service providers for children, adolescents and their families, Aarons (2004) found higher educational status, less experience and working in inpatient settings were all associated with more positive attitudes toward EBP. In the same sample, the association of organisational culture and climate on EBP attitudes was also explored (Aarons & Sawitzky, 2006). It was found that workers in organisations considered to have more constructive cultures and workers earlier in their professional careers had more positive attitudes towards adopting EBP. However, the predictors accounted for only 8.6% of the variance in attitudes, suggesting many unmeasured factors also account for attitudes. The authors argued that 'having a positively perceived local opinion leader who can influence organizational culture and who can introduce and guide change in practice may facilitate receptivity to change in provider behavior' (Aarons & Sawitzky, 2006, p. 68).

Managers will often encounter acceptance of EBP as a principle or practice ideal but with minimal commitment to practice change. In a survey of 649 occupational therapists in Australia, 88% agreed or strongly agreed that EBP improved client care (Bennett et al., 2003). However, 39% had rarely or not at all relied on current research evidence in their practice over the previous two months. Further, research evidence was used to inform clinical decision making for an estimated average of only 42% of the time. A quarter of those surveyed agreed or strongly agreed that EBP was of limited value in occupational therapy because there was not enough research evidence. Almost a third thought that although adoption of EBP was worthwhile it placed too many demands on their workload. Consistent with these findings, the main barrier to implementing EBP was a lack of time (92%) followed by not enough evidence (63%). Lack of skills for locating evidence, lack of computing resources and poor access to research were all endorsed by at least half of respondents as often or very often being barriers to implementing EBP. A lack of skills for understanding research was endorsed by 45% of participants. Although a third had already received training in EBP over half felt that further training was needed. Most (82%) felt that short in-service presentations and workshops would be useful training format along with brief written information (79%) and web-based resources (76%) (Bennett et al., 2003).

## Strategies and activities to promote EBP

So, what is the evidence base for successful implementation of EBP in mental health services? While there is a great deal of strong evidence for particular treatments for mental health problems (e.g. Drake et al., 2005; Goodheart et al., 2006) there is relatively little evidence about what the most effective strategies are for implementing EBP in mental health services. To our knowledge there have been no randomised controlled trials testing EBP implementation strategies. However, the studies outlined in earlier sections of this chapter do provide us with some guidance, as does research from other areas of health. The general medical literature suggests that the use of multiple strategies to overcome barriers to implementation is likely to be more effective than a single intervention (e.g. Grimshaw & Russell, 1993). Changing complex practice behaviours is likely to be more difficult than changing relatively simple behaviours (Torrey & Gorman, 2005). Several studies have addressed what is needed to transfer training into practice and these too provide some guidelines (e.g. Milne et al., 2000; Deane et al., 2006). For example, the following increase the probability of transfer success: support from management at all levels; new practice is not too dissimilar from prior practice; changes are clearly communicated, cued, checked and positively reinforced (Deane et al., 2006).

Panzano and Herman (2005) described a simple formula for thinking about factors that determine the success of implementing new practices. Implementation success is viewed as 'a function of know-how, motivation, and the opportunity to learn' (p. 265). Staff need the opportunity to develop new knowledge and skills. They need to have either internal (e.g. work satisfaction, values) or external motivations (e.g. success stories, respect from peers, promotion) to implement the behaviour change. Finally, the opportunity to implement a particular EBP may require overcoming barriers such as lack of time or other resources (e.g. transport, equipment, staff). Managers in leadership positions have a major role in all three components of know-how, motivation and opportunity. Panzano and Herman (2005, p. 268) summarise leaders' tasks as:

- communicate a vision
- guide stakeholders through the decision process
- articulate goals
- develop and implement a plan to work towards goals
- monitor progress towards goals
- implement education and training programmes
- establish reward structures to keep staff motivated
- remove barriers to day-to-day implementation.

In addition to these leadership tasks, research related to staff attitudes and perceived barriers suggests other activities that managers might also consider in introducing EBP (Box 12.2).

---

**Box 12.2  Strategies for promoting an EBP culture.**

- Create a culture by initiating conversations about evidence. This can begin informally during team meetings, case reviews, oto.
- Introduce routine client progress measurement and ensure that results are readily available to clinicians
- Be sure to nurture workers early in their professional careers toward EBP not only because they appear to be more open to this, but also because there is risk that they will fall into the 'custom and practice' of an organisation which may or may not follow EBP
- Model critical consideration of evidence in your own clinical work (e.g. by referring to evidence when reviewing cases. Doing this creates a culture of openness)
- Educate about the role of clinical judgement and client preferences in EBP (see earlier section). Staff are likely to be less resistant to EBP when they appreciate that these two factors are important components
- Ensure that staff have access to information and resources that will support EBP (see suggested resources below). Arrange appropriate access to resources to do this ahead of time and ensure that staff have both sufficient training and sufficient access to utilise internet-based resources
- Anticipate attitudinal and practical barriers to implementation of EBP and avoid rigid or unnecessarily prescriptive responses. Allowing some flexibility in implementation will most likely result in clinicians viewing a strategy as 'useable', however, it is important to ensure that flexibility does not result in loss of fidelity to a degree likely to compromise the effectiveness of an intervention
- Start with small changes to practice to help establish a culture of responding to evidence, then move to more substantial projects if needed
- Continue to emphasise the importance of therapeutic relationship in conjunction with implementation of EBP
- Reinforce EBP through direct praise and highlight success stories
- Where training to develop EBP is needed allocate appropriate resources so this can be achieved. Advocate to make funding available if needed

## Sources of information about EBP

In the focus groups by Nelson et al. (2006) practitioners were asked where they got their information about treatments. The most common source of information was from professional colleagues and supervisors. This was typically an informal process. Workshops and other training sessions were also frequently cited sources. Books were also frequently used but a major difficulty was finding sufficient time to read them. Information on the internet was often mentioned but little detail about specific search strategies was provided. The practitioners generally found the literature overwhelming in its volume and complexity and wanted more accessible summaries, particularly those that emphasised how to translate findings into different clinical settings.

Although practitioners indicate that in-service presentations and brief summaries of research evidence are valued (e.g. Bennett et al., 2003), passive educational approaches alone are unlikely to lead to practice change (Torrey & Gorman, 2005). There is a need for active, participatory approaches which include practice, direct feedback, and ongoing supervision, support and/or incentives. One powerful incentive is seeing positive change in clients and it has been recommended that 'telling success stories' is a strategy to support implementation of new behaviours in practice (Torrey & Gorman, 2005).

Below are a range of specific resources or sources of information that can support EBP (Box 12.3). However, there is a need to make sure these resources are tied to an ongoing process of active education, implementation and review.

---

**Box 12.3   Resources to assist in implementation of EBP.**

- In-service presentations or workshops on EBP
- Brief written summaries of evidence in particular domains
- Bibliographic databases such as Medline, Psychinfo, CINAHL (Cumulative Index for Nursing and Allied Health). PubMed is a bibliographic database freely available over the internet and contains Medline as part of its content
- Tutorials to learn how to use these bibliographic databases (e.g. CINAHL, www.mclibrary.duke.edu/training/cinahlovid, accessed 17 March 2007)
- The *Database of Systematic Reviews* in the *Cochrane Library* online
- Relationships with university academics or other health providers with interests in EBP
- Journal clubs (small groups that meet on a regular basis to discuss recent publications in areas of shared interests)
- Synthesised one-page summaries, which are available from some journals e.g. *Evidence-based Medicine, Evidence-based Mental Health*. The Cochrane database also provides one-page abstracts of reviews with a 'Plain language summary'
- Online tutorials on EBP (Duke University)
- An excellent chapter on the research process and steps for practice to become evidence-based can be found in Mueser & Drake (2005)

---

# Conclusion

The use of EBP is a key element of service quality improvement and a means both of fulfilling our professional obligations to clients and the wider public and also of ensuring professional development of our staff. Developing, promoting and supporting a culture of EBP is a core responsibility for mental health service managers. Implementing EBP is much more complex than implementing ESTs and managers need a sophisticated understanding of EBP. We think that this is best achieved through consideration of the APA formulation. The introduction of ESTs forms part of EBP, but managers need to ensure that any EST introduced as a service-wide intervention meets the eight requirements we have set out in this chapter. Managers can play a key role in developing EBP but need to be aware of both the resource requirements and the more subtle cultural and interpersonal issues that are likely to be critical to success or failure in development of a service with a strong EBP culture.

# References

Aarons, G. A. (2004). Mental health provider attitudes toward adoption of evidence-based practice: the Evidence-Based Practice Attitude Scale (EBPAS). *Mental Health Services Research*, 6, 61–74.

Aarons, G. A. & Sawitzky, A. C. (2006). Organizational culture and climate and mental health provider attitudes toward evidence-based practice. *Psychological Services*, 3, 61–72.

American Psychological Association (APA) Division of Clinical Psychology (1995). Training in and dissemination of empirically-validated psychological treatments: Report and recommendations. *The Clinical Psychologist*, 48, 3–27.

APA Presidential Task Force on Evidence-Based Practice (2006). Evidence-based practice in psychology. *American Psychologist*, 61, 271–285.

Bennett, S., Tooth, L., McKenna, K., Rodger, S., Strong, J., Ziviani, J., Mickan, S. & Gibson, L. (2003). Perceptions of evidence-based practice: a survey of Australian occupational therapists. *Australian Occupational Therapy Journal*, 50, 13–22.

Bohart, A. C., O'Hara, M. & Leitner, L. M. (1998). Empirically violated treatments: disenfranchisement of humanistic and other psychotherapies. *Psychotherapy Research*, 8, 141–157.

Burgess, P. & Pirkis, J. (1999). The currency of case management: benefits and costs. *Current Opinion in Psychiatry*, 12, 195–199.

Clarke, G. N., Herinckx, H. A., Kinney, R. F., Paulson, R. I., Cutler, D. L., Lewis, K. & Oxman, E. (2000). Psychiatric hospitalizations, arrests, emergency room visits, and homelessness of clients with serious and persistent mental illness: findings from a randomized trial of two ACT programs vs. usual care. *Mental Health Services Research*, 2, 155–164.

Deane, F. P., Crowe, T. P., King, R., Kavanagh, D. J. & Oades, L. G. (2006). Challenges in implementing evidence-based practice into mental health services. *Australian Health Review*, 30, 305–309.

Drake, R. E., Merrens, M. R. & Lynde, D. E. (eds) (2005). *Evidence-based Mental Health Practice: A Textbook*. New York: Norton.

Duan, N., Braslow, J., Weisz, J. & Wells, K. (2001). Fidelity, adherence, and robustness of interventions. *Psychiatric Services*, 52, 413.

Flay, B., Biglan, A., Boruch, R., Castro, F., Gottfredson, D., Kellam, S., Moscicki, E., Schinke, S., Valentine, J. & Ji, P. (2005). Standards of evidence: criteria for efficacy, effectiveness and dissemination. *Prevention Science*, 6, 151–175.

Goodheart, C. D., Kazdin, A. E. & Sternberg, R. J. (eds) (2006). *Evidence-based Psychotherapy: Where Practice and Research Meet.* Washington, DC: American Psychological Association.

Grimshaw, J. M. & Russell, I. T. (1993). Effect of clinical guidelines on medical practice: a systematic review of rigorous evaluations. *Lancet*, 342, 1317–1322.

Henry, W. P. (1998). Science, politics, and the politics of science: the use and misuse of empirically validated treatment research. *Psychotherapy Research*, 8, 126–140.

King, R. (1998). Evidence based practice, where is the evidence? *Australian Psychologist*, 33, 83–88.

King, R. (2006). Intensive case management: a critical re-appraisal of the scientific evidence for effectiveness. *Administration and Policy in Mental Health and Mental Health Services Research*, 33, 529–535.

Lambert, M. J., Harmon, C., Slade, K., Whipple, J. L. & Hawkins, E. J. (2005). Providing feedback to psychotherapists on their patients' progress: clinical results and practice suggestions. *Journal of Clinical Psychology*, 61, 165–174.

McGrew, J. H., Bond, G. R., Dietzen, L. L. & Salyers, M. (1994). Measuring the fidelity of implementation of a mental health program model. *Journal of Consulting and Clinical Psychology*, 62, 670–678.

Messer, S. (2004). Evidence-based practice: beyond empirically supported treatments. *Professional Psychology: Research and Practice*, 35, 580–588.

Milne, D., Gorenski, O., Westerman, C. & Leck, C. (2000). What does it take to transfer training? *Psychiatric Rehabilitation Skills*, 4, 259–281.

Mueser, K. T. & Drake, R. E. (2005). How does a practice become evidence-based? In: Drake, R. E., Merrens, M. R. & Lynde, D. E. (eds) *Evidence-based Mental Health Practice: A Textbook*. New York: Norton, pp. 217–242.

Nelson, T. D., Steel, R. G. & Mize, J. A. (2006). Practitioner attitudes toward evidence-based practice: themes and challenges. *Administration and Policy in Mental Health*, 33, 398–409.

Norcross, J. C., Koocher, G. P. & Garofalo, A. (2006). Discredited psychological treatments and tests: a Delphi poll. *Professional Psychology: Research and Practice*, 37, 515–522.

Panzano, P. & Herman, L. (2005). Developing and sustaining evidence-based systems of mental health services. In: Drake, R. E., Merrens, M. R. & Lynde, D. E. (eds) *Evidence-based Mental Health Practice: A Textbook*. New York: Norton, pp. 243–272.

Parker, G. (2007). What is the place of psychological treatments in mood disorders? *International Journal of Neuropsychopharmacology*, 10, 137–145.

Pirkis, J., Burgess, P., Coombs, T., Clarke, A., Jones-Ellis, D. & Dickson, R. (2005). Routine measurement of outcomes in Australia's public sector mental health services. *Australia and New Zealand Health Policy*. www.anzhealthpolicy.com/content/2/1/8 (accessed 17 May 2008).

Sackett, D. L., Richardson, W. S., Rosenberg, W. & Haynes, R. B. (1997). *Evidence-based Medicine: How to Practice and Teach EBM*. New York: Churchill Livingstone.

Torrey, W. C. & Gorman, P. G. (2005). Closing the gap between what services are and what they could be. In: Drake, R. E., Merrens, M. R. & Lynde, D. E. (eds) *Evidence-based Mental Health Practice: A Textbook*. New York: Norton, pp. 167–187.

Wampold, B. E., Minami, T., Baskin, T. W. & Callen Tierney, S. (2002). A meta-(re)analysis of the effects of cognitive therapy versus 'other therapies' for depression. *Journal of the Affective Disorders*, 68, 159–165.

Westen, D., Novotny, C. & Thompson-Brenner, H. (2004). The empirical status of empirically supported psychotherapies: assumptions, findings, and reporting in controlled clinical trials. *Psychological Bulletin*, 130, 631–663.

# Index

600

① 6 tables

② $\frac{300}{40} \times 5 = 3.75$ millitus

③ 100   0.9%
    20 drops per ml

④ —

⑤ —

⑥ $30 \div 15 = 2$ tab

⑦ $\frac{10mg^2}{5} \times 5 = 10mls$

⑧ 50ml — 15 minutes
   1hr = 60mins
    Set @ $50 \div 60 = 0.10ml$

⑨ $\frac{525}{100} = 5.25$

⑩ 20mg

S Ss
safe
secure
specific
shaved
supple

Models of security
by service

* Locked Rehab.

PICU
AIMS Rehab
Forensic

**Higher**

OXFORD

# GCSE
# Maths
# for OCR

SPECIFICATION A

## Jayne Kranat
*Series editor*

Mike Heylings
Marguerite Appleton
Clare Plass

# OXFORD
## UNIVERSITY PRESS

Great Clarendon Street, Oxford OX2 6DP

Oxford University Press is a department of the University of Oxford. It furthers the University's objective of excellence in research, scholarship, and education by publishing worldwide in

Oxford   New York

Auckland  Cape Town  Dar es Salaam  Hong Kong  Karachi
Kuala Lumpur  Madrid  Melbourne  Mexico City  Nairobi
New Delhi  Shanghai  Taipei  Toronto

With offices in

Argentina  Austria  Brazil  Chile  Czech Republic  France  Greece
Guatemala  Hungary  Italy  Japan  Poland  Portugal  Singapore
South Korea  Switzerland  Thailand  Turkey  Ukraine  Vietnam

Oxford is a registered trade mark of Oxford University Press
in the UK and in certain other countries

© Oxford University Press 2010

The moral rights of the author have been asserted

Database right Oxford University Press (maker)

First published 2010

British Library Cataloguing in Publication Data

Data available

ISBN: 978-0-19-913928-6
10 9 8 7 6 5 4 3 2 1

Printed in Spain by Cayfosa (Impresia Iberica)

We are grateful to the following for permission to reproduce copyright material:

Front cover: Cathy Keifer/iStockphoto.com; zxcynosure/iStockphoto.com; Oscar E. Gutierrez/iStockphoto.com; nel4/iStock.

p2-3: Kuzma/Shutterstock; p6: OUP/Digital Vision; p12-13: Harish Tyagi/epa/Corbis; p31: Craig Barhorst/Shutterstock; p35-35: Czintos Ödön/Dreamstime.com; p52-53: Joggie Botma/Dreamstime; p59: photobank.ch/Shutterstock; p62-63: MARKABOND/Shutterstock; p65: Dmitriy Shironosov/Dreamstime.com;  p74-75: 4774344sean/Dreamstime; p81: Orhan Çam/Shutterstock; p82: OUP/Photodisc; p87: OUP/Corel; p94-95: Dgareri/Dreamstime; p110-111: Soleg1974/Dreamstime; p101: Vadim Ponomarenko/Shutterstock; p122: 2009EUROVision/Shutterstock; p130-131: The London Art Archive/Alamy; p123: Britvich/Dreamstime.com; p134: Koshevnyk/Shutterstock; p146-147: Doug Steley A/Alamy; p155: Philip Lange/Shutterstock; p164-165: Ivan Cholakov/Dreamstime; p176-177: Doug Steley A/Alamy; p194-195: Juan Fuertes/Shutterstock; p203: Rachelle Burnside/Shutterstock; p208-209: Andres Rodriguez/Dreamstime; p224-225: John Rawsterne/Shutterstock; p229: OUP/Digital Vision; p238-239: MasPix/Alamy; p246-247: SHOUT/Alamy; p252: Sciencephotos/Alamy; p255: Sciencephotos/Alamy; p256: Anthony Baggett/Dreamstime.com; p260-261: Jason Hawkes/Corbis; p268: OUP/Ingram; p274-275: Saniphoto/Dreamstime.com; p294-295: Doug Steley A/Alamy; p307: Odyssei/Dreamstime.com; p312-313: Ivonne Wierink/Shutterstock; p320: Verity Johnson/Shutterstock;

p321: Richard Nowitz/Getty Images; p326-327: Kuzma/Shutterstock; p334: Patrimonio Designs Limited/Shutterstock & Sabino Parente/Shutterstock; p337: Filippo Prono/Dreamstime.com; p344-345: Idrutu/Dreamstime.com; p351: Vlad Turchenko/Dreamstime.com; p356-357: NTERFOTO/Alamy; p371: Sebastian Kaulitzki/Shutterstock; p378-379: Slobodan Djajic/Dreamstime; p381: OUP/Score by Aflo.

CASE STUDY 1 RECYCLING
Feng Yu/Dreamstime.com; iStockphoto.com; Christophe Testi/Dreamstime.com; Lobke Peers/Shutterstock; Sailorr/Dreamstime.com; Zentilia/Dreamstime.com.

CASE STUDY 2 HOLIDAY
iStockphoto.com; Ben Renard-wiart /Dreamstime.com; Bruce Hempell /Dreamstime.com; Rider of the storm/Dreamstime.com; Elifranssens/Dreamstime.com; Ben Renard-wiart/Dreamstime.com; Grondin Julien/Dreamstime.com; Ben Mcleish/Dreamstime.com; c./Shutterstock.

CASE STUDY 3 BUSINESS
iStockphoto.com; Christophe Testi/Dreamstime.com; Alex Varlakov/Dreamstime.com; Yang Jay/Dreamstime.com; Design56/Dreamstime.com; Tatiana Popova/Shutterstock; Condor 36/Shutterstock.

CASE STUDY 4 SANDWICH SHOP
Christophe Testi/Dreamstime.com; Andrzej Tokarski/Dreamstime.com; Christopher Elwell/Dreamstime.com; 350jb/Dreamstime.com; Branislav Senic/Dreamstime.com; Yeko Photo Studio/Shutterstock; Studiotouch/Shutterstock.

CASE STUDY 5 WEATHER
Science Photo Library

CASE STUDY 6 RADIO MATHS
Feng Yu/Dreamstime.com; Digital Vision/Getty Images; Giraffarte/Dreamstime.com.

CASE STUDY 7 SPORT
Jim Cooper/Getty Images; Danny De Bruyne/Dreamstime.com; Feng Yu/Shutterstock; Mike Flippo/Shutterstock.

CASE STUDY 8 ART
Andry A/Alamsyah/Alamy; Eduardo Miller/Shutterstock; Michael Mcdonald/Dreamstime.com; www.lucypringle.co.uk; Zaznoba/Dreamstime.com.

The publisher would also like to thank Anna Cox for her work in creating the case studies. The charts on pages 144–5 are reproduced courtesy of the Meteorological Office; the bar chart on page 196 is reproduced courtesy of Defra; the data on page 150 is reproduced courtesy of the IAAF.

# About this book

In official partnership with OCR, this book has been specifically written to help you achieve your highest potential in your GCSE Mathematics course for OCR Specification A. It is designed for students who are expecting to enter for the Higher tier.

The authors are experienced teachers and examiners who have an excellent understanding of the OCR specifications and so are well qualified to help you successfully meet your objectives.

The book is made up of chapters that are based on OCR Specification A, and is organised clearly into the three units that will make up your assessment:

| | | |
|---|---|---|
| **Unit A** | (25% of the qualification) | **pages 2 – 129** |
| **Unit B** | (25% of the qualification) | **pages 130 – 249** |
| **Unit C** | (50% of the qualification) | **pages 250 – 401** |

The **functional elements of mathematics** and **problem-solving** are integrated throughout.

- In particular there are **rich tasks**, which provide an investigative lead-in to the topics – you may need to study some of the techniques in order to be able to complete them properly
- There are also **case studies**, which allow you to apply your GCSE knowledge in a variety of engaging contexts.

**Levels of demand** are signposted in the exercises, so you can gauge the difficulty level of each topic and monitor your progress throughout the course.

Also integrated into this book are the new **assessment objectives**:

**AO1** recall and use their knowledge of the prescribed content
**AO2** select and apply mathematical methods in a range of contexts
**AO3** interpret and analyse problems and generate strategies to solve them

The **summary assessments** contain questions in the style of the new examinations, with a particular emphasis on these new assessment objectives, so that you can be thoroughly prepared.

Finally, you will notice an asterix that looks like this: *

This shows opportunities for **Quality of Written Communication**, which you will be assessed on in Units B and C. Please note that the use of this asterix is simply to give an indication of the types of question that may contain a QWC element, and these examples should not be considered to be exclusive or exhaustive.

Best wishes with your GCSE Maths – we hope you enjoy your course and achieve success!

# Contents

# Finding your way around this book

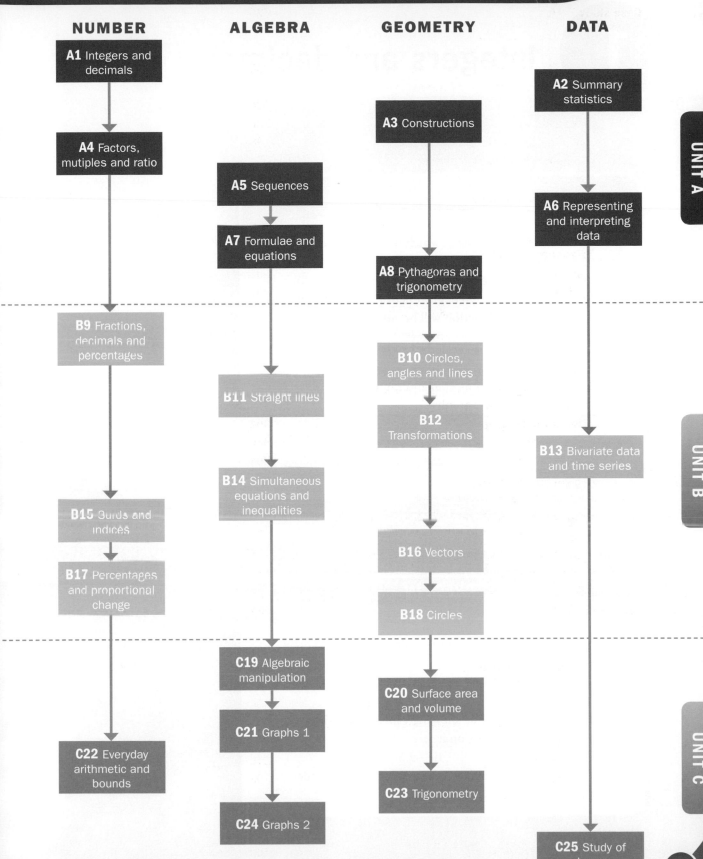

**NUMBER**

**A1** Integers and decimals

**A4** Factors, mutiples and ratio

**B9** Fractions, decimals and percentages

**B15** Surds and indices

**B17** Percentages and proportional change

**C22** Everyday arithmetic and bounds

**ALGEBRA**

**A5** Sequences

**A7** Formulae and equations

**B11** Straight lines

**B14** Simultaneous equations and inequalities

**C19** Algebraic manipulation

**C21** Graphs 1

**C24** Graphs 2

**GEOMETRY**

**A3** Constructions

**A8** Pythagoras and trigonometry

**B10** Circles, angles and lines

**B12** Transformations

**B16** Vectors

**B18** Circles

**C20** Surface area and volume

**C23** Trigonometry

**DATA**

**A2** Summary statistics

**A6** Representing and interpreting data

**B13** Bivariate data and time series

**C25** Study of chance

UNIT A

UNIT B

UNIT C

# 1 Integers and decimals

## INTRODUCTION

There are lots of professions in which it is vital to perform mental calculations. These include doctors working out the dose of medicine to give a patient, pilots checking the fuel required for a flight, or civil engineers calculating the stresses and strains that a construction will be subjected to.

**What's the point?**
If doctors, pilots and engineers don't check that their answers are sensible, things could go badly wrong.

## CHECK IN

1 Write in words the value of the digit 4 in each of these numbers.

    **a** 4506    **b** 23 409    **c** 200.45    **d** 13.054

2 **a** Sketch a number line showing values from −5 to +5 and mark these numbers on it.

    **i** −3    **ii** +4    **iii** −2.5    **iv** 0

  **b** Write this set of directed numbers in ascending order.

    +5,  −2.4,  −3,  +6,  0,  +1.5,  −1.8

**What I should know**

Key stage 3

**What I will learn**

- Calculate with negative numbers
- Round numbers to significant figures
- How to use a calculator effectively

**What this leads to**

A9

## RICH TASK

How many hamsters would weigh the same as an elephant?
How much food would an elephant-sized hamster
need to eat?
How big would the cage for an elephant-sized hamster
need to be?

# Using numbers

- Understand integers and place value

Simple arithmetic is used every day, worldwide, by people and machines.
The following exercise explores bar codes and other number investigations.

The standard international bar code number contains 13 digits.

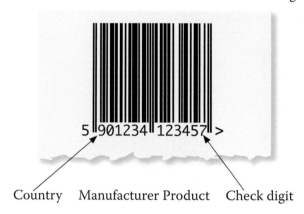

5 901234 123457 >

Country   Manufacturer Product   Check digit

The final digit of a bar code is the check digit.
The check digit lets the scanner determine if it scanned the number correctly or not.

| To find the check digit: | |
|---|---|
| → Read all the numbers other than the check digit from right to left | 5, 4, 3, 2, 1, 4, 3, 2, 1, 0, 9 |
| → Find the sum of digits in 'odd' positions | 5 + 3 + 1 + 3 + 1 + 9 = 22 |
| → Multiply this total by 3 | 22 × 3 = 66 (A) |
| → Find the sum of digits in 'even' positions | 4 + 2 + 4 + 2 + 0 + 5 = 17 (E) |
| → Find overall total (A + E) | 66 + 17 = 83 |
| → Total + check digit = next multiple of 10 | 83 + 7 = 90 ✓ |

A bar code can vary in the number of digits it contains:

0 36000 29145 2

0 4 9 5 5 1 0 6

LOW

1 Find out if these check digits on international bar codes have been given correctly.

a
0 123456 789010

b
4 903726 884816

c
3 200000 003774

2 Find out if you can use the same process of check digits for these non-international bar codes.

a
0 36000 29145 2

b
47000 06200

c
4 9 3 8 6 2 3 3

The first barcode was used in the UK in October 1979. The barcode was invented in the USA, where its first use in a shop was in 1974. It took a further five years to make its way to the UK.

3 ☆ **PROBLEM** ☆

Your school is raising money for charity.
Your class has decided to produce and sell soap.
You will be making different sizes of soap with different scents.
Devise a bar code system to identify each product that you will sell.
Remember that in general every item as well as every size of packaging (single or multipack) needs a different bar code.

4 **RICH TASK**

Write down the largest and smallest three-digit number that you can make with the digits:

        1      8      2

Subtract the smallest number from the largest number.
Using the three digits in this answer, repeat the process until you obtain the same three-digit number.

Choose another set of three different digits to start the process.
Why can the final three-digit number always be divided exactly by 99?

What would happen if you began with two digits?
What would happen if you began with four digits?

# Directed numbers

• Add, subtract, multiply and divide integers

In very cold weather the temperature drops below freezing.
In degrees Celsius these temperatures are negative numbers.

→ **Directed numbers are numbers with a + or – sign attached.**
→ **When a number has no sign, the number is positive.**

**You should already know that**

→ adding a negative number gives a smaller number      $4 + -2 = 4 - 2 = 2$
→ subtracting a negative number gives a bigger number   $4 - -2 = 4 + 2 = 6$
→ multiplying or dividing a positive number
  by a negative number gives a negative number      $4 \times -2 = -8$      $4 \div -2 = -2$
→ multiplying or dividing a negative number
  by a negative number gives a positive number      $-4 \times -2 = 8$      $-4 \div -2 = 2$

## Exercise A1.2

MEDIUM

1   Work out
   **a**   $7 + -9$         **b**   $-9 + 10$         **c**   $-8 - 11$         **d**   $-7 - -15$
   **e**   $-9 \times 3$         **f**   $-10 \times -2$         **g**   $-12 \div -3$         **h**   $15 \div -5$
   **i**   $5 - 4(6 \times -3)$         **j**   $27 - 3(60 \div 12)$         **k**   $4 - (3^2)$

2   Use the formula $y = \dfrac{x-5}{2x}$ to find the value of $y$ when

   **a**   $x = -4$         **b**   $x = -6$         **c**   $x = -0.5$

3   ☆ **PROBLEM** ☆

   There are 18 questions in a quiz.
   A correct answer scores 4 points. An incorrect answer scores $-3$ points.
   A question not answered scores nothing. It is possible to have a negative total.
   **a**   What are the maximum and minimum points that you could score on the quiz?
   **b**   A pupil answers 7 of the questions. 3 are correct.
       Explain why this pupil's total score is zero.
   **c**   Write down three different ways in which a pupil could have a total score of 12 points.

4   **RICH TASK**

   Some numbers are smaller than their cubes. For example $2 < 2^3$
   **a**   Which numbers are equal to their cubes?
   **b**   Some numbers are bigger than their cubes. Describe this set of numbers.

# Decimal places and significant figures

- Round numbers to a specified degree of accuracy

Numbers are **rounded** when it is not appropriate to give an answer that is too precise.

Numbers can be rounded:

- to the nearest unit, 10, 100 or 1000
- to a number of **decimal places** → count the digits after the decimal point
- to a number of **significant figures** → count from the first non-zero digit from the left.

| → **To round a number to a specified number of decimal places or significant figures:** | 3.147 to | ... | 2 d.p. | ... | 2 s.f. |
|---|---|---|---|---|---|
| • **Look at the first digit to be discarded** | | | 3.147 | | 3.147 |
| • **If it is 5 or greater, increase the previous digit by 1** | | | 3.15 | | |
| • **If it is less than 5, the previous digit stays the same.** | | | | | 3.1 |

A zero trapped between digits or at the right-hand end of a number will count as a significant figure.
So 3.0652 = 3.07 to 3 s.f.

**EXAMPLE**

1 Round:
   a 3.8946 to 2 decimal places (2 d.p.)
   b 5362 to 3 significant figures (3 s.f.)
   c 0.04625 to 3 s.f.
2 Work out £25.99 ÷ 7
3 A shelf 2 m long is filled with files 42 cm wide. How many files are there?

You round down here as you will not be able to fit in a fifth file.

**ANSWER**

1 a 2 d.p. so leave **2** digits after the decimal point. 3.8946 = 3.**89** to 2 d.p.
   b 3 s.f. so use the first **3** non-zero digits. 5362 = **5360** to 3 sig figs
   c 3 s.f. so use the first 3 non-zero digits. The next digit is 5 or more so round the 2 up. 0.04**625** = 0.0**463** to 3 sig figs
2 25.99 ÷ 7 = 3.712857...     Answer £3.71
3 200 ÷ 42 = 4.7619...     Answer 4 files

p. 132

Questions 2 and 3 in the example show that you use different types of rounding in different contexts.

## Exercise A1.3

MEDIUM LOW

1 Write down the numbers correct to the number of decimal places stated.

   a 19.372 to 2 d.p.
   b 19.372 to 1 d.p.
   c 0.007519 to 5 d.p.
   d 0.007519 to 3 d.p.
   e 153.2617 to 3 d.p.
   f 153.2617 to 2 d.p.

2 Write down the numbers correct to the number of significant figures stated.

   a 76286 to 2 s.f.
   b 76286 to 3 s.f.
   c 23403 to 3 s.f.
   d 57961 to 3 s.f.
   e 46320 to 2 s.f.
   f 23.403 to 4 s.f.

- Enter complex calculations and use function keys for reciprocals, squares and powers

A scientific calculator will usually work out sums in the standard **order of operations**.

**EXAMPLE**

Calculate

a $\dfrac{(4.2-1.7)^2}{10}$  b $\dfrac{19.1\times 3}{\sqrt{12\times 3}}+2$

**ANSWER**

First work out the **brackets**

a $\dfrac{2.5^2}{10}$  b $\dfrac{19.1\times 3}{\sqrt{36}}+2$

Next work out **powers** or **roots**

a $\dfrac{6.25}{10}$  b $\dfrac{19.1\times 3}{6}+2$

Then **multiplication** and **division**

a $= 0.625$  b $\dfrac{57.3}{6}+2$

$9.55 + 2$

Finally **addition** and **subtraction**

$= 11.55$

There are some special keys on your calculator that will make calculating simpler.

> You may need to put some numbers in brackets before you use these special keys.

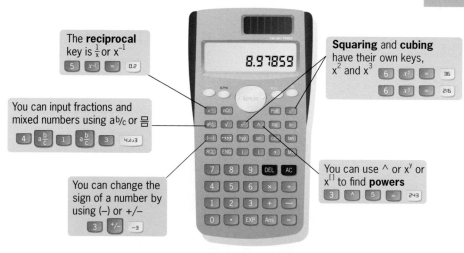

The **reciprocal** key is $\frac{1}{x}$ or $x^{-1}$

**Squaring** and **cubing** have their own keys, $x^2$ and $x^3$

You can input fractions and mixed numbers using $a^{b}/_{c}$ or ⊟

You can change the sign of a number by using (–) or +/–

You can use ^ or $x^y$ or $x^{[]}$ to find **powers**

The **reciprocal** of a number is often useful in calculations

The reciprocal of $n$ is $\dfrac{1}{n}$  The reciprocal of 7 is $\dfrac{1}{7}$

The reciprocal of $\dfrac{a}{b}$ is $\dfrac{b}{a}$  The reciprocal of $\dfrac{4}{5}$ is $\dfrac{5}{4}$

Remember to check that your answer is sensible using approximation.

## Exercise A1.4

1 Calculate (where necessary, give your answer to 2 d.p.).

   a $12 + \frac{14.7}{0.3}$

   b $5.7^2 - \sqrt{75}$

   c $\frac{1}{0.8^2}$

   d $\frac{2^3}{5^2 - 2}$

   e $\frac{7.6}{12.5 - 6.8}$

   f $\left(\frac{5}{0.4}\right)^2$

   g $\frac{45}{(0.3)^2}$

   h $\sqrt{36 + (4.5)^2}$

2 Calculate the following by
   i  Writing down all the figures shown on your calculator
   ii Giving your answer to the specified number of decimal places or significant figures.

   a $\frac{7.92 \times 1.71}{4.2 + 3.6}$ correct to 1 d.p.

   b $\frac{4.72 + 1.4}{1.4^2}$ correct to 2 d.p.

   c $\frac{3.14 - 8.16}{8.25 \times 3.18}$ correct to 2 d.p.

   d $\frac{16.5 \times 10.3}{8.25 + 5.15}$ correct to 1 d.p.

   e $\sqrt{4.5 + 3.2^2}$ correct to 3 s.f.

   f $\sqrt{25.3 - 2.7^3}$ correct to 2 s.f.

3 Calculate the reciprocal of the following numbers.
   a 4     b 9     c 2.5     d 3.6     e 0.2

   f 0.16     g $\frac{1}{2}$     h $\frac{1}{4}$     i $\frac{2}{5}$

4 Find these quantities by using the power key on your calculator.
   a $6^4$     b $5^7$     c $10^5$
   d $8^6$     e $4.5^4$     f $0.4^6$

5 ☆ ACTIVITY ☆

   Investigate the keys on your calculator. Choose four keys that you were previously unfamiliar with and write brief instructions for each one with an example.

# Summary and assessment

## CHECK OUT

**You should now be able to**
- use the four operations with directed numbers
- round numbers using
  - ➤ significant figures
  - ➤ decimal places
- use a calculator effectively.

### Exam-style question

Work out $\dfrac{14.3 \times 1.2}{3.3 + 6.1}$

a  Write down all the numbers on your calculator display.
b  Give your answer correct to 2 decimal places.

Using your calculator efficiently means showing less working.

Remember to round answers given to so many decimal places or significant figures.

**Demelza's answer:**
Type into your calculator this sequence

$(14.3 \times 1.2) \div (3.3 + 6.1) =$

a  1.825531915

b  1.83

It may be helpful to put brackets around the numerator and brackets around the denominator when using your calculator.

## Exam practice

**1 a** Work out $\dfrac{7 \cdot 2 + 9 \cdot 3}{(3 \cdot 1)^2}$

Write down all the numbers on your calculator display.

**b** Give your answer correct to 1 significant figure.

*(2 marks)*

**2** What is the reciprocal of 0·45?

*(1 mark)*

**\*3** There is a gravitational force of attraction between a planet and a person standing on that planet's surface. This means that people will have a different weight on each planet.
The table gives the multiplication factor for your weight on different surfaces.

| PLANET | Multiply your Earth weight by: |
|---|---|
| Mercury | 0·4 |
| Venus | 0·9 |
| Earth | 1 |
| Moon | 0·17 |
| Mars | 0·4 |
| Jupiter | 2·5 |
| Saturn | 1·1 |
| Uranus | 0·8 |
| Neptune | 1·2 |
| Pluto | 0·01 |

If your doctor told your aunt that weighing 75 kg makes her 12 kg overweight, on which planet would this be an acceptable weight? Justify your answer.

*(3 marks)*

# 2 Summary statistics

## INTRODUCTION

In the run-up to a general election, opinion polls are taken of which political party people are likely to vote for. The results of just a thousand people's voting intentions are taken very seriously by the media and the politicians.

**What's the point?**
Statistics allow people and organisations to make sense of large amounts of data, so that they can appreciate opinions and trends, and therefore make informed decisions.

## CHECK IN

1 Nicola and Maddy wanted to find out how many people catch flu in December. Nicola asked 100 people in the town centre one morning. Maddy looked up flu statistics on the internet.
   a Who collected primary data and who collected secondary data?
   b Explain the difference between primary and secondary data.

2 Lee drew this tally table to collect data on hours of TV people watch:
   a Explain why it would be difficult to write a tally mark for
      i 4 hours  ii 2 hours.
   b How could the difficulties discussed in part **a** be overcome?

| TV hours | Frequency |
|---|---|
| 3 – 4 | |
| 4 – 5 | |
| more than 5 | |

3 Find
   a $\frac{1}{2}$ of 45  b $\frac{1}{2}$ of (41 + 1)  c $\frac{1}{4}$ of 24  d $\frac{3}{4}$ of (27 + 1)

| What I should know | What I will learn | What this leads to |
|---|---|---|
| Key stage 3 | ■ Use the data handling cycle<br>■ Calculate summary statistics<br>■ Draw and use stem and leaf diagrams and box and whisker plots<br>■ Design a questionnaire | A6 |

## RICH TASK

What is the average height of pupils at your school?

Are the boys taller than the girls?

Are the pupils who live near the school taller than the pupils who live further away?

Investigate and write a report on your results

- Understand and use the handling data cycle

Thao wants to investigate: Just how good is your memory?
She collects 25 objects and lays them out in a square grid.

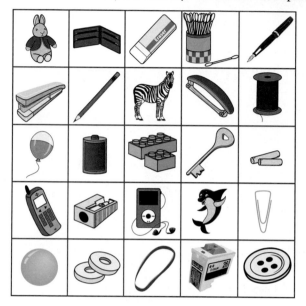

☆ **ACTIVITY** ☆

Look at the objects for 30 seconds. How many objects can you recall?

**Planning** an investigation is the first part of the **handling data cycle**.
The second part is **collecting data**.

Design & plan → Collect the data → Process & represent → Interpret & discuss → (back to Design & plan)

This is part of the **data collection sheet** Thao used to collect data on memory.

Thao records the time taken for a small grid of 9 objects and also the number recalled for all 25 objects.

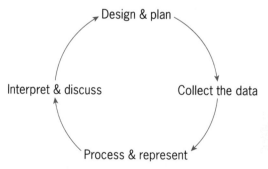

| Gender Male(M) Female(F) | Age | Nine objects time (seconds) | 25 objects number recalled | 1st object recalled |
|---|---|---|---|---|
| M | 15 | 74 | 13 | iPod |

Thao plans to collate some of her results in a **two-way table**.

| Number recalled / Gender | 0–5 | 6–10 | 11–15 | 16–20 | 21–25 |
|---|---|---|---|---|---|
| Male | | | | | |
| Female | | | | | |

You can collect data:

→ **In surveys where you ask questions of everyone, or from a sample of the population.**
→ **In experiments such as observations in science or geography.**

### Exercise A2.1

MEDIUM LOW

1 Design a suitable data collection sheet in the form of a two-way table for the following surveys.

   a Katy is doing a survey to find out how often people go to the cinema and how much they spend.

   b James wants to know which flavour crisps he should stock in the school tuck shop.
   He also wants to know which year groups prefer which flavours.

   c Merlin wants to find out how far people would travel to see their favourite band perform, and how much they would spend on a ticket to watch them.

2 The table shows the distribution of blood groups amongst the population of some countries in the mid-1980s.

| % blood group / Country | A | B | AB | O |
|---|---|---|---|---|
| England | 42 | 8 | 3 | 47 |
| Ireland | 32 | 11 | 3 | 54 |
| Scotland | 35 | 11 | 3 | 51 |

People from Wales are thought to be closely related to the Scots and Irish.

   a What percentage of Welsh people would you expect to have blood group B?

   b What other problems could you investigate from this data?

**Continued ➤**

* 3 The table gives information on the number of prescription
items per 1000 patients.

| | Age | 0–4 | 0–15 | 16–24 | 25–34 | 35–44 | 45–54 | 55–64 | 65–74 | 75–84 | 85+ |
|---|---|---|---|---|---|---|---|---|---|---|---|
| | Year | | | | | | | | | | |
| Males | 1994 | 1691 | 714 | 550 | 386 | 404 | 407 | 536 | 737 | 913 | 1050 |
| | 1995 | 1805 | 823 | 636 | 437 | 444 | 451 | 576 | 784 | 940 | 1120 |
| | 1996 | 1727 | 702 | 597 | 404 | 412 | 428 | 582 | 767 | 927 | 1081 |
| | 1997 | 1656 | 713 | 571 | 404 | 418 | 431 | 571 | 764 | 937 | 1010 |
| | 1998 | 1403 | 606 | 539 | 359 | 372 | 391 | 519 | 709 | 850 | 1002 |
| Females | 1994 | 1529 | 834 | 853 | 812 | 770 | 735 | 799 | 852 | 879 | 1012 |
| | 1995 | 1631 | 948 | 964 | 898 | 830 | 782 | 866 | 905 | 910 | 1056 |
| | 1996 | 1541 | 829 | 897 | 841 | 780 | 753 | 843 | 892 | 933 | 1067 |
| | 1997 | 1495 | 831 | 898 | 841 | 791 | 754 | 852 | 901 | 952 | 1069 |
| | 1998 | 1259 | 724 | 811 | 757 | 703 | 687 | 775 | 849 | 910 | 1038 |

Adapted from Key Health Statistics from General Practice 1998
Office for National Statistics

a How do you think the data were collected: survey or experiment?
b Who do you think the data were collected from?
c Describe fully how the survey or experiment may have been
carried out.
d What type of problem could you be investigating that might
use these data?

- Understand and use the handling data cycle

Here is some of the **primary data** collected by Thao in her survey.

This is **continuous data** – you can measure it on a scale

This is **discrete data** – you can count it

This is **qualititative data** – you can describe it

| Gender<br>Male (M)<br>Female (F) | Age | Nine objects<br>Time<br>(seconds) | 25 objects<br>Number<br>recalled | First object<br>recalled |
|---|---|---|---|---|
| M | 15 | 74 | 13 | iPod |
| M | 15 | 103 | 20 | Rabbit |
| F | 15 | 64 | 15 | Rabbit |
| F | 15 | 58 | 9 | iPod |
| M | 15 | 58 | 18 | Rabbit |
| M | 15 | 50 | 16 | Elastic band |
| M | 15 | 35 | 13 | Ball |
| F | 15 | 64 | 14 | Button |
| F | 15 | 60 | 13 | Phone |

**REMEMBER:**

- **Primary data** is data that you collect yourself.
- **Secondary data** is data that someone else has collected.

When she collected her data, Thao should have considered:

→ **Data can be biased, if not everyone has an equal chance to be part of the survey.**

Thao may have only asked her friends.

→ **In a random sample everyone has an equal chance of being chosen.**

Thao may have picked names at random from a hat, or numbered everyone and chosen random numbers.

She should have also considered how many people to include in her survey. The more the better!

→ **Increasing the sample size generally leads to better results.**

There are other methods of sampling for a survey:

> → In a systematic sample every *n*th value from a list is chosen.
> → In a stratified sample everyone is grouped, for example by gender or age, and a random sample chosen in proportion to the group size.

James carries out a survey to find out if people in his town enjoy sport.
He stands outside a football ground and surveys people's opinions as they go in to watch a match.
Write down two reasons why this is not a good sample to use.

**ANSWER**
- People who watch football usually enjoy sport
- More men than women go to watch football so the survey could be gender biased.

### Exercise A2.2

MEDIUM

1  State whether each type of data is discrete or continuous.

   **a  i**  How long you take to finish in a cross country race and
      **ii**  Your finishing position in the race.
   **b  i**  The weight of a parcel and  **ii**  the cost of its postage.
   **c  i**  The number of eggs and  **ii**  the amount of sugar needed in a cake recipe.
   **d  i**  The stars in the galaxy and  **ii**  the distance of each star from Earth.

\*2  James wants to know which flavour crisps he should stock in the school tuck shop.
   He carries out a random sample of students from only Year 11 at his school.

   **a**  Explain why this sample could be biased.
   **b**  There are 1000 students in his school. James wants to take a sample of 50 students.
      Describe how James could find
      **i**  a random sample  **ii**  a systematic sample.

\*3  Shakira carries out a survey to find the most popular band in her school year.
   There are 160 girls and 40 boys in her school year.
   She carries out a random sample containing 20 girls and 30 boys.

   **a**  Explain why this sample could be biased.
   **b**  Shakira decides that a sample of 20 girls and 30 boys is biased and decides instead to take a stratified sample of 50 students in proportion to gender.
      **i**  How many students are in her school year altogether?

**ii** What **proportion** of these are girls? (give your answer as a fraction).

**iii** With a sample of 50 students, use your answer to **ii** to work out how many girls should be in Shakira's sample.

**iv** Use your answer to **iii** to work out how many boys there will be in Shakira's sample.

**\* 4** To find out more about antibiotic prescriptions (see data in exercise A2.1 question 3), a local GP wanted to find out if his patients were aware that a course of antibiotic prescriptions should be completed.

**a** Explain why he should not just ask patients visiting the surgery.

**b** The largest users of prescriptions are the 0–4 age range.
Which age range should he ask to capture information about this age range completing a course of antibiotics?

**c** Describe how the GP may choose a sample of patients to ask.

**\*5** Thao believes that people can be trained to improve their memory.
Design an experiment and/or survey for Thao to use to test this theory.
Remember to include where appropriate:

- Sample size
- How you would choose the sample
- Data collection sheet.

**6** ☆ **CHALLENGE** ☆

The table shows information about age and gender of 600 members at a sports centre.

| Age | Under 16 | 16–18 |
|------|----------|-------|
| Girls | 140 | 96 |
| Boys | 205 | 159 |

A sample of 90 members is to be chosen stratified by both age and gender.
Consider how many of each age and each gender should be included in the sample. How could you work it out accurately?

- Compare distributions, using measures of average and spread

Thao records the time taken to recall nine objects by a group of 11-year-olds. She draws this **stem-and-leaf diagram**.

| 12 | 1 |
|----|---|
| 11 | 3  6 |
| 10 | 6  9 |
| 9 | 1  2  5 |
| 8 | 1  3  4  4 |
| 7 | 2  3  6  8  9 |
| 6 | 0  0  2  7  7 |
| 5 | 6  6  6 |
| 4 | 4  6 |

Key: 7 | 2 means 72 seconds

Thao summarises the data with the following statistics:

| Range | $121 - 44 = 77$ |
|-------|-----------------|
| Mode | 56 |
| Median | 78 |
| Mean | $2127 \div 27 = 78.8$ |
| IQR | $92 - 60 = 32$ |

Can you check her statistics?

**REMEMBER:**

- **Range** is the difference between the largest and smallest values
- **Mode** is the most common value
- **Mean** is calculated by adding all the value and dividing by the number of values
- **Median** the middle number when the values are listed in order
- **Interquartile range** (IQR) is the difference between the **upper** and **lower quartiles**

To work out the **quartiles:**
Lower quartile (LQ) = the value that is $\frac{1}{4}$ of the way along.
Upper quartile (UQ) = value that is $\frac{3}{4}$ of the way along.
There are 27 values.
LQ = 7th value = 60
UQ = 21st value = 92
so IQR = $92 - 60 = 32$

You can use **back-to-back stem-and-leaf diagrams** to make comparisons.

**EXAMPLE**

38 students answered a survey question about time spent on the internet one evening.

| Girls | | Boys |
|------:|:-:|:-----|
| 8 7 | 3 | |
| 9 7 5 4 4 3 2 1 | 4 | 1 4 8 |
| 8 6 6 5 3 2 1 | 5 | 3 3 4 6 7 7 |
| 2 1 | 6 | 1 3 5 6 9 |
| | 7 | 0 2 2 5 9 |

Key: 1 | 5 | 3 means
Girls 51 minutes; Boys 53 minutes

Compare the times taken by boys and girls.

**ANSWER**

Median: Girls 49 minutes; Boys 61 minutes
Interquartile range Girls 13 minutes;
Boys 17 minutes
Range: Girls 25 minutes; Boys 38 minutes
The data shows that on average boys spent longer on the internet, but the time spent by the boys was more varied. You can also see this just by looking at the **shape** of the diagrams.

**Girls**
LQ  = 5th value = 43
UQ = 15th value = 56
IQR = 13 minutes

**Boys**
LQ  = 5th value = 53
UQ = 15th value = 70
IQR = 17 minutes

1 The reaction times of a sample of boys and girls is represented in this stem-and-leaf diagram.

| Boys | | Girls |
|---|---|---|
| 8 8 8 6 2 2 | 3 | |
| 7 5 4 2 | 4 | 0 3 4 6 8 |
| 9 8 7 6 3 2 | 5 | 2 2 5 6 9 |
| 8 6 4 2 1 | 6 | 2 3 3 5 6 7 |
| 2 1 | 7 | 2 3 4 6 7 |
| | 8 | 0 2 |

Key: 2 | 4 | 0 means
Boys 4.2 seconds; Girls 4.0 seconds

- To find the position of the LQ, add 1 to the number of items, then divide by 4
- There are 23 girls, so $\frac{1}{4}(23+1) = 6$

The LQ is the 6th item. This is 5.2 seconds.

  a Find summary statistics for these data:
     i range   ii mode   iii median   iv mean   v IQR
  b Compare the reaction times of boys and girls.

*2 Here are the survey results for the times in minutes taken for a sample of students to complete two jigsaw puzzles.

| Puzzle P: | 13 | 17 | 19 | 10 | 8 | 22 | 31 | 11 | 24 | 27 |
|---|---|---|---|---|---|---|---|---|---|---|
| | 6 | 37 | 18 | 12 | 29 | 14 | 8 | 17 | 9 | |

| Puzzle Z: | 28 | 21 | 29 | 15 | 12 | 9 | 32 | 17 | 18 | 11 |
|---|---|---|---|---|---|---|---|---|---|---|
| | 19 | 16 | 8 | 33 | 24 | 14 | 25 | 17 | 23 | |

  a Draw stem-and-leaf diagrams to represent these data.
  b For each puzzle, work out:
     i the range          ii the mode            iii the mean
     iv the median        v the interquartile range
  c Which of the jigsaws is more difficult? Justify your answer.

When you draw a **stem-and-leaf diagram** you need to:
- Choose a **stem** appropriate for your data
- Order the **leaves**
- Write a **key** to explain the data.

3 A group of students takes a fitness test.
  25 girls and 52 boys take the test.
  The average fitness score for the girls is 6.4.
  The average fitness score for the boys is 9.2.
  Work out the average fitness score for the whole group.

4 ☆ CHALLENGE ☆

The mean mark in a statistics test for class 10Z was 84%.
There are 32 students in class 10Z.
12 of these students are girls.
Their mean mark in the test was 93%.
Work out the mean mark in the statistics test for the boys in class 10Z.

- Draw and produce box plots for continuous data

Using Thao's data for 11-year-olds' memory time, you can draw a **box-and-whisker plot**.

These are sometimes just called **box plots**.

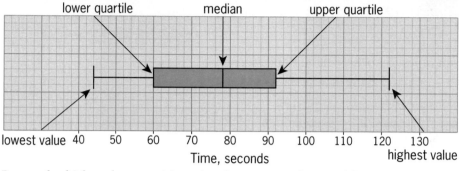

lower quartile        median        upper quartile

lowest value  40    50    60    70    80    90    100   110   120   130

Time, seconds        highest value

 p. 82

Box-and-whisker plots provide a visual summary of a set of data.
They also allow you to identify **skewness**.
The position of the median in the central box determines the skewness.

| Positive skew | Symmetrical | Negative skew |
|---|---|---|
| 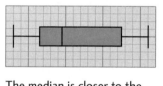 | 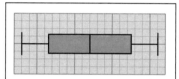 | 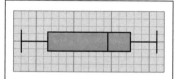 |
| The median is closer to the lower quartile. | The median is central in the box. | The median is closer to the upper quartile. |

A **positive skew** means the tail of higher values is longer than the tail of lower values.
A **negative skew** means the tail of lower values is longer than the tail of higher values.

## EXAMPLE

Famida kept a record of the number of minutes per day she spent searching the internet every day for one month.

Draw a box-and-whisker diagram and use it to comment on any skewness in the data. Describe briefly what it means.

| 40 | 26 | 75 | 84 | 33 | 39 | 28 | 66 | 67 | 71 | 80 |
|---|---|---|---|---|---|---|---|---|---|---|
| 37 | 56 | 47 | 63 | 49 | 41 | 44 | 58 | 59 | 43 | |
| 73 | 55 | 59 | 43 | 61 | 38 | 29 | 30 | 57 | 60 | |

**ANSWER**

The diagram shows that there is negative skew.
Although the central 50% ranges between 39 and 63, the times are skewed towards the higher value.

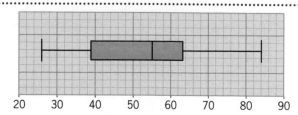

20    30    40    50    60    70    80    90

\* For each set of data in questions 1 to 5, draw a box-and-whisker plot to represent the results and comment on any skewness shown.

**1** Nick summarised the test results of a group of students:

> Lowest mark 41%    Lower quartile 54%    Median 60%
> Highest mark 84%    Upper quartile 70%

**2** Taz recorded the reaction times to the nearest tenth of a second of a class of students. He summarised the data as shown:

> Quickest time 3.2    Lower quartile 3.7    Median 4.4
> Upper quartile 7.5    Slowest time 9.6

**3** Michelle summarised the heights of girls in Year 10:

> Smallest 148 cm    Lower quartile 154 cm    Median 157 cm
> Tallest 177 cm    Upper quartile 162 cm

**4** The stem-and-leaf diagram shows the times taken, in seconds, to swim 25 m by a class of students.

```
 9 | 6
10 | 0 1 3 5 7 7 9
11 | 1 2 3 4 8 8 9 9
12 | 4 6 7 8
13 | 3 8
14 | 0
```
Key: 12 | 4 means 124 seconds

**5** Keith recorded the time taken in minutes to solve the crossword puzzle in a newspaper every day for one month.

| 12 | 24 | 21 | 16 | 8 | 9 | 3 | 31 | 18 | 27 | 35 |
|----|----|----|----|---|---|----|----|----|----|----|
| 41 | 26 | 12 | 17 | 6 | 5 | 19 | 29 | 32 | 37 | |
| 15 | 22 | 10 | 33 | 11 | 7 | 20 | 27 | 29 | 34 | |

- Compare distributions and make inferences

## RICH TASK

Thao says that 15-year-old boys have a quicker recall than 15-year-old girls.
Use the box-and-whisker plots to present a convincing argument for or against.

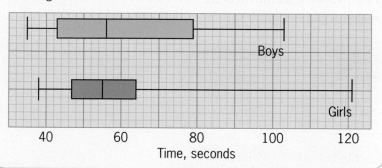

p. 82

→ **Box-and-whisker plots can be used to compare two or more sets of data.**

Make four comparisons between the heights of boys and girls in this sample of Year 9 students.

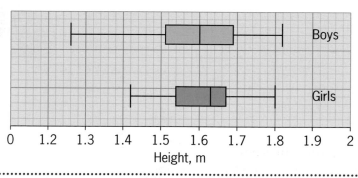

Do not compare specific values such as lowest values or UQ. Always compare like measures from each graph such as medians, IQRs, ranges, skewness.

UQ = Upper quartile
LQ = Lower quartile
IQR = Inter quartile range

### ANSWER

1. On average the girls are taller than the boys since the girls' median is greater than the boys'.
2. Heights of boys are more varied than heights of girls since the range for boys is greater than for girls.
3. IQR for boys is greater than IQR for girls, which means the middle half of heights has a wider spread for boys than for girls.
4. Median for boys' heights is central in box so boys' data is not skewed. Median for girls is nearer UQ than LQ so girls' heights are negatively skewed. There are more short girls at the bottom end than there are tall girls at the top end.

**Unit A**

**\* 1** **a** Draw box-and-whisker plots to represent the percentages
achieved in two tests by a sample of students.

**b** Write down all similarities and differences between the test results shown by the graphs.

| Test A: | 38 | 37 | 62 | 45 | 42 | 55 | 56 | 61 | 49 | 52 |
|---------|----|----|----|----|----|----|----|----|----|----|
|         | 47 | 58 | 43 | 51 | 44 | 56 | 41 | 44 | 53 |    |

| Test A: | 38 | 37 | 62 | 45 | 42 | 55 | 56 | 61 | 49 | 52 |
|---------|----|----|----|----|----|----|----|----|----|----|
|         | 47 | 58 | 43 | 51 | 44 | 56 | 41 | 44 | 53 |    |

**\* 2** **a** Draw box-and-whisker plots to represent the IQ scores of the two classes X and Y.

**b** Use statistics to present a convincing argument to show that
students from one class have, in general, a higher IQ.

| X: | 105 | 123 | 131 | 117 | 118 | 104 | 98 | 96 | 103 | 112 | 110 |
|----|-----|-----|-----|-----|-----|-----|----|----|-----|-----|-----|
|    | 117 | 126 | 129 | 123 | 109 | 108 | 115 | 99 | 89 | 121 |    |
|    | 134 | 106 | 105 | 122 | 124 | 116 | 110 | 118 | 115 | 130 |    |

| Y: | 118 | 119 | 104 | 121 | 126 | 118 | 109 | 97 | 114 | 129 | 130 |
|----|-----|-----|-----|-----|-----|-----|----|----|-----|-----|-----|
|    | 107 | 116 | 87 | 93 | 128 | 121 | 118 | 113 | 103 | 102 |    |
|    | 114 | 107 | 131 | 99 | 106 | 124 | 132 | 119 | 126 | 114 |    |

**\* 3** Claire says that older girls spend longer on the phone than younger girls.
How does the diagram support Claire's statement?

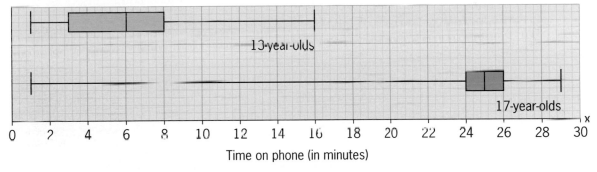

**\* 4** Charlie says that girls have quicker reaction times than boys.
Explain why this diagram might or might not support his view.

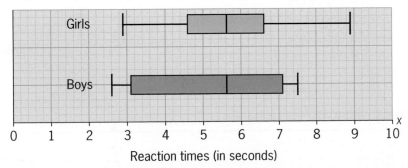

# Summary statistics from frequency tables A2.6

- Compare distributions and make inferences

Thao draws these tables to compare the number of objects recalled by 15-year-olds and 11-year-olds.

| Number recalled 15-year-olds | 13 | 14 | 15 | 16 | 17 | 18 | 19 |
|---|---|---|---|---|---|---|---|
| Frequency | 3 | 2 | 7 | 4 | 3 | 6 | 2 |

| Number recalled 11-year-olds | 11 | 12 | 13 | 14 | 15 | 16 | 17 |
|---|---|---|---|---|---|---|---|
| Frequency | 1 | 1 | 2 | 3 | 5 | 8 | 7 |

## RICH TASK

Thao says that the recall of both age groups is the same. On what evidence is she basing her conclusion?
How can you use the tables to present a convincing argument that 15-year-olds can recall more objects than 11-year-olds?

**EXAMPLE**

The table shows the length of answers in a crossword puzzle.
For these data, work out:

**a** the mode
**b** the median
**c** the mean
**d** the IQR
**e** the range.

| Word length | Frequency |
|---|---|
| 4 | 3 |
| 5 | 5 |
| 6 | 7 |
| 7 | 8 |
| 8 | 3 |
| 9 | 1 |
| Total | 27 |

**ANSWER**

**a** Mode = 7 — words with 7 letters have the highest frequency

**b** Median = 6 — total number of words = 27 (total frequency)
$\frac{1}{2}(27 + 1) = 14$th word

**c** Mean = 168 ÷ 27 = 6.2
- Count the total number of letters (168) (add a column to the table as shown on the right)
- Divide by the total number of words.

**d** IQR = 7 − 5 = 2
$\frac{1}{4}(27 + 1) = 7$ — 7th word — LQ = 5
21st word — UQ = 7

**e** Range = 5 — longest − shortest word length — 9 − 4 = 5

| Word length × frequency |
|---|
| 4 × 3 = 12 |
| 5 × 5 = 25 |
| 6 × 7 = 42 |
| 7 × 8 = 56 |
| 8 × 3 = 24 |
| 9 × 1 = 9 |
| 168 |

## Exercise A2.6

1 The data sets give information about the length of words in four different crosswords.

Work out these summary statistics for each crossword:

i  mode      ii  median      iii  mean
iv  range     v  interquartile range

a

| Word length | Frequency |
|---|---|
| 4 | 8 |
| 5 | 4 |
| 6 | 9 |
| 7 | 5 |
| 8 | 5 |

b

| Word length | Frequency |
|---|---|
| 3 | 4 |
| 4 | 6 |
| 5 | 9 |
| 6 | 6 |
| 7 | 4 |

c

| Word length | Frequency |
|---|---|
| 4 | 7 |
| 5 | 3 |
| 6 | 4 |
| 7 | 2 |
| 8 | 3 |
| 9 | 6 |
| 10 | 2 |

d

| Word length | Frequency |
|---|---|
| 3 | 5 |
| 4 | 5 |
| 5 | 7 |
| 6 | 8 |
| 7 | 6 |
| 8 | 4 |
| 9 | 2 |

* 2 The tables show the number of objects recalled by 15-year-old boys and girls in Thao's survey.

| Number recalled Boys | Frequency |
|---|---|
| 13 | 2 |
| 14 | 1 |
| 15 | 2 |
| 16 | 2 |
| 17 | 1 |
| 18 | 4 |
| 19 | 1 |

| Number recalled Girls | Frequency |
|---|---|
| 13 | 1 |
| 14 | 1 |
| 15 | 5 |
| 16 | 2 |
| 17 | 2 |
| 18 | 3 |
| 19 | 1 |

Thao believes that girls have better recall than boys.

a  Explain, using summary statistics, why she may be correct.
b  Can you find evidence for the boys to have better recall than the girls?

Unit A

# Grouped data

- Estimate the median and mean for large data sets

Large data sets of **continuous data** are often presented in a **grouped frequency table**. Actual data values are usually unknown so only **estimates** of summary statistics can be found.

**EXAMPLE**

The table shows the times taken, to the nearest minute, by a group of students to solve a crossword puzzle.
For these data:
a  Find the modal class
b  Find the class containing the median
c  Work out an estimate for the mean
d  Estimate the maximum possible range.

| Time, $t$, minutes | Frequency |
|---|---|
| $5 < t \leq 10$ | 2 |
| $10 < t \leq 15$ | 14 |
| $15 < t \leq 20$ | 13 |
| $20 < t \leq 25$ | 6 |
| $25 < t \leq 30$ | 1 |

**ANSWER**

a  Modal class = $10 < t \leq 15$

Look for the highest frequency – this is 14
14 students took between 10 & 15 minutes
so $10 < t \leq 15$ is the modal class

b  Class containing median

$15 < t \leq 20$

Total number of students = 36 (total frequency)
$\frac{1}{2}(36 + 1) = 18\frac{1}{2}$th, look for 18th & 19th students
Adding frequencies: 2 + 14 = 16; 16 + 13 = 29
18th & 19th students both took between 15 & 20 minutes

c  Mean = total time ÷ total number of students
- Multiply the midpoint of each class by the frequency.
- Find the total (580) – this is the *estimated* total number of minutes.
- Divide by the total number of students.

Mean = 580 ÷ 36 = 16.1

| Time, $t$, minutes | Frequency | Midpoint | Midpoint × frequency |
|---|---|---|---|
| $5 < t \leq 10$ | 2 | 7.5 | 7.5 × 2 = 15 |
| $10 < t \leq 15$ | 14 | 12.5 | 12.5 × 14 = 175 |
| $15 < t \leq 20$ | 13 | 17.5 | 17.5 × 13 = 227.5 |
| $20 < t \leq 25$ | 6 | 22.5 | 22.5 × 6 = 135 |
| $25 < t \leq 30$ | 1 | 27.5 | 27.5 × 1 = 27.5 |
| Total | 36 | | 580 |

d  Range = 30 – 5
        = 25

Longest possible 30 minutes
Shortest possible 5 minutes

You do not need to work out all three averages each time – instead, try to choose the most appropriate one.

> → **If the data looks fairly symmetrical or evenly spread, the best average to use is the mean**
> → **If there are a few extreme values in the data a better average to use would be the median.**

An estimated median can be found from a **cumulative frequency graph**. See page 82.

## Exercise A2.7

**MEDIUM**

*1 Alfie kept a record of his monthly mobile phone bills for one year.

   **a** Write down the class interval that contains the median.

   **b** Calculate an estimate for the mean cost of Alfie's mobile phone bill.

   **c** Give a reason why the mean is a better average to use.

| Phone bill, £ (B) | Frequency |
|---|---|
| $10 < B \le 20$ | 5 |
| $20 < B \le 30$ | 4 |
| $30 < B < 40$ | 2 |
| $40 < B \le 50$ | 1 |

*2 A garden centre gave discount to its staff.
It kept a record of how much each staff member spent during one month.

   **a** Calculate an estimate for the mean amount of money spent at the garden centre by its staff.

   **b** Write down the class interval that contains the median.

The manager of the garden centre did not include the amount he spent at the garden centre that month. He spent £250.

   **c** If this amount spent were included, would the class interval in which the median lies change? Explain your answer.

| Monies spent, £ (M) | Frequency |
|---|---|
| $0 < M \le 40$ | 11 |
| $40 < M \le 80$ | 8 |
| $80 < M \le 120$ | 8 |
| $120 < M \le 160$ | 9 |
| $160 < M \le 200$ | 3 |
| $200 < M \le 240$ | 1 |

*3 David carried out a survey to find the distance travelled to work by 120 teachers and by 120 office workers.

Teachers

| Distance, d, km | Frequency |
|---|---|
| $0 < d \le 5$ | 12 |
| $5 < d \le 10$ | 33 |
| $10 < d \le 15$ | 48 |
| $15 < d \le 20$ | 20 |
| $20 < d \le 25$ | 7 |

Office workers

| Distance, d, km | Frequency |
|---|---|
| $0 < d \le 5$ | 2 |
| $5 < d \le 10$ | 21 |
| $10 < d \le 15$ | 51 |
| $15 < d \le 20$ | 28 |
| $20 < d \le 25$ | 18 |

Work out summary statistics for each data set and use them to justify or refute David's conclusion that teachers live closer to their work place than office workers.

● Design and use data collection sheets

---

## RICH TASK

Look at this questionnaire:

> Please complete the following questionnaire
>
> 1 Do you own or rent your home?
> ☐ Own    ☐ Rent
>
> 2 Are you happy with the refuse collection services supplied by the council?
> ☐ Yes very    ☐ Yes they are okay    ☐ Mostly happy    ☐ No opinion
>
> 3 When was the last time you contacted the council offices?
> ☐ In the last week    ☐ In the last month    ☐ In the last year    ☐ Never

➤ What problem might the answers to this questionnaire be trying to address?
➤ Who do you think is asking the questions?
➤ Do you think it is possible to answer all or any of the questions?
➤ What other answers do you think should be included in each question? Why?
➤ Can you tick more than one answer box in any of the questions?

A **questionnaire** can find out data from individuals. Questions can have a set of suggested responses or be open to any answer.

How old are you?
☐ Under 10    ☐ 11–15    ☐ 15–18    ☐ Over 18

This is not a good question as a 10-year-old cannot answer and a 15-year-old can tick two boxes.

→ **Questions in a questionnaire should:**
  • **use clear language**
  • **be unambiguous**
  • **be free from bias**
  • **be useful and relevant to your survey.**
**Here is an example of a leading question:**

'Do you listen to a lot of music?' is ambiguous because 'a lot' means different things to different people.

Questions that begin with 'Do you agree …' tend to bias people to agree with the statement.

'Do you agree that Kasabian is the best band of 2009?'   yes ☐

**\* 1** A radio station made some changes to the style of breakfast radio show.
They asked this question in a questionnaire:

> What do you think of the new breakfast radio show?
> ☐ Fantastic          ☐ Good

**a** Write down what might be wrong with this question.
This is another question on the questionnaire:

> How long do you listen to the radio?
> ☐ Less than 10 minutes     ☐ 1 hour     ☐ 1–2 hours

**b** Write down three things that are wrong with this question.
**c** Write a question to find out how long people listen to the breakfast radio show on a weekday. Remember to include some response boxes.

**\* 2** Merlin wants to find out how far people would travel to see their favourite band perform.
He writes this question:

> How far would you travel to see your favourite band?
> ☐ Less than 1 mile     ☐ 5–10 miles     ☐ any distance

**a  i** Write down what is wrong with this question.
**ii** Design a better question for Merlin to use.
You should include some response boxes.

Merlin also wants to find out how much people would pay for a ticket to see their favourite band.
**b** Design a question for Merlin to use. You should include some response boxes.

**\* 3** Design a questionnaire to help an independent cinema manager find out

- how often people visit the cinema
- how much they spend on cinema snacks and drinks
- and what would encourage visitors to spend more.

## CHECK OUT

**You should now be able to**
- classify types of data
- find a sample
- find mean, median, mode
- find quartiles and interquartile range
- draw and use stem-and-leaf diagrams
- draw and use box-and-whisker plots
- write questions for questionnaires
- apply the handling data cycle.

### Exam-style question

The box-and-whisker plots show the scores awarded by judges of dancers in a dance competition.
Mark says that the girls are better dancers than the boys.
Explain how the diagram may or may not support Mark's view.

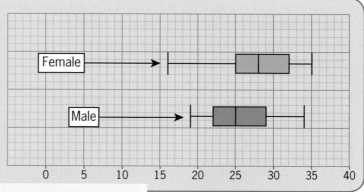

When you compare data sets, you compare summary values such as medians in both or interquartile ranges or ranges.

Be precise in your use of statistical language.

**Shea's answer:**

The boy's median score, 25 is lower than the girl's median score, 28; so on average, girls are better than boys. This supports Mark's view.

However, the girl's range (35 − 16 = 19) is larger than the boy's range (34 − 19 = 15) so the boy's dancing scores are more consistent. This doesn't support Mark's view.

Do not be tempted to compare single values such as the lowest values in both or unlike values such as the lower quartile in one data set with the median in the other data set.

Explain your conclusions with reference to the data.

## Exam practice

1 Edith drew this table to show the length of each track on her iPod.

| Time (*m* minutes) | Number of tracks |
|---|---|
| $2 < m \leq 3$ | 7 |
| $3 < m \leq 4$ | 40 |
| $4 < m \leq 5$ | 38 |
| $5 < m \leq 6$ | 13 |
| $6 < m \leq 7$ | 2 |

   a  Calculate the mean length of the tracks on Edith's iPod.

   b  Which class contains the median?

*(5 marks)*

2 In a football competition decisions during the games were made by the officials. There were 62 referees, 176 assistant referees and 62 fourth officials.
A survey was to be carried out after the competition finished.
A representative sample is to be chosen.
Explain why it would be difficult to choose a stratified sample of 80.

*(3 marks)*

\* 3 Mr Graham gave his students a test.
He summarised their test percentages in a back-to-back stem and-leaf diagram.

| Boys | | Girls |
|---|---|---|
| 6 | 8 | 8 9 |
| 7 | 7 | 2 |
| 6 6 0 | 6 | 2 3 |
| 1 | 5 | 1 7 7 |
| 2 | 4 | 3 |

Key: 2 | 4 | 3 means
Boys 42%, Girls 43%

Comment on whether the boys or the girls performed better in the test, justifying your answer.

*(4 marks)*

# 3 Constructions

## INTRODUCTION

When a company grows in size and opens a new branch in a different town, they need to find a suitable location for their distribution warehouse. In an effort to save transport costs they try to choose a site which has good transport links and which is as close as possible to each branch.

**What's the point?**
By applying some basic geometry in their planning, companies can make their operations more efficient, thereby saving themselves a lot of money.

## CHECK IN

1 Use a protractor to measure these angles.

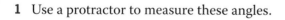

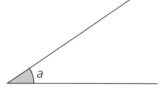

2 Use compasses to draw
   a a circle with radius 3 cm      b an arc with radius 5 cm.

3 a Draw a square $ABCD$ with sides 4 cm.
   b Draw a pair of arcs, each with radius 3 cm, centred on each of the four corners of $ABCD$.
   c Join together the points where the arcs cut the sides of the square to form an octagon.

**Orientation**

| What I should know | What I will learn | What this leads to |
|---|---|---|
| Key stage 3 | ■ Read scales accurately<br>■ Convert between metric and imperial measurements<br>■ Construct triangles<br>■ Construct loci | A8 |

## RICH TASK

A rectangular field is 80 m long and 60 m wide. An electric fence goes from one corner to the opposite corner along the main diagonal.

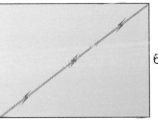

80 m

60 m

A goat is tethered somewhere in the field. The goat can be tethered in different ways.

Fixed point          Between two fixed posts

Running tether

Investigate where the goat should be positioned and how it should be tethered so that it has access to the most grass.

- Convert measurements, know approximate equivalents between metric and imperial systems, read scales and make estimates

→ **The metric system** of measurement is a decimal system because conversions between units are all based on powers of 10. This is the most widely used system of measurement around the world.

| Length | Mass | Volume and capacity |
|---|---|---|
| 1 cm = 10 mm | 1 gram = 1000 mg | 1 litre = 1000 ml |
| 1 metre = 100 cm | 1 kg = 1000 grams | 1 litre = 1000 cm³ |
| 1 metre = 1000 mm | 1 tonne = 1000 kg | 1 ml = 1 cm³ |
| 1 km = 1000 metres | | |

milli- means 'thousandth';
centi- means 'hundredth';
kilo- means 'thousand'.

The **imperial system** is a traditional system of measurement and has developed in Britain over a thousand years.

| Length | Mass | Volume and capacity |
|---|---|---|
| 1 foot = 12 inches | 1 stone = 14 pounds (lb) | 1 gallon = 8 pints |
| 1 yard = 3 feet | | |

There has been some controversy in the UK over which system of measurement to use. With both systems frequently being used, it is useful to be able to convert between the two.

| Length | Mass | Volume and capacity |
|---|---|---|
| 1 foot ≈ 30 cm | 1 pound (lb) ≈ $\frac{1}{2}$ kg | 1 gallon ≈ $4\frac{1}{2}$ litres |
| 5 miles ≈ 8 km | 1 kg ≈ $2\frac{1}{4}$ pounds | 1 pint ≈ $\frac{1}{2}$ litre |
| 1 metre = 1.1 yards | | 1 litre ≈ $1\frac{3}{4}$ pints |

The symbol ≈ means 'approximately equal to'.

A long-distance runner collapsed after running 9.65 km.
While running, he lost 1800 grams in mass and he drank
2000 ml of water.
Convert these measurements to metres, kilograms and pints.

**ANSWER**

9.65 km = 9.65 × 1000 = 9650 metres

1800 grams = 1800 ÷ 1000 = 1.8 kg

2000 ml = 2 litres ≈ 2 × $1\frac{3}{4}$ = $3\frac{1}{2}$ pints

## Exercise A3.1

LOW

1 **a** The man in this diagram is about 2 metres tall.
   Estimate, without measuring, the height
   (in metres) of
   **i** the street lamp
   **ii** the tallest tree
   **iii** the office block.
  **b** Make new imperial estimates (in feet and inches)
   based on the man's height of 6 feet.

2 Write the readings for these lettered arrows.

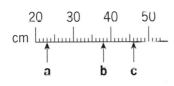

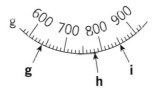

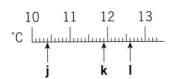

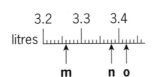

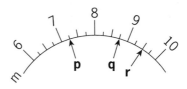

3 The largest standard size of paper (called A0) is a rectangular sheet
   1189 mm by 841 mm. What are these measurements in metres?

**Continued ➤**

4  I buy a bottle of milk and a carton of ice-cream and note the volumes, masses and heights of their containers. Copy and complete this table.

| | Volume | | Mass | | Height | |
|---|---|---|---|---|---|---|
| | litres | ml | grams | kg | metres | mm |
| Milk | 2.27 | | 2400 | | 0.32 | |
| Ice-cream | | 2500 | | 1.47 | | 150 |

5  a  Find approximate metric equivalents for
   **i**  2 feet        **ii**  15 miles        **iii**  5 lbs
   **iv**  6 gallons        **v**  4 pints
   b  Find approximate imperial equivalents for
   **i**  100 cm        **ii**  40 km        **iii**  8 kg
   **iv**  18 litres        **v**  2 litres

6  Amit Patel weighed 87 kg before his diet and 75 kg after his diet. Convert these two masses to pounds (lb) and find how many pounds he lost, giving your answer to the nearest whole number.

7  ★ CHALLENGE ★

A family go to the seaside by car. They travel 160 miles using 18 litres of petrol.
   a  How many kilometres did they travel? What was their petrol consumption in km per litre?
   b  How many gallons of petrol did they use? What was their petrol consumption in miles per gallon?

8  **RICH TASK**

Research the history of the metric system. Where, when and why was it invented?
Which countries have not adopted it as their official system of measurement?

9  **RICH TASK**

Can you find connections between the metre, the equator, the North Pole and the speed of light?

# Constructing triangles

- Construct triangles accurately and use constructions in various contexts

You can draw triangles accurately with ruler and protractor if you know

> → **two sides and the angle between them   (SAS)**
> → **two angles and the side between them   (ASA).**

You can draw triangles accurately without a protractor if you know all three sides.

---

**EXAMPLE**

Draw the triangle ABC with sides of 8 cm, 7 cm and 6.5 cm.
Find the height, $h$, of the triangle.

**ANSWER**

Draw AB = 8 cm.
With your compass point on A, draw arc Y (set the compasses at 7 cm).
With your compass point on B, draw arc Z (set the compasses at 6.5 cm).
Label point C where Y and Z cross.
A ruler gives the height $h$ as 5.4 cm.

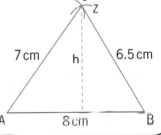

---

> → **You can construct an angle of 60° without a protractor by constructing an equilateral triangle using compasses.**

---

**EXAMPLE**

Construct an equilateral triangle LMN.
Check that each angle is 60°.

**ANSWER**

Choose any length for the side of the triangle (say 5 cm).
Draw one side LM and then use compasses, opened to 5 cm, to draw two arcs to find the third vertex N.
Use a protractor on each vertex to check that all three angles are 60°.

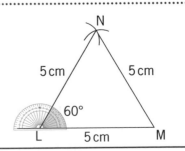

---

## Exercise A3.2

1 Here are sketches of four triangles. Draw each triangle accurately.
   Measure the three angles of each triangle. How can you check your accuracy?

   **a**

   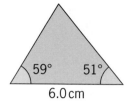

   59°   51°
   6.0 cm

   **b**

   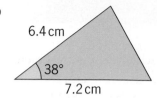

   6.4 cm
   38°
   7.2 cm

   **c**

   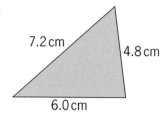

   7.2 cm
   4.8 cm
   6.0 cm

   **d**

   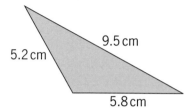

   9.5 cm
   5.2 cm
   5.8 cm

2 The villages Aird, A and Craig, C are 7.5 km apart.
   The mountain Ben More, B makes angles 62° and 53° as
   shown in this sketch. Use a scale of 1 cm = 1 km and draw
   triangle ABC accurately. Find the distances AB and CB to the
   nearest 0.1 km.

   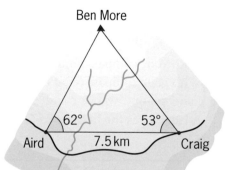

   Ben More

   62°   53°
   Aird   7.5 km   Craig

3 The angles of elevation of a mountain top T from points P and
   Q are 12° and 24°. P and Q are 4.8 km apart. Draw triangle PQT
   accurately. Find the height $h$ of the mountain.

   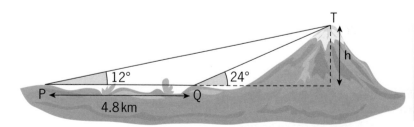

   T
   h
   12°   24°
   P ←————→ Q
   4.8 km

   > The angle of elevation is the
   > angle between the horizontal
   > and the line of sight if you
   > stand and look at T from points
   > P or Q.

4 A telegraph pole 5.7 metres tall is held by a wire fixed to its top
   and to a point in the ground 2.7 metres from the foot of the pole.
   The wire is 6.5 metres long. Is the pole vertical?

**5** As the crow flies, Acomb is 2.5 miles from Barlby and 2.0 miles from Cawood.
Barlby is 1.5 miles from Cawood.
If Acomb is due north of Cawood, in what direction is Barlby from Cawood?
Is this the only possible solution?

**6** Triangle ABC is equilateral with sides of 5 cm. Triangles
PAB, QBC and RCA are also equilateral. Construct these four
equilateral triangles without using a protractor. If triangle PQR
is cut out and folded so that corners P, Q and R meet, what 3-D
shape is made?

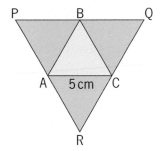

**7** A bridge has a cross-section of five equilateral triangles. Make
an accurate drawing of the bridge to a scale of 1 cm = 2 metres
without using a protractor.
What is the span (width) of the bridge in metres?

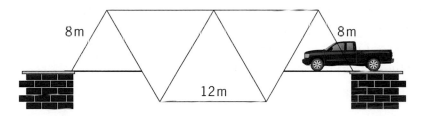

**\*8** Write your partner a description of a triangle that you want them
to draw. Is the triangle the one you expected?

**\*9** A canal has straight banks. How can you measure its width
without crossing it?

**10** **RICH TASK**

Triangle ABC has AB = 6 cm and angle A = 40°.
If BC = 4 cm, is angle C unique?

**11** **RICH TASK**

Can you draw this triangle accurately?
Explain your findings.

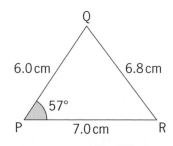

# More constructions

- Use ruler and compasses to find midpoints and bisectors and to construct perpendiculars

A ruler and compasses allow you to construct accurate geometrical shapes.

- You can bisect a line and find its midpoint.

  With compass point on end A, draw two arcs P.
  With compass point on end B, draw two arcs Q (use the same compass setting).
  Join the intersections X and Y of arcs P and Q.

  The line XY is the perpendicular bisector of AB.
  Point M is the midpoint of AB.

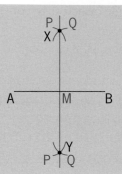

- You can bisect an angle.

  With compass point on A, draw arcs P and Q,
  With compass point on P, draw arc R (you can change the setting).
  With compass point on Q, draw arc S (do not change the setting from R).
  Label the intersection X of R and S.

  The line AX is the bisector of angle A.

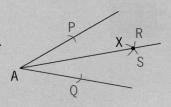

- You can construct a perpendicular from point to a line.
  X is the point from which the perpendicular is to be drawn.

  With compass point on X, draw arcs P and Q.
  With compass point on P, draw arc R.
  With compass point on Q, draw arc S.
  Join point X to the intersection Y of arcs R and S.

  The line XY is perpendicular to the line AB.

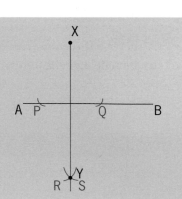

1   a   Construct the perpendicular bisector of line AB which is
8 cm long. Label the midpoint M of AB. Check your results
with a ruler and protractor.

     b   On axes labelled from 0 to 8, construct the perpendicular
bisector of the line joining points (1, 3) and (7, 4).

2   a   Draw any **obtuse** angle A. Construct the angle bisector of
angle A. Check your result with a protractor.

     b   Use angle bisectors to construct angles of 30° and 45°.

3   a   Draw line AB 8 cm long. Mark any point X on line AB.
Construct a line through X which is perpendicular to line AB.
Check your result with a protractor.

     b   On axes labelled from 0 to 8, draw the line through A(2, 2) and
B(8, 5). Construct a perpendicular to line AB at the point X(6, 4).

4   A hiker at X wants to reach the A832.
Trace this map and construct his
shortest route.

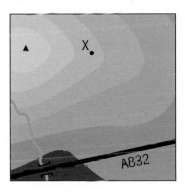

**5**   **RICH TASK**

Construct the angle bisectors of any triangle. What do you
notice? Label a point as an Incentre and draw an incircle.
Construct the three perpendicular bisectors of the sides
of any triangle. Label a point as a circumcentre and draw a
circumcircle.

# Loci

- Find loci which give paths or regions in two dimensions

A locus is a set of points which obey a rule.
The points may lie on a line or they may lie inside a region.

> The word 'loci' is the plural of the Latin word 'locus' which means 'a place'.

## RICH TASK

Jamie wants to pass through an opening in an electrified fence so that he is always as far from gate post P as he is from gate post Q. Sketch the path he must take.

**EXAMPLE**

A dog is tethered by a lead 3 metres long to a point P which is 2 metres from the corner of two walls. Find the region which the dog can reach.

**ANSWER**

At full stretch, the dog can reach points 3 metres from P. These points lie on the arc of a circle with P as centre. When **not** at full stretch, the dog is inside this arc. The shaded area gives the region that the dog can reach.

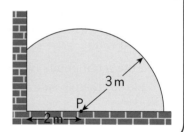

## Exercise A3.4

**MEDIUM**

1 In each case, sketch the locus of point X and describe it in words. A point X moves on a flat surface so that it is:

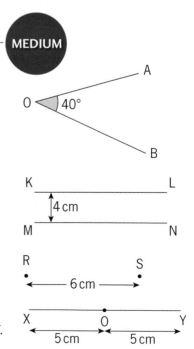

a always 6 cm from a fixed point P
b always less than 6 cm from a fixed point P
c the same distance from line OA as it is from line OB
d nearer to line OA than it is to line OB

e the same distance from line KL as it is from line MN
f nearer to line KL than line MN

g equidistant from two fixed points R and S, 6 cm apart
h nearer to point R than it is to point S

i less than 5 cm from point O but more than 3 cm from line XY.

**2** LM and MN are two walls of a house.

The owner wants to pave that part of the garden which is either less than 3 metres from wall LM or which is less than 3 metres from point P in wall MN. Make a scale drawing to find the part of the garden which will be paved.

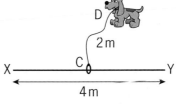

**3** A dog's running lead CD is 2 metres long.
It can slide along the fixed wire XY.
Use a scale of 1 cm = 1 metre and construct the locus of all the points that the dog can reach.

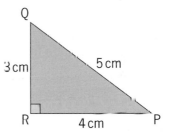

**4** **a** Draw this triangle accurately.
Find the locus of all points inside the triangle which are nearer to RP than they are to QP.
   **b** Draw another diagram for the locus of all points inside the triangle which are nearer to P than they are to R.

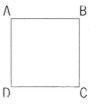

**5** Find the set of points inside square ABCD which are both nearer to side AB than to side AD, and **also** nearer to D than to C.

**6** ☆ **CHALLENGE** ☆

   **a** Point A is fixed 4 cm from the straight line LM.
   A variable point P moves so that it is always as far from the line LM as it is from point A. Sketch the locus of P.

   **b** Draw the graph of the curve $y = \frac{1}{4}x^2$ accurately for $-10 \leq x \leq 10$ on squared paper with the same scale on both axes. Mark the point A(0, 1) and the line $y = -1$ as line LM. Take various positions of point P on the graph and show that this curve satisfies the conditions of the locus in part **a**.

**7** **RICH TASK**

Explore the locus of points on the edges of rolling objects. Here are some examples.
   ● Roll a coin along a ruler.
   ● Imagine a cubical box being rolled, face by face, along a floor.
   ● Imagine a garden roller being rolled up steps.
   ● What are hypocycloids? What is the rotary car engine? Find animations of them on the internet.

# Maps and bearings

**A3.5**

• Interpret maps and use bearings

## RICH TASK

Design a course for racing yachts. The yachts must sail round the corners of a square of side 5 km. The first leg is towards the prevailing wind (blowing from 060°). Give the bearings of the other three legs. If a yacht averages a speed of 18 km/h, estimate how long it takes to get round the course.

From your current position, you can fix a distant point by knowing its distance and direction from you.

> These requirements are also those needed to define a vector. See page 242.

You can give the distance by using the scale of a map.
You can give the direction using either the compass points, such as *south-west* or, more accurately, a 3-figure bearing.

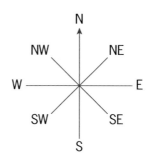

> A bearing always needs three figures. For example, the direction NE is the bearing 045°.

A **bearing** is always measured **clockwise** from the **north**.

**EXAMPLE**

Give directions for an aircraft flying from Cardiff to Oxford via Gloucester.

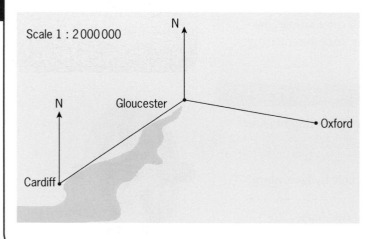

Scale 1 : 2 000 000

**ANSWER**

The scale means that 1 cm on the map stands for 2 000 000 cm = 20 000 m = 20 km in reality.
Use ruler and scale to find distances and use a protractor to find bearings.
The plane flies 4 × 20 = 80 km on a bearing of 056° from Cardiff to Gloucester, and then flies 3.5 × 20 = 70 km on a bearing of 100° from Gloucester to Oxford.

> Divide by 100 and then again by 1000 to change cm to km.

1 This map of the Irish Sea has a scale of 1:4000000.
  a Find the distances in km between
     i Belfast and Carlisle
     ii Dublin and Douglas
  b An aircraft flies from Dublin to Belfast and then to Liverpool.
     Find the distance and bearing for each leg of the flight.

2 Give a three-figure bearing for these compass directions:
  a due west
  b north east
  c south west.

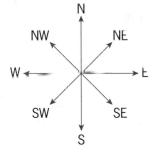

3 Manchester is 40 km from Preston on a bearing of 140°.
  Liverpool is 45 km from Preston on a bearing of 210°.
  Lancaster is 32 km from Preston on a bearing of 345°.
  Use a scale of 1:1000000 to make a scale drawing of these cities.
  What is the shortest distance between
  a Manchester and Liverpool
  b Manchester and Lancaster?

4 A business jet leaves London to fly 340 km to Paris on a bearing
  of 148°. From Paris it flies 470 km to Frankfurt on a bearing of
  070° and then 320 km on a bearing of 180° to Zurich. Finally,
  it flies from Zurich 750 km to Bordeaux on a bearing of 252°.
  Using a scale of 1:10000000, find the distance and bearing
  directly from London to Bordeaux.

5 The bearing of N from M is $x$°. What is the bearing of M from N?

6 The bearings of B and C from A are 060° and 110° respectively.
  The bearing of C from B is 140°. Find the bearing of A from B and from C.

7 ☆ **CHALLENGE** ☆

Frank flew his light aircraft at 300 km h$^{-1}$ on a bearing of 075° in a
wind which was blowing at 60 km h$^{-1}$ on a bearing of 290°. What was
his speed and direction relative to the ground?

The wind is travelling **towards** a
direction of 290°.

## CHECK OUT

**You should now be able to**

- construct triangles and other 2-D shapes
- use ruler and compasses for constructions including loci
- use bearings.

**Exam-style question**

Construct a triangle as follows:

The two longest sides are 9 cm and 7 cm.

The smallest angle is 30°.

Use facts you know about triangles to draw a sketch.

Construct an angle of 60° and then construct the angle bisector to find 30°.

Always leave the construction lines.

Extend the second side to 9 cm with a ruler or compasses.

**Saul's answer:**

The smallest angle in a triangle is opposite the smallest side

30° angle must lie between the two longer sides

Draw one of the sides using a ruler.

Use a ruler or compasses to draw the base of the triangle length of 7 cm.

Join the two arcs to complete the triangle.

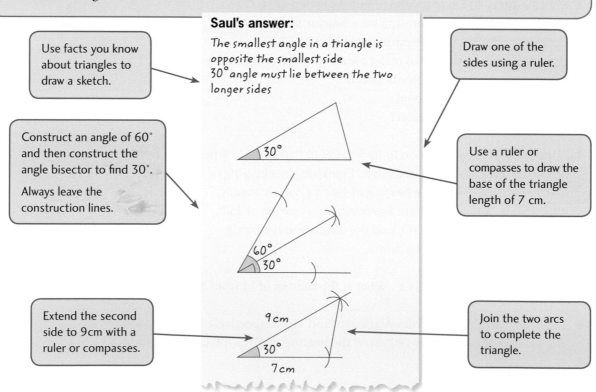

1   Treasure is buried 3 m from a tree T and 7 m from a gatepost G.
    The tree and the gatepost are 6 m apart.
    Draw a diagram to show where the treasure could be buried.

    (*3 marks*)

2   Use ruler and compasses only to construct a regular
    hexagon of side length 4 cm.                    (*4 marks*)

3   The map shows part of the United Kingdom.
    The map scale is 1 cm = 50 km.

    a   Work out the actual distance and bearing of Truro from
        Exeter.
    b   Work out the distance and bearing of the distance
        from Cambridge to Hereford via Birmingham.

        (*6 marks*)

Mathematics is used widely in sport, particularly when taking measurements and recording results.

Here are the results and wind speeds for the fastest thirteen all-time 100m Men's sprinters as of 20th September 2009:

| Rank | Time (s) | Wind speed (m/s) | Athlete | Nation | Date |
|---|---|---|---|---|---|
| | | | | JAM | 16/08/2009 |
| 1 | 9.58 | +0.9 | Bolt | USA | 20/09/2009 |
| 2 | 9.69 | +2.0 | Gay | JAM | 02/09/2008 |
| 3 | 9.72 | +0.2 | Powell | USA | 16/06/1999 |
| 4 | 9.79 | +0.1 | Greene | CAN | 27/07/1996 |
| 5 | 9.84 | +0.7 | Bailey | CAN | 22/08/1999 |
| | | +0.2 | Surin | USA | 06/07/1994 |
| 7 | 9.85 | +1.2 | Burrell | USA | 22/08/2004 |
| | | +0.6 | Gatlin | NIG | 12/05/2006 |
| | | +1.7 | Fasuba | USA | 25/08/1991 |
| 10 | 9.86 | +1.2 | Lewis | NAM | 03/07/1996 |
| | | −0.4 | Fredericks | TRI | 19/04/1998 |
| | | +1.8 | Boldon | POR | 22/08/2004 |
| | | +0.6 | Obikwelu | | |

What level of accuracy is reported for
a) the result times    b) the wind speeds?

Plot a time–series graph for these results. Can you see any trend? When (if ever) do you think the 9.50s barrier will be broken? Explain your answer referring to the data.

What is the    a) fastest    b) slowest
actual time that each of the athletes could have run to give their reported result?

# FASTEST TEN ALL-TIME 100m WOMEN'S SPRINTERS
## AS OF 20th SEPTEMBER 2009:

NEWS    PHOTOS    VIDEO    AUDIO

By Date    By Event    Entry List    Medal Table    Placing Table    Entry Standards

**CHOOSE YOUR COUNTRY!**
Select a country

Here are the results and wind speeds for the fastest ten all-time 100m Women's sprinters as of 20th September 2009:

| Rank | Time (s) | Wind speed (m/s) | Athlete | Nation | Date |
|---|---|---|---|---|---|
| 1 | 10.49 | 0.0 | Griffith-Joyner | USA | 16/07/1988 |
| 2 | 10.64 | +1.2 | Jeter | USA | 20/09/2009 |
| 3 | 10.65 | +1.1 | Jones | USA | 12/09/1998 |
| 4 | 10.73 | +0.1 | Fraser | JAM | 17/08/2009 |
| 5 | | +2.0 | Arron | FRA | 17/08/1998 |
| 6 | 10.74 | +1.3 | Ottey | JAM | 07/09/1996 |
| 7 | 10.75 | +0.4 | Stewart | JAM | 10/07/2009 |
| 8 | 10.76 | +1.7 | Ashford | USA | 22/08/1984 |
| 9 | 10.77 | +0.9 | Privalova | RUS | 06/07/1994 |
| | | +0.7 | Lalova | BUL | 19/06/2004 |

Florence Griffith-Joyner's World Record is quoted as being 'probably strongly wind assisted' because it is suspected that the wind speed measurer was faulty.

Comment on this, referring to the data and using your diagrams and statistics.

Use time-series diagrams and statistics to compare the Women's and Men's results. Refer to any trends you notice.

A maximum tail wind of +2.0m/s is allowed for 'wind legal' results. Head winds are not taken into account.

Tail winds follow the athlete and are recorded as +ve.

Head winds act against the athlete and are recorded as −ve.

Draw a scatter diagram of result time against wind speed for
a) the Men's results          b) the Women's results.

Do you think there is any correlation between wind speed and time? Justify your response by referring to the data.

# 4 Factors, multiples and ratio

## INTRODUCTION

The golden ratio, *phi*, has been considered the most pleasing to the eye. The ancient Egyptians used it in the construction of the pyramids and the Greeks used it in their architecture. The golden ratio is a ratio of length to width in rectangles of 1.6180339887 : 1

**What's the point?**
The concept of proportion is vital to art and architecture. Evidence of proportion can be seen in many works of art and architecture, especially in ancient Greece and Rome.

## CHECK IN

1  Write all the factors of 24.

2  Write the first six multiples of 13.

3  Write the first 10 prime numbers.

4  Work out
   a  $3^2 \times 5$        b  $2^2 \times 5^2$

**Orientation**

| What I should know | What I will learn | What this leads to |
|---|---|---|
| Key stage 3 | ■ Find prime factors<br>■ Divide an amount into a given ratio | B9 |

## RICH TASK

Your height is about the same as three times around your head.
Investigate.

# Prime factors

- Use highest common factors, least common multiples and prime factor decomposition

## ☆ ACTIVITY ☆

Take turns to choose two numbers from the grid, which have not yet been picked. Score all factors that are common to both your chosen numbers.
**The winner:** The player with the highest score when all numbers on the grid have been used.

| 1 | 2 | 3 | 4 | 5 | 6 |
|----|----|----|----|----|----|
| 7 | 8 | 9 | 10 | 11 | 12 |
| 13 | 14 | 15 | 16 | 17 | 18 |
| 19 | 20 | 21 | 22 | 23 | 24 |
| 25 | 26 | 27 | 28 | 29 | 30 |
| 31 | 32 | 33 | 34 | 35 | 36 |

During the game see if you can answer these questions:
- **i**  What number will always be scored by the first player? Why?
- **ii**  What sort of numbers can achieve the highest scores?
- **iii**  List the numbers with exactly two factors.
  What is the name given to this type of number?
- **iv**  What type of number has an odd number of factors? Why?
- **v**  How can you check that all the numbers have been accounted for?

 p. 228

**For example:**
Cathy chooses 24 and 20.
Factors of 24 are 1, 2, 3, 4, 6, 8, 12, 24.
Factors of 20 are 1, 2, 4, 5, 10, 20.
Common factors are 1, 2, 4.
Cathy scores 1 + 2 + 4 = 7.

Dave chooses 35 and 15.
Factors of 35 are 1, 5, 7, 35.
Factors of 15 are 1, 3, 5, 15.
Common factors are 1, 5.
Dave scores 1 + 5 = 6.

→ **Numbers can be written as a product of their prime factors.**

Prime factors are factors that are also prime numbers.

You can find prime factors by dividing.

**EXAMPLE**

Write 5544 as a product of prime factors.

**ANSWER**

Start with dividing by 2: $5544 \div 2 = 2772$
Keep dividing until it will not divide exactly: $2772 \div 2 = 1386$
$1386 \div 2 = 693$
Then move to the next prime number (3): $693 \div 3 = 231$
$231 \div 3 = 77$
5 won't work, so try 7: $77 \div 7 = 11$
Stop when you get a prime number answer: 11
Write your number as a product of primes:
$5544 = 2 \times 2 \times 2 \times 3 \times 3 \times 7 \times 11$

In the **factor tree method**
- Write the number as the product of two smaller numbers
- Keep breaking the numbers down until you get to prime numbers

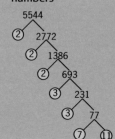

You can use the product of prime factors to find the **highest common factor** (HCF) and **least common multiple** (LCM).

> → **The HCF of a set of numbers is the largest number that will divide into all of the numbers exactly.**
> → **The LCM of a set of numbers is the smallest number that all of the numbers will divide into exactly.**

**EXAMPLE**

Find the HCF and LCM of 24 and 20.

**ANSWER**

First write 24 and 20 as the product of prime factors:
$$24 = 2 \times 2 \times 2 \times 3 \qquad 20 = 2 \times 2 \times 5$$
Arrange the products in two overlapping circles:

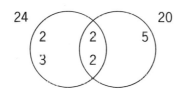

*If more than one of the same prime factor is needed in the product you must list them all.*

The HCF of 24 and 20 is 4
$(2 \times 2 = 4)$

The LCM of 24 and 20 is 120
$(2 \times 3 \times 2 \times 2 \times 5 = 120)$

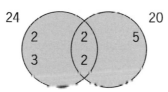

## Exercise A4.1

MEDIUM

1  Write each number as a product of prime factors.
   a  48   b  27   c  54   d  120
   e  72   f  294   g  371

2  For the following pairs of numbers find   **i** the LCM   **ii** the HCF.
   a  54 and 48   b  120 and 99   c  72 and 94   d  49 and 28   e  65 and 30

3  **RICH TASK**

   A prime number is a number with exactly two factors.
   a  Explain why the square of a prime number has exactly three factors.
   The numbers 6, 8, 10, 15 and 27 all have exactly four factors.
   b  Give description(s), with reasons, of numbers that have exactly four factors.

- Use ratio notation, including reduction to its simplest form

This is the **Fibonacci sequence:**

1  1  2  3  5  8  13  21  34  ...

The first two numbers are 1 and 1.
The third number is 1+1 = 2.
The fourth number is 1+2 = 3,
and so on.

## RICH TASK

Continue the sequence of Fibonacci numbers and write adjacent pairs
as **ratios** in the **unitary form** 1 : $n$.
The first four have been done for you:

   1:1    1:2    2:3 = 1:1.5    3:5 = 1:1.666

What happens to the ratio of adjacent Fibonacci numbers?

Use the internet to find out
about the **golden ratio.**

- → A ratio is a way of showing a relationship between two or
  more numbers.
- → A ratio in its simplest form has integer values that cannot be
  cancelled further.
- → You use the unitary form **1 : $n$** or **$n$ : 1** to compare ratios.

## RICH TASK

"Why is A4 paper A4?"
A sheet of A3 paper folded in half is the size of A4 paper.
Fold A4 paper in half and the paper size is A5 and so on.
So the length of one paper size will be the width of the next size bigger.

Measure the length and width of A3, A4, A5 and A6 paper.
Find the ratio width : length for each paper size.
What do you find?

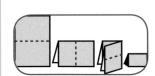

1 ☆ ACTIVITY ☆

Using the digits
    0  1  2  3  4  5  6  7  8  9

Step 1: Choose three of these digits
Step 2: Add them up and call the total A.
Step 3: Make all possible two-digit numbers
        from the three chosen digits in step 1.
        Add them up and call the total B.
Step 4: Find the ratio A : B in the form 1 : n.

**For example:**
Step 1    Choose 2  8  5
Step 2    $A = 2 + 8 + 5 = 15$
Step 3    The possible two-
          digit numbers are
          28  25  82  85  52  58
          $B = 28 + 25 + 82 +$
          $85 + 52 + 58 = 330$
Step 4    $A : B = 15 : 330$
                $= 1 : 22$

**a  i**   Choose your own set of three digits and find the ratio $A : B$
       using steps 1 to 4.

   **ii**  Choose a different set of three numbers and find the
       ratio $A : B$.

   **iii** What do you notice about the example and your answers
       to **i** and **ii**?

Use symbols to explain why
this might always happen.

**b  i**   Choose four of the numbers from the list.
       Work through steps 1 to 4 using these numbers and find the
       ratio $A : B$.
       (Remember to work systematically to find all possible two-digit
       numbers in step 3.)

   **ii**  Choose a different set of four numbers and find the
       ratio $A : B$.

   **iii** Choose a third set of four numbers and find the
       ratio $A : B$.

   **iv**  What do you notice about your answers to **i**, **ii** and **iii**?

**c  i**   Choose a set of five numbers from the list and use these to find
       the ratio $A : B$.

   **ii**  Compare and comment on your answers to **a i**, **b i** and **c i**.

# Using ratio

- Know the links between ratio and fraction notation
- Divide a quantity into a given ratio

## RICH TASK

Marvin is exactly four years older than his brother Fred.
The ratio of their ages is $3:1$.
How old are Marvin and Fred?
How old will they both be when the ratio of their ages becomes $3:2$?

You can use ratio to share amounts.

---

**EXAMPLE**

Share £75 in the ratio $4:1$

**ANSWER**

$4 + 1 = 5$      First find the number of equal parts that the money will be divided into

$75 \div 5 = £15$      Find one part

$4:1 = 60:15$      Multiply the numbers in the ratio to find each share

---

**EXAMPLE**

£3000 is divided between Tom, Dick and Harry in the ratio
     $T:D:H = 2:3:5$
How much do they each get?

**ANSWER**

$2 + 3 + 5 = 10 \Rightarrow 3000 \div 10 = £300$
$\Rightarrow 2:3:5 = 600:900:1500$

Tom gets £600, Dick gets £900 and Harry gets £1500

---

**EXAMPLE**

Harriet and Oliver have a joint birthday party. The number of guests they are allowed to invite is in the ratio
     Harriet : Oliver = $5:3$
Harriet invites 20 guests. How many are invited in total?

**ANSWER**

$20 \div 5 = 4$      First find what one part is worth

$3 + 5 = 8$      Work out the total number of equal parts

Total number invited
$= 8 \times 4 = 32$      Multiply to find the total

---

Working with ratio can be linked to work with fractions.

In the last example, the ratio Harriet : Oliver = $5:3$
The fraction of guests invited by Harriet is $\frac{5}{8}$.
The fraction invited by Oliver is $\frac{3}{8}$.

There is more work on fractions in Chapter 9.

**1** Share the following amounts in the given ratios.
  **a** £48 in the ratio 1:5       **b** £64 in the ratio 7:1
  **c** £108 in the ratio 2:7      **d** £96 in the ratio 7:5
  **e** £420 in the ratio 1:2:4    **f** £425 in the ratio 3:6:8

**2** Petra and Sam took part in a sponsored swim.
The amounts they raised were in the ratio 5:3. Petra raised £75.50.
How much did Sam raise?

**3** Jenny and Mike share prize money in the ratio 3:2.
Jenny gets £12.60.
How much does Mike get?

**4** In a 400 g tin of tuna there are 250 calories.
How many calories would there be in a 150 g tin of tuna?

**5** A 160 g cereal bar has 220 calories.
How many calories will there be in a 100 g cereal bar?

**6** A melon medley is made by mixing honeydew and cantaloupe
melons in the ratio 3 : 5 by weight. The weight of honeydew melon
is 255 g.
What is the total weight of the melon in the melon medley?

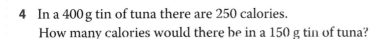

**7** ☆ **PROBLEM** ☆

Joshua is 12 years old and Reuben is 9 years old.
  **a** When Joshua is 18 years old, what will the ratio of
     Joshua's age to Reuben's age be? Write this ratio as simply as
     possible.
  **b** When Reuben is 18 years old, what will the ratio of Joshua's age to
     Reuben's age be? Write this ratio as simply as possible.
  **c** Find the ages of Joshua and Reuben when the ratio of their ages
     was 2:1.

**8** **RICH TASK**

  **a** **i** Choose a passage of writing in any novel (about 10 lines of writing), and count the
       number of times the letter E appears and the number of times the letter T appears.
     **ii** Work out the ratio E:T. (You may want to express this as a unitary ratio.)
  **b** In a standard *Scrabble* set there are 12 E's and 6 T's. Work out the ratio E:T.
     Compare your ratio with your answer to **a i**. Comment on what you notice.
  **c** Combine your total number of E's and T's from **b** with the totals from one or more
     people. Work out the new ratio E:T. Comment on your answer.

# Summary and assessment

## CHECK OUT

**You should now be able to**
- find least common multiple and highest common factor
- write numbers as a product of prime factors
- use ratio.

---

\* **Exam-style question**

PrintsRUs develops 35 mm films in two sizes.
Compact size: 5 inches by 3·5 inches.
Large size: 7 inches by 5 inches.
Are the print sizes in the same ratio to each other?
Justify your answer.

**Dayle's answer:**
Ratio of the compact size
5 : 3.5 = 1 : 0.7

Ratio of large size
7 : 5 = 1 : 0.714

0.7 is nearly the same as 0.714

The print sizes are not exactly in the same ratio.

However if the sizes had been rounded then the ratio might have been the same.

Think about what mathematics you need to use.

You justify or explain answers using mathematics as well as words.

Work out the ratios of each size the same way so that you can compare them.

Comment on your working to answer the question.

## Exam practice

1   Write 84 as a product of prime factors.

(*2 marks*)

2   Two numbers have highest common factor (HCF) 15 and least
    common multiple (LCM) 90.
    One of the numbers is 30. What is the other number?

(*2 marks*)

3   a   A bathroom tile has two colours, purple and green,
        in its design.
        The ratio purple : green is 3 : 2.
        What fraction of the tile is purple?

    b   In another tile design, $\frac{5}{8}$ is coloured yellow and the remainder
        is white.
        What is the ratio yellow : white?

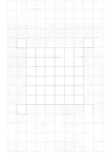

(*3 marks*)

## INTRODUCTION

There are lots of different types of sequences in mathematics from the most basic arithmetic sequences such as the set of even numbers, to the curious Fibonacci sequence which can be used to describe many patterns of growth in the natural world, through to the elegant and complex world of fractal geometry.

**What's the point?**
Sequences allow us to find patterns in nature, so that we can predict its behaviour and understand it better.

## CHECK IN

1 Complete the next two values in each pattern

 **a**  2, 4, 6, 8, …   **b**  100, 94, 88, 82, 76, …

 **c**  1, 2, 4, 7, 11, …  **d**  10, 7, 4, 1, …

 **e**  3, 6, 12, 24, …  **f**  $1, \frac{1}{2}, \frac{1}{3}, \frac{1}{4}, \frac{1}{5}, …$

2 Given that $n = 3$, put these expressions in ascending order.

 $2n + 7$   $4(n - 1)$   $2n^2$   $\frac{9}{n} + 15$   $15 - n$

3 This pattern has been shown in three different ways. It has a special name. What is it called? Describe how it got this name.

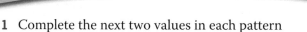

| 1 | 4 | 9 | 16 |
|---|---|---|---|
| 1 × 1 | 2 × 2 | 3 × 3 | 4 × 4 |

| What I should know | What I will learn | What this leads to |
|---|---|---|
| Key stage 3 | ■ Generate sequences<br>■ Find the general term of a sequence<br>■ Understand square and triangle numbers | Careers in finance and computing. |

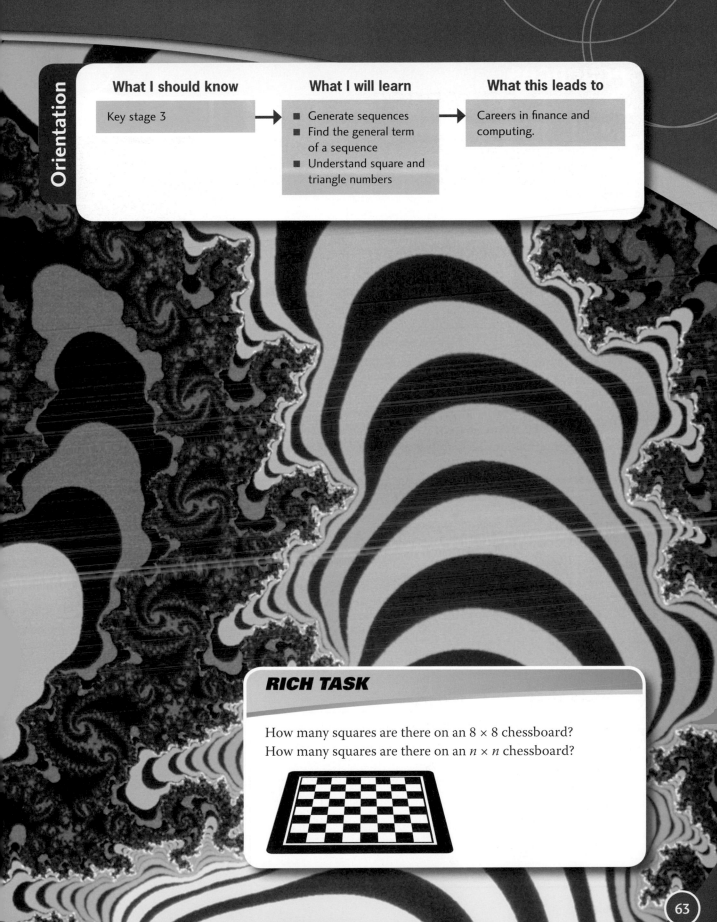

## RICH TASK

How many squares are there on an 8 × 8 chessboard?

How many squares are there on an $n \times n$ chessboard?

# Sequences

- Generate terms of a sequence given the general term
- Describe the behaviour of a sequence

## RICH TASK

A plant grows one leaf per shoot.
After 24 hours, any shoot on the plant can produce one new shoot.

How many leaves would the plant have after one week?

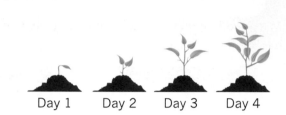

Day 1   Day 2   Day 3   Day 4

→ **A sequence is a set of numbers or elements that are connected by a rule.**

→ **The general term T($n$) of a sequence is a formula that allows you to find any term in the sequence.**

T(1) is the first term, T(2) is the second term and so on.

---

**EXAMPLE**

Generate the first five terms of each of these sequences.

**a**  T($n$) = $5n - 2$     **b**  T($n$) = $3(n + 1)$

**ANSWER**

**a**  T($n$) = $5n - 2$
   T(1) = 5(1) − 2 = 3
   T(2) = 5(2) − 2 = 8
   T(3) = 5(3) − 2 = 13
   T(4) = 5(4) − 2 = 18
   T(5) = 5(5) − 2 = 23
   First five terms are
   3, 8, 13, 18, 23, …

**b**  T($n$) = $3(n + 1)$
   T(1) = 3(1 + 1) = 6
   T(2) = 3(2 + 1) = 9
   T(3) = 3(3 + 1) = 12
   T(4) = 3(4 + 1) = 15
   T(5) = 3(5 + 1) = 18
   First five terms are
   6, 9, 12, 15, 18, …

---

**EXAMPLE**

Find the value of $n$ that generates the term given from this sequence. T($n$) = $3(n + 1)$; T($n$) = 75

**ANSWER**

$3(n + 1) = 75$
  $3n + 3 = 75$    Multiply out brackets
      $3n = 72$    Subtract 3
       $n = 24$    Divide by 3

1 Generate the first five terms of each of these linear sequences.

   a   $3n$                b   $4n + 1$

   c   $7n - 3$           d   $5(n + 1)$

   e   $2(n - 3)$        f   $\frac{n}{10}$

   g   $5 - n$            h   $99 - 9n$

2 Match each of these formulae to their general term. The first one has been done for you.

| Formula |
| --- |
| 3, 6, 9, 12, 15, ... |
| 5, 11, 17, 23, 29, ... |
| 7, 11, 15, 19, 23, ... |
| 46, 42, 38, 34, 30, ... |

| General term |
| --- |
| $50 - 4n$ |
| $4n + 3$ |
| $3n$ |
| $6n - 1$ |

Generate the first few terms of each sequence.

3 Find the value of $n$ that generates the term given from each of these sequences.

   a   $T(n) = 6n + 5$, $T(n) = 53$      b   $T(n) = 5n - 2$; $T(n) = 73$

   c   $T(n) = 3(n + 4)$; $T(n) = 75$     d   $T(n) = 100 - 2n$; $T(n) = 82$

4 Write the next three terms for each of these sequences. In each case, find the 20th term (but without writing out all 20 terms).

   a   10, 12, 14, 16, ...          b   5, 8, 11, 14, 17, ...

5  **RICH TASK**

When two people meet and shake hands they perform one handshake.

Andy, Ben and Carl meet. Each person shakes hands once with his two friends. They perform three handshakes.

Use a sketch to check this.

David joins the group. Each person shakes hands once with all his friends. How many handshakes are now performed?

Investigate the number of handshakes if the group continues to grow.

- Generate and describe sequences and relate them to geometrical patterns
- Generate terms of a sequence given the general term

## RICH TASK

A crate of fruit contains one layer of apples arranged in a square of side $n$, where $n$ is an integer.

An apple towards the centre of the crate has rotted.

After 24 hours, any rotten apple causes the four apples that surround it to rot. Investigate the number of rotten apples.

Square of side 5

Day 1    Day 2    Day 3

Each term in the sequence of **square numbers** can be represented as a square pattern of dots.

T(1) = 1    T(2) = 4    T(3) = 9    T(4) = 16

→ **The general or $n$th term of the sequence of square numbers is T($n$) = $n^2$**

Here are the first four terms in the sequence of **triangular numbers**:

T(1) = 1    T(2) = 3    T(3) = 6    T(4) = 10

To find the 5th triangular number add a row of 5 dots to the 4th triangle.

You can find a general formula using rectangles.

T(1) + T(1) = 1 × 2    T(2) + T(2) = 2 × 3    T(3) + T(3) = 3 × 4    T(4) + T(4) = 4 × 5

The number of dots in the $n$th rectangle is $n \times (n + 1)$.

$$T(n) + T(n) = n(n + 1)$$
$$2T(n) = n(n + 1)$$

→ **The general or $n$th term of the sequence of triangular numbers is T($n$) = $\frac{1}{2}n(n + 1)$**

1  Here is a number pattern.

$$1^2 = 1$$
$$2^2 = 1 + 3$$
$$3^2 = 1 + 3 + 5$$
$$4^2 = 1 + 3 + 5 + 7$$

> Work out the relationship between the number being squared and the last odd number being summed.

a  Write the next three lines.
b  Find the value of $t$ if  $100^2 = 1 + 3 + 5 + \ldots + t$
c  Work out the sum of the odd numbers from 1 to 49.

*2  You can write some numbers as the difference between two square numbers. For example  $7 = 16 - 9 = 4^2 - 3^2$

> Use 0 as a square number so that, for example, $1 = 1^2 - 0^2$

a  Write 12 as the difference between two square numbers.
b  Write 15 as the difference between two square numbers in two different ways.
c  Write, in ascending order, all the even numbers up to and including 20 that can be written as the difference between two square numbers. Describe any patterns that you see.

3  Look at this number pattern involving the triangular numbers.

$$1 = 1$$
$$3 = 1 + 2$$
$$6 = 1 + 2 + 3$$
$$10 = 1 + 2 + 3 + 4$$

> The $n$th term of the sequence of triangular numbers is
> $T(n) = \frac{1}{2}n(n + 1)$

The $n$th triangular number is equal to the sum of the first $n$ whole numbers.

You can write $\sum n = \frac{1}{2}n(n + 1)$ where $\sum n$ means 'the sum of the first $n$ whole numbers'. Use this formula to find the sum of the whole numbers from one to

a  10    b  20    c  99    d  200    e  1000.

*4  Phil asks his Dad for some pocket money and is offered two options.

> **Option 1**  1p on the first day, 2p on the second day, 3p on the third day and so on for one year.
> **Option 2**  £10 per week for one year.

Advise Phil on which option to choose, showing the total amount of pocket money that he would receive in each case.

# The general term

- Generate terms of a sequence given the general term
- Write and justify the general or $n$th term of a sequence

## RICH TASK

Arrange these cards to create several different sequences. You do not have to use all the cards each time.
For each sequence, generate the first five terms. Comment on the behaviour of each sequence.
What if you introduced cards containing brackets?

| $T(n) =$ | 1 | n |
| $x^n$ | − | 2 | ÷ |

→ **The general or $n$th term of a sequence allows you to find any term by substituting its position into a formula.**
**For example, the sequence of cube numbers**
**can be written in the form**
**where $T(1) = 1^3$, $T(2) = 2^3$, $T(3) = 3^3$, ...**

1, 8, 27, 64, 125, ...
$1^3$, $2^3$, $27^3$, $64^3$, $125^3$, ...
so $T(n) = n^3$

**EXAMPLE**

Find the $n$th term of the sequence 4, 9, 14, 19, 24, ...

**ANSWER**

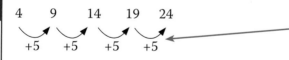

4    9    14    19    24

+5    +5    +5    +5

> The difference between consecutive terms is 5.
> The $n$th term involves the 5 times table.
> For the 5 times table, the $n$th term is $T(n) = 5n$

| Position number, $n$ | 1 | 2 | 3 | 4 | 5 |
| 5 times table, $5n$ | 5 | 10 | 15 | 20 | 25 |
| $n$th term, $T(n)$ | 4 | 9 | 14 | 19 | 24 |

$\times 5$

$-1$

> A linear sequence occurs when the differences between consecutive terms are constant.

In words the $n$th term is 'multiply the position number by 5 and subtract 1'
As a formula        $T(n) = 5n - 1$

→ **The $n$th term of a linear sequence is of the form $T(n) = an + b$ where $a$ is the difference between consecutive terms.**

## Exercise A5.3

**1** Copy and complete the working below to find the *n*th term of the sequence 1, 4, 7, 10, 13, …

1    4    7    10    13

+__    +__    +__    +__

| Position number, *n* | 1 | 2 | 3 | 4 | 5 |
|---|---|---|---|---|---|
| __times table, __*n* |  |  |  |  |  |
| *n*th term, T(*n*) | 1 | 4 | 7 | 10 | 13 |

×__

−__

The *n*th term is T(*n*) =_____.

**2** Find the *n*th term of each of these sequences.

    **a** 7, 14, 21, 28, 35, …    **b** 5, 8, 11, 14, 17, …    **c** 14, 18, 22, 26, 30, …

    **d** 5, 11, 17, 23, 29, …    **e** 8, 18, 28, 38, 48, …    **f** 25, 30, 35, 40, 45, …

    **g** −6, −2, 2, 6, 10, …    **h** 2.2, 2.4, 2.6, 2.8, 3.0, …    **i** 99, 98, 97, 96, 95, …

    **j** 45, 40, 35, 30, 25, …    **k** 1, −3, −7, −11, −15, …

**3** **RICH TASK**

Write three linear sequences that have a third term of 12.
For each sequence, find
    **a** the *n*th term    **b** T(100)

**4** Using the information given for each sequence, find
    **i** the *n*th term   **ii** the first five terms.
    **a** T(8) = 34, T(9) = 37, T(10) = 40    **b** T(20) = 155, T(21) = 163, T(22) = 171
    **c** T(10) = 53, T(12) = 63

**5** ☆ CHALLENGE ☆

*n* = height, T(*n*) = number of dots
Isla and Flora both write a formula for the number of dots in each diagram.
Isla writes T(*n*) = *n*(*n* + 2).    Flora writes T(*n*) = $n^2$ + 2*n*.
Who is correct? Explain your answer.

- Find the *n*th term of a sequence
- Justify the form of the *n*th term by referring to the context in which it was generated

## RICH TASK

Copy the table and add two more completed columns. Make sketch diagrams to help you. Explain how to find the number of diagonals of an octagon using a term-to-term rule.

A square has 2 diagonals.

A pentagon has 5 diagonals.

| Number of sides | 1 | 2 | 3 | 4 | 5 |
|---|---|---|---|---|---|
| Number of diagonals | – | – | 0 | 2 | 5 |

EXAMPLE

Find a rule that relates the number of triangles, *n*, to the number of matchsticks, *m*. Explain why the rule works by referring to the diagrams.

1 triangle       2 triangles       3 triangles

**ANSWER**

The number of matchsticks is 3, 5, 7, 9, …

The difference between consecutive terms is 2. The formula involves the 2 times table.

| Number of triangles, *n* | 1 | 2 | 3 | 4 |
|---|---|---|---|---|
| 2 times table, 2*n* | 2 | 4 | 6 | 8 |
| Number of matchsticks, *m* | 3 | 5 | 7 | 9 |

× 2

+1

In words       'to find the number of matchsticks, *m*, multiply the number of triangles, *n*, by 2 and add 1'

As a formula     $m = 2n + 1$

The formula works because each new triangle requires 2 matchsticks plus 1 matchstick to close the first triangle.

**Exercise A5.4**

*1  Find a rule that relates the number of pentagons, *n*, to the number of matchsticks, *m*.
Explain why the rule works by referring to the diagrams.

  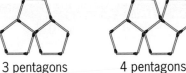

1 pentagon    2 pentagons    3 pentagons    4 pentagons

*2  **a**  Find a rule that connects the number of red tiles, *r*, to the number of white tiles, *w*.

**b**  Use your formula to find the number of white tiles surrounding 50 red tiles.

**c**  Explain why your formula works.

*3

1 triangle    2 triangles    3 triangles    4 triangles

The formula that connects the number of triangles, *t*, to the number of coloured straws, *s* is    $s = 3t + 2$

Explain why this formula works.

4  Hydrocarbons consist of hydrogen (H) and carbon (C) atoms bonded together. Most of the compounds in crude oil are hydrocarbons.

  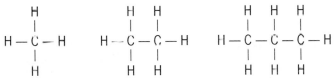

Methane $CH_4$    Ethane $C_2H_6$    Propane $C_3H_8$

**a**  Write a formula to relate the number of carbon atoms (C) to hydrogen atoms (H).

**b**  Use your formula to copy and complete this statement:
'Octane has the chemical formula $C_8H_\square$'

**c**  Investigate the names and chemical formulae of other linear hydrocarbons.

5  ☆ **CHALLENGE** ☆

Find a rule that relates the height of each rectangle, *h*, to the number of tiles, *t*, by inspecting the diagrams.

# Summary and assessment

## CHECK OUT

**You should now be able to**

- generate terms of a sequence using term-to-term and position-to-term rules
- describe the *n*th term of a sequence
- generate common integer sequences.

### Exam-style question

Four numbers in a sequence are given by

$2n + 1 \quad 2n + 5 \quad 2n + 9 \quad 2n + 13$

**a** Explain why the numbers in this sequence are odd numbers.

**b** Write down the term-to-term rule for numbers in this sequence.

'Explain' may mean that you do some mathematics, but you may also need to write an explanation.

It is helpful to show your thinking.

**Shipa's answer:**

**a** All the numbers in the sequence are 2 times a number plus an odd number.

2 x a whole number = an even number

An even number + an odd number = an odd number

So the numbers in the sequence will always be odd.

To explain it is not always enough to give an example.

For *n* = 1 the sequence is 3, 7, 11, 13

This is not enough for an explanation.

**b** The difference between each pair of numbers is 4

$(2n + 5) - (2n + 1) = 4$

$(2n + 9) - (2n + 5) = 4$ etc

The term-to-term rule is +4

## Exam practice

**1 a** Write down the next two terms in this sequence

4   7   10   13   ____   ____

**b** Describe, in words, the rules for continuing this sequence

3   6   12   24   ____   ____

**c** The $n$th term of a sequence is $n^2 + 1$.

Write down the first three terms of this sequence.

*(6 marks)*

**2** Ellen has left the kitchen sink almost full with water and the kitchen tap is still on.

The distances, in mm, from the water level to the top of the sink, measured each minute are:

37      34      31      28

If the tap is not switched off, how much longer will it take for the sink to overflow?

*(3 marks)*

**\*3** A sequence is formed by counting the number of diagonals, $d$, formed in polygons with $p$ sides.

The first three polygons and number of diagonals in the sequence are as follows:

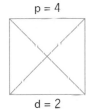
p = 4
d = 2

p = 5
d = 5

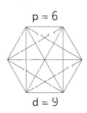
p = 6
d = 9

**a** Find the next two values in this sequence.

**b** Find a rule to find the number of diagonals $d$ in a polygon with $p$ sides and explain why your rule only works for $p \geq 4$.

*(6 marks)*

# 6 Representing and interpreting data

## CHECK IN

1 Calculate

   a $\frac{1}{2}$ of 124     b $\frac{1}{2}$ of 140     c $\frac{1}{4}$ of 240

   d $\frac{1}{4}$ of 180     e $\frac{3}{4}$ of 136     f $\frac{3}{4}$ of 144

Use this graph showing the cost per day to hire a power tool for questions **2** and **3**.

2 How much does it cost to hire the power tool for
   a 3 days     b 5 days?

3 Mike has £40.
   What is the maximum number of days he can hire the power tool?

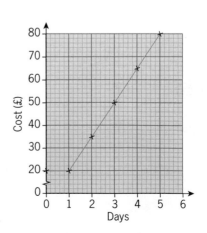

| What I should know | What I will learn | What this leads to |
|---|---|---|
| **A2** Key stage 3 | ■ Draw frequency diagrams, cumulative frequency diagrams and box plots<br>■ Draw histograms | B13 |

### RICH TASK

The taller you are the heavier you are.

Investigate if this statement is true by looking at different age groups.

# Frequency diagrams

- Draw and produce frequency diagrams
- Identify the modal class for grouped data

You can use a **frequency diagram** to represent continuous data.

Thao shows a tray of nine objects for exactly 20 seconds to a large sample of men and women.
She summarises the time they took to recall all nine objects in these tables.

Men

| Time, $t$ seconds | Frequency |
|---|---|
| $0 < t \leq 20$ | 5 |
| $20 < t \leq 40$ | 11 |
| $40 < t \leq 60$ | 13 |
| $60 < t \leq 80$ | 20 |
| $80 < t \leq 100$ | 16 |
| $100 < t \leq 120$ | 7 |

Women

| Time, $t$ seconds | Frequency |
|---|---|
| $0 < t \leq 20$ | 7 |
| $20 < t \leq 40$ | 22 |
| $40 < t \leq 60$ | 18 |
| $60 < t \leq 80$ | 16 |
| $80 < t \leq 100$ | 6 |
| $100 < t \leq 120$ | 3 |

Draw frequency diagrams to represent the times taken by the men and the women. Use the diagrams to compare the times taken.

**ANSWER**

Plot coordinates using the **midpoint** of each class: (10, 5), (30, 11) and so on.

> The midpoint is a representative value for each class.

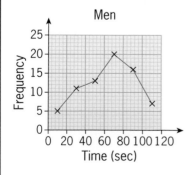

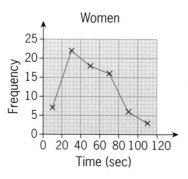

> These diagrams are often called frequency polygons.

The men tended to take longer than the women to recall the objects as the modal class for men, 60–80, is higher than for women, 20–40. The ranges are broadly similar as both men and women have times within 0–20 seconds and 100–120 seconds.

You can compare continuous distributions by:
- **modal class** – compare where the graph peaks (not how high the peak is)
- **range** – compare the ranges of class intervals

**EXAMPLE**

Here is part of a report that appeared in a school magazine.

Year 7 pupils are spending twice as long on homework each night as Year 10 pupils

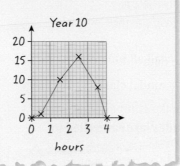

Is the report fair?

**ANSWER**

No: the year 7 modal class is 3 to 4 hours, whereas the year 10 modal class is 2 to 3 hours. The range of time spent on homework is the same.

## Exercise A6.1

**MEDIUM**

*1  David carried out a survey to find the time taken by 120 teachers and 120 office workers to travel home from work.

Teachers

| Time, t, minutes | Frequency |
| --- | --- |
| 0 < t ≤ 10 | 12 |
| 10 < t ≤ 20 | 33 |
| 20 < t ≤ 30 | 48 |
| 30 < t ≤ 40 | 20 |
| 40 < t ≤ 50 | 7 |

Office workers

| Time, t, minutes | Frequency |
| --- | --- |
| 10 < t ≤ 20 | 2 |
| 20 < t ≤ 30 | 21 |
| 30 < t ≤ 40 | 51 |
| 40 < t ≤ 50 | 28 |
| 50 < t ≤ 60 | 18 |

a  Draw frequency polygons for these data
b  Work out for each data set the
   i  modal class          ii  range
c  Use your answers to **b** and make comparisons, with reasons, between the time taken by the teachers and office workers to travel home from work.

**Continued ➤**

*2 Jayne kept a daily record of the number of miles she travelled in her car during two months.

December

| Miles travelled (m) | Frequency |
|---|---|
| 0 < m ≤ 20 | 3 |
| 20 < m ≤ 40 | 8 |
| 40 < m ≤ 60 | 10 |
| 60 < m ≤ 80 | 6 |
| 80 < m ≤ 100 | 4 |

January

| Miles travelled (m) | Frequency |
|---|---|
| 0 < m ≤ 20 | 0 |
| 20 < m ≤ 40 | 5 |
| 40 < m ≤ 60 | 12 |
| 60 < m ≤ 80 | 8 |
| 80 < m ≤ 100 | 6 |

a   Draw frequency polygons for these data

b   Work out for each data set the   i   modal class      ii   range

c   Use your answers to **a** and **b** and make comparisons, with reasons, between the number of miles Jayne travelled in December and January.

*3 Two different companies, Duracomp and Powerblast, claim that their batteries are the ones to buy. The tables show the times that samples of batteries from these two companies lasted.

Duracomp

| Time, t hours | Frequency |
|---|---|
| 0 < t ≤ 5 | 8 |
| 5 < t ≤ 10 | 6 |
| 10 < t ≤ 15 | 7 |
| 15 < t ≤ 20 | 5 |
| 20 < t ≤ 25 | 0 |
| 25 < t ≤ 30 | 4 |

Powerblast

| Time, t hours | Frequency |
|---|---|
| 0 < t ≤ 5 | 3 |
| 5 < t ≤ 10 | 9 |
| 10 < t ≤ 15 | 7 |
| 15 < t ≤ 20 | 8 |
| 20 < t ≤ 25 | 2 |
| 25 < t ≤ 30 | 1 |

a   Draw frequency polygons to represent these data

b   By finding different and appropriate measures, comment on the claims made by these two companies giving reasons for your comments. Decide which of the two companies you would recommend.

**ADDITIONAL TASK:**

Draw a histogram for the Duracomp data, on the same diagram as the frequency polygon. How do the two types of diagram relate to each other?

**\*4** These two graphs were drawn to summarise the football premiership points score for two different years.

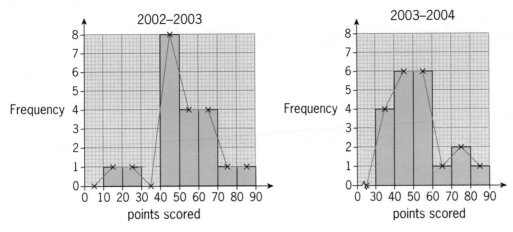

The following news report was written about one of these two years.

> 57 $\frac{1}{2}$ points were achieved on average with a range of 67 by teams in the premiership this season

Which year was being reported on? Give a reason for your choice.

**\*5** These two graphs summarise the distances travelled by representatives at two different firms.

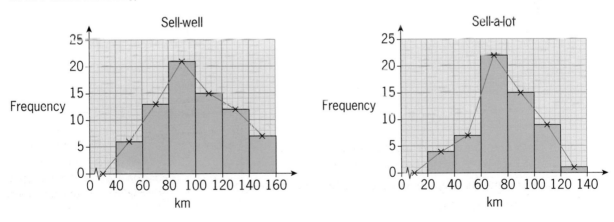

The following news report was written about one of the two firms.

> On average sales representatives at the firm travel 60km per day
> The range of distances travelled is 116km

Which firm was being reported on?

# Cumulative frequency diagrams

- Draw and produce cumulative frequency tables and diagrams

Thao wants to represent and analyse the men's recall time for all nine objects.
First she finds the **cumulative frequency** of the data which is a running
total of the frequencies.

| Time, $t$ seconds | Frequency |
|---|---|
| $0 < t \le 20$ | 5 |
| $20 < t \le 40$ | 14 |
| $40 < t \le 60$ | 19 |
| $60 < t \le 80$ | 28 |
| $80 < t \le 100$ | 14 |
| $100 < t \le 120$ | 8 |

| Time, $t$ seconds | Cumulative frequency |
|---|---|
| $0 < t \le 20$ | 5 |
| $0 < t \le 40$ | (5 + 14) = 19 |
| $0 < t \le 60$ | (19 + 19) = 38 |
| $0 < t \le 80$ | (38 + 28) = 66 |
| $0 < t \le 100$ | (66 + 14) = 80 |
| $0 < t \le 120$ | (80 + 8) = 88 |

Add frequencies to get cumulative frequency

Thao draws a **cumulative frequency polygon** of the data, joining points with
straight lines. She could alternatively draw a **cumulative frequency curve**.

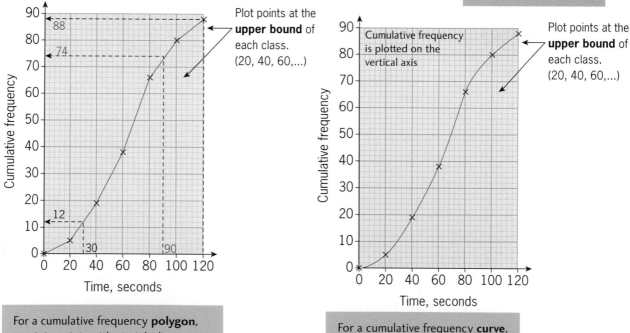

Plot points at the **upper bound** of each class. (20, 40, 60,...)

Cumulative frequency is plotted on the vertical axis

Plot points at the **upper bound** of each class. (20, 40, 60,...)

For a cumulative frequency **polygon**, you join points with straight lines.

For a cumulative frequency **curve**, join points with a smooth curve.

Thao uses her cumulative frequency diagram to find **estimates**.
Looking at the cumulative frequency polygon she estimates that…
12 people took less than 30 seconds to recall all nine objects.
14 people (88–74) took longer than 90 seconds.

## Exercise A6.2

**1** For each of the following draw a cumulative frequency diagram (remember to draw a cumulative frequency table first), and use your diagram to find estimates.

**a** The heights of 100 girls are given in the table.

| Height, $h$, cm | $145 \leq h < 150$ | $150 \leq h < 155$ | $155 \leq h < 160$ | $160 \leq h < 165$ | $165 \leq h < 170$ |
|---|---|---|---|---|---|
| Frequency | 9 | 27 | 45 | 16 | 3 |

Estimate the number of girls with height
**i** less than 154 cm       **ii** greater than 162 cm.

**b** The table gives information about the ages of teachers in a school.

| Age, $A$ | $20 \leq A < 30$ | $30 \leq A < 40$ | $40 \leq A < 50$ | $50 \leq A < 60$ | $60 \leq A < 70$ |
|---|---|---|---|---|---|
| Frequency | 22 | 35 | 53 | 25 | 15 |

Estimate the number of teachers who are aged
**i** less than 25       **ii** over 45.

**c** The table gives information about the weight of a sample of cats and kittens.

| Weight, $w$ grams | Frequency |
|---|---|
| $1500 \leq w < 2000$ | 7 |
| $2000 \leq w < 2500$ | 23 |
| $2500 \leq w < 3000$ | 34 |
| $3000 \leq w < 3500$ | 25 |
| $3500 \leq w < 4000$ | 11 |

Estimate how many cats and kittens weighed
**i** less than 2600 g       **ii** over 3300 g.

**2** 1200 runners competed in a half marathon. The fastest time was 63 minutes. The first 120 runners finished the race in less than 90 minutes. A total of 280 runners finished the race in less than 2 hours. Another 420 runners took longer than 2 hours, but less than $2\frac{1}{2}$ hours. Only 50 runners took longer than 3 hours and the slowest 3 hours 26 minutes.

Estimate, from a cumulative frequency diagram,
**i** how many runners completed the race within 2 hours 45 minutes
**ii** how long it took the first 500 runners to complete the half marathon.

★ **DISCUSSION** ★

Which type of graph is likely to give more accurate estimates: a cumulative frequency curve, or a cumulative frequency polygon?

- Draw and produce box plots
- Find the quartiles for large data sets

Thao uses her cumulative frequency graph to find the **median** and **quartiles**.

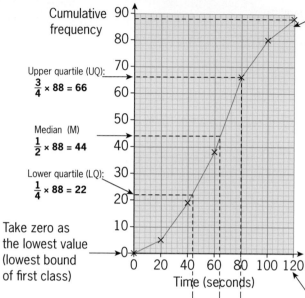

Cumulative frequency

Upper quartile (UQ):
$\frac{3}{4} \times 88 = 66$

Median (M)
$\frac{1}{2} \times 88 = 44$

Lower quartile (LQ):
$\frac{1}{4} \times 88 = 22$

Take 120 as the highest value (upper bound of last class)

The median is 64, not 44. Use the vertical axis to locate the median and quartiles, then use the horizontal axis to find the actual values.

She finds these statistics from the graph:
LQ = 44
M  = 64
UQ = 80

Thao then draws a **box-and-whisker** diagram or **box plot**.

Take zero as the lowest value (lowest bound of first class)

A box plot just shows the median, quartiles and extreme values.

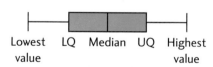

Use the median and quartiles from the graph to draw the vertical lines of the box.

Read along this axis for the actual values of the median and quartiles

p. 24

Lowest value   LQ   Median   UQ   Highest value

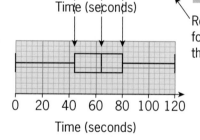

0   20   40   60   80   100   120
Time (seconds)

---

## RICH TASK

Jodie and Fred each recorded the heights of the same sample of sunflowers.

Use the information to draw bo-and-whisker diagrams, and comment on the differences and similarities that are shown by recording the information differently.

You will first need to draw cumulative frequency diagrams to find the median and quartiles.

| Jodie | |
|---|---|
| Height, $h$ cm | Frequency |
| $50 \le h < 70$ | 7 |
| $70 \le h < 90$ | 33 |
| $90 \le h < 110$ | 49 |
| $110 \le h < 130$ | 21 |
| $130 \le h < 150$ | 10 |

| Fred | |
|---|---|
| Height, $h$ cm | Frequency |
| $50 \le h < 75$ | 12 |
| $75 \le h < 100$ | 50 |
| $100 \le h < 125$ | 41 |
| $125 \le h < 150$ | 7 |

Unit A

*1  Nick surveys the waiting times for patients at a local surgery for
both dentists and doctors.
Draw box-and-whisker diagrams and **compare** the waiting times
for the doctors and dentists.

In comparing these data sets
you should compare the
medians, and also the IQR to
see which is more variable.

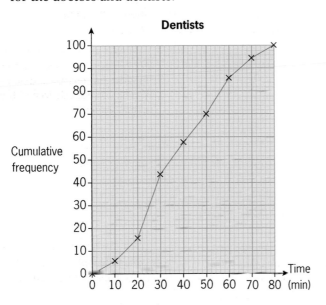

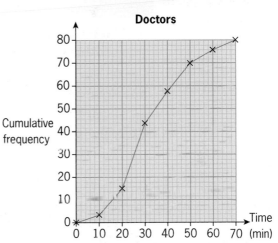

*2  The cumulative frequency graphs show the number of correctly
answered general knowledge questions for two groups of adults.

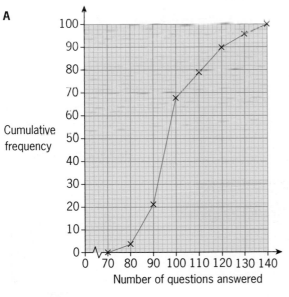

A team of five is chosen from each group to compete in a quiz.
Decide with reasons which group may perform better in the quiz.

- Draw and produce histograms for grouped continuous data
- Understand and use frequency density

Jenny and Robert timed how long 5-year-olds took to complete a simple puzzle.
They presented the same data, each using a **histogram** in different ways.

| Time, $t$ seconds | Frequency |
|---|---|
| $0 < t \le 10$ | 11 |
| $10 < t \le 20$ | 27 |
| $20 < t \le 30$ | 32 |
| $30 < t \le 40$ | 17 |
| $40 < t \le 50$ | 8 |
| $50 < t \le 60$ | 5 |

Jenny chooses equal class intervals with a width of 10

| Time, $t$ seconds | Frequency |
|---|---|
| $0 < t \le 10$ | 11 |
| $10 < t \le 15$ | 12 |
| $15 < t \le 20$ | 15 |
| $20 < t \le 25$ | 22 |
| $25 < t \le 35$ | 17 |
| $35 < t \le 45$ | 14 |
| $45 < t \le 60$ | 9 |

Robert chooses unequal class intervals, with different widths

Jenny divides each frequency by 10 to find the **frequency density**

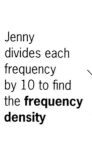
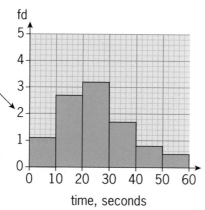

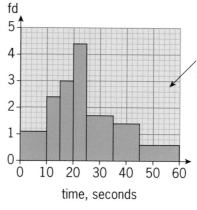

Robert divides each frequency by the class width to find his frequency densities.

→ The area of each bar in a histogram represents frequency.
→ The height of each bar is the frequency density.

$$\text{Frequency density} = \frac{\text{frequency}}{\text{class width}}$$

This table shows how Robert calculated his frequency densities.

| Time, $t$ seconds | Frequency | Class width | F ÷ CW | Frequency density |
|---|---|---|---|---|
| $0 < t \le 10$ | 11 | 10 | 11 ÷ 10 | 1.1 |
| $10 < t \le 15$ | 12 | 5 | 12 ÷ 5 | 2.4 |
| $15 < t \le 20$ | 15 | 5 | 15 ÷ 5 | 3 |
| $20 < t \le 25$ | 22 | 5 | 22 ÷ 5 | 4.4 |
| $25 < t \le 35$ | 17 | 10 | 17 ÷ 10 | 1.7 |
| $35 < t \le 45$ | 14 | 10 | 14 ÷ 10 | 1.4 |
| $45 < t \le 60$ | 9 | 15 | 9 ÷ 15 | 0.6 |

The histogram shows the time spent on the internet one evening by a sample of students.

a Estimate the number of students that spent longer than 50 minutes on the internet.

b How many students were included in the sample?

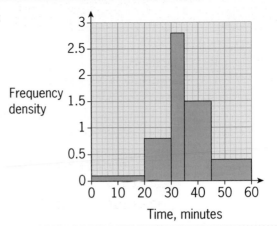

Frequency density

Time, minutes

**ANSWER**

a Area that represents > 50 minutes is part of the last bar only.
Bar height × width of required part of the bar    $0.4 \times 10 = 4$
4 students spent longer than 50 minutes on the internet.

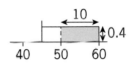

b $(0.1 \times 20) + (0.8 \times 10) + (2.8 \times 5) + (1.5 \times 10) + (0.4 \times 15) = 2 + 8 + 14 + 15 + 6 = 45$
45 students were included in the sample.

The incomplete table and histogram give some information about the length of phone calls that Wendy makes at work on one day.

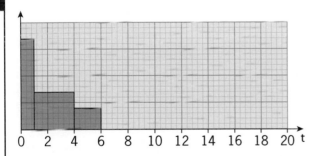

| Time, $t$, minutes | Frequency |
|---|---|
| $0 \leq t < 1$ | 17 |
| $1 \leq t < 4$ | |
| $4 \leq t < 6$ | |
| $6 \leq t < 10$ | 12 |
| $10 \leq t < 20$ | 10 |

a Use the information in the histogram to find the missing frequencies in the table.

b Complete the histogram.

*Continued* ➤

**ANSWER**

a  $0 \leq t < 1$   frequency density: $\frac{17}{1} = 17$

 $1 \leq t < 4$   frequency: $7 \times 3 = 21$ calls
 $4 \leq t < 6$   frequency: $4 \times 2 = 8$ calls

b

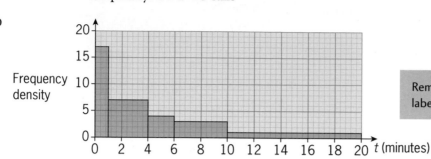

Frequency density

Remember to scale and label the vertical axis.

### Exercise A6.4

**HIGH**

1  For each part
   - draw tables to find the frequency densities
   - draw a histogram to represent the information
   - find estimates from the data.

   a  Jimmy recorded the amount spent by the first 100 customers in his shop one Saturday.
   Estimate the number of customers who spent more than £50.

   | Amount spent £$A$ | Frequency |
   |---|---|
   | $0 \leq A < 5$ | 6 |
   | $5 \leq A < 10$ | 10 |
   | $10 \leq A < 20$ | 23 |
   | $20 \leq A < 40$ | 29 |
   | $40 \leq A < 60$ | 24 |
   | $60 \leq A < 100$ | 8 |

   b  Andy summarised the information he collected on distance travelled to work by a sample of office workers.
   Estimate the number of office workers who travelled less than 8 miles to work.

   | Distance, $d$ miles | Frequency |
   |---|---|
   | $0 \leq d < 2$ | 8 |
   | $2 \leq d < 5$ | 15 |
   | $5 \leq d < 10$ | 27 |
   | $10 \leq d < 20$ | 44 |
   | $20 \leq d < 30$ | 6 |

   c  Elizabeth recorded the distance swum by children in a sponsored swim.
   Estimate the number of children who swam
   i   less than 1 kilometre
   ii  more than 2 kilometres.

   | Distance, $d$ km | Frequency |
   |---|---|
   | $0.1 \leq d < 0.2$ | 3 |
   | $0.2 \leq d < 0.5$ | 12 |
   | $0.5 \leq d < 1$ | 22 |
   | $1 \leq d < 2$ | 25 |
   | $2 \leq d < 5$ | 18 |

**2** The histogram shows the time spent watching TV one evening by a sample of students.

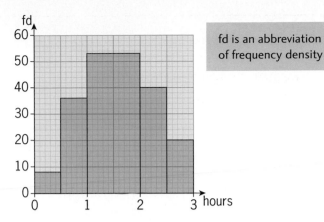

fd is an abbreviation of frequency density

**a** How many students spent longer than $2\frac{1}{2}$ hours watching TV?

**b** Copy and complete the frequency table for these data.

**c** How many students were in the sample?

| Time, $t$ hours | $0 \le t < 0.5$ | $0.5 \le t < 1$ | $1 \le t < 2$ | $2 \le t < 2.5$ | $2.5 \le t < 3$ |
|---|---|---|---|---|---|
| Frequency | | | | | |

**3** The histogram shows the distance $d$ that teachers at a particular school travel to work each day.

**a** How many teachers travel 5–10 km?

**b** Draw and complete a frequency table for these data.

**c** How many teachers were in the sample?

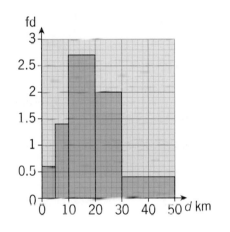

**4** The incomplete table and histogram give some information about the weight, in grams, of a sample of apples.

| Weight, $g$ grams | Frequency |
|---|---|
| $120 \le g < 140$ | 8 |
| $140 \le g < 150$ | 6 |
| $150 \le g < 155$ | |
| $155 \le g < 160$ | |
| $160 \le g < 165$ | |
| $165 \le g < 175$ | 16 |
| $175 \le g < 185$ | 12 |
| $185 \le g < 200$ | 6 |

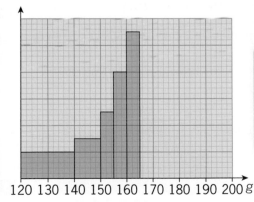

**a** Use the information in the histogram to copy and complete the table.

**b** Copy and complete the histogram.

- Compare distributions and make inferences

## ☆ ACTIVITY ☆

Ursula collects data on the times taken by a sample of boys and a sample of girls to complete a sudoku puzzle. She draws two histograms to summarise her results.
Compare the times taken by the boys and the girls.

Compare the modal classes – these are the bars with greatest area.

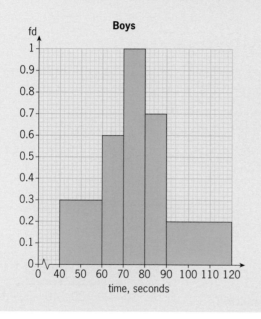

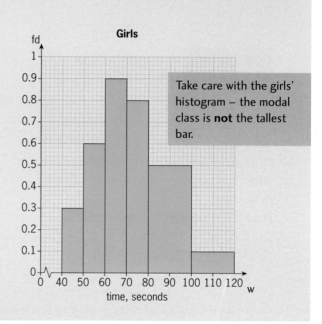

Take care with the girls' histogram – the modal class is **not** the tallest bar.

→ **The modal class is given by the bar on a histogram with greatest area.**

The shape of a histogram can indicate if the distribution is **skewed**.

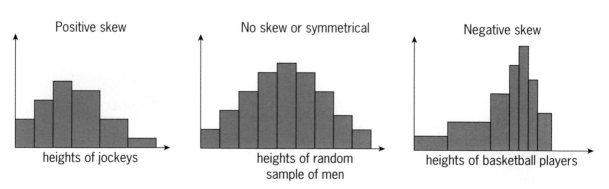

You can use **skewness,** along with summary statistics, to compare distributions. In the sudoku activity above, both distributions are positively skewed, the girls more than the boys. This means that the girls' times are more clustered towards the lower end than the boys, implying that girls are faster.

*1 Compare the heights of two samples of boys of different ages as summarised in these histograms.

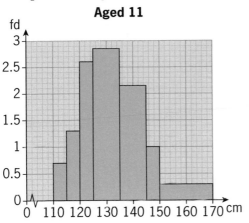

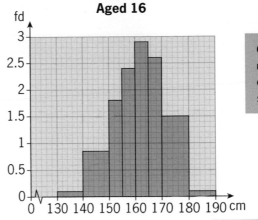

Compare modal class and skewness.

*2 Compare the weights of samples of apples and of pears as summarised in these histograms.

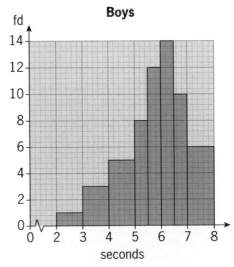

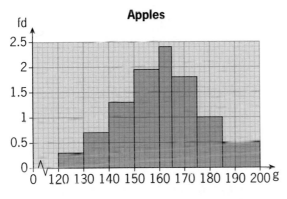

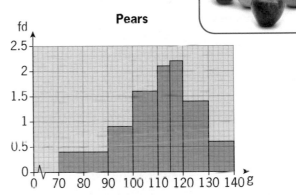

*3 Compare the reaction times of girls and boys as summarised in these histograms.

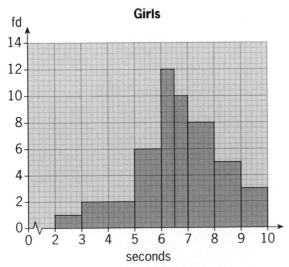

**CHECK OUT**

**You should now be able to draw and interpret**
- frequency diagrams
- cumulative frequency diagrams
- box-and-whisker plots from cumulative frequency diagrams
- histograms.

*

**Exam-style question**

The histogram shows the speeds of 180 vehicles travelling along a stretch of road in the UK.

**a** Use the histogram to determine the likely speed restriction for that stretch of road.

**b** Should the time of day that the speeds were recorded have any effect on your answer?

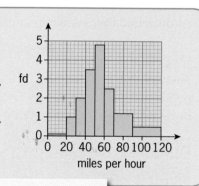

**Anja's answer:**

a   Road speeds range from below 20 mph to 120 mph.
    Positive skew with very few below 40mph so speed restriction likely to be higher than 40 mph.
    Anything above 70 is speeding, but these need to be accounted for in calculations
    Modal class 50 – 60; this suggests the speed restriction is 60mph. There are 26 + 24 + 15 = 65 drivers going above 60; about 1/3 of the speeds recorded
    Speed restriction 60mph, if most drivers law abiding

b   Time of day may make a difference as at peak traffic times, cars cannot always travel up to the limit of the road.

Think about the context of the question and use it in your answers.

Look at the shape of the graph and comment on what it tells you.

Back up final answers with the maths.

Work out summary statistics and comment on what they imply.

## Exam practice

**1** Reuben kept a daily record of the time in minutes he cycled during two months. The table summarises the data for July.

| Time (*m*, minutes) | Frequency |
|---|---|
| $0 < m \leq 5$ | 6 |
| $5 < m \leq 10$ | 11 |
| $10 < m \leq 15$ | 10 |
| $15 < m \leq 20$ | 4 |

**a** Draw a frequency polygon for these data.

**b** This frequency polygon represents the data Reuben collected for August.
Write down one similarity and one difference between the daily times for which Reuben cycled during July and August.

Frequency

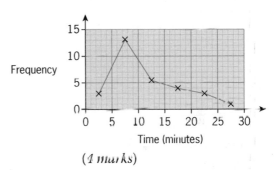

*(4 marks)*

**2** The mob run is a cross-country event that all Year 7 and Year 8 pupils take part in at a school. Chris summarised the times taken by the pupils to complete the mob run in this table.

| Time (*t*, minutes) | Frequency |
|---|---|
| $15 < t \leq 20$ | 16 |
| $20 < t \leq 24$ | 46 |
| $24 < t \leq 26$ | 27 |
| $26 < t \leq 28$ | 40 |
| $28 < t \leq 30$ | 31 |
| $30 < t \leq 35$ | 72 |
| $35 < t \leq 40$ | 8 |

Draw a histogram to represent these data.

*(4 marks)*

**3** 112 runners completed a cross-country race. The fastest time was 18 minutes.
22 runners finished the race in less than 30 minutes.
A total of 57 runners finished the race in less than 40 minutes.
Another 45 runners took more than 40 minutes but less than 50 minutes.
The last runner to complete the race finished in 67 minutes.

**a** Draw a cumulative frequency diagram to represent these data.

**b** Use your diagram to draw a box-and-whisker plot.

*(6 marks)*

# Case study 2: Sandwich shop

The manager of a catering company can use data about customer numbers in order to spot trends in customer behaviour and to plan for the future.

## Simply Sandwiches

Simply **andwiches**

wiches, paninis, baguettes and salads

## Simply Sandwiches

Customer numbers at 'Simply sandwiches' takeaway over a given two-week period were:

| Day | Number of Customers | |
|---|---|---|
| | Week 1 | Week 2 |
| Monday | 50 | 54 |
| Tuesday | 68 | 60 |
| Wednesday | 47 | 53 |
| Thursday | 58 | 57 |
| Friday | 52 | 56 |
| Saturday | 76 | 70 |
| Total | | |

## Simply Sandwiches

Work out an appropriate average number of customers for

a)  each day of the week
b)  the whole week in total.

How does your answer to a) differ if

c)  you exclude Saturdays
d)  a 24-person coach trip arrives on the second Wednesday?

Construct a pie chart to show what percentage of customers visited the sandwich shop on each day during this two-week period.

Comment on the spread of the data, referring to the data and your chart.

This frequency polygon shows customer numbers during each hour on the first Saturday, the busiest day during this two-week period:

What was the busiest/quietest time of day?

What can you say about the relationship between time of day and customer numbers? Would you expect every day of the week to have a similar pattern?

Justify your answers referring to the data.

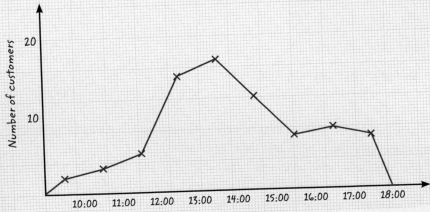

t Check

CHECK NUMBER

GUESTS   143001

How do you think the manager could use such data about customer numbers?

A manager can use data about customer numbers to estimate how much stock to order each week. In reality, limitations due to space and the shelf life of products also apply.

In the second week of the two-week period at 'Simply sandwiches', total percentage sales of the different varieties of sandwiches were:

| Variety | Ham | Cheese | Hummous | Tuna | Chicken |
|---------|-----|--------|---------|------|---------|
| % sales | 26 | 18 | 10 | 15 | 31 |

How many of each sandwich were sold during this week? (assuming every customer bought one sandwich)

The manager does a weekly stocktake every Sunday before placing the order for the following week.

The stocktake figures for this week were:

| Product | Bread | Ham | Cheese | Hummous | Tuna | Chicken |
|---------|-------|-----|--------|---------|------|---------|
| Stock (packs) | 0 | 2.5 | 3 | 2 | 1.5 | 1 |

**Note that:**

Each loaf of bread makes 20 sandwiches;

Each pack of ham, cheese and chicken contains 10 portions;

Each tub of hummous contains 8 portions;

Each can of tuna contains 14 portions.

Use the information given to estimate the amount of each product that the manager should order to last for the following week.

Record your estimations in a table.

The stock will be delivered on Wednesday.

A coach trip of 24 people arrives unexpectedly and places the following order on Tuesday, before the new stock arrives.

| Sandwich | Ham | Cheese | Hummous | Tuna | Chicken |
|----------|-----|--------|---------|------|---------|
| Quantity | 4 | 7 | 5 | 3 | 5 |

Would 'Simply sandwiches' be able to cater for this order?

How would you advise the manager to prepare for such situations in the future?

*Simply Sandwiches*

sandwiches, paninis, baguettes and salads

# Formulae and equations

## INTRODUCTION

Calculating the cost of using a mobile phone, or the amount of fuel burned off by a racing car, are all examples of mathematical equations. Mathematicians turn problems in the real world into mathematical equations which they know how to solve.

**What's the point?**
Learning how to solve equations allows complicated real-life problems to be solved. Formula 1 engineers use complex mathematical equations to predict the effect on performance of their cars when they make technical modifications.

## CHECK IN

1 Work out these multiplications and divisions mentally.
   a $15 \times 3$    b $4 \times 13$    c $(-2) \times 13$    d $14 \times 14$
   e $56 \div 8$    f $91 \div 7$    g $150 \div (-3)$    h $1200 \div 40$

2 Explain why the answer to each calculation is 15.
   a $9 + 3 \times 2$    b $18 - 9 \div 3$    c $(3 + 2) \times 3$    d $3^3 - 4 \times 3$

3 Find the highest common factor of these number pairs.
   a 6 and 9    b 8 and 12    c 20 and 30    d 12 and 18
   e 24 and 52    f 50 and 75    g 99 and 132    h 7 and 14

**What I should know**

Key stage 3

**What I will learn**

- Solve equations
- Derive formulae
- Rearrange formulae

**What this leads to**

B11

## RICH TASK

In this diagram the equation $3x + 2 = 17$ has been changed in different ways, but all of these ways still give the same solution, $x = 5$.

Describe each change to the equation.

Continue each change for at least one more step.

Invent some changes of your own.

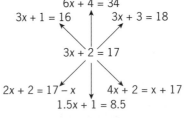

$$6x + 4 = 34$$
$$3x + 1 = 16 \qquad 3x + 3 = 18$$
$$3x + 2 = 17$$
$$2x + 2 = 17 - x \qquad 4x + 2 = x + 17$$
$$1.5x + 1 = 8.5$$

# Using and deriving formulae

- Substitute into formulae from mathematics and other subjects
- Derive a formula

## RICH TASK

Flora makes a tower using three blue cubes. Then she paints the outside of the tower red.

How many faces are red? What if the tower is made using 10 cubes? 100 cubes?

Flora knocks the tower down. How many blue faces can she see?

**EXAMPLE**

Find the volume of this cylinder.
Use the formula $V = \pi r^2 h$
Give your answer in terms of $\pi$.

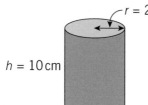

$r = 2.5\,\text{cm}$

$h = 10\,\text{cm}$

**ANSWER**

Substitute $r = 2.5$ and $h = 10$ into
$V = \pi r^2 h$

p. 330

$$V = \pi \times 2.5^2 \times 10$$
$$= \pi \times 6.25 \times 10$$
$$= 62.5\pi \ \text{cm}^3$$

**EXAMPLE**

In a garden, four circles of lawn are surrounded by flowerbeds. The garden is square of side $4x$ m.

**a** Derive a formula for the area of the flowerbeds.

**b** Calculate the area of the flowerbeds if the garden is a square of side 8 m.

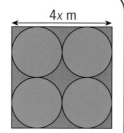

$4x$ m

**ANSWER**

**a** Area of garden $= 4x \times 4x$      Area of lawn $= 4 \times \pi r^2$
$\qquad\qquad\qquad = 16x^2$ $\qquad\qquad\qquad\quad = 4 \times \pi \times x^2$
$\qquad\qquad\qquad\qquad\qquad\qquad\qquad\qquad\quad = 4\pi x^2$

The radius of one circle of lawn is $4x \div 4 = x$

Area of flowerbeds = area of garden − area of lawn
$\qquad\qquad\qquad\qquad\quad = 16x^2 - 4\pi x^2$
$\qquad\qquad\qquad\qquad\quad = 4x^2(4 - \pi)$

You can factorise the formula.

**b** Area of flowerbeds $= 4x^2(4 - \pi)$
$\qquad\qquad\qquad\qquad\quad = 16(4 - \pi)$
$\qquad\qquad\qquad\qquad\quad = 13.7345 \ldots = 13.7\ \text{m}^2$ (3 s.f.)

The square is of side 8 m. Hence, the radius of one circle is $8 \div 4 = 2$ m and $x = 2$

MEDIUM

**1** Find the volume, $V$, of each shape using the formula given.

**a**

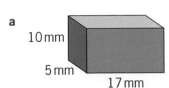

10 mm
5 mm
17 mm

**b**

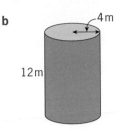

4 m
12 m

**c**

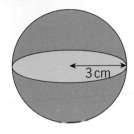

3 cm

$$V = lwh$$

where $l$ is the length, $w$ is width and $h$ is the height of the cuboid.

$$V = \pi r^2 h$$

where $r$ is the radius of the circle and $h$ is the height of the cylinder.

$$V = \frac{4}{3}\pi r^3$$

where $r$ is the radius of the sphere.

**2** Write a formula for the area, $A$, of each of these shapes.

**a**

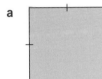

$l$

**b**

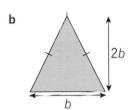

$2b$
$b$

**c**

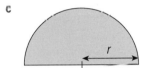

$r$

**3** A circular pond is surrounded by paving.
The radius of the pond is $x$ m.

**a** Show that a formula for the area, $A$, of the paving is
$$A = x^2(4 - \pi)$$

The expanded version is $A = 4x^2 - \pi x^2$

**b** Calculate the area of the paving if the pond has a radius of 2 m.

$x$ m

**4** A square stained glass window is made of red and yellow glass.
The window is of side $k$ m.

**a** Show that a formula for the area, $R$, of the red glass is
$$R = \frac{1}{4}\pi k^2$$

**b** Write a formula for the area, $Y$, of the yellow glass.

**c** Use your formula to find the area of the yellow glass if the window is a square of side 4 m.

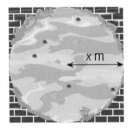

$k$

# Rearranging formulae

A7.2

- Change the subject of a formula
- Use real-life formulae

## RICH TASK

Here is a formula to convert $C$ degrees Celsius to $F$ degrees Fahrenheit.

$$F = \frac{9}{5}C + 32$$

Can you find a temperature at which the Celsius and Fahrenheit readings are the same?

→ **You can use inverse operations to change the subject of a formula.**

**EXAMPLE**

Rearrange the formula $C = \pi d$ to make $d$ the subject.

**ANSWER**

$C = \pi d$ The formula reads 'start with $d$ and multiply by $\pi$ to get $C$'.

$\frac{C}{\pi} = d$ The inverse of 'multiply by $\pi$' is 'divide by $\pi$'.

$d$ is now the subject because it is on its own.

**EXAMPLE**

Rearrange the formula $a = bx + c$ to make $x$ the subject.

**ANSWER**

$a = bx + c$ Start with $x$, multiply by $b$ and add $c$ to get $a$

$a - c = bx$ Subtract $c$ from both sides

$\frac{a - c}{b} = x$ Divide both sides by $b$

$x = \frac{a - c}{b}$

**EXAMPLE**

**a** Rearrange the formula

$V = \pi r^2 h$ to make $r$ the subject.

**b** Find $r$ when $V = 125\text{ cm}^3$ and $h = 10$ cm.

**ANSWER**

**a** $V = \pi r^2 h$

$\frac{V}{\pi h} = r^2$ Divide both sides by $\pi h$

$\sqrt{\frac{V}{\pi h}} = r$ Square root both sides

**b** $r = \sqrt{\frac{125}{\pi \times 10}}$

$r = 1.994711 \ldots$

$r = 2.0$ (2 s.f.)

## Exercise A7.2

**1** Make $x$ the subject of these formulae.

   **a** $x + t = k$       **b** $w = x + y - z$    **c** $10a = x - a$    **d** $a = x + bc$

   **e** $t = x + p^2$      **f** $gh + k = x - f$   **g** $p = \sqrt{q} + x$    **h** $a + b = a + x$

**2** Make $y$ the subject of these formulae.

   **a** $a = by$         **b** $k = \dfrac{y}{t}$      **c** $p = qy + r$    **d** $wy = x - z$

   **e** $b = ay + c^2$    **f** $\dfrac{y}{k} = m + n$    **g** $t^2 = \dfrac{y}{g - h}$    **h** $mny = k + t$

**3** A British recipe for toad-in-the-hole (sausages in batter) uses
a cooking temperature of 220 °C. A formula to convert degrees
Celsius to degrees Fahrenheit is

$$F = \frac{9}{5}C + 32$$

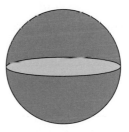

   **a** Caitlin's American oven uses degrees Fahrenheit. Work out
the temperature at which Caitlin should cook toad-in-the-hole.

   **b** Rearrange the formula to make $C$ the subject.

   **c** Key lime pie (an American dessert) requires a cooking temperature
of 350 °F. Work out the temperature in degrees Celsius. Give your
answer to a sensible degree of accuracy.

**4** Make $a$ the subject of these formulae.

   **a** $a^2 = x$        **b** $k - u^3 - t$      **c** $x = a^2 y$      **d** $\dfrac{a^2}{m} = n$

   **e** $\sqrt{a} = t$      **f** $\sqrt{a} + q = p$    **g** $2k = \sqrt{a}$    **h** $b - \sqrt[3]{u}$

**5** A formula for the volume of a sphere is

$$V = \frac{4}{3}\pi r^3$$

   **a** Rearrange this formula to make $r$ the subject.

   **b** Hence find the radius of a sphere with volume 300π cm³.
Give your answer to 3 significant figures.

**\*6** Victoria has got all of her mathematics homework on rearranging
formulae wrong. Copy out each question and explain the mistakes in each one.

   a         $y = 2x + c$     b  $xt - k = y$     c  $x^2 y = C$

             $y + c = 2x$          $t - k = \dfrac{y}{x}$       $xy = \sqrt{C}$

       $y + c - x = x$                  $x = \dfrac{\sqrt{C}}{y}$

                            $t = \dfrac{y - k}{x}$

- Construct and solve linear equations

## RICH TASK

In the pyramid, each box is the sum of the two boxes directly below. Work out the missing numbers and complete the pyramid.
What if the numbers on the bottom row are in a different order?
What if the bottom row has four boxes?

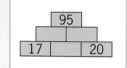

→ **To solve a linear equation, find the value of the unknown using inverse operations.**

A linear equation can be simplified to the form $ax + b = c$.

Solve these equations.
**a** $3(2x + 5) = 39$
**b** $\frac{x}{4} - 3 = 2$

**ANSWER**

You must perform the same operation on both sides of the equation.

**a** $3(2x + 5) = 39$

$6x + 15 = 39$    Expand the brackets

$6x = 24$    Subtract 15 from both sides

$x = 4$    Divide both sides by 6

**b** $\frac{x}{4} - 3 = 2$

$\frac{x}{4} = 5$    Add 3 to both sides

$x = 20$    Multiply both sides by 4

You can **derive** an equation to solve a problem.

*Derive* means deduce from the information given.

Find the angles of this triangle.

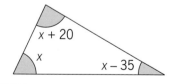

**ANSWER**

Use the fact that the angles of a triangle sum to 180°.

$x + (x + 20) + (x - 35) = 180$

$3x - 15 = 180$    Collect like terms

$3x = 195$    Add 15 to both sides

$x = 65$

The angles are 30°, 65° and 85°.

p. 278 ▶

## Exercise A7.3

**1** Solve these equations.

a $2x + 10 = 18$  b $16 = 3y - 5$  c $4t - 6 = 6$  d $11 + 8k = 11$

e $60 = 7p - 10$  f $2q + 5 = 6$  g $3g + 12 = 14$  h $6 = 10a - 3$

**2** Solve these equations.

a $2(x + 4) = 10$  b $5(3 + y) = 30$  c $\dfrac{a}{5} + 2 = 3$  d $\dfrac{2b - 5}{3} = 3$

e $20 = 4(2m - 1)$  f $\dfrac{n}{7} - 3 = 1$  g $8 = \dfrac{7k - 2}{5}$  h $3(7 + 4t) = 21$

**\*3** Form an equation and solve it to find the dimensions of each rectangle.

a
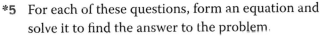
perimeter = 48 cm  2x − 1

5x + 4

b
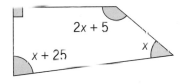
area = 32 cm²  4

3x − 7

**4** Solve these equations.

a $3(x + 4) + 5(x + 1) = 25$  b $4(k - 3) + 7(k + 2) = 35$

c $2(2t + 5) + 3(t - 1) = 42$  d $6(2k - 1) + 4(3k - 2) = 34$

e $5(3a - 2) - 2(4a + 1) = 16$  f $8(2b + 3) - 4(3b - 5) = 60$

> Expand the brackets and collect like terms. Take care with the negatives!

**\*5** For each of these questions, form an equation and solve it to find the answer to the problem.

a Find the size of the angles of this quadrilateral.

b Vivienne has three children. Victoria is twice as old as Jonathan and Jamie is one year younger than Victoria. The sum of their ages is 19. Find the ages of Vivienne's children.

$2x + 5$

$x$

$x + 25$

**6** Solve these equations.

a $5 - a = 3$  b $10 - 3n = 4$  c $1 = 6 - 5b$  d $3(7 - 2m) = 9$

e $8 - \dfrac{q}{2} = 5$  f $20 = 5(10 - 3x)$  g $15 - \dfrac{p}{4} = 10$  h $\dfrac{11 - 5x}{3} = 2$

> Take care with the negative terms.

**7** ☆ **CHALLENGE** ☆

For each of these questions, form an equation and solve it to find the answer to the problem.

a Jason has £50. He buys 4 brake pads for his mountain bike and is given £22 change. Work out the cost of each brake pad.

b Jason cycles to work and back in 66 minutes. On the way there he cycles at an average speed of 20 km/h and on the way back at an average speed of 24 km/h. Find the distance to Jason's work.

# Linear equations 2

- Form and solve linear equations with unknowns on both sides

## RICH TASK

Here is a two-way flow diagram.
For any value of $k$, you can choose to follow either the left or the right path.

Can you find a value of $k$ for which the left and right paths give the same value of $n$?

Can you make up a similar two-way flow diagram?

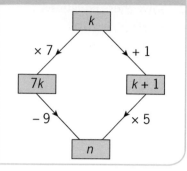

In the equation $\quad 3x + 4 = 2x + 9$

the unknown value, $x$, appears on both the left-hand and right-hand sides.

To solve the equation you have to get the unknown on one side only.

### EXAMPLE

Solve these equations.

**a** $5x + 3 = 9x - 5$

**b** $2(3a - 5) = 4(a + 3)$

#### ANSWER

**a** $5x + 3 = 9x - 5$

$\quad 3 = 4x - 5 \qquad$ – 5x from both sides

$\quad 8 = 4x \qquad$ + 5 to both sides

$\quad 2 = x \qquad$ ÷ by 4 on both sides

$\quad x = 2$

**b** $2(3a - 5) = 4(a + 3)$

$\quad 6a - 10 = 4a + 12 \qquad$ Expand the **brackets**

$\quad 2a - 10 = 12 \qquad$ – 4a from both sides

$\quad 2a = 22 \qquad$ + 10 to both sides

$\quad a = 11 \qquad$ ÷ by 2 on both sides

### EXAMPLE

Find the length of this rectangle.

$20 - 3t$

$5t + 4$

#### ANSWER

The two lengths of the rectangle are equal.

$\quad 20 - 3t = 5t + 4$

$\quad 20 = 8t + 4 \qquad$ + 3t to both sides

$\quad 16 = 8t \qquad$ – 4 from both sides

$\quad 2 = t \qquad$ ÷ by 8 on both sides

Substitute $t = 2$: $\qquad 5t + 4 = 5(2) + 4 = 14$

The length of the rectangle is 14 units.

To check your answer substitute $t = 2$ into $20 - 3t$. Try it and see what you get.

**1** Solve these equations with unknowns on both sides.

   **a** $2x + 3 = x + 10$     **b** $3k + 5 = k + 9$     **c** $8n - 3 = 4n + 1$

   **d** $3t - 2 = 7(t + 2)$    **e** $5(a - 2) = 9a - 2$    **f** $3(2p - 1) = 2p - 7$

**2** Samantha made two mistakes in each of the questions on her mathematics homework. Copy out her homework and correct each question as though you are her teacher.

   a  $2(x + 4) = 3x + 7$    b  $3x + 4 = 12 - x$    c  $5 - x = 4 - 3x$

         $2x + 4 = 3x + 7$         $2x + 4 = 12$          $5 + 2x = 4$

            $4 = x + 7$              $2x = 16$            $2x = 1$

              $x = 11$                $x = 8$             $x = 2$

**3** Solve these equations.

   **a** $2x + 1 = 10 - x$     **b** $5t - 6 = 1 - 2t$     **c** $17 - 4y = 3y - 4$

   **d** $2(a - 1) = 4 - a$    **e** $3k - 4 = 2(3 - k)$    **f** $5b - 8 = 2(10 - b)$

   **g** $8(p + 2) = 4(4 - p)$    **h** $5 - d = 9 - 2d$     **i** $3 - 4q = 13 - 6q$

   **j** $10 - 3m = 2(2 - m)$    **k** $3(3 - r) = 5(1 - r)$    **l** $4(1 - 3n) = 2(7 - n)$

**\*4** For each of these questions, form an equation and solve it to find the number that I am thinking of.

   **a** I think of a number, multiply it by 10 and subtract 4. I get the same answer as when I add 1 to my number and then multiply by 3.

   **b** I think of a number, double it and then subtract it *from* 15. I get the same answer as when I multiply my number by 5 and add 1.

   **c** I think of a number, multiply it by 4 and subtract it from 30. I get the same answer as if I subtract my number from 9 and then double it.

**\*5** For each of these questions, form an equation and solve it to find the answer to the problem.

   **a**

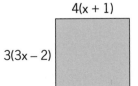

$4(x + 1)$

$3(3x - 2)$

Find the length of a side of this square.

   **b**

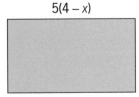

$5(4 - x)$

$7x - 4$

Find the length of this rectangle.

# Equations with fractions

● Form and solve linear equations involving fractions

## RICH TASK

In the lens formula, $u$ is the distance of the object from the lens, $v$ is the distance of the image from the lens and $f$ is the focal length. Investigate the lens formula

$$\frac{1}{u} + \frac{1}{v} = \frac{1}{f}$$

A student wrote $\frac{1}{u} + \frac{1}{v} = \frac{2}{u+v}$. Is the student correct? If not, show why.

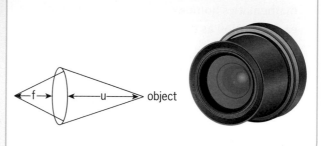

→ **You can solve an equation with a fraction on each side by 'cross-multiplying'.**

**EXAMPLE**

Solve $\dfrac{3x+7}{4} = \dfrac{5x-3}{3}$

**ANSWER**

| | |
|---|---|
| $3x + 7 = \dfrac{4(5x-3)}{3}$ | Multiply both sides by 4 |
| $3(3x + 7) = 4(5x - 3)$ | Multiply both sides by 3 |
| $9x + 21 = 20x - 12$ | Expand the brackets |
| $21 = 11x - 12$ | Subtract $9x$ from both sides |
| $33 = 11x$ | Add 12 to both sides |
| $x = 3$ | Divide both sides by 11 |

You can do these two steps together; this is cross-multiplying

$$3(3x + 7) = 4(5x - 3)$$
$$\quad 4 \qquad\qquad 3$$

In some cases the algebraic term is in the denominator.

**EXAMPLE**

Solve these equations.

**a** $\dfrac{4}{x} = \dfrac{2}{3}$  **b** $\dfrac{10}{y} - 3 = 2$

**ANSWER**

**a**

| | |
|---|---|
| $\dfrac{4}{x} = \dfrac{2}{3}$ | One fraction on each side so cross-multiply |
| $4 \times 3 = 2 \times x$ | |
| $12 = 2x$ | |
| $x = 6$ | Divide both sides by 2 |

**b**

| | |
|---|---|
| $\dfrac{10}{y} - 3 = 2$ | |
| $\dfrac{10}{y} = 5$ | Add 3 to both sides |
| $10 = 5y$ | Multiply both sides by $y$ |
| $y = 2$ | Divide both sides by 5 |

## Exercise A7.5

**1** Solve these equations involving a fraction on one side.

**a** $\dfrac{a}{3} = 9$    **b** $12 = \dfrac{x}{3}$    **c** $\dfrac{2b}{5} = 1$    **d** $2 = \dfrac{3y}{4}$

**e** $\dfrac{f}{4} + 7 = 10$    **f** $3 = \dfrac{m}{5} + 1$    **g** $\dfrac{g}{2} - 3 = -5$    **h** $-1 = 2 + \dfrac{n}{3}$

**i** $\dfrac{p-7}{2} = 1$    **j** $\dfrac{5t-1}{3} = 3$    **k** $3 = \dfrac{10-q}{2}$    **l** $\dfrac{3(5-k)}{2} = 3$

**2** Solve these equations where the algebraic term is in the denominator.

**a** $\dfrac{10}{x} = 5$    **b** $3 = \dfrac{21}{a}$    **c** $-4 = \dfrac{20}{p}$    **d** $5 = \dfrac{7}{m}$

**e** $\dfrac{8}{y} + 7 = 9$    **f** $5 = \dfrac{12}{b} - 1$    **g** $-3 = \dfrac{6}{q} - 5$    **h** $9 - \dfrac{7}{n} = 5$

**i** $\dfrac{8}{f-1} = 4$    **j** $\dfrac{20}{3g+4} = 5$    **k** $\dfrac{12}{7-2k} = -4$    **l** $\dfrac{6}{4-5t} = 2$

**3** Solve these equations by cross multiplying.

**a** $\dfrac{4}{a} = \dfrac{2}{5}$    **b** $\dfrac{2}{3} = \dfrac{10}{b}$    **c** $\dfrac{x}{4} = \dfrac{x+3}{7}$    **d** $\dfrac{y-5}{3} = \dfrac{y-1}{5}$

**e** $\dfrac{7q-1}{5} = \dfrac{5q+1}{4}$    **f** $\dfrac{2n+5}{3} = \dfrac{5(n-1)}{4}$    **g** $\dfrac{6}{m+5} = \dfrac{2}{m-1}$    **h** $\dfrac{4}{n+5} = \dfrac{5}{3n+1}$

**\*4** For each of these questions, form an equation and solve it to find the number that I am thinking of.

  **a** I think of a number, add 5 and divide by 7. I get the same answer as when I subtract 1 from my number and divide by 4.

  **b** I think of a number, double it and divide by 3. I get the same answer as when I add 10 to my number and divide by 4.

  **c** I think of a number and divide it *into* 20. I get the same answer as when I subtract 2 from my number and divide it *into* 12.

**5** If these trapezia have the same area, find the lengths of the parallel sides.

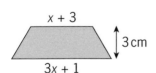
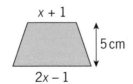

**6** ☆ **CHALLENGE** ☆

The size of an exterior angle of a regular $n$-sided polygon is given by $\dfrac{360}{n}$.

  **a** Write an expression for the interior angle of a regular $n$-sided polygon.

  **b** Write and solve an equation to find the number of sides of a polygon with an interior angle measuring
    **i** 108°    **ii** 140°    **iii** 156°

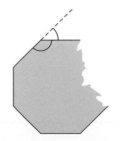

# Further rearranging formulae

- Change the subject of a formula
- Use real-life formulae

## RICH TASK

An isosceles triangle has base = 6 cm and height = 10 cm.
Work out the value of $x$ and hence the area of the square.

Write a formula for the area of the triangle as the sum of its component parts.

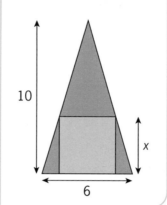

Alternatively, use ratio as introduced in Chapter 4 (number), or similar triangles as described in Chapter 16 (geometry).

---

**EXAMPLE**

Rearrange these formulae to make $x$ the subject.

**a** $k = b - ax$

**b** $\dfrac{m}{x} + n = t$

**ANSWER**

**a**    $k = b - ax$

$k + ax = b$        Add $ax$ to both sides

$ax = b - k$        Subtract $k$ from both sides

$x = \dfrac{b - k}{a}$        Divide both sides by $a$

**b**    $\dfrac{m}{x} + n = t$

$\dfrac{m}{x} = t - n$        Subtract $n$ from both sides

$m = x(t - n)$        Multiply both sides by $x$

$x = \dfrac{m}{t - n}$        Divide both sides by $t - n$

---

**EXAMPLE**

Rearrange these formulae to make $x$ the subject.

**a** $px + m = qx + n$

**b** $a(x + k) = b(t - x)$

**ANSWER**

**a** $px + m = qx + n$

$px - qx = n - m$        Collect the terms in $x$ on one side

$x(p - q) = n - m$        Factorise to isolate the term in $x$

$x = \dfrac{n - m}{p - q}$        Divide both sides by $p - q$

**b** $a(x + k) = b(t - x)$

$ax + ak = bt - bx$        Expand both brackets

$ax + bx = bt - ak$        Collect the terms in $x$

$x(a + b) = bt - ak$        Factorise the left-hand side

$x = \dfrac{bt - ak}{a + b}$        Divide both sides by $a + b$

*1  Isla and Kia rearrange the formula

$$k = t(x - y)$$

in order to make $x$ the subject. Here are their solutions.

ISLA  $x = \dfrac{k + ty}{t}$     KIA  $x = \dfrac{k}{t} + y$

Which solution is correct? Or are they both correct? Explain your answer.

2  Make $x$ the subject of these formulae involving brackets.

  **a**  $x(a + b) = y$     **b**  $t = p(x + q)$     **c**  $n^2 = m(x - k)$     **d**  $w = x(k^2 - y)$

  **e**  $p = \pi(a + x)$     **f**  $a = \frac{1}{2}(x - y)$     **g**  $\frac{1}{5}(x + gh) = g$     **h**  $s - \frac{1}{\pi}(x - k^2)$

> Decide whether or not you need to expand the brackets.

3  Rearrange these formulae to make $y$ the subject.

  **a**  $b = a - y$     **b**  $p^2 = q - y$     **c**  $ab - y = t$     **d**  $r - k - ay$

  **e**  $n - ky = m$     **f**  $d = q(p - y)$     **g**  $h(x - y) = k^2$     **h**  $n = \frac{1}{k}(m - y)$

4  The formula $a = \frac{1}{t}(v - u)$ connects the variables

  $a$ = acceleration, $t$ = time, $v$ = final velocity and $u$ = initial velocity.

  **a**  Rearrange this formula to make $u$ the subject.

  **b**  A train is travelling at a constant acceleration of 1.5 m/s². The train passes signal box A and 10 seconds later enters station B at a velocity of 32 m/s. Find the velocity of the train when it passes signal box A.

5  Make $k$ the subject of these formulae.

  **a**  $\dfrac{a}{k} = b$     **b**  $p = \dfrac{t}{k}$     **c**  $t = \dfrac{mn}{k}$     **d**  $r = \dfrac{d}{kt}$

  **e**  $\dfrac{w}{x} = \dfrac{y}{k}$     **f**  $a = \dfrac{p}{k} + q$     **g**  $\dfrac{h}{k} - z = y^2$     **h**  $\dfrac{m}{n + k} = p$

6  **a**  Rearrange the formula $s = \dfrac{d}{t}$ where $s$ = speed, $d$ = distance and $t$ = time to make $t$ the subject.

  **b**  A car travels 28 miles at an average speed of 40 mph. Work out the time taken.

7  Rearrange these formulae to make $x$ the subject.

  **a**  $ax + b = px + q$     **b**  $mx - n = wx - z$     **c**  $cx - a = b - dx$

  **d**  $g(x + 1) = f - x$     **e**  $k(x - c) = r(d - x)$     **f**  $\dfrac{x - k}{x + 2} = c$

8  Make $t$ the subject of this formula.   $a - \dfrac{x}{t} = b$

## CHECK OUT

**You should now be able to**
- derive a formula
- change the subject of a formula
- set up and solve linear equations.

**Exam-style question**

Mo thinks of a number $x$.

Multiplying the number by 5 and subtracting 4 gives the same answer as multiplying the number by 3 and adding 2.

Write down an equation in $x$ and solve it to find the number.

Read the information in the question and write it out using maths symbols.

Using trial and improvement to find $x$ means you will not have fully answered the question.

**Leo's answer:**

$x \times 5 - 4$
$x \times 3 + 2$
$5x - 4 = 3x + 2$
$5x - 3x = 2 + 4$
$2x = 6$
$x = 3$

Collect like terms, showing your working to solve the equation.

## Exam practice

1 Solve

   a $\frac{3}{5}x - 2 = 7$

   b $4(3x - 2) = 3(x + 6)$

   c $\frac{x-2}{2} + \frac{x+5}{5} = \frac{4-x}{4}$

   *(9 marks)*

2 This is a formula to change British shoe size, $b$, into European shoe size, $e$.

   $e = \frac{5}{4}b + 32$

   Rearrange the formula to make $b$ the subject.

   *(3 marks)*

3 The first three numbers in a sequence are

   $2n + 1$, $2n + 3$ and $2n + 5$.

   a Write down an expression for the fourth number in this sequence.

   The sum of the first and fourth numbers in the sequence is 44.

   b Form an equation in $n$ and solve it to find the first number in this sequence.

   *(5 marks)*

## INTRODUCTION

Mountain rescue teams need to find the shortest distance to an accident in the mountains. They can calculate the distance on a map from their starting place to the accident using Pythagoras' theorem.

**What's the point?**

Knowing the shortest distance between two locations enables people to get to their destination quicker – in some circumstances this can save lives.

## CHECK IN

1  Calculate

    **a** $7^2$      **b** $4^2 + 6^2$      **c** $3^2 + 5^2$      **d** $8^2 - 4^2$

    **e** $7^2 - 2^2$      **f** $9^2 - 1^2$      **g** $\sqrt{13^2 - 12^2}$      **h** $\sqrt{25^2 - 24^2}$

2  Rearrange these equations to make $x$ the subject.

    **a** $y = \dfrac{x}{6}$      **b** $y = \dfrac{x}{5}$      **c** $y = \dfrac{x}{10}$

    **d** $y = \dfrac{2}{x}$      **e** $y = \dfrac{5}{x}$      **f** $y = \dfrac{8}{x}$

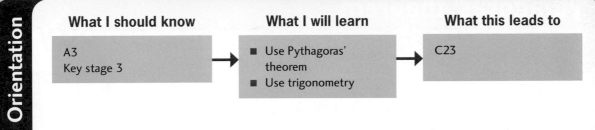

**What I should know**

A3
Key stage 3

**What I will learn**

- Use Pythagoras' theorem
- Use trigonometry

**What this leads to**

C23

## RICH TASK

A stretch of motorway 6 km long is being built close to two towns.

Assuming all roads are perfectly straight, where would you place the junction so that the distance from the motorway to each town was the same?

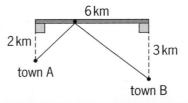

6 km

2 km

town A

3 km

town B

# Pythagoras' theorem

- Understand and use Pythagoras' theorem

You use Pythagoras' theorem to calculate one side of a right-angled triangle when you know the other two sides.

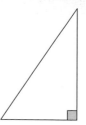

A floor is covered with small triangular tiles.
Patterns are drawn on the floor.
Each pattern has a coloured triangle with squares on its sides.
Count the tiles in each square for each pattern.
Enter your results in a copy of this table.

| Pattern | Number of tiles inside | | |
| | a small square | the other small square | the large square |
|---|---|---|---|
| A | | | |
| B | 8 | 8 | 16 |
| C | | | |
| D | | | |

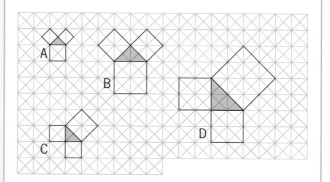

Draw some more patterns of your own like these.
What do you notice about the total number of tiles in the two small squares?

## RICH TASK

Draw any right-angled triangle ABC and squares X and Y accurately.

Split Y into four equal parts as shown, where O is the centre of square Y, DE is parallel to AB and FG is perpendicular to DE.

Cut out X and the four parts of Y.

Can you arrange these five pieces to make the square Z on side AB?

What can you say about the areas of X, Y and Z?

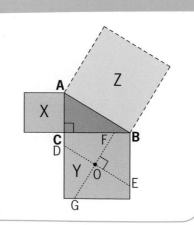

→ **Pythagoras' theorem says that:**
**the area of the square on the hypotenuse**
**is equal to the sum of the areas of the**
**squares on the two shorter sides.**
**Area of Z = Area of X + Area of Y**

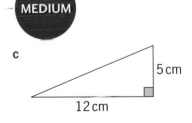

The hypotenuse is the longest
side. It is opposite the right
angle.

**Investigation** Search on
the internet for a proof of
Pythagoras' theorem.

→ $c^2 = a^2 + b^2$

**EXAMPLE**

a  Find the length $c$.
   Give your answer to 1 d.p.

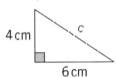
4 cm, 6 cm, $c$

b  Find the length $a$.

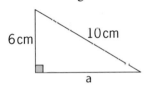
6 cm, 10 cm, $a$

**ANSWER**

a  $c^2 = a^2 + b^2$
   $c^2 = 6^2 + 4^2$
   $\quad = 36 + 16$
   $\quad = 52$
   $c = \sqrt{52} = 7.2$ cm (1 d.p.)

b  Pythagoras' theorem gives
   $10^2 = a^2 + 6^2$
   $100 = a^2 + 36$
   $\quad a^2 = 100 - 36 = 64$
   So  $a = \sqrt{64} = 8$ cm

## Exercise A8.1

**MEDIUM**

1  Find the hypotenuse in each of these right-angled triangles.

a
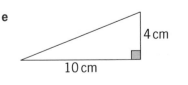
3 cm, 4 cm

b
8 cm, 15 cm

c
5 cm, 12 cm

d
5 cm, 9 cm

e
4 cm, 10 cm

f
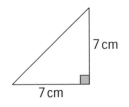
7 cm, 7 cm

**Continued ➤**

**2** Find the missing side in each of these right-angled triangles.

**a**
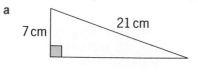
7 cm    21 cm

**b**

24 cm    26 cm

**c**
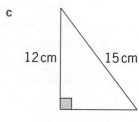
12 cm    15 cm

**d**
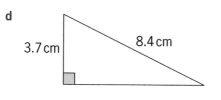
3.7 cm    8.4 cm

**e**
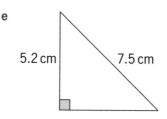
5.2 cm    7.5 cm

**f**
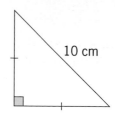
10 cm

**3** A telegraph pole 6 metres tall is held in place by a sloping wire as shown. Calculate the length, $x$, of the wire.

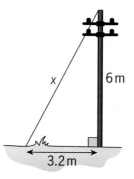
$x$    6 m
3.2 m

**4** A skier drops a vertical distance of 0.9 km as he skis 3.6 km down a steep hill. Calculate the horizontal distance, $d$, that he covers.

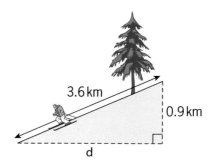
3.6 km    0.9 km
$d$

**5** A ladder 6 metres long leans against a wall to reach a window. The foot of the ladder is 2 metres from bottom of the wall. Calculate the height, $h$, of the window above ground level.

**6** A hiker walks 6 miles due north and then 2.5 miles due east. Calculate the shortest distance, $d$, that he now is from his starting point.

**7** Calculate the height of an equilateral triangle of side 8 cm.

**8** A rhombus of side 3.9 cm has a diagonal 3.0 cm long. Find the length of its other diagonal.

**9** Calculate the shortest distance between each pair of points.
**i** $(0, 4), (3, 8)$       **ii** $(4, 5), (7, 2)$       **iii** $(8, 9), (20, 14)$
**iv** $(2, 6), (18, 18)$     **v** $(4, 9), (14, 19)$     **vi** $(a, b), (c, d)$

**10** The largest possible circle is drawn to fit inside a square of side 20 cm. Four identical small circles just fit into the gaps in the four corners. Find the diameters of the small circles.

**11 ✩ CHALLENGE ✩**

   **a** A square of side $x$ is inscribed in a semicircle of radius $r$.

      Prove that $x = \dfrac{2r}{\sqrt{5}}$.

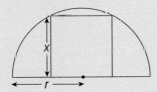

   **b** A rectangle with sides $x$ and $y$ is inscribed in a semicircle of radius 10 cm.

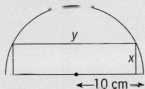

      Find an expression for the area $A$ of the rectangle in terms of $x$.
      By substituting values of $x$, draw the graph of $A$ against $x$.
      Find the value of $x$ which gives a maximum value for $A$.

- Use scale drawing and a calculator to find the tangent of an angle

**Angle A = 72°**

This triangle has angle A = 72°. The table suggests possible lengths for side AB.

Working in groups

> → **draw these triangles accurately**
> → **measure the length of side BC**
> → **find how many times longer BC is than AB.**

Enter results in a copy of this table.

What do you notice?

| AB, cm | BC, cm | BC ÷ AB |
|--------|--------|---------|
| 2      |        |         |
| 2.5    |        |         |
| 3      |        |         |
| 3.5    |        |         |
| 4      |        |         |

**Angle A = 64°**

Repeat the activity with angle A = 64°.

Let AB take the same values (or any other values of your choice).

Work in groups.

Answer the question *How many times longer is* BC *than* AB?

Enter your results in a similar table.

What do you notice?

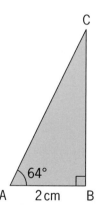

**Other values of angle A**

Repeat the activity for angle A = 56°, 45° and 27°.

For each angle, answer the question *How many times longer is* BC *than* AB?

**Summary of results**

You found the answer to *How many times longer is side* BC *than side* AB? by working out $\frac{BC}{AC}$. This ratio is called the **tangent** of angle A.

It is written in short as $\textbf{tan A} = \frac{BC}{AC}$.

You have found that, for a given angle, **tan A** has the same value regardless of the size of the triangle.

You can check your results using your calculator, for example, to find the tangent of 72° use

Enter your results from your scale drawings and your calculator in a copy of this table.

| Angle A | | 72° | 64° | 56° | 45° | 27° | 0° |
|---|---|---|---|---|---|---|---|
| tan A | from scale drawing | | | | | | |
| | from calculator | | | | | | |

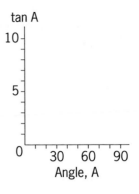

Draw a graph of these results on axes labelled as here. Describe the shape of the graph and say what is special about tan 45° and tan 90°.

## Exercise A8.2

**MEDIUM HIGH**

1 These four triangles are drawn accurately.
Measure sides AB and BC and calculate the ratio $\frac{BC}{AB}$ as a decimal. Measure angle A and use your calculator (or your graph) to find tan A. Compare tan A with your value of $\frac{BC}{AB}$.

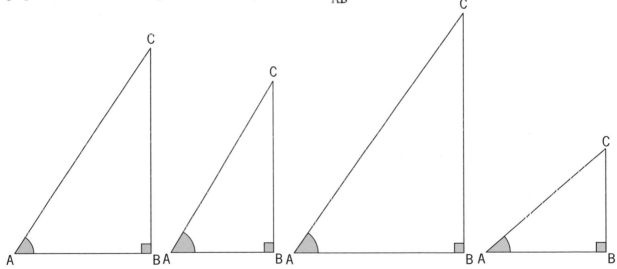

2 Draw right-angled triangles ABC accurately with AB = 2 cm and angle A equal to

a 68°　　　b 51°　　c 42°　　d 31°

Use the triangles to find approximate values for tan A.
Check each answer using your calculator.

- Use tangents to find sides and angles.

## RICH TASK

When you see road-signs for steep hills, what do the numbers mean?
What are the steepest gradients that a cyclist or a car can climb up?
Where are the steepest roads in England and Wales?

In this triangle, the longest side, AC, is the **hypotenuse**.
Side BC is opposite angle A and is called the **opposite** side.
Side AB is next to angle A and is called the **adjacent** side.
You already know that $\tan A = \frac{BC}{AB}$,

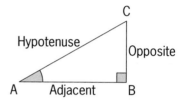

so you can now write $\tan A = \dfrac{\text{Opposite side}}{\text{Adjacent side}}$ for any triangle.

You use this definition for finding both sides and angles.

**EXAMPLE**

**Finding the opposite side**

From where you are standing, the top of a hill makes an angle of elevation of 12°. The hill is 4 km away from you. Calculate its height, $h$.

**ANSWER**

$\tan 12° = \dfrac{\text{opposite}}{\text{adjacent}} = \dfrac{h}{4}$

Multiply both sides by 4

$$h = 4 \times \tan 12°$$
$$= 4 \times 0.21255...$$
$$= 0.85022...$$
$$= 0.850 \text{ km (to 3 s.f.)}$$

The height of the hill is 850 metres.

EXAMPLE

## Finding an angle

A tree 15 metres tall casts a shadow 8 metres long. Calculate the elevation of the sun (to the nearest degree).

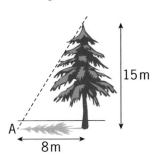

15 m

A

8 m

**ANSWER**

$\tan A = \dfrac{15}{8} = 1.875$

You can use the invese function $\tan^{-1}$ to find the angle whose tangent is 1.875. You can write $A = \tan^{-1} 1.875$

Use [Inv] [tan] [1] [.] [8] [7] [5] [=]

A = 61.9°

> INV TAN on some calculators is SHIFT TAN. Think of INV TAN as finding 'the angle whose tangent is' 1.875

The angle of elevation of the sun is 62°.

> Check by finding tan 61.9°.

## Exercise A8.3

**MEDIUM HIGH**

1 Calculate the lettered lengths in these triangles in cm to 1 decimal place.

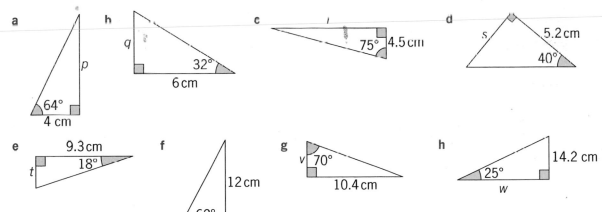

**a** 64°, 4 cm, p

**b** q, 32°, 6 cm

**c** 75°, 4.5 cm

**d** s, 5.2 cm, 40°

**e** 9.3 cm, 18°, t

**f** 12 cm, 62°, n

**g** v, 70°, 10.4 cm

**h** 14.2 cm, 25°, w

2 You stand 150 metres from the bottom of a church spire. The angle of elevation of its top is 25°. How high is the spire?

3 A boat is 450 metres from a vertical cliff. The angle of elevation of the cliff-top from the boat is 13°. Find the height of the cliff.

4 When the altitude of the sun is 42°, a radio mast casts a shadow 24.5 metres long. Find the height of the mast.

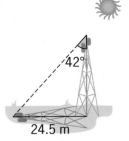

42°

24.5 m

**Continued** ➤

**5** Calculate the lettered angles in these triangles to the nearest 0.1°.

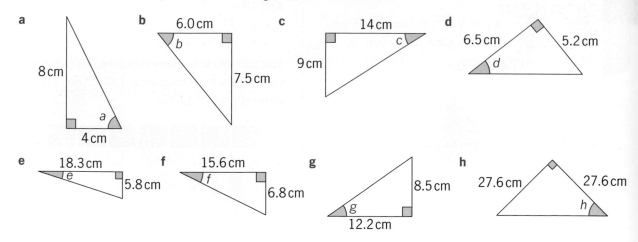

**a** 8 cm, 4 cm, *a*

**b** 6.0 cm, 7.5 cm, *b*

**c** 14 cm, 9 cm, *c*

**d** 6.5 cm, 5.2 cm, *d*

**e** 18.3 cm, 5.8 cm, *e*

**f** 15.6 cm, 6.8 cm, *f*

**g** 8.5 cm, 12.2 cm, *g*

**h** 27.6 cm, 27.6 cm, *h*

**6** A ladder leans against a wall with its foot 2.0 metres from the bottom of the wall. If the top of the ladder is 6.4 metres above ground, find the angle of inclination of the ladder to the ground.

**7** You stand 16 metres from the bottom of a factory chimney 32 metres high. What is the angle of elevation of its top?

**8** A cog railway climbs a mountain so that it rises vertically 2.5 metres for every for 6.5 metres travelled horizontally. Find the angle to the horizontal at which it is climbing.

**9** ☆ **CHALLENGE** ☆

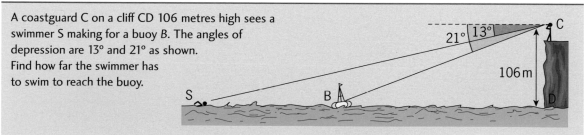

A coastguard C on a cliff CD 106 metres high sees a swimmer S making for a buoy *B*. The angles of depression are 13° and 21° as shown. Find how far the swimmer has to swim to reach the buoy.

**10** ☆ **CHALLENGE** ☆

Calculate the height *h* of this triangle.

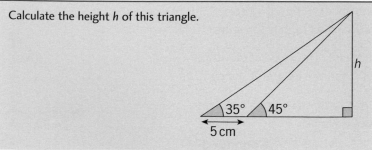

35° 45° 5 cm *h*

# Sine and cosine of an angle

- Use sine and cosine to calculate sides and angles of right-angled triangles

If you choose the opposite and adjacent sides of a right-angled triangle, you already know that their ratio is the tangent of angle A. The two other ratios are called the sine and the cosine of angle A.

> Sine and cosine are written, in short, as sin and cos.

$$\rightarrow \quad \sin A = \frac{\text{Opposite side}}{\text{Hypotenuse}} \qquad \cos A = \frac{\text{Adjacent side}}{\text{Hypotenuse}}$$

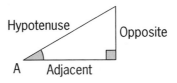

You can find sides and angles as you did with tan A.

**EXAMPLE**

Find the missing sides.

**a**

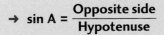

**b**

**c**

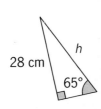

**ANSWER**

**a**  $\sin 32° = \dfrac{a}{14}$

$14 \times \sin 32° = a$

$a = 7.42 \text{ cm (3 s.f.)}$

> Use the sin key on your calculator.

**b**  $\cos 22° = \dfrac{b}{8}$

$9 \times \cos 22° = b$

$b = 8.34 \text{ cm (3 s.f.)}$

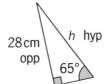

> Use the cos key on your calculator.

**c**  $\sin 65° = \dfrac{28}{h}$

$h = \dfrac{28}{\sin 65}$

$h = 30.9 \text{ cm (3 s.f.)}$

> To find the hypotenuse, you will always need to divide by either sin or cos.

You can use trigonometry to solve real-life problems.

Ornsay on the Isle of Skye is 10.5 km from Armadale on a bearing of $x°$. If Ornsay is 9.0 km further north than Armadale, what is the value of $x$?

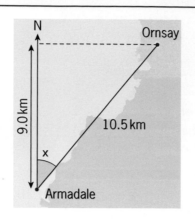

**ANSWER**

You know the adjacent side, 9.0 km, and the hypotenuse, 10.5 km.

So   $\cos x = \dfrac{9.0}{10.5}$

    $= 0.8571...$

Use Inv  Cos

$x = 31.0$

The bearing of Ornsay from Armadale is 031°.

## Exercise A8.4

**MEDIUM HIGH**

1   Find the lettered sides in these triangles to the nearest 0.1 cm.

**a**

$p$   35°   4 cm

**b**
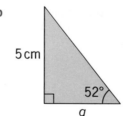
5 cm   52°   $q$

**c**
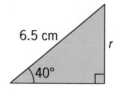
6.5 cm   40°   $r$

**d**

5.8 cm   49°   $s$

**e**
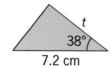
$t$   38°   7.2 cm

**f**
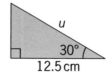
$u$   30°   12.5 cm

2   A kite flies in a strong wind at the end of 72 metres of string which rises at 32° to the horizontal. How high is the kite to the nearest metre?

3   A radio mast is held vertical by a 36-metre wire which slopes at 65° to the ground. One end of the wire is fixed to the top of the mast. How far is the other end fixed from the bottom?

4   An aeroplane takes off and climbs for 3.6 km at an angle of 28°. How far has its shadow travelled horizontally?

Assume the sun is vertically above the aircraft.

**5** A mountain railway climbs 5.2 km of a track at 8° to the horizontal. What height does it climb in metres?

**6** An equilateral triangle has sides 6 cm long. Find the height of the triangle.

**7** Find the lettered angles in these triangles to the nearest 0.1°.

**a**
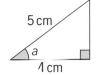
5 cm
*a*
4 cm

**b**

7 cm
*b*
5 cm

**c**
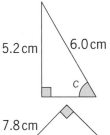
5.2 cm    6.0 cm
*c*

**d**

4.5 cm
*d*
3.6 cm

**e**

5.2 cm
*e*
6.8 cm

**f**
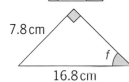
7.8 cm
*f*
16.8 cm

**8** An 8-metre ladder leans against a wall so its foot is 3 metres from the bottom of the wall. At what angle is it inclined to the horizontal?

**9** A road over the Alps rises steadily uphill for 9.0 km, climbing a vertical height of 1.4 km.
What angle does the road make with the horizontal?

**10** This diagram gives the cross-section of a metal-framed tent.
Calculate the distance AB across the floor.

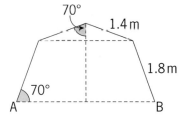
70°
1.4 m
1.8 m
70°
A          B

**11** **RICH TASK**

Construct a table of the values of sine and cosine for 0° ≤ θ ≤ 90°.

| Angle, θ° | 0 | 10 | 20 | ...... |
|-----------|---|----|----|--------|
| sin θ | | | | |
| cos θ | | | | |

Draw graphs of sin θ and cos θ for 0° ≤ θ ≤ 90°.
Describe the transformation which maps one of the graphs onto the other.
What do you notice about sin 30° and cos 60°?

θ is the symbol for the Greek letter 'theta'.

# The right-angled triangle

• Choose between sine, cosine and tangent and use all three ratios with Pythagoras' theorem

In any right-angled triangle, you can use

> → $\sin \alpha = \dfrac{\text{opposite}}{\text{hypotenuse}}$
>
> → $\cos \alpha = \dfrac{\text{adjacent}}{\text{hypotenuse}}$
>
> → $\tan \alpha = \dfrac{\text{opposite}}{\text{adjacent}}$ and
>
> → $(\text{hypotenuse})^2 = (\text{adjacent})^2 + (\text{opposite})^2$

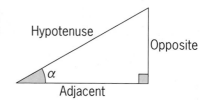

p. 348

When deciding which ratio to use,

> → imagine yourself at the angle which you are interested in (e.g. 30°)
> → name the three sides of the triangle from this angle
> → choose the two sides you are involved with (adjacent and hypotenuse)
> → decide which ratio you need (cos).

**Find x.**

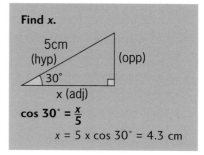

$\cos 30° = \dfrac{x}{5}$

$x = 5 \times \cos 30° = 4.3$ cm

**EXAMPLE**

A radio mast LN is held vertical by four wires symmetrically fixed as shown. Calculate

**a** the distance AB between the two fixing points

**b** the angle $\alpha$ between wire AL and the ground.

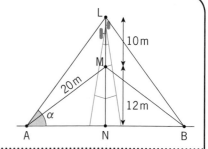

**ANSWER**

**a** In triangle AMN, Pythagoras' theorem gives
$$AM^2 = AN^2 + MN^2$$
$$20^2 = AN^2 + 12^2$$
Subtract $12^2$ from both sides
$$AN^2 = 20^2 - 12^2 = 400 - 144 = 256$$
$$AN = \sqrt{256} = 16$$
The distance AB $= 2 \times 16 = 32$ metres

**b** In triangle ALN,
$$\tan \alpha = \frac{\text{Opposite}}{\text{Adjacent}} = \frac{LN}{AN} = \frac{22}{16} = 1.375$$

Use

Angle $\alpha = 53.97 = 54°$ to the nearest degree

Work out the angle $\theta$ between the diagonal and the base in this cuboid.

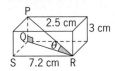

**ANSWER**

SRQ and PQR are right-angled triangles:

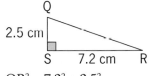 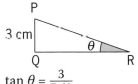

$QR^2 = 7.2^2 + 2.5^2$

$QR = \sqrt{58.09}$

$\quad = 7.62$ cm

$\tan \theta = \dfrac{3}{7.62}$

$\theta = 21.49 \approx 21°$

Use Pythagoras in SRQ to find QR.

Use trigonometry to find $\theta$ in triangle PQR.

---

## Exercise A8.5

**MEDIUM HIGH**

1  Find the lettered lengths and angles in these diagrams.
   Give answers to 3 significant figures.

**a** 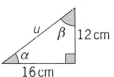  **b** 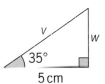  **c** 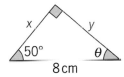  **d**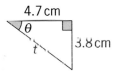

**e** 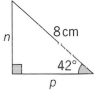  **f** 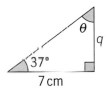  **g** 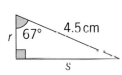  **h**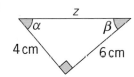

2  Calculate the lengths $x$ and $y$ and the angle $\alpha$ in these diagrams.

**a** 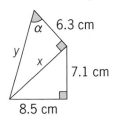  **b** 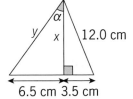  **c**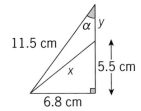

3  Calculate the length of the hypotenuse in this triangle when
   **a**  $\theta = 48°$, $x = 8.7$ cm      **b**  $\theta = 52°$, $x = 6.4$ cm
   **c**  $\theta = 67°$, $y = 9.25$ cm     **d**  $\theta = 31°$, $y = 12.7$ cm

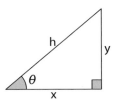

**Continued ➤**

**4** A railway track rises 120 metres vertically on an incline at 9° to the horizontal. How long is the track?

**5** How long are the diagonals of a square of side 6 cm?

**6** A triangle has sides of 12 cm, 12 cm and 10 cm. Calculate its angles.

**7** A square of side 4 cm contains triangle ABC as shown. Calculate the sides of the triangle and hence prove that triangle ABC is right-angled.

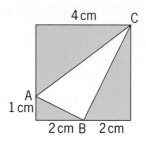

**8** Four identical coins of radius 1.5 cm touch each other so their centres are at the corners of a square. Calculate the radius of the largest coin that can be placed in the space between the four coins.

**9** Askham is 6 km from Boston on a bearing of 020°. Culham is 8 km from Boston on a bearing of 110°. Find
   **a** the distance      **b** the bearing of Culham from Askham.

**10** A room has the shape of a cuboid with the dimensions shown. Calculate the length AG of the longest rod which can be stored in this room.

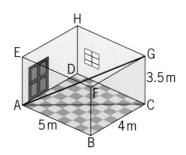

**11** Calculate the length of the longest rod which can be placed in a box which has
   **a** length 25 cm, width 20 cm and height 15 cm
   **b** a square cross-section of side 12 cm and a height of 15 cm
   **c** the shape of a cube with a capacity of 1 litre.

**12** This rectangular ski-slope runs downhill as it drops vertically 85 metres.
A skier traverses in a straight line from P to R.
How far does she ski?

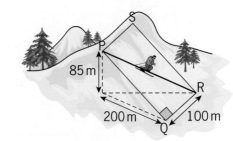

**13** A rod MN has its lower end N on the ground and its upper end M in the crack between two vertical walls as shown. Calculate the length of the rod.

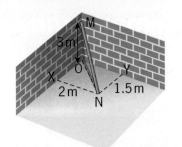

**14** A tree TU stands directly opposite point P on a straight river bank. From point Q on the river bank, angle UQP is 38° and angle TQU is 27°.
If PQ is 12 metres, find the height of the tree.

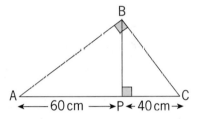

T is the top of the tree

**15** *RICH TASK*

  a   Right-angled triangle ABC is split into two other right-angled triangles by the line BP such that AP is 60 cm and PC is 40 cm.
       Find the other sides of triangle ABC.

  b   If AP : PC = $x : y$ and AC = 1 metre, can you generalise your results for the lengths of sides AB and BC?

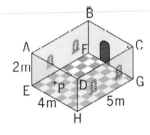

**16** *RICH TASK*

A spider sits at the middle point P of my living room wall.
It sees a fly in corner C.
Find the shortest distance the spider must travel to reach C.

**17** *RICH TASK*

Four circles of radius 1 metre fit into a square frame without overlapping. What is the size of the smallest possible frame?
Find the smallest possible rectangular frame which will just hold three of these circles without overlapping.

## CHECK OUT

**You should now be able to**
- use Pythagoras theorem in 2-D and 3-D problems
- use trigonometry in problems involving right-angled triangles.

*

**Exam-style question**

Edina and Patsy are estimating the height of the same tree.
Edina stands 20 m from the tree and measures the angle of elevation of the treetop as 52°.
Patsy stands 28 m from the tree and measures the angle of elevation of the treetop as 43°.
Can they both be correct?

**Jiao's answer:**

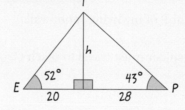

Draw a diagram or diagrams.

Work out separately the height of the tree for Edina's measurements and for Patsy's measurements.

For Edina

$\tan 52 = \dfrac{h}{20}$; $h = 20 \times \tan 52 = 25.6$m

For Patsy

$\tan 43 = \dfrac{h}{20}$; $h = 28 \times \tan 43 = 26.1$m

While both answers are not exactly the same, they are the same to 2 significant figures

Edina and Patsy could both be correct

Compare the answers, thinking about how accurate you can be with measuring angles.

Give a reason for your final answer based on the maths.

## Exam practice

**1  a**  Work out the length PQ.

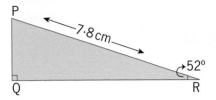

**b**  Work out angle $x$.

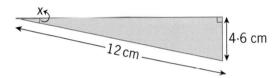

*(6 marks)*

**\*2**  Use this equilateral triangle to show that $\cos 60° = \dfrac{1}{2}$.

*(3 marks)*

**3**  Following restoration work the top of the Tower of Pisa is 55·8 m from the ground leaning at an angle of 4°.
What is the height of the tower?

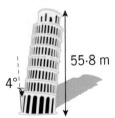

55·8 m

4°

*(3 marks)*

# 9 Fractions, decimals and percentages

## CHECK IN

1 Cancel each of these fractions down to their simplest terms.

a $\frac{2}{4}$    b $\frac{15}{20}$    c $\frac{8}{10}$    d $\frac{95}{100}$    e $\frac{6}{8}$

2 Write a decimal equivalent to each of these fractions.

a $\frac{3}{4}$    b $\frac{2}{5}$    c $\frac{7}{10}$    d $\frac{9}{20}$    e $\frac{17}{100}$

3 Write a fraction equivalent to each of these decimals.

a 0.5    b 0.25    c 0.3    d 0.8    e 0.45

4 Write notes to show how you would find a mental estimate for each of these calculations.

a 19.2 × 28.9                    b 355.72 ÷ 58.91

c 1206 − 816                     d 6987 + 6039

**Orientation**

| What I should know | What I will learn | What this leads to |
|---|---|---|
| A4 | ■ Calculate using decimals and percentages<br>■ Multiply, divide, add and subtract fractions | C17 |

## RICH TASK

In this diagram a square has been divided into different-sized pieces.
Calculate the fraction or percentage of the whole square that each piece represents.

- Estimate answers to problems involving decimals

The latest paperback novels are on sale at a supermarket for £3.79 each. How many can Keith buy for £21?

Keith could calculate 21 ÷ 3.79, but does he need the exact answer? 3.79 rounds up to 4.

**p. 7**
21 ÷ 4 is more than 5 so Keith can buy 5 books.

You can use estimation to solve problems. Be careful with rounding.

> → **When multiplying, compensate by making one number bigger and one smaller**    $3.4 \times 4.4 \rightarrow 3 \times 5 = 15$
> → **When dividing, compensate by making both numbers bigger or both smaller**    $3.4 \div 4.4 \rightarrow 3 \div 4 = 0.75$

You would need to be careful if the amount were £23. A sensible estimate might be 24 ÷ 4 = 6.

Check how accurate these estimates are.

**EXAMPLE**

Estimate    **a** $\dfrac{3.2 \times 49}{3.8 - 1.9}$    **b** $\dfrac{6.1^2}{8.7 \times 2.3}$

**ANSWER**

**a** $\dfrac{3.2 \times 49}{3.8 - 1.9} \approx \dfrac{3 \times 50}{4 - 2} = \dfrac{150}{2} = 75$

**b** $\dfrac{6.1^2}{8.7 \times 2.3} \approx \dfrac{6^2}{9 \times 2} = \dfrac{36}{18} = 2$

≈ means 'approximately equal to'.

Check how accurate these estimates are.

You can often use place value for mental arithmetic calculations.

**EXAMPLE**

Given that $430 \times 5.8 = 2494$ find

**a** $43\,000 \times 58$    **b** $0.43 \times 58$    **c** $24\,940 \div 43$

**ANSWER**

**a** 100 times bigger × 10 times bigger → answer is 1000 times bigger
$43\,000 \times 58 = 2\,494\,000$

**b** 1000 times smaller × 10 times bigger → answer is 100 times smaller
$0.43 \times 58 = 24.94$

**c** $2494 \div 430 = 5.8$
10 times bigger ÷ 10 times smaller → answer is 100 times bigger
$24\,940 \div 43 = 580$

Use estimation to check that the order of your answer is correct.

$\div \dfrac{1}{10}$ is the same as $\times 10$
($\dfrac{1}{10}$ and 10 are reciprocals)

Doubling and halving are also useful strategies.

Work out   **a**   $4.68 \times 50$     **b**   $20.04 \div 0.8$

**ANSWER**

**a**   $4.68 \times 50 = 2.34 \times 100 = 234$

**b**   $20.04 \div 0.8 = 200.4 \div 8 = 200.4 \times \dfrac{1}{8}$

$\qquad = 100.2 \times \dfrac{1}{4} = 50.1 \times \dfrac{1}{2} = 25.05$

Double one number and halve another number when multiplying.

You can combine strategies.

Unit B

## Exercise B9.1

MEDIUM

1   Work out

    a   $375 \times 54$      b   $16 \times 6$      c   $48 \times 52$

    d   $1.32 \div 0.4$      e   $5.17 \div 0.06$      f   $29 \div 0.8$

This exercise is to be completed without a calculator.

2   a   Given $87 \times 132 = 11484$, find    **i**   $11484 \div 870$    **ii**   $114.84 \div 132$

    b   Given $93 \times 214 = 19\,902$, find    **i**   $199.02 \div 9.3$    **ii**   $9300 \times 0.00214$

    c   Given $76 \times 45 = 3420$, find    **i**   $342 \div 0.045$    **ii**   $342 \div 7600$

    d   Given $32 \times 225 = 7200$, find    **i**   $72 \div 3.2$    **ii**   $0.0032 \times 2250$

3   Estimate

    a   $\dfrac{2.2 \times 3.7}{4.5 - 1.9}$      b   $\dfrac{39 \times 203}{77}$      c   $\dfrac{11.2 + 6.7}{3.25 \times 2.9}$      d   $\dfrac{7.3^2}{9.7 - 4.1}$

    e   $\sqrt{36 + (4.5^2)}$      f   $\dfrac{19.8}{2.8 + 5.9^2}$      g   $\dfrac{2 \times 623.25}{12.6 + 87.22}$      h   $\dfrac{\sqrt{24.7}}{98.1 - 26}$

    i   $\dfrac{\sqrt{40095}}{9.87^2}$      j   $\dfrac{610 \times 4.98}{0.213}$      k   $\dfrac{7.6}{12.5 - 6.8}$      l   $\left(\dfrac{5}{0.4}\right)^2$

4   a   Estimate the number of sticks of rock costing £1.29 each that can be bought with £10.

    b   Chris has £16.72 credit left on his mobile phone.

       Estimate the number of games he can download if each game costs £1.35

5   ☆ **PROBLEM** ☆

Dave is making a garden patio.
The patio is 3.2 m by 4.8 m.
The patio slabs are 0.8 m by 0.5 m.

Estimate the number of patio slabs that Dave needs.

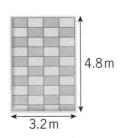

4.8 m

3.2 m

# Fractions, decimals and percentages

- Convert between fractions, decimals and percentages

## ☆ ACTIVITY ☆

This old ruler shows one inch divided into tenths and sixteenths. The complete ruler is 6 inches long.

Which divisions on the sixteenths scale line up exactly with divisions on the tenths scale? List them all.

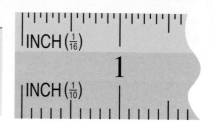

## Converting between fractions and decimals

➜ **To write a fraction as a decimal, divide the numerator by the denominator.**

$\frac{1}{4} = 1 \div 4 = 0.25$

$\frac{2}{5} = 2 \div 5 = 0.4$

Fraction — Decimal

Percentage

➜ **To write a decimal as a fraction, count the number of places after the decimal point.**

0.75 **Two** places after the decimal point So $0.75 = \frac{75}{100} = \frac{3}{4}$

0.6 **One** place after the decimal point So $0.6 = \frac{6}{10} = \frac{3}{5}$

Look at a place value table:

| Units | . | $\frac{1}{10}$ | $\frac{1}{100}$ | |
|---|---|---|---|---|
| 0 | . | 7 | 5 | |
| 0 | . | 6 | | |

## Converting between fractions/decimals and percentages

Percentage means parts of 100 $\Rightarrow$ $25\% = \frac{25}{100} \left(= \frac{1}{4}\right)$

The fraction – decimal – percentage equivalent is $\frac{1}{4} = 0.25 = 25\%$

➜ **To write a decimal as a percentage, multiply by 100%**

$0.23 = 0.23 \times 100\% = 23\%$
$0.07 = 0.07 \times 100\% = 7\%$

Fraction — Decimal

Percentage

p. 252

➜ **To write a percentage as a decimal or a fraction, divide by 100**

$20\% = 20 \div 100 = 0.2$

$0.2 = \frac{2}{10} = \frac{1}{5}$

$\Rightarrow 20\% = 0.2 = \frac{1}{5}$

$14\% = 14 \div 100 = 0.14$

$0.14 = \frac{14}{100} = \frac{7}{50}$

$\Rightarrow 14\% = 0.14 = \frac{7}{50}$

Which of these fractions is nearest to $\frac{1}{2}$?

$$\frac{6}{10} \qquad \frac{11}{20} \qquad \frac{13}{30} \qquad \frac{21}{40}$$

**ANSWER**

$$\frac{6}{10} = \frac{72}{120} \qquad \frac{11}{20} = \frac{66}{120} \qquad \frac{13}{30} = \frac{52}{120} \qquad \frac{21}{40} = \frac{63}{120}$$

$\frac{63}{120}$ is closest to $\frac{1}{2}$ $\left(\frac{60}{120}\right)$

The LCM of 10, 20, 30 and 40 is 120

### Exercise B9.2

MEDIUM LOW

1 Which of these fractions is closest to $\frac{1}{2}$?

$$\frac{3}{8} \qquad \frac{15}{32} \qquad \frac{29}{64}$$

This exercise is to be completed without a calculator.

*2 Which of these amounts would you prefer to have:
$\frac{3}{8}$ of £500 or $\frac{3}{4}$ of £250?

Justify your answer.

3 Work out
   a  5% of 320      b  4% of 300
   c  55% of 120     d  62% of 20

4 Work out
   a  $0.3 \times 0.2$      b  $0.4 \times 1.2$      c  $0.03 \times 0.5$
   d  $0.6 \times 0.1$      e  $0.04 \times 0.15$     f  $1.2 \div 0.4$
   g  $15.6 \div 0.3$       h  $10.9 \div 0.04$       i  $15 \div 0.15$

5 Choose from this list:
   0.2      0.15      0.4      0.08      0.02      5
   a  two numbers that give the lowest possible product
   b  two numbers that give an answer 10 in a division sum:
   _____ ÷ _____ = 10

6 Which is larger, 25% of 60 or 20% of 70? Show your working.

7 Which is smaller, 50% of 30 or 40% of 40? Show your working.

8 a  Work out   i   10% of 250     ii   5% of 500
   b  Explain why the answers are the same.

9 a  25% of a number is 100. What is the number?
   b  10% of a number is 35. What is the number?

# Calculating with fractions

- Add and subtract fractions
- Multiply and divide a fraction by an integer

## ★ ACTIVITY ★

Look at this rectangle. How many squares is

- $\frac{1}{2}$ of the rectangle
- $\frac{1}{3}$ of the rectangle
- $\frac{1}{6}$ of the rectangle?

Explain why $\frac{1}{2} + \frac{1}{3} + \frac{1}{6} = 1$

→ **To add or subtract fractions, they must have the same denominator. If they don't, you can change them so that they do.**

**EXAMPLE**

Work out    **a** $\frac{2}{5} + \frac{1}{4}$    **b** $\frac{5}{6} - \frac{3}{8}$

**ANSWER**

**a** $\frac{2}{5} = \frac{8}{20}$    $\frac{1}{4} = \frac{5}{20}$

$\frac{2}{5} + \frac{1}{4} = \frac{8}{20} + \frac{5}{20}$

$= \frac{13}{20}$

**b** $\frac{5}{6} = \frac{20}{24}$    $\frac{3}{8} = \frac{9}{24}$

$\frac{5}{6} - \frac{3}{8} = \frac{20}{24} - \frac{9}{24}$

$= \frac{11}{24}$

You can multiply and divide fractions.

Jenny has $\frac{1}{3}$ of a cake. She gives Joel $\frac{1}{2}$ of her $\frac{1}{3}$.

What fraction does Joel get?

$\frac{1}{2}$ of $\frac{1}{3} = \frac{1}{2} \times \frac{1}{3} = \frac{1}{6} \Rightarrow$ Joel gets $\frac{1}{6}$ of the cake

→ **To multiply fractions, multiply the numerators and multiply the denominators**

**EXAMPLE**

Work out

**a** $\frac{2}{7} \times \frac{4}{5}$    **b** $\frac{3}{8} \times \frac{7}{9}$    **c** $\frac{3}{4}$ of 84

**ANSWER**

**a** $\frac{2}{7} \times \frac{4}{5} = \frac{2 \times 4}{7 \times 5} = \frac{8}{35}$    **b** $\frac{3}{8} \times \frac{7}{9} = \frac{3^{1} \times 7}{8 \times 9^{3}} = \frac{1 \times 7}{8 \times 3} = \frac{7}{24}$

**c** $\frac{3}{4}$ of 84 = 3 × 84 ÷ 4 = 63

Katy wanted to share £40 equally between two friends.
She could do either of these sums:

£40 ÷ 2 = £20      $\frac{1}{2}$ of £40 = £20

**REMEMBER:**

'Of' means multiply.

**Fractions, decimals and percentages**

→ **Dividing by 2 is the same as multiplying by $\frac{1}{2}$**

- **2 and $\frac{1}{2}$ are reciprocals**
- **Similarly, ÷ 5 is the same as × $\frac{1}{5}$**
- **÷ $\frac{4}{5}$ is the same as × $\frac{5}{4}$**

→ **To divide by a fraction, change from ÷ to × and use the reciprocal fraction.**

**EXAMPLE**

Work out

a $\frac{2}{15} \div \frac{1}{3}$    b $\frac{1}{8} \div \frac{2}{3}$

**ANSWER**

a $\frac{2}{15} \div \frac{1}{3} = \frac{2}{15} \times \frac{3}{1} = \frac{6}{15} = \frac{2}{5}$    b $\frac{1}{8} \div \frac{2}{3} = \frac{1}{8} \times \frac{3}{2} = \frac{3}{16}$

## Exercise B9.3

**MEDIUM**

1 Add these fractions. Give your answers in their simplest form.

a $\frac{3}{8} + \frac{1}{8}$    b $\frac{3}{8} + \frac{5}{16}$    c $\frac{2}{7} + \frac{1}{10}$    d $\frac{2}{5} + \frac{7}{12}$

> This exercise is to be completed without a calculator.

2 Subtract these fractions. Give your answers in their simplest form.

a $\frac{5}{8} - \frac{3}{8}$    b $\frac{8}{9} - \frac{8}{27}$    c $\frac{3}{10} - \frac{1}{5}$    d $\frac{2}{3} - \frac{1}{4}$

3 Multiply these fractions. Give your answers in their simplest form.

a $\frac{2}{3} \times \frac{1}{4}$    b $\frac{2}{7} \times \frac{3}{10}$    c $\frac{4}{5} \times \frac{6}{7}$    d $\frac{4}{9} \times \frac{3}{8}$

4 Work out these fractions of amounts.

a $\frac{1}{4}$ of £90    b $\frac{3}{5}$ of £35    c $\frac{5}{8}$ of £16    d $\frac{2}{3}$ of £24

5 What fraction of £500 is left after deducting $\frac{1}{5}$ of £500 and $\frac{1}{2}$ of £500?

6 Divide these fractions. Give your answers in their simplest form.

a $\frac{2}{5} \div 4$    b $\frac{1}{2} \div 2$    c $\frac{3}{4} \div 5$    d $\frac{9}{10} \div 6$

e $\frac{1}{5} \div \frac{1}{2}$    f $\frac{2}{9} \div \frac{1}{4}$    g $\frac{5}{16} \div \frac{1}{3}$    h $\frac{3}{10} \div \frac{2}{5}$

7 ☆ **PROBLEM** ☆

a Choose from this list: $\frac{1}{2}$ $\frac{3}{8}$ $\frac{2}{5}$ $\frac{4}{7}$ $\frac{1}{10}$

   i two fractions that have the lowest product
   ii three fractions that add up to 1.

b Choose from this list: $\frac{5}{8}$ $\frac{1}{2}$ $\frac{1}{5}$ $\frac{2}{7}$ $\frac{3}{10}$

   i two fractions that have the lowest product
   ii three fractions that add up to 1.

# Mixed numbers

- Use efficient methods to calculate with fractions

> → An **improper fraction** has the numerator (top) greater than the denominator (bottom). For example $\frac{10}{7}$ or $\frac{3}{2}$.
> → A **mixed number** contains a whole number part and a fraction part. For example $2\frac{1}{5}$ or $5\frac{3}{8}$
> → To calculate with **mixed numbers**, change them to **improper fractions** first.

**EXAMPLE**

Work out these fraction sums. Give your answer as a mixed number.

**a** $4\frac{1}{2} + 2\frac{3}{5}$　　　　　　　　**b** $5\frac{1}{6} - 2\frac{3}{4}$

**ANSWER**

**a** $4\frac{1}{2} = \frac{9}{2}$　　　　$4 \times 2 + 1 = 9$

$2\frac{3}{5} = \frac{13}{5}$　　　　$2 \times 5 + 3 = 13$

$4\frac{1}{2} + 2\frac{3}{5} = \frac{9}{2} + \frac{13}{5}$

$= \frac{45}{10} + \frac{26}{10}$

$= \frac{71}{10} = 7\frac{1}{10}$

**b** $5\frac{1}{6} - 2\frac{3}{4} = \frac{31}{6} - \frac{11}{4}$

$= \frac{62}{12} - \frac{33}{12}$

$= \frac{29}{12} = 2\frac{5}{12}$

**EXAMPLE**

Karl catches two fish. The first weighs $2\frac{1}{4}$ pounds.
The second fish weighs $1\frac{1}{2}$ times as much as the first fish.
How much does the second fish weigh?

**ANSWER**

$\frac{1}{2}$ of $2\frac{1}{4} = 1\frac{1}{8}$　　　Find $\frac{1}{2}$ of the weight of the first fish

$2\frac{1}{4} + 1\frac{1}{8} = \frac{9}{4} + \frac{9}{8}$　　　Then add weights

$= \frac{18}{8} + \frac{9}{8}$

$= \frac{27}{8} = 3\frac{3}{8}$

The second fish weighs $3\frac{3}{8}$ lb.

You get the same answer if you multiply the two fractions
$2\frac{1}{4} \times 1\frac{1}{2} = \frac{9}{4} \times \frac{3}{2} = \frac{27}{8} = 3\frac{3}{8}$

You can write the unit for pounds as lb. Always give the units in your answer.

Work out $3\frac{1}{5} \div 1\frac{7}{10}$

**ANSWER**

$3\frac{1}{5} \div 1\frac{7}{10} = \frac{16}{5} \div \frac{17}{10}$     First change to improper fractions

$= \frac{16}{\cancel{5}^{1}} \times \frac{\cancel{10}^{2}}{17}$     Cancel factors if you can

$= \frac{32}{17} = 1\frac{15}{17}$     Write your answer as a mixed number

## Exercise B9.4

**MEDIUM**

1   Work out these fractions of amounts.
Give your answer as a mixed number.

> This exercise is to be completed without a calculator.

   a   $\frac{2}{5} \times 4$      b   $\frac{3}{4} \times 10$      c   $\frac{5}{6} \times 9$      d   $\frac{1}{4} \times 3$

   e   $\frac{5}{6} \times 11$      f   $\frac{2}{3} \times 4$      g   $2\frac{1}{2} \times 5$      h   $\frac{2}{7} \times 3$

2   Work out these fraction additions.
Give your answer in its simplest form.

   a   $1\frac{2}{5} + 2\frac{3}{8}$      b   $9\frac{1}{2} + 2\frac{1}{4}$      c   $2\frac{3}{4} + 5\frac{1}{3}$      d   $1\frac{9}{10} + 3\frac{1}{2}$

3   Work out these fraction subtractions.
Give your answer as a mixed number.

   a   $2\frac{1}{2} - \frac{4}{13}$      b   $2\frac{1}{4} - \frac{3}{5}$      c   $1\frac{5}{6} - 2\frac{1}{4}$      d   $1\frac{3}{4} - 2\frac{2}{3}$

4   Work out these multiplications.
Give your answer as a mixed number.

   a   $2\frac{1}{4} \times \frac{3}{5}$      b   $1\frac{5}{6} \times \frac{4}{11}$      c   $\frac{2}{3} \times 1\frac{1}{4}$

> **RICH TASK**
>
> Work out
>
> a   $1, \; 1 \times \frac{1}{2}, \; 1 \times \frac{1}{2} \times \frac{1}{4}, \cdots$
>
> What happens to the product with each successive multiplication?
>
> b   $1, \; 1 \div \frac{1}{2}, \; 1 \div \frac{1}{4}, \cdots$
>
> What happens to the answer with each successive division?

5   A photograph is $12\frac{1}{2}$ cm wide and $17\frac{1}{5}$ cm long.
Work out the area of the photograph.

6   Work out these divisions.
Give your answer in its simplest form.

   a   $1\frac{2}{5} \div 4\frac{1}{2}$      b   $1\frac{1}{2} \div 3\frac{4}{5}$      c   $2\frac{3}{4} \div 1\frac{5}{6}$

   d   $3\frac{1}{3} \div 4\frac{1}{4}$      e   $4\frac{2}{9} \div 1\frac{1}{3}$      f   $3\frac{1}{6} \div 2\frac{3}{5}$

# Recurring decimals

- Convert a recurring decimal to a fraction

→ Recurring decimals **contain digits that repeat over and over again.**

Dots above the recurring digits show how the decimal recurs:

$\frac{7}{9}$ = 0.77777...     = 0.$\dot{7}$         Only 7 repeats

$\frac{1}{15}$ = 0.06666...     = 0.0$\dot{6}$         6 repeats but not 0

$\frac{16}{33}$ = 0.48484...     = 0.$\dot{4}\dot{8}$         4 and 8 both repeat

$\frac{1}{7}$ = 0.14285714...   = 0.$\dot{1}$42857$\dot{7}$   A group of 6 digits repeats

**REMEMBER:**

To convert a fraction to a decimal, just divide:

$\frac{7}{9}$ = 7 ÷ 9 = 0.77777...

You can change a recurring decimal to a fraction by eliminating the recurring

**EXAMPLE**

Write as a fraction   **a** 0.0$\dot{4}$   **b** 0.4$\dot{9}\dot{2}$

× 100 so that the decimal part matches the original decimal part.

**ANSWER**

- Multiply by a power of 10:   **a** 100 × 0.0$\dot{4}$ = 4.0404...   **b** 1000 × 0.4$\dot{9}\dot{2}$ = 492.49249
- Subtract the original amount:   4.0404... – 0.0404 = 4       492.49249... – 0.49249 = 492
- Write how many lots of
  the decimal remain:       99 × 0.0$\dot{4}$ = 4       999 × 0.4$\dot{9}\dot{2}$ = 492
- Turn into a fraction:       0.0$\dot{4}$ = $\frac{4}{99}$       0.4$\dot{9}\dot{2}$ = $\frac{492}{999}$ = $\frac{164}{333}$

× 1000 so that the decimal part matches the original.

Try the same method with 0.5$\dot{7}$.
→ **Multiply it by 100. Multiply it also by 10.**
→ **Take the second quantity from the first quantity.**

## RICH TASK

These fractions all make **terminating decimals.**

$\frac{1}{2}$ = 0.5       $\frac{1}{5}$ = 0.2       $\frac{3}{10}$ = 0.3

$\frac{7}{25}$ = 0.28     $\frac{9}{40}$ = 0.225     $\frac{3}{8}$ = 0.375

Break the denominators down into their prime factors. What do they all have in common?

A **terminating decimal** has a finite number of decimal digits.

**Fractions, decimals and percentages**

> → **Fractions with denominators that can be written as products of only the prime numbers 2 and 5 are represented by terminating decimals.**

## Exercise B9.5

MEDIUM

*1 a Work out all the ninths fractions as decimals:
$\frac{1}{9}, \frac{2}{9}, \frac{3}{9}, \dots$

b Write down anything you notice.

> This exercise is to be completed without a calculator.

*2 a Work out the elevenths fractions as decimals:
$\frac{1}{11} \quad \frac{2}{11} \quad \frac{3}{11} \quad \frac{4}{11} \quad \frac{5}{11} \quad \frac{6}{11} \quad \frac{7}{11} \quad \frac{8}{11} \quad \frac{9}{11} \quad \frac{10}{11}$

b What do you notice about these decimals?

c Which is closer to $\frac{1}{2}$: $0.\dot{3}\dot{6}$ or $0.\dot{6}\dot{3}$? Justify your answer.

*3 a Which of these fractions can be expressed as a recurring decimal?
$\frac{3}{5}, \frac{3}{15}, \frac{3}{25}, \frac{3}{35}$
Explain how you know.

b Which of these fractions is not a recurring decimal:
$\frac{6}{27} \quad \frac{6}{30} \quad \frac{6}{33} \quad \frac{6}{36}$
Without working them out, explain how you decided.

*4 a Write these fractions as recurring decimals.
**i** $\frac{2}{9}$    **ii** $\frac{2}{90}$    **iii** $\frac{2}{900}$    **iv** $\frac{2}{9000}$

b Comment on any patterns you can see and explain why this happens.

5 Write these recurring decimals as fractions.
a $0.3\dot{7}$    b $0.1\dot{8}$    c $0.\dot{6}\dot{5}$    d $0.5\dot{6}\dot{7}$
e $0.\dot{1}23\dot{4}$    f $0.007\dot{6}$    g $0.0\dot{1}0\dot{3}$

6 **RICH TASK**

Work out $\frac{22}{7}$ as a decimal.

Now work out $4 - \frac{4}{3} + \frac{4}{5} - \frac{4}{7} + \frac{4}{9} - \frac{4}{11} + \cdots$

Continue this sum following the same pattern with the signs and the denominators. What special number do you find?

## CHECK OUT

You should now be able to
- use estimation and mental calculation
- perform calculations using fractions, decimals and percentages without a calculator
- understand that in some cases a fraction is exact where a decimal may not be
- convert recurring decimals to exact fractions.

*

**Exam-style question**

Which of the following is a recurring decimal?

$\frac{9}{15}$  $\frac{15}{20}$  $\frac{20}{25}$  $\frac{25}{30}$

Write down how you know that the other fractions do not recur, without converting them to decimals.

You will not have a calculator for this type of question.

Fractions are easier to deal with when given in their lowest terms.

**Liz's answer:**

Cancelling the fractions to lowest terms

$\frac{9}{15} = \frac{3}{5}$       $\frac{15}{20} = \frac{3}{4}$

$\frac{20}{25} = \frac{4}{5}$       $\frac{25}{30} = \frac{5}{6}$

$\frac{25}{30}$ is a recurring decimal

The other fractions do not recur since when cancelled to lowest terms they have denominators whose numbers are products of only 2 and 5

You may need to write a sentence to explain your thinking.

Thinking about the types of fractions that do not make recurring decimals.

## Exam practice

1  Work out
$$3\frac{4}{7} \div 1\frac{2}{7}$$

*(3 marks)*

2  Find the fractions equivalent to the following recurring decimals.

a  $0.0\dot{5}$

b  $0.\dot{3}\dot{1}$

*(4 marks)*

*3  A school librarian is given £400 to spend one year.

She wants to take out two magazine subscriptions for one year. One subscription costs £11·99 per month and the other £7·99 per month.

She also wants to buy a daily newspaper each day the school is open. The newspaper costs 80p per day and the school opens on 195 days.

Estimate whether or not she has enough money to pay for the magazine subscriptions and the newspaper.

*(4 marks)*

# Case study 3: Weather

Before creating a weather forecast, data is collected from all over the world to give information about the current conditions. A supercomputer and knowledge about the atmosphere, the Earth's surface and the oceans are then used to create the forecast.

Write down the temperature shown on each of these thermometers:

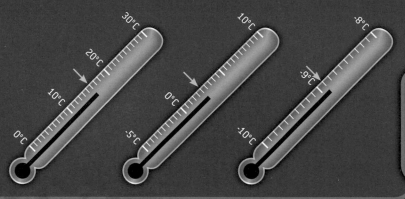

Each day, the Met Office receives and uses around half a million observations.

These tables show the national and UK weather records, last updated 24th November 2008:

| HIGHEST DAILY TEMPERATURE RECORDS | | | |
|---|---|---|---|
| England | 38.5 °C | 10 August 2003 | Faversham (Kent) |
| Wales | 35.2 °C | 2 August 1990 | Hawarden Bridge (Flintshire) |
| Scotland | 32.9 °C | 9 August 2003 | Greycrook (Scottish Borders) |
| Northern Ireland | 30.8 °C | 30 June 1976 12 July 1983 | Knockarevan (County Fermanagh) Shaw's Bridge, Belfast (County Antrim) |

| LOWEST DAILY TEMPERATURE RECORDS | | | |
|---|---|---|---|
| Scotland | -27.2 °C | 11 February 1895 10 January 1982 30 December 1995 | Braemar (Aberdeenshire) Braemar (Aberdeenshire) Altnaharra (Highland) |
| England | -26.1°C | 10 January 1982 | Newport (Shropshire) |
| Wales | -23.3 °C | 21 January 1940 | Rhayader (Powys) |
| Northern Ireland | -17.5 °C | 1 January 1979 | Magherally (County Down) |

Calcuate the difference (in °C) between the maximum and minimum temperatures for each of the nations shown.

Use the internet to find out if these records have since been broken.

Wind direction is measured in tens of degrees relative to true North and is always given from where the wind is blowing. In the UK, wind speed is measured in knots, where 1 knot = 1.15mph, or in terms of the Beaufort Scale.

Look up the Beaufort Scale on the internet. Use it to describe the weather shown on this map.

Describe the wind speed (in knots) and direction (in tens of degrees and in words) shown by each of the arrows shown on this map:

▲
(12)
24
indicates a mean wind of 12 m.p.h., coming from the south, gusting 24 m.p.h.

Observed data can be used to make predictions, but there is always some level of uncertainty. This graph shows the range of uncertainty in temperature in Exeter with some indication of the most probable values:

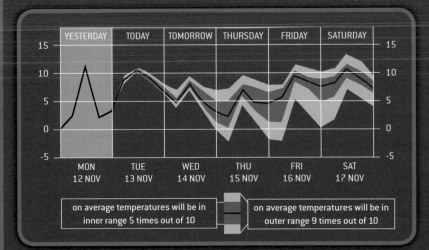

on average temperatures will be in inner range 5 times out of 10

on average temperatures will be in outer range 9 times out of 10

What predictions do you think a weather forecaster would have made about the temperature in Exeter during the week shown?

Justify your response by referring to the graph.

## INTRODUCTION

In everyday life you usually rely on experience to decide if something is true. In mathematics you start with something you already know is true and use steps of logical reasoning to show how it follows that something else is true. Mathematical proofs are essential and central to every part of higher level mathematics.

**What's the point?**
The skills used in being able to set out a logical train of thinking lie at the heart of every mathematician's work.

## CHECK IN

1 Work out the missing angles.

137°

a

123°

98°  b

2 Work out the missing angle in these shapes.

a

46°    32°

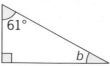

61°

b

**Orientation**

| What I should know | What I will learn | What this leads to |
|---|---|---|
| A3 | ■ Recognise different angles.<br>■ Use circle theorems<br>■ Find angles in polygons | C18 |

### RICH TASK

Investigate the angles and lengths
formed when a circle is cut by two lines.
(Hint: Look for similar triangles.)
Try to prove any results you find.

- Revise and use basic facts about angles

## RICH TASK

At 3 o'clock the hands of a clock are at right angles. How long will it be before the two hands are once again at right angles?

You should know these angle facts:

**Vertically opposite angles**

$a = b$

**Corresponding angles**

$a = b$

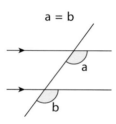

**Alternate angles**

$a = b$

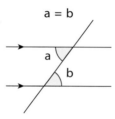

How are the ancient Babylonians who lived in modern Iraq associated with a 360° turn?

These angle facts can be used in a variety of problems.

---

**EXAMPLE**

Find the lettered angles made by the girders of this crane.

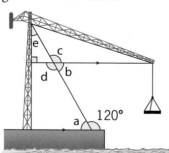

120°

**ANSWER**

$a = 180 - 120 = 60°$    (*a* and 120° make a straight line)

$b = 60°$    (*a* and *b* corresponding angles)

$d = 180 - 60 = 120°$    (*b* and *d* make a straight line)

$c = 120°$    (*c* and *d* vertically opposite)

$e = 180 - 90 - 60 = 30°$    (angle sum of a triangle)

MEDIUM

*Calculate the lettered angles. Angles given the same letter are equal.
Justify the steps in your working clearly.

1

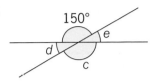

150°

e

d

c

2

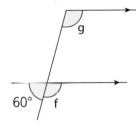

g

60°  f

3

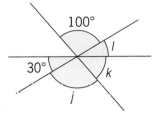

100°

l

30°

k

j

4

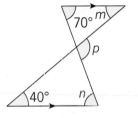

70° m

p

40°

n

5

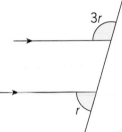

3r

r

6

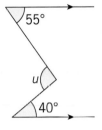

55°

u

40°

7

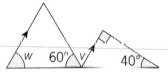

w   60°  v

40°

8

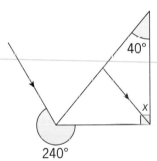

40°

x

240°

9  ☆ **CHALLENGE** ☆

Place two mirrors at an angle α with a pin P symmetrically between
them. Starting with α = 180°, reduce α and count the greatest number,
n, of pins you can see (including P itself) for different values of α.
Draw a graph of n against α.

- Revise various facts about triangles and quadrilaterals and prove some of them

## RICH TASK

A baby bouncer is attached in a doorframe with sides AB and CD elastic and BC rigid. The baby bounces vertically. Find a relationship between angles *x* and *y* and draw its graph. Which part of the graph gives the only practical possibilities for the baby?

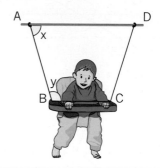

You already know this theorem, but you may not know how to prove it.

A theorem is a statement of a fact which has been proved.

The sum of the angles of any triangle is 180°.

**Proof**

Let the angles of triangle ABC be *a*, *b* and *c*.
Draw a line DE through C parallel to AB.
So   DĈA = *a* (alternate angles)
and   EĈB = *b* (alternate angles).
At point C on the straight line DE, *a* + *c* + *b* = 180°.
So the three angles of any triangle ABC add up to 180°.

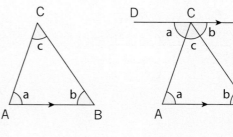

Can you use this theorem to prove two more theorems?

An exterior angle of a triangle is equal to the sum of the two opposite interior angles.

This theorem states that the exterior angle *z* = *a* + *c*.

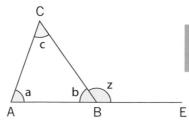

The sum of the interior angles of any quadrilateral is 360°.

This theorem states that *a* + *b* + *c* + *d* = 360°.

This symmetrical footbridge is made from steel girders.
Find the size of angle $x$.

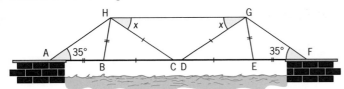

**ANSWER**

$\triangle$ABH is isosceles, so A$\hat{B}$H = $180 - 2 \times 35 = 110°$
On straight line ABC, H$\hat{B}$C = $180 - 110 = 70°$
$\triangle$HBC is isosceles, so B$\hat{C}$H = $180 - 2 \times 70 = 40°$
On straight line BCD, D$\hat{C}$H = $180 - 40 = 140°$
In quadrilateral HCDG, $x + x + 140 + 140 = 360°$
Angle $x = \frac{1}{2}(360 - 280) = 40°$

## Exercise B10.2

MEDIUM
LOW

Find the lettered angles.

1
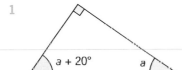

2
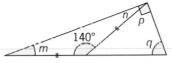

3
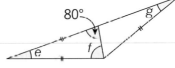

4
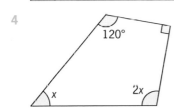

5
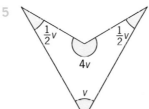

6
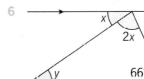

7
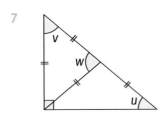

8
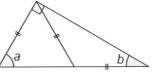

9
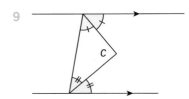

10 Triangle ABC has angle B which is 10° greater than angle A and
angle C which is 20° less than angle A. Find angle C.

11 As you visit the four angles of a quadrilateral in turn,
each angle is double the previous angle. Find all the angles.

**Continued** ▷

**12** A quadrilateral has two sides parallel and two of its angles are 50° and 120°. Find its other two angles.

Find the lettered angles in these diagrams. Angles marked with the same letter are equal.

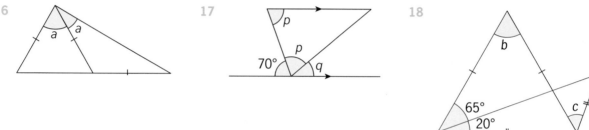

13

14

15

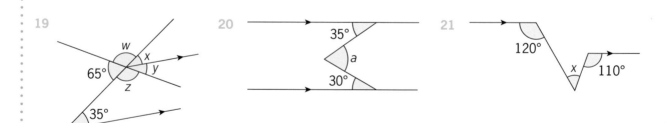

16

17

18

19

20

21

**22** A quadrilateral has a right angle, two equal angles and a fourth angle 20° bigger than these two. Write the sizes of all the angles.

**Circles, angles and lines**

# Angles in polygons

- Revise the properties and angles of polygons (including quadrilaterals)

★ ACTIVITY ★

Here are the names of the common **quadrilaterals**.

| Square | Rectangle | Parallelogram |
|---|---|---|
| Trapezium | Rhombus | Kite |

The **properties** of quadrilaterals tell you about their sides and angles. Draw an example of each of these quadrilaterals and say which of them **must** have

- all sides equal
- all angles equal
- both pairs of opposite sides equal
- both pairs of opposite sides parallel
- both pairs of opposite angles equal

- both diagonals equal
- diagonals which are perpendicular
- diagonals which bisect each other.

What other properties can you list?

'Quad' means 'four' in words such as quad-bike, quadruplets, quadrangle.

Polygons are 2-D shapes with straight edges.
Polygons can be split into triangles by joining one corner to all other corners, as for this hexagon.
The sum of the angles of a polygon can be found from the angles of these triangles.
Sum of angles of a hexagon = 4 × 180° = 720°

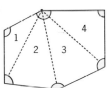

Poly- comes from the Greek word for 'many'.

**EXAMPLE**

The design of an arrow head is based on a hexagon with two angles of 100°, an angle of 70° and three other equal angles, $\alpha$.
Calculate the value of the interior angles $\alpha$ and the exterior angles $\beta$.

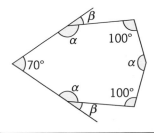

**ANSWER**

The sum of the six interior angles =
$2 \times 100° + 70° + 3 \times \alpha = 720°$
So   $3\alpha = 720 - 200 - 70 = 450°$
Interior angle $\alpha = 450 \div 3 = 150°$
and exterior angle $\beta = 180 - \alpha = 180 - 150 = 30°$

## RICH TASK

You can find the sum of the interior angles of any polygon.

For an octagon    For a pentagon

6 triangles, and 6 × 180° = 1080°   3 triangles, and 3 × 180° = 540°

Can you find a general rule?

### Exercise B10.3

MEDIUM

1   Copy and complete for regular polygons.

| Polygon | Number of sides | Each interior angle | Each exterior angle | Sum of all interior angles |
|---|---|---|---|---|
| Triangle | 3 | | | 180° |
| Quadrilateral | 4 | | | |
| Pentagon | 5 | | | |
| Hexagon | 6 | | | |
| Octagon | 8 | | | |
| Decagon | 10 | | | |

2   Find the lettered interior and exterior angles.

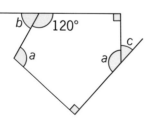

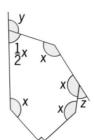

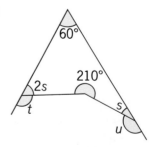

3   a   A hexagon has three angles of $x°$ each, an angle of $x + 29°$, an angle of $x - 10°$ and a
further angle which is double the smallest angle. Find all the angles.

   b   A pentagon has two angles the same size and three equal angles which are each 10° bigger.
Find all the angles.

4   A pentagon has four equal angles and a fifth angle of 100°.
It is used in the design of a star.
Calculate the angles at the points of the star.

5  A regular polygon has all its sides and angles equal.
   Draw a regular pentagon and regular octagon by dividing two
   circles of radius 5 cm into equal parts.
   Measure their interior and exterior angles and check your answers by calculation.

   a   What is the size of one exterior angle of a regular polygon if it has
       **i**  12 sides    **ii**  36 sides    **iii**  20 sides    **iv**  18 sides?
   b   Find the size of each exterior angle and each interior angle of a regular polygon with
       **i**  9 sides    **ii**  15 sides    **iii**  24 sides    **iv**  30 sides.

6   **RICH TASK**

   Find formulae to calculate
   a   the sum of all the interior angles of any *n*-sided polygon
   b   one interior angle and one exterior angle of a regular *n*-sided polygon.
   Calculate an interior angle and an exterior angle of a regular icosagon.

7   Two frame tents have these cross-sections.
    Calculate the values of *m* and *n*.

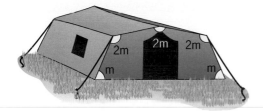
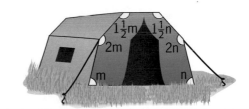

8   A garden pond has the shape of a heptagon.
    Calculate the value of *x*.

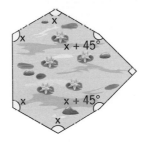

9   **RICH TASK**

   A regular *n*-sided polygon has an interior angle, $\alpha$.
   Copy and complete this table for increasing values of *n*.
   Draw a graph of $\alpha$ against *n*.
   Explain what is happening as *n* gets larger.

   | No of sides, n | 3 | 4 | 5 | ... |
   |---|---|---|---|---|
   | Interior angle, $\alpha$ | | | | |

10  **Research**
   Islamic art, like the ancient art of the Greeks and Romans, uses
   geometric patterns. Find some tessellations used in the
   Alhambra palace in Spain. Use the internet to explore the
   modern-day work of Roger Penrose and M. C. Escher.

Angles in polygons

Unit B

# Circle theorems 1

- Understand and use symmetry properties of circles

How many lines of symmetry does a circle have?

When radii, tangents or chords are drawn on a circle, the whole shape may still have a line of symmetry.

 p. 270

There are three particular cases.

A radius is drawn at the point T
where a tangent touches a circle.
Where is the line of symmetry of the shape?
What can you say about angles $a_1$ and $a_2$?
Is the radius OT perpendicular to the tangent?

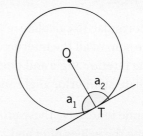

If the tangent at T moves towards O, it becomes the chord PQ.

A perpendicular line is drawn from the centre of the circle O to a chord PQ to meet the chord at point M.
Where is the line of symmetry of the shape?
What can you say about
i   angles $a_1$ and $a_2$
ii  triangles OMP and OMQ
iii the lines PM and QM?
Does the perpendicular line bisect the chord?

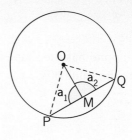

Two tangents XP and XQ are drawn to a circle from an external point X.
Where is the line of symmetry of the shape?
What can you say about
i   angles $a_1$ and $a_2$
ii  angles $b_1$ and $b_2$
iii triangles OXP and OXQ
iv  the lengths XP and XQ?

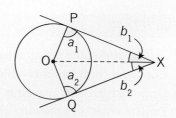

The conclusions are:
- the angle between a tangent and a radius is 90°
- the perpendicular from the centre to a chord bisects the chord
- two tangents meeting at an external point are equal in length.

A garden sprinkler waters a circle of radius 3 metres.
The water just reaches the far edge of a straight path which is 1 metre wide.
What length of the nearer edge of the path is sprinkled?

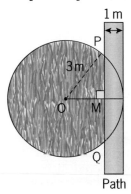

**ANSWER**

By symmetry, triangle OMP is right-angled at point M.
OP = 3 metres and OM = 3 − 1 = 2 metres
Pythagoras' theorem gives    $OP^2 = OM^2 + PM^2$
$$3^2 = 2^2 + PM^2$$
$$PM^2 = 9 - 4 = 5$$
$$PM = \sqrt{5} = 2.236...$$
By symmetry, M is the midpoint of PQ
So    PQ = 2 × 2.236 ..... = 4.47 (to 2 d.p.)
The nearer edge of the path is sprinkled along 4.47 metres.

## Exercise B10.4

MEDIUM HIGH

Find the lettered angles in these diagrams.

1

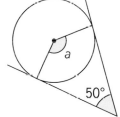

2

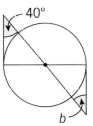

3

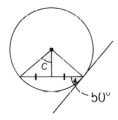

4

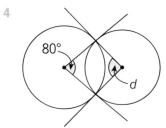

5

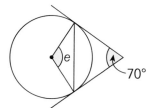

6

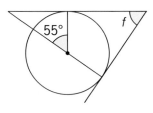

**Continued** ➤

Circle theorems 1    157

**7**

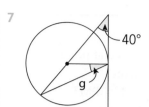

40°

g

**8**

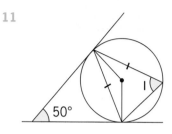

40°

70°

h

**9**

25°

i

**10**

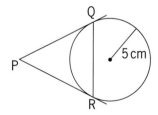

j

70°

**11**

50°

l

12  A satellite is positioned to stay 100 km directly above the
North Pole. An explorer walks due south from the pole
keeping the satellite in view.
How far is he from the satellite when he can no longer see it?

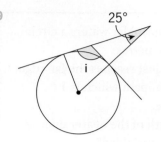

The earth's radius is about
6378 km

13  Two tangents of length 12 cm are drawn from an external point P
to a circle of radius 5 cm to touch the circle at points Q and R.
Calculate the length of chord QR.

Q

P

5 cm

R

# Circle theorems 2

- Prove five theorems and use them to calculate angles in circles

In this circle, the arc XY subtends an angle $\alpha$ at the centre O and an angle $\beta$ at any point P on the circumference.

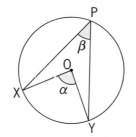

The word *subtends* means *stretches beneath*.

You can prove a relationship between angles $\alpha$ and $\beta$.

## *Proof*

Extend the line PO and make two triangles.

In triangle OXP, $\quad a_1 = O\hat{X}P + O\hat{P}X$
$$= 2 \times O\hat{P}X = 2b_1$$
Similarly, in triangle OYP, $a_2 = 2b_2$

By addition, $a_1 + a_2 = 2b_1 + 2b_2 = 2(b_1 + b_2)$

so $\qquad X\hat{O}Y = 2 \times X\hat{P}Y$ or $\alpha = 2\beta$

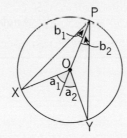

or ...
the angle at the centre is twice the angle at the circumference

→ **The angle subtended at the centre is twice the angle subtended at any point on the circumference.**

This theorem can be extended.

### ☆ ACTIVITY ☆

Imagine points X and Y moving further apart so that the arc XY becomes a semicircle.
XOY is now a straight line and a diameter of the circle.
What are the values of angles $\alpha$ and $\beta$ now?

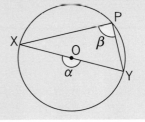

This result can be made into a theorem:

→ **The angle subtended at the circumference in a semicircle is a right angle.**

Now consider a cyclic quadrilateral $XP_1YP_2$ as shown.
Using the earlier theorem, obtuse angle $\beta_1 = 2 \times \beta_1$
and reflex angle $\beta_2 = 2 \times \beta_2$

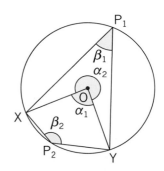

Addition gives

$$\beta_1 + \beta_2 = 2\beta_1 + 2\beta_2$$
$$= 2(\beta_1 + \beta_2)$$

But $\beta_1 + \beta_2 = 360°$, so $\beta_1 + \beta_2 = 180°$.
This result can be expressed as a theorem:

A *cyclic quadrilateral* is one which has its four vertices on the circumference of a circle.

→ **Opposite angles in a cyclic quadrilateral add up to 180°.**

Find angle $\theta$ where the circle has centre O.

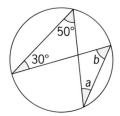

**ANSWER**

$O\hat{S}Q = 30°$     base angles in isosceles triangle

$Q\hat{O}S = 180 - 2 \times 30 = 120°$     angle sum of triangle

$Q\hat{P}S = \frac{1}{2} \times 120 = 60°$     angles on circumference and at centre

Angle $\theta = Q\hat{R}S = 180 - 60 = 120°$     cyclic quadrilateral

## Exercise B10.5

MEDIUM HIGH

1 Find the lettered angles.

a

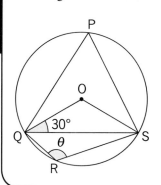

b

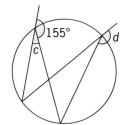

c

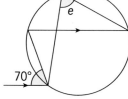

d

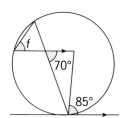

e

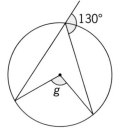

f

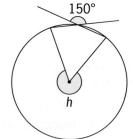

g

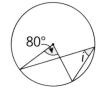

h

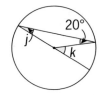

i

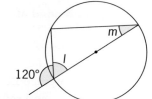

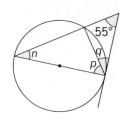

j

k

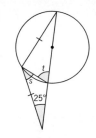

l

2   Find the lettered angles in these diagrams. Where marked, O is the centre of the circle and T is the point at which a tangent touches the circle.

a
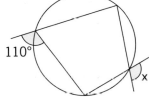

b
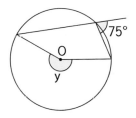

c
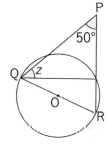

d
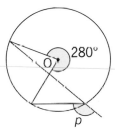

e
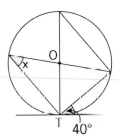

f
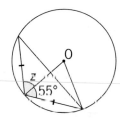

3   **RICH TASK**

An unusual snooker table has a circular shape. You hit a ball from any point to strike the circumference of the circle at point P such that the direction of motion makes an angle $\theta$ with the tangent at P. Assuming that the ball bounces off at the same angle $\theta$, what values of $\theta$ make the snooker ball travel the same route over and order again? What shapes does the ball describe in these cases?

What happens when $\theta$ takes other values?

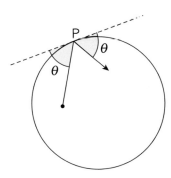

## CHECK OUT

You should now be able to
- solve problems using angles in parallel lines and in polygons
- prove and use circle theorems.

**Exam-style question**

The diagram shows an irregular hexagon. Angle $y$ is $\frac{3}{4}$ angle $x$.

x   x

y        y

126°   x

Work out angle $x$ and angle $y$.

**Carla's answer:**

Find the sum of the interior angles in a hexagon by dividing the shape into triangles.

Work out the total angles in the hexagon shown.

4 triangles
Sum interior angles = 4 × 180 = 720°

Sum interior angles in shape
$x + x + y + x + y + 126 = 3x + 2y + 126$

$3x + 2y + 126 = 720; 3x + 2y = 594$

Use the information given
angle $y$ is $\frac{3}{4}$ angle $x$
to find a relationship between $x$ and $y$.

$y$ is $\frac{3}{4}x$ so $4y = 3x$

Substitute to find $x$ and $y$.

$4y + 2y = 594; 6y = 594; y = 99°$

$3x = 4y; 3x = 4 × 99; x = 132°$

## Exam practice

*1 Find the size of angle $x$ and angle $y$.
Write down a reason for each answer.

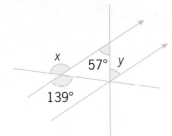

(4 marks)

*2 a Find the missing angles. Give a reason for each answer.

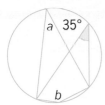

b Explain why C is not the centre of the circle.

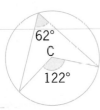

(6 marks)

3 This shape is made from five congruent isosceles triangles with a regular pentagon at its centre.

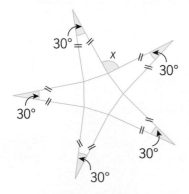

Find the size of angle $x$.

(4 marks)

# 11 Straight lines

## INTRODUCTION

When you hire a car the price increases in equal amounts for each extra day of hiring. This is an example of a linear function and the graph will be a straight line.

**What's the point?**

Linear functions occur commonly in man-made situations, such as in currency conversion and in working out tariffs and charges. Using linear graphs can help you to solve real-life problems quickly and efficiently.

## CHECK IN

1 Plot these sets of points on a graph, joining them to produce a line in each case.

 **i** $(3, 1), (3, 2), (3, 3)$    **ii** $(1, -2), (2, -2), (3, -2)$
 **iii** $(1, 3), (2, 5), (3, 7)$    **iv** $(1, 4), (2, 3), (3, 2)$

2 Convert these improper fractions to mixed numbers and vice versa.

 a $\dfrac{13}{2}$    b $\dfrac{21}{4}$    c $\dfrac{33}{7}$    d $-\dfrac{100}{11}$

 e $2\dfrac{1}{3}$    f $7\dfrac{1}{2}$    g $5\dfrac{3}{4}$    h $-4\dfrac{3}{8}$

3 Find the value of the unknown in each equation.

 a $9 = 3n + 3$    b $6 = 1 + 5m$    c $10p - 4 = 1$

## What I should know

A7

## What I will learn

- Find the equation of a straight line
- Interpret graphs
- Identify equations

## What this leads to

B14

## RICH TASK

You can draw squares in different orientations on a square dotty grid.

Investigate the relationship between the gradients of adjacent sides of squares.
What gradients are possible for the sides of squares drawn on a 6 × 6 dotty grid?

# Linear graphs

- Generate points and plot graphs of linear functions

## RICH TASK

Arrange these cards to create a variety of different linear functions. You do not have to use all the cards each time. For each linear function, generate three coordinate pairs and plot the corresponding graph. Comment on its shape.

p. 362

A linear function is of the form $y = ax + b$,
where $a$ and $b$ are constants.

$y = 5$, $y = 3x - 2$ and $5x + 2y = 1$ are linear functions.
$y = x^2$, $y = x^2 - 2x - 3$ and $y = x^3 + 1$ are not linear functions.

How could you define a linear function to others in your class?

→ **The graph of a linear function is always a straight line.**

### EXAMPLE

Plot the graphs of $y = 2$ and $y = 2x + 1$ on a set of coordinate axes and write the point of intersection.

**ANSWER**

Choose three values for $x$ (say 0, 1, 2) to give you three pairs of coordinates.

$y = 2$

| x | 0 | 1 | 2 |
|---|---|---|---|
| y | 2 | 2 | 2 |

All the $y$-values are 2.

$y = 2x + 1$

| x | 0 | 1 | 2 |
|---|---|---|---|
| y | 1 | 3 | 5 |

Each $y$-value is double the $x$-value, add 1.

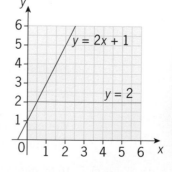

You can draw a straight line with two points, but you also need a third point to check your line is correct.

The point of intersection is $\left( \frac{1}{2}, 2 \right)$.

In the previous example, you can see that the graph of $y = 2$ is a horizontal line.

→ **If $c$ is a constant, functions of the form $y = c$ produce horizontal line graphs.**
   **Similarly, functions of the form $x = c$ produce vertical line graphs.**

**Straight lines**

## Exercise B11.1

1

$y = 3x - 5$    $x = 3$    $y = x^2 + 2x$    $y = 2x$

$y = x^3$    $y = 0$    $x = 10$    $y = x$

Select the functions that produce

a    horizontal straight-line graphs
b    vertical straight-line graphs
c    diagonal straight lines
d    curved graphs.

> 'Diagonal' here means not horizontal nor vertical.

2    a    For each given function, copy and complete the table of values.

**i** $y = 2$

| x | 0 | 1 | 2 |
|---|---|---|---|
| y |   |   |   |

**ii** $y = 3x$

| x | 0 | 1 | 2 |
|---|---|---|---|
| y |   |   |   |

**iii** $y = 2x - 1$

| x | 0 | 1 | 2 |
|---|---|---|---|
| y |   |   |   |

**iv** $y = 3 - 2x$

| x | 0 | 1 | 2 |
|---|---|---|---|
| y |   |   |   |

b    Plot these graphs on a set of coordinate axes with values from −8 to +8.

3    A quadrilateral has vertices at the points (1, 2), (1, 5), (4, 5) and (4, 2).

> Draw a sketch to help you!

a    What type of quadrilateral is this?
b    Write the equations of the four straight lines that make up the sides of this shape.

4    The point (2, 4) lies on the graph of the linear function $y = 3x - 2$.
a    Write the coordinates of another point that lies on this graph.
b    The point (6, y) lies on this graph. Find the value of y.
c    The point (x, 10) lies on this graph. Find the value of x.

*5    a    Plot these graphs on the same set of coordinate axes.

> Choose x-values from −2 to 2.

   **i** $y = 2x - 3$    **ii** $y = 2x$    **iii** $y = 2x + 5$

b    Write what you notice about these graphs.
c    Write a linear function whose graph is parallel to the line $y = 3x$.

*6    a    Plot these graphs on the same set of coordinate axes.

> Choose x-values from −2 to 2.

   **i** $y = \frac{1}{2}x + 1$    **ii** $y = 2x + 1$    **iii** $y = 5x + 1$

b    Write what you notice about these graphs.
c    Write a linear function whose graph is steeper than the line $y = 3x$.

# Gradients and *y*-intercepts

- Find the gradient and *y*-intercept of a straight line

## RICH TASK

Copy and complete this arithmagon.
Each square must contain the gradient of the line joining the two points given in the surrounding circles.
Can you create an arithmagon of your own to swap with a partner?

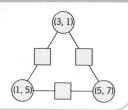

→ **Gradient is a measure of the steepness or slope of a straight line.**

**The gradient is 2. This means that for every 1 unit across you move 2 units up.**

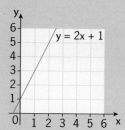

**The gradient is $-\frac{1}{2}$. This means that for every 1 unit across you move $\frac{1}{2}$ a unit down.**

→ **The gradient, *m*, of the line joining the points $(x_1, y_1)$ and $(x_2, y_2)$ is given by**

$$m = \frac{y_2 - y_1}{x_2 - x_1}$$

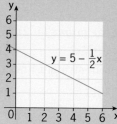

$$\text{Gradient} = \frac{\text{change in } y\text{-direction}}{\text{change in } x\text{-direction}}$$

→ **The *y*-intercept, *c*, is the point at which a straight line cuts the *y*-axis. The point has coordinates (0, *c*).**

**EXAMPLE**

Find the gradient and *y*-intercept of the straight line joining the points $(-1, -1)$ and $(1, 5)$.

**ANSWER**

A sketch of the line is:

Gradient $= m = \dfrac{5 - (-1)}{1 - (-1)} = \dfrac{6}{2} = 3$

By inspecting the diagram, the line cuts the *y*-axis at 2. The coordinates of the *y*-intercept are (0, 2).

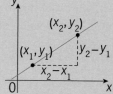

Change in *y*-direction is +6

Change in *x*-direction is +2

1 Find the gradient and $y$-intercept of each of these lines.

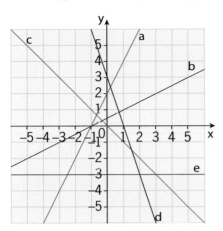

2 Find the gradients of the line segments joining these pairs of points.
   a (1, 3) to (4, 9)   b (2, 7) to (6, 23)   c (−5, 5) to (−2, 2)
   d (−2, 0) to (4, 3)   e (−2, 4) to (5, −10)   f (1, 2) to (13, 6)
   g (−4, 1) to (4, −3)   h (−10, 2) to (5, 2)
   What can you say about the line segment in part h?

3 For each of these linear functions
   i  Plot a straight-line graph
   ii  Write the gradient and $y$-intercept
   iii  Compare the equation of the line with the gradient and
       $y$-intercept and write what you notice.

   a $y = 3x + 5$   b $y = 2x − 3$   c $y = \frac{1}{2}x + 1$   d $y = 3 − x$

4 On a set of coordinate axes from −5 to +5, draw lines that fit
   these descriptions.
   a Has a gradient of 2 and cuts the $y$-axis at 1.
   b Has a $y$-intercept at (0, −1) and a gradient of $\frac{1}{2}$.
   c Has a gradient of −3 and cuts the $y$-axis at (0, 4).

5 a The gradient of the line joining (5, $t$) to (8, 3$t$) is 4.
      Find the value of $t$ and hence the given coordinates.
   b The gradient of the line joining ($k$, 4$k$) to (3$k$, 20) is 3.
      Find the value of $k$ and hence the given coordinates.

# Equation of a straight line

- Find the equation of a straight line in the form $y = mx + c$

→ **The equation of a straight-line graph can be written in the form $y = mx + c$ where $m$ is the gradient and $(0, c)$ are the coordinates of the $y$-intercept.**

**EXAMPLE**

A straight line has equation    **a**   $y = 3x - 1$     **b**   $x + 4y = 12$
Write   **i**   the gradient   **ii**   the $y$-intercept.

**ANSWER**

**a**   $y = 3x - 1$

Compare with $y = mx + c$.

$m = 3, c = -1$

So, **i**   gradient = 3     **ii**   $y$-intercept = $(0, -1)$

**b**   The equation $x + 4y = 12$ is in implicit form. Rearrange the equation to make $y$ the subject.

$$x + 4y = 12$$
$$4y = 12 - x \quad \text{Subtract } x \text{ from both sides}$$
$$y = 3 - \frac{1}{4}x \quad \text{Divide both sides by 4}$$

> When $y$ is the subject, an equation is in explicit form. When $y$ is *not* the subject, an equation is in implicit form.

In explicit form    $y = -\frac{1}{4}x + 3$    Reorder the equation for easy comparison to $y = mx + c$

Comparing gives   **i**   Gradient = $-\frac{1}{4}$   **ii**   $y$-intercept $(0, 3)$

## RICH TASK

- Explore parallel straight lines.
  What can you say about their gradients?
- Explore perpendicular straight lines.
  What can you say about their gradients?

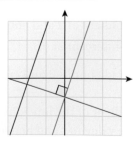

**You should find the following key points.**
→ **The gradients of parallel lines are equal.**
→ **The gradients of perpendicular lines multiply to give −1.**

## Exercise B11.3

1  Copy and complete the table for each of these equations.

| Equation | Gradient | Coordinates of y-intercept |
|----------|----------|----------------------------|
|          |          |                            |

a  $y = 2x + 5$     b  $y = 7x - 1$     c  $y = 3x$     d  $y = \frac{1}{3}x + 2$

e  $y - 4(x - 3)$     f  $2y = x - 3$     g  $x + 4y = 12$     h  $3x + 4y = 8$

2  Match each line with its equation.

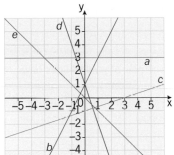

$y = \frac{1}{3}x - 1$

$y = 3$

$y = -x$

$y = 1 - 3x$

$y = 2x + 1$

3  Write the equations of these straight lines.
   a  Line A has a gradient of 3 and y-intercept at (0, 1).
   b  Line B cuts the y-axis at −5 and has a gradient of 1.
   c  Line C is parallel to the line $2y = x + 2$ and has a y-intercept at (0, −3).
   d  Line D is perpendicular to the line $y = 5 - \frac{1}{3}x$ and cuts the y-axis at −2.

*4  Are these statements true or false? Explain your answers.
   a  The lines $y = 5$ and $x = -3$ are parallel.
   b  The lines $y = 5x - 1$ and $2y - 10x = 1$ do not intersect.
   c  The lines $y = 2x + 1$ and $2y = 6 - x$ meet at right angles.
   d  The line $y = \frac{1}{2}x$ and the line passing through the points (0, 2) and (3, 8) are perpendicular.

5  It is thought that two variables, $k$ and $t$, are related by an equation of the form $t = mk + c$. The table shows some values of these variables.

| k | 1   | 3   | 3.5  | 4.2 | 5.6  |
|---|-----|-----|------|-----|------|
| t | 3.5 | 6.5 | 7.25 | 8.3 | 10.4 |

   a  Plot a graph of this information.
   b  Use your graph or the values in the table to determine the gradient of the line.
   c  Write the equation of the line relating the variables $k$ and $t$.

# Identifying equations

- Use knowledge of the properties of straight-line graphs to find equations

## RICH TASK

Can you draw these squares? Write the equations of the lines that you use.

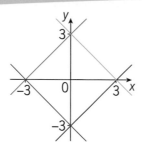

If one pair of parallel lines have the equations $y = x + k$ and $y = x - k$, find the equations of the other pair.

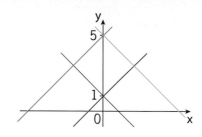

If one pair of parallel lines have the equations $y = mx + c$ and $y = mx + d$, where $m$ is positive, find the equations of the other pair.

→ **To write the equation of a straight line you need the gradient, $m$, and the $y$-intercept, $c$. Substitute these values into the general equation $y = mx + c$.**

→ **You can find the equation of a straight line given the gradient and a point on the line.**

**EXAMPLE**

A line is parallel to $3y = x + 3$ and passes through $(3, 5)$. Write the equation of this line.

**ANSWER**

The equation $3y = x + 3$ is in implicit form. Rearrange the equation to make $y$ the subject.

This equation is in explicit form ⟶ $y = \frac{1}{3}x + 1$      Divide both sides by 3

This line has a gradient of $\frac{1}{3}$. A line parallel to this line will also have a gradient of $\frac{1}{3}$.

Substituting the gradient, $m = \frac{1}{3}$ into $y = mx + c$ gives $y = \frac{1}{3}x + c$

Then susbstitute the values $x = 3$ and $y = 5$ into

$y = \frac{1}{3}x + c$      The line passes through $(3, 5)$

$5 = \frac{1}{3} \times 3 + c$

$5 = 1 + c$

$c = 4$      Subtract 1 from both sides

The equation of the line is $y = \frac{1}{3}x + 4$.

→ **You can find the equation of a straight line given two points on the line.**

A line passes through the points $(-1, 4)$ and $(2, 10)$. Write the equation of this line.

**ANSWER**

Gradient $= m = \dfrac{10 - 4}{2 - (-1)} = \dfrac{6}{3} = 2$

Substituting the gradient, $m = 2$ into $y = mx + c$ gives $y = 2x + c$

Substituting the values $x = -1$ and $y = 4$ gives

$$4 = 2 \times -1 + c$$
$$4 = -2 + c$$

Add 2 to both sides $\quad c = 6$

> Substitute the other point into $y = 2x + 6$ to check.
> $10 = 2 \times 2 + 6$. Correct.

The equation of the line is $y = 2x + 6$.

## Exercise B11.4

MEDIUM HIGH

1 Which of these lines passes through the point $(2, -1)$?

| Line | $y = x - 3$ | $x + y = 1$ | $y = 2x$ | $y = 2x - 3$ | $y = \dfrac{3}{2}x - 4$ |
|---|---|---|---|---|---|
| ✓ or ✗ | | | | | |

2 Write the equation of each of these lines.

| Line A | Line B | Line C | Line D |
|---|---|---|---|
| Gradient = 3 | Gradient = −2 | Gradient = 2 | Gradient = $\dfrac{1}{4}$ |
| $y$-intercept = $(0, 2)$ | $y$-intercept = $(0, 5)$ | Passes through $(1, -3)$ | Passes through $(8, -1)$ |

3 Write the equation of each of these lines.

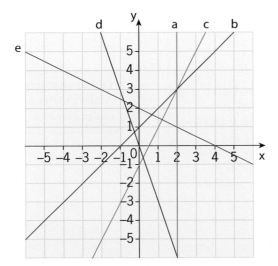

4 Write the equations of the lines joining these points.

a $(0, 1)$ and $(3, 7)$    b $(2, 8)$ and $(4, 18)$

c $(4, 3)$ and $(12, 7)$    d $(5, -1)$ and $(10, 0)$

e $(1, 3)$ and $(7, -3)$    f $(-1, 13)$ and $(3, 1)$

g $(-2, 6)$ and $(2, -4)$    h $(-3, 3)$ and $\left(1, 1\dfrac{2}{3}\right)$

## CHECK OUT

You should now be able to
- draw straight lines
- find and use gradient and *y*-intercept of straight lines.

**Exam-style question**

Look at this diagram.

**a** Explain why the gradient of the lines joining A and D, and B and C, is 0.

**b** What is the gradient of the line joining
   **i** A and B    **ii** C and D?

**c** Explain how this tells you that the shape ABCD is a parallelogram.

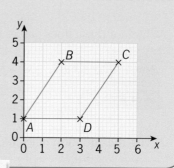

**Jane's answer:**

**a** AD and BC are both horizontal lines and the gradient of a horizontal line is zero

**b** **i** A(0, 1) B(2, 4)

Gradient AB = $\dfrac{1-4}{0-2} = \dfrac{-3}{-2} = \dfrac{3}{2}$

**ii** C(5, 4) D(3, 1)

Gradient CD = $\dfrac{4-1}{5-3} = \dfrac{3}{2}$

**c** Gradient of AB = gradient of CD So AB is parallel to CD & AB is opposite CD. We were told that gradients of AD and BC are the same and they are opposite sides. A four-sided shape with two pairs of parallel sides is a parallelogram, so ABCD is a parallelogram

All the information you need will be on the diagram.

Write explanations that are complete, clear and concise.

Explain means that you have to use words as well as numbers.

Explain what your results show in your explanation.

## Exam practice

*1  a  Find the equation of the line that passes through the points (1, 5) and (0, 2).

Another line has equation $x + 3y = 5$.

  b  Explain, without drawing, how you can tell whether this line is
  - parallel,
  - perpendicular
  - or neither parallel nor perpendicular to the first line.

*(5 marks)*

*2  Three straight lines intersect to form a triangle.
The equations of these straight lines are
$$y = 2x - 5 \qquad y = 5x + 2 \qquad x + 2y = 5$$
Is the triangle right-angled? Justify your answer.

*(3 marks)*

3  AB is the diameter of a circle.
A is the point $(-2, 8)$. B is the point $(0, -2)$.

Work out
  a  The gradient of the line AB
  b  The equation of the diameter that is perpendicular to the diameter AB

*(7 marks)*

## INTRODUCTION

When you play a computer game the way your character moves around the screen can be described by mathematical transformations. Combinations of these transformations, often taking place in 3-D worlds, allow the characters to move in many different ways.

**What's the point?**

Mathematicians use transformations not just to move shapes but also to move graphs and statistics. This helps them match the mathematics to real-life situations.

## CHECK IN

1 Write the coordinates of the points A–E.

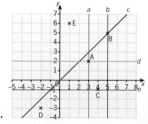

2 Write the equations of the lines a–e.

# Orientation

| What I should know | What I will learn | What this leads to |
| --- | --- | --- |
| Key stage 3 | ■ Find images of reflected shapes<br>■ Find the images of rotated shapes<br>■ Translate and enlarge shapes | C20 |

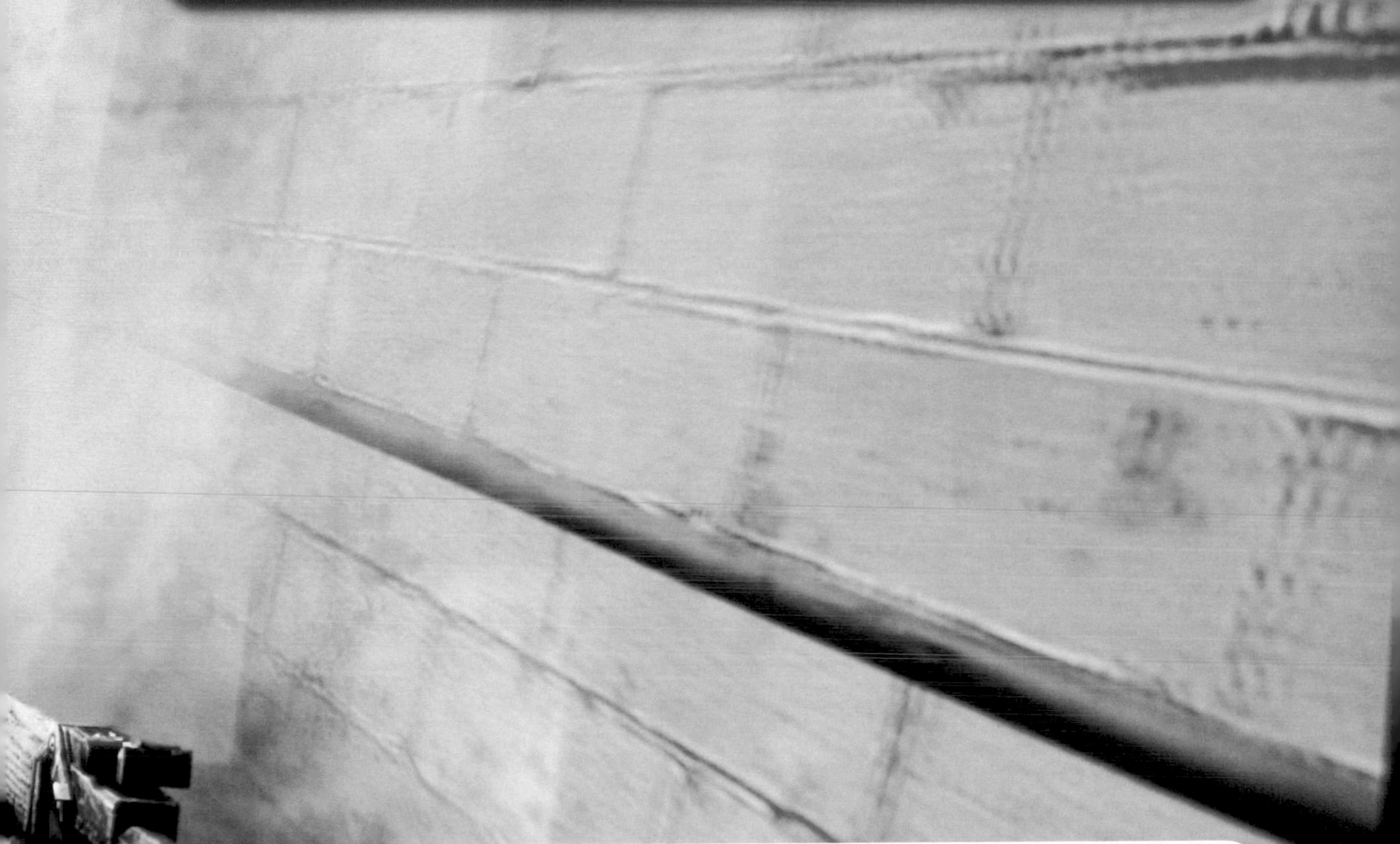

## RICH TASK

You will need some square dotty paper for this investigation.

This diagram shows a quadrilateral with an area of 4 cm². There are six dots on the perimeter of the quadrilateral and 2 dots inside the perimeter.

Investigate.

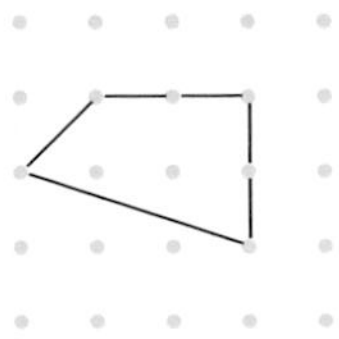

# Reflections and rotations

• Know how to reflect and rotate a shape

When a shape is reflected in a **mirror line**, every point maps onto its image by moving at right angles to the mirror line for the same distance beyond the mirror.

To find a mirror line, joint object points to their image points. Find the midpoints. These midpoints are on the mirror line.

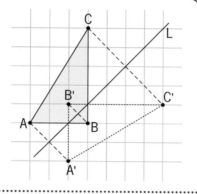

**EXAMPLE**

Reflect triangle ABC in line L.

**ANSWER**

Map each corner of the object triangle ABC onto its image A′B′C′ by counting diagonal distances at right angles to line L. Join the image points A′, B′ and C′.

> When the object shape crosses the mirror line, the mirror-line acts as a double-sided mirror.

When a shape is rotated, you need to know:

→ the **centre** of rotation
→ the **angle** of rotation
→ the **direction** of rotation.

> An anticlockwise angle of rotation is positive; clockwise is negative.

You can use tracing paper to help you do rotations.

Triangle A is rotated through 90° clockwise about point P onto its image A′.

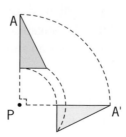

> You can check a rotation by using compasses to draw some of the paths traced out.

1 Copy this diagram.

  a  Reflect the triangle T in the line $x = 2$.
Label the image U.

  b  Reflect the triangle T in the line $y = 1$.
Label the image V.

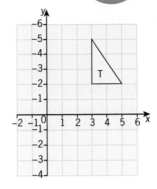

2 Copy this diagram.

  a  Reflect the kite K in the line $x = -1$.
Label the image L.

  b  Reflect the kite K in the line $y = 1$.
Label the image M.

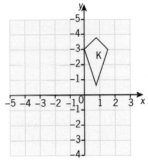

3 Copy this diagram.

  a  Rotate the triangle T through 180° about (0, 0).
Label the image U.

  b  Rotate the triangle T through 180° about (2, 2).
Label the image V.

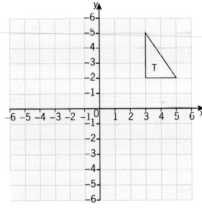

* 4 Copy this diagram.

  a  Rotate shape P through −90° about (2, 1).
Label the image Q.

  b  Rotate image Q through −90° about (2, 1).
Label the image R.

  c  Rotate shape P through 180° about (2, 1).
What do you notice?
Explain why this happens.

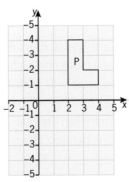

**Continued** ➤

5   Draw triangles C and D and their images C' and
    D' onto axes labelled from 0 to 10.
    Find their mirror lines.
    Repeat for triangle T and its image T' on new axes.

| Object triangle | Image triangle |
|---|---|
| C(2, 0) (6, 4) (8, 3) | C'(2, 4) (6, 0) (8, 1) |
| D(2, 10) (6, 10) (6, 8) | D'(7, 5) (7, 9) (5, 9) |
| T(2, 4) (3, 8) (5, 7) | T'(5, 0) (10, 1) (9, 3) |

6   For each triangle, label axes from 0 to 8.
    Draw each triangle and its image after a rotation
    of 90° clockwise about the centre. Use tracing
    paper to help you.

| | Triangle | Centre of rotation |
|---|---|---|
| a | (1, 4) (1, 7) (6, 7) | (4, 3) |
| b | (2, 2) (2, 7) (5, 2) | (3, 4) |
| c | (1, 6) (4, 6) (4, 1) | (4, 4) |

7   On axes labelled from 0 to 12, draw the shape S with vertices
    (5, 4) (5, 10), (11, 10) and (8, 4). Mark the point C (6, 6) as the
    centre of rotation.
    Find the images of S after anticlockwise rotations
    about C of 90°, 180° and 270°.

8   The square with corners (1, 2), (1, 6), (5, 6), (5, 2) can be rotated
    onto the square (7, 2), (7, 6), (11, 6), (11, 2) using several
    different centres of rotation.
    Find the possible rotations and describe them fully.

9   ***RICH TASK***

    Two identical squares S and T overlap so that one corner of
    T is at the centre of S. With S fixed, T rotates about the
    centre of S. Explain why, as T rotates, the area of overlap of
    T and S is constant.

10   ***RICH TASK***

    a   Cog A has 30 teeth and cog B has 10 teeth. What is the
        gear ratio?
        If B rotates at constant speed, describe the rotation of A.
    b   A typical bicycle has a front chainwheel (where the
        pedals and crank are attached) with 40 teeth and a rear
        gear with 10 teeth for cycling on level ground.
        How would you change the rear gear to make it suitable
        for climbing uphill? What gear ratios are involved?

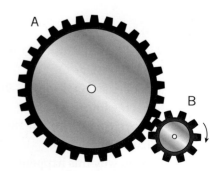

Know how to translate a shape using a vector

## RICH TASK

Two mirrors M and N are 6 cm apart. A flag F is placed 2 cm in front of M.
The image of F in M is reflected in N to give the final image F′.
a   What transformation maps F directly onto F′ ? How is this transformation affected by different positions of F?
b   Describe the transformation fully if the mirrors are *a* cm apart and F is *x* cm from M.

When a shape is translated, it moves from one position to another without turning.
You can describe its motion
   by giving the distance it moves and its direction
   *or* by using a grid and giving how far it moves up or down and left or right.

Aircraft A translates onto aircraft B, the translation is described by:

*either* **5 km on a bearing of 053°**

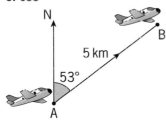

**or 4 km right and 3 km up the grid.**

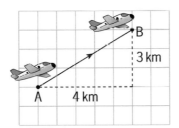

When using a grid, this movement can be written as the

vector, $\begin{pmatrix} 4 \\ 3 \end{pmatrix}$

$\begin{pmatrix} 4 \\ 3 \end{pmatrix}$ — top number means 4 squares **right**

bottom number means 3 squares **up**

In general, the vector

$\begin{pmatrix} x \\ y \end{pmatrix}$ means

*x* units right (+) or *x* units left ( − )
*y* units up (+)    or *y* units down ( − ).

p. 242

Triangle A'B'C' is the image of triangle ABC under a translation. Find the vector of the translation.

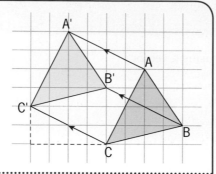

**ANSWER**

Corner A moves 4 squares left and 2 squares up to reach its image A'.

So the vector is $\begin{pmatrix} -4 \\ +2 \end{pmatrix}$, or simply $\begin{pmatrix} -4 \\ 2 \end{pmatrix}$.

The same vector describes the move from B to B' or from C to C'.

## Exercise B12.2

MEDIUM

*1 A group of students travel between these seaside resorts, over sea and land. Find the length and direction of the three vectors which describe each journey.

a
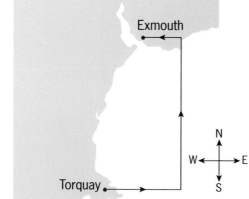

b
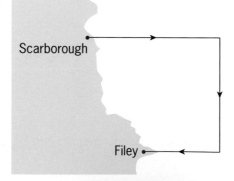

Scale 1 cm : 4 km

2 Write the vectors of the translations which map

a P onto Q
b P onto R
c Q onto R
d Q onto P.

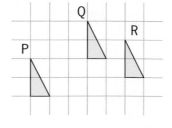

3 The cursor on a computer screen is programmed for three translations T, U and V, given by the vectors $\begin{pmatrix} 4 \\ 2 \end{pmatrix}$, $\begin{pmatrix} -1 \\ 3 \end{pmatrix}$ and $\begin{pmatrix} 2 \\ -2 \end{pmatrix}$ respectively.

Take any starting point on a square grid and subject it to three successive translations T, U and V, one after the other, in any order. Explore whether the position of the final image depends on the order of the three translations. What single translation has the same overall effect?

4 ### RICH TASK

The Romans are famous for their tiled floors, many of which survive to this day.
Which of these tiles will tessellate by using only translations?
Give some of the vectors of your translations.

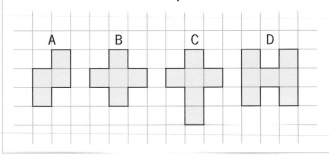

5 ### ☆ CHALLENGE ☆

Find how a knight moves in chess.
Use vectors to describe all possible moves from a square.
Find the least number of moves needed to land on other squares.
(In this diagram, to reach the numbered squares needs 1 and 2 moves.) Is there any pattern to your answers?

# Combining transformations

- Combine two transformations and find an equivalent single transformation

An object shape can be mapped onto its final image in two steps using a second transformation after the first transformation.

**EXAMPLE**

The shape S is firstly reflected in the line L onto its image S'. S' is then reflected in line M onto the image S". Describe the single transformation which maps S directly onto S" in one step.

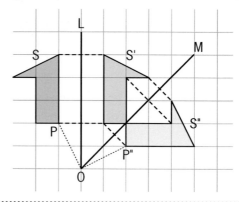

**ANSWER**

S can be transformed directly onto S" by a rotation.

Draw shape S on tracing paper.

With your pencil point on O, rotate S onto S". Line OP rotates through 90° onto line OP".

So the single transformation is a clockwise rotation of 90° about point O.

## Exercise B12.3

MEDIUM

1 a Shape S is reflected in line L onto its image S′.

Shape S′ is reflected in line M onto a second image S″.

Find the positions of S′ and S″.

Give full details of the *single* transformation which maps S onto S″.

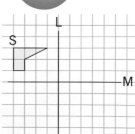

b Repeat part a with these new positions for lines L and M.

Describe the single transformation in full.

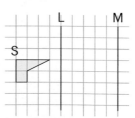

2  Trapezium T with vertices (1, 7), (4, 7), (4, 4) and (1, 3) is reflected in the line $y = x$ onto its image U. U is reflected in the $x$-axis onto a new image V. Draw the positions of T, U and V on axes labelled from −8 to 8. Describe fully the transformation which maps T onto V in one step.

3  Give full details of the single transformation which is equivalent to
   a  a reflection in the line $x = 3$, followed by a reflection in the line $x = 7$
   b  a reflection in the line $x = 3$, followed by a reflection in the line $y = 5$
   c  a half-turn about the point (4, 4), followed by a half-turn about the point (6, 4)
   d  a half-turn about the point (4, 4), followed by a half-turn about the point (7, 5)
   e  a half-turn about the point (4, 4), followed by a 90° clockwise turn about (7, 5).

4  Describe fully all the possible transformations which map
   a  rectangle R directly onto rectangle R'
   b  square S directly onto square S'.

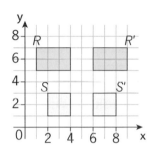

5  A crate with a rectangular cross-section ABCD is rotated 90° clockwise about corner A to stand vertically on the floor. It is then rotated 90° clockwise three more times in succession about corners B, C and D.
   Give full details of the single transformation which is equivalent to these four rotations.

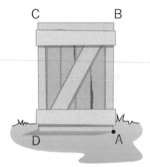

6  **RICH TASK**

   A triangular speedboat course has three equal length legs defined by three translations. The vector for the first leg is $\begin{pmatrix} 3 \\ 4 \end{pmatrix}$. The course starts and finishes at the same point.

   Calculate the possible vectors for the other two legs.

7  **RICH TASK**

   A knight in chess moves using a translation of 2 units and 1 unit in perpendicular directions. What size of square can a knight cross in two moves from one corner to the opposite corner? What is the smallest number of moves to go from one corner to the opposite corner on a $n \times n$ chess board?

- Recognise congruent shapes and similar shapes

Congruent shapes will fit on top of each other exactly.
These two quadrilaterals have both sides and angles which are the same size.
The quadrilaterals are congruent.

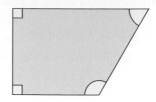

Similar figures have the same shape but different sizes.
These two triangles have the same angles (so their shape is the same) but triangle A has all sides twice as long as triangle B (so their sizes are different).
The triangles are similar.

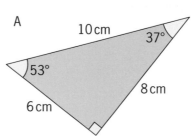

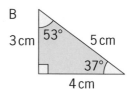

Enlarging a shape creates a similar figure.

Enlargements are commonly used in photography and film-making. They are also used in many design processes such a graphic design and in industries such as advertising and map-making.

> In mathematics, the word *similar* has this specific meaning. Everyday English uses the word less precisely.

**EXAMPLE**

A street light L is 2 metres above the roof AB of a lorry and it casts a shadow of the lorry on the road.
If the lorry is 4 metres tall and 2.5 metres wide, find the width PQ of the shadow.

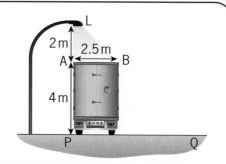

**ANSWER**

Triangle LPQ is an enlargement of triangle LAB with L as centre.

LA enlarges onto LP so the length scale factor of the enlargement is $\frac{LP}{LA} = \frac{4+2}{2} = 3$.

PQ is the image of AB, so the width PQ = 3 × 2.5 = 7.5 metres

## Exercise B12.4

**MEDIUM**

1   If a transformation preserves lengths and angles, the object and image are exactly the same shape and size. The object and image are *congruent*.
    If the image has the same shape but not the same size as the object, the object and image are *similar*.

Are object and image *congruent* or *similar* for these transformations? Copy this table and enter *yes* or *no* in each cell.

| Object and image are... | Reflection | Rotation | Translation | Enlargement |
|---|---|---|---|---|
| Congruent/similar | | | | |

2   Look at the angles and the sides of these shapes.
    Decide if the pairs of shapes are similar or not.

a
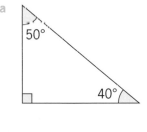
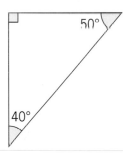

b
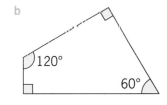

3   On axes labelled from 0 to 12, draw these pairs of triangles.
    Use ruler and protractor to measure sides and angles to decide if the pairs of triangles are *congruent, similar* or neither.

| | First triangle | Second triangle |
|---|---|---|
| a | (1, 8)(4, 1)(10, 5) | (5, 3)(9, 9)(2, 12) |
| b | (1, 1)(6, 1)(3, 7) | (12, 1)(12, 11)(0, 5) |
| c | (1, 4)(10, 2)(8, 12) | (1, 9)(7, 1)(12, 7) |
| d | (1, 8)(8, 7)(11, 0) | (4, 1)(12, 11)(5, 8) |

4   Find the lettered angles and decide if triangles PQR and PST are similar (or not).

a
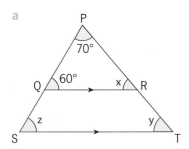

b
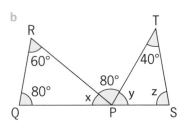

c
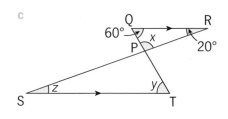

5 A manufacturer makes trousers based on this shape for the child's size. Draw an enlargement (scale factor 2) on squared paper to create a template for adults.

If each square of this diagram represents 10 cm, find the overall height of the adults' trousers.

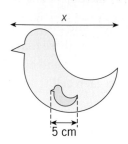

6 a This logo for a farm selling eggs involves an enlargement with scale factor 4. Find the value of $x$.

b An enlargement of the whole logo is painted so that it just fits on a rectangular board which is 1 metre long.

What are the lengths on the board of the two hens?

7 a A post 2.5 metres high casts a shadow 2 metres long in sunlight. At the same time, a street light has a shadow 6 metres long. Find the height, $h$, of the street light.

b At night when the street light is lit, how long is the shadow of the post, if the post and street light are 8 metres apart?

8 You print a photograph as a rectangle $7'' \times 5''$. You have two picture frames you can use. Frame A is 180 mm × 130 mm. Frame B is 210 mm × 150 mm. Which of these frames is the better fit?

The symbol ″ is used for *inches*.

9 Photographs are printed to many standard sizes. A popular size is $6'' \times 4''$. Other popular sizes are $12'' \times 8''$, $18'' \times 12''$, $10'' \times 8''$ and $7'' \times 5''$. Which of these sizes are true enlargements of the original $6'' \times 4''$ print and which will need the original photograph to be cropped? Research the size of posters which can be made from prints. Are poster sizes true enlargements?

10 ☆ **CHALLENGE** ☆

On a sunny day, how can you use a metre-rule held vertically on level ground to find the height of a tall tree or a tall building?
Explain how you use an 'angle of elevation' in your method.
What connections are there with the tangent of this angle?

# Enlargements

- Find the scale factor and centre of an enlargement

The word enlargement is used in photography when a picture is increased in size.
An old fashioned projector passes light through a small image to make a larger image on a screen.

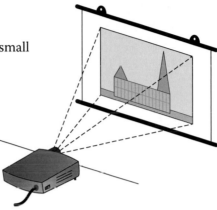

A mathematical enlargement has rays from a centre passing through the object to reach the image.
The scale factor is the number of times that the image is further away than the object from the centre.

> Most projectors nowadays do not work quite like this as they are digital.

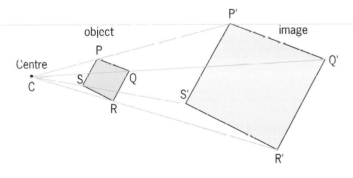

p. 302

Point P′ on the image is 6 cm from the centre C. Point P on the object is 2 cm from the centre C. P′ is 3 times further away than P from C because $3 \times 2\,\text{cm} = 6\,\text{cm}$.
So the scale factor of the enlargement is $\frac{6}{2} = 3$.

> The object and image are similar.

The scale factor is also the number of times that the length of any side has been increased.
Side PQ is 1.5 cm long and its image P′Q′ is 4.5 cm long.
So the scale factor is 3 because $3 \times 1.5\,\text{cm} = 4.5\,\text{cm}$.

## RICH TASK

An enlargement scale factor 2 means that the lengths double.
An enlargement scale factor 1.5 means that the lengths are multiplied by $1\frac{1}{2}$.

What do you think an enlargement scale factor $\frac{1}{2}$ means?

Explore fractional scale factors.

### Exercise B12.5

MEDIUM

1   On axes labelled from 0 to 24, draw these object shapes.
    Find their images using the given centres of enlargement
    and scale factors.

On the grid, you can draw 'rays' with your ruler by counting squares across and up like a vector.

| | Object shape | Centre | Scale factor |
|---|---|---|---|
| a | (3, 3)(5, 3)(3, 6) | (2, 0) | 2 |
| b | (12, 4)(14, 6)(11, 7) | (9, 6) | 3 |
| c | (4, 17)(8, 17)(8, 19)(4, 20) | (5, 18) | 2 |
| d | (16, 23)(24, 23)(20, 19) | (20, 11) | $\frac{1}{2}$ |

On new axes, find the image of this object shape.

| | Object shape | Centre | Scale factor |
|---|---|---|---|
| e | (1, 1)(13, 1)(4, 10) | (7, 4) | $\frac{1}{3}$ |

2   On axes labelled from 0 to 24, draw these pairs of objects and images.
    For each pair, find where possible
    i   the centre                        ii   the scale factor of the enlargement.

| | Object | Image |
|---|---|---|
| a | (2, 2)(4, 2)(4, 4) | (4, 1)(8, 1)(8, 5) |
| b | (14, 3)(15, 6)(13, 6) | (18, 7)(21, 16)(15, 16) |
| c | (4, 8)(6, 8)(5, 10)(4, 10) | (1, 11)(9, 11)(5, 19)(1, 19) |
| d | (4, 23)(5, 23)(5, 24)(3, 24) | (9, 19)(17, 19)(17, 24)(11, 24) |

3   Write the scale factors for these enlargements as fractions.

> Even though the image is smaller, mathematicians still use the word *enlargement*.

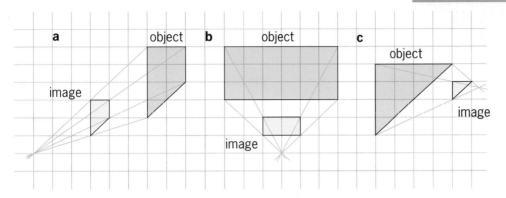

Unit B

4   For each pair of shapes, draw a diagram to find the centre and the scale factor of the enlargement.
   a   *Object* (3, 1)(3, 5)(9, 5)        *Image* (2, 4)(2, 6)(5, 6)
   b   *Object* (0, 12)(8, 16)(4, 0)   *Image* (4, 6)(3, 9)(5, 10)

5   A film is shown in a community centre on a screen 7 metres wide. The projector uses a roll of film 35 mm wide. What is the scale factor of the enlargement?

6   ☆ CHALLENGE ☆

Explore sizes of paper from the smallest size A10 to the largest A0. If an A4 sheet is enlarged to A3 size, what is the scale factor? What are the scale factors when using other sizes of paper? Do you notice anything special?

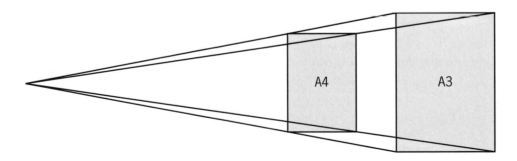

# More enlargements

- Find an image when an object is enlarged using positive and negative scale factors

---

**RICH TASK**

A pinhole camera of width $x$ cm photographs an object $w$ metres away and produces an image $z$ cm high.

Find an expression for the height $h$ metres of the object.

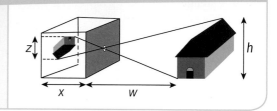

---

When you know the centre and scale factor of an enlargement, you can find the image of an object shape.

This triangle T can be enlarged using the centre C with a scale factor of 2.
Draw 'rays' from C through the corners of T and extend them.
Use a ruler to mark the corners of the image *2 times* further away from C than the object.
Join the corners in order to draw the image T'.

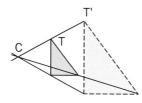

A scale factor can be negative. When triangle T is enlarged with a scale factor of −2, the image T" is 2 times further away from C but in the opposite direction and therefore upside down.

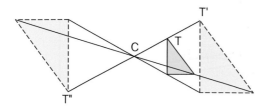

1 Make exact copies of these shapes on blank paper. With the lettered points as centres of enlargement use the given scale factors to draw images of the shapes.

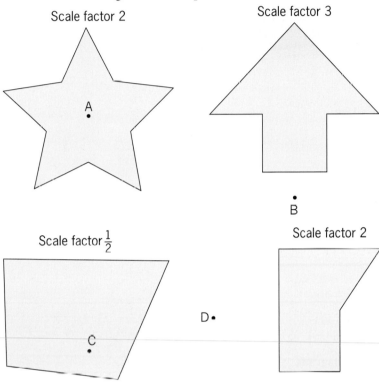

Scale factor 2

Scale factor 3

A

B

Scale factor $\frac{1}{2}$

Scale factor 2

C

D

2 On axes labelled from 0 to 24, draw these object shapes. Find their images using the given centres of enlargement and scale factors.

| | Object shape | Centre | Scale factor |
|---|---|---|---|
| a | (2, 23)(5, 23)(3, 20)(2, 21) | (7, 21) | −2 |
| b | (18, 4)(18, 7)(20, 7) | (19, 6) | −3 |
| c | (7, 11)(7, 15)(13, 15)(13, 13) | (15, 13) | $-\frac{1}{2}$ |

3 On axes labelled from 0 to 26, draw the object triangle (9, 10), (12, 10), (11, 12) and four images after enlargements using the centre (8, 8) and scale factors of 2, 4, −1 and −2.

*4 Triangle ABC maps onto triangle LMN under an enlargement, where L, M and N are the midpoints of the sides of triangle ABC. Find the scale factor and describe the position of the centre of the enlargement, P.
Explain why point P is also the centre of gravity of triangle ABC.

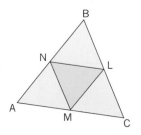

## CHECK OUT

You should now be able to

- understand congruence and similarity
- transform 2-D shapes using
  - ➤ reflection
  - ➤ rotation
  - ➤ translation
  - ➤ enlargement
- describe transformations and combinations of transformations.

*

### Exam-style question

An equilateral triangle YPQ is drawn
inside a square WXYZ as shown in the diagram.
Explain why triangles PYZ and QYX are congruent,
and show that WPQ is isosceles.

Use facts that you know about angles and side lengths in squares and equilateral triangles.

Use angle and line facts you know about isosceles triangles to finish the question.

**Andy's answer:**

PY = QY as the triangle PQY is equilateral

Angle at Z = angle at X = 90° as they are at the corners of a square

ZY = XY as they are sides of a square

PYZ and QYX must be congruent

This means ZP = XQ

So, PW = QW as they are the remainder of the sides of the square

WPQ has two sides the same so is isosceles

Use the facts to give a reason about every statement you make.

Remember to write a statement that answers the question.

## Exam practice

1   The diagram shows triangles R, S and T.

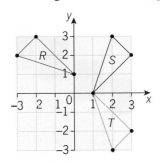

a   Describe fully the single transformation that maps
   i   triangle S onto triangle T     ii   triangle S onto triangle R
b   Is it possible to describe a single transformation to map
   triangle R onto triangle T?
   If yes, describe it, if no explain why not.

(*7 marks*)

2   The diagram shows a trapezium T.
   a   Copy the diagram with axes scaled from −5 to 5 and enlarge T with
      i   scale factor $\frac{1}{2}$ centre (0, 0). Label the image F.
      ii   scale factor −1 centre (0, 0). Label the image G.
   b   Write down the single transformation that would map T onto G.

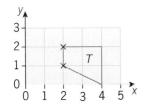

(*6 marks*)

3   Ben played a round of golf.
   On the diagram the dotted lines show the positions of
   the golf ball after each stroke at the first hole.
   a   Describe each movement of the golf ball from
      position to position.
   b   Write down the vector that the golf ball would
      have to travel if the golfer hit a hole-in-one stroke.

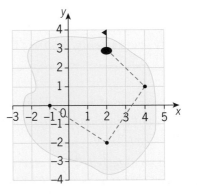

(*5 marks*)

# Case study 4: Recycling

Recycling waste materials has become an important part of everyday life now that our focus on protecting the environment is stronger than ever.

This time-series chart shows the amounts of different materials recycled from households in England between 1997/98 and 2007/8.

What can you say about the different types of materials being recycled by households in England during this time? Do you notice any trends? Justify your response by referring to the data.

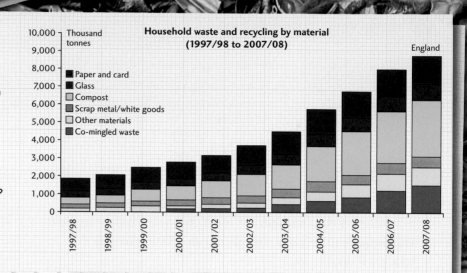

**Household waste and recycling by material (1997/98 to 2007/08)**

England

- Paper and card
- Glass
- Compost
- Scrap metal/white goods
- Other materials
- Co-mingled waste

Copy and complete this table, using the data in the chart.

| Year | 1997/98 | 1998/99 | 1999/00 | 2000/01 | 2001/02 | 2002/03 | 2003/04 | 2004/05 | 2005/06 | 2006/07 | 2007/08 |
|---|---|---|---|---|---|---|---|---|---|---|---|
| Co-mingled waste (amount) | 0 | 0 | 0 | | 221 | 268 | 469 | | | 1241 | 1563 |
| Co-mingled waste (% of total) | 0.00 | 0.00 | | 7.33 | 6.94 | 7.16 | | | 12.65 | 15.39 | |
| Other materials (amount) | 230 | 257 | 355 | | 235 | 269 | 385 | 516 | | | 989 |
| Other materials (% of total) | 12.31 | 12.27 | | 5.94 | 7.38 | | | 8.92 | 10.74 | | |
| Scrap metal/white goods (amount) | 231 | 253 | 265 | | 369 | 419 | 465 | 577 | | 601 | 598 |
| Scrap metal/white goods (% of total) | 12.36 | 12.08 | | 11.02 | 11.58 | 11.20 | | 9.97 | 7.83 | 7.45 | |
| Compost (amount) | 383 | | 668 | | 954 | 1189 | 1362 | 1960 | | 2895 | 3189 |
| Compost (% of total) | 20.49 | 21.68 | | 28.38 | 29.94 | 31.78 | | 33.88 | 35.89 | 35.90 | |
| Glass (amount) | 335 | 347 | 383 | | 426 | 470 | 568 | 670 | 760 | | 902 |
| Glass (% of total) | 17.92 | 16.57 | | 14.12 | 13.37 | 12.56 | | 11.58 | 11.18 | 10.42 | |
| Paper and card (amount) | 690 | 783 | 842 | | 1126 | 1272 | | 1406 | | 1535 | 1599 |
| Paper and card (% of total) | 36.92 | 37.39 | | 33.21 | 30.10 | | | 24.30 | 21.70 | 19.04 | |
| Total recycled (1000 tonnes) | | | 2513 | 2812 | 3186 | | | | | 8063 | |

Compare the three largest components of recycled waste in 1997/98 and 2007/08. Can you think of any explanation for the difference? Justify your response, referring to the data.

A total of 25.3 million tonnes of household waste was collected in England in 2007/08, what percentage of this collected waste was re-used, recycled or composted?

The amount of household waste NOT re-used, recycled or composted was 7.0% lower in 2007/08 than in 2006/07. What was the total amount of household waste collected in tonnes in 2006/07?

Can you think of any reason for the trend shown by this data?

In 2007 the government set a target to reduce the amount of household waste in England not re-used, recycled or composted to 15.8 million tonnes. Do you think that this was a realistic target? Justify your response by referring to the data.

Manufacturers are responsible for designing packaging that is as environmentally friendly as possible whilst also protecting the product.

A company sells its own brand of baked beans in cans made of steel. The weight of these cans has been reduced by 13% every 10 years over the past 50 years. 50 years ago a can weighed 112g. What is the weight of a new can? By what proportion has the weight of a can changed over the last 50 years?

Glass milk bottles are 50% lighter than they were 50 years ago.

As well as reducing the consumption of raw materials, lighter packaging also saves money in other ways such as transport costs.

A supermarket sells tomatoes in packs of six. The packaging consists of a plastic tray with a lid as shown.

Given that on average this variety of tomato is spherical with a radius of 3cm, on average what percentage of the available volume of each package is empty?

Do you think that not having packaging would risk the quality of the tomatoes?

19cm

13cm

2cm

6cm

12cm

18cm

The product/pack ratio compares the weight of the packaging with the weight of the product it contains. Companies use this ratio to assess the suitability of the packaging used for each of their products. They often express it as a percentage to show how much of the overall weight is contributed by the packaging.

Look at some of the packaging you have at home. Could it be adapted to use less material without increasing the risk of damage to the product? If so, how?

How does the packaging used for perishable goods (e.g. food) differ from that used for non-perishable goods (e.g. electrical items)?

Research some well-known manufacturing companies on the Internet to find out about their packaging guidelines. Do they have different rules for different products (e.g. perishable/non-perishable goods)?

## INTRODUCTION

Over 30% of the numbers in everyday use begin with the digit 1. 'Benford's law', as this fact is called, makes it possible to detect when a list of numbers has been falsified. This is particularly useful in fraud investigations for detecting 'made-up' entries on claim forms and expense accounts.

**What's the point?**

Recognising patterns in numbers and measures helps us to make sense of a world that is increasingly swamped with data.

## CHECK IN

1 Draw a grid with both axes from −4 to 5.
  Draw these points on the grid.
  a (2, 4)   b (1, −3)   c (5, −3)   d (−2, 2)
  e (−4, −1)   f (0, 3)   g (4, 0)   h (0, −1)

2 Find the midpoint of each pair of numbers.
  a 5 and 15   b 20 and 30   c 0 and 40
  d 10 and 15   e 25 and 30

| What I should know | What I will learn | What this leads to |
|---|---|---|
| A6 | ■ Draw and use scatter graphs and understand correlation<br>■ Draw and use time series graphs | Careers involving statistics include environmental statistics, medical statistics, social policy, actuarial science… |

## RICH TASK

What is the most likely time during a football game for a team to score a goal?

It is frequently stated by football commentators that teams are most likely to concede a goal within five minutes of scoring a goal themselves. Is this true?

Investigate and write a report on your results.

# Scatter graphs

- Draw and interpret scatter graphs

A survey was conducted on a sample of people who live at different altitudes, to measure their lung capacity. The scatter graph shows the results.

## RICH TASK

Does where you live affect your lung capacity?

Is there any other data that could have been collected?

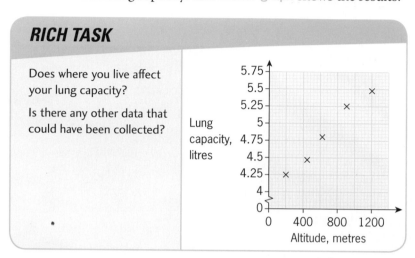

→ **A scatter graph can be used to represent paired data.**

**EXAMPLE**

Freddie carried out an experiment to find how high his power ball would bounce.

| Drop height, cm | 30 | 40 | 50 | 60 | 70 | 80 | 90 | 100 |
|---|---|---|---|---|---|---|---|---|
| Bounce height, cm | 27 | 48 | 53 | 62 | 69 | 89 | 102 | 110 |

Paired data is data that is collected for two variables that may be linked.

Draw a scatter graph to represent these data.

**ANSWER**

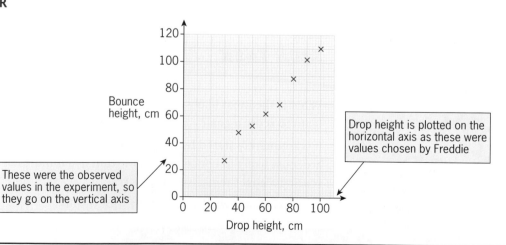

These were the observed values in the experiment, so they go on the vertical axis

Drop height is plotted on the horizontal axis as these were values chosen by Freddie

1 Draw a scatter graph to represent the data recorded by Iain on the percentages achieved in Statistics and Mathematics exams by 10 students.

| Statistics % | 78 | 82 | 74 | 75 | 93 | 70 | 66 | 62 | 77 | 89 |
|---|---|---|---|---|---|---|---|---|---|---|
| Mathematics % | 70 | 76 | 61 | 70 | 89 | 65 | 59 | 58 | 73 | 82 |

*2 Carrie conducted an experiment to find out if height and arm span are related. She measured the heights and arm spans of eight of her friends.

| Height (cm) | 136 | 158 | 126 | 131 | 149 | 157 | 143 | 152 |
|---|---|---|---|---|---|---|---|---|
| Arm span (cm) | 134 | 146 | 122 | 130 | 147 | 150 | 134 | 145 |

a  Draw a scatter graph to represent these data.
b  Anthropometric data is the name given to data collected about body measurements. What paired data might be useful to collect for bicycle design?

*3 Read the information and answer the questions that follow.
Louise recorded information about the average number of minutes per day spent playing computer games and reaction time.

| Minutes per day spent playing computer games | 40 | 60 | 75 | 40 | 35 | 20 | 80 | 50 | 45 |
|---|---|---|---|---|---|---|---|---|---|
| Reaction time, seconds | 5.2 | 4.3 | 3.9 | 5.5 | 6.0 | 7.2 | 3.6 | 4.8 | 5.0 |

Barry carried out an experiment to find the reaction time of volunteers after they had consumed alcohol.

| Units of alcohol | 2.5 | 9.0 | 5.0 | 3.5 | 4.5 | 8.5 | 7.5 | 6.0 | 2.0 | 7.0 | 8.0 |
|---|---|---|---|---|---|---|---|---|---|---|---|
| Reaction time (s) | 3.6 | 9.2 | 4.7 | 4.8 | 3.4 | 8.8 | 7.5 | 4.7 | 1.4 | 7.3 | 9.2 |

Jordan recorded the reaction times, in seconds, of a group of students when woken at 3 a.m. one morning and their reaction time at mid-morning on another day.

| 3 a.m. reaction time | 5.3 | 4.6 | 7.8 | 7.9 | 8.4 | 7.0 | 5.8 | 6.6 | 5.0 | 9.5 |
|---|---|---|---|---|---|---|---|---|---|---|
| Mid-morning reaction time | 3.7 | 3.1 | 6.2 | 6.5 | 7.0 | 5.7 | 4.5 | 4.7 | 3.3 | 7.8 |

a  Draw three scatter graphs to represent the information collected by Louise, Barry and Jordan.
b  What can you say about the effects of computer games, alcohol and sleep on reaction time?

# Correlation

- Appreciate correlation
- Distinguish between positive, negative and zero correlation

→ **A scatter graph shows you if there is correlation between two variables.**

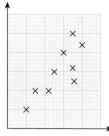

Positive correlation

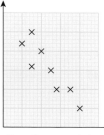

Negative correlation

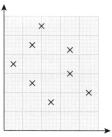

No correlation

**EXAMPLE**

Jon collected these data from a beach cafe on eight consecutive days one summer.

| Midday temperature, °C | 15 | 22 | 21 | 18 | 20 | 19 | 20 | 17 |
|---|---|---|---|---|---|---|---|---|
| Ice-cream sales, £ | 100 | 154 | 139 | 122 | 140 | 132 | 135 | 115 |
| Cold drinks sales, £ | 82 | 112 | 105 | 94 | 108 | 96 | 107 | 92 |

Comment on the relationship between the midday temperature and sales at the cafe, using appropriate scatter graphs.

**ANSWER**

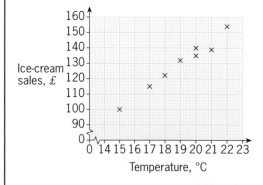

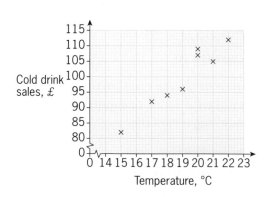

Both graphs show positive correlation.
The correlation is stronger between temperature and ice-cream sales than between temperature and cold drink sales.
The graphs show that as the temperature increases, the sales of ice-cream increase and the sales of cold drinks increase.

What would a scatter graph of cold drink sales vs ice-cream sales look like?

## Exercise B13.2

MEDIUM

*1 The graph shows the results of the survey on altitude and lung capacity described on page 200.
Write down the correlation shown by the graph, and describe the relationship shown by the variables.

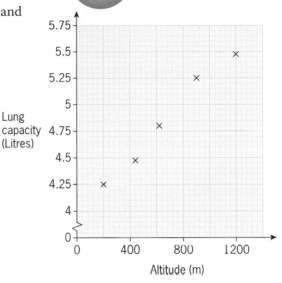

*2 For each of the graphs you drew in exercise B13.1 questions 1 and 2
   a Describe any correlation shown by the graph
   b Describe the relationship shown between the variables.

*3 Emma recorded how long it took a group of friends to write their name with their right hand and with their left hand.

| Right-hand time taken, seconds | 4.6 | 6.5 | 7.2 | 4.8 | 5.8 | 6.2 | 4.8 | 9.8 | 4.6 | 1.0 | 6.8 | 7.0 |
|---|---|---|---|---|---|---|---|---|---|---|---|---|
| Left-hand time taken, seconds | 6.2 | 8.4 | 9.6 | 6.4 | 7.0 | 7.5 | 6.6 | 6.5 | 6.6 | 6.0 | 8.5 | 9.2 |

   a Draw a scatter graph of these data.
   b Describe the correlation shown.
   c Describe the relationship between the times taken to write your name with each hand.

*4 The table shows the place, year, magnitude (measured on the Richter scale) and number of deaths (to the nearest 500) of major earthquakes between 1900 and 1940.

| Place | USA | Chile | Italy | Italy | China | Japan | China | China | India | Chile | Turkey |
|---|---|---|---|---|---|---|---|---|---|---|---|
| Year | 1906 | 1906 | 1908 | 1915 | 1920 | 1923 | 1927 | 1932 | 1935 | 1939 | 1939 |
| Magnitude | 8.3 | 8.6 | 7.5 | 7.5 | 8.6 | 8.3 | 8.3 | 7.6 | 7.5 | 7.8 | 7.9 |
| Number of deaths (000's) | 0.5 | 20 | 120 | 30 | 180 | 143 | 200 | 70 | 60 | 30 | 23 |

Draw an appropriate scatter graph to investigate whether the number of deaths is related to the magnitude of the earthquake as measured on the Richter scale. Explain what you find.

Unit B

# Lines of best fit

- Draw lines of best fit and understand what these represent

When a scatter graph shows correlation you can often draw a
line of best fit.

The table gives the marks earned in two exams by 10 students.

| Maths % | 70 | 76 | 61 | 70 | 89 | 65 | 59 | 58 | 73 | 82 |
|---|---|---|---|---|---|---|---|---|---|---|
| Statistics % | 78 | 82 | 74 | 75 | 93 | 70 | 66 | 62 | 77 | 89 |

a Draw a scatter graph for the data.
b Describe the correlation and the relationship shown.
c Draw a line of best fit.
d Predict the statistics mark for a student who scored 62% in
Maths.

One way to draw a line of best
fit is 'by eye':
- Find the mean of each
  variable
- Plot the means as a single
  point M (maths 70.3,
  statistics 76.6)
- Draw a straight line through
  M, with half the data points
  above and half below the line.

**ANSWER**

a, c See graph.

b Positive correlation. Students who
scored higher in Maths also tended
to score higher in Statistics.

c Maths mean: $\frac{703}{10}$ = 70.3

Statistics mean: $\frac{766}{10}$ = 76.6

d Predicted Statistics mark =70%

A line of best
fit need not
pass through
the origin.

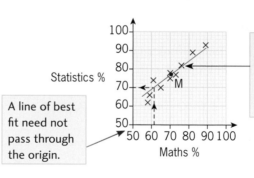

The line of best
fit may not pass
though any of the
points, but will be
close to them.

Sometimes data do not
appear to follow a straight
line, but they  do follow a
curve. This graph shows
the annual heating costs
and the number of rooms
in a survey of hotels.

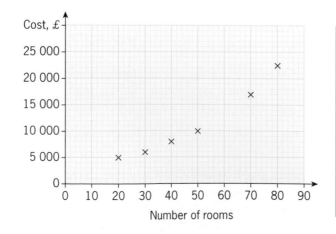

This is an example
of **non-linear
correlation**.
You can often
change a curve
into a straight
line by plotting an
appropriate graph.
Non-linear curves
are deal with in
Chapter 21.

## Exercise B13.3

1   The graphs show the information collected by Jon on midday temperature and sales of cold drinks and ice-cream at a beach cafe.

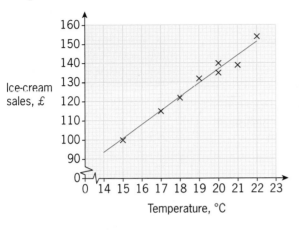
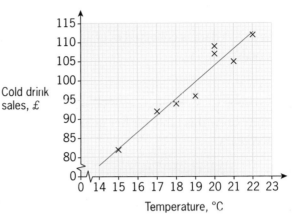

Use the graphs to estimate

a   Ice-cream sales when the midday temperature is 16 °C

b   Cold drink sales when the midday temperature is 18.5 °C.

*2   The graph shows the altitude of the location where a sample of men live and their lung capacity.

a   Estimate the lung capacity for a man living at an altitude of 720 m.

b   Explain why it may not be sensible to use the graph to estimate the lung capacity of
   i   a man living at an altitude of 1500 m,
   ii   a woman.

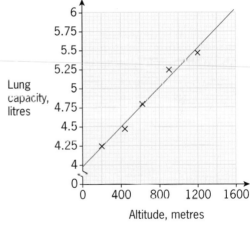

*3   The table shows the average life span, in years, and average gestation period, in days, for some mammals.

| Mammal | Black bear | Cat | Goat | Hamster | Horse | Lion | Mouse | Pig | Rabbit | Red fox | Sheep | Squirrel |
|---|---|---|---|---|---|---|---|---|---|---|---|---|
| Life span years | 18 | 15 | 8 | 4 | 24 | 15 | 3 | 10 | 5 | 3 | 12 | 10 |
| Gestation days | 210 | 63 | 145 | 16 | 336 | 106 | 21 | 114 | 31 | 52 | 150 | 44 |

a   Use the data to draw a scatter graph and estimate
   i   the life span of a guinea pig, gestation period 68 days
   ii   the gestation period of a tiger, life span 16 years.

b   Discuss the reliability of your results with reference to animal size.

Lines of best fit   205

Unit B

# Time series

● Draw and interpret line graphs for time series

Time series data is collected over a period of time at regular intervals.

Common real-life examples of time series data are utility bills, unemployment rates, and average house prices.

**EXAMPLE**

Jenny drew this table for her quarterly gas bills over a period of two years.

|  | Jan–March | April–June | July–Sept | Oct–Dec |
|---|---|---|---|---|
| **2008** | £65 | £38 | £24 | £60 |
| **2009** | £68 | £42 | £30 | £68 |

a  Draw a time series graph to represent these data.

b  Describe the annual changes in Jenny's gas bill shown by the graph.

c  Roughly what would you expect the 2010 April–June gas bill to be?

Explain your answer.

**ANSWER**

a

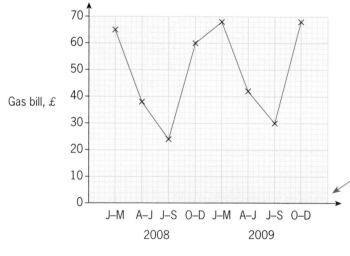

Time is on the horizontal axis.

b  The bills are highest in the January–March quarter in each year and are lowest in the July–September quarter each year.

c  The bill for April–June 2010 may be in the range £45–£50, because the 2009 prices are all higher than in 2008.

## Exercise B13.4

Draw a time series graph to represent the information given in each question.

Describe what is shown in each time series graph.

1   The table shows information about Richard's monthly mobile phone bill.

| Jan | Feb | Mar | Apr | May | Jun | Jul | Aug | Sep | Oct | Nov | Dec |
|-----|-----|-----|-----|-----|-----|-----|-----|-----|-----|-----|-----|
| £12 | £14 | £10 | £18 | £16 | £22 | £13 | £10 | £15 | £15 | £17 | £20 |

2   The table shows information about Luigi's quarterly electricity bills over a two-year period.

|      | Jan–Mar | Apr–Jun | Jul–Sep | Oct–Dec |
|------|---------|---------|---------|---------|
| 2004 | £55     | £24     | £21     | £46     |
| 2005 | £59     | £28     | £23     | £50     |

3   The table shows information about monthly ice-cream sales at Haroun's shop during one year.

| Jan | Feb | Mar | Apr | May | Jun | Jul | Aug | Sep | Oct | Nov | Dec |
|-----|-----|-----|-----|-----|-----|-----|-----|-----|-----|-----|-----|
| £16 | £10 | £8  | £16 | £22 | £36 | £48 | £50 | £12 | £15 | £16 | £39 |

4   Tasmin kept a record of how much money she had earned from odd jobs during three years.

|      | Jan–Apr | May–Aug | Sep–Dec |
|------|---------|---------|---------|
| 2007 | £15     | £39     | £27     |
| 2008 | £21     | £45     | £30     |
| 2009 | £24     | £54     | £42     |

5   Alec kept a record of his quarterly expenses over a period of two years.

|      | Jan–Mar | Apr–Jun | Jul–Sep | Oct–Dec |
|------|---------|---------|---------|---------|
| 2004 | £47     | £56     | £33     | £18     |
| 2005 | £39     | £48     | £29     | £16     |

## CHECK OUT

You should now be able to draw and interpret
- scatter graphs
- time series graphs.

**Exam-style question**

Two samples of students with similar alcohol, smoking and exercise patterns took part in a survey on pulse rates, in beats per minute, before and after exercise.

Males

| Before | 82 | 70 | 96 | 86 | 74 | 75 | 72 | 85 |
|--------|----|----|----|----|----|----|----|----|
| After | 140 | 96 | 152 | 150 | 98 | 130 | 119 | 120 |

Females

| Before | 78 | 88 | 76 | 80 | 78 | 60 | 65 | 75 |
|--------|----|----|----|----|----|----|----|----|
| After | 130 | 140 | 100 | 135 | 120 | 90 | 104 | 116 |

Draw scatter graphs to represent these data.
Comment on any differences and similarities shown between male and female pulse rate.

Use the same scales on both graphs to make comparisons easier.

Draw separate diagrams next to each other.

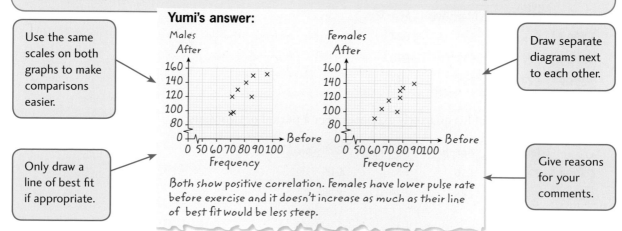

**Yumi's answer:**

Only draw a line of best fit if appropriate.

Give reasons for your comments.

Both show positive correlation. Females have lower pulse rate before exercise and it doesn't increase as much as their line of best fit would be less steep.

## Exam practice

1  The table gives the mean monthly temperature in °C for
   July in Northern Ireland from 1996 to 2007.

| 1996 | 1997 | 1998 | 1999 | 2000 | 2001 | 2002 | 2003 | 2004 | 2005 | 2006 | 2007 |
|------|------|------|------|------|------|------|------|------|------|------|------|
| 14·2 | 14·9 | 13·7 | 15·5 | 14·4 | 14·3 | 13·6 | 15·6 | 13·8 | 15·0 | 16·7 | 13·9 |

Draw a time series graph to show these data.
Describe what the graph is showing.

*(3 marks)*

2  The table gives the number of marriages, to the nearest hundred,
   in the UK for each month during 1992 and 1993.

|      | January | February | March  | April  | May     | June   |
|------|---------|----------|--------|--------|---------|--------|
| 1992 | 8500    | 15900*   | 15700  | 22700  | 33900*  | 32500  |
| 1993 | 9200    | 11900    | 15400  | 22300  | 32800*  | 33100  |

|      | July    | August | September | October | November | December |
|------|---------|--------|-----------|---------|----------|----------|
| 1992 | 37800   | 49100  | 41600     | 26200   | 13900    | 13800    |
| 1993 | 41900*  | 40200  | 40000     | 25200   | 13500    | 14200    |

The numbers with a * are the months where there were five Saturdays.
Draw a time series graph to display this data and comment on
any trends shown.

*(4 marks)*

*3  A simulation was carried out into two different types of queuing in a bank.
   Queuing method A: A single queue line forms and people wait for next free counter.
   Queuing method B: Queue lines form for individual counters.
   The people taking part in the simulation had the following waiting times
   in minutes.

| A | 1 | 7 | 3 | 0 | 0 | 6 | 8 | 6 | 7 | 1 | 2 | 5 | 2 | 9 | 3 |
| B | 1 | 6 | 0 | 1 | 0 | 4 | 6 | 3 | 4 | 5 | 1 | 6 | 4 | 5 | 3 |

Calculate summary statistics for the data.
Comment on which method you think is best for queuing.

*(6 marks)*

## INTRODUCTION

In the business world, people try to maximise profits. They often do this by maximising productivity and minimising costs. However, there are lots of factors (called constraints) such as the number of workers, the capacity of their factories, cost of materials etc., which affect these things. The different constraints are represented as straight-line graphs and a process called linear programming is used to find the optimal solution.

**What's the point?**

Many problems in the real world are about obtaining the best results within given constraints – from comparing the price plans of different mobile phones to choosing the most cost-effective way of spending your time. Plotting linear functions and solving simultaneous equations lies at the heart of many real-life decision-making situations.

## CHECK IN

1   You will have met some formulae before. Match each formula with the information that it is designed to find.

2   Solve each equation to find the value of $x$.
   a   $3x - 2 = 15$        b   $4(4x - 5) = 20$        c   $3x^2 = 75$
   d   $5\sqrt{x} = 20$        e   $x^3 + 1 = 9$        f   $10 - x = 8$

| Formula: | To find: |
|---|---|
| $A = lw$ | Area of triangle |
| $A = \pi r^2$ | Volume of a cuboid |
| $a^2 + b^2 = c^2$ | Area of a rectangle |
| $V = lwh$ | Area of a circle |
| $A = \frac{1}{2}bh$ | Length of sides in a right-angled triangle |

3   Copy and complete the table of coordinates and use it to draw a graph of the line.
   a   $y = 3x + 2$        b   $2x + y = 12$

| x | 1 | 2 | 3 |
|---|---|---|---|
| y |   |   |   |

| x | -1 | 0 |   |
|---|---|---|---|
| y |   |   | 0 |

**Orientation**

| What I should know | What I will learn | What this leads to |
|---|---|---|
| B11 | ■ Represent inequalities<br>■ Solve simultaneous equations | C19 and C21 |

## RICH TASK

In a store there are a range of different mobile phone packages available.

Package 1    Pay as you go 10p per minute

Package 2    £5 per month and then all calls at 5p per minute

Package 3    £12 per month, with a 100 mins of free calls, and then all calls at 3p per minute

Package 4    £25 per month, with 600 mins of free calls, and then all calls at 2p per minute.

Which package is the best value for money?

# Simultaneous equations

- Solve a pair of simultaneous equations by eliminating one variable

### RICH TASK

In an arithmagon, the sum of each pair of circles is given in the square between them.
Can you find the missing numbers?
Can you find a way of solving any such problem?

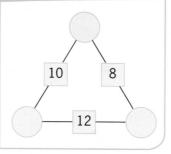

At a school summer fete, Lynda is in charge of the stationery stall.
A gust of wind blows away the price labels for the pens and pencils.
Philip says 'I bought 2 pencils and 2 pens and spent 56p'.
Lily says 'I bought 5 pencils and 2 pens and spent 80p'.
Lynda can use this information to rewrite the price labels.

Write this information as a pair of equations. Let $p$ = the cost in pence of a pencil and $q$ = the cost in pence of a pen.

| Philip: | $2p + 2q = 56$ | (1) |
| Lily: | $5p + 2q = 80$ | (2) |

Subtracting equation (1) from equation (2) gives

| (2) – (1) | $3p = 24$ | |
| | $p = 8$ | The cost of a pencil is 8p. |

> You could try (1) – (2) but it would give awkward negatives. Try it!

Substituting the cost of a pencil into equation (1) gives

p. 100

| In (1) | $16 + 2q = 56$ | |
| | $2q = 40$ | |
| | $q = 20$ | The cost of a pen is 20p. |

> Check these solutions by substituting into the unused equation.
> In (2), $5 \times 8 + 2 \times 20 = 80$. This is correct.

→ **Two or more equations that have a common solution are called simultaneous equations.**

→ **You can eliminate one of the variables by adding or subtracting the equations.**

**Simultaneous equations and inequalities**

Solve these pairs of simultaneous equations.   **a**   $3x + 2y = 17$   **b**   $3a - 4b = 1$
$x + 2y = 7$         $2a + 4b = 14$

**ANSWER**

**a**

| | | |
|---|---|---|
| | $3x + 2y = 17$ | (1) |
| | $x + 2y = 7$ | (2) |
| $(1) - (2)$ | $2x = 10$ | – to lose $y$ |
| | $x = 5$ | ÷ 2 on both sides |
| In (2) | $5 + 2y = 7$ | |
| | $2y = 2$ | – 5 from both sides |
| | $y = 1$ | ÷ 2 on both sides |

Check in (1)   $3 \times 5 + 2 \times 1 = 17$. Correct!
The solutions are $x = 5$ and $y = 1$.

**b**

| | | |
|---|---|---|
| | $3a - 4b = 1$ | (1) |
| | $2a + 4b = 14$ | (2) |
| $(1) + (2)$ | $5a = 15$ | + to lose $b$ |
| | $a = 3$ | ÷ 5 on both sides |
| In (2) | $6 + 4b = 14$ | |
| | $4b = 8$ | – 6 from both sides |
| | $b = 2$ | ÷ 4 on both sides |

Check in (1)   $3 \times 3 - 4 \times 2 = 1$. Correct!
The solutions are $a = 3$ and $b = 2$.

## Exercise B14.1

MEDIUM
HIGH

1  Solve these pairs of simultaneous equations.

a   $x + 3y = 10$
    $x + 2y = 7$

b   $4a + 2b = 8$
    $4a + 3b = 10$

c   $3p + 5q = 21$
    $3p + 3q = 15$

d   $5m + 3n = 25$
    $2m + 3n = 19$

e   $5c + d = 22$
    $c + d = 6$

f   $2t + k = 9$
    $2t + 4k = 24$

g   $2x + 5y = 8$
    $7x + 5y = 3$

h   $5a + 2b = 4$
    $8a + 2b = 10$

2  Solve these pairs of simultaneous equations.

a   $2x + y = 9$
    $x - y = 3$

b   $4p - 2q = 6$
    $2p + 2q = 6$

c   $c - 3d = 0$
    $5c + 3d = 36$

d   $6m + 5n = 23$
    $2m - 5n = 1$

e   $2a + 7b = 18$
    $-2a + 3b = 2$

f   $3t + 4k = 17$
    $-3t + k = -7$

g   $6x + 5y = 2$
    $3x - 5y = 16$

h   $8p - 2q = 2$
    $4p + 2q = -14$

3  Solve these pairs of simultaneous equations. You will need to decide
whether to add or subtract the equations.

a   $2a + 3b = 21$
    $10a - 3b = 15$

b   $7p + 2q = 19$
    $2p + 2q = 14$

c   $c - d = 7$
    $6c + d = 28$

d   $3k + 4t = 5$
    $5k - 4t = 3$

e   $4m + 7n = 30$
    $4m - n = 14$

f   $x + 3y = 3$
    $-x + 6y = 0$

g   $5a + 8b = 1$
    $5a - 2b = -19$

h   $3p - 2q = 14$
    $3p - q = 13$

4  Victoria treated some friends and visited the same café twice. Here are her receipts.

**TONED CAFE**

32, CHAPEL MARKET, LONDON, N12 8PU
02.05.09  5.46pm  Bill No. 546574

| ITEM | QUANTITY |
|---|---|
| Cappuccinos | 2 |
| Americanos | 3 |
| **Total Cost** | **£8.70** |

**TONED CAFE**

32, CHAPEL MARKET, LONDON, N12 8PU
10.05.09  5.39pm  Bill No. 547731

| ITEM | QUANTITY |
|---|---|
| Cappuccinos | 2 |
| Americanos | 7 |
| **Total Cost** | **£15.10** |

Find the cost of a cappuccino and an americano.

- Solve a pair of simultaneous equations by eliminating one variable

## RICH TASK

Find the value of each colour and hence the missing column total.

44  39  46  ?

Gemma cannot find her leaflet detailing the costs on her new mobile phone tariff.

Last week she sent 4 text messages and 3 picture messages at a cost of £1.20.

This week she sent 8 text messages and 2 picture messages at a cost of £1.60.

Gemma can use this information to work out the cost of each text and picture message.

Write the information as a pair of simultaneous equations.

Let $t$ = text and $p$ = picture message.
Last week: $\quad 4t + 3p = 120 \quad$ (1)
This week: $\quad 8t + 2p = 160 \quad$ (2)

Change the cost in pounds to pence for ease of calculation.

In this pair of simultaneous equations the coefficients of each variable are different.

> → **To eliminate a variable you may need to multiply one or both equations by an appropriate number before adding or subtracting.**

Multiply equation (1) by 2 $\quad 8t + 6p = 240 \quad$ (3)
$\qquad\qquad\qquad\qquad 8t + 2p = 160 \quad$ (2)  the coefficient of $t$
$\qquad\quad$ (3) − (2) $\qquad\quad 4p = 80 \qquad$ are now the same.
$\qquad\qquad\qquad\qquad\quad p = 20$

Substituting $p = 20$ in (1) gives $\quad 4t + 60 = 120$
$\qquad\qquad\qquad\qquad\qquad\qquad\qquad t = 15$

The cost of a text is 15p and the cost of a picture message is 20p.

Check these solutions by substituting into the unused equation.
In (2), $8 \times 15 + 2 \times 20 = 160$. This is correct.

Solve this pair of simultaneous equations.
$$2x + 3y = 5$$
$$5x - 2y = 22$$

**ANSWER**

| | | | |
|---|---|---|---|
| | | $2x + 3y = 5$ | (1) |
| | | $5x - 2y = 22$ | (2) |
| Multiply both equations | (1) × 2 | $4x + 6y = 10$ | (3) |
| | (2) × 3 | $15x - 6y = 66$ | (4) |
| | (3) + (4) | $19x = 76$ so $x = 4$ | |
| | In (1) | $8 + 3y = 5$ | |
| | | $3y = -3$ so $y = -1$ | |

The solution is $x = 4$, $y = -1$.

> The coefficients of y are now the same.

> Check these solutions by substituting into the unused equation.
> In (2), $5 \times 4 - 2 \times -1 = 22$.
> This is correct.

## Exercise B14.2

**MEDIUM HIGH**

1 Solve these pairs of simultaneous equations by multiplying one equation by a suitable number.

a $3x + y = 9$
$4x + 2y = 14$

b $a + 2b - 7$
$4a + 3b = 23$

c $5p + 3q = 31$
$2p - q = 8$

d $4m - 2n = 6$
$7m + n = 15$

e $3m - 2n = 1$
$m - 3n = -9$

f $6t - 2k = 14$
$2t + 5k = 16$

g $2x + 8y = 12$
$7x + 4y = -6$

h $3a - 2b = 19$
$12a - 5b = 70$

2 Solve these pairs of simultaneous equations by multiplying both equations.

a $3x - 2y = 8$
$2x + 3y = 14$

b $5p - 2q = 0$
$2p + 3q = 19$

c $2a + 5b = 29$
$7a + 2b = 55$

d $4m + 2n = 10$
$3m + 5n = 4$

e $2t - 3k = 17$
$7t + 4k - 16$

f $8p - 7q = 6$
$5p + 3q = -11$

g $2a + 8b = 14$
$3a + 3b = 16\frac{1}{2}$

h $3x + 6y = 6$
$7x + 4y = -1$

3 Find the values of the symbols in each of these puzzles.

a

b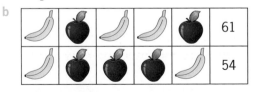

> The last column is the **sum total** of the value of the symbols.

4 a At a charity event, Edward charges 10p per badge and 15p per rosette.
   He sells a total of 75 items and raises £9.10. How many badges did Edward sell?

   b Jacob needs to transport himself and 34 friends to a party by taxi.
   He uses both black cabs that can carry 5 people and minicabs that can
   carry 3 people. If Jacob orders 9 taxis, how many of each type does he use?

   c A straight line has equation $ax + by = 4$. The line passes through the points (2, 5) and (4, 8).
   i Find the values of $a$ and $b$.
   ii Write the gradient and $y$-intercept of this line.

# Graphical solutions

- Solve a pair of simultaneous equations using a graphical method
- Form and solve linear simultaneous equations to solve problems

## RICH TASK

| $2x + y = -11$ | $x + 3y = 7$ | $7y - x = 13$ | $2y - x = -2$ |

These four straight-line graphs intersect each other once.
Write the number of intersections.
Three of these lines enclose a triangle in the first quadrant. Write the equations of these three lines.

The point (2, 3) lies on both the lines $x + y = 5$ and $2x - y = 1$.

The solution of the simultaneous equations
$$x + y = 5$$
and $\quad 2x - y = 1 \quad$ is $x = 2$, $y = 3$.

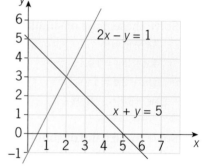

p. 166

→ **The solution to a pair of simultaneous equations is the point of intersection of their graphs.**

p. 292

**EXAMPLE**

Use a graphical method to solve this pair of simultaneous equations.
$$2x + y = 4$$
$$x - y = -1$$

### ANSWER

Draw the line given by $2x + y = 4$.

| $x$ | 0 | 1 | 2 |
|---|---|---|---|
| $y$ | 4 | 2 | 0 |

Draw the line given by $x - y = -1$.

| $x$ | 0 | 1 | 2 |
|---|---|---|---|
| $y$ | 1 | 2 | 3 |

The lines intersect at the point (1, 2).
The solution is $x = 1$, $y = 2$.

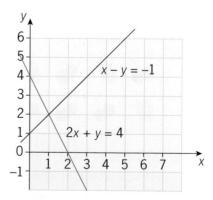

Check that these values satisfy the equations:
$2 \times 1 + 2 = 4$ and $1 - 2 = -1$
Correct!

1  a  Use the graph to solve these pairs of simultaneous equations.

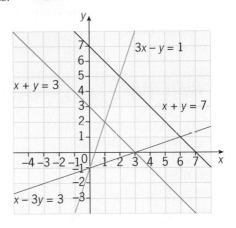

   **i**   $x + y = 7$
       $3x - y = 1$

   **ii**  $x + y = 3$
       $3x - y = 1$

   **iii**  $x + y = 7$
       $x - 3y = 3$

   **iv**  $x + y = 3$
       $x - 3y = 3$

  b  Explain why the simultaneous equations $x + y = 3$ and $x + y = 7$ have no solution.

2  a  Use the graph to write pairs of simultaneous equations that have these solutions.

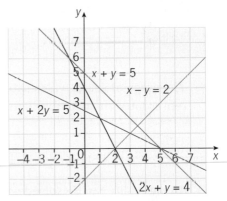

   **i**   $x = 1, y = 2$

   **ii**  $x = 2, y = 0$

   **iii**  $x = -1, y = 6$

   **iv**  $x = 3, y = 1$

   **v**   $x = 5, y = 0$

   **vi**  $x = 3\frac{1}{2}, y = 1\frac{1}{2}$

  b  Solve each pair of simultaneous equations algebraically and confirm the solutions.

3  Solve these simultaneous equations graphically.

  a   $x + y = 2$      b   $x + y = 7$      c   $x - y = -5$      d   $2x - y = 7$
      $3x - y = 2$        $x - 2y = 1$        $2x + y = 8$        $3x + y = 8$

4  Use a graphical method to solve these problems.

  a  Twice one number plus another is 12. The sum of the numbers is 7. Find the two numbers.

  b  If you take three times William's age from twice Alexander's age the result is 2. The difference between their ages is 3. How old are Alexander and William?

5  ☆ **CHALLENGE** ☆

  Can you write a pair of simultaneous equations that have more than one solution? Think about the graphs of such equations.

# Representing inequalities

- Solve linear inequalities, representing the solution on a number line

## RICH TASK

The Greek philosopher Plutarch is credited with finding all the rectangles which have an area equal to their perimeter.
Find these rectangles and use an algebraic method to prove that you have found all of them.

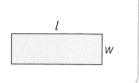

→ **An inequality is a mathematical sentence involving an inequality symbol.**

< means 'less than'          ≤ means 'less than or equal to'
> means 'greater than'       ≥ means 'greater than or equal to'

→ **The range of values which satisfy an inequality can be represented on a number line.**

$a < 5$

3  4  5  6  7

$d \geq 2$

0  1  2  3  4

An open circle means that the value at the end of the range is not included. A solid circle means that it is included.

→ **An inequality can be solved using inverse operations.**

$$5x - 7 \leq 33$$
$$5x \leq 40 \qquad \text{Add 7 to both sides}$$
$$x \leq 8 \qquad \text{Divide both sides by 5}$$

→ **If you multiply or divide an inequality by a negative number, you must reverse the inequality symbol.**
**$-5 < 10$ is true but multiplying by $-1$ gives $5 > -10$.**

Notice that the sign has been reversed to make the inequality true.

**EXAMPLE**

Solve these inequalities and represent the solution on a number line.
a  $7(x - 3) > 3x - 1$          b  $10 - 3x \leq 22$

**ANSWER**

a  $7(x - 3) > 3x - 1$
$7x - 21 > 3x - 1$  Multiply out brackets
$4x - 21 > -1$  Subtract $3x$ from both sides
$4x > 20$  Add 21 to both sides
$x > 5$  Divide both sides by 4

3  4  5  6  7

b  $10 - 3x \leq 22$
$-3x \leq 12$  Subtract 10 from both sides
$x \geq -4$  Divide both sides by $-3$.

Sign is reversed.

$-6$  $-5$  $-4$  $-3$  $-2$

**Simultaneous equations and inequalities**

## Exercise B14.4

**MEDIUM**

1 Write these notices as inequalities, defining any variables that you use. The first one has been done for you.

a

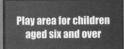

Play area for children aged six and over

b

Long Flume you must be at least 1.2 m to ride!

c

Maximum speed on site

**5**

mph

d

Children under 5 eat for free

$a \geq 6$ where $a$ is age in years

2 Write these inequalities, using $x$ to represent the variable.

a
1 2 3 4 5

b
–1 0 1 2 3

c
–5 –4 –3 –2 –1

d
–3 –2 –1 0 1

e
2 1 0 1 2 3

f
–4 –3 –2 –1 0 1

3 Represent these inequalities on a number line.

a $x \geq 1$   b $x < 5$   c $x > -8$   d $4 \leq x$

e $-12 \geq x$   f $1 \leq x \leq 5$   g $-3 \leq x < 0$   h $-10 < x \leq -8$

4 If $x$ is an integer, list all possible solutions for each of these inequalities.

a $2 < x < 5$   b $0 < x < 6$   c $-6 \leq x < 3$   d $-2 < x \leq 1$

e $1 < x < 2$   f $2 \leq 2x < 5$   g $-1 \leq \frac{x}{2} \leq 0$   h $3 \leq -3x < 12$

5 Solve these inequalities.

a $5x \leq 15$   b $10y > 50$   c $-2a > 6$   d $\frac{q}{7} \geq 3$

e $\frac{n}{-4} < 3$   f $t + 12 < 15$   g $p - 7 \geq 5$   h $3b + 7 < 19$

i $8k - 4 \leq 20$   j $17 \geq 2y + 5$   k $2(x + 1) > 10$   l $-3 \leq \frac{m}{6} - 5$

6 Solve these inequalities, representing each solution on a number line.

a $5x + 2 \leq 3x + 10$   b $6y - 5 \geq 2y + 11$   c $10n - 8 > 3n - 1$

d $3(b - 1) > 7b - 11$   e $8t - 3 \geq 5(t + 3)$   f $3(k + 3) < 8(k - 2)$

g $\frac{m + 2}{5} \leq \frac{m - 2}{3}$   h $\frac{a - 2}{2} < \frac{a - 8}{5}$

7 Find the range of values of $x$ that satisfy both inequalities.

a $5x - 3 \leq 12$ and $-3x < 3$   b $6(x - 2) \geq -3$ and $-4x > -20$

8 Solve these inequalities.

a $8 \leq 2x \leq x + 7$   b $3a + 1 < 5a \leq 2(a + 6)$

c $y < 5y + 2 \leq 2(y + 4)$   d $3b - 6 \leq 7b + 2 < 2(2b + 7)$

Split each into two separate inequalities then solve each one.

Unit B

# Regions

- Solve linear inequalities in one variable using a graphical method

## RICH TASK

Is the mean of the squares of two numbers greater than or less than the square of their means?
Use algebra and inequality symbols to justify your answer.

→ **An inequality can be represented as a region on a set of coordinate axes.**

The unshaded region is the set of all points that satisfy the inequality $x > 1$.

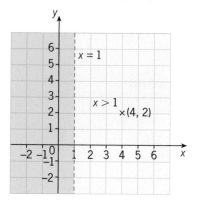

The broken line $x = 1$ indicates that the points on this line are not included in the region.

The unshaded region is the set of all points that satisfy the inequality $y \leq -2$.

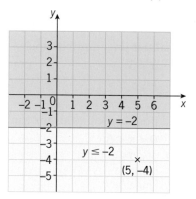

The solid line $y = -2$ indicates that the points on this line are included in the region.

---

**EXAMPLE**

Draw a graph to represent the regions given by these inequalities.

**a**  $x \leq 4$ and $y > -3$          **b**  $1 \leq y < 4$

**ANSWER**

**a**

Draw the lines $x = 4$ and $y = -3$ then show the required region unshaded.

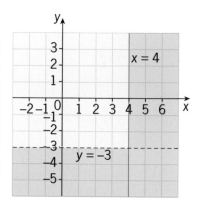

**b**

Choose a point and check. The point $(-1, 2)$ has a $y$-coordinate between 1 and 4

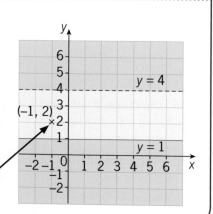

---

**Simultaneous equations and inequalities**

1 Use inequalities to describe the unshaded region. Take care with the broken lines.

a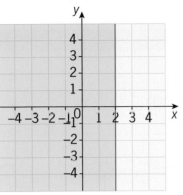

b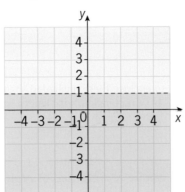

c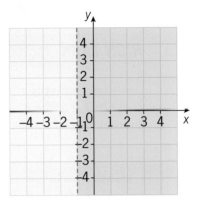

d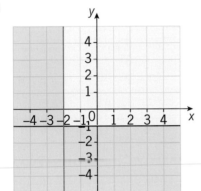

e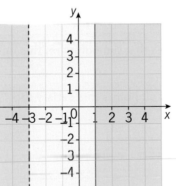

f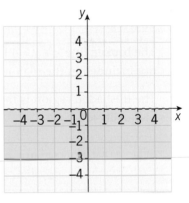

2 Draw a sketch graph to represent each of these inequalities.
Leave the required region unshaded.

a $x \geq 2$
b $y < 1$
c $x < -2$
d $y \leq 3$

e $1 \leq x \leq 3$
f $-2 \leq x < 2$
g $0 < y \leq 4$
h $-5 < y < -3$

i $x \geq 0$ and $y > 0$
j $x < 2$ and $y \geq -1$

3 Draw a sketch graph to represent each of these inequalities.
Leave the required region unshaded.

a $-1 \leq x \leq 5$ and $y > -2$
b $-3 < y \leq 0$ and $x < 1$

c $1 < x < 2$ and $y < 0$
d $-4 \leq y < 4$ and $x \geq -3$

4 Draw regions to deduce all the possible integer pairs that satisfy
the following description:
The first number is greater than −3 but less than 1.
The second number is greater than or equal to 0 but less than 3.

# Inequalities in two variables

- Solve inequalities in two variables using a graphical method

## RICH TASK

Draw graphs and write inequalities to enclose these unshaded shapes:

**a**   a square of side 2 units    **b**   a rectangle whose length is 3 × its width

**c**   a right-angled triangle    **d**   an isosceles triangle.

→ **Inequalities in two variables can be represented as regions on a set of coordinate axes.**

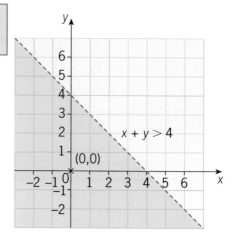

This region represents the inequality $x + y > 4$.

The broken line $x + y = 4$ indicates that the points on this line are not included in the region.

The unshaded region is the set of all points that satisfy the inequality $x + y > 4$.

**EXAMPLE**

Draw a graph to represent the region given by the inequalities $x < 2$, $y \geq 1$ and $y \leq 2x + 1$.

### ANSWER

To begin with, ignore the inequality symbols and draw the lines $x = 2$, $y = 1$ and $y = 2x + 1$.

Generate points for the line $y = 2x + 1$

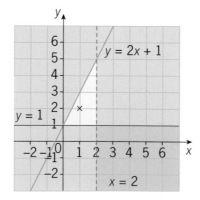

| x | 0 | 1 | 2 |
|---|---|---|---|
| y | 1 | 3 | 5 |

Use a broken or dashed line for < and >.
Use an unbroken or solid line for ≤ and ≥.

Choose the point $(1, 2)$ and substitute into $y \leq 2x + 1$.

Is it true that $2 \leq 2 \times 1 + 1$? Yes!

Thus the region containing the point $(1, 2)$ is unshaded.

1 Use inequalities to describe the unshaded region.

a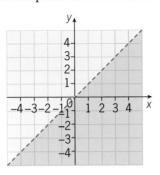

b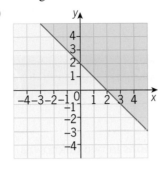

c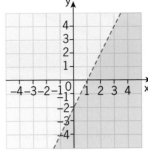

2 Draw a sketch graph to represent each of these inequalities, leaving the required region unshaded.

a $y \leq 2x$  b $y \geq x + 1$  c $y < 2x - 1$  d $x + y \leq 5$

e $y \leq 3x + 2$  f $x + 2y < 4$  g $4y > x + 4$  h $4x - 3y \leq 12$

3 Use incqualities to describe the unshaded region.

a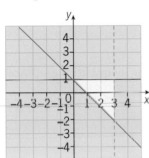

b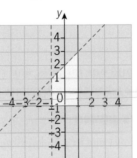

c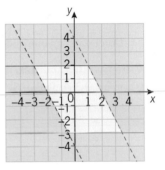

4 Draw a sketch graph to represent each of these inequalities, leaving the required region unshaded. Describe the shape that you have drawn.

a $x \geq 0$, $y \geq 0$ and $2x + y \leq 4$

b $y > -1$, $y < x + 2$ and $x + y < 6$

c $-3 < y < 1$, $x > -4$ and $y < 1 - 2x$

d $-2 \leq x < 3$, $2y \leq x + 2$ and $2y \geq x - 6$

5 ☆ **CHALLENGE** ☆

Harry has £100 to spend on CDs. Bargain basement CDs cost £6 and chart CDs cost £10. Harry wants to buy at least 10 CDs but will not buy more bargain basement CDs than chart CDs. Let $x$ be the number of bargain basement CDs and $y$ be the number of chart CDs that Harry buys.

a Show that the following inequalities model these conditions.

$3x + 5y \leq 50$, $x + y \geq 10$ and $x \leq y$

b Draw a graph to represent these inequalities, shading out any unwanted regions.

c List all of the points that satisfy the given conditions.

d How many of each type of CD should Harry buy if he decides to spend all of his money?

Unit B

## CHECK OUT

You should now be able to

- solve simultaneous linear equations in two unknowns, including using a graphical solution
- solve linear inequalities in one or two unknowns
- represent linear inequalities on a number line or graphically.

### Exam-style question

Standard creepiness rule for dating:

Don't date anyone under $(\frac{1}{2}$ age $+ 7)$

Write two inequalities, one for boys and one for girls, and represent your inequalities graphically. When are boys and girls the same age when the creepiness rule applies?

Decide on a strategy and make it clear how you are working.

Use previous answers, such as graphs, to answer questions.

Show your method and thoughts clearly.

You sometimes need both maths and words.

**Tim's answer:**

Let boy's age be y and girl's age be x.

Boys must be older than half girl's age + 7

$y > \frac{x}{2} + 7$

The same rule works for the girls

$x > \frac{y}{2} + 7$

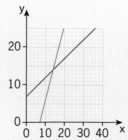

Graphs meet at (14, 14)
The creepiness rule gives the same age for boys and girls aged 14

## Exam practice

1   The grid shows the lines $x + y = 5$ and $y = 2x + 1$

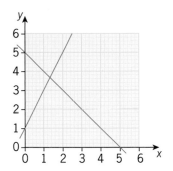

a   Write down the solution of the simultaneous equations
$x + y = 5$
$y = 2x + 1$

b   Solve algebraically
$2x - 3y = 7$
$3x + 2y = -2 \cdot 5$

                                                    (*5 marks*)

2   a   **i**  Solve this inequality     $2x - 3 \geq 12$
        **ii** Represent your solutions on a number line.

    b   Write down all the integer values that satisfy $7 \leq 3x < 24$

                                                    (*5 marks*)

3   Josh does a local paper round delivering newspapers and flyers.
    One week he was paid £6·50 for delivering 50 newspapers and
    200 flyers.
    The next week he was paid £6·80 for delivering 40 newspapers
    and 240 flyers.
    How much was Josh paid the following week for delivering 65
    newspapers and 127 flyers?

                                                    (*5 marks*)

# 15 Indices and surds

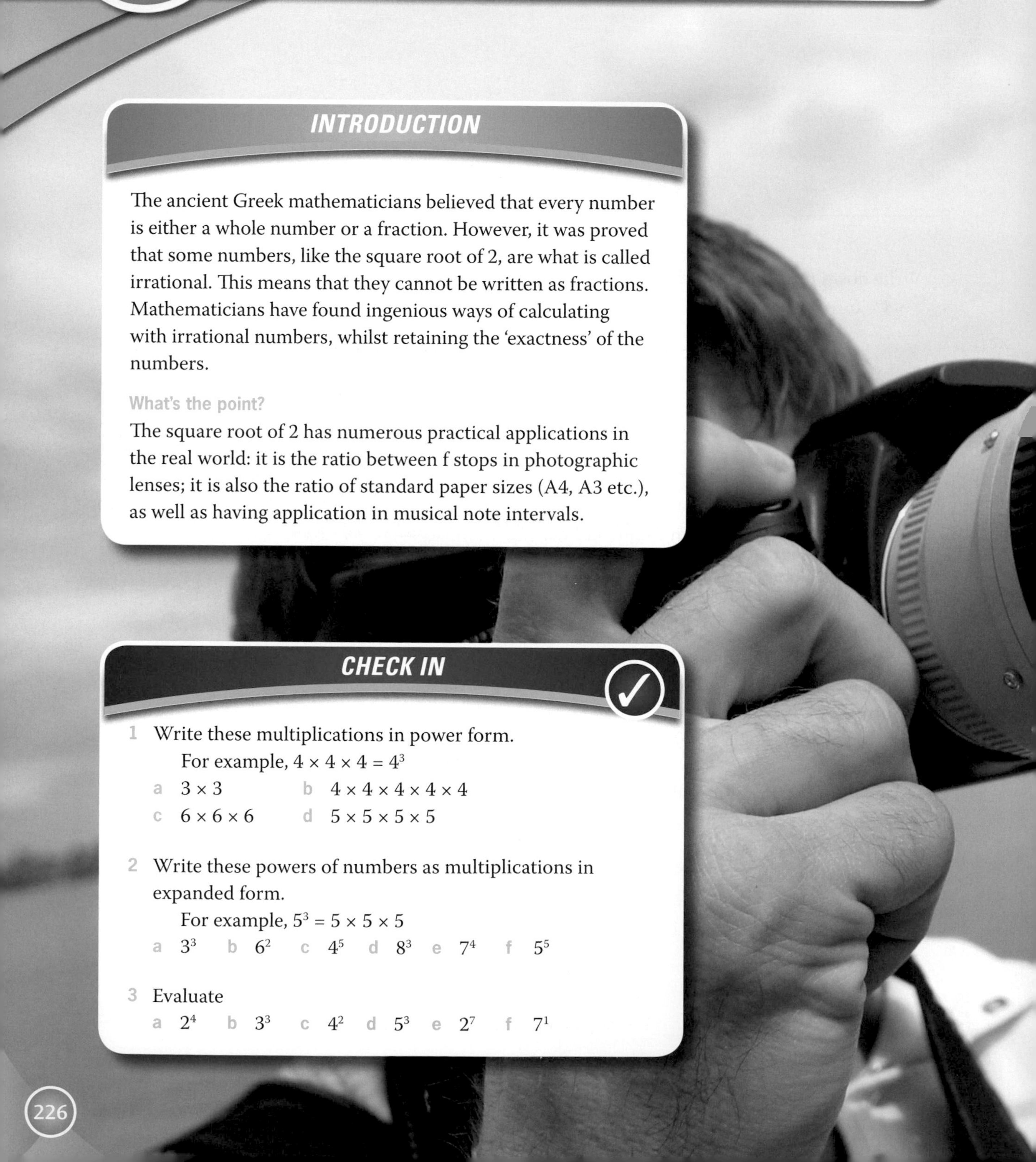

## INTRODUCTION

The ancient Greek mathematicians believed that every number is either a whole number or a fraction. However, it was proved that some numbers, like the square root of 2, are what is called irrational. This means that they cannot be written as fractions. Mathematicians have found ingenious ways of calculating with irrational numbers, whilst retaining the 'exactness' of the numbers.

**What's the point?**

The square root of 2 has numerous practical applications in the real world: it is the ratio between f stops in photographic lenses; it is also the ratio of standard paper sizes (A4, A3 etc.), as well as having application in musical note intervals.

## CHECK IN

1 Write these multiplications in power form.

For example, $4 \times 4 \times 4 = 4^3$

a $3 \times 3$      b $4 \times 4 \times 4 \times 4 \times 4$

c $6 \times 6 \times 6$      d $5 \times 5 \times 5 \times 5$

2 Write these powers of numbers as multiplications in expanded form.

For example, $5^3 = 5 \times 5 \times 5$

a $3^3$   b $6^2$   c $4^5$   d $8^3$   e $7^4$   f $5^5$

3 Evaluate

a $2^4$   b $3^3$   c $4^2$   d $5^3$   e $2^7$   f $7^1$

**What I should know**

A1

**What I will learn**

- Simplify surds
- Use index notation and index laws

**What this leads to**

C22

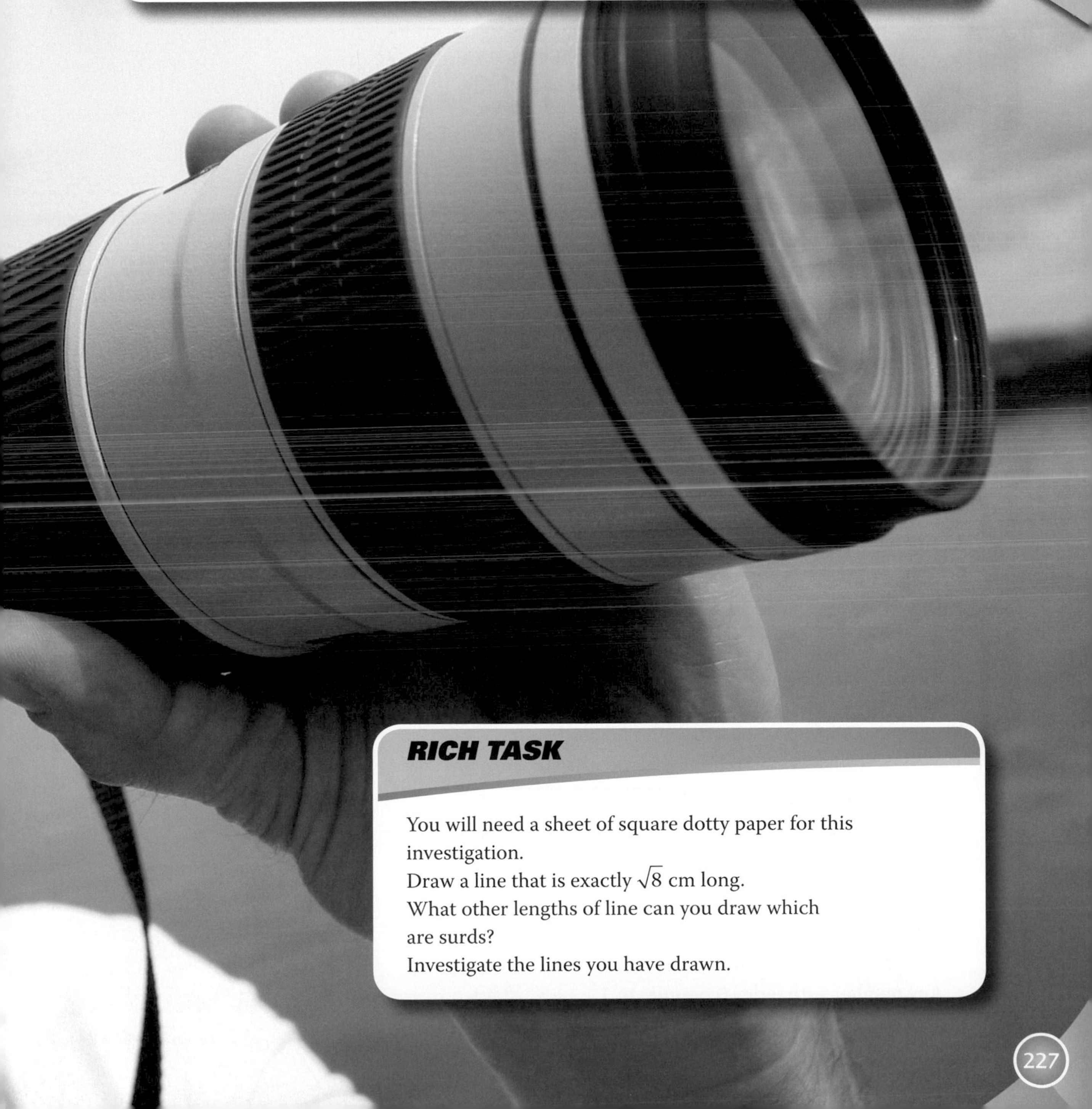

## RICH TASK

You will need a sheet of square dotty paper for this investigation.

Draw a line that is exactly $\sqrt{8}$ cm long.

What other lengths of line can you draw which are surds?

Investigate the lines you have drawn.

# Indices

- Use index notation for simple integer powers
- Use index laws for multiplication and division of integer powers

Indices provide a quick way to show multiplication by the same number repeatedly.

p. 54

**EXAMPLE**

**a** Simplify    **i**   $3 \times 3 \times 3 \times 3 \times 3$    **ii**   $6 \times 6 \times 6 \times 6$
**b** Write 504 as a product of prime factors in index form.

**ANSWER**

**a**   **i**   $3 \times 3 \times 3 \times 3 \times 3 = 3^5$    **ii**   $6 \times 6 \times 6 \times 6 = 6^4$
**b**   $504 = 2 \times 2 \times 2 \times 3 \times 3 \times 7$
      $= 2^3 \times 3^2 \times 7$

## RICH TASK

**a** Work out $2^2 \times 2^3$ as   **i**   an ordinary number    **ii**   a power of 2
**b** Work out $3^6 \div 3^2$ as   **i**   an ordinary number    **ii**   a power of 3
**c** Try multiplying and dividing other powers. Write down anything you notice.

This leads to two important rules of indices:

- Add the indices when multiplying powers of the same number   $a^m \times a^n = a^{m+n}$
- Subtract the indices when dividing powers of the same number   $a^m \div a^n = a^{m-n}$

**EXAMPLE**

Simplify    **a**   $3^2 \times 3^6$    **b**   $5^{12} \div 5^3$    **c**   $3^3 \times 5^2$

**ANSWER**

**a**   $3^2 \times 3^6 = 3^{2+6} = 3^8$      **b**   $5^{12} \div 5^3 = 5^{12-3} = 5^9$
**c**   $3^3 \times 5^2$ cannot be simplified as the numbers 3 and 5 are not the same

But you can work out
$3^3 \times 5^2 = 27 \times 25 = 675$

## RICH TASK

Work out $5^3 \div 5^3$   **i**   as an ordinary number    **ii**   as a power of 5
Try with other numbers and powers. Write down anything you notice.

→ **Any number with index 0 is equal to 1**      $a^0 = 1$

$a^0$ follows a pattern:
$a^3 = a \times a \times a$
$a^2 = a \times a \ (\div a)$
$a^1 = a \quad (\div a)$
$a^0 = 1 \quad (\div a)$

## Exercise B15.1

MEDIUM

1 Choose, if possible, from each of these sets of numbers
   a $1^7$  $2^6$  $3^4$  $4^3$  $5^3$
   b $1^9$  $4^6$  $9^3$  $16^3$  $25^2$  $7^3$
   i    The largest number
   ii   A number that is not a square number
   iii  Two equal numbers.

This exercise is to be completed without a calculator.

Unit B

2 Write as a product of prime factors in index form
   a  48    b  42    c  600    d  1280    e  735

3 Simplify, give your answers as indices.
   a  $7^4 \times 7^5$          b  $3^6 \times 3^2$          c  $8^5 \times 8^4$
   d  $15^1 \times 15^7$        e  $4^6 \times 4^6$          f  $3^8 \div 3^2$
   g  $8^{12} \div 8^{11}$      h  $9^7 \div 9^2$            i  $6^8 \div 6^4$

4 a  Write down the values of $x$ and $y$ if
         $256 = 16^x$ and $256 = 4^y$
   b  Write down the value of $k$ if
      i   $64 = 2^k$         ii   $81 = 3^k$

5 a  You are given $3^7 = 2187$. Work out $3^6$
   b  You are given $4^9 = 262\,144$. Work out $4^8$
   c  You are given $2^{12} = 4096$. Work out   i   $2^{11}$     ii   $2^{13}$
   d  You are given $10^5 = 100\,000$. Work out $10^{10}$

6 Write down, giving your answer in index form
   a  half of $2^{18}$       b  a third of $3^{12}$        c  a quarter of $4^8$

7 Write down   a  $8^0$      b  $756^0$

8

$6^0 = 1$        $6^1 = 6$        $6^2 = 36$        $6^3 = 216$
$6^4 = 1296$   $6^5 = 7776$   $6^6 = 46\,656$

Use the table to:
   a  Explain why $36 \times 216 = 7776$        b  Work out $\dfrac{46\,656}{36}$

# Fractional and negative indices

- Use index laws with fractional and negative powers

## RICH TASK

**a** Use the rule of indices $a^m \times a^n = a^{m+n}$
to work out $16^{\frac{1}{2}} \times 16^{\frac{1}{2}}$

**b** Write down the value of $\sqrt{16} \times \sqrt{16}$

**c** Explain why $16^{\frac{1}{2}} = \sqrt{16}$
Try with other numbers.

---

→ **The index $\frac{1}{2}$ means 'square root'** $\qquad a^{\frac{1}{2}} = \sqrt{a}$

→ **The index $\frac{1}{3}$ means 'cube root'** $\qquad a^{\frac{1}{n}} = \sqrt[n]{a}$

**Generally,**

→ **A fractional index $\frac{1}{n}$ means 'nth root'** $\qquad a^{\frac{1}{n}} = \sqrt[n]{a}$

## RICH TASK

**a** Use the rule of indices $a^m \div a^n = a^{m-n}$
to work out $5^3 \div 5^4$

**b** Write down the value of $\dfrac{5 \times 5 \times 5}{5 \times 5 \times 5 \times 5}$ as a fraction.

**c** Explain why $\frac{1}{5} = 5^{-1}$. Try with other numbers.

---

→ **A negative index means reciprocal** $\qquad a^{-n} = \dfrac{1}{a^n}$

---

You can combine these rules to work out indices.

$$9^{-2} = \frac{1}{9^2} = \frac{1}{81} \qquad 25^{-\frac{1}{2}} = \frac{1}{25^{\frac{1}{2}}} = \frac{1}{5}$$

There is another useful rule of indices:
$$(2^4)^3 = 2^4 \times 2^4 \times 2^4 = 2^{12}$$

---

→ **To raise a number in index form to a power multiply the indices $(a^m)^n = a^{mn}$**

**a** Write $125^2$ as a power of 5   **b** Work out $4^{-\frac{5}{2}}$

**ANSWER**

**a** $125 = 5^3$   $(125)^2 = (5^3)^2 = 5^6$   **b** $4^{-\frac{5}{2}} = \dfrac{1}{4^{\frac{5}{2}}}$

$$= \dfrac{1}{\left(4^{\frac{1}{2}}\right)^5} = \dfrac{1}{2^5} = \dfrac{1}{32}$$

$4^{\frac{1}{2}} = \left(2^2\right)^{\frac{1}{2}} = 2^{2 \times \frac{1}{2}}$ or $2^1$

## Exercise B15.2

HIGH

**1** Work out

| | | | |
|---|---|---|---|
| **a** $64^{\frac{1}{2}}$ | **b** $64^{\frac{1}{3}}$ | **c** $169^{\frac{1}{2}}$ | **d** $81^{\frac{1}{4}}$ |
| **e** $225^{\frac{1}{2}}$ | **f** $9^{0.5}$ | **g** $81^{0.25}$ | **h** $81^{0.5}$ |
| **i** $16^{0.25}$ | **j** $32^{0.2}$ | **k** $4^{-2}$ | **l** $94^{-1}$ |
| **m** $2^{-4}$ | **n** $5^{-3}$ | **o** $10^{-5}$ | **p** $9^{-\frac{1}{2}}$ |
| **q** $27^{-\frac{1}{3}}$ | **r** $32^{-\frac{1}{5}}$ | **s** $0.01^{-\frac{1}{2}}$ | **t** $1000^{-\frac{1}{3}}$ |

This exercise is to be completed without a calculator.
Where appropriate give your answers as fractions.

**2** Write as a single power

**a** $(7^3)^2$   **b** $(17^3)^5$   **c** $(6^7)^2$   **d** $(12^4)^3$   **e** $(5^3)^{-2}$

**3** Work out

**a** $(8)^{-\frac{2}{3}}$   **b** $\left(\dfrac{1}{4}\right)^{\frac{1}{2}}$   **c** $(125)^{-\frac{4}{3}}$   **d** $\left(\dfrac{1}{9}\right)^{\frac{3}{2}}$   **e** $(4)^{-\frac{5}{2}}$

**4** Work out

**a** $25^{0.5} \times 6^{-2}$   **b** $49^{-\frac{1}{2}} \times 7^{-2}$   **c** $4^{-2} \times 9^{0.5}$   **d** $4^{0.5} \div 5^2$   **e** $7^{-1} \div \left(\dfrac{1}{5}\right)^2$

**5** Express 81   **a** as a power of 9   **b** as a power of 3

**6** **a** Express $8^p$ as a power of 2.
   **b** Find the exact value of $p$ when $2^4 \times 8^p = 2^6$

**7** ☆ **PROBLEM** ☆

Pond lilies are introduced into a pond.
The weight of pond lilies, $p$ grams, in the pond $t$ days later is given by $p = 5 + 2^t$.
**a** Work out the weight of pond lilies in the pond after 3 days.
**b** **i** Write down an equation that could be used to find the number of days it takes for the weight of pond lilies to reach 133 grams.
   **ii** Work out the number of days it takes for the weight of pond lilies to reach 133 grams.

• Use surds in exact calculations without a calculator

## RICH TASK

Find the exact length of the side x.

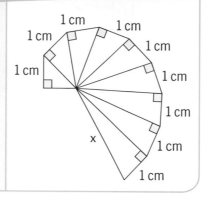

1 cm
1 cm
1 cm
1 cm
1 cm
1 cm
1 cm
1 cm
x
1 cm

> The first triangle is isosceles.

Some square roots have exact values.

$$\sqrt{4} = 2 \qquad \sqrt{25} = 5$$

Other square roots such as $\sqrt{2}$, $\sqrt{3}$ and $\sqrt{12}$ are not whole numbers. They are known as surds.

> Try working them out on your calculator. They are **irrational numbers** – the decimal digits go on for ever without recurring.

## RICH TASK

Work out    **a**   **i**   $\sqrt{9} \times \sqrt{9}$     **ii**   $\sqrt{81}$

          **b**   **i**   $\sqrt{4} \times \sqrt{25}$    **ii**   $\sqrt{100}$

Write down anything you notice.

→ $\sqrt{a} \times \sqrt{b} = \sqrt{a \times b}$

> A surd multiplied by itself gives the number inside the root:
> $\sqrt{a} \times \sqrt{a} = a$

This rule is very useful for simplifying surds.

Working backwards

$$\sqrt{36} = \sqrt{(4 \times 9)} = \sqrt{4} \times \sqrt{9} = 2 \times 3 = 6$$

$$\sqrt{45} = \sqrt{(9 \times 5)} = \sqrt{9} \times \sqrt{5} = 3\sqrt{5}$$

→ **Surds are given in their simplest form when the smallest possible integer is written inside the square root sign.**

Express in the simplest form

**a** $\sqrt{32}$                 **b** $\sqrt{150}$

**ANSWER**

**a** $\sqrt{32} = \sqrt{(16 \times 2)}$
$= \sqrt{16} \times \sqrt{2} = 4\sqrt{2}$

**b** $\sqrt{150} = \sqrt{(25 \times 6)}$
$= \sqrt{25} \times \sqrt{6} = 5\sqrt{6}$

> When simplifying surds look for **square numbers**.

## Exercise B15.3

**HIGH**

> This exercise is to be completed without a calculator.

1   Evaluate

   a   $\left(\sqrt{10}\right)^2$        b   $\left(\sqrt{7}\right)^2$        c   $\left(\sqrt{2}\right)^4$

   d   $\left(\sqrt{0.5}\right)^2$       e   $\left(\sqrt{3}\right)^4$        f   $\left(\sqrt{80}\right)^2$

2   Express in the simplest form

   a   $\sqrt{99}$          b   $\sqrt{60}$         c   $\sqrt{75}$

   d   $\sqrt{200}$        e   $\sqrt{125}$       f   $\sqrt{128}$

3   Evaluate

   a   $\sqrt{5} \times \sqrt{3} \times \sqrt{15}$     b   $\sqrt{2} \times \sqrt{7} \times \sqrt{14}$

   c   $\sqrt{3} \times \sqrt{12}$            d   $\sqrt{6} \times \sqrt{30}$

4   Given that $q = \sqrt{2}$ and $r = \sqrt{8}$, evaluate

   a   $q^3 r$           b   $\sqrt{qr}$         c   $(qr)^2$

5   Given that $s = \sqrt{3}$ and $t = \sqrt{6}$, simplify

   a   $st$            b   $st^3$          c   $(st)^{-2}$

6   **RICH TASK**

   a   Use this equilateral triangle to show that $\sin 60° = \dfrac{\sqrt{3}}{2}$

   b   Use the triangle to find in surd form the exact values of

     **i**   $\cos 30°$    **ii**   $\tan 30°$    **iii**   $\tan 60°$

   c   Draw an appropriate right-angled triangle and find in surd form the exact value of

     **i**   $\sin 45°$    **ii**   $\cos 45°$

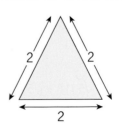

# Simplifying surds

- Use surds in exact calculations without a calculator
- Rationalise a denominator

A fraction where the denominator is a surd is *not* in its simplest form.

→ **To rationalise a denominator, multiply numerator and denominator by the denominator.**

$$\frac{19}{\sqrt{5}} = \frac{19}{\sqrt{5}} \times \frac{\sqrt{5}}{\sqrt{5}} = \frac{19\sqrt{5}}{5}$$

Use a calculator to check that the fractions are the same.

**EXAMPLE**

Simplify    **a** $\dfrac{20}{\sqrt{5}}$      **b** $\dfrac{2+\sqrt{3}}{\sqrt{3}}$

**ANSWER**

**a** $\dfrac{20}{\sqrt{5}} = \dfrac{20}{\sqrt{5}} \times \dfrac{\sqrt{5}}{\sqrt{5}} = \dfrac{20\sqrt{5}}{5} = 4\sqrt{5}$

**b** $\dfrac{2+\sqrt{3}}{\sqrt{3}} = \dfrac{2+\sqrt{3}}{\sqrt{3}} \times \dfrac{\sqrt{3}}{\sqrt{3}} = \dfrac{\sqrt{3}(2+\sqrt{3})}{3} = \dfrac{3+2\sqrt{3}}{3}$

The next example shows how to multiply numbers containing surds. You will need to know how to multiply two brackets together.

p. 282

**EXAMPLE**

Simplify      **a** $\left(3+\sqrt{2}\right)^2$      **b** $\left(8-\sqrt{5}\right)\left(8+\sqrt{5}\right)$

**ANSWER**

**a** $\left(3+\sqrt{2}\right)\left(3+\sqrt{2}\right)$

$= 9 + 3\sqrt{2} + 3\sqrt{2} + 2 = 11 + 6\sqrt{2}$

Using a grid like this can help with **expanding brackets**.

| × | 3 | $\sqrt{2}$ |
|---|---|---|
| **3** | 9 | $3\sqrt{2}$ |
| $\sqrt{2}$ | $3\sqrt{2}$ | 2 |

**b** $\left(8-\sqrt{5}\right)\left(8+\sqrt{5}\right)$

$= 64 + 8\sqrt{5} - 8\sqrt{5} - 5 = 59$

| × | 8 | $-\sqrt{5}$ |
|---|---|---|
| **8** | 64 | $-8\sqrt{5}$ |
| $\sqrt{5}$ | $8\sqrt{5}$ | $-5$ |

Multiply every term in one bracket by every term in the other bracket.

$(3 + \sqrt{2})\,(3 + \sqrt{2})$

## RICH TASK

This is a method to find an approximate value for $\sqrt{5}$.

The nearest integer to $\sqrt{5}$ is 2

$$\sqrt{5} - 2 < \frac{1}{2}$$

Square both sides

$$\left(\sqrt{5} - 2\right)^2 < \left(\frac{1}{2}\right)^2$$

$$9 - 4\sqrt{5} < \frac{1}{4}$$

Square both sides again

$$\left(9 - 4\sqrt{5}\right)^2 < \left(\frac{1}{4}\right)^2$$

$$161 - 72\sqrt{5} < \frac{1}{16}$$

$$\sqrt{5} \approx \frac{161}{72}$$

i    Try to explain each stage of the method.
ii   What would happen if you continued to square both sides of the inequality?
iii  Use this method to find an approximate value for $\sqrt{2}$.
iv   Can you use this method to find an approximate value for $\sqrt{3}$?

## Exercise B15.4

**HIGH**

1  Evaluate

> This exercise is to be completed without a calculator.

a  $\dfrac{\sqrt{18}}{\sqrt{2}}$    b  $\dfrac{\sqrt{12}}{\sqrt{3}}$    c  $\dfrac{\sqrt{125}}{\sqrt{5}}$    d  $\dfrac{\sqrt{80}}{\sqrt{5}}$

e  $\dfrac{\sqrt{32}}{\sqrt{2}}$    f  $\dfrac{\sqrt{98}}{\sqrt{2}}$    g  $\sqrt{2\tfrac{1}{4}}$    h  $\sqrt{1\tfrac{7}{9}}$

2  Write in the form $a\sqrt{b}$, where $a$ and $b$ are integers.

a  $\dfrac{12}{\sqrt{3}}$    b  $\dfrac{21}{\sqrt{3}}$    c  $\dfrac{15}{\sqrt{5}}$    d  $\dfrac{36}{\sqrt{2}}$    e  $\dfrac{35}{\sqrt{7}}$    f  $\dfrac{50}{\sqrt{5}}$

3  Simplify

a  $\left(7 + \sqrt{3}\right)\left(7 - \sqrt{3}\right)$    b  $\left(2 - \sqrt{5}\right)\left(2 + \sqrt{5}\right)$    c  $\left(\sqrt{2} + \sqrt{18}\right)^2$    d  $\left(\sqrt{27} - \sqrt{3}\right)^2$

e  $\left(5 - \sqrt{6}\right)^2$    f  $\left(2 - \sqrt{7}\right)^2$    g  $\left(3 - \sqrt{2}\right)^2$    h  $\dfrac{4 + \sqrt{3}}{\sqrt{3}}$    i  $\dfrac{3 + \sqrt{7}}{\sqrt{7}}$

4  Show that    a  $\left(\sqrt{2} + \dfrac{1}{\sqrt{2}}\right)^2 = 4.5$    b  $\left(\sqrt{5} + \dfrac{1}{\sqrt{5}}\right)^2 = 7.2$

5  ☆ **PROBLEM** ☆

> Two squares are such that their areas are in the ratio $1:3$
> The side of the larger square is 12 cm.
> What is the side of the smaller square?
> Give your answer in the form $a\sqrt{b}$, where $a$ and $b$ are integers.

6  ☆ **PROBLEM** ☆

> The numbers $A$, $B$ and $C$ are such that    $B^2 = A \times C$.
>
> a   Find the number $C$ if   $A = \sqrt{3}$ and   $B = 1 - \sqrt{3}$
>     Give your answer in the form $p + q\sqrt{3}$ where $p$ and $q$ are numbers.
> b   Explain why it would not be possible to find $B$ if
>     $A = \sqrt{5}$   and   $C = 1 - \sqrt{5}$

## CHECK OUT

You should now be able to:

- use indices in calculations
- use surds in exact calculations
- rationalise a denominator.

## Exam-style question

Given that $16^{\frac{3}{4}} \times 8^{-\frac{1}{3}} = 2^p$, find the value of $p$.

**Rupa's answer:**

$$16^{\frac{3}{4}} = (2^4)^{\frac{3}{4}} = 2^3$$

$$8^{-\frac{1}{3}} = (2^3)^{-\frac{1}{3}} = 2^{-1}$$

$$16^{\frac{3}{4}} \times 8^{-\frac{1}{3}} = 2^3 \times 2^{-1} = 2^2$$

$$2^p = 2^2 \qquad p = 2$$

You will not have a calculator for this type of question.

Write each number so that the base numbers are the same.

Work out each index.

Solve the equation.

## Exam practice

1   Evaluate.
   a   $25^{0.5} \times 4^{-2}$
   b   $(2 - \sqrt{3})(2 + \sqrt{3})$
   c   $\sqrt{18} \times \sqrt{18}$

   *(6 marks)*

2   Solve.
   $16x^3 = 2$

   *(2 marks)*

3   Australian broadsheet paper has length 841 mm.
   Its sides are in the ratio $1 : \sqrt{2}$.
   The broadsheet is folded in half.
   Work out the length and width of this paper size,
   giving your answer in surd form.

   *(3 marks)*

# Case study 5: Business

One out of every two small businesses goes bust within its first two years of trading. Mathematics can be applied to reduce the risk of failure for a business as well as to maximise its profits.

A manager needs to know how much cash is coming into and going out of the business.
Accountants must set a suitable budget that includes realistic performance targets, and limits expenditure to what the business can afford.

## Example

Annie sells hand made cards at a monthly craft fair. She has two ranges of cards; standard and deluxe.
The production costs and selling prices per card are:

| | Materials used | Time to make | Wages paid | Selling price | Profit |
|---|---|---|---|---|---|
| Standard | £0.30 | 15 minutes | £1.00 | £2.55 | £1.25 |
| Deluxe | £0.20 | 30 minutes | £2.00 | £3.60 | £1.40 |

This is Annie's cash flow budget for her first three craft fairs (some of the information is missing):

| | January (£) | February (£) | March (£) |
|---|---|---|---|
| Standard card sales | 45.90 | 40.80 | |
| Deluxe card sales | 43.20 | | 32.40 |
| TOTAL INCOME | 89.10 | 91.20 | 93.60 |
| | | | |
| Materials used | 7.80 | 7.60 | 9.00 |
| Wages | | | |
| Craft fair fees | 10.00 | 10.00 | 10.00 |
| Advertising | 5.00 | 5.00 | 5.00 |
| TOTAL EXPENDITURE | 64.80 | | |
| | | | |
| NET CASH SURPLUS/DEFICIT | 24.30 | | |
| CASH BALANCE BROUGHT FORWARD | - | 24.30 | |
| CASH BALANCE TO CARRY FORWARD | 24.30 | | |

How many of each type of card did Annie sell in each of the three months?
Calculate her spend on materials and wages for each month.

The net surplus (profit) or net deficit (loss) is calculated using the formula Balance = Income − Expenditure
Copy the table and complete the missing values.

On separate copies of the table template, show how the cash flow could change if
* the craft fair fees were increased to £15
* the cost of the materials used to make each type of card increased by 40%
* Annie sold the cards at a discount price of 20% off each type of card.

Investigate how other changes to costs/income might affect Annie's cash flow.

Managers can use mathematical models to make decisions about their business. These techniques are widely used in production planning to obtain the maximum profit or to incur the minimum cost in a given situation.

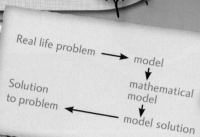

Real life problem ⟶ model

model ↓

Solution to problem ⟵ mathematical model

model solution

Annie wants to know how much of each type of card she should produce in order to maximise her profits in a particular month. She has £9.00 cash available for materials and a maximum of £50 to spend on wages for that month.

Use s to represent the number of standard cards, and d to represent the number of deluxe cards.

For the material costs, you have $0.3s + 0.2d \leq 9$

For the wage costs, you have $s + 2d \leq 50$

The aim is to maximise the profit, £P, where

$P = 1.25s + 1.40d - 15$

The '– 15' is for the fixed costs.

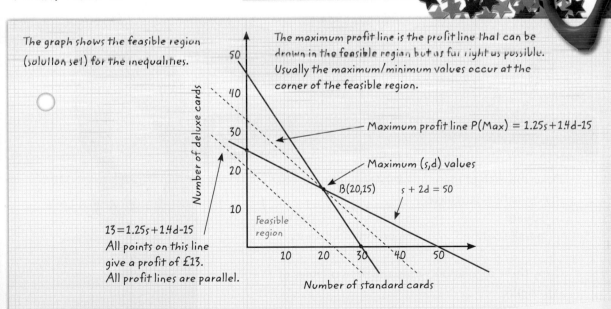

The graph shows the feasible region (solution set) for the inequalities.

The maximum profit line is the profit line that can be drawn in the feasible region but as far right as possible. Usually the maximum/minimum values occur at the corner of the feasible region.

Number of deluxe cards

Maximum profit line P(Max) = 1.25s + 1.4d - 15

Maximum (s,d) values

B(20,15)    s + 2d = 50

$13 = 1.25s + 1.4d - 15$
All points on this line give a profit of £13. All profit lines are parallel.

Feasible region

Number of standard cards

Annie should make 20 standard and 15 deluxe cards, which would give her a profit of £31.00.

Given these constraints, investigate how changes to the production costs and selling prices might affect the maximum possible profit.

For another month, Annie has only £8.00 cash available for materials and a maximum of £40 to spend on wages. Using the method shown, calculate the maximum possible profit and the number of standard and deluxe cards Annie should make to achieve this value.

How do you think you would need to adapt the method to find the minimum amount Annie would need to spend on materials to guarantee a specified minimum profit and wage for a given month?

# 16 Vectors

## INTRODUCTION

Vectors are commonly used in computer graphics, where the information required to compose the image is stored as mathematical equations.

**What's the point?**

Computer-generated images are widely used in the entertainment industry, as well as having application in scientific research and industrial design.

## CHECK IN

1 Describe each of these quadrilaterals using precise mathematical language:

   a  square         b  rhombus     c  rectangle

   d  parallelogram   e  trapezium   f  kite

2 Copy these regular polygons and draw all lines of symmetry.

   a                b                c

**What I should know**

B12

**What I will learn**

- Use vector notation
- Use vectors to solve problems in algebra and geometry

**What this leads to**

Careers in engineering and meteorology

## RICH TASK

In a triangle ABC, P, Q, and R are the midpoints of the sides AB, BC and CA respectively. Show that the lines joining AQ, BR and CP all meet at a point which is two-thirds of the distance along each line from the vertex.

# Introducing vectors

- Use vector notation and manipulate vectors

p. 181

A **vector** has both a *size* (or *magnitude*) and a *direction*.
But a **scalar** has only a *size* and no direction.
A vector can be shown as an arrow and written
as $\mathbf{XY}$, $\overrightarrow{XY}$, $\mathbf{a}$ or $\underset{\sim}{a}$.

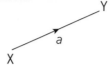

A translation can be expressed as a **vector**. But the area of a shape is a **scalar**.

Vectors can be added together by placing
arrows tip-to-tail.
The order does not matter.
So $\underset{\sim}{a} + \underset{\sim}{b} = \underset{\sim}{r}$   and   $\underset{\sim}{b} + \underset{\sim}{a} = \underset{\sim}{r}$
The vector $\underset{\sim}{r}$ is called the **resultant**.

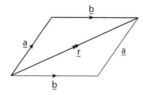

When three vectors are added, the resultant is always the same regardless of the order of the addition.

Also $\underset{\sim}{a} + (\underset{\sim}{b} + \underset{\sim}{c}) = (\underset{\sim}{a} + \underset{\sim}{b}) + \underset{\sim}{c}$

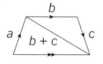

The negative of a vector is in the opposite
direction. So subtracting a vector is the same
as adding its negative.

Multiplying a vector by a number increases
its size but does not change its direction.

In this diagram, $\underset{\sim}{a} - \underset{\sim}{b} = \underset{\sim}{a} + (-\underset{\sim}{b}) = \underset{\sim}{r}$

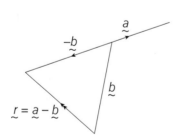

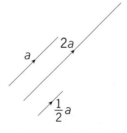

## EXAMPLE

On this grid,
**i** express the
vectors **OI** and
**OV** in terms of
**a** and **b**

**ii** find the resultant
of $2\mathbf{a} - \mathbf{b}$.

**ANSWER**

**i**  OI = OM + MI = $\mathbf{a}$ + (−$\mathbf{b}$) = $\mathbf{a}$ − $\mathbf{b}$
    OV = OL + LV = (−$\mathbf{a}$) + 2$\mathbf{b}$ = 2$\mathbf{b}$ − $\mathbf{a}$

**ii**  $2\mathbf{a} - \mathbf{b}$ = ON + NJ = OJ

If you start from K instead of O,
then $2\mathbf{a} - \mathbf{b}$ = KH.
What other values could $2\mathbf{a} - \mathbf{b}$ have?

1 On the same grid as used in the previous example,
  a express these vectors in terms of **a** and **b**.
    **i** ON        **ii** OW        **iii** OC
    **iv** OY        **v** OP        **vi** OB
  b find the resultant of
    **i** $a + 2b$      **ii** $2a + b$      **iii** $a - 2b$
    **iv** $b - a$      **v** $-b - a$      **vi** $-2a - b$

2 The grid on the right contains vectors **a** to **p**. Are these
statements *true* or *false* ?
  a $c = 2a$      b $p = 2a$      c $g = 3d$      d $j = -2d$
  e $f = 2e$      f $m = 2b$      g $i = 2h$      h $n = \frac{1}{2}h$
  i $k = \frac{1}{2}h$      j $i = -4k$      k $c = -\frac{1}{2}f$      l $p = -c$
  m $n = k$      n $d = \frac{1}{3}g$

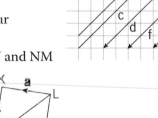

3 Write the vectors **b** to **h** in terms of vector **a**.

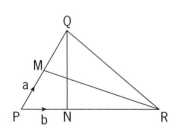

4 Write these vectors in terms of **a** and **b**, simplifying your
answers where possible.
  a OV, OW and WO      b PR and QR      c LN and NM

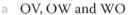

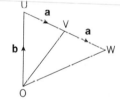 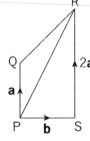 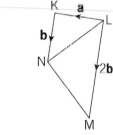

5 In triangle PQR, M is the midpoint of PQ and PN : NR = 1 : 2.
Find, in terms of **a** and **b**, the vectors
  a **MQ**      b **PQ**      c **NR**      d **PR**
  e **NQ**      f **MR**      g **QR**      h **RQ**

6 A small aircraft aims to fly on a bearing of 030° at a speed of 90 mph in a
wind blowing due east at 50 mph. Make a scale drawing to find its actual
speed relative to the ground. Check your answer by calculation.
In what circumstances would its ground speed be **a** greatest, **b** least?

7 **RICH TASK**

A man can swim at 10 metres per minute relative to the water in a river flowing at
8 metres per minute. Explain how he can swim straight across the river.

# Vector geometry

- Use vectors in different forms to solve problems in algebra and geometry

The components of a vector on a square grid are the two parts of the vector parallel to the $x$- and $y$-directions, so the components of $\mathbf{a} = \begin{pmatrix} 1 \\ 3 \end{pmatrix}$ are 1 and 3.

On this grid, $\mathbf{a} + \mathbf{b} = \begin{pmatrix} 1 \\ 3 \end{pmatrix} + \begin{pmatrix} 2 \\ 2 \end{pmatrix} = \begin{pmatrix} 3 \\ 5 \end{pmatrix}$

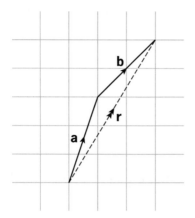

where 3 and 5 are the components of the resultant $\mathbf{r}$. What are the components of $\mathbf{a} - \mathbf{b}$?

You can multiply column vectors.

$$3\begin{pmatrix} 2 \\ -1 \end{pmatrix} = \begin{pmatrix} 3 \times 2 \\ 3 \times -1 \end{pmatrix} = \begin{pmatrix} 6 \\ -3 \end{pmatrix}$$

**EXAMPLE**

Find the components $p$ and $q$ in the vector equation

$$2\begin{pmatrix} 3 \\ 1 \end{pmatrix} - \begin{pmatrix} p \\ 4 \end{pmatrix} + 2\begin{pmatrix} -2 \\ q \end{pmatrix} = \begin{pmatrix} 1 \\ 6 \end{pmatrix}$$

**ANSWER**

For the $x$-components,
$(2 \times 3) - p + (2 \times -2) = 1$
$6 - p - 4 = 1$
$p = 1$

For the $y$-components,
$(2 \times 1) - 4 + (2 \times q) = 6$
$2 - 4 + 2q = 6$
$q = 4$

→ **Two vectors a and b are parallel if one is a multiple of the other or a = kb**

so $\begin{pmatrix} 6 \\ 2 \end{pmatrix}$ is parallel to $\begin{pmatrix} 3 \\ 1 \end{pmatrix}$ because $\begin{pmatrix} 6 \\ 2 \end{pmatrix} = 2\begin{pmatrix} 3 \\ 1 \end{pmatrix}$     a   b

**a** Given that **OA** = **a** and **OB** = **b**, find the vector **OM** where M is the midpoint of AB.

**b** If $\mathbf{a} = \begin{pmatrix} 3 \\ 2 \end{pmatrix}$ and $\mathbf{b} = \begin{pmatrix} 9 \\ -8 \end{pmatrix}$, find the coordinates of M.

**ANSWER**

**a** *First method*

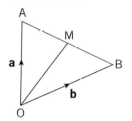

**a** *Second method*

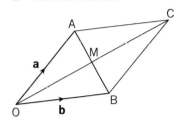

$\mathbf{AB} = \mathbf{AO} + \mathbf{OB} = -\mathbf{a} + \mathbf{b} = \mathbf{b} - \mathbf{a}$

$\mathbf{AM} = \frac{1}{2}\mathbf{AB} = \frac{1}{2}(\mathbf{b} - \mathbf{a})$

So $\mathbf{OM} = \mathbf{OA} + \mathbf{AM} = \mathbf{a} + \frac{1}{2}(\mathbf{b} - \mathbf{a})$

$= \frac{1}{2}(\mathbf{a} + \mathbf{b})$

Consider the parallelogram OACB.

$\mathbf{OC} = \mathbf{OA} + \mathbf{AC} = \mathbf{OA} + \mathbf{OB} = \mathbf{a} + \mathbf{b}$

M is the midpoint of OC

So $\mathbf{OM} = \frac{1}{2}\mathbf{OC} = \frac{1}{2}(\mathbf{a} + \mathbf{b})$

**b** $\mathbf{OM} = \frac{1}{2}\left( \begin{pmatrix} 3 \\ 2 \end{pmatrix} + \begin{pmatrix} 9 \\ -8 \end{pmatrix} \right) = \frac{1}{2}\begin{pmatrix} 12 \\ -6 \end{pmatrix} = \begin{pmatrix} 6 \\ -3 \end{pmatrix}$

The point M has coordinates (6, −3).

## Exercise B16.2

**HIGH**

**1** Given that $\mathbf{a} = \begin{pmatrix} 3 \\ 1 \end{pmatrix}$, $\mathbf{b} = \begin{pmatrix} -2 \\ 4 \end{pmatrix}$ and $\mathbf{c} = \begin{pmatrix} 0 \\ -3 \end{pmatrix}$, find

  a   $\mathbf{a} + \mathbf{b}$      b   $\mathbf{a} + \mathbf{b} - \mathbf{c}$      c   $2\mathbf{b} + 3\mathbf{c}$      d   $2(\mathbf{a} - \mathbf{c}) + \frac{1}{2}\mathbf{b}$

**2** Three tug boats are pulling an ocean liner. The forces in their tow ropes are $\begin{pmatrix} 2 \\ 8 \end{pmatrix}$, $\begin{pmatrix} 9 \\ 1 \end{pmatrix}$ and $\begin{pmatrix} 4 \\ -5 \end{pmatrix}$.

Find the resultant force on the liner.

**3** These six vectors can be arranged into three pairs of parallel vectors. Find the pairs which are parallel.

$\begin{pmatrix} 2 \\ 4 \end{pmatrix}$ $\begin{pmatrix} 2 \\ -3 \end{pmatrix}$ $\begin{pmatrix} 1 \\ 2 \end{pmatrix}$ $\begin{pmatrix} 4 \\ -1 \end{pmatrix}$ $\begin{pmatrix} -2 \\ 3 \end{pmatrix}$ $\begin{pmatrix} -2 \\ \frac{1}{2} \end{pmatrix}$

**Continued** ▶

Unit B

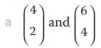

4 Find the vector **OM** for the midpoint of PQ when **OP** and **OQ** are

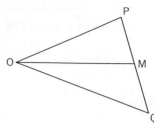

a $\begin{pmatrix} 4 \\ 2 \end{pmatrix}$ and $\begin{pmatrix} 6 \\ 4 \end{pmatrix}$     b $\begin{pmatrix} 3 \\ -1 \end{pmatrix}$ and $\begin{pmatrix} -1 \\ 7 \end{pmatrix}$     c $\begin{pmatrix} 0 \\ 5 \end{pmatrix}$ and $\begin{pmatrix} -2 \\ -1 \end{pmatrix}$

5 Find the lettered components in these vector equations.

a $\begin{pmatrix} p \\ 3 \end{pmatrix} + \begin{pmatrix} 5 \\ q \end{pmatrix} - \begin{pmatrix} 2 \\ 1 \end{pmatrix} = \begin{pmatrix} 8 \\ 5 \end{pmatrix}$     b $2\begin{pmatrix} 3 \\ m \end{pmatrix} - \begin{pmatrix} 1 \\ 6 \end{pmatrix} + \begin{pmatrix} n \\ 0 \end{pmatrix} = \begin{pmatrix} 9 \\ 4 \end{pmatrix}$

c $2\begin{pmatrix} c+1 \\ 3 \end{pmatrix} - 3\begin{pmatrix} c-1 \\ d \end{pmatrix} = \begin{pmatrix} 0 \\ 9 \end{pmatrix}$     d $\begin{pmatrix} 3u \\ 1 \end{pmatrix} + \begin{pmatrix} 4 \\ 5u \end{pmatrix} - \begin{pmatrix} v \\ v \end{pmatrix} = \begin{pmatrix} 4 \\ 7 \end{pmatrix}$

6 a The resultant of three vectors has components 5 and 4 as given in this equation. Find the unknown vector.

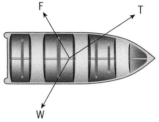

$$\begin{pmatrix} 2 \\ 3 \end{pmatrix} + \begin{pmatrix} x \\ y \end{pmatrix} + \begin{pmatrix} -1 \\ 2 \end{pmatrix} = \begin{pmatrix} 5 \\ 4 \end{pmatrix}$$

b A rowing boat is held at rest by a combination of the tension $\mathbf{T} = \begin{pmatrix} 6 \\ 1 \end{pmatrix}$ in a rope,

the force of the tide $\mathbf{F} = \begin{pmatrix} -2 \\ 2 \end{pmatrix}$ and the force of the wind **W**. Find the vector **W**.

7 **RICH TASK**

Design an orienteering course on a square grid to cover a total of 10 km. The course is to have 4 legs and the first leg is $\begin{pmatrix} 2 \\ 2 \end{pmatrix}$ km.

8 O is the origin and OABC is a parallelogram.

If $\mathbf{OA} = \begin{pmatrix} 3 \\ 5 \end{pmatrix}$ and $\mathbf{AB} = \begin{pmatrix} 4 \\ -1 \end{pmatrix}$, find

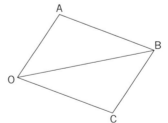

a the vectors **OB** and **OC**
b the coordinates of the points B and C.

9 The parallelogram OPQR has O as the origin. $\mathbf{OP} = \begin{pmatrix} 8 \\ 6 \end{pmatrix}$ and $\mathbf{OR} = \begin{pmatrix} 12 \\ -2 \end{pmatrix}$.

Find   a   **OQ**
      b   **OM**, where M is the midpoint of PR.

What can you deduce from your two answers about the diagonals of this parallelogram?

**10** Triangle OEF has $\mathbf{OE} = \begin{pmatrix} 6 \\ 10 \end{pmatrix}$ and $\mathbf{OF} = \begin{pmatrix} 8 \\ 1 \end{pmatrix}$, where O is the origin
and M and N are the midpoints of lines OE and OF.
Write these vectors in component form.
  a **OM**    b **ON**    c **MN**    d **EF**
What two facts can you deduce about the lines MN and EF?

**THINK:**
What are their sizes?
What are their directions?

**11** A straight railway line across open moorland passes through the
origin O in the direction $\mathbf{b} = \begin{pmatrix} 4 \\ 1 \end{pmatrix}$. A troop of soldiers leaves O and
walks to point A where $\mathbf{OA} = \begin{pmatrix} 2 \\ 5 \end{pmatrix}$. They then turn and walk parallel to the railway.
Show that the troop will pass through the point $(x, 8)$ and find the value of $x$.

**12** Two ships $S_1$ and $S_2$ leave port P at the same time travelling with velocities
of $\begin{pmatrix} 2 \\ 5 \end{pmatrix}$ km h$^{-1}$ and $\begin{pmatrix} 4 \\ 1 \end{pmatrix}$ km h$^{-1}$. The position of a lighthouse L is given by
$\mathbf{PL} = \begin{pmatrix} 10 \\ y \end{pmatrix}$ km. After $t$ hours, the line $S_1S_2$ has L as its midpoint.
Find the values of $t$ and $y$.

**13** The regular hexagon OABCDE has $\mathbf{OA} = \mathbf{a}$ and $\mathbf{OE} = \mathbf{e}$ where O is the origin.
The diagonals of the hexagon intersect at the point M.
Find, in terms of **a** and **e**,
  a **AM**    b **OM**    c **AB**    d **OD**    e **AC**
What do you deduce about the lines AC and OD?

**14** A quadrilateral WXYZ has points S, T, U and V as the
midpoints of its sides as shown.
If $\mathbf{WS} = \mathbf{p}$, $\mathbf{XT} = \mathbf{q}$ and $\mathbf{YU} = \mathbf{r}$, find in terms of **p**, **q** and **r**
  a **ST**    b **WZ**    c **VU**
Make a deduction about the lines ST and VU.
What do you deduce about quadrilateral STUV?

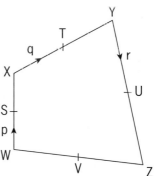

**15** ☆**CHALLENGE**☆

Triangle OAB has O as the origin, points M and N as the midpoints
of OA and OB respectively, **OA** = **a** and **OB** = **b**.
Points X and Y lie on AN and BM respectively such that
NX : XA = 1 : 3 and MY : YB = 1 : 3.
Find OX and OY to prove that X and Y are the same point.
What do you deduce about the three medians of any triangle?
What is the connection with the centre of gravity of a triangular piece
of card?
Cut out such a card and demonstrate your result.

The median joins a vertex of a
triangle to the midpoint of the
opposite side.

Unit B

You should now be able to

- understand and use vector notation
- represent vectors graphically
- calculate with vectors
- solve simple geometrical problems in 2-D using vector methods.

## Exam-style question

PQRS is a parallelogram. $\overrightarrow{PQ} = \mathbf{q}$. $\overrightarrow{PS} = \mathbf{s}$.
W, X, Y and Z are the midpoints of the sides
PQ, QR, RS and SP respectively.
Show that WXYZ is parallelogram.

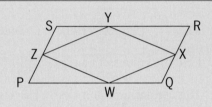

### Ruby's answer:

A parallelogram has opposite sides parallel

Need to show that
$\overrightarrow{WZ} = \overrightarrow{XY}$ and $\overrightarrow{WX} = \overrightarrow{ZY}$

$WZ = WP + PZ = -\frac{1}{2}q + \frac{1}{2}s$

$XY = XQ + QP + PS + SY$

$\quad = -\frac{1}{2}s - q + s + \frac{1}{2}q = -\frac{1}{2}q + \frac{1}{2}s$

So $\overrightarrow{WZ} = \overrightarrow{XY}$

$WX = WQ + QX = \frac{1}{2}q + \frac{1}{2}s$

$ZY = ZS + SY = \frac{1}{2}s + \frac{1}{2}q$

So $\overrightarrow{WX} = \overrightarrow{ZY}$

WXYZ is a parallelogram

Decide what facts about a parallelogram make it a special type of quadrilateral.

Use your knowledge of parallel lines to find the vectors.

Travel round the shape from point to point and add the vectors as you go.

Remember to make a final statement to show that you know the sides are the same.

## Exam practice

*1  OAB is a triangle.

$\overrightarrow{OA} = \mathbf{a}$

$\overrightarrow{OB} = 2\mathbf{b}$

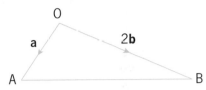

a  Write down, in terms of **a** and **b**, the vector $\overrightarrow{AB}$.

b  X is the midpoint of OA. Y is the midpoint of OB.

Write down, in terms of **a** and **b**, the vector $\overrightarrow{XY}$.

c  Describe fully the relationship between AB and XY.

*(3 marks)*

*2  Claire draws a parallelogram ABCD with $\overrightarrow{AB} = \begin{pmatrix} 5 \\ 12 \end{pmatrix}$ and $\overrightarrow{BC} = \begin{pmatrix} 13 \\ 0 \end{pmatrix}$.

Give a more precise mathematical name for the parallelogram that Claire has drawn, justifying your answer.

*(4 marks)*

3  The diagram shows a maze.

The maze is made from 18 squares and 4 triangles.

The lines on the diagram represent the paths that you can walk along.

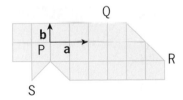

Write down in terms of **a** and **b** the vector that represents walking through the maze from

a  P to Q    b  Q to R    c  R to S    d  S to P

*(4 marks)*

## INTRODUCTION

In a lake, the proportion of lilies of a particular colour depends on the conditions, such as the temperature and acidity of the water, the amount and distribution of sunlight, and the presence of other flora and fauna.

**What's the point?**

Ratio and proportion are important in biology because they allow comparison of species that might be living in harmony or competition.

## CHECK IN

1   Gill and Paul share £500 between them.
    Gill gets four times as much as Paul.
    How much does each person get?

2   In a sale, you can buy three items for the price of two.
    What percentage decrease on the original price does this represent?

| What I should know | What I will learn | What this leads to |
|---|---|---|
| B9 | ■ Calculate percentage increases and decreases<br>■ Calculate exponential growth and decay<br>■ Calculate direct and inverse proportion | Aspects of everyday life involving financial management |

## RICH TASK

A type of purple paint is made up of blue and red paint in the ratio 1:3.

Another type is in the ratio 1:7.

You can mix the two together to get different shades of purple.

How many tins of each do you need to achieve a mix of

a 1:5   b 1:4?

What other mixes can you get? Are there any mixes that you can't get?

Experiment with a few different shades and report your findings.

- Solve percentage problems, including increase and decrease

### ☆ PROBLEM ☆

A trader buys £600 of fresh cut flowers to sell at a market stall.
The stall costs £70 for the day.
80% of the flowers are sold at 30% profit.
With an hour left the trader reduces his prices by 50% and sells
75% of the remaining flowers.
Did the trader make a profit or loss and by how much?

**EXAMPLE**

**a** Work out the sale price of a necklace bought for £150 and sold at a 64% profit.
**b** Work out the sale price of a dress costing £80 reduced by 35% in a sale.

**ANSWER**

**a** 64% of 150 = $\frac{64}{100} \times 150 = 96$

150 + 96 = 246    The sale price is £246.

A one-step solution: 100% + 64% = 164% = 1.64  **1.64** × 150 = £246

**b** 35% of 80 = $\frac{35}{100} \times 80 = 28$    Sale price 80 − 28 = £52

A one-step solution: 100% − 35% = 65% = 0.65  **0.65** × 80 = £52

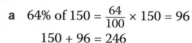

The numbers in **bold** are the **decimal multipliers**.

p. 134

→ **To find an amount after**
**an increase of $r$%, multiply the amount by (100 + $r$)%**
**a decrease of $r$%, multiply the amount by (100 − $r$)%.**

**EXAMPLE**

Rob adds 40% for profit to the price he pays for bicycles in his cycle shop.
He sells bicycles to friends at a discount of 25% of the selling price.
What percentage profit or loss is made on a bicycle bought for £370 and sold to a friend?

**ANSWER**

40% profit, so multiply by 1.4    1.4 × 370 = £518 selling price
25% discount, so multiply by 0.75    0.75 × 518 = £388.50
Profit 388.50 − 370 = £18.50    % profit $\frac{18.50}{370} \times 100 = 5\%$

There is a quicker way to solve this. Can you work it out?

## Exercise C17.1

1 Work out the sale price of
   a a camera that cost £480 and is reduced by 22% in a sale
   b a toy that cost £89 and is reduced in a sale by 45%.

2 What is the selling price of a bag of sweets bought for 25p and sold for 40% profit?

3 Jules is paid an annual salary of £34 900.
   She is given a pay rise of 3.2%.
   What is her new annual salary?

4 ☆ PROBLEM ☆

   A company wanted to promote 200 g chocolate bars with a special offer.
   These chocolate bars normally cost 164 pence.
   The company could choose to
   i increase the amount of chocolate in the bar by 25% or
   ii reduce the price of the bar by 25%.

   Which should they choose to give customers the better deal?

5 **RICH TASK**

   Find the effect on price of:
   i a 10% increase followed by a 10% decrease
   ii a 10% decrease followed by a 10% increase
   iii a 10% increase followed by another 10% increase
   iv a 10% decrease followed by another 10% decrease

   Take a good guess at first, then use real numbers to arrive at the answers. Justify your responses clearly.

6 ☆ PROBLEM ☆

   A manufacturer running a promotion on a bottle of lemonade
   investigates increasing the contents and reducing the price.
   Assume the usual size bottle is 1 litre (1000 ml) and costs £2.
   a Compare the effect of increasing contents by 10% and reducing
      prices by 10%.
   b Repeat the comparison using
      i 20%     ii 40%     iii 50%.
   c Comment on your answers in a and b.
   d If the contents were increased by 25%, what price reduction on
      the usual size bottle would give the same quantity of lemonade
      per penny?

# Reverse percentages

- Calculate an original amount in reverse percentage problems

### ☆ PROBLEM ☆

On a holiday to the USA, Gareth paid \$519.92 in total for a model aircraft engine. The state where he bought it added sales tax at 7.2%. How much would he have paid in a neighbouring state where the tax was 2.8%?

Sales taxes in the USA are added on to the price of goods or services purchased. Sales tax is a percentage of the sale price.

You often need to find an original amount after a percentage change.

**EXAMPLE**

In a restaurant, Ralph is presented with a bill of £139.50, which includes 12.5% service charge. To check the bill was correct, Ralph needs to find the original amount.
What is the amount of the bill excluding service charge?

**ANSWER**

| | | |
|---|---|---|
| Start with 112.5%: | £139.50 | 112.5% = 100% + 12.5% |
| Find 1%: | 139.50 ÷ 112.5 = 1.24 | |
| Now find 100%: | 1.24 × 100 = 124 | |

The bill exclusive of service charge is £124.

You can do this in a single step:
139.50 ÷ 1.125 = 124
Think about why this works.

**EXAMPLE**

A car's value **depreciates** by 10% each year.
At one year old Louise's car is valued at £16 650.
How much was Louise's car when new?

**ANSWER**

| | | |
|---|---|---|
| Start with 90%: | 16 650 | 90% = 100% − 10% |
| Find 1%: | 16 650 ÷ 90 = 185 | |
| Now find 100%: | 185 × 100 = 18 500 | |

Louise's car was £18 500 when new.

You can do this in a single step:
16 650 ÷ 0.9 = 18 850

→ **To find an original amount after a percentage increase:**
   **÷ (100 + increase%) × 100**
→ **To find an original amount after a percentage decrease:**
   **÷ (100 − decrease%) × 100**

## Exercise C17.2

MEDIUM HIGH

1   In a sale prices were reduced by 30%.
    The sale price of a dress is £22.40.
    What was the price of the dress before the sale?

2   In a sale the price of a handbag is reduced by 35%.
    The sale price of the handbag is £55.25.
    What was the original price of the handbag?

3   One American state adds tax at 5% to the price of goods.
    A bill of £154.56 includes tax at 5%.
    How much of the bill is tax?

4   One day a shop sold 387 books.
    This was an increase of 7.5% on the number of books sold the
    previous day.
    How many books did the shop sell on the previous day?

5   The cost of a holiday was reduced by 5% when booking online.
    The cost of the holiday after the reduction was £856.90.
    What was the cost of the holiday before the reduction?

6   In a sale the price of a pair of shoes is reduced by 45%.
    The sale price of the shoes is £24.75.
    What was the original price of the shoes?

7   A dealer added 64% to the price he paid for a diamond bracelet
    before reselling it.
    The dealer sold the bracelet for £1394.
    Work out the price the dealer paid for the bracelet.

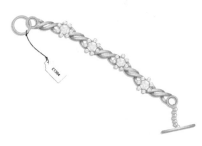

8   Martha made ice-lollies from fruit juice.
    When the fruit juice was frozen its volume increased by 12%.
    The volume of the frozen ice-lollies was 728 cm$^3$.
    Calculate the volume of the fruit juice before it was frozen.

9   A property was purchased for £535 600 including stamp duty at 4%.
    Stamp duty is calculated as a percentage of the purchase price.
    Work out the price the property was purchased for before stamp
    duty was added.

- Represent repeated percentage change using a multiplier

## RICH TASK

An ordinary piece of paper is about 0.081 mm thick.
**i**   Take a sheet of ordinary A4 paper and fold it in half.
**ii**  Fold it a second time and then a third – it should now be the thickness of a fingernail
**iii** Continue folding in half for as long as you can.
**iv**  How many folds is it possible to make?
**v**   How thick is the paper at each fold?
**vi**  How many folds would you make before the paper thickness reaches 970 km, the straight-line distance from Lands End to John O'Groats?

Exponential change occurs when you repeatedly multiply by a fixed value less than or greater than 1.

**Compound interest** is an everyday example of repeated percentage change. It is earned on the total amount in an account at any time, not just the initial amount.

---

**EXAMPLE**

£11 000 is invested in a savings account.
7% compound interest is paid annually.
**a**   How much is in the account after 3 years?
**b**   How long does it take for the investment to exceed £15 000?

**ANSWER**

**a**   After 1 year      $11\,000 \times 1.07 = £11\,770$
       After 2 years     $11\,770 \times 1.07 = £12\,593.90$
       After 3 years     $12\,593.90 \times 1.07 = £13\,475.47$
                          to the nearest penny

**b**   Use trial and improvement:
       $11\,000 \times (1.07)^4 = 14\,418.76$    less than 15 000
       $11\,000 \times (1.07)^5 = 15\,428.07$    greater than 15 000
       It takes five years.

> Here is a one-step solution:
> $11\,000 \times (1.07)^3 = £13\,475.47$

**Depreciation** is another everyday example of exponential change.

---

**EXAMPLE**

A car bought for £36 000 **depreciates** in value by 10% each year.
How much is the car worth after 6 years?

**ANSWER**

$100\% - 10\% = 90\% = 0.9$        $36\,000 \times (0.9)^6 = £19\,131.88$
The car is worth £19 100 after six years.

> → **For an initial amount *A* that increases or decreases at a rate *b*% for *n* years:**
> exponential growth = $A \times (100\% + b\%)^n$
> exponential decay = $A \times (100\% - b\%)^n$

## Exercise C17.3

HIGH

1 A bouncy ball is dropped from a height of 6 m.
   After each bounce it rises to 90% of its previous height.
   a To what height does it rise after one bounce?
   b How many times does it bounce altogether before the height is less than 4 m?

2 The population of a species of small mammal on an island increases at a rate of 12% per year. One year the population was 1.5 million.
   a What size will the population be in
     i 4 years' time    ii 7 years' time?
   b How long will it take for the population to quadruple in size?

3 The population of a rare species of bird is falling at a rate of 8% per year. One year the population was 28 000.
   a What size will the population be in
     i 2 years' time    ii 8 years' time?
   b The population reaches a critical point when the numbers drop below 5000. In how many years will this be?

4 £19 000 is invested in a savings account. 6.95% compound interest is paid annually.
   a How much is in the account after
     i 2 years           ii 5 years?
   b How long does it take for the investment to more than double?

5 A savings plan offers an annual rate of 6% compound interest, paid monthly.
   Jayne opened this savings plan and paid in £250 per month.
   How much was it worth at the end of one year?

6 ☆ **PROBLEM** ☆

   > Sara has £2000 to invest for 5 years. She could put the money into a savings account paying compound interest at
   > i 4.6% paid annually   ii 4.5% paid monthly
   >
   > Which savings account would you advise Sara to invest her money in? Would you give different advice if the money was to be invested for a longer period of time?

# Direct proportion

- Set up and use equations to solve problems involving direct proportion

→ **Two quantities with a constant ratio between them are in direct proportion.** The symbol for **proportionality** is ∝

As one quantity doubles the other doubles too.

**EXAMPLE**

The distance travelled, $d$, by a cyclist is in direct proportion to the number of revolutions, $r$, made by a bicycle wheel.
Josh travels 11 m for 5 revolutions of the wheel.
 a Find an equation connection $d$ and $r$.
 b How far does Josh travel when the wheel makes 18 revolutions?
 c Josh cycles 4.84 km to college each day.
How many revolutions of the wheel is that?

**ANSWER**

 a $d \propto r$          $d$ is in proportion to $r$

    So $d = k \times r$, or $d = kr$    where $k$ is a constant to be found

    When $d = 11$, $r = 5$

        $11 = k \times 5$      Substitute into $d = kr$

         $k = \dfrac{11}{5}$

    So the equation is $d = \dfrac{11}{5} r$

 b When $r = 18$      $d = 2.2 \times 18 = 39.6$ m

 c $d = 4.84$ km $= 4840$ m

    $11 \times r = 5 \times 4840$    ⇨    $r = 2200$ revolutions

If, $d \propto r$
then $d$ is **some multiple** of $r$
$k$ is the multiple to be found.

$k$ is called the **constant of proportionality**.

Alternatively,
$d = 2.2\, r$    or    $5d = 11r$

→ **A quantity $A$ can be in direct proportion to the square of another quantity $B$.**
**You can write $A \propto B^2$, or $A = kB^2$, where $k$ is a constant.**

**EXAMPLE**

$y$ is proportional to the square of $x$ and $y = 15$ when $x = 4$.
 a Find an equation connecting $y$ and $x$.
 b Find the value of $y$ when $x = 2$     c Find the values of $x$ when $y = 0.6$

**ANSWER**

 a Write the proportionality:     $y \propto x^2$ ⇨ $y = k \times x^2$

    Substitute the numbers to find $k$:    $15 = k \times 4^2$ ⇨ $k = \dfrac{15}{16}$

    Write the equation:          $y = \dfrac{15}{16} x^2$

 b $y = \dfrac{15}{16} \times 2^2$    ⇨    $y = \dfrac{15}{4}$     c $0.6 = \dfrac{15}{16} x^2$     ⇨     $x^2 = 0.64$

                                                                      $x = \pm\, 0.8$

## Exercise C17.4

1  $y$ is proportional to $x$ and $y = 18$ when $x = 3$.
   a  Find an equation connecting $y$ and $x$.
   b  Find the value of $y$ when $x = 7$.

2  $y$ is proportional to $x$ and $y = 12$ when $x = 8$.
   a  Find an equation connecting $y$ and $x$.
   b  Find the value of $y$ when $x = 5$.

3  The extension of a spring, $e$, is proportional to the mass, $m$, hung from the spring.
   When a mass of 4 kg is hung from a spring its extension is 5 cm
   a  Find an equation connecting $e$ and $m$.
   b  Work out
      i   the mass hung when $e = 2$ cm
      ii  the extension when $m = 5$ kg.

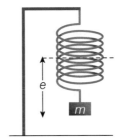

4  $y$ is proportional to the cube of $x$ and $y = 4$ when $x = 2$.
   a  Find an equation connecting $y$ and $x$.
   b  Find the value of $y$ when $x = 3$.

5  The energy stored in a spring, $E$, is proportional to the square of its extension, $e$.
   When $E = 240$, $e = 4$.
   a  Find an equation connecting $E$ and $e$.
   b  Find the value of  i  $E$ when $e = 8$    ii  $e$ when $E = 375$.

6  The energy of a moving object, $E$, is proportional to the square of its speed, $v$.
   $E = 40$ when $v = 5$.
   a  Find an equation connecting $E$ and $v$.
   b  Find the value of  i  $E$ when $v = 4$    ii  $v$ when $E = 160$.

7  The area of a circle is in direct proportion to the square of the radius of the circle.
   Write down the constant of proportionality.

8  The volume of a sphere is in direct proportion to the cube of its radius.
   Write down the constant of proportionality.

# Inverse proportion

- Set up and use equations to solve problems involving inverse proportion

## RICH TASK

Radio stations are located by wavelength and frequency.
The product of wavelength, $\lambda$ metres, and frequency, $f$ hertz, is a constant value.

As frequency increases, wavelength decreases.
As frequency decreases, wavelength increases.

Radio 1 FM operates on 97–99 megahertz at a wavelength of 3 m.
Verify that the constant value is the speed of light, 300 million m/s.

1 megahertz = 1 000 000 hertz

→ **When variables are in inverse proportion, one increases at the same rate that the other decreases.**

→ **If $y$ is inversely proportional to $x$, then $y \propto \dfrac{1}{x}$ and $y = \dfrac{k}{x}$**

$k$ is the constant of proportionality.

For example, the time taken $t$ to build a wall is inversely proportional to the number of bricklayers $b$.
So $b \propto \dfrac{1}{t}$, and an equation linking $b$ and $t$ is $b = \dfrac{k}{t}$, where $k$ is a constant.
If you now know that, say, 5 bricklayers take 4 hours, you can work out $k$:
$5 = \dfrac{k}{4} \Rightarrow k = 5 \times 4 = 20$ and $b = \dfrac{20}{t}$

Given this information, how long would it take 8 bricklayers to build the wall?

→ **If $y$ is inversely proportional to the square of $x$, then $y \propto \dfrac{1}{x^2}$ and $y = \dfrac{k}{x^2}$**

**EXAMPLE**

The intensity of light, $I$, on an object is inversely proportional to the square of the distance, $d$, from the light source.
$I = 4$ units when $d = 5$ m.
a Find an equation connecting $I$ and $d$.
b Find the value of   **i**  $I$ when $d = 2$ m   **ii**  $d$ when $I = \dfrac{1}{4}$ units.

ANSWER

a  $I \propto \dfrac{1}{d^2}$        $I = \dfrac{k}{d^2}$        b  **i**  $I = \dfrac{100}{2^2}$        $I = 25$

   $4 = \dfrac{k}{5^2}$        $k = 100$        **ii**  $\dfrac{1}{4} = \dfrac{100}{d^2}$        $d^2 = 400$        $d = 20$ m

   $I = \dfrac{100}{d^2}$   or   $d^2 I = 100$

**Percentages and proportional change**

## Exercise C17.5

1   $y$ is inversely proportional to $x$ and $y = 5$ when $x = 4$.
    a   Find an equation connecting $y$ and $x$.
    b   Find the value of $y$ when $x = 30$.

2   $y$ is inversely proportional to $x$ and $y = 0.25$ when $x = 4.8$.
    a   Find an equation connecting $y$ and $x$.
    b   Find the value of $y$ when $x = 1.6$.

3   A septic tank can be emptied in 10 hours using 4 pumps.
    a   How many pumps would be needed to empty the tank in 2 hours?
    b   How long would it take to empty the tank if only 3 pumps were available?

Septic pump

4   At constant temperature, the volume of gas is inversely proportional to its pressure. When $P = 200 \text{ N/m}^2$, $V = 4 \text{ m}^3$.
    a   Find an equation connecting $P$ and $V$.
    b   Find the volume of gas when the pressure is $250 \text{ N/m}^2$.
    c   Find the pressure when the volume of gas is $4.8 \text{ m}^3$.

5   $y$ is inversely proportional to the square root of $x$ and $y = 5$ when $x = 9$.
    a   Find an equation connecting $y$ and $x$.
    b   Find
        i   $y$ when $x = 4$       ii   $x$ when $y = 1.5$.

6   $y$ is inversely proportional to $x^2$ and $y = 4$ when $x = 0.5$.
    a   Find an equation connecting $y$ and $x$.
    b   Find
        i   $y$ when $x = 6$       ii   $x$ when $y = 25$.

7   The force of attraction, $F$, between two magnets is inversely proportional to the square of the distance, $d$, between them. $F = 3$ newtons when $d = 2$ cm.
    a   Find an equation connecting $F$ and $d$.
    b   Find the value of
        i   $F$ when $d = 0.5$ cm       ii   $d$ when $F = 0.75$ newtons.

You should now be able to
- calculate with percentages in problem solving
- solve problems involving reverse percentages
- solve problems involving exponential growth and decay
- use direct and inverse proportion in problem solving.

**Exam-style question**

2000 of a species of toad was introduced to an island.

The number of this species of toad, $t$, on the island after $y$ years is given by
$$t = 2000(1 \cdot 16)^y$$

**a** What is the annual percentage increase in the toad population?

**b** How many of this species of toad will be on the island after 3 years?
Give your answer to a sensible degree of accuracy.

**c** How long will it take for the toad population to double?

The question is about exponential growth.

Other sensible answers could be 3100 or 3000.

**Bill's answer:**

a After 1 year $t = 2000 \times 1.16$
The annual percentage increase is 16%

b $2000 \times (1.16)^3 = 3121.792$
After 3 years 3120 toads

c $4000 = 2000 \times (1.16)^y$
$2 = (1.16)^y$
$y = 5$

It will take 5 years.

Think about what each part of the equation means.

You can solve this using trial and improvement.

## Exam practice

1   The price of a dress is reduced in a sale by 35%.
    The sale price is £66·30.
    Calculate the original price of the dress.

    *(3 marks)*

*2   A recipe for carrot cake uses 100 g of carrot, 80 g of walnuts
    and 2 eggs.
    Gareth picks a carrot weighing 285 g.

    He wants to use all the carrot to make a cake.
    a   What weight of walnuts should he use?
    b   How many eggs should he use?
    Show how you arrive at your answer.

    *(3 marks)*

3   A photograph's image is projected on to a wall from a viewfinder.
    The image projected on a wall varies directly with the distance
    of the viewfinder from the wall.
    The image is 27 cm high when the viewfinder is 72 cm from
    the wall.

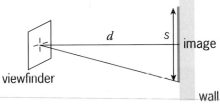

    a   Find an equation connecting the image size, $s$, and the
        distance, $d$, of the viewfinder from the wall.
    b   How far away from the wall does the viewfinder need to
        be for the image to be 42 cm high?

    *(5 marks)*

## INTRODUCTION

Neolithic people in Europe created some wonderful megalithic strutures between around 3000–2000 BC, including stone circles. A popular theory is that these circular monuments worked as astronomical calendars, being aligned with important events such as solstice sunrises. Stonehenge in Wiltshire is a particularly awesome example.

**What's the point?**
Prehistoric monuments show us that the circle was as important a shape thousands of years ago as it is today.

## CHECK IN

1 These shapes are drawn on a centimetre square grid.

a    b    c

   For shapes *a* to *c*
   　i　write the length of each side in cm.
   　　Hence find the perimeter in cm.
   　ii　calculate the area of the shape in cm²

2 a Draw a net of this cube
   b Hence calculate its surface area
   c Calculate its volume.

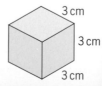

3 cm
3 cm
3 cm

| What I should know | What I will learn | What this leads to |
|---|---|---|
| B10 | ■ Find the perimeter and area of shapes ■ Calculate scale factors | Careers in manufacturing and industrial design |

## RICH TASK

Here are two ways of drawing a triangle within a 6-point circle.

How many triangles can be drawn altogether?
Investigate circles with different numbers of points.

# Area and perimeter of compound shapes  C18.1

- Calculate and use perimeters and areas of basic shapes and compound shapes

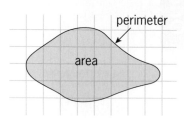

→ The **perimeter** of a shape is the total distance around its edge.
→ **Area** is a measure of the amount of space enclosed by a shape.

Irregular areas can be found by counting squares on a grid.
Areas of basic shapes can be found using **formulae**.

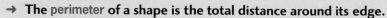

| Rectangle | Triangle | Trapezium | Parallelogram |

$A = lw$

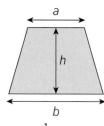

$A = \frac{1}{2}bh$

$A = \frac{1}{2}h(a+b)$

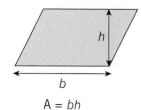

$A = bh$

Compound shapes are made by combining basic shapes.

**EXAMPLE**

**a** Find the perimeter of this field.

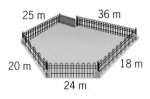

**b** Calculate the area of this field.

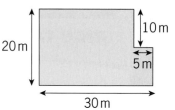

**ANSWER**

**a** The perimeter
= 20 + 25 + 36 + 18 + 24
= 123 metres

**b** Split into two shapes:

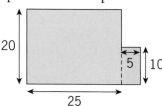

Area = 20 × 25 + 5 × 10
= 550 m²

1   Calculate **i**   the perimeter **ii**   the area of these shapes.
    All measurements are in centimetres.

a
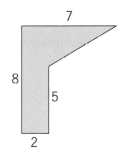

b
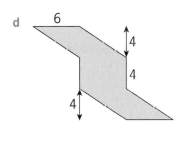

c
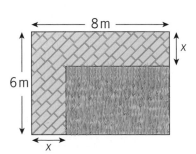

d

2   Mr Wagstaff is making a lawn for his house.
    Find the cost of laying turf if each square metre costs £8.10.

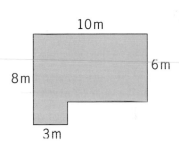

3   A trapezium has an area of 40 cm², a height of 5 cm and two
    parallel sides of 10 cm and *x* cm. Find the value of *x*.

4   A rectangular garden 8 metres by 6 metres has a paved area
    *x* metres wide along two sides as shown.
    If the paved area is half the area of the garden, find *x*.

Unit C

# Circumference and area of a circle

- Calculate circumference and area of a circle

→ **The perimeter of a circle is called its circumference.**
→ **An arc of a circle is the part of the circumference between two points.**

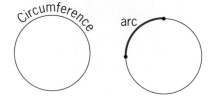

Three pieces of string with lengths equal to the diameter $d$ will fit around the circumference of a circle and leave a small gap.

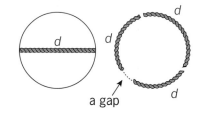

a gap

So the circumference,
$C = (3 \text{ and a bit}) \times$ the diameter
$= 3.14 \times$ the diameter

The 3 and a bit is a number $\approx$ 3.14159265..... and its exact value cannot be written as a decimal. It is written as the Greek letter $\pi$.

→ **$C = \pi d$ or $C = 2\pi r$**
→ **The area of a circle, $A = \pi r^2$**

Since $d = 2 \times r$

## RICH TASK

The radius of this circle and the sides of this square are 4 cm long.

Draw and cut out several of these squares. How many squares do you need to cover the circle? You will need to trim the squares and try to fill any gaps.

Repeat with other sizes of circle.
What do you conclude?

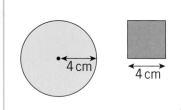

4 cm      4 cm

---

**EXAMPLE**

An Olympic gold medal has a diameter of 7 cm.
Calculate its area to the nearest cm². (Use $\pi = 3.14$.)

**ANSWER**

Its radius is $\frac{1}{2} \times 7 = 3.5$ cm
Its area is $\pi \times r^2 = 3.14 \times 3.5^2 = 3.14 \times 12.25 = 38$ cm²
(to nearest cm²)

7 cm

---

**EXAMPLE**

The distance around this circular pond is 20 metres.
Find its radius, in metres, to 2 d.p.

**ANSWER**

$C = 20 \quad C = 2\pi r$

$r = \dfrac{C}{2\pi} = \dfrac{20}{2\pi} = 3.18$ m

20 m

Pond

---

## Exercise C18.2

1 Calculate the circumference of a circle (to the nearest whole cm) with
   a  a diameter of 5 cm     b  a diameter of 8 cm
   c  a radius of 3 cm       d  a radius of 10 cm.

2 A bicycle has wheels of diameter 40 cm.
   a  How far forward does the bicycle move when its wheels go round once?
   b  How many rotations of the wheels are there in a ride of 2 km?

3 A donkey is tethered to a rope 12 metres long.
   What area of grass can it eat?

4 A circular carpet is 4.6 metres across. What is its area?

5 A circular helipad (for landing a helicopter) has a radius of 14 metres.
   The cost of building the helipad is £85 per square metre.
   Find
   a  the area of the helipad to the nearest square metre
   b  the cost of building it to the nearest £100.

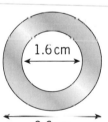

14 m

6 A metal washer has the external and internal diameters shown.
   Find
   a  the external and internal radii
   b  the area of the hole in the washer
   c  the area of the washer.

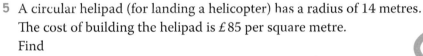

1.6 cm

2.6 cm

7 Find the diameter of a circle with a circumference of 50 cm.

8 The edge of a circular coffee table is 2 metres long.
   Find its diameter in centimetres.

9 What is the radius of a 10 pence coin, if its face has an area of 6.15 cm²?

10 A semicircular window is fitted with a sheet of glass of area 9 m².
   Find the radius of the window.

11 This semicircular protractor has a perimeter of 25.7 cm.
   Find its radius, $r$ cm.

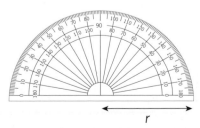

$r$

Unit C

# Sectors of circles

- Calculate perimeters and areas of sectors of circles

A sector is a fraction of a circle.

p. 156

- A **sector** of a circle is bounded by an arc and two radii.

- The area of a sector
$$= \frac{\theta}{360} \times \text{the area of circle} = \frac{\theta}{360} \times \pi r^2$$

- The length $L$ of an arc of the circle $= \frac{\theta}{360} \times 2\pi r$, where $\theta$ is the angle at the centre of the circle.

**EXAMPLE**

A school's athletics ground has an area for the javelin. Find the perimeter of the area set aside for the javelin (exclude the throwing area).

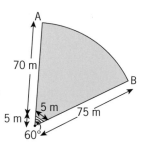

**ANSWER**

The length of arc AB $= \frac{60}{360} \times 2 \times \pi \times 75$

$= 78.5$ metres

So the perimeter required $= 70 + 5 + 70 + 78.5$

$= 223.5$ metres

**EXAMPLE**

The sector AOB is cut out of a circular piece of card and the radii OA and OB are brought together to make a hollow cone.

Find

**a** the curved surface area of the cone

**b** the diameter of the base of the cone.

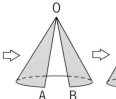

**ANSWER**

**a** Surface area of cone = area of sector

$$= \frac{240}{360} \times \pi \times 9^2$$

$$= 170 \text{ cm}^2$$

**b** Circumference of base = length of arc AB

$$\pi \times d = \frac{240}{360} \times 2 \times \pi \times 9$$

Diameter $d = \frac{240}{360} \times 2 \times 9 = 12$ cm

1 Calculate the area of the sector and the length of its arc with
the angle $\theta$ at the centre and the given dimension.
  a  $\theta = 72°$, radius = 6 cm
  b  $\theta = 135°$, diameter = 16 cm
  c  $\theta = 270°$, radius = 9 cm
  d  $\theta = 28°$, diameter = 20 cm.

2 Calculate the length $L$ of an arc of a circle when the arc subtends
an angle $\theta$ at the centre of a circle with the given dimensions.
  a  $\theta = 120°$, radius = 5 cm
  b  $\theta = 45°$, diameter = 12 cm
  c  $\theta = 215°$, radius = 8 cm
  d  $\theta = 132°$, diameter = 24 cm.

3 A pie chart of diameter 8 cm shows how students come to school.
The sector for those using a bus has an angle of 150°.
  a  What fraction (in its lowest terms) of all the students use a bus?
  b  What is the area of this sector?

4 A circular box of radius 7 cm contained six cream cheeses.
Two of them have been eaten. What is the area of the base of
the box which can be seen when the lid is taken off?

5 Calculate
  a  the area of sector OAB
  b  the length OM
  c  the area of the shaded segment

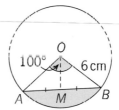

6 An equilateral triangle is inscribed in a circle of radius 20 cm.
Calculate the area bounded by one of its sides and the
circumference of the circle.

7 A ice-cream cornet wrapper is made from thin card
having the shape of this sector. Calculate
  a  the area of the card
  b  the diameter of the top of the cornet
  c  the height of the cornet.

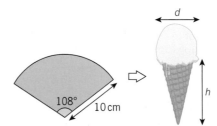

8 An arc of a circle is 25 cm long and it subtends an angle of 50°
at the centre of the circle. Calculate the circle's radius.

9 A school's athletics ground has a shot-put area of 118 m² in the shape
of the sector of a circle. If the radius of the sector is 15 metres,
find the angle at its centre.

Unit C

## Exam-style question

Work out the area of a regular hexagon of side length 4 cm, giving your answer in surd form.

Use facts you know about a regular hexagon to make the shape simpler.

Find the area of one triangle and then the area of the hexagon.

**Amir's answer:**

Dividing a regular hexagon from the centre gives 6 congruent equilateral triangles

$h^2 = 4^2 - 2^2 = 12$
$h = \sqrt{12} = 2\sqrt{3}$

Area of one triangle
$= \frac{1}{2} \times 4 \times 2\sqrt{3} = 4\sqrt{3}$

Area of hexagon $= 6 \times 4\sqrt{3}$
$= 24\sqrt{3}$ cm$^2$

Use Pythagoras' theorem to find the height of one hexagon.

Work in surd form as this is how you need to give your final answer.

## Exam practice

1 Congruent isosceles triangles are cut from each corner of a
rectangle to form a regular octagon.

The octagon has perimeter $p$ cm.
Work out, in terms of $p$, the exact lengths of the sides of one
isosceles triangle.

*(3 marks)*

2 An earring is made from two circles as shown.

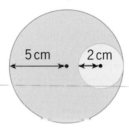

5 cm    2 cm

Work out the shaded area giving your answer in terms of $\pi$.

*(3 marks)*

3 A design is made using one large circle and four small circles.
The small circles are all the same size.
The large circle just fits inside a square of length 8 cm and the
small circles just fit into the corners of the square as shown.

When the design is drawn, work out the area of the square that
is not used in the design.

*(7 marks)*

# Case study 6: Holiday

Mathematics can help you to plan and budget for a holiday, as well as to understand currency, temperature and other units of measure at your destination.

## holiday

Paris

**LOUISE'S** family are planning to go on holiday. Her parents will pay for the trip, but she must raise her own spending money.

---

**1** How much money could Louise save in the three months from March to May if she hired a DVD once a week instead of going to the cinema?

**2** A neighbour offers to pay Louise £10 per week if she takes her dog for a 30-minute walk every weekday before school.

What hourly rate of pay does this represent?

How much would Louise earn if she walked the dog every weekday throughout March, April and May?

**3** Louise's brother sold 20 of his CDs and 11 of his DVDs to raise his holiday money. In the first month he sold 9 CDs and 4 DVDs for a total of £36.50. In the second month he sold 5 CDs and 5 DVDs for a total of £30.

How much money does he raise from selling all of the CDs and DVDs?

---

VALID FOR DATE OF PERFORMANCE ONLY
MANAGEMENT RESERVES THE RIGHT TO REFUSE ADMISSION

Screen 13    **Cinemaland**
29/11/09         CINEMAS
17:50
A GOOD NIGHT      £4.50

YOU WERE SERVED BY DS AT TERMINAL 4. PAID BY: Cash

Hire charge
£1.99 per film!     SIGN UP
                    NOW!!
4 easy steps to online

How could you raise money towards a holiday fund or to buy a new item? How long would it take you to reach your target amount?

GREAT BRITAIN
16. 6
09
POST OFFICE

30P

If you are going on holiday outside of the UK, then you will need to convert your money from £ Sterling to the local currency of your destination. Many European countries now use the Euro, €.

Suppose that you are charged £70 (with no commission) to buy 91.7EUR.

What is the exchange rate? Give your answer as a ratio £ Sterling : Euro.

Some companies charge a commission fee to exchange currency. With an added charge of 1%, how many Euros would you now receive (at the same exchange rate) for £70?

In 2000 Tim went on a holiday to France and Germany. To prepare for his trip he bought 700 French Francs (FRF) and 100 German Deutsche Marks (DEM) for £99.86. He was then given 200 FRF and 40 DEM as a present from his parents, who paid £32.23 for this currency. Calculate the unit per £ Sterling (GBP) rates for the FRF and the GEM (assuming that the rates were the same for both Tim and his parents).

Use the Internet to research the conversion rates used to convert the national currencies to the Euro in 2002. How did this affect the strength of the currencies of the Eurozone compared to the GBP? Compare this to today's unit per GBP exchange rate.

Deciding on your method of transport is an important part of planning a holiday.

Some travel options between Oxford and Paris are shown.

**1**

| Class STD | Outward SATURDAY 06:36 ARRIVE 07:37 | RETURN MONDAY 17:14 ARRIVE 18:14 |
| From OXFORD | | |
| To BIRMINGHAM INT. | | Price £21.00 |

2–PART RETURN

ECONOMY
Boarding Pass

PASSENGER
LOUISE
FROM
BIRMINGHAM INT (BHX)
TO
PARIS (CDG)
OUTWARD SAT 0920, ARRIVE 1150
RETURN MON 1555, ARRIVE 1625

| SEAT 50K | ADDITIONAL INFO COST: £115.16 |

**2**

Oxford
Buses
Route 777

Valid From:
**Oxford**

Valid To:
**London Heathrow**

Outward depart every hour and half hour.
Return every hour and half hour.

Adult Single £25

PA____
LOUISE
FROM
LONDON HEATHROW
TO
PARIS (CDG)
OUTWARD SAT 0955, ARRIVE 1210
RETURN MON 1610, ARRIVE 1625

| SEAT 50K | ADDITIONAL INFO COST: £136.37 |

**3**

| Class STD | Outward SATURDAY 08:01 ARRIVE 09:29 | RETURN MONDAY 19:20 ARRIVE 20:49 |
| From OXFORD | | |
| To LONDON ST. PANCRAS | | Price £14.00 |

2–PART RETURN

TICKET RESERVATION
**EUROSTAR**

**01 ADULT**

| DEPARTURE SAT 10:25 ARRIVE 13:47 | FROM LONDON ST. PANCRAS | TO PARIS | RETURN MON 17:13 ARRIVE 18:34 | CLASS 2 |

TRAIN 9141  ES          COACH 4       SEAT 44
01 SEAT    Non Smkg                   CARRIL

ELGAR/MXTHPFWU    10080 U066      IV248500394 VO
95389899543495
BW RT30AD 152485003940 RWXASE

PRICE £104.00

4244A2

101007 12H59    PNR/IYFFS0 1/1

----

**WHICH** travel option would you choose? Explain your response with reference to the travel times and costs. All times given are local. Paris is in the time zone GMT + 1 hour.

The foreign travel legs of the same journey options can be paid for in Euros for the following prices:

Return flight BHX to Paris CDG 151.49€; return Eurostar journey 130€, return flight London Heathrow to Paris CDG 162.82€.

How does each of the prices in Euros compare with the corresponding price in GBP?

*Explore travel options from your hometown to different destinations. Be careful, there are some times hidden costs such as additional taxes and fees.*

■ Different countries often use different units of measure for quantities such as temperature.

An internet site states that the maximum and minimum temperatures in Rome on a particular day are 34°C (93°F) and 22°C (63°F) respectively. The formula used to convert temperatures is of the form $°C = aF° + b$ where $a$ and $b$ are constants.

Use the information to set up two simultaneous equations involving $a$ and $b$.

Hence find the values of $a$ and $b$ and derive the formula used by the website.

*What are the maximum and minimum temperatures in your home town today? Use the formula in the example to convert the temperatures you have found from °C to °F.*

STREET MAP
# Paris
1:13,000 and 1:8,600

# Algebraic manipulation

## INTRODUCTION

Algebra is a generalisation of arithmetic. By generalising for all possible cases, it enables us to save a lot of time in performing calculations. In the modern world, machines often perform billions of calculations per second. Algebra, including quadratic functions, enables them to do this.

**What's the point?**
Engineers and scientists use quadratic expressions to model and explain the behaviour of events and activities in real life. Without quadratic expressions there wouldn't be aircraft, mobile phones or satellite TV.

## CHECK IN

1 Simplify each of the following, where possible.

   a  $5x + 2x$             b  $4a + 5b + a + 11b$

   c  $6y + 4$               d  $11x + x^2 + 15x + x^2$

2 Expand each of the following.

   a  $3(x + 2)$             b  $5(y - 8)$

   c  $x(x + 5)$           d  $3p(2p + 4)$

3 Simplify the following using the rules of indices.

   a  $5^6 \times 5^4$          b  $2^5 \times 2^{-3}$

   c  $4^6 \div 4^2$          d  $6^{10} \div 6^{-4}$

   e  $(7^2)^3$             f  $(5^{-2})^{-3}$

| What I should know | What I will learn | What this leads to |
|---|---|---|
| B14 | ■ Manipulate algebraic expressions<br>■ Complete the square<br>■ Factorise double brackets | C21 |

## RICH TASK

A square grid is numbered from 1 to 100.

A 2 × 2 square is shaded in as shown on the grid.
The numbers in the opposite corners of the 2 × 2 square are multiplied together.
Investigate.

| 1 | 2 | 3 | 4 | 5 | 6 | 7 | 8 | 9 | 10 |
|---|---|---|---|---|---|---|---|---|---|
| 11 | 12 | 13 | 14 | 15 | 16 | 17 | 18 | 19 | 20 |
| 21 | 22 | 23 | 24 | 25 | 26 | 27 | 28 | 29 | 30 |
| 31 | 32 | 33 | 34 | 35 | 36 | 37 | 38 | 39 | 40 |
| 41 | 42 | 43 | 44 | 45 | 46 | 47 | 48 | 49 | 50 |
| 51 | 52 | 53 | 54 | 55 | 56 | 57 | 58 | 59 | 60 |
| 61 | 62 | 63 | 64 | 65 | 66 | 67 | 68 | 69 | 70 |
| 71 | 72 | 73 | 74 | 75 | 76 | 77 | 78 | 79 | 80 |
| 81 | 82 | 83 | 84 | 85 | 86 | 87 | 88 | 89 | 90 |
| 91 | 92 | 93 | 94 | 95 | 96 | 97 | 98 | 99 | 100 |

# Simplifying expressions

- Manipulate algebraic expressions by collecting like terms

## RICH TASK

Pick a number from the page of a calendar. Add to it the numbers directly above and below. Repeat for different starting numbers.

What do you notice about this total compared to the starting number? Why does this happen? Prove it.

Investigate different totals and starting positions.

Did you know that there is always at least one Friday the 13th in a year?

p.100

- $5x + 3y$ is an **expression**. It is not an **equation** since it has no equals sign. This expression has two terms, $5x$ and $3y$.
- Expressions involving addition and/or subtraction can be **simplified** by collecting **like terms** together.

| Like terms such as $5x$ and $3x$ can be collected | Unlike terms cannot be collected together | Take care with minus signs | Some terms do not immediately seem alike | Other terms seem alike but are not |
|---|---|---|---|---|
| $5x + 3x = 8x$ | $2x + 3y$ <br> No simpler form | $5x + 8y - 7x + 4y$ <br> $= 12y - 2x$ | $4ab + 2ba = 6ab$ | $2x + 3x^2$ <br> No simpler form |

- Expressions involving multiplication and/or division are simplified in a different way. It may help to simplify the numbers or **coefficients** first and then the symbols or **variables**.

Simplify each of the following expressions.

**a** $5x \times 2y$ **b** $3m \times 2m \times 5m$ **c** $\dfrac{15ab}{5a}$

**ANSWER**

**a** $5 \times 2 = 10$

$x \times y = xy$

$5x \times 2y = 10xy$

**b** $3 \times 2 \times 5 = 30$

$m \times m \times m = m^3$

$3m \times 2m \times 5m = 30m^3$

**c** $15 \div 5 = 3$

$\dfrac{ab}{a} = \dfrac{\cancel{a} \times b}{\cancel{a}} = b$

$\dfrac{15ab}{5a} = 3b$

Multiplying by $a$ is the opposite of dividing by $a$ so you can cancel the $a$'s.

- You can use the rules of indices to simplify expressions.

**EXAMPLE**

Simplify each of the following expressions.

**a** $3p^6 \times 4p^{-2}$      **b** $\dfrac{12a^{10}}{4a^6}$      **c** $(5x^3)^2$

**ANSWER**

**a** $3p^6 \times 4p^{-2} = 12p^4$      **b** $\dfrac{12a^{10}}{4a^6} = 3a^4$      **c** $(5x^3)^2 = 25x^6$

## Exercise C19.1

MEDIUM
HIGH

1 For each expression given in the grid below, find, where possible, its simplified form.

| | | | |
|---|---|---|---|
| $2a + 3b + 7a - 4b$ | $2 \times m$ | $5p + 4$ | $2c + 8c - c$ |
| $3m \times 4n$ | $x^2 + x^2$ | $\dfrac{8xy}{4}$ | $4xy + 8x$ |
| $12mn + 3nm$ | $2b \times 3b$ | $\dfrac{20abc}{5ac}$ | $\dfrac{14x^2y}{7xy}$ |
| $5k \times 2k \times 4k$ | $\dfrac{15(xy)^2}{3x}$ | $5x + 8x^2$ | $\dfrac{\pi r^2 h}{2\pi r}$ |

2 Simplify each of the following.

   **a** $x^2 \times x^3$    **b** $x^4 \div x^2$    **c** $x^3 \times x$    **d** $x^5 \div x$    **e** $y^3 \times y^{10}$

   **f** $k^8 \div k^5$    **g** $(n^3)^4$    **h** $g^8 \times g^{-5}$    **i** $\dfrac{b^{-2}}{b^4}$

   **j** $(g^{-4})^3$    **k** $j^{-4} \times j^{-2}$    **l** $(t^{-5})^{-2}$    **m** $\dfrac{n^{-8}}{n^{-6}}$

3 Simplify each of the following fully.

   **a** $4h^4 \times 3h^7$    **b** $\dfrac{15p^3}{5p}$    **c** $(2m^8)^2$    **d** $6r^3 \times 6r^{-4}$

   **e** $(3h^{-3})^3$    **f** $\dfrac{9b^3}{3b^{-5}}$    **g** $\dfrac{(3m^3 \times 2m^7)^2}{18m}$    **h** $\dfrac{18(f^{-4})^4}{9f^{-16}}$

4 Show that the expression $(4p^4)^3 \div (8p^7)^2$ simplifies to $\dfrac{1}{p^2}$

5 Ben is constructing a box to hold an expensive statue whose base is square. The base must fit snugly into the box to keep it upright. The height of the statue is twice the cube of the length of its base. Given that Ben's box is a cuboid, write an expression for its volume. For what height of statue will the box's volume exceed 0.064 m³?

6 ☆ **CHALLENGE** ☆

> True or false? $3^x \times 3^y$ simplifies to give $9^{x+y}$. Explain.

**DID YOU KNOW..?**

The Maitreya project is planning a 150 m high bronze Buddha statue in Kushinagar, Uttar Pradesh in India. It will be a place for tourists and Buddhists alike and is being designed to last into the next millennium.

Unit C

# Expanding and factorising

- Manipulate algebraic expressions by expanding and factorising

## RICH TASK

Choose a two-digit integer. Form another two-digit integer by reversing the digits. Now subtract the smaller value from the larger one. Repeat this for different values. What do you notice? Why? Prove this. What would happen with three-digit integers?

$$\begin{array}{r} 75 \\ -\ 57 \\ \hline 18 \end{array}$$

→ **To expand a bracket you multiply every term in the bracket by the term outside. Take care when there is a negative outside the bracket.**

Multiply **every** term. A common error is to write $5(x - 4) = 5x - 4$

**EXAMPLE**

Expand each of the following, simplifying your answer where possible
a $5(x - 4)$  b $y(y + 9) + y(y - 4)$  c $2(x + 5) - (x - 9)$

**ANSWER**

a $5(x - 4) = 5 \times x - 5 \times 4$
  $= 5x - 20$

b $y(y + 9) + y(y - 4) = y \times y + y \times 9 + y \times y - y \times 4$
  $= y^2 + 9y + y^2 - 4y$
  $= 2y^2 + 5y$

c $2(x + 5) - (x - 9) = 2x + 10 - x + 9$
  $= x + 19$

→ **The opposite of expanding is called factorising.**

**EXAMPLE**

Factorise fully by finding all common factors.
a $3x + 9$  b $10a - 15a^3$  c $4y + 16xy$

**ANSWER**

a $3x + 9 = 3(x + 3)$  b $10a - 15a^3 = 5a(2 - 3a^2)$
c $4y + 16xy = 4y(1 + 4x)$

Check your factorisation by expanding.

- Factorisation can be used to simplify fractions.

$$\frac{x^2 - 5x}{x} = \frac{x(x - 5)}{x} = \frac{\cancel{x}(x - 5)}{\cancel{x}} = x - 5$$

$\frac{6x}{3}$ cancels to $2x$ since it contains multiplication and division only but $\frac{6 + 3x}{3}$ requires factorising first since it contains addition and division.

**Algebraic manipulation**

## Exercise C19.2

1 Expand and simplify each of the following.

   a   $4(5x + 8)$            b   $3p(4p - 7)$

   c   $2m(5 - 2m)$        d   $4(2y + 9) + 3(3y - 2)$

   e   $5x(3x + 2y - 9)$      f   $5(t + 9) - 2(3t - 7)$

   g   $(7h + 9) - (4h - 7)$    h   $x(3x^2 + x^3)$

\*2 A rectangle has length $x - 3$ and width 5 cm.

   a   Explain why the perimeter of this rectangle can be written as $2(x - 3) + 10$. Expand and simplify this expression.

   b   Write a simplified expression for the area of this rectangle.

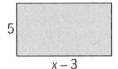

3 Factorise each of the following by finding common factors.

   a   $3x + 6y + 9z$          b   $10p - 15$

   c   $5xy + 7x$             d   $6mn + 9mt$

   e   $16x^2 - 12xy$         f   $3p + 9pq$

   g   $7xy - 56x^2$          h   $3x^2 + 12x^3 - 6x$

   i   $3(m + n) + (m + n)^2$    j   $4(p - q) + (p - q)^3$

   k   $ax + bx + ay + by$

> Factorise means find factors.
>
> Since $15 = 3 \times 5$ then 3 and 5 are factors of 15.
>
> Since $5x = 5 \times x$ then 5 and $x$ are factors of $5x$.

\*4 Show that a factorised expression for the shaded area is $2(x + 30)$.

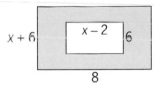

5 Simplify each of the following fractions.

   a   $\dfrac{9x}{3}$          b   $\dfrac{27xy}{3y}$         c   $\dfrac{2x + 4}{2}$

   d   $\dfrac{5x - 10}{15}$     e   $\dfrac{x^2 + 4x}{x}$      f   $\dfrac{2y^3 - 6y^2}{4y}$

6 ☆ **CHALLENGE** ☆

> Write down any three consecutive integers. Find the difference between the sum of the last two integers and the sum of the first two integers. Repeat for other values. What do you notice? Explain this and use algebra to prove why this happens.

# Expanding double brackets

- Expand the product of two linear expressions

## RICH TASK

Write an expression for the area of the large white square. Repeat for the area of each white triangle.

Hence, write a formula for $c^2$, the area of the coloured square. Expand and simplify your answer.

Have you seen your answer before? Could it have been achieved in any other way?

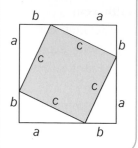

You can expand double brackets by multiplying each term in one bracket by each term in the other ... a useful way to check you have multiplied all the terms is F.O.I.L.

p. 234

**F** ... Firsts
**O** ... Outers
**I** ... Inners
**L** ... Lasts

e.g.

$$F \quad L$$
$$(x + 7) \quad (x - 4)$$
$$O \quad I$$

$$(x + 7)(x - 4) = x^2 - 4x + 7x - 28$$
$$= x^2 + 3x - 28$$

---

**EXAMPLE**

Expand each of the following.

**a** $(x + 3)(x + 4)$     **b** $(y - 5)(y - 2)$     **c** $(3x - 2)(2x + 4)$

**ANSWER**

**a** $(x + 3)(x + 4) = x^2 + 3x + 4x + 12$
$$= x^2 - 7x + 12$$

**b** $(y - 5)(y - 2) = y^2 - 2y - 5y + 10$
$$= y^2 - 7y + 10$$

**c** $(3x - 2)(2x + 4) = 6x^2 + 12x - 4x - 8$
$$= 6x^2 + 8x - 8$$

---

- Double brackets are often found "in disguise".
  $(x + 5)^2$ is a double bracket since it means $(x + 5)(x + 5)$.
  $(x + 5)^2 = (x + 5)(x + 5) = x^2 + 5x + 5x + 25$
  $$= x^2 + 10x + 25$$
- Double brackets are often found when solving equations.

> A common error is to expand $(x + 5)^2$ like this:
>
> $(x + 5)^2 = x^2 + 25$ **X**

1   Expand and simplify each of the following.
   a   $(x + 5)(x + 2)$
   b   $(y + 4)(y + 11)$
   c   $(x + 5)(x - 3)$
   d   $(p - 9)(p + 7)$
   e   $(m + 8)^2$
   f   $(y - 7)(y + 7)$

*2   Jed has expanded all of her double brackets incorrectly. Explain
   what Jed has done wrong in each case.

$(x+4)^2 = x^2 + 16$         $(x+7)(x+2) = x^2 + 2x + 7x + 9$

$(x-2)(x-3) = x^2 - 3x - 2x - 6$     $(x+2)(x-3) = x^2 - 3x + 2x - 1$

3   Expand and simplify each of the following.
   a   $(2x + 8)(x + 3)$
   b   $(3p + 2)(4p + 5)$
   c   $(3m - 7)(2m - 6)$
   d   $(5y - 9)(2y + 7)$
   e   $(3t - 2)^2$
   f   $(x + 4)(x - 6) + (x + 3)^2$

4   Find an expression for the difference in area between these two rectangles.

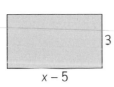

3

$x - 5$

$2x - 1$

$x + 7$

5   Solve each of the following equations.
   a   $(x + 3)(x + 2) = (x + 5)^2$
   b   $(2x + 1)(x + 4) = 2x(x + 5)$

6   A vertical tower is supported by a taut cable.
   If the foot of the cable is 8 metres from the
   base of the tower and the cable is 2 metres
   longer than the tower is high, find the height
   of the tower.

8 m

7   ☆ **CHALLENGE** ☆

   a   Show that $(x + 1)(x + 2)(x + 3) = x^3 + 6x^2 + 11x + 6$.

   b   Now expand $(y - 3)^3$.

   c   True or false? The product of any two consecutive odd integers is
       always one less than a multiple of four.

Unit C

- Manipulate algebraic expressions by factorising quadratic expressions

## RICH TASK

Investigate the difference obtained between the squares of any two consecutive integers. What do you notice?
Prove that this is always the case. Extend your investigation to the difference between the squares of two integers that differ by two, three, ...

$$12^2 = 144$$
$$11^2 = 121$$
$$144 - 121 = 23$$

The opposite of expanding double brackets is factorising them.

expand

$(x + 3)(x + 5)$ = $x^2$ + $8x$ + $15$

factorise     $3 + 5$   $3 \times 5$

**EXAMPLE**

Factorise the following expressions into double brackets.
a $x^2 + 9x + 14$    b $x^2 - 5x - 36$

**ANSWER**

a $x^2 + 9x + 14 = (x + 2)(x + 7)$    b $x^2 - 5x - 36 = (x - 9)(x + 4)$

2 + 7   2 × 7                          −9 + 4  −9 × 4

Here is a harder example.

**EXAMPLE**

Factorise the following expressions into double brackets.
a $3x^2 + 26x + 16$    b $5x^2 + 34x - 7$

**ANSWER**

a $3x^2 + 26x + 16$
$= 3x^2 + 2x + 24x + 16$
$= x(3x + 2) + 8(3x + 2)$
$= (3x + 2)(x + 8)$

b $5x^2 + 34x - 7$
$= 5x^2 + 35x - 1x - 7$
$= 5x(x + 7) - 1(x + 7)$
$= (5x - 1)(x + 7)$

Notice the change of signs as you remove a factor of −1.

There is a special case called the 'difference of two squares' (or D.O.T.S).

**EXAMPLE**

Factorise the following expressions into double brackets.
a $x^2 - 16$    b $9y^2 - 25$

**ANSWER**

a $x^2 - 16 = (x + 4)(x - 4)$    b $9y^2 - 25 = (3y + 5)(3y - 5)$

To factorise D.O.T.S., each term must be square rooted.

1 Factorise each of the following using double brackets.

  a $x^2 + 7x + 10$      b $x^2 + 8x + 15$      c $x^2 + 8x + 12$      d $x^2 + 12x + 35$

  e $x^2 - 3x - 10$      f $x^2 - 2x - 35$      g $x^2 - 8x + 15$      h $x^2 - x - 20$

  i $x^2 - 8x - 240$     j $x^2 + 3x - 108$     k $x^2 - 10x + 25$     l $x^2 - 6 - x$

2 Factorise each of the following fully.

  a $2x^2 + 5x + 3$      b $3x^2 + 8x + 4$      c $2x^2 + 7x + 5$      d $2x^2 + 11x + 12$

  e $3x^2 + 7x + 2$      f $2x^2 + 7x + 3$      g $2x^2 + x - 21$      h $3x^2 - 5x - 2$

  i $4x^2 - 23x + 15$    j $6x^2 - 19x + 3$    k $12x^2 + 23x + 10$    l $8x^2 - 10x - 3$

  m $6x^2 - 27x + 30$   n $6x^2 + 7x - 3$     o $18x^2 + 21x - 4$

3 Factorise these expressions.

  a $x^2 - 100$        b $y^2 - 16$        c $p^2 - 144$       d $k^2 - 64$

  e $x^2 - \dfrac{1}{4}$        f $y^2 - \dfrac{16}{25}$       g $n^2 - 2500$      h $49 - t^2$

  i $4x^2 - 25$       j $9y^2 - 121$      k $16m^2 - \dfrac{1}{4}$     l $400p^2 - 169$

4 Factorise each of the following using the correct type or types
of factorisation.

  a $16a^2 - 9b^2$        b $x^2 - 11x + 28$     c $2x^2 + 11x - 21$

  d $x^3 + 3x^2 - 18x$    e $5ab + 10(ab)^2$     f $10 - 3x - x^2$

  g $10 - 10x^2$        h $2y + y^2 - 63$      i $2x^3 - 132x$

  j $6x^2 + 6 - 13x$     k $x^4 - y^4$

5 By first factorising, simplify each of the following algebraic fractions.

  a $\dfrac{x^2 + 5x + 6}{x + 3}$       b $\dfrac{x^2 - 7x + 12}{2x - 8}$       c $\dfrac{x^2 - 9}{x + 3}$

  d $\dfrac{2x^2 + 9x + 4}{4x + 2}$      e $\dfrac{x^2 - 16}{(x - 4)^2}$      f $\dfrac{3x^2 + 4x + 1}{9x^2 - 1}$

> **Hint for question 5a:**
> $x^2 + 5x + 6 = (x + 2)(x + 3)$
> Now cancel top and bottom.

6 Work out the following without a calculator by using the
difference of two squares.

  a $101^2 - 99^2$       b $10\,006^2 - 9994^2$      c $100^2 - 99^2$

7 ☆ **CHALLENGE** ☆

Without using a calculator, find the
missing side of this triangle.

Leave your answer in surd form.

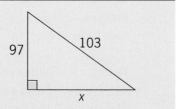

Unit C

# Solving quadratic equations

- Solve simple quadratic equations by factorisation

## RICH TASK

In three years' time Alex's age will be the square of his age three years ago. How old is Alex?
Can you find similar relationships for differences other than three years?

Here are some **quadratic equations**:
$$3x^2 + 5x - 2 = 0 \qquad x^2 = 25 \qquad 2x^2 - 6x = 3$$

> → **A quadratic equation can be written in the form**
> $$ax^2 + bx + c = 0 \qquad \text{where } a, b \text{ and } c \text{ are constants.}$$

 p. 316

You can solve a quadratic equation by factorising.

---

**EXAMPLE**

Solve the following quadratic equations.
**a** $x^2 = 4x$  **b** $x^2 - 7x + 12 = 0$  **c** $x^2 = 16$

**ANSWER**

**a** $x^2 = 4x$  **b** $x^2 - 7x + 12 = 0$  **c** $x^2 = 16$
 $x^2 - 4x = 0$    $x^2 - 16 = 0$     ← Make each equation = 0
 $x(x - 4) = 0$  $(x - 3)(x - 4) = 0$  $(x - 4)(x + 4) = 0$ ← Factorise
Either $x = 0$  Either $x - 3 = 0$  Either $x - 4 = 0$
     So    $x = 3$  So    $x = 4$     ← Make each factor = 0 in turn
Or $x - 4 = 0$  Or   $x - 4 = 0$  Or    $x + 4 = 0$
So    $x = 4$  So     $x = 4$  So     $x = -4$

---

**EXAMPLE**

The area of this rectangle is 54 cm². Find its dimensions.

*x + 2*

*x − 1*

**ANSWER**

Area = length × width so   $(x + 2)(x - 1) = 54$
$$x^2 - x + 2x - 2 = 54$$
Equation = 0     $x^2 + x - 56 = 0$
Factorise      $(x + 8)(x - 7) = 0$
Each factor = 0   Either $x + 8 = 0$ or $x - 7 = 0$
           Hence, $x = -8$ or $x = 7$

Reject $x = -8$ since you cannot have a length of $-8 + 2 = -6$ and a width of $-8 - 1 = -9$.
Hence, $x = 7$ and length is $7 + 2 = 9$ cm
and width is $7 - 1 = 8$ cm

---

## Exercise C19.5

1 Solve these quadratic equations by first finding a common factor.

a $x^2 - 5x = 0$  b $x^2 + 9x = 0$

c $2x^2 - 7x = 0$  d $3x^2 - 6x = 0$

e $x^2 = 9x$  f $x^2 = 7x$

g $12x = x^2$  h $6x - x^2 = 0$

> Do not confuse the vocabulary used:
>
> *Factorise* means to put into *brackets* and do not go any further.
>
> *Solve* means to find out the values that $x$ can take.

2 Solve these quadratic equations using double brackets.

a $x^2 + 7x + 12 = 0$  b $x^2 + 8x + 12 = 0$

c $x^2 + 12x + 36 = 0$  d $x^2 + 2x - 15 = 0$

e $x^2 + 5x - 14 = 0$  f $x^2 - 4x - 5 = 0$

g $x^2 - 5x + 6 = 0$  h $x^2 - 10x + 25 = 0$

i $2x^2 + 7x + 3 = 0$  j $3x^2 + 7x + 2 = 0$

k $2y^2 + 11y + 12 = 0$  l $6x^2 + 7x + 2 = 0$

m $x^2 = 8x - 12$  n $2x^2 + 7x = 15$

o $0 = 5y - 6 - y^2$  p $x(x + 10) + 21 = 0$

3 Solve these quadratic equations using the difference of two squares.

a $x^2 - 49 = 0$  b $y^2 - 64 = 0$  c $9x^2 - 4 = 0$

d $4x^2 - 1 = 0$  e $x^2 = 144$  f $4y^2 = 25$

4 Solve these quadratic equations using your choice of factorisation.

a $3x^2 - x = 0$  b $x^2 - 2x - 15 = 0$  c $3x^2 - 11x + 6 = 0$

d $9y^2 - 25 = 0$  e $16 - 9w^2$  f $20r^2 = 7x + 3$

5 Solve

a $\dfrac{x + 3}{3} = \dfrac{8}{x - 2}$  b $10x = 1 + \dfrac{3}{x}$

6 A rectangular garden has a perimeter of 68 m. A path of 26 m cuts diagonally across the garden. Find the dimensions of the garden.

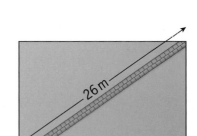

26 m

7 ☆ CHALLENGE ☆

**a** Use examples to show that squaring a number does not always produce a result that is larger than the starting number. Prove, using algebra, that there are only two numbers whose square is equal to itself.

**b** Solve $x^4 - 13x^2 + 36 = 0$

Unit C

# Completing the square

- Solve simple quadratic equations by completing the square

## RICH TASK

Think of a number, square it, subtract twice the number you started with and add 2. Can the final value ever be negative?

- Some quadratics factorise into squared brackets directly:
$$x^2 + 2x + 1 \equiv (x + 1)(x + 1) \equiv (x + 1)^2$$
$$x^2 + 4x + 4 \equiv (x + 2)(x + 2) \equiv (x + 2)^2$$
You can use this pattern to write other quadratics in this way but you may need to compensate.
$$x^2 + 6x + 10 = (x + 3)^2 + 1$$
Note that the 3 in the bracket is half of 6, the $x$-coefficient.

> → **A quadratic expression in the form $x^2 + bx + c$ can be rewritten in factorised form like this: $(x + p)^2 + q$.**

This is called **completing the square**.

Notice that the number in the squared bracket is half of the coefficient of the original $x$-term.

Think of compensating with squares:

$x + 3$

| | $x + 3$ | |
|---|---|---|
| $x + 3$ | Area = $x^2 + 6x + 9$ | + $\boxed{1}$ |

$$x^2 + 6x + 10 = (x + 3)^2 + 1$$

**EXAMPLE**

**a** Complete the square on each of the following expressions.
  **i** $x^2 - 10x + 4$    **ii** $x^2 + 3x - 1$

**b** Solve $x^2 + 12x + 27 = 0$ using completing the square.

**ANSWER**

**a i** $x^2 - 10x + 4 = (x - 5)^2 + q$    **ii** $x^2 + 3x - 1 = \left(x + \frac{3}{2}\right)^2 + q$

$\qquad = (x - 5)^2 - 21$    $\qquad = \left(x + \frac{3}{2}\right)^2 - \frac{13}{4}$

**b** $x^2 + 12x + 27 = 0 \quad \rightarrow \quad (x + 6)^2 - 9 = 0$
$\qquad\qquad\qquad (x + 6)^2 = 9$
$\qquad\qquad$ Either $x + 6 = 3$ or $x + 6 = -3$
$\qquad$ So $\quad x = -3 \qquad$ or $x = -9$

Half of $-10$ is $-5$
$(x - 5)^2 = x^2 - 10x + 25$ so you subtract 21 to get 4.

With odd coefficients it may be best to work with fractions.

Positive numbers have two square roots
e.g. $\sqrt{9}$ is 3 or $-3$

What is the minimum value of $x^2 + 8x + 19$ and for what value of $x$ does this minimum occur?

**ANSWER**

$x^2 + 8x + 19 = (x + 4)^2 + 3$

The smallest possible square number is zero so the minimum value of the expression is $0 + 3 = 3$

$(x + 4)^2$ is zero when $x = -4$

## Exercise C19.6

**HIGH**

1 Complete the square on these quadratic expressions.

   a $x^2 + 4x + 6$      b $y^2 + 8x + 15$      c $x^2 + 6x + 9$      d $x^2 + 10x + 27$

   e $y^2 + 4y$      f $x^2 + 12x + 10$      g $x^2 + 14x + 30$      h $x^2 + 4x - 5$

   i $y^2 + 8x - 3$      j $x^2 + 3x + 4$

2 Write these expressions in the form $(x + p)^2 + q$

   a $x^2 + 20x + 50$      b $x^2 - 5 + 16x$      c $x^2 - 9x - 11$

3 Solve these quadratics by completing the square.

   a $x^2 - 12x + 20 = 0$      b $y^2 + 2y - 15 = 0$      c $x^2 - 4x - 5 = 0$

   d $x^2 + 2x + 1 = 0$      e $m^2 + 2m - 63 = 0$      f $x^2 - 14x + 49 = 0$

   g $y^2 - 8y = 0$      h $x^2 = 1 - 12x$      i $x(x + 3) = 88$

   j $(x + 1)^2 - 2x(x - 2) = 10$

4 Find the minimum possible value of each of these expressions and state the value of $x$ which would give rise to this minimum value.

   a $x^2 + 6x + 10$      b $x^2 - 8x + 14$      c $x^2 - 12x - 4$      d $x^2 + 5x + 1$

*5 Use completing the square to explain why

   a $x^2 + 4x + 10 \geq 6$      b $x^2 + 8x + 17 = 0$ has no solutions

*6 The area of painting A is twice the area of painting B. Show that $x^2 + 2x - 15 = 0$ and use completing the square to find the dimensions of each picture.

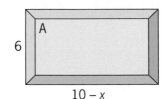
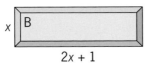

7 ☆ **CHALLENGE** ☆

A farmer has 1000 metres of fencing and wishes to fence a rectangular field in which to keep her animals. Investigate the size of the rectangle that would give the maximum area of the field and use completing the square to prove that no larger area is possible.

# The quadratic equation formula

- Solve simple quadratic equations using the quadratic equation formula

## RICH TASK

Two sisters were born a year apart to the exact day.
How old are they when the product of their ages is 20? Or 30?
Why could this product never be 40? Prove it.
Investigate other possible and impossible products that are multiples of 10.

Some quadratic equations do not factorise.

→ **All quadratic equations of the form $ax^2 + bx + c = 0$ can be solved using the quadratic equation formula**
$$x = \frac{-b \pm \sqrt{b^2 - 4ac}}{2a}$$

You can use completing the square on the equation $ax^2 + bx + c = 0$ to reach this formula.

In the above formula, ± means 'plus or minus'.

**EXAMPLE**

Solve the equation $2x^2 - 5x - 6 = 0$, giving your answers to two decimal places.

You get exact answers when you can factorise so the request for decimal solutions is a hint that you should use the formula.

**ANSWER**

$2x^2 - 5x - 6 = 0$        so    $a = 2, b = -5, c = -6$

$x = \dfrac{-b \pm \sqrt{b^2 - 4ac}}{2a}$

$x = \dfrac{5 \pm \sqrt{(-5)^2 - 4 \times 2 \times (-6)}}{2 \times 2}$

$b = -5$ so $-b = 5$

$x = \dfrac{5 \pm \sqrt{73}}{4}$

$x = 3.3860009...$ or $x = -0.8860009...$

$x = 3.39$ or $x = -0.89$ (to 2 decimal places)

→ **Equations involving fractions can be tackled by multiplying all terms by the denominators.**

Solve $\dfrac{5}{x+3} + x = 4$

**ANSWER**

$\dfrac{5}{x+3} + x = 4$ ... multiply all terms by $(x+3)$ ... $5 + x(x+3) = 4(x+3)$

$5 + x^2 + 3x = 4x + 12$

$x^2 - x - 7 = 0$ $\qquad x = \dfrac{1 \pm \sqrt{(-1)^2 - (4 \times 1 \times -7)}}{2} = \dfrac{1 \pm \sqrt{29}}{2}$

$x = 3.19258...$ or $x = -2.19258...$

You could do

$\dfrac{5}{x+3} + x = 4$

$\dfrac{5}{x+3} = 4 - x$

And then use cross-multiplication since you have fraction = fraction. A universal method for all fraction equations is to multiply through by any denominators present.

## Exercise C19.7

**HIGH**

1 Solve these quadratic equations using the quadratic equation formula. Where necessary, give your answers to 3 significant figures.

  a $\quad 3x^2 + 10x + 6 = 0$      b $\quad 5x^2 - 6x + 1 = 0$

  c $\quad 2x^2 - 7x - 15 = 0$      d $\quad x^2 + 4x + 1 = 0$

  e $\quad 2x^2 + 6x - 1 = 0$      f $\quad 6y^2 - 11y - 5 = 0$

  g $\quad 3x^2 = 10x - 3$        h $\quad 6x + 2x^2 - 1 = 0$

2 Solve these equations using the quadratic formula. Give your answers to 3 significant figures.

  a $\quad x(x + 4) = 9$        b $\quad 2x(x + 1) - x(x + 1) = 11$

  c $\quad (3x)^2 = 8x + 3$

3 A rectangle has dimensions as shown.

  a $\quad$ Write an expression for the area of this rectangle.

  b $\quad$ Given that the area of this rectangle is 20 cm², show that
$\qquad x^2 + 5x - 34 = 0$

  c $\quad$ Find the dimensions of the rectangle, giving your lengths to two decimal places.

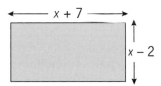

4 Solve the following equations.

  a $\quad \dfrac{5}{x} + 3x = 35$        b $\quad \dfrac{3}{x} + \dfrac{4}{x+1} = 3$

  c $\quad \dfrac{5}{x+2} + \dfrac{2}{x-1} = 4$        d $\quad \dfrac{3}{x-2} - \dfrac{2}{x+3} = 2$

**REMEMBER:**

**Don't forget** that the equation needs to be in the form $ax^2 + bx + c = 0$ first.

5 ☆ **CHALLENGE** ☆

Solve $2x^2 + 11x + 12 = 0$ using the formula. Repeat for $2x^2 + 11x + 10 = 0$. Now try and solve both via factorisation. What do you notice? Investigate which part of the quadratic formula tells us whether or not a quadratic will factorise.

- Solve simultaneous linear and quadratic equations

### RICH TASK

Investigate the graph of the equation $x^2 + y^2 = r^2$, where $r$ is a constant.

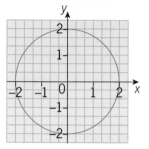

→ **Substitution can be used to solve simultaneous equations where one equation is linear and the other quadratic.**

**EXAMPLE**

Solve the simultaneous equations $x + 2y = 7$
$x^2 + y = 11$

**ANSWER**

*Linear equation:* $\quad x + 2y = 7 \rightarrow x = 7 - 2y$

*Quadratic equation:* $\quad x^2 + y = 11$
$$(7 - 2y)^2 + y = 11$$
$$49 - 28y + 4y^2 + y = 11$$
$$4y^2 - 27y + 38 = 0$$
$$(4y - 19)(y - 2) = 0$$

Either $\quad 4y - 19 = 0 \rightarrow y = 4\frac{3}{4} \rightarrow x = 7 - 2 \times 4\frac{3}{4} = -2\frac{1}{2}$

Or $\quad y - 2 = 0 \rightarrow y = 2 \rightarrow x = 7 - 2 \times 2 = 3$

The solutions are $\left(-2\frac{1}{2}, 4\frac{3}{4}\right)$ and $(3, 2)$.

> Rearrange the linear equation to make $x$ the subject.

> Substitute into the quadratic equation.

p. 362

p. 214

→ **Solving a pair of simultaneous equations is equivalent to finding the coordinate(s) of their point(s) of intersection.**

**EXAMPLE**

The diagram shows the graphs $y = x - 1$ and $y = x^2 - x - 3$. Find the two points of intersection.

p. 316

**ANSWER**

$y = x - 1$ and $y = x^2 - x - 3$
$$x - 1 = x^2 - x - 3$$
$$0 = x^2 - 2x - 2$$
$$x = \frac{2 \pm \sqrt{12}}{2}$$
$x = 2.732...$ and $x = -0.7320...$

$\therefore y = 1.732...$ and $y = -1.7320...$

The points are $(2.73, 1.73)$ and $(-0.73, -1.73)$ (to 3 s.f.)

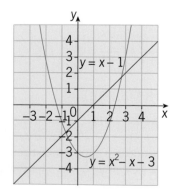

1 Solve these pairs of simultaneous equations.

  a  $x^2 + y = 55$        b  $x + y^2 = 32$

     $y = 6$               $x = 7$

  c  $x^2 - 3y = 73$      d  $x - y^2 = 3$

     $y = 9$                $x = 7$

2 Solve these equations simultaneously.

  a  $y = x + 4$         b  $y = 2x - 2$

     $y = x^2 - 2x$        $y = x^2 - 1$

  c  $x = 9y - 4$       d  $2x + y = 1$

     $x = 2y^2$           $x^2 + y^2 = 1$

3 Solve these equations simultaneously.

  a  $y = 5x - 8$        b  $p = 2q$

     $y = x^2 - 3x + 7$     $p^2 + 3pq = 10$

4 The diagram shows the graphs $y = x^2 - 2x - 8$ and $y = 3x - 2$.

  a  The graphs intersect at two points. Use algebra to find the coordinates of these points.

  b  Use the diagram to confirm that the coordinates you have found are correct.

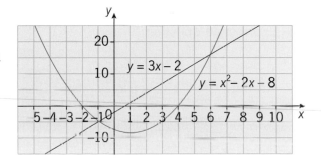

6 A room is made up of two square sections.
The area of carpet needed to cover the entire room is 25 m². By writing and solving, simultaneously, one linear and one quadratic equation, find the dimensions of the room.

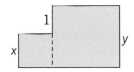

7 ☆ **CHALLENGE** ☆

  Solve the following pair of simultaneous equations.

$$xy = 15$$
$$xy^3 = 135$$

Unit C

## CHECK OUT

You should now be able to
- expand and simplifying the product of two linear expressions
- factorise quadratic expressions
- solve quadratic equations by factorising, completing the square and by formula
- solve simultaneous linear and quadratic equations.

**Exam-style question**

The length of the shortest side of a right-angled triangle is $x$ mm.
The hypotenuse is 12 mm longer than the shortest side.
The third side is 10·5 mm longer than the shortest side.

Form an equation in $x$ and solve it to find the length of the shortest side of the triangle.

**Kevin's answer:**

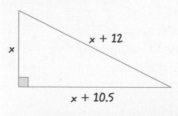

$x + 12$

$x$

$x + 10.5$

$$x^2 + (x+10.5)^2 = (x+12)^2$$
$$x^2 + x^2 + 21x + 110.25 = x^2 + 24x + 144$$
$$x^2 - 3x - 33.75 = 0$$
$$4x^2 - 12x - 135 = 0$$
$$(2x + 9)(2x - 15) = 0$$

$2x + 9 = 0$ : negative answer & $x$ cannot be negative
$2x - 15 = 0$ : $x = 7.5$
Shortest side 7.5 mm

A diagram may be useful to explain the question.

Explain why a solution will not work, don't just ignore it.

Read the information in the question and write it out using maths symbols.

You may need to use mathematics from other parts of the course.

## Exam practice

1 **a** Solve these quadratic equations.

    **i** $x^2 - 7x - 30 = 0$     **ii** $x^2 - 4x - 1 = 0$

  **b** **i** Find the integers $a$ and $b$ such that $x^2 + 6x + 2 = (x + a)^2 + b$

    **ii** Hence solve $x^2 + 6x + 2 = 0$ leaving the roots in surd form.

*(10 marks)*

*2 A circle has equation $x^2 + y^2 = 50$.

A straight line has equation $y + x = 10$.

Find, algebraically, where the circle and line intersect and describe the relationship between the circle and the line, giving a reason for your answer.

*(7 marks)*

3 Martha throws a ball to Nathan who catches it.

Nathan and Martha are standing 6 m apart.

The ball is thrown at a height of 1 m above the ground.

The ball follows a curve with equation $y = 1 \cdot 5 - \dfrac{1}{k}(3 - x)^2$.

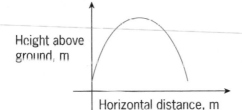

a **Show** that $k = 18$.

b Find the height of the ball above ground when it has travelled a horizontal distance of $1 \cdot 2$ m.

*(4 marks)*

# 20 Surface area and volume

## INTRODUCTION

Many of the man-made shapes we see in everyday life are cuboids, particularly in packaging.

**What's the point?**

Cuboids are easy to assemble, and most importantly they stack up without leaving any gaps. This makes them more economical and practical for packaging and transporting goods.

## CHECK IN

1 Calculate the area of each shape.

a

5 cm
8 cm

b

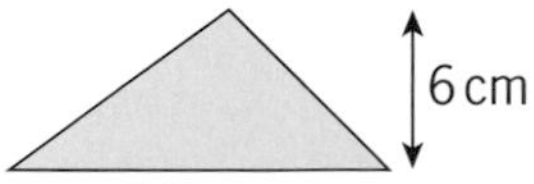
6 cm
10 cm

2 Evaluate

a $25 \times 10$  b $63 \times 100$  c $4.1 \times 10$
d $2.5 \times 100$  e $3.5 \times 1000$  f $40 \div 10$
g $56 \div 10$  h $4000 \div 100$  i $410 \div 100$
j $5200 \div 1000$

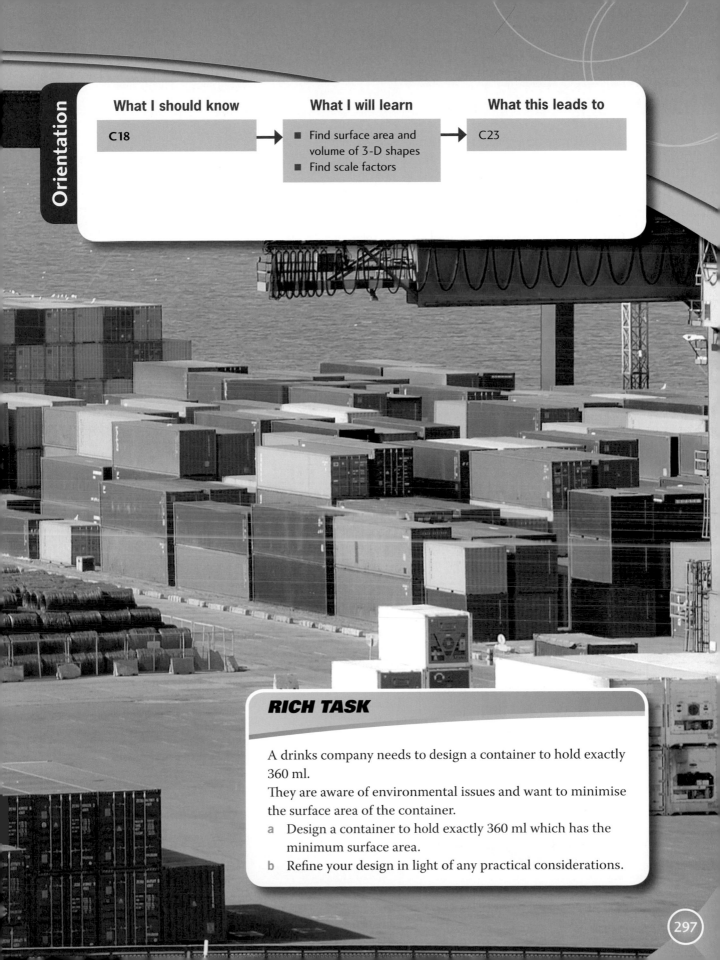

## Orientation

| What I should know | What I will learn | What this leads to |
|---|---|---|
| C18 | ■ Find surface area and volume of 3-D shapes<br>■ Find scale factors | C23 |

### RICH TASK

A drinks company needs to design a container to hold exactly 360 ml.

They are aware of environmental issues and want to minimise the surface area of the container.

a Design a container to hold exactly 360 ml which has the minimum surface area.

b Refine your design in light of any practical considerations.

# Surface area of prisms

- Calculate and use the surface area of 3-D shapes

## RICH TASK

Find a cuboid that will hold a minimum of 1000 cm³ and has the least surface area.

Cuboids are prisms.

The surface area of a 3-D object is the total area of all its faces.
You should be able to find the surface area of the objects on the right.

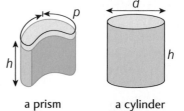

a cuboid          a prism          a cylinder

Cuboids have only **plane** (flat) faces.
The **curved** faces of other objects are found using formulae:

Take care with hollow open objects. For example, a cylindrical tube has no ends, just a curved surface.

| Object | Prism | Cylinder |
|---|---|---|
| Curved surface area | $p \times h$ | $\pi d \times h$ or $2\pi r \times h$ |

The curved face of a prism and a cylinder can be opened out into a rectangle of area $p \times h$ or $\pi d \times h$ respectively, where $p$, $d$ and $h$ are perimeter, diameter and height.

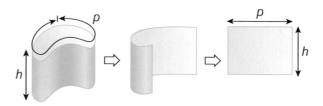

### EXAMPLE

A tin of beans has a total surface area of 380 cm². If the ends of the tin have a diameter of 8.0 cm, find the height of the tin.

**ANSWER**

The total surface area is found by adding the areas of the curved face and the two circular ends.

Area of one end = $\pi r^2 = \pi \times 4^2 = 16\pi$
Area of the curved face = $\pi dh = \pi \times 8 \times h = 8\pi h$
Total surface area gives  $380 = 2 \times 16\pi + 8\pi h$
$\qquad\qquad\qquad\qquad 380 = 100.5 + 25.1 \times h$
Subtract 100.5 from both sides  $279.5 = 25.1 \times h$

Divide both sides by 25.1  $\qquad h = \frac{279.5}{25.1} = 11.1$

The height, $h$, of the tin is 11.1 cm.

This is a **closed** cylinder. In a question like this, sketch your shape and decide whether it has open or closed end faces.

## Exercise C20.1

1 Here is the net of a cuboid.
   Find its surface area.

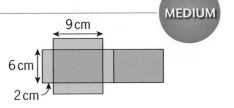

9 cm
6 cm
2 cm

2 Find the surface area of
   a a tin of tomatoes of height 12 cm and radius 5 cm.
   b an unopened box of tissues of length 18 cm, width 10 cm and height 12 cm.

3 Draw nets for these two prisms and
   find their surface areas.
   The dimensions are in centimetres.

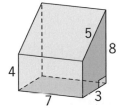
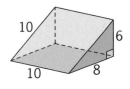

10
10
6
8

5
8
4
7
3

4 A gardener makes a frame for his seedlings from sheets of wood.
   The frame has four sides and is open at the top and the bottom.
   a Find the area of the wood that he needs.
   b If the wood costs £12.45 per m², how much will the frame cost?
   c He makes a glass top for the frame from glass costing
      £6.50 per m². How much will the glass cost?

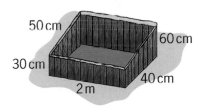

50 cm
60 cm
30 cm
40 cm
2 m

5 A hollow cylindrical tube and a solid cylinder both have a radius
   of 5 cm and outer surface area of 400 cm². Find their lengths.

6 The surface area of a closed cylinder is 1 m². It is 1 metre long.
   Find    a its radius to the nearest centimetre
           b its exact radius in terms of π.

7 **RICH TASK**

   An open box (without a lid) is 15 cm long, 10 cm wide and
   5 cm high. It is made from a net which is cut in one piece
   from a larger rectangular sheet of cardboard.
   a Find the area of the net and the dimensions of the smallest
      possible rectangular sheet.
   b What percentage of the sheet is wasted in making the net?

8 **RICH TASK**

   A hollow cuboid must hold 1 litre of liquid. Suggest
   different possible dimensions for the cuboid. Which of your
   suggestions has the smallest surface area?
   What is special about this particular cuboid?

Unit C

# Surface area of other shapes

• Calculate and use the surface area of 3-D shapes

You know how to find the surface area of a prism, including a cylinder. You also need to be able to find the surface area of other shapes.

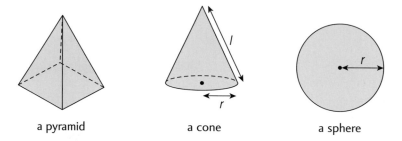

a pyramid          a cone          a sphere

Pyramids have only **plane** (flat) faces.
The area of the **curved** faces of a cone and a sphere can be found using these formulae:

| Object | Cone | Sphere |
|---|---|---|
| **Curved surface area** | $\pi r l$ | $4\pi r^2$ |

## Exercise C20.2

**HIGH**

1 Here is the net of a square-based pyramid.
Find its surface area.

6 cm

4 cm  4 cm

4 cm

2 Find the surface area of
  a  a tennis ball of radius 3.5 cm
  b  a solid cone with a base radius of 5 cm and a slant height of 12 cm
  c  a solid cone with a base radius of 5 cm and a vertical height of 12 cm.

**3** The geography department's globe of the Earth has a surface area of 3000 cm². Find its radius.

**4** Law 2 of Association Football specifies the circumference of a soccer ball. If its surface area is 1560 cm², find its circumference.

**5** Given that each base radius is 5 cm,
calculate the vertical height of
  **a** a hollow cone with a surface area of $60\pi$ cm²
  **b** a solid cone with a surface area of $95\pi$ cm²

**6** A solid pyramid has a base 10 cm square and its total surface area is 360 cm². Calculate its vertical height.

**7** The Great Pyramid of Giza in Egypt is built on a square base with sides 230 metres. Its four sloping faces have a total area of 85 500 m². Calculate the length, $x$, of each sloping edge of the pyramid.

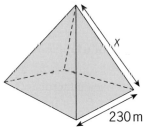

230 m

> ### RICH TASK
>
> A manufacturer of tin cans stamps out three pieces from a rectangular sheet – two circular ends and one rectangular piece to make the curved surface of the tin.
> How should he arrange the three pieces for the rectangular sheet to be as small as possible (and so waste as little of it as possible)?

# Length, area and volume scale factors

● Find and use length and area scale factors

Here is an enlargement.
Look at the sides. The **sizes** of the two triangles
are different.
The sides of the image = 2 × the sides of the object
The length **scale factor** is 2.

p. 189

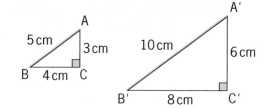

Calculate the **perimeters** of the triangles.

The perimeter of triangle ABC = 5 + 4 + 3
$$= 12 \text{ cm}$$

The perimeter of triangle A′B′C′ = 10 + 8 + 6
$$= 24 \text{ cm}$$

The perimeter scale factor is 2.

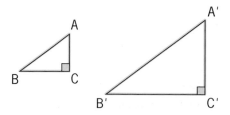

Calculate the **areas** of the triangles.

The area of object triangle
$$\text{ABC} = \tfrac{1}{2} \times 3 \times 4 = 6 \text{ cm}^2$$

The area of image triangle
$$\text{A′B′C′} = \tfrac{1}{2} \times 6 \times 8$$
$$= 24 \text{ cm}^2$$

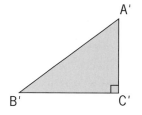

The area of the image = 4 × the area of the object.
The area scale factor is 4.

You can fit four object triangles
into the image triangle.

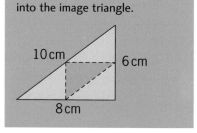

## RICH TASK

Here is an enlargement in
three dimensions.
What is the scale factor of
enlargement for
i    the length of each edge
ii   the area of each face
iii  the volume of the shape?

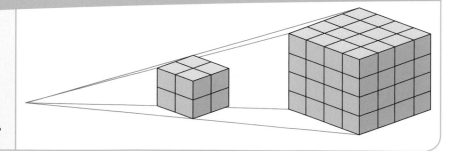

→ **If an enlargement has a length scale factor of *m*,**
  ➤ **then the perimeter scale factor is *m***
  ➤ **the area scale factor is *m*².**
  ➤ **the volume scale factor is *m*³.**

## Exercise C20.3

1  a  Draw a graph and label both axes from 0 to 8. Draw the object
      triangle (2, 3), (4, 3), (3, 2) and image triangle (2, 6), (6, 6), (4, 4).
      Find the centre of enlargement, the length scale factor and
      the area scale factor.

   b  Repeat on new axes labelled from 0 to 10 with the object
      shape (2, 2), (2, 4), (3, 4), (3, 2) and the image shape
      (4, 4), (4, 10), (7, 10), (7, 4).

2  An advert in a magazine has an area of 15 cm².
   An enlargement of the advert three times longer and wider
   appears in a newspaper. Find the area of the newspaper advert.

3  The large cuboid is an enlargement of the small cuboid.
   a  How many times longer are the edges?
      Write down the length scale factor.
   b  How many times bigger has the area of the top become?
      Write down the area scale factor.
   c  How many small cuboids fit into the large cuboid?
      Write down the volume scale factor.
   d  Check that the scale factors follow the pattern of $m$, $m^2$ and $m^3$.

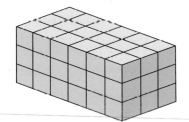

4  Two similar oil drums have heights of 60 cm and 180 cm.
   The smaller drum holds 30 litres of oil. Find
   a  the length scale factor
   b  the volume scale factor
   c  how much oil is in the larger drum.

5  ☆ **CHALLENGE** ☆

   The V&A Museum in London sell copies of paintings. You can buy
   paintings by Toulouse-Lautrec as posters (75 cm by 50 cm) and as
   prints (30 cm by 20 cm).
   Are the posters a mathematical enlargement of the prints? What are
   the length and area scale factors?

# Measures of area and volume

- Convert area measures and volume measures to different units

1 millimetre (1 mm) enlarged by a factor of 10 becomes 1 centimetre (1 cm).

This diagram shows a square with sides of 1 mm enlarged using a length scale factor of 10.

For 10 rows of 10 squares, you need $10^2 = 10 \times 10 = 100$ small squares to make the large square.

> → **$1\,cm^2 = 10^2\,mm^2 = 100\,mm^2$**

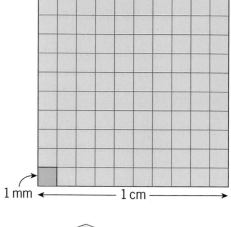

1 mm ← 1 cm →

This diagram shows a cube with edges of 1 mm enlarged using a length scale factor of 10.

It needs $10^3 = 10 \times 10 \times 10 = 1000$ small cubes to make the large cube.

> → **$1\,cm^3 = 10^3\,mm^3 = 1000\,mm^3$**

There is a similar relationship for metres and centimetres.
1 metre = 100 cm so

> → **for area,**      **$1\,m^2 = 100^2\,cm^2 = 10\,000\,cm^2$**
> → **for volume,**    **$1\,m^3 = 100^3\,cm^3 = 1\,000\,000\,cm^3$**

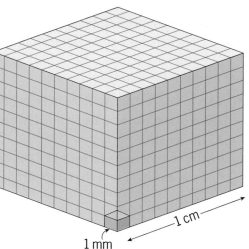

1 cm

1 mm

**EXAMPLE**

Change    **a**   6.4 m² to cm²      **b**   350 mm³ to cm³.

**ANSWER**

**a**   $1 m^2 = 100^2\,cm^2 = 10\,000\,cm^2$
     So 6.4 m² = 6.4 × 10 000 cm²
           = 64 000 cm²

**b**   $1\,cm^3 = 10^3\,mm^3 = 1000\,mm^3$
     So 350 mm³ = 350 ÷ 1000 cm³
           = 0.35 cm³

## Exercise C20.4

1   Use the conversion 1 cm = 10 mm to change
    a   i   8 cm to mm          ii   6 cm² to mm²      iii  2 cm³ to mm³
    b   i   35 mm to cm         ii   140 mm² to cm²    iii  500 mm³ to cm³

2   Use the conversion 1metre = 100 cm to change
    a   i   8 metres to cm      ii   3 m² to cm²       iii  5 m³ to cm³
    b   i   750 cm to metres    ii   8500 cm² to m²    iii  412 000 cm³ to m³

3   a   i   A thermometer's mercury column is 4.6 cm long.
            What is this length in mm?
        ii  A finger nail has an area of 1.3 cm².
            What is its area in mm² ?
        iii My contact lens case has a volume of 0.35 cm³.
            Find its volume in mm³.
    b   i   A sheet of paper is 0.32 metres long.
            What is the length in centimetres?
        ii  A sheet of glass has an area of 0.025 m².
            Find this area in cm².
        iii A crate of goods has a volume of 0.75 m³.
            What is this volume in cm³?
    c   i   How long is a 3 km bike ride in metres?
        ii  What is the area of a 2 km² nature reserve in square metres?
        iii The reservoir next to Heathrow Airport holds 15 900 000 m³
            of water. How many cubic kilometres is this?

4   Use the length conversion 1 km = 1000 metres in this problem.
    A nature reserve has a lake with a perimeter of 7.4 km and a surface
    area of 2.1 square kilometres. The lake has an estimated volume
    of 5 000 000 cubic metres.
    Find   a   the perimeter of the lake in metres
           b   its surface area in square metres
           c   its estimated volume in cubic kilometres.

5   Wembley Stadium has the world's longest single span
    of 315 metres across its roof. The roof has an area of 44 500 m².
    The stadium encloses a volume of 4 000 000 (4 million)
    cubic metres.
    Find   a   the length of its span in kilometres
           b   the area of the roof in square kilometres
           c   the volume of the stadium in cubic kilometres.

# Calculating volumes

- Calculate and use the volumes of 3-D shapes

You need to be able to find the volumes of these shapes.

> A *right* pyramid has its vertex directly above the centre of its base.

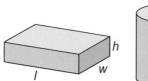

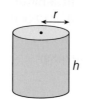

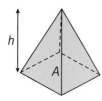
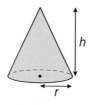

The volumes are found using formulae:

| Object | Cuboid | Prism | Cylinder | Pyramid | Cone | Sphere |
|--------|--------|-------|----------|---------|------|--------|
| Volume | $l \times w \times h$ | $A \times h$ | $\pi r^2 \times h$ | $\frac{1}{3}A \times h$ | $\frac{1}{3}\pi r^2 \times h$ | $\frac{4}{3}\pi r^3$ |

**EXAMPLE**

A firework in the shape of a rectangular-based pyramid is filled with combustible chemicals. Find its volume.

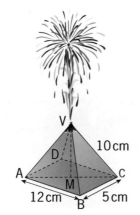

**ANSWER**

Its base has an area $A = 12 \times 5 = 60 \, \text{cm}^2$.
The vertical height $h$ of the firework is needed.

Pythagoras' theorem gives:

$$\text{in } \triangle ABC, \; AC^2 = 12^2 + 5^2 = 144 + 25 = 169$$
$$AC = \sqrt{169} = 13 \, \text{cm}$$
$$\text{in } \triangle AMV, \; MV^2 = 10^2 - 6.5^2 = 100 - 42.25 = 57.75$$
$$MV = \sqrt{57.75}$$

So the height of the firework, $h$ is 7.6 cm
Its volume $V = \frac{1}{3}A \times h = \frac{1}{3} \times 60 \times \sqrt{57.75} = 152 \, \text{cm}^3$ (3 s.f.)

1   An open tank 12.5 metres by 8.2 metres catches rainwater. If the level rises 3 cm during a storm, how many litres of rainwater has it collected?

2   A cylindrical bottle of olive oil says *1 litre* on the label. The bottle's inner diameter is 10.4 cm and its height is 11.8 cm. Should you complain about the labelling?

3   A solid piece of wood is hollowed out to create an open container.
    Calculate the percentage of wood cut away.

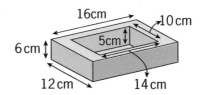
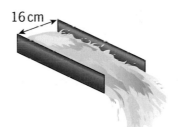

4   Water 9 cm deep flows down a rectangular duct 16 cm wide at a speed of 150 cm per second. How long will it take to fill a tank of capacity 5400 litres?

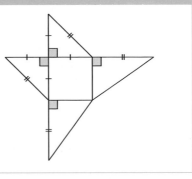

5   **RICH TASK**

Find the dimensions of all the different cuboids which each have
- a volume of 1 litre
- dimensions which are a whole number of centimetres
- a base with both length and width in multiples of 10 cm.
Which of your answers would suit a pack of ready-made custard?

6   **RICH TASK**

Here is a net of square-based pyramid.
Make three identical pyramids using this net.
(The base can be any size.)
Fit the pyramids together to make a cube.
What does this tell you about the volume of one of the pyramids? How does this relate to the volume formulae for a pyramid and a cone?

**Continued** ➤

Unit C

**7** Find the volume of

a a cylindrical vase of radius 12 cm and height 18 cm

b an ice-cream cone of radius 8 cm and vertical height 12 cm

c an ice-cream cone of radius 8 cm and slant height 12 cm

d a ball-bearing of radius 0.7 cm

e a pyramid with a 12 cm square base and height 8 cm

f the L-shaped steel beam shown on the right.

**8** Half a litre of cream is sold in a cylindrical tube of radius 3 cm. Calculate its length.

**9** You want to buy a new fridge. It must have a base 50 cm by 40 cm.
The model you like has a volume of 160 litres.
Will this model fit under a worktop of height 85 cm?

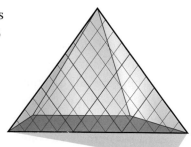

**10** The official size of a netball is one with a circumference of 70 cm. Find its volume in litres (to 2 s.f.).

**11** **RICH TASK**

> You have two identical beakers of diameter 8 cm.
> One beaker contains water 7 cm deep.
> The other contains a small lump of metal.
> How can you find the volume of the metal using only a ruler?

**12** A snooker ball has a volume of 75.8 cm³. Find its diameter.

**13** a A metal cube has a volume of half a litre. How long are the edges of the cube?

b The metal is melted and used to make ten equal spherical ball-bearings. Find their radius.

**14** La Pyramide du Louvre is a modern glass building in Paris which is the entrance to the Louvre Museum. It has a vertical height of 20.6 metres and a volume of 8410 m³.
Find the length of the sides of its square base.

**15** The Egyptian pyramid of Khafra has a square base of side 215.2 metres and a volume of 2.22 million cubic metres. Calculate its height and the length of its sloping edges.

**16** ☆ **CHALLENGE** ☆

A litre of milk is packed for sale in a container in the shape of a regular tetrahedron.
Calculate the length of the edges of the tetrahedron.

**17** *RICH TASK*

A sector of a circle of radius $R$ has an angle $\theta$ at its centre. The sector is used to make a cone.

a   Find the volume $V$ of the cone in terms of $R$ and $\theta$.

b   Use computer software to find values of $\theta$ and to draw a graph of $V$ against $\theta$. Does $V$ have a maximum value? (Take $R = 1$)

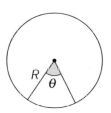

# Volumes of complex shapes

**C20.6**

- Calculate and use the volumes of more complex shapes including frustums

More complex shapes can be made from basic shapes.

**EXAMPLE**

A metal peg is made from a hemisphere and cone as shown.
Find its volume as a multiple of $\pi$.

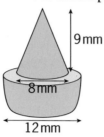

9 mm

8 mm

12 mm

**ANSWER**

Volume of peg $= \frac{1}{2} \times \frac{4}{3} \times \pi \times 6^3 + \frac{1}{3} \times \pi \times 4^2 \times 9$

$= 144\pi + 48\pi$

$= 192\pi \text{ mm}^3$

A **frustum** is part of a pyramid or cone.
It is the part left when you slice off the top by a plane parallel to the base.

The volume of a frustum $V$ is the volume of the original pyramid less the volume removed.

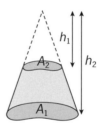

$h_1$

$A_2$ $h_2$

$A_1$

➜ So $V = \frac{1}{3}A_1h_1 - \frac{1}{3}A_2h_2$

A frustum is a *truncated pyramid* (truncated means 'chopped off').

**EXAMPLE**

A bobbin for holding yarn has the shape of a truncated cone with the given dimensions. Find its volume in terms of $\pi$.

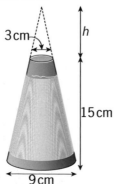

3 cm

h

15 cm

9 cm

**ANSWER**

Let the height of the cone removed be $h$.
To find the volume, we need the overall height of the original cone $= h + 15$ cm.
The length scale factor of the enlargement is $\frac{h+15}{h} = \frac{9}{3} = 3$
So $h + 15 = 3 \times h$
$h = 7.5$
and the original overall height $= h + 15 = 22.5$ cm

The volume of the bobbin $= \frac{1}{3}\pi\left(\frac{9}{2}\right)^2 22.5 - \frac{1}{3}\pi\left(\frac{3}{2}\right)^2 7.5$

$= \frac{585}{4}\pi \text{ cm}^3$

1 Calculate the volume and surface area of these solids.
   All dimensions are in centimetres. Give your answers in terms of $\pi$.

**a**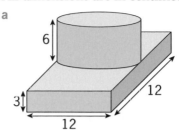

**b**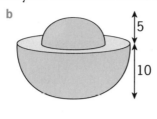

**c**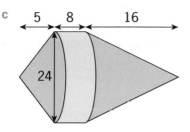

2 Three metal spheres of diameter 2 cm are dropped into a beaker
  of water of diameter 8 cm. By how much does the water level rise?

3 Calculate the volume of these frustums.

**a**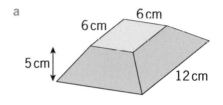

**b**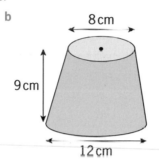

**c**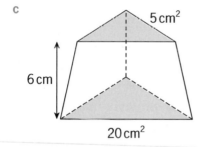

4 This bucket is made from a truncated cone.
   **a** Calculate its volume in litres.
   **b** How much water is needed to fill it to half its height?

5 **RICH TASK**

   The first stage of a multi-stage rocket (such as
   the US Saturn rocket) is made from a cone,
   a cylinder and a frustum.
   Calculate the volume and exterior surface area
   of this first stage.
   Do some research on space rockets and find
   what other shapes are used in their construction.
   What is the 'fairing' of a rocket?

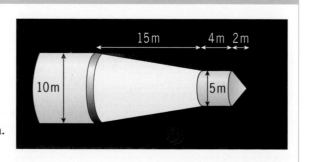

Unit C

## CHECK OUT

You should now be able to
- solve problems involving surface area and volume of
  - ➤ prisms
  - ➤ pyramids
  - ➤ cylinder
  - ➤ cones, including frustums
  - ➤ spheres
- understand the effect of enlargement on area and volume.

*

### Exam-style question

The volume of a cuboid is 80 cm³.
The cuboid has square ends.
The sides of the cuboid are all integer (whole number) values.
**a** Work out the possible dimensions of the cuboid.
**b** Work out
  **i** the smallest possible surface area
  **ii** explain, without working out other surface areas, why this must be the smallest.

**Sammy's answer:**

a Volume = area square × length

Start with how to find the volume.

All lengths are integers, so look for square number that is a factor of the volume
Possibilities are 1, 4, 16

Use the area of a square to find possible integer values; list them all.

Possible dimensions are
1, 1, 80 or 2, 2, 20 or 4, 4, 5

Think about what the different cuboids will look like.

b i Cuboid 4, 4, 5
SA = 2×(4×4) + 4×(4×5) = 112 cm²

Reading the whole of part **b** will save you time.

ii Smallest surface area when the cuboid is closest to a cube

### Exam practice

1  The diagram shows the net of a cone.

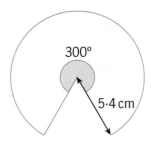

300°

5·4 cm

Calculate the volume of the cone.

*(5 marks)*

2  A paper case for cakes is in the shape of a frustum.
A shop sells two sizes of paper cases, which are mathematically similar.
The radius of the smaller case is 1·2 cm; the radius of the larger paper case is 2·4 cm.

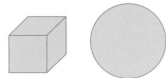

The larger paper case holds 100 cm³.
How much can the smaller paper case hold?

*(2 marks)*

3  The centre of a golf ball is made from a solid block of rubber in the shape of a cube.
The block of rubber is heated and pressed to form a sphere.

The radius of the sphere is 2 cm.
Work out the side length of the cube.

*(4 marks)*

# 21  Graphs

## CHECK IN

1  Given that $x = 3$, find the value of the following expressions.

   a  $x^2 - 1$        b  $2x^2$

   c  $x^2 - 4x$      d  $x^2 + x + 2$

   Repeat for $x = -3$

2  Plot graphs of these linear functions.
   Choose values of $x$ from $-2$ to $2$.

   a  $y = 2x - 1$     b  $y = 3 - x$

3  Sketch a graph to show each situation.

   a  your height as you age from a baby to a 20-year-old

   b  the temperature of a cup of tea as it is left to stand for half an hour.

| What I should know | What I will learn | What this leads to |
|---|---|---|
| B14 | ■ Plot quadratic curves ■ Solve quadratic equations by graph | Courses and careers in business and finance |

## RICH TASK

Investigate the gradient of the curve $y = x^2$ at different points along the curve.

A tangent is a line that touches the curve at one point. The tangent to the curve at any given point allows the gradient of the curve to be calculated at that point. Here the tangent has been drawn at the point (2, 4).

- Generate points and plot graphs of quadratic functions

## RICH TASK

Vince's personal best at throwing a javelin is 30 metres. His throw can be modelled using the equation $y = x(30 - x)$, where $x$ is the horizontal distance covered and $y$ is the vertical distance covered, both in metres. Using a graph, find out the height that Vince's javelin reaches. If Vince's personal best increases to 40 metres and the equation becomes $y = x(40 - x)$, how does the height reached change? Investigate the height change for each 10-metre improvement made.

p. 292

→ A **quadratic graph** forms a characteristic U-shaped curve, or **parabola**.

**EXAMPLE**

By completing the table, plot the graph $y = x^2 - 1$ for $-3 \leq x \leq 3$.

**ANSWER**

Plot $(-3, 8)$, $(-2, 3)$, ..., $(3, 8)$ and join smoothly.

| x | −3 | −2 | −1 | 0 | 1 | 2 | 3 |
|---|---|---|---|---|---|---|---|
| x² | 9 | 4 | 1 | 0 | 1 | 4 | 9 |
| −1 | −1 | −1 | −1 | −1 | −1 | −1 | −1 |
| y | 8 | 3 | 0 | −1 | 0 | 3 | 8 |

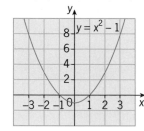

You should plot at least seven points.

→ A parabola has a **maximum** or **minimum point** and a **vertical line of symmetry**.

**EXAMPLE**

Plot the curve $y = 2x - x^2$ and give the coordinates of its maximum point and the equation of its line of symmetry.

**ANSWER**

| x | −3 | −2 | −1 | 0 | 1 | 2 | 3 |
|---|---|---|---|---|---|---|---|
| 2x | −6 | −4 | −2 | 0 | 2 | 4 | 6 |
| −x² | −9 | −4 | −1 | 0 | −1 | −4 | −9 |
| y | −15 | −8 | −3 | 0 | 1 | 0 | −3 |

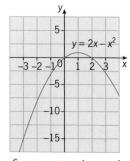

Add the first three values in each column to get the value of $y$.

The coordinates of the maximum point are $(1, 1)$ and the equation of the line of symmetry is $x = 1$.

## Exercise C21.1

1 For each equation listed below, copy and complete the table of coordinates and use your values to plot the curve for this equation.

   a  $y = x^2 - 2$

| $x$ | -3 | -2 | -1 | 0 | 1 | 2 | 3 |
|---|---|---|---|---|---|---|---|
| $x^2$ | | | 1 | | | | 9 |
| -2 | | | -2 | | | | -2 |
| $y$ | | | -1 | | | | 7 |

   b  $y = 2x^2$

| $x$ | -3 | -2 | -1 | 0 | 1 | 2 | 3 |
|---|---|---|---|---|---|---|---|
| $y$ | | | | | | 8 | |

   c  $y = x^2 - 2x$

| $x$ | -3 | -2 | -1 | 0 | 1 | 2 | 3 |
|---|---|---|---|---|---|---|---|
| $x^2$ | 9 | | | | | 4 | |
| $-2x$ | 6 | | | | | -4 | |
| $y$ | 15 | | | | | 0 | |

   d  $y = 5 - x^2$

| $x$ | -3 | -2 | -1 | 0 | 1 | 2 | 3 |
|---|---|---|---|---|---|---|---|
| 5 | 5 | 5 | 5 | 5 | 5 | 5 | 5 |
| $-x^2$ | | | | | | -4 | |
| $y$ | | | | | | 1 | |

2 For each equation given below
   i   Make a table of $x$-values from −4 to +4 and find the corresponding $y$ values.
   ii  Plot your points on a suitably sized set of axes and join them to form a smooth parabola.
   iii Write down the coordinate of the minimum point and the equation of the line of symmetry of
      a  $y = 3x^2 + 2$     b  $y = x^2 + 2x - 1$
      c  $y = x^2 - 4x$      d  $y = (x + 2)(x - 1)$

3 A ball is thrown and its path follows the curve given by the equation $y = 4x - x^2$, where $y$ is the height, in metres, and $x$ is the time from release, in seconds. Using a graph, find the height reached by the ball and the time taken for it to return to the ground.

4 ☆ CHALLENGE ☆

Plot the curve $y = x^2 + 5x + 6$ and write down the coordinates of the points where the graph intersects the $x$-axis. Now solve $x^2 + 5x + 6 = 0$. What do you notice? Why? Repeat with the curves:

$$y = x^2 - 7x + 12 \qquad y = 2x^2 - x - 1 \qquad y = x^2 - 3x - 1$$

5 **RICH TASK**

Parabolas have either a maximum or a minimum point. By investigating quadratic graphs, try to find a rule for whether an equation will give a maximum or a minimum point. How would you describe the shape of each type of graph?

Unit C

- Apply to the quadratic graph $y = f(x)$ the transformations $f(x) + a$ and $f(x + a)$

→ **The function notation $f(x) = \ldots$ is sometimes used instead of $y = \ldots$ as it makes it easier to keep track of the values of inputs and outputs.**

If $f(x) = x^2 - 1$ then $f(3) = 3^2 - 1 = 8$ and $f(-2) = (-2)^2 - 1 = 4 - 1 = 3$

**EXAMPLE**

Given that $f(x) = x^2$, plot this function together with $y = f(x) + 2$ and $y = f(x) - 1$. Describe how $f(x)$ has been transformed.

**ANSWER**

$f(x) = x^2$ First plot $y = x^2$ ( in red)
$f(x) + 2 = x^2 + 2$
Now plot $y = x^2 + 2$ (in green)

$y = f(x - 1) = x^2 - 1$         Now plot $y = x^2 - 1$(in blue)

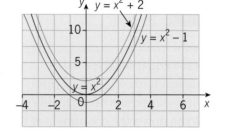

$y = f(x) + 2$ is a **translation** of $f(x)$ by 2 units upwards, or $\begin{pmatrix} 0 \\ 2 \end{pmatrix}$.

$f(x) - 1$ is a translation of $f(x)$ by 1 unit downwards, or $\begin{pmatrix} 0 \\ -1 \end{pmatrix}$.

p. 372

→ **In general, $y = f(x) + a$ represents a translation of $y = f(x)$ through $\begin{pmatrix} 0 \\ a \end{pmatrix}$.**

p. 181

## RICH TASK

Again taking $f(x) = x^2$, plot the functions
$y = f(x + 3)$ and $y = f(x - 4)$. Use the same axes as shown.
Describe how $y = f(x)$ has been transformed.
Can you describe the effect of $y = f(x + a)$?

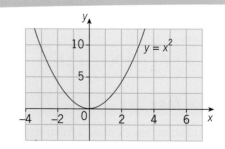

→ **In general, $y = f(x + a)$ represents a translation of $y = f(x)$ through $\begin{pmatrix} -a \\ 0 \end{pmatrix}$.**

## Exercise C21.2

1   a   On one set of axes, plot the graphs $y = x^2$, $y = x^2 + 3$ and $y = x^2 - 2$.
    b   Describe, using a column vector, the translation from $y = x^2$
        to $y = x^2 + 3$ and also $y = x^2$ to $y = x^2 - 2$.

2   Repeat question 1 for $y = x^2$, $y = (x + 1)^2$ and $y = (x - 2)^2$.

3   Copy the following function machine, changing each ? for a value.

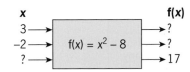

4   Given that $f(x) = x^2 + 4x + 5$, find the following values.
    a   $f(2)$      b   $f(4)$      c   $f(-3)$
    d   the values of $x$ for which $f(x) = 10$

5   Match the following graphs with their equations and, for the graph left over,
    write down its equation.

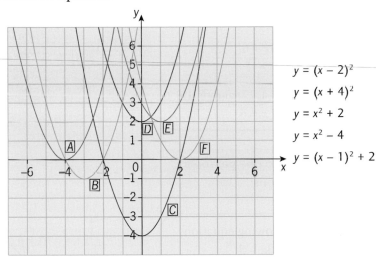

$y = (x - 2)^2$

$y = (x + 4)^2$

$y = x^2 + 2$

$y = x^2 - 4$

$y = (x - 1)^2 + 2$

*6   Given that $f(x) = x^2$, write each equation given in question 5 using
    function notation. Describe the transformation from $f(x)$ to each equation.

7   ☆ **CHALLENGE** ☆

> Using hand-drawn graphs or a computer graph package if available,
> investigate the transformations $y = af(x)$ and $y = f(ax)$, given that
> $f(x) = x^2$.

# Solving quadratic equations by graph

- Find approximate solutions of quadratic functions

## RICH TASK

I think of a number, subtract 2, square this and add 4. This gives me the same answer as when I add 5 to my original number.
Show, using graphs, that there are two possible starting numbers.
What if I add 6 instead of 5 to my original number: are there still two solutions? Investigate how the size of the number I add alters how many solutions I get.

→ **Quadratic equations can be approximately solved graphically.**

**EXAMPLE**

Solve the following equations graphically.
a $x^2 - 5x + 6 = 0$      b $x^2 - 5x + 6 = 12$

**ANSWER**

a Plot $y = x^2 - 5x + 6$ and $y = 0$

  Intersection $(2, 0)$ and $(3, 0)$
  So $x = 2$ and $x = 3$

b Plot $y = x^2 - 5x + 6$ and $y = 12$

  Intersection $(-1, 12)$ and $(6, 12)$
  So $x = -1$ and $x = 6$

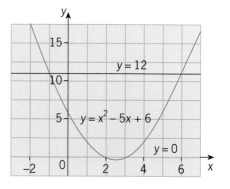

→ **Plotting a parabola accurately takes time so one parabola can be used to solve several related equations.**

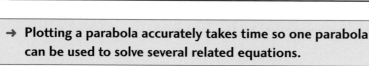

**EXAMPLE**

Using the graph $f(x) = x^2 - 4x + 3$, solve the following equations.
a $x^2 - 4x + 3 = x - 1$      b $x^2 - 2x + 2 = 3x - 3$

**ANSWER**

a Plot $y = x - 1$ in addition

b $x^2 - 2x + 2 = 3x - 3$
  Rearrange to include $x^2 - 4x + 3$
  $x^2 - 4x + 3 = x - 2$
  Plot $y = x - 2$ in addition

a Intersection $(1, 0)$ and $(4, 3)$

  So $x = 1$ and $x = 4$

b Intersection $\approx (1.4, -0.6)$ and $(3.6, 1.6)$

  So $x \approx 1.4$ and $x \approx 3.6$

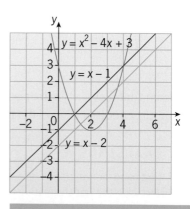

All of the equations contain $x$ as the variable so you need to state the values of $x$ as your solutions, not $y$.

1 Use the graphs to find approximate solutions of
   these equations.
   a $x^2 - 2x - 3 = 2$  b $x^2 - 2x - 3 = -3$
   c $x^2 - 2x - 3 = 0$  d $x^2 - 2x - 3 = x + 1$

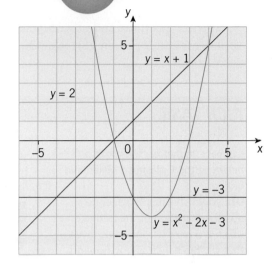

2 a Use the table of values to plot $y = x^2 - x - 6$.
   b By adding appropriate lines to your graph, find the
     approximate solutions of
     i $x^2 - x - 6 = 0$  ii $x^2 - x - 6 = 3$
     iii $x^2 - x - 6 = -4$  iv $x^2 = x + 6$

| $x$ | –3 | –2 | –1 | 0 | 1 | 2 | 3 | 4 |
|-----|----|----|----|---|----|---|---|---|
| $x^2$ |  |  |  |  | 1 |  |  |  |
| $-x$ |  |  |  |  | –1 |  |  |  |
| –6 |  |  |  |  | –6 |  |  |  |
| $y$ |  |  |  |  | –6 |  |  |  |

3 Use the graphs to find approximate solutions to
   these equations.
   a $x^2 + 2x - 3 = 0$  b $x^2 + 2x - 3 = x + 1$
   c $x^2 + 2x - 5 = 0$  d $x^2 + x = 0$

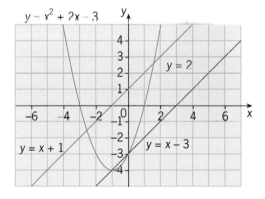

4 Which graph, if any, would you need to add to the grid in
   question 3 in order to solve each of these equations?
   a $x^2 + 2x = 3$  b $x^2 + x = 5$  c $x^2 + x - 2 = 0$

5 ☆ CHALLENGE ☆

   Draw the graph $f(x) = 2^x$ for $-4 \leq x \leq 4$ and use your graph to solve
   the following equations.

   a $2^x = 3$  b $2^x = x^2$  c $2^x + 4x = 2$

Unit C

# Real-life quadratic graphs

- Construct quadratic and other functions from real-life problems and plot their corresponding graphs

### RICH TASK

Estimate, in metres, the width and height of the Gateshead Millennium bridge.
Use your estimates to generate a possible equation of the bridge, which is a parabola in shape, given that $y$ is the height and $x$ the width.

**EXAMPLE**

The path of a shot as it is put can be modelled using the equation $y = 2x - \frac{1}{5}x^2$, where $x$ is the horizontal distance and $y$ is the vertical distance from the point of release.

**a** Plot the path of the shot.

**b** Use your graph to determine the height and distance achieved in this throw.

**ANSWER**

**a**

| $x$ | 0 | 2 | 4 | 6 | 8 | 10 |
|---|---|---|---|---|---|---|
| $2x$ | 0 | 4 | 8 | 12 | 16 | 20 |
| $-\frac{1}{5}x^2$ | 0 | $-\frac{4}{5}$ | $-3\frac{1}{5}$ | $-7\frac{1}{5}$ | $-12\frac{4}{5}$ | $-20$ |
| $y$ | 0 | $3\frac{1}{5}$ | $4\frac{4}{5}$ | $4\frac{4}{5}$ | $3\frac{1}{5}$ | 0 |

You need about seven points to plot a parabola.

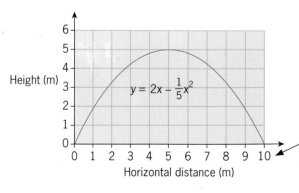

$y = 2x - \frac{1}{5}x^2$

Height (m)

Horizontal distance (m)

Label each axis with the quantities that it represents in real life.

**b** The shot reaches a height of 5 metres. The shot travels a distance of 10 metres.

## Exercise C21.4

1 A ball is thrown in the air. Its height, $y$ metres, after $x$ seconds is given by the equation $y = 25x - 5x^2$.

  a By copying and completing the table, plot a graph to show the path of the ball over five seconds.

  b Find the coordinates of the highest point of your graph and explain what this means in real life.

  c When does the ball hit the ground?

  d If we let $x = 10$ then $y$ is $-250$. Explain why this is impossible in real life.

| x | 0 | 1 | 2 | 3 | 4 | 5 |
|-----|---|---|---|-----|---|---|
| 25x | | | | | | |
| −5x² | | | | −45 | | |
| y | | | | | | |

2 A satellite dish at the University of Saskatchewan in Canada controls a satellite launched in 1995. Its cross-section is a parabola in shape and given by the equation $y = \frac{1}{45}(x^2 - 81)$.

  a Using values of $x$ from $-11$ to $+11$, plot the cross-section of the satellite dish.

  b The dish is 22 metres wide. How deep is it?

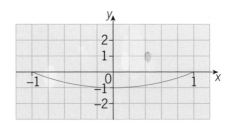

**DID YOU KNOW...?**

The Ben-Gurion National Solar Energy centre in Israel houses the largest solar dish whose cross-section is parabolic in shape. This can produce clean, renewable energy.

3 A rectangular conservatory is being built on a house. The base walls of the conservatory have a total length of 50 metres.

House

  a If the width of the conservatory is $x$ metres, write an expression using $x$ for its length.

  b If $y$ is the area of the conservatory, write an equation for $y$ in terms of $x$.

  c Use your answer to part b to plot a graph of area $y$ against width $x$.

  d Use your graph to find the largest possible area of this conservatory and explain why, in real life, a homeowner may wish to maximise area.

4 ☆ **CHALLENGE** ☆

The graph shows the cross-section of a large umbrella. Find the equation of this cross-section and explain the measurements used on each axis.

Real-life quadratic graphs

# Summary and assessment

## CHECK OUT

You should now be able to
- draw graphs of quadratic functions and use graphs to solve linear and quadratic equations simultaneously
- transform functions
- draw and interpret real-life quadratic graphs.

### Exam-style question

**a** Draw the graph of $y = x^2 - 5x + 3$ for $0 \le x \le 5$.

**b** On the same graph draw the line $y = x - 3$

**c** Explain why you can use your graphs to solve $x^2 - 6x + 6 = 0$

**Lin's answer:**

a&b

| x | 0 | 1 | 2 | 2.5 | 3 | 4 | 5 |
|---|---|---|---|-----|---|---|---|
| y | 3 | −1 | −3 | −3.25 | −3 | −1 | 3 |

Use a table to find points to plot.

A quadratic will not have a straight line joining points: work out the middle value if needed.

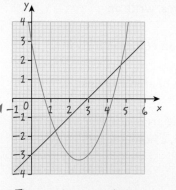

Plot points and join with a curve, not straight lines.

c The graphs cross when
$y = x^2 - 5x + 3$
and $y = x - 3$ meet; that is when
$x^2 - 5x + 3 = x - 3$
and rearranging gives
$x^2 - 5x - x + 3 + 3 = 0$
$x^2 - 6x + 6 = 0$ as required

An explanation can sometimes mean showing maths calculations.

## Exam practice

1  The diagram shows the graph of the function $y = f(x)$

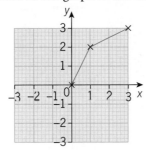

Sketch the following functions.    a  $y = f(x + 2)$    b  $y = 2f(x)$

*(2 marks)*

2  A jet of water from a fountain follows a path that can be
described by the equation

$$y = 2 + 3x - \frac{3}{4}x^2$$

where $y$ is the height of the water above ground level and $x$ is the
distance of the water jet from the fountain.

a  Draw the graph of $y = 2 + 3x - \frac{3}{4}x^2$ for $0 \leq x \leq 5$

b  The fountain is 2 m above ground level. The water jet lands in a pool whose
surface is 1·5 m below the level of the fountain.
On the same diagram, draw a suitable line and use your graph to estimate
how far from the fountain the jet lands in the pool.

*(6 marks)*

*3  The stopping distance of a car can be estimated using the formula $y = \frac{x^2}{25} + \frac{3x}{25}$
where $y$ is the stopping distance in metres and $x$ is the speed of the car in km/h.

The table gives stopping distance for speeds up to 50 km/h.

| x | 0 | 10 | 20 | 30 | 40 | 50 |
|---|---|----|----|----|----|----|
| y | 0 | 5·2 | 18·4 | 39·6 | 68·8 | 106 |

a  Draw the graph of $y = \frac{x^2}{25} + \frac{3x}{25}$ for speeds up to 50 km/h.

b  Use your graph to estimate the stopping distance for a car travelling at 35 km/h.

c  A driver claimed that he was travelling at 44 km/h.
Skid marks of 80 m were measured on the road.
Is the driver's claim correct? Justify your answer.

*(5 marks)*

# Case study 7: Art

Graffiti artists often sketch their designs before projecting them onto the surface. They sometimes use grids or parts of their body as measuring tools to help them copy the proportions accurately.

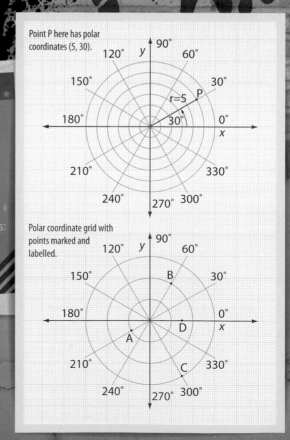

1. A graffiti artist projects an image from a sketchpad of length 20cm and height 14.8cm onto a wall of length 6m.

   a.  What scale factor is being used?
   b.  What is the height of the graffiti wall?

The artist's hand-span is 150mm.

   c.  What are the dimensions of the wall in terms of hands?
   d.  If a 1cm square grid was used in the sketch, what size would the grid squares be on the graffiti wall?
   e.  What effect does the enlargement have on the area of the graffiti image?

## Polar *coordinates* ★ ★ ★ ★

Graffiti designs often involve arcs and spirals. You can plot these on a polar grid using polar coordinates.

Polar coordinates describe the position of a point, **P**, in terms of **r**, the distance P is from the origin and ϑ, the angle that the line **OP** makes with the horizontal axis. **P** has polar coordinates (**r**, ϑ).

2. a. Match points **A**, **B** and **C** with their polar coordinates:
     i. (2, 60)    ii. (1, 210)    iii. (3, 300)

   b. Write down the polar coordinates of point **D**.

Point P here has polar coordinates (5, 30).

Polar coordinate grid with points marked and labelled.

*Plot and label some other points on a polar coordinate grid.*

Crop circles are geometric patterns that are displayed in crop fields. They are often based on circles and spirals.

Polar coordinate grid with red circle and blue spiral.

Circle $r = a$
Spiral $r = 0.025$

90°

180°

0   $a$

270°

3. This diagram shows a circle (red) and a spiral (blue) through 360°

a. What is the radius of the circle?
The circle has an equation of the form $r = a$ where $a$ is a constant.

b. What is the value of $a$?
The radius of the spiral increases by 0.025 units every degree.

c. How many units does the radius increase by in total?
The spiral has an equation of the form $r = k\theta$ where $k$ is a constant.

d. What is the value of $k$?

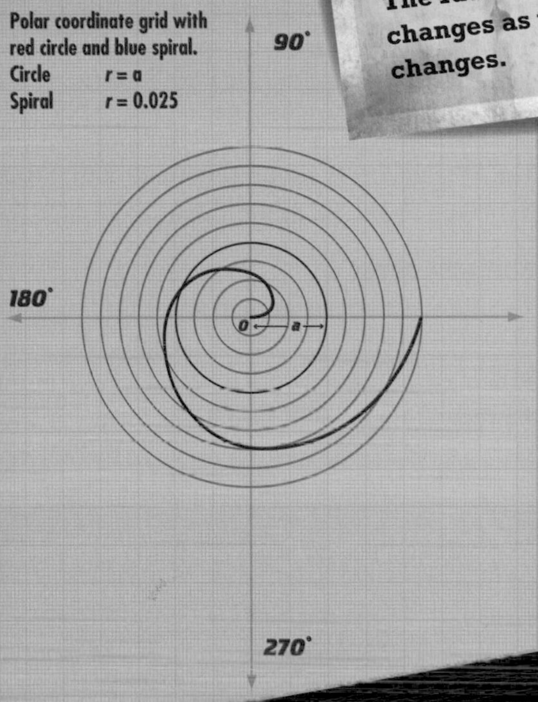

4. Use a polar coordinate grid to sketch

a. a circle with the equation $r = 5$

b. a semi-circle (starting at 90°) with equation $r = 3$

c. a spiral, starting at the origin, with equation $r = 0.01\theta$

This crop circle was found in Wiltshire in 2006.

5. Which parts of the design are based on
   a. a circle
   b. a spiral?

Explain your answers, referring to the radii.

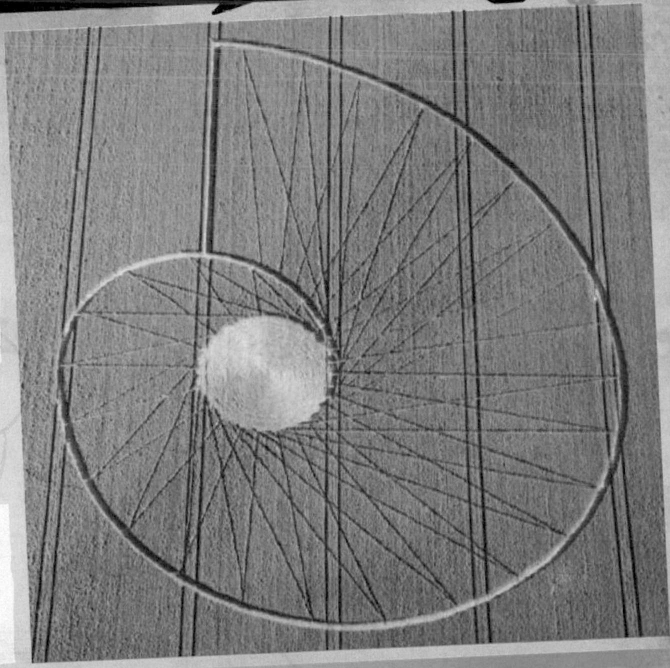

Study some photos of crop circles.

What geometric shapes do they contain?

CREATE YOUR OWN CROP CIRCLE DESIGNS WITH SPIRALS AND ARCS USING A POLAR GRID.

327

# 22 Everyday arithmetic and bounds

## INTRODUCTION

The M32 galaxy is about 22 000 000 000 000 000 000 km from Earth. The light from that galaxy has taken about 2.3 million years to reach Earth, so we are effectively looking back in time!

**What's the point?**

The numbers are so large in space that they are often measured in terms of how far light travels in a year. This is called a light year.

When astronomers work with such large numbers they need a much handier way of expressing them. Standard index form was invented so that a number like the distance of the M32 galaxy can be written down in the much more useful form of $2.2 \times 10^{19}$ km.

## CHECK IN

1 Write notes to show how you could carry out these additions and subtractions mentally.

   a  $23 + 97$     b  $234 - 96$     c  $46 + 44$     d  $973 - 708$

2 Show how you could use a column method to work these out.

   a  $3775 + 663$     b  $2886 - 909$     c  $3775 - 2918$     d  $5549 + 8675$

3 Write notes to show how you could carry out these multiplications and divisions mentally.

   a  $21 \times 7$     b  $101 \times 15$     c  $8320 \div 8$     d  $7350 \div 21$

4 Show how you can calculate these multiplications and divisions using a written method.

   a  $325 \times 36$     b  $4356 \times 18$     c  $3485 \div 17$     d  $889 \times 76$

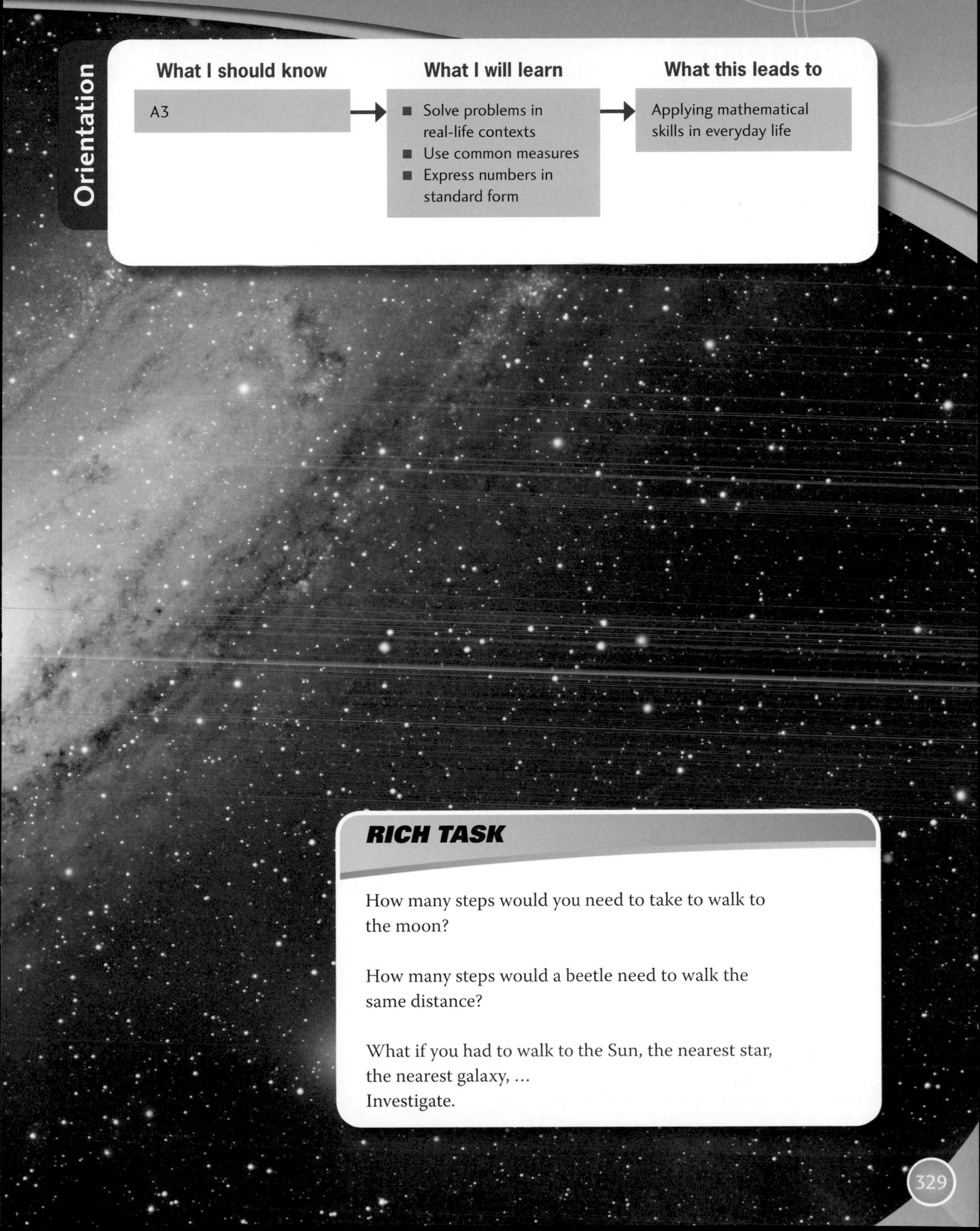

Orientation

| What I should know | What I will learn | What this leads to |
| --- | --- | --- |
| A3 | ■ Solve problems in real-life contexts<br>■ Use common measures<br>■ Express numbers in standard form | Applying mathematical skills in everyday life |

## RICH TASK

How many steps would you need to take to walk to the moon?

How many steps would a beetle need to walk the same distance?

What if you had to walk to the Sun, the nearest star, the nearest galaxy, …
Investigate.

# Using formulae

- Explore and solve problems in real-life contexts

## RICH TASK

Two different formulae are proposed to calculate the required child's dosage for a medicine.

$$\text{Child dose} = \frac{\text{Age (years)} \times \text{adult dose}}{\text{Age (years)} + 12} \qquad \text{Child dose} = \frac{\text{Age (months)} \times \text{adult dose}}{150}$$

Suppose you prescribed medicine for a 6-year-old, where the adult dose is 30 mg. Will it make any difference which formula you use?
Suppose the child was aged 10 years, what difference will there be?
Try some other ages – can you find the age of the child for which there is no difference?

Medicine Bottle

**Formulae** are used in everyday life.

One formula you may be familiar with is changing temperature in °F to °C.

p. 96

$$C = \frac{5}{9}(F - 32)$$

You may need this to convert cooking temperatures from old recipe books.

Other formulae include those used to calculate interest on savings or money borrowed.

$$A = P\left(1 + \frac{r}{n}\right)^{nt}$$

You may need these if you want to borrow money to buy a car.

## EXAMPLE

Davina is making a circuit for her amplifier.
She puts two resistors in parallel in the circuit.
The total resistance for two resistors in parallel is found using the formula

$$R_{\text{Total}} = \frac{R_1 \times R_2}{R_1 + R_2}$$

$R_1$ is the value of one resistor
$R_2$ the value of the other resistor

Calculate the total resistance in Davina's circuit if she uses resistors with values 1.5 ohms and 2.2 ohms.

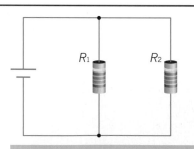

The units of resistance are ohms.

### ANSWER

$$R_{\text{Total}} = \frac{1.5 \times 2.2}{1.5 + 2.2} = \frac{3.3}{3.7} = 0.89189\ldots$$

The total resistance is 0.89 ohms to 2 d.p.

## ☆ PROBLEM ☆

Another formula for two resistors in parallel is

$$\frac{1}{R_T} = \frac{1}{R_1} + \frac{1}{R_2}$$

Convince a partner that the formulae

$\frac{1}{R_T} = \frac{1}{R_1} + \frac{1}{R_2}$ and $R_T = \frac{R_1 \times R_2}{R_1 + R_2}$ are the same.

## Exercise C22.1

MEDIUM

1 a A formula for changing degrees Fahrenheit (°F) into degrees Celsius (°C) is

$$C = (F - 32) \times \frac{5}{9}$$

Calculate the temperature in °C for a temperature in °F of
**i** 40°  **ii** 98.4°  **iii** 30°

b A formula for changing °C into °F is

$$F = \frac{9}{5} \times C + 32$$

Calculate the temperature in °F for a temperature in °C of
**i** 22°  **ii** −5°  **iii** −2°

**REMEMBER:**

| | |
|---|---|
| 1 stone | = 14 pounds |
| 2.2 pounds | = 1 kilogram |
| 1 foot | = 12 inches |
| 1 inch | = 2.54 centimetres |

\* 2 The formula to calculate a person's body mass index (BMI) is

$$BMI = \frac{m}{h^2} \qquad \text{where } m \text{ is the person's mass in kilograms}$$
$$h \text{ is the person's height in metres.}$$

To be healthy the BMI should be in the range
19–25.

John is 5 feet 9 inches tall and his mass is $12\frac{1}{2}$ stones.
To estimate his BMI John just doubles his mass in pounds.

Calculate John's BMI using the formula and show how John's method
puts him in the healthy range, when his true BMI is not healthy.

3 ☆ CHALLENGE ☆

A formula to calculate a child's medicine dose based on the child's
body surface area (BSA) is

$$\text{Child dose} = \frac{BSA}{1.7} \times \text{adult dose}$$

a Calculate the child dose for a child with BSA = 0.67
where the adult dose is 40 mg.

A formula to calculate BSA is given by
$$BSA = W^{0.5} \times H^{0.42} \times 0.0235$$
where $W$ = weight in kg, $H$ = height in cm.

b A doctor prescribed a 10 mg dose for a child of weight 28 kg and
height 76 cm.
If the adult dose is 35 mg, has the doctor prescribed the correct
dose?

# Everyday arithmetic

- Explore and solve problems that use common measures

Numbers are everywhere: in the media, on the internet, on food packaging and so on. You need to make sense of the information – you won't need all of it!

**EXAMPLE**

The table gives the guideline daily amounts of calories needed by boys and girls of different ages.

| Gender \ Age | 11 – 14 | 15 – 18 | Adult |
|---|---|---|---|
| Male | 2220 | 2750 | 2550 |
| Female | 1845 | 2110 | 1940 |

You burn 750 calories for each hour of exercise.
You lose one pound of fat for each 3500 calories burnt.

Alex takes in an average 3050 calories each day.
How long does Alex need to exercise each day if
i   Alex is a 21-year-old man and doesn't wish to lose any weight
ii  Alex is a 17-year-old girl and wants to lose $\frac{1}{2}$ pound of fat each day?

**ANSWER**

i   A male aged 21 needs 2550 calories.
   $3050 - 2550 = 500$
   500 extra calories need to be burnt to maintain weight.
   $500 \div 750 = \frac{2}{3}$ of an hour     $\frac{2}{3}$ of 60 = 40 minutes
   Alex needs to do 40 minutes exercise each day.

ii  A female aged 17 needs 2110 calories.
   $3050 - 2110 = 940$
   Alex wants to lose $\frac{1}{2}$ lb of fat daily     $\frac{1}{2}$ of 3500 = 1750
   Alex needs to burn an extra $1750 + 940 = 2690$ calories each day.

   $2690 \div 750 = 3.586...$       $0.586... \times 60 = 35.2$ minutes
   Alex needs to do 3 hours 35 minutes exercise each day.

A sensible answer here would be around $3\frac{1}{2}$ hours.

| When answering problems involving everyday arithmetic | |
|---|---|
| • Read the question twice | work out what you need to do |
| • Perform one step at a time | you cannot always go directly to an answer |
| • Use the numbers in the question | rounding at the start often leads to errors |
| • Avoid rounding intermediate answers | if you have a calculator |
| • Give your final answer to a sensible degree of accuracy | look at the numbers you started with |
| • Use sensible units | relate back to the problem |

## Exercise C22.2

MEDIUM LOW

1   Josh painted his bedroom.

Write down the three missing values in his paint bill.

2   Prices in a shop are given on the price tag in two currencies, pounds and euros.
A handbag is priced as £39 and €55; a pair of shoes is priced as £64 and €90.
What exchange rate is being used?

| Purchase No: 1 | | Red: 22 |
|---|---|---|
| **Name of Item** | **Unit price** | **Amount** |
| 4 tins silk emulsion | @ £18.99 | £ _____ |
| _____ tins gloss | @ £ 8.50 | £ _____ |
| | Total | £ 101.46 |

3   A pair of jeans is priced at €125 in Paris.
The identical jeans are priced at $180 in New York and £110 in London.
On a day when the exchange rates are £1 = €1.15 and £1 = $1.75, which place is the cheapest to purchase the jeans?

4   ☆ PROBLEM ☆

San Francisco uses Pacific Daylight Time (PDT).
PDT is eight hours behind British Summer Time (BST).
A flight leaves London on Monday at 11:15 BST and arrives in San Francisco at 14:00 PDT the same day.
On the return flight to London, a tail wind means that the flight time is one hour less.
The return flight leaves San Francisco on Tuesday at 15:40 PDT.
What time does the flight arrive in London?

5   **RICH TASK**

Is it possible to celebrate New Year in two different capital cities on the same night?
If you leave London after the midnight celebration, would you be able to arrive in a different country before midnight to celebrate New Year again?

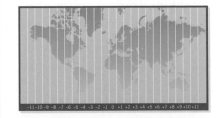

- Explore and solve problems that use compound measures

## ☆ PROBLEM ☆

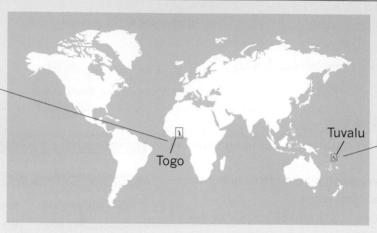

Togo has an area of 21 853 square miles, and the population was 6 762 000 people in 2009.

Tuvalu

The Tuvalu islands cover 9.9 square miles, and had a population of 9810 people in 2009.

Togo

Which place is more crowded?

You can use **compound measures**, such as speed, density and rates, to make comparisons.

**EXAMPLE**

Gareth and Eric drive 150 miles in separate cars. Gareth begins the journey 30 minutes after Eric. Eric travels at an average speed of 50 miles per hour.
How fast does Gareth need to go to arrive at the same time as Eric?

**ANSWER**

$$\text{Speed} = \frac{\text{distance}}{\text{time}}$$

$$50 = \frac{150}{\text{time}} \quad \Rightarrow \quad \text{Time taken} = \frac{150}{50} = 3 \text{ hours}$$

$3$ hours $- 30$ minutes $= 2\frac{1}{2}$ hours $\quad 150 \div 2\frac{1}{2} = 60$

Gareth needs to travel at an average speed of 60 miles per hour.

## RICH TASK

Imagine identical-sized boxes, one filled with marshmallows and the other filled with sugar. Which box is heavier?

Density compares mass with volume.

→ Density = $\frac{\text{mass}}{\text{volume}}$

a  Work out the density of a 3 kg lump of metal with volume 1.5 m³.

b  Work out the density of a pane of glass weighing 1.8 kg with a volume 6000 cm³.

c  The density of cork is 0.25 g/cm³. Find the volume of a piece of cork with mass 110 g.

ANSWER

a  Density = $\frac{m}{v} = \frac{3}{1.5} = 2$ kg/m³

b  1.8 kg = 18 000 g

   Density = $\frac{18\,000}{6000} = 3$ g/cm³

c  $V = \frac{m}{d} = \frac{110}{0.25}$

   = 440 cm³

### Exercise C22.3

MEDIUM

1  a  Work out the average speed of a cyclist riding
      i   48 km in 2 hours 30 minutes    ii   30 km in 1 hour 45 minutes.
   b  Work out the average speed of a car travelling
      i   100 miles in 1 hour 15 minutes  ii  60 miles in 50 minutes.

2  What is the average speed of a runner who runs
   a  a marathon (26 miles) in 3 hours 30 minutes
   b  a half-marathon (13 miles) in 2 hours 40 minutes?

3  The winner of the 2006 Tour De France completed the 3639 km course in 89 hours 39 minutes. What was his average speed?

4  A cheetah runs at a speed of 120 km per hour. At this speed how far does it go in 2 minutes?

5  a  Work out the volume of a gold bar with volume 0.6 m³ (the density of gold is 19 300 kg/m³).
   b  The density of sunflower oil is 0.92 g/cm³. What is the mass of 2 litres of oil?

6  Armenia had a population of 2 967 004 in 2009, and covers an area of 11 484 square miles. What was the population density of Armenia in 2009?

Armenia

7  Water drips out of a tap at the rate of 2 ml per second. How long does it take before 5 litres of water are lost?

# Standard form

- Explore and solve problems that use standard form

## ☆ PROBLEM ☆

Tom builds two electric circuits.
In one circuit there is a capacitor of 40 nanofarads and a resistor of 10 ohms. In the other circuit the capacitor is 2 microfarads and the resistor 1 mega ohm.
Which circuit has the greater capacitor?
Which one has the greater resistance?

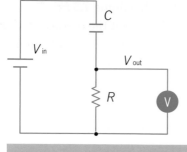

→ **A number in standard form is written as $A \times 10^n$**
   **where $1 \le A < 10$**
→ **To write a number in standard form,**
   - **write as a number between 1 and 10 (this is $A$)**
   - **multiply by a power of 10 (this is $n$).**

You should know the **decimal system** as powers of 10, for large numbers:

| | |
|---|---|
| 10 | $= 10^1$ |
| 100 | $= 10^2$ |
| 1000 | $= 10^3$ |
| 10 000 | $= 10^4$ |
| 100 000 | $= 10^5$ |
| 1 000 000 | $= 10^6$ |

Also for small numbers:

| | |
|---|---|
| 1 | $= 10^0$ |
| 0.1 | $= 10^{-1}$ |
| 0.01 | $= 10^{-2}$ |
| 0.001 | $= 10^{-3}$ |
| 0.000 1 | $= 10^{-4}$ |
| 0.000 01 | $= 10^{-5}$ |

**EXAMPLE**

Write these numbers in standard form.
**a**  2 300 000          **b**  5006          **c**  0.000 435

**ANSWER**

**a**  $2 300 000 = 2.3 \times 10^6$          $10^6 = 1 000 000$
**b**  $5006 = 5.006 \times 10^3$          $10^3 = 1000$
**c**  $0.000 435 = 4.35 \times 10^{-4}$          $10^{-4} = 0.0001$

**EXAMPLE**

Write these as normal numbers.
**a**  $1.47 \times 10^8$          **b**  $6.05 \times 10^{-5}$

**ANSWER**

**a**  $1.47 \times 10^8 = 147 000 000$          **b**  $6.05 \times 10^{-5} = 0.000 060 5$

Many quantities in science involve numbers in standard form.

**EXAMPLE**

The diameter of Venus is $1.2 \times 10^4$ km.
The diameter of Saturn is $1.2 \times 10^5$ km.
Which planet has the larger diameter and by how much?

**ANSWER**

The larger the power of 10 the larger the number, so Saturn is bigger. Saturn has diameter 10 times bigger than Venus.

## Exercise C22.4

**MEDIUM HIGH**

1 Which of these numbers are given in standard form?
  a  $2.3 \times 10^3$      b  $12 \times 10^3$      c  $9.998 \times 10^4$
  d  $0.1 \times 10^7$      e  $1.002 \times 10^2$    f  $4 \times 10^{-2}$

> The first number must be between 1 and 10.

2 Write these as normal numbers.
  a  $4.7 \times 10^3$      b  $2.3 \times 10^8$      c  $7.9 \times 10^{-5}$
  d  $1.25 \times 10^4$     e  $2.05 \times 10^5$     f  $4.9 \times 10^{-6}$
  g  $9.02 \times 10^{-3}$  h  $7 \times 10^{-6}$

3 Write these numbers in standard form.
  a  56 000              b  8 700 000           c  5503
  d  100 000             e  0.004               f  0.0056
  g  0.000 002 04        h  500 006

4 The speed of light is 300 million m/s.
  Write this as a number in standard form.

5 The diameter of the sun is $8.65 \times 10^5$ miles.
  Write this as a normal number.

6 How many seconds are there in
  a  one hour           b  one day?
  Write your answers in standard form.

7 Write these fractions in standard form.
  a  $\dfrac{1}{50\,000}$         b  $\dfrac{1}{4000}$

  c  $\dfrac{1}{25\,000}$         d  $\dfrac{1}{10\,000\,000}$

8 ☆ **PROBLEM** ☆

> The American value for a billion is $1 \times 10^9$.
> The British value for a billion is $1 \times 10^{12}$.
> How many times smaller is an American billion than a British billion?

*9 Explain how you can know that $8.9 \times 10^6$ is smaller than $1.2 \times 10^7$
  without writing out the normal numbers.

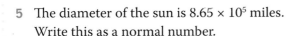
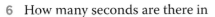

# Calculations in standard form

- Calculate with standard index form

## ☆ PROBLEM ☆

Supan is building an electronic circuit with a time delay switch.
He uses a formula:
Time delay = 0.7 x $R$ x $C$
where $R$ is resistance in ohms, $C$ is capacity in farads.
a What is the time delay for a circuit with
$R = 4 \times 10^4$ ohms and $C = 9 \times 10^{-5}$ farads?
Suppose the time delay needs to be 5 seconds.
b What value resistance would Supan use if he were to keep the
same capacity?
c What value capacitance would Supan use if he were to keep the
same resistance?

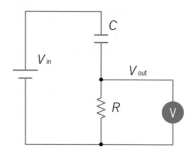

You can multiply and divide in standard form.

p. 228

$(3.7 \times 10^4) \times (2.2 \times 10^6)$ $=$ $3.7 \times 2.2 \times 10^{4+6} = 8.14 \times 10^{10}$

$(3 \times 10^2) \times (6 \times 10^{-7})$ $=$ $3 \times 6 \times 10^{2+-7} = 18 \times 10^{-5}$
$=$ $1.8 \times 10^{-4}$

Use the rules of indices.

$(7.2 \times 10^2) \div (3 \times 10^5)$ $=$ $7.2 \div 3 \times 10^{2-5} = 2.4 \times 10^{-3}$

$(6 \times 10^5) \div (2 \times 10^{-6})$ $=$ $6 \div 2 \times 10^{5--6} = 3 \times 10^{11}$

You can also add and subtract in standard form.

$(6 \times 10^5) + (3 \times 10^4)$ $=$ $(6 \times 10^5) + (0.3 \times 10^5)$
$=$ $6.3 \times 10^5$

$(4.7 \times 10^5) - (8 \times 10^3)$ $=$ $(4.7 \times 10^5) - (0.08 \times 10^5)$
$=$ $4.62 \times 10^5$

Write the numbers with the
same power of 10.

$(1.6 \times 10^4) - (9 \times 10^3)$ $=$ $(1.6 \times 10^4) - (0.9 \times 10^4)$
$=$ $0.7 \times 10^4 = 7 \times 10^3$

You can use a calculator for standard form.

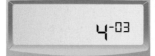

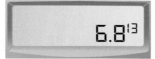

Use the [EXP] or [E] key on
your calculator.

$4 \times 10^{-3}$ can be displayed as $4^{-03}$      $6.8 \times 10^{13}$ can be displayed as $6.8^{13}$

**Everyday arithmetic and bounds**

## Exercise C22.5

1 Work out, giving your answers in standard form.
   a $(4 \times 10^5) \times (2 \times 10^3)$        b $(4 \times 10^5) \times (8 \times 10^2)$
   c $(7.5 \times 10^4) \times (2 \times 10^6)$       d $(6.5 \times 10^2) \times (3 \times 10^{-6})$
   e $(7 \times 10^{-5}) \times (5 \times 10^4)$       f $(6 \times 10^{-4}) \times (9 \times 10^{-7})$

2 Work out, giving your answers in standard form.
   a $(4 \times 10^5) \div (2 \times 10^3)$        b $(4 \times 10^2) \div (2 \times 10^7)$
   c $(8 \times 10^5) \div (5 \times 10^{-3})$       d $(6 \times 10^{-5}) : (2 \times 10^{-4})$
   e $(3 \times 10^5) \div (6 \times 10^3)$       f $(1.2 \times 10^{-5}) \div (3 \times 10^9)$

3 Work out, without a calculator, giving your answers in standard form.
   a $\sqrt{9 \times 10^8}$        b $\sqrt{4 \times 10^6}$
   c $\sqrt{2.5 \times 10^9}$       d $\sqrt{9 \times 10^{-8}}$

4 Work out, giving your answers in standard form.
   a $(4 \times 10^5) + (4 \times 10^4)$        b $(5.7 \times 10^5) + (2 \times 10^3)$
   c $(4.5 \times 10^6) - (2 \times 10^2)$       d $(4.8 \times 10^5) - (4.8 \times 10^4)$
   e $(4 \times 10^2) + (2 \times 10^{-2})$       f $(5.4 \times 10^5) - (2.9 \times 10^5)$

5 a An oxygen atom has a mass of $2.7 \times 10^{-23}$ grams.
     How heavy would 800 oxygen atoms be?
   b The mass of a carbon atom is $2 \times 10^{-23}$ g.
     How many carbon atoms are there in 8 g of carbon?

6 There are $6.02 \times 10^{23}$ atoms in 1 gram of hydrogen.
   a Find the number of atoms in 10 kg of hydrogen.
   b Helium atoms weigh twice as much as hydrogen atoms.
     How many atoms are there in one gram of helium?

7 The diameter of the moon is $3.5 \times 10^3$ km.
   a The diameter of the sun is 400 times the diameter of the moon.
     Work out the diameter of the sun.
     Give your answer in standard form.
   b The diameter of the earth is $1.3 \times 10^4$ km.
     How many times smaller is the diameter of the moon than the diameter of the earth?

- Recognise limitations in the accuracy of data and measurements

## ☆ PROBLEM ☆

These are the distances, given to the nearest mile, between junctions on a motorway.

A car's instruments indicate that there is 27 miles of fuel remaining in the tank as the car passes junction 17.
The next service station is at junction 11.
Is it possible that the car will reach the service station before the fuel runs out?

Measurements are only as accurate as the measuring instrument you use.
All measurements contain some degree of **error**.

| You can measure with a ruler to the nearest mm. | Kitchen scales measure ingredients to the nearest 5 grams. |

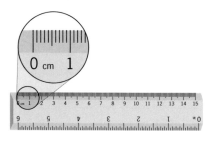

→ **The error in measuring a quantity is $\pm\frac{1}{2}$ of the unit that the measurement is accurate to.**
→ **When measurements are put together, the effect of the error is sometimes increased.**

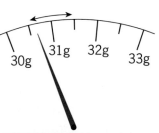

The measurement could be anything from $30\frac{1}{2}g \rightarrow 31\frac{1}{2}g$

**a** Two jugs of water are poured into a bowl. One jug contains 6 litres to the nearest litre, the other jug contains 10 litres to the nearest litre. What are the minimum and maximum amounts of water poured into the bowl?

**b** Two lengths of wood are measured to be 80 cm and 50 cm to the nearest 10 cm. What are the maximum and minimum differences in their length?

**ANSWER**

**a** $6 \pm \frac{1}{2}$ litre:   from 5.5 to 6.5 litres     $10 \pm \frac{1}{2}$ litre:   from 9.5 to 10.5 litres

Maximum 6.5 + 10.5 = 17 litres     Minimum 5.5 + 9.5 = 15 litres

**b** $80 \pm \frac{1}{2} \times 10$ cm;   from 75 to 85 cm     $50 \pm \frac{1}{2} \times 10$ cm;   from 45 to 55 cm

Maximum difference 85 − 45 = 40 cm     Minimum difference 75 − 55 = 20 cm

## Exercise C22.6

MEDIUM HIGH

1   Write down the range of possible values of these measurements.

| | | | | | |
|---|---|---|---|---|---|
| **a** | 28 cm | to the nearest cm | **b** | 48 g | to the nearest gram |
| **c** | 112 g | to the nearest gram | **d** | 560 cm | to the nearest 10 cm |
| **e** | 9350 km | to the nearest 10 km | **f** | 9350 km | to the nearest 50 km |
| **g** | 520 miles | to the nearest 20 miles | **h** | 420 m | to the nearest 10 m |
| **i** | 43.6 s | to the nearest tenth of a second | **j** | 5.2 g | to the nearest tenth of a gram |
| **k** | 7.3 cm | to the nearest tenth of a cm | **l** | 40 m | to the nearest m |

**\*2**   Swinley School had a sports day at the end of the school year.

 **a**   In the high jump competition a distance jumped was recorded as 154 cm to the nearest cm.
 Could the distance jumped have been higher than 1.54 m?
 Explain your answer.

 **b**   The 100 m sprint was won in a time of 16.7 seconds measured to the nearest tenth of a second.
 Between what two values does this time actually lie?

 **c**   In the long jump competition, a distance jumped was recorded as 4.37 m to the nearest cm.
 Could the distance jumped have been longer than 4.37 m?
 Explain your answer.

3   What are the maximum and minimum weights of

 **a**   8 eggs that each weigh 22 g to the nearest gram

 **b**   10 cups that each weigh 240 g to the nearest 10 g

 **c**   6 parcels that each weigh 2500 g to the nearest 100 g?

4   A lift can carry 5 people and a maximum of 350 kg.
 Will it definitely be able to carry 5 people with these weights, all given to the nearest kg:

 65 kg        73 kg        77 kg        64 kg        70 kg

5   Work out the maximum possible difference in the circumferences of two trees measured as 69.2 cm and 41.5 cm, both given to 1 d.p.

Unit C

# Further bounds

- Calculate upper and lower bounds of calculation

### ★ PROBLEM ★

Ali walks at a speed of 2 m/s, given to 1 significant figure.
The distance from home to the station is 540 m to the nearest 10 m.
The train leaves in 5 minutes to the nearest minute.
Is it certain that Ali will catch the train?

Bounds of calculation allow you to work out best or worst case scenarios.

**EXAMPLE**

A hoist can lift 1400 kg, given to 2 significant figures.
A standard packing case weighs 80 kg, to 2 s.f.
How many standard packing cases can the hoist safely lift?

**ANSWER**

1400 to 2 s.f.     ⇨     range 1350 to 1450
80 to 2 s.f.     ⇨     range 75 to 85
Divide by the mass of the packing case, and take the worst case scenario:
$1350 \div 85 = 15.8\ldots$
The hoist can safely lift 15 packing cases.

> Think about the context when rounding final answers.

**EXAMPLE**

A square-based cuboid holds a volume of 12 000 cm³
to 2 s.f.
The height of the cuboid is 18 cm to the nearest cm.
What is the maximum length the square could be?

**ANSWER**

$V = x^2 h$            $x^2 = \dfrac{V}{h}$

$V$ ranges from 11 500 to 12 500
$h$ ranges from 17.5 to 18.5
Maximum length:     $V_{max} \div h_{min}$
$x^2 = 12\,500 \div 17.5$     ⇨     $x = \sqrt{714.28}\ldots = 26.7\ldots$
So the maximum length is 27 cm (to nearest cm).

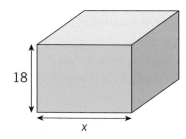

## Exercise C22.7

1   A sack of flour weighs 25 kg measured to the nearest kg.
    It is used to fill bags that contain 500 g of flour measured to the
    nearest 10 g.
    Find the maximum number of bags that could be filled.

2   The length of a running track is 100 m to the nearest metre.
    Andi runs the length of the track.
    Her time is recorded as 23 seconds to the nearest second.
    What is Andi's greatest possible average speed?

3   A lorry is 3.8 m high to the nearest 0.1 m.
    It is driven under a bridge 4.28 m high to the nearest cm.

    a   What is the least possible clearance of the lorry as it
        travels under the bridge?

    The lorry tail lift can carry a safe working load of 1200 kg, to the
    nearest 50 kg.
    It is used to load boxes that weigh 36 kg, to the nearest kg.

    b   What is the maximum number of boxes it can be sure to lift
        safely?

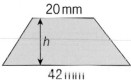

3.8 m

4   A trapezium has area 610 mm² to 2 significant figures.
    It has parallel sides 20 mm and 42 mm, each to the nearest
    millimetre.
    Calculate the lower bound of the height, $h$, of the trapezium.

20 mm

$h$

42 mm

5   In an experiment a toy car is pushed down an incline.
    The toy car travelled 180 cm to the nearest 10 cm, and it took
    7 seconds to the nearest second.
    Work out the maximum average speed of the toy car.

6   **RICH TASK**

    A circular hole has diameter 42 mm.
    A square peg will just fit into the hole.
    Find the length of a side of the square.

## CHECK OUT

You should now be able to
- use arithmetic to solve problems involving measures such as time, money, mass, length, area and volume
- use arithmetic to solve problems involving compound measures such as speed and density
- calculate with standard form
- use error in measurement to solve problems.

### Exam-style question

The load an estate car can safely carry, excluding people, is 300 kg given to the nearest 10 kg.
Potatoes are picked and loaded into 25 kg sacks given to the nearest kg.
What is the maximum number of sacks of potatoes this car can carry?

Think about what calculation you will do.

**Liu's answer:**
To find the number of sacks calculate:
 Load ÷ sacks

To be safe use:

Minimum load the car can carry 300 to nearest 10, minimum is 295
&
Maximum weight of each sack 25 to nearest 1, maximum is 25.5

$295 ÷ 25.5 = 11.56....$

Safe maximum number is 11 sacks

Decide whether you need to work with upper bounds or lower bounds.

Do the calculation.

To be safe, round down, even though the number after the decimal point is 5.

## Exam practice

1   A brand of washing powder costs £4·50 for a 2 kg box. On the box
    is written:

    'Enough powder for 25 washes'

    A new box size is produced to contain enough powder for 30 washes.
    The cost of the new box size is 1p per wash cheaper than the 2 kg box.

    How much is the new box size and what will it cost?
    Show your working.

    (*5 mark*)

2   A light year is approximately $9·46 \times 10^{12}$ km.
    Earth is approximately $1·5 \times 10^{8}$ km from the sun.

    How many light years is Earth from the sun?
    Give your answer in standard form.

    (*2 mark*)

3   A sack of coffee beans weighs 6·5 kg to the nearest 500 g.
    It is used to fill bags that contain 100 g of coffee beans
    measured to the nearest 5 g.

    Find the maximum number of bags that could be filled.

    (*4 mark*)

## INTRODUCTION

Once a right-angled triangle can be seen in a particular situation or problem, a mathematician only needs two pieces of information from which any other lengths or angles can then be calculated. Amongst many other things this allows them to calculate the heights of mountains.

**What's the point?**
Pilots have to learn how to navigate without the use of GPS. They use celestial navigation with the stars as fixed points and calculate the angles that two separate stars make with the horizon. They look up the position of the stars on their charts and then they can use trigonometry to calculate their position. This technique has been used for centuries to enable sailors to navigate across the widest oceans.

## CHECK IN

1 Use Pythagoras' theorem to find the missing side in these triangles.

a

b

c

d

2 Use trigonometry to find the shaded angles in question 1.

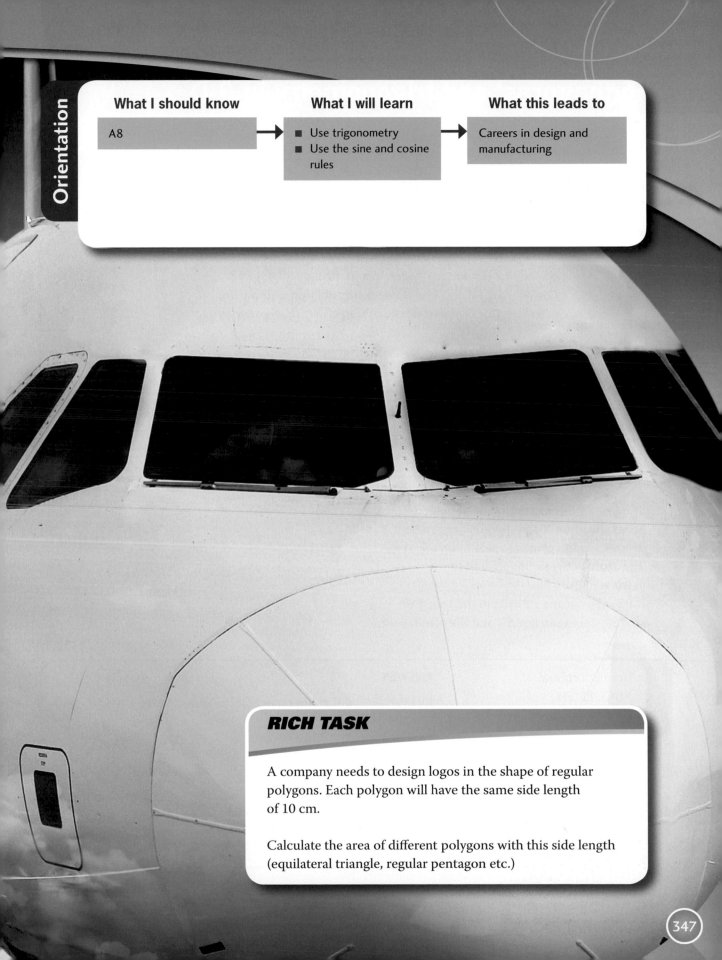

| What I should know | What I will learn | What this leads to |
|---|---|---|
| A8 | ■ Use trigonometry<br>■ Use the sine and cosine rules | Careers in design and manufacturing |

## RICH TASK

A company needs to design logos in the shape of regular polygons. Each polygon will have the same side length of 10 cm.

Calculate the area of different polygons with this side length (equilateral triangle, regular pentagon etc.)

**C23.1**

- Use trigonometry to solve 3-D problems

**p. 124**

In 3-D situations, you can use trigonometry and Pythagoras' theorem when right-angled triangles are involved.

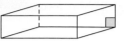

**EXAMPLE**

I stand at point B and see an aircraft landing at airport A.
The angle of elevation of the aircraft from B is 24°.
Find its angle of elevation, $\alpha$, from the airport.

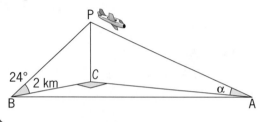

**ANSWER**

In $\triangle BPC$, $\tan 24° = \dfrac{PC}{2}$

So the height of the aircraft,
PC = 2 × tan 24° = 0.89 km
In $\triangle BCA$, $AC^2 = 2.5^2 - 2^2 = 6.25 - 4 = 2.25$
So $AC = \sqrt{2.25} = 1.5$ km

In $\triangle PCA$, $\tan \alpha = \dfrac{PC}{CA} = \dfrac{0.89}{1.5} = 0.593....$

Using [ Inv ] [ tan ], the angle of elevation, $\alpha = 30.7°$

---

The line ST intersects a plane at point S.
From any point P, a perpendicular can be dropped to the plane to meet the plane at P′.
The angle between line ST and the plane is $P\hat{S}P'$.
If PS = 10 cm and PP′ = 3 cm then $\sin P\hat{S}P' = \dfrac{3}{10} = 0.3$
so $P\hat{S}P'$ (between line ST and the plane) = 17.5°

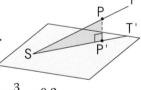

Imagine a light vertically above the plane so that line ST′ is the shadow of line ST and point P′ is the shadow of point P.

---

**EXAMPLE**

Here is a cuboid ABCDEFGH.
Find the length EC to 1 d.p.

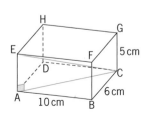

**ANSWER**

Imagine the right-angled triangle ACE.
First find length AC by using Pythagoras on $\triangle ABC$:
$AC^2 = 10^2 + 6^2 = 136$
$AC = \sqrt{136}$
Now find EC using Pythagoras on $\triangle ACE$:
$EC^2 = 5^2 + 136 = 161$
$EC = \sqrt{161} = 12.7$ cm (1 d.p.)

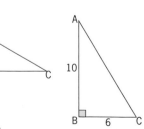

1   A square sports area has a floodlight L
    on top of a pole CL, 8 metres high,
    at corner C.
    Calculate the angle of elevation, α,
    of light L from corner A.

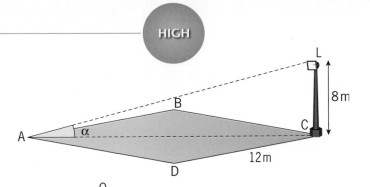

2   A vertical radio mast PQ 30 metres tall is anchored
    by four wires from the midpoint M of the mast
    to the ground at the corners of a square of
    side 11 metres.
    Calculate the angle between any wire and
    the ground.

3   At point P, Rev Jenkins is 50 metres due south of a
    church spire S. He walks to
    point Q which is 40 metres due east of the spire.
    Calculate
    a   the height of the spire, RS
    b   the angle of elevation of S from Q.

4   A rod AB is propped in the corner of a room as shown.
    Find the angle between
    a   the rod and the floor
    b   the rod and the wall XCZ.

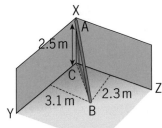

5   **RICH TASK**

    Find an expression in $x$ for the distance between the
    midpoints of the opposite edges, of length $x$, of a regular
    tetrahedron.

Unit C

● Use the sine rule to calculate sides and angles in any triangle

## RICH TASK

In this diagram, can you find the height $h$ in both $\triangle ABP$ and $\triangle CBP$ in terms of $a$, $c$, $\hat{A}$ and $\hat{C}$?

p. 121

What do your two answers tell you about $\dfrac{a}{\sin A}$?

If you drop a perpendicular from C to AB instead, can you find $\dfrac{a}{\sin A}$ another way?

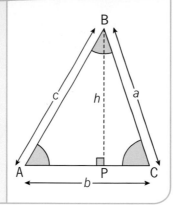

Label angle A opposite side $a$ and similarly for angles B and C.

Your answers give you the sine rule for $\triangle ABC$, which is:

→ **either** $\dfrac{a}{\sin A} = \dfrac{b}{\sin B} = \dfrac{c}{\sin C}$ **(better for finding lengths)**

→ **or** $\dfrac{\sin A}{a} = \dfrac{\sin B}{b} = \dfrac{\sin C}{c}$ **(better for finding angles).**

The sine rule enables you to calculate sides and angles in triangles which are **not** right-angled.

You can use the sine rule to find angles.

$$\frac{\sin A}{7} = \frac{\sin 50°}{8} \Rightarrow \sin A = \frac{7 \sin 50}{8}$$

Sin A = 0.67

A = 42°

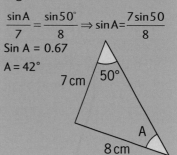

**EXAMPLE**

A soldier at point A sees a tower B on a bearing of 030°.
After walking 5 miles due north, the same tower is now on a bearing of 100°. Find the distance AB.

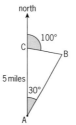

**ANSWER**

Angle ACB = 180 − 100 = 80° and angle ABC = 100 − 30 = 70°

In $\triangle ABC$, the sine rule gives $\dfrac{AB}{\sin 80°} = \dfrac{5}{\sin 70°}$

So the distance AB = $\dfrac{5 \times \sin 80°}{\sin 70°}$ = 5.24 miles

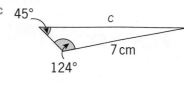

**1** Find the lettered sides and angles in these triangles.
All lengths are in centimetres

**a**

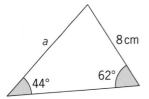

**b**

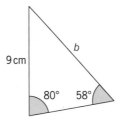

**c**

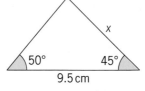

**d**

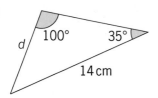

**e**

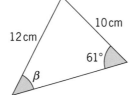

**f**

**g**

**2** A vertical mast ST stands on a sloping hillside.
Point P is downhill of S so that angle
SPT is 25°.
If angle TSP is 120°, calculate the height
*h* of the mast.

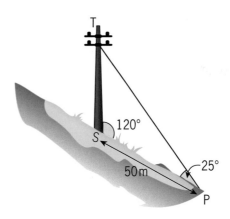

**3**

**RICH TASK**

Zeb walks the 25 metres between points B and C on
a river bank. He sees a point A on the other bank and
measures angles B̂ and Ĉ.
How can he calculate the width of the river?

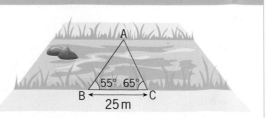

**Unit C**

# The cosine rule

* Use the cosine rule to calculate sides and angles in any triangle

## RICH TASK

Triangle ABC has been split into two right-angled triangles.
Can you use Pythagoras' theorem in these triangles to find

* an expression for $c^2$ involving $h$, $b$, $c$ and $\cos A$
* an expression for $a^2$ involving $h$, $b$, $c$ and $\cos A$?

Find an expression $a^2 - c^2$ and simplify it to make $a^2$ the subject.

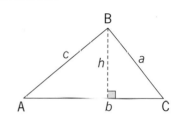

You have derived the cosine rule, which is:

* $a^2 = b^2 + c^2 - 2bc \cos A$

p. 121

**You can use the cosine rule to:**
* calculate one side of any triangle if you know the other two sides and the included angle
* find an angle of a triangle if you know all three sides.

Can you use your algebra skills to rearrange the cosine rule to make $\cos A$ the subject?

**EXAMPLE**

A boat B intended to sail 12 miles to port P. But the tide takes it 11° off course and it reaches a jetty J after 10 miles. Find the distance JP.

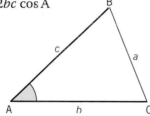

Three small islands A, B and C are separated by the distances shown. If A is due north of C, find the bearing of B from C to the nearest degree.

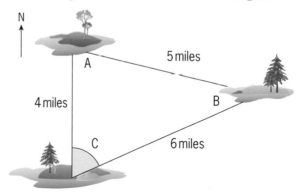

**ANSWER**

The cosine rule gives
$$JP^2 = 12^2 + 10^2 - 2 \times 12 \times 10 \times \cos 11°$$
$$= 144 + 100 - 235.6$$
$$= 8.4$$
The distance JP = $\sqrt{8.4}$ = 2.9 miles

The cosine rule gives
$$5^2 = 4^2 + 6^2 - 2 \times 4 \times 6 \times \cos C$$
$$25 = 52 - 48\cos C$$
$$\cos C = \frac{52 - 25}{48} = 0.5625$$
Angle C = 55.8°
The bearing of B from C is 056°

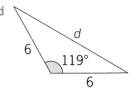

HIGH

1  Calculate the lettered sides and angles in these triangles.
   All lengths are in centimetres.

**a**
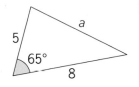
5

$a$

65°

8

**b**
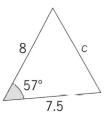
6

108°

9

$b$

**c**
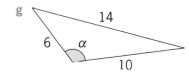
8

$c$

57°

7.5

**d**
6

$d$

119°

6

**e**
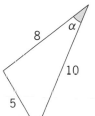
8

$\alpha$

10

5

**f**
14

$\theta$

12

10

**g**
14

6

$\alpha$

10

**h**
24

10

$\theta$

27

2  A kite is held in position in the air by two ropes 50 m
   and 40 m long. The ropes are fixed 80 m apart at ground level.
   Find the angle between the ropes.

3  Part of the practice green of a golf course
   has three holes these distances apart.
   Calculate the lettered angles.

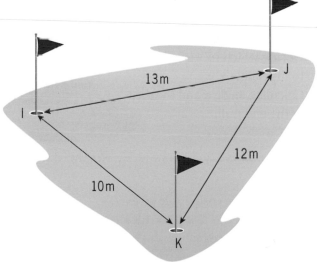

13 m

12 m

10 m

I

J

K

4  **RICH TASK**

   a  Three edges of a cube meet at point. The midpoints of
      these edges are joined to make a triangle. What size are
      the angles of this triangle?

   b  A cuboid has edges 10 cm, 20 cm and 30 cm long. Three
      edges meet at point. Calculate the angles of the triangle
      formed by joining the midpoints of these three edges.

Unit C

- Apply the sine and cosine rules to solve problems

You should find that, using two sides and the included angle,

→ **the area of ΔABC = $\frac{1}{2} ab \sin C$**

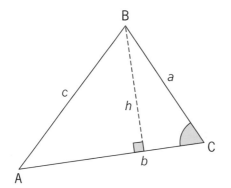

By dropping a perpendicular from B to AC in ΔABC, can you find the height $h$ of ΔABC in terms of $a$ and angle C?
Can you then find the area of ΔABC?

**EXAMPLE**

The end wall of a tent has the dimensions shown.
Decide which rule is needed to find angle $\alpha$.
Calculate angle $\alpha$ and the area of the end wall.

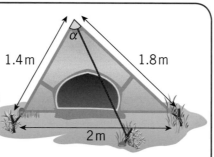

**ANSWER**

Choosing the cosine rule gives
$2^2 = 1.4^2 + 1.8^2 - 2 \times 1.4 \times 1.8 \times \cos \alpha$
$4 = 5.2 - 5.04 \cos \alpha$
$\cos \alpha = \frac{5.2 - 4}{5.04} = 0.238 \ldots$

Angle, $\alpha = 76.2°$
So, the area of the end face
$= \frac{1}{2} \times 1.4 \times 1.8 \times \sin 76.2°$
$= 1.22 \text{ m}^2$

Do you have enough information to work with **two pairs** of sides and angles?
So, can you use the sine rule to find angle $\alpha$?
Can you work with two sides and an included angle?

1 Find the lettered lengths and angles and also the areas of these
triangles.

a
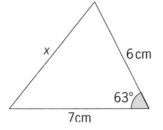
x
6 cm
63°
7 cm

b
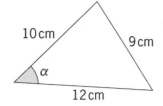
10 cm
9 cm
α
12 cm

c
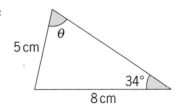
5 cm
θ
34°
8 cm

2 Calculate all the unknown lengths and angles in these triangles
and the area of each triangle.

a
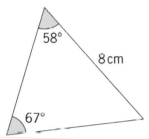
58°
8 cm
67°

b
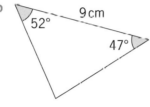
52°
9 cm
47°

c
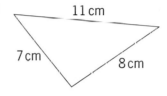
11 cm
7 cm
8 cm

3 Three lighthouses L, M and N protect ships from a shoal of
rocks. M is 6 km from L on a bearing of 080°.
N is on a bearing of 125° from L. M is on a bearing
of 333° from N.
Calculate the distances of N from both L and M and find the
area of ΔLMN.

4 **RICH TASK**

A regular tetrahedron of edge $a$ has a face in contact with a
horizontal table.
a Calculate the angle between any sloping edge and the base
face.
b The tetrahedron is sliced vertically along a plane of
symmetry. Calculate the area which is exposed by the cut.

A regular tetrahedron has more
than one vertical plane of
symmetry.

Unit C

## CHECK OUT

**You should now be able to**
- use trigonometrical relationships in 3-D contexts
- solve problems in 2-D and 3-D using sine rule and cosine rule
- calculate the area of a triangle using the formula $A = \frac{1}{2}ab\sin C$
- use Pythagoras' theorem in 3-D.

### Exam-style question

The hands on a clock are 9 cm and 12 cm long.

What is the distance between the tips of the hands at 7 o'clock?

**Esme's answer:**

Use the clock face to find the angle between the hands.

Angle between each pair of number
$360 \div 12 = 30°$

Draw a new diagram with all the information you know. Mark on the diagram what you want to find.

Angle between 7 and 12 $= 5 \times 30 = 150°$

Choose the appropriate method and solve. Take care with cosine rule.

Use BIDMAS.

$d^2 = 9^2 + 12^2 - 2 \times 9 \times 12 \cos 150°$
$d^2 = 81 + 144 - (-187.06)$
$d^2 = 412.06$
$d = 20.3 \text{ cm}$

Don't round too early, only round the final answer.

## Exam practice

1 Work out the area of triangle ABC.

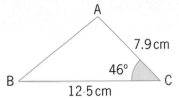

(2 marks)

2 In triangle PQR, PQ = 11 cm, PR = 15·2 cm and angle R = 38°.
   a Tom draws PQR as an acute-angled triangle.

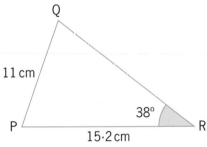

   Calculate angle Q in Tom's triangle.

   b Josh draws triangle PQR with angle Q obtuse.

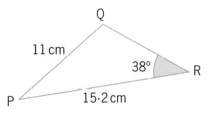

   Write down the size of angle Q in Josh's triangle.
   Explain how you found your answer.

(5 marks)

3 Two windsurfers Jo and Kevin are surfing at sea.
   They are travelling around a buoy in opposite directions when
   the wind drops.
   Jo is 18 m on a bearing of 124° from the buoy.
   Kevin is 12 m on a bearing of 252° from the buoy.
   Work out the distance Jo and Kevin are apart.

(4 marks)

# 24 Graphs 2

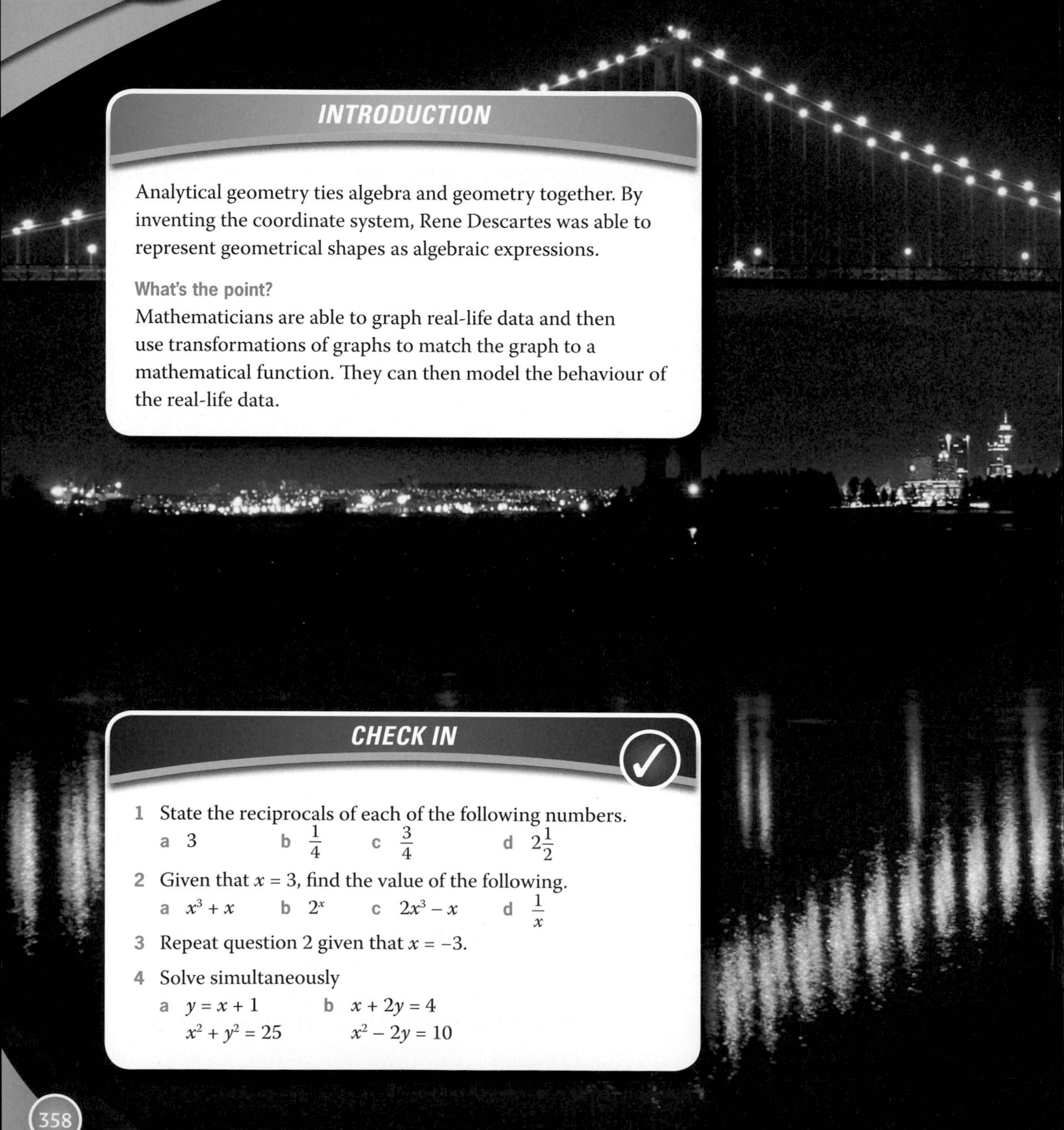

## INTRODUCTION

Analytical geometry ties algebra and geometry together. By inventing the coordinate system, Rene Descartes was able to represent geometrical shapes as algebraic expressions.

**What's the point?**

Mathematicians are able to graph real-life data and then use transformations of graphs to match the graph to a mathematical function. They can then model the behaviour of the real-life data.

## CHECK IN

1 State the reciprocals of each of the following numbers.

   a 3     b $\frac{1}{4}$   c $\frac{3}{4}$    d $2\frac{1}{2}$

2 Given that $x = 3$, find the value of the following.

   a $x^3 + x$   b $2^x$   c $2x^3 - x$   d $\frac{1}{x}$

3 Repeat question 2 given that $x = -3$.

4 Solve simultaneously

   a $y = x + 1$     b $x + 2y = 4$

     $x^2 + y^2 = 25$     $x^2 - 2y = 10$

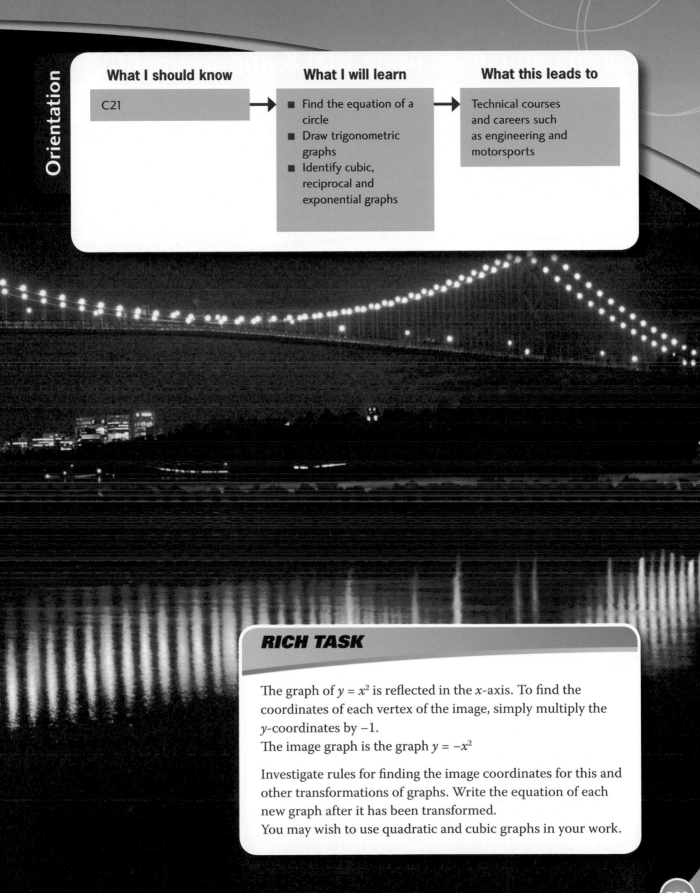

## What I should know

C21

## What I will learn

- Find the equation of a circle
- Draw trigonometric graphs
- Identify cubic, reciprocal and exponential graphs

## What this leads to

Technical courses and careers such as engineering and motorsports

### RICH TASK

The graph of $y = x^2$ is reflected in the $x$-axis. To find the coordinates of each vertex of the image, simply multiply the $y$-coordinates by $-1$.

The image graph is the graph $y = -x^2$

Investigate rules for finding the image coordinates for this and other transformations of graphs. Write the equation of each new graph after it has been transformed.

You may wish to use quadratic and cubic graphs in your work.

# Solving equations using trial & improvement C24.1

- Use systematic trial and improvement to find approximate solutions of equations

Some equations cannot be solved easily using algebra. You can solve them approximately using **trial and improvement**.

**EXAMPLE**

Solve the equation $x^3 - x = 100$, giving your answer correct to one decimal place.

**ANSWER**

| $x$ | $x^3$ | $x^3 - x$ | Comment |
|---|---|---|---|
| 4 | 64 | 60 | Too small |
| 5 | 125 | 120 | Too large |
| 4.5 | 91.125 | 86.625 | Too small |
| 4.7 | 103.823 | 99.123 | Too small |
| 4.8 | 110.592 | 105.792 | Too large |
| 4.75 | 107.171... | 102.421... | Too large |

Use an ordered table of trials. "Sandwich" the answer between two consecutive whole numbers, then two consecutive numbers with 1 d.p. etc.

The solution is between $x = 4.7$ and $x = 4.75$, so $x = 4.7$ correct to 1 d.p.

You need to work to one more d.p. than is required in your answer.

You may have to construct the equation to be solved from given information.

**EXAMPLE**

The volume of this cuboid is 2184 cm³. Find its exact dimensions.

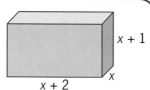

$x + 1$
$x + 2$
$x$

**ANSWER**

Volume = length × width × height = $x \times (x + 1) \times (x + 2)$
Hence, $x(x + 1)(x + 2) = 2184$

Remember to use the rules of algebra correctly when writing your expressions:
$x \times x + 1 \times x + 2$ is not the same as
$x \times (x + 1) \times (x + 2)$
because of BIDMAS.

| $x$ | $x + 1$ | $x + 2$ | $x(x + 1)(x + 2)$ | Comment |
|---|---|---|---|---|
| 10 | 11 | 12 | 1320 | Too small |
| 11 | 12 | 13 | 1716 | Too small |
| 12 | 13 | 14 | 2184 | Correct |

The dimensions of the cuboid are 12 cm by 13 cm by 14 cm.

## Exercise C24.1

1   Find the exact solutions to the following equations using trial and improvement.

   a   $x^2 + x = 72$          b   $x^3 - x = 210$
   c   $x(x + 2) = 675$        d   $x^3 + 2x^2 + 3 = 444$

*2   Write an equation for each problem. Use trial and improvement to solve each one.

   a   The area of this rectangle is 192 cm².
       Find the dimensions of the rectangle.
   b   The product of three consecutive numbers is 9240.
       Find the numbers.
   c   The volume of a cuboid is 990 cm³. Its width is 1 cm more than its length and its height is 1 cm more than its width.
       Find its dimensions.

The answers to question 2 are all exact numbers.

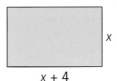

*3   Two students used trial and improvement to solve $x^2 + 3x = 60$ to one decimal place. List all of the mistakes that each student has made.

| $x$ | $x^2$ | $3x$ | $x^2 + 3x$ |
|---|---|---|---|
| 6 | 36 | 18 | 54 |
| 6.8 | 46.24 | 20.4 | 66.64 |
| 6.2 | 38.44 | 18.6 | 57.04 |
| 6.4 | 40.96 | 19.2 | 60.16 |

$x = 60.16$

| $x$ | $x^2$ | $3x$ | $x^2 + 3x$ |
|---|---|---|---|
| 6 | 36 | 18 | 54 |
| 7 | 49 | 21 | 70 |
| 6.3 | 39.69 | 18.9 | 58.59 |
| 6.4 | 40.96 | 19.2 | 60.16 |
| 6.35 | 40.3225 | 19.05 | 59.3725 |
| 6.36 | 40.4496 | 19.08 | 59.5296 |
| 6.37 | 40.5769 | 19.11 | 59.6869 |
| 6.38 | 40.7044 | 19.14 | 59.8444 |
| 6.39 | 40.8321 | 19.17 | 60.0021 |

$x = 6.4$

4   Use trial and improvement to solve the following equations to one decimal place.

   a   $x^2 + 4x = 100$          b   $x^3 - x = 700$
   c   $5x^2 + 3x = 90$          d   $y(y - 2) = 220$

5   ☆ CHALLENGE ☆

   The cube of a number is forty times its square root.
   Find the number to one decimal place.

# Linear and quadratic graphs

• Find the intersection points of the graphs of a linear and a quadratic function

## RICH TASK

The diagram shows the graph
$$y = x^2 - 4x + 3$$
Use the diagram to find the two solutions of the simultaneous equations
$$y = x^2 - 4x + 3$$
$$y = x + 1$$
Investigate the number of solutions for
$$y = x^2 - 4x + 3$$
$$y = x + a$$
where $a$ is an integer.

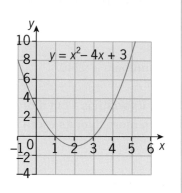

You can solve two simultaneous equations, one of which is linear and the other quadratic, by drawing a graph. The solutions are at the points of intersection.

p. 292

**EXAMPLE**

Solve these simultaneous equations graphically.
$$y = x^2 - 3x - 4$$
$$y = 2x + 2$$

> This question could be phrased as "Solve graphically $x^2 - 3x - 4 = 2x + 2$"

**ANSWER**

Plot the graphs $y = x^2 - 3x - 4$ and $y = 2x + 2$

| x | −2 | −1 | 0 | 1 | 2 | 3 | 4 | 5 | 6 | 7 |
|------|------|------|------|------|------|------|------|------|------|------|
| $x^2$ | 4 | 1 | 0 | 1 | 4 | 9 | 16 | 25 | 36 | 49 |
| −3x | 6 | 3 | 0 | −3 | −6 | −9 | −12 | −15 | −18 | −21 |
| −4 | −4 | −4 | −4 | −4 | −4 | −4 | −4 | −4 | −4 | −4 |
| y | 6 | 0 | −4 | −6 | −6 | −4 | 0 | 6 | 14 | 24 |

| x | 1 | 2 | 3 |
|---|---|---|---|
| y | 4 | 6 | 8 |

The graphs intersect at (−1, 0) and (6, 14).
The solutions to $y = x^2 - 3x - 4$ and $y = 2x + 2$ are $x = -1$ and $x = 6$

> The equations only involve x, not y, so only give the x-coordinate as your solution.

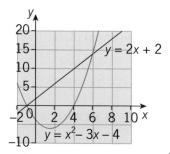

Solutions found graphically may only be approximate since you cannot read off a value exactly. However, exact solutions can be found using an algebraic method. In the previous example, you can substitute the linear equation into the quadratic.

$$y = x^2 - 3x - 4 \ldots \text{quadratic} \qquad y = 2x + 2 \ldots \text{linear}$$

$$2x + 2 = x^2 - 3x - 4$$
$$0 = x^2 - 5x - 6$$
$$0 = (x - 6)(x + 1)$$

So $x = 6$ or $x = -1$

## Exercise C24.2

1  Use the graphs on the right to find the (approximate) solutions of these pairs of simultaneous equations.

   a  $y = x^2 - 2x - 5$    b  $y = x^2 - 2x - 5$    c  $y = x^2 - 2x - 5$
      $y - x - 1$              $y = -2x - 1$         $y = 2x - 3$

2  a  By completing the following table of values, plot the graph
      $y = x^2 - 4x - 1$

| x | −1 | 0 | 1 | 2 | 3 | 4 | 5 |
|---|---|---|---|---|---|---|---|
| $x^2$ | | | | 4 | | | |
| $-4x$ | | | | −8 | | | |
| $-1$ | | | | −1 | | | |
| y | | | | −5 | | | |

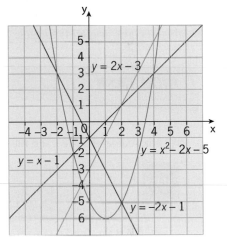

▲ Question 1

   b  By adding suitable line graphs to your diagram, solve the following pairs of simultaneous equations graphically.

      i  $y = x^2 - 4x - 1$    ii  $y = x^2 - 4x - 1$    iii  $y = x^2 - 4x - 1$
         $y = x - 2$           $y = \frac{1}{2}(x - 4)$       $x + 2y = 4$

   c  Using graphs that you have already drawn, solve $x^2 - 5x + 1 = 0$

3  a  By drawing suitable graphs, solve these simultaneous equations graphically.
      $$y = x^2 - 4x + 9$$
      $$y = 2x + 1$$

   b  Confirm your solutions using algebra.

4  Confirm your solutions to question 1 algebraically.

5  ☆ CHALLENGE ☆

   The solution to a linear and quadratic simultaneous equation pair is $x = -2$ and $x = 0$. Try to find a pair of equations that fit.

# Trigonometric graphs

- Plot the graphs of the circular functions $y = \sin x$ and $y = \cos x$
- Recognise the characteristic shapes of these functions

In **right-angled** triangles, two angles are always acute.

In **obtuse-angled** triangles, one angle is always obtuse.

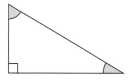

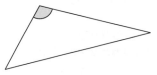

You can use the sine and cosine functions to find lengths and angles in right-angled triangles.

The sine and cosine functions can also be used for obtuse-angled triangles.

## RICH TASK

### Part 1

Here is a table of angle $x$ and the sine of $x$ (or sin $x$), partially completed.

| x° | 0 | 45 | 90 | 135 | 180 | 225 | 270 | 315 | 360 |
|---|---|---|---|---|---|---|---|---|---|
| **sin x°** | 0 | 0.71 | 1 | 0.71 | 0 | | | | |

**a** Use the sine key on your calculator to complete the table, giving values of sin $x$ to 2 d.p. where appropriate.

The table of values can be used to draw a graph of sin $x$ against $x$. Here is the graph, partially completed.

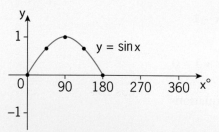

**b** Copy the axes, with $x$ from 0° to 360° and $y$ from −1 to 1. Complete the graph for the values in the table.

### Part 2

Repeat the activity in Part 1 for the cosine function. Use values of $x$ from 0° to 360° as before.

Try to describe the two graphs you have drawn, using precise mathematical language.

Here is the graph of $y = \sin x$ for values of $x$ between 0° and 360°.

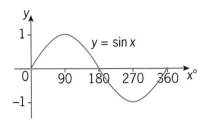

Here is the graph of $y = \cos x$ for values of $x$ between 0° and 360°.

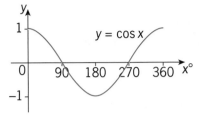

The shape of these curves is often described as sinusoidal.

→ **The graph of $y = \sin x$ ranges between −1 and 1.**
→ **The graph has rotational symmetry of order 2.**

→ **The graph of $y = \cos x$ ranges between −1 and 1.**
→ **The graph has a line of symmetry at 180°.**

Unit C

## Exercise C24.3

You will need to have drawn graphs of $y = \sin x$ and $y = \cos x$ for values of $x$ between 0° and 360° to do this exercise.

1 Use the graph of $y = \sin x$ to find the sine of these angles. Use a calculator to check the accuracy of your answers.

a sin 30°    b sin 150°    c sin 45°    d sin 225°    e sin 315°    f sin 90°

2 Use the graph of $y = \cos x$ to work out the cosine of each angle. Use a calculator to check the accuracy of your answers.

a cos 60°    b cos 140°    c cos 45°    d cos 225°    e cos 315°    f cos 90°

3 Use the graph of $y = \sin x$ to find the other angle between 0° and 360° with sine the same value as

a sin 50°    b sin 68°    c sin 140°    d sin 217°    e sin 262°    f sin 98°

4 Use the graph of $y = \cos x$ to find the other angle between 0° and 360° with cosine the same value as

a cos 30°    b cos 66°    c cos 150°    d cos 237°    e cos 164°    f cos 78°

5 **RICH TASK**

What would happen if you extended the values of $x$ beyond 0° to 360°?
Try some values on your calculator and plot them on an extended version of the graphs – you could use graphing software or a graphics calculator.

6 **RICH TASK**

The graphs of $\sin x$ and $\cos x$ look very similar to each other. What transformation would map the graph of $\sin x$ to the graph of $\cos x$?

Trigonometric graphs

# Cubic graphs

- Plot graphs of simple cubic functions
- Recognise the characteristic shape of cubic functions

Cubics contain $x^3$ as the highest power.

The simplest cubic function is $y = x^3$ or $f(x) = x^3$

Choose values of $x$ from $-3$ to $3$:

| $x$ | $-3$ | $-2$ | $-1$ | 0 | 1 | 2 | 3 |
|-----|------|------|------|---|---|---|---|
| $y$ | $-27$ | $-8$ | $-1$ | 0 | 1 | 8 | 27 |

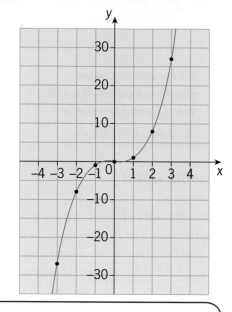

**EXAMPLE**

Plot the graph $y = x^3 - 2x^2 + 3$ for values of $x$ in the range $-3 \leq x \leq 3$.

**ANSWER**

Construct a table of values.

| $x$ | $-3$ | $-2$ | $-1$ | 0 | 1 | 2 | 3 |
|-----|------|------|------|---|---|---|---|
| $x^3$ | $-27$ | $-8$ | $-1$ | 0 | 1 | 8 | 27 |
| $-2x^2$ | $-18$ | $-8$ | $-2$ | 0 | 2 | 8 | 18 |
| $+3$ | $+3$ | $+3$ | $+3$ | $+3$ | $+3$ | $+3$ | $+3$ |
| $y$ | $-42$ | $-13$ | 0 | 3 | 6 | 19 | 48 |

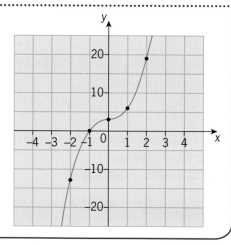

In general, the characteristic shape of a cubic curve is 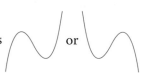 or

1  Match an equation from the top row of the table with its graph
   shape from the bottom row.

| $y = x^2 + 2$ | $y = 2$ | $y = x + 2$ | $y = 2 - x^2$ | $y = x^3 + 2$ | $x = 2$ |
|---|---|---|---|---|---|
| A | B | C | D | E | F |

2  Copy and complete the table of values for each cubic function
   and use your values to plot the graph of the given function.

a  $y = x^3 + x + 2$

| $x$ | −3 | −2 | −1 | 0 | 1 | 2 | 3 |
|---|---|---|---|---|---|---|---|
| $x^3$ | | | −1 | | | | |
| $+x$ | | | | | | | |
| $2$ | 2 | 2 | 2 | 2 | 2 | 2 | 2 |
| $y$ | | | 0 | | | | |

b  $y = -x^3$

| $x$ | −3 | −2 | −1 | 0 | 1 | 2 | 3 |
|---|---|---|---|---|---|---|---|
| $y$ | | | | | | −8 | |

c  $y = x^3 - x^2 + 3$

| $x$ | −3 | −2 | −1 | 0 | 1 | 2 | 3 |
|---|---|---|---|---|---|---|---|
| $x^3$ | | | | | | 8 | |
| $-x^2$ | | | | | | −4 | |
| $3$ | | | | | | 3 | |
| $y$ | | | | | | 7 | |

> To find $-x^2$ square the number
> first and then multiply by −1.

3  a  Plot the graph of $f(x) = x^3 - 2x^2 + x - 3$ for $-3 \le x \le 3$.
   b  Use your graph to find
      i   $x$ when $f(x) = -20$    ii   $f(1.8)$

4  Look at these equations.

| $y = 2(x + 1)$ | $x = 4$ | $y = 3x + 2$ | $y = x^3 - 2$ | $y = 2x^2$ |
|---|---|---|---|---|

   a  Which graph passes through the origin?
   b  Which two graphs are not straight lines?
   c  Which graphs intersect at the point (2, 6)?
   d  Which graph is perpendicular to the $x$-axis?

**DID YOU KNOW...?**
cubic equations
are used in the
designs for roller
coasters.

5  ☆ **CHALLENGE** ☆

   Plot the graph $y = (x - 1)(x + 1)(x + 2)$ and write down the
   coordinates of the points where this graph intersects the $x$-axis.
   Use what you have found to sketch $y = (x - 10)(x - 5)(x + 12)$

Unit C

# Reciprocal graphs

- Plot graphs of simple reciprocal functions
- Recognise the characteristic shape of reciprocal functions

## RICH TASK

List all of the pairs of integers whose product is 24. Don't forget negatives. For example, 1 × 24, 3 × 8, 8 × 3, (−2) × (−12).
Plot and join all of your pairs on a set of axes, where $x$ is one number from the pair and $y$ the other. What is the equation of your graph?
Investigate such graphs for numbers other than 24.

p. 8

→ Reciprocal graphs involve the reciprocal function $y = \dfrac{1}{x}$.
They have a characteristic shape called a hyperbola.

The reciprocal of 5 is $\dfrac{1}{5}$.

### EXAMPLE

Plot $f(x) = \dfrac{1}{x}$ for $-10 \le x \le 10$.

**ANSWER**

| x | −10 | −8 | −6 | −4 | −2 | 0 | 2 | 4 | 6 | 8 | 10 |
|---|---|---|---|---|---|---|---|---|---|---|---|
| y | $-\frac{1}{10}$ | $-\frac{1}{8}$ | $-\frac{1}{6}$ | $-\frac{1}{4}$ | $-\frac{1}{2}$ | NOT DEFINED | $\frac{1}{2}$ | $\frac{1}{4}$ | $\frac{1}{6}$ | $\frac{1}{8}$ | $\frac{1}{10}$ |

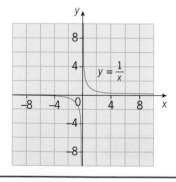

As $x$ gets large $y$ gets small and vice versa.
$x$ cannot take the value of zero since we cannot evaluate $\dfrac{1}{0}$. The same is true for $y$. Hence, the $x$-axis and the $y$-axis are both asymptotes. The graph will get close to but never touch an asymptote.

### EXAMPLE

The graph $y = \dfrac{2}{x} + 1$ is shown. Write down the equations of the asymptotes.

**ANSWER**

The graph is not defined when $x = 0$ and when $y = 1$.
The asymptotes are $x = 0$ and $y = 1$.

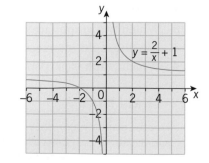

1 Three of the equations given below would form a hyperbola when plotted. Find these three equations.

| $f(x) = \dfrac{2}{x}$ | $y = x^2 - 1$ | $y = \dfrac{3}{x} - 1$ | $y = 2x - 1$ | $y = x^3 - 1$ | $y = \dfrac{1}{x+1}$ |

State the shape of the remaining three functions.

2 For each of the following functions
   i Copy and complete the table of values
   ii Draw suitable axes and plot each graph, joining your points with a smooth curve in each case
   iii Write down the equations of any asymptotes.

**DID YOU KNOW...?**
a hyperbola is formed by taking a slice through two cones joined vertex to vertex. You could research different sections through a cone that give you ellipses, parabolas and circles.

a $y = \dfrac{12}{x}$

| x | −6 | −5 | −4 | −3 | −2 | −1 | 0 | 1 | 2 | 3 | 4 | 5 | 6 |
|---|----|----|----|----|----|----|---|---|---|---|---|---|---|
| y |    |    |    |    |    |    |   |   |   | 3 |   |   |   |

b $f(x) = \dfrac{20}{x} + 1$

| x | −5 | −4 | −3 | −2 | −1 | 0 | 1 | 2 | 3 | 4 | 5 |
|---|----|----|----|----|----|---|---|---|---|---|---|
| y |    | $-5\frac{2}{3}$ |    |    |    |   |   |   |   | 6 |   |

c $y = \dfrac{12}{x-2}$

| x     | −4 | −3 | −2 | −1 | 0 | 1 | 2 | 3 | 4 | 5 | 6 | 7 | 8 |
|-------|----|----|----|----|---|---|---|---|---|---|---|---|---|
| x − 2 |    |    | −4 |    |   |   |   |   |   |   | 4 |   |   |
| y     |    |    | −3 |    |   |   |   |   |   |   | 3 |   |   |

3 Draw the graph of $f(x) = \dfrac{4}{x}$ and use your graph to approximate the value of $x$ for which $f(x) = 1.9$.

4 It takes one man 10 days to build a conservatory. Plot a graph of how long it would take up to 10 men to build this same conservatory and find the equation of your graph.

5 ☆ **CHALLENGE** ☆

Solve these simultaneous equations graphically   $y = \dfrac{8}{x}$
$y = x + 2$

Unit C

# Exponential graphs

- Plot graphs of simple exponential functions
- Recognise the characteristic shape of exponential functions

## RICH TASK

The half-life of a quantity whose value decreases with time is the interval required for the quantity to decay to half of its initial value. Carbon-14 has a half-life of 5730 years. Sketch a graph of the amount of carbon-14 remaining over time for an initial quantity of 500 grams and explain why there will always be some carbon-14 present.

→ **Exponential functions can be written in the form $y = ka^x$, where $k$ and $a$ are constants, and $a > 0$.**

The graphs of exponential functions have a characteristic shape.

**EXAMPLE**

Plot the graph of $y = 2^x$ for $-4 \leq x \leq 4$ and use it to find the approximate value of $2^{3.5}$

**ANSWER**

| $x$ | −4 | −3 | −2 | −1 | 0 | 1 | 2 | 3 | 4 |
|---|---|---|---|---|---|---|---|---|---|
| $y$ | $\frac{1}{16}$ | $\frac{1}{8}$ | $\frac{1}{4}$ | $\frac{1}{2}$ | 1 | 2 | 4 | 8 | 16 |

When $x = 3.5$, $y \approx 11$, so $2^{3.5} \approx 11$

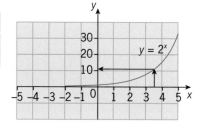

As $x$ gets larger, $y$ gets larger and vice versa. Since $2^x$ can never be zero, the $x$-axis is an asymptote.

→ **Exponential curves can be used to model some real-life situations.**

**EXAMPLE**

The graph shows the population $P$ of a village over time $t$ years. Given that $P = ab^t$, find the values of $a$ and $b$.

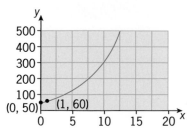

**ANSWER**

Using $P = ab^t$

At $(0, 50)$  $\qquad 50 = a \times b^0$

so $a = 50$

At $(1, 60)$  $\qquad 60 = a \times b^1$

so $60 = 50b^1$

so $b = 1.2$

## Exercise C24.6

HIGH

**\*1** Bacteria reproduce by splitting in two. Beginning with one bacterium, this splits, after one hour, to make two bacteria and these split, after a further hour, to make four bacteria and so on.

a  Copy and complete the table to show the number of bacteria over a period of 10 hours.

| Time | 0 | 1 | 2 | 3 | 4 | 5 | 6 | 7 | 8 | 9 | 10 |
|---|---|---|---|---|---|---|---|---|---|---|---|
| Bacteria | 1 | 2 | 4 | | | | | | | | |

**DID YOU KNOW...?**
bacteria with an average doubling time of 20 minutes can produce a billion new cells in just 10 hours.

b  Plot a graph to show the number of bacteria over time.

c  Use your graph to estimate how long it takes for there to be 1000 bacteria.

d  Can you suggest an equation for your graph?

e  How would the graph differ if a new strain of bacteria was discovered that splits into three to reproduce? Sketch your graph.

**2**  Copy and complete the following tables of values and use them to plot an exponential graph in each case.

a  $y = 3^x$

| x | -4 | -3 | -2 | -1 | 0 | 1 | 2 | 3 | 4 |
|---|---|---|---|---|---|---|---|---|---|
| y | | | $\frac{1}{9}$ | | | | 9 | | |

You may have to work these out without a calculator. If a calculator is allowed, remember your power button. Here are two possible variations.

$\wedge$     $x^y$

b  $y = \left(\frac{1}{2}\right)^x$

| x | -4 | -3 | -2 | -1 | 0 | 1 | 2 | 3 | 4 |
|---|---|---|---|---|---|---|---|---|---|
| y | | | | | | | $\frac{1}{4}$ | | |

c  $y = 2^{-x}$

| x | -4 | -3 | -2 | -1 | 0 | 1 | 2 | 3 | 4 |
|---|---|---|---|---|---|---|---|---|---|
| y | | 4 | | | | | | | |

**3**  The population $P$, over time $t$ years, of a herd of elephants living in a Thai jungle is modelled using the formula $P = 4 \times 1.5^t$.

a  What is the initial population of the herd?

b  What is the population of the herd after
   i  1 year
   ii  2 years?

c  Plot a graph of $P$ against $t$ for a 10-year period and use it to find the point in time at which the herd exceeded 100 elephants.

Unit C

- Transform the graph of $y = f(x)$ for linear, quadratic, sine and cosine functions

Here is the graph of $y = f(x) = x^2$

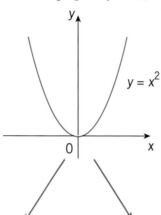

$y = x^2$

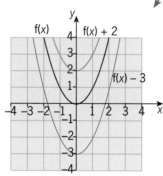

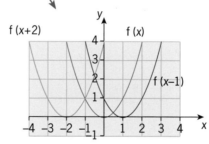

Here are $y = f(x) + 2 = x^2 + 2$
and $y = f(x) - 3 = x^2 - 3$

Here are $y = f(x + 2) = (x + 2)^2$
and $y = f(x - 1) = (x - 1)^2$

## RICH TASK

p. 318

By using graphical software, confirm these graphs and try a few more, using functions of your own.
Describe anything you notice.

In general,
→ $y = f(x) + a$ is a translation of $\begin{pmatrix} 0 \\ a \end{pmatrix}$ on $y = f(x)$

→ $y = f(x + a)$ a is a translation of $\begin{pmatrix} -a \\ 0 \end{pmatrix}$ on $y = f(x)$

1   Translate the function f($x$) = 2$x$ + 1 as described in parts **a** to **d**.

   **a**   $y$ = f($x$) + 2    **b**   $y$ = f($x$) − 1    **c**   $y$ = f($x$ + 3)    **d**   $y$ = f($x$ − 2)

   Draw each graph accurately on the same set of axes, choosing your scale carefully.

2   The graph of $y$ = f($x$) is transformed. Match each of the transformed functions
   **a**–**d** with one of the graphs A–D.

   **a**   $y$ = f($x$) + 1

   **b**   $y$ = f($x$) + 2

   **c**   $y$ = f($x$) − 2

   **d**   $y$ = f($x$) − 1

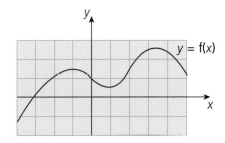

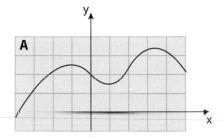

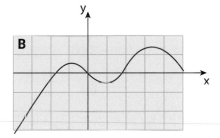

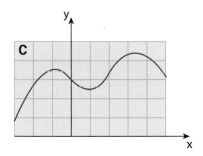

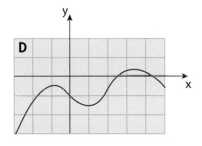

3   **RICH TASK**

   How would you need to transform the graph of f($x$) = cos $x$ to
   get sin $x$?

   What constant would you need to use?

Unit C

• Transform the graph of $y = f(x)$ for linear, quadratic, sine and cosine functions

Here is the graph of $y = f(x) = \sin x$

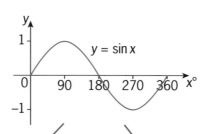

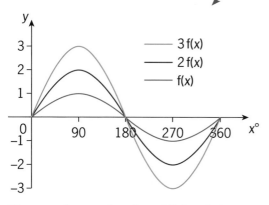

Here are the graphs of $y = 2f(x) = 2 \sin x$
and $y = 3f(x) = 3 \sin x$

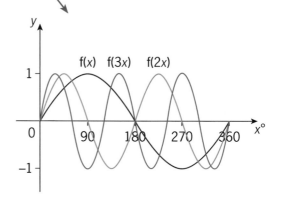

Here are the graphs of $y = f(2x) = \sin 2x$
and $y = f(3x) = \sin 3x$

## RICH TASK

By using graphical software, confirm these graphs and try a few more, using functions of your own.
Describe anything you notice.

→ $y = af(x)$ is a stretch parallel to the $y$-axis of $y = f(x)$ by a scale factor of a.
→ $y = f(ax)$ is a stretch parallel to the $x$-axis of $y = f(x)$ by a scale factor of $\frac{1}{a}$.

## Exercise C24.8

**1** This is a sketch of the graph $y = \sin x$.
On separate diagrams sketch the graphs of
  **a** $y = \sin 2x$ for angles 0° to 360°
  **b** $y = 2 \sin x$ for angles 0° to 360°
  **c** $y = -2 + \sin x$ for angles 0° to 360°

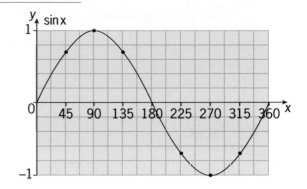

**2** This is a sketch of the graph $y = \cos x$.
On separate diagrams sketch the graphs of
  **a** $y = \cos \frac{1}{2} x$ for angles 0° to 360°
  **b** $y = \frac{1}{2} \cos x$ for angles 0° to 360°
  **c** $y = \cos (x - 60°)$ for angles 0° to 360°

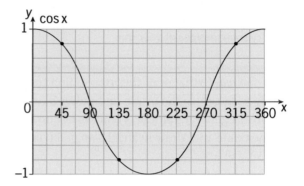

**3** The graph shows the function f($x$).

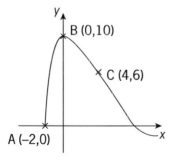

Where will the points A, B and C be translated to under these transformations?
  **a** f($2x$)          **b** $f\left(\frac{1}{2}x\right)$          **c** f($4x$)

  **d** f($-x$)          **e** f($2x$) + 5

# The equation of a circle

- Construct the graph of the circle $x^2 + y^2 = r^2$ which has radius $r$ and is centred at the origin

> You will not be assessed on this topic but it is included for your interest.

## RICH TASK

Can you create, using an ICT graphical package, these patterns that all involve circles, by entering suitable equations into the software?

Try some designs of your own.

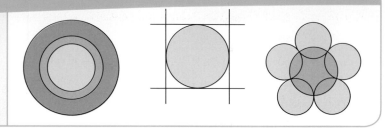

You can use Pythagoras' theorem to find the equation of a circle with centre the origin and radius 3 units.

Choose a general point $(x, y)$ on the circumference of the circle and draw in a right-angled triangle, so that

$$x^2 + y^2 = 3^2$$
$$x^2 + y^2 = 9$$

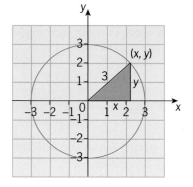

➡ **You can generalise to give the equation of any circle with centre (0, 0) and radius $r$. This is**

$$x^2 + y^2 = r^2$$

---

**EXAMPLE**

Find the equations of the following circles.

a  Centre $(0, 0)$, radius 5      b  Centre the origin, radius $\frac{3}{4}$

..............................................................

**ANSWER**

a  $x^2 + y^2 = 5^2$          b  $x^2 + y^2 = \left(\frac{3}{4}\right)^2$

   $x^2 + y^2 = 25$            $x^2 + y^2 = \frac{9}{16}$

---

**EXAMPLE**

Describe the following circles.

a  $x^2 + y^2 = 100$          b  $x^2 + y^2 = 50$

..............................................................

**ANSWER**

a  Centre $(0, 0)$, radius $\sqrt{100} = 10$    b  Centre $(0, 0)$, radius $\sqrt{50}$

> Leaving the radius in surd form as $\sqrt{50}$ means that it is exact and you do not need to round off a decimal, which would give an approximate answer only.

1 Write down the equations of these circles.

   a  Centre the origin, radius 4       b  Centre the origin, radius 6

   c  Centre the origin, radius $\frac{1}{2}$     d  Centre $(0, 0)$, radius 0.4

   e  Centre $(0, 0)$, radius 13      f  Centre the origin, radius $\sqrt{7}$

2 Write down the centre and radius of the following circles.

   a  $x^2 + y^2 = 49$     b  $x^2 + y^2 = 144$     c  $x^2 + y^2 = 225$

   d  $x^2 + y^2 = 10$     e  $x^2 + y^2 = \frac{16}{25}$     f  $x^2 + y^2 = 0.09$

3 Find the equations of the circles shown in the diagram below.

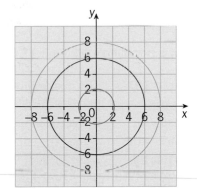

4 Where do the circles $x^2 + y^2 = 9$ and $x^2 + y^2 = 25$ intersect?

> Imagine or draw a diagram.

5  a  Plot the circle $x^2 + y^2 = 16$

   b  By drawing the line $x = 3$ onto the same diagram, state how
      many times the circle $x^2 + y^2 = 16$ and the line $x = 3$ intersect.

   c  How many times do these equation pairs intersect?

     **i**  $x^2 + y^2 = 16$    **ii**  $x^2 + y^2 = 25$    **iii**  $x^2 + y^2 = 16$

          $y = 2$              $x = 6$              $y = x$

6  a  Explain how you know that the point $(3, 4)$ lies on the circle
      $x^2 + y^2 = 25$

   b  Match each circle equation with one point that lies on it.

| Circle | $x^2 + y^2 = 16$ | $x^2 + y^2 = 169$ | $x^2 + y^2 = 10$ | $x^2 + y^2 = 100$ |
|---|---|---|---|---|
| Point | $(5, 12)$ | $(6, 8)$ | $(2, \sqrt{12})$ | $(1, 3)$ |

# Points in three dimensions

- Understand and use coordinates of points in three dimensions

## RICH TASK

Compare a road atlas for planning a car journey, the maps in a school atlas, and an OS map in the Explorer or Landranger series.
How do these maps fix positions?
How do they use squares and grid lines?
Which maps give you heights – of some points, of all points?
What do some maps have on them to give heights of all points?
Discuss which maps are best for which purpose.

The position of a point in **1-D** needs just one coordinate on one axis.
The coordinate of point $P$ is $x = 2$.

The position of a point in **2-D** needs two coordinates on two axes. The coordinates for point $Q$ are (2, 3). Which is the $x$-coordinate and which is the $y$-coordinate?

The position of a point in **3-D** needs a third axis which gives the vertical height off the base plane. The coordinates of point $R$ are (2, 3, 4). Which of these is the $z$-coordinate?

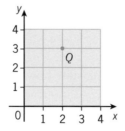

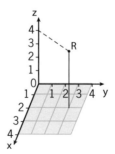

Write down the coordinates of

**a**    the top $T$ of the church tower which is 60 metres above ground level

**b**    the end $E$ of the nave roof which is 40 metres above ground level.

······················································

### ANSWER

$T$ is the point (30, 20, 60)
$E$ is the point (30, 70, 40)

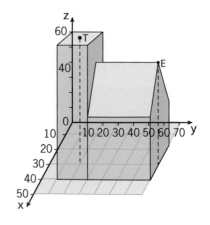

# Exercise C24.10

1 This diagram shows the tall buildings in a town.
Write the three coordinates for the lettered points *A* to *F*
indicated by the red dots.
Clock tower *A* is 30 metres high.
Office block *B* is 50 metres high.
Crane *C* is 60 metres high.
Church spire *D* is 20 metres high.
Factory chimney *E* is 75 metres high.
Radio mast *F* is 40 metres high.

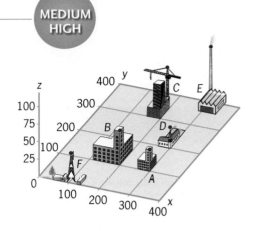

2 This map shows a coastline. The contours on land are
at 10-metre intervals.
Write the 3-D coordinates of the lettered points *A* to *L*.

3 The next map also shows a coastline.
Its contours at 50-metre intervals are both above and below
sea-level.
  a Write the 3-D coordinates of the lettered points *A* to *J*.
  b Copy and complete these coordinates for the unlettered
points.

(40, 50, ....)     (80, 20, ....)
(20, ...., 100)    (5, ...., 150)
(...., 5, 0)       (...., 50, 50)
(75, ...., −50)    (50, 5, ....)

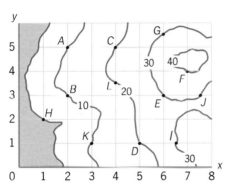

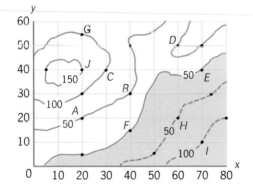

4  ### RICH TASK

Learn how to give a 6-figure grid reference for any place in
the UK on the National Grid. You could use the internet or
geography reference books.

5  ### RICH TASK

Learn how to play
3-D noughts and crosses.

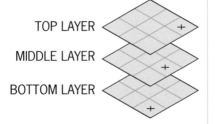

TOP LAYER

MIDDLE LAYER

BOTTOM LAYER

You have to say the three
coordinates each time you place
a nought or a cross.

**Unit C**

# Summary and assessment

## CHECK OUT

**You should now be able to**
- use systematic trial and improvement to solve equations
- draw and interpret graphs for
  - ➤ cubic functions
  - ➤ reciprocal functions
  - ➤ exponential functions
  - ➤ trigonometric functions.

**Exam-style question**

Use trial and improvement to solve this equation

$$3^x = 17$$

Give your answer to one decimal place.

Show all your trials and their outcomes.

**Sally's answer:**

$3^2 = 9; 3^3 = 27$
try values of between 2 and 3

$3^{2.5} = 15.5....$ too low
$3^{2.6} = 17.3....$ too high
$3^{2.55} = 16.4....$ too low

Values of 2.55 and 2.6 give results below and above 17

Value of x lies between 2.55 and 2.6
To one decimal place x = 2.6

Decide on a strategy and explain your thinking.

Give your final answer in the form asked for.

Show all your working clearly.

Justify your answer.

## Exam practice

1 The diagram shows part of the graph of $y = x^3 + 3x^2 + 1$

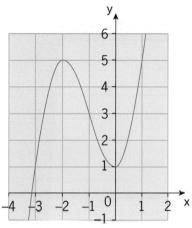

  a  Use the graph to find the values of $x$ when $y = 3$.

  b  What straight line should be drawn on the graph to solve
     $x^3 + 3x^2 - 2x = 0$?

*(4 marks)*

2  a  Draw the graph of $y = \dfrac{8}{x}$ for $-8 \le x \le 8$.

  b  On the same axes draw the line $y = x$.

  c  Show why you can use these graphs to find the square root of 8.

*(6 marks)*

3 Team Quizzers took part in a quiz.
In round one they scored $x$ points.
Their round two score, also $x$, was cubed and added to their score
from round one.
The total was almost 465 points.

If points are awarded to one decimal place, find how many points
were scored in round one.

*(4 marks)*

# Case study 8: Radio maths

Mathematics can be used to explain how radio transmission works.

Radio transmitters use continuous sine waves to send and receive information such as music or speech.

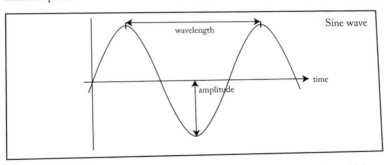

The Frequency is the number of waves transmitted per second, measured in hertz (Hz).

| 1 kilohertz | = 1 kHz | = 1,000 Hz |
|---|---|---|
| 1 megahertz | = 1 MHz | = 1,000,000 Hz |
| 1 gigahertz | = 1 GHz | = 1,000,000,000 Hz |

Use standard index form to express
a. 35 GHz in kilohertz
b. 300 Hz in megahertz.

For a sound wave, the larger the amplitude, the louder the sound.
A higher frequency gives a sound with a higher pitch.

Compare the sound produced by these waves. Comment on their pitch and volume, referring to the diagrams.

a.
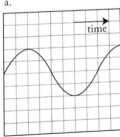

b.
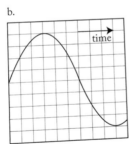

c.
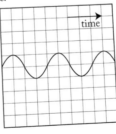

The original sound wave carrying the music or speech is not a sine wave.
The radio transmitter must encode the information on to a sine wave before it can be sent.
Two ways of doing this are by varying the sine waves amplitude (AM radio) or its frequency (FM radio).

AM radio stations transmit on frequencies between 535 kHz and 1700 kHz.

*640 on the AM dial stands for 640 kHz.*

FM radio stations transmit on frequencies between 88 mHz and 108 mHz.

*88.7 FM stands for 88,700,000 Hz.*

Maths FM transmits on the frequency 93.2 FM with a wavelength of 3.22m.

a. What is the frequency of the radio station in

   i. MHz    ii. Hz    iii. GHz?

   Give your answers in standard index form.

Maths AM transmits on a frequency of 930kHz. The wave speed is the same as for Maths FM.

b. What is the wavelength used by Maths AM?

The frequency (in kHz) of another radio station, Radio Alpha, is equal to its wavelength in metres.

c. Is this radio station on the AM or FM dial?
   Justify your answer and write down its AM or FM frequency.

**Mathematics can also be applied to plan and produce radio programmes.**

DJ Cool uses this wheel diagram to plan his hour-long show:

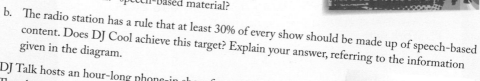

a. How many minutes of the show are taken up by
   i. music    ii. speech-based material?

b. The radio station has a rule that at least 30% of every show should be made up of speech-based content. Does DJ Cool achieve this target? Explain your answer, referring to the information given in the diagram.

DJ Talk hosts an hour-long phone-in show from 4pm.
The phone-in makes up 75% of the show. The news report is at 4pm and the weather forecast is at 4:45pm. 5-minute music sections are spread throughout the show.

c. Draw a wheel diagram to show how DJ Talk's show might look.

Investigate the frequency and wavelengths used by the radio stations that you and your friends and family listen to.

Consider some of the radio shows that you and your friends and family listen to. Do they use a format that could be shown on a wheel?

## INTRODUCTION

There are many things in life which are uncertain. Will it be sunny tomorrow? Will my football team win the Premier League? Will I be able to afford a house in the future? The mathematics used to deal with uncertainty is called probability.

**What's the point?**

When the Met Office gives a weather forecast, they use a complex mathematical model of the earth's climate to predict the probability of sunshine in a particular region.

## CHECK IN

1  Work out

   a  $1 - 0.45$       b  $1 - 0.96$       c  $1 - 0.28$

   d  $1 - 0.375$      e  $0.2 + 0.4$       f  $0.3 + 0.04$

   g  $0.65 + 0.25$     h  $0.7 + 0.05$      i  $0.5 \times 0.36$

   j  $0.25 \times 0.68$     k  $0.64 \times 0.3$      l  $0.16 \times 0.75$

2  Work out

   a  $1 - \dfrac{5}{6}$        b  $1 - \dfrac{1}{5}$        c  $1 - \dfrac{7}{9}$

   d  $2 - 1\dfrac{1}{4}$      e  $\dfrac{1}{5} + \dfrac{2}{3}$      f  $\dfrac{3}{4} + \dfrac{1}{6}$

   g  $\dfrac{2}{3} \times \dfrac{5}{6}$      h  $\dfrac{2}{9} \times \dfrac{4}{5}$

**What I should know**

Key stage 3
B9

**What I will learn**

- Calculate experimental and theoretical probability
- Identify mutually exclusive outcomes
- Draw tree diagrams

**What this leads to**

Life choices involving uncertainty

## RICH TASK

Inside a bag are three cards with the letters A, N and D written on them.

You are allowed to pick one card from the bag and then replace the card in the bag.

How many cards will you have picked before you have all the letters to spell the word AND?

# Probability

- Use the vocabulary of probability
- Understand and use the probability scale

At a fete there are two silver money-trees.
There are five envelopes left on each tree.
The envelopes on each tree contain 50p, 25p, 20p, 10p and 5p respectively.
To choose an envelope from the money tree costs 25p each time.

On a money-tree, the amounts would not be written on the envelopes, otherwise people would just choose the highest amount!

## RICH TASK

Reuben decides to choose two envelopes, one from each tree.
To help find out if he is wise to play the game, he lists the **set of all possible outcomes** in a **sample space diagram**.
He believes that he will receive more money than he paid. Is he correct?

|      | 5p  | 10p | 20p | 25p | 50p  |
|------|-----|-----|-----|-----|------|
| 5p   | 10p | 15p | 25p | 30p | 55p  |
| 10p  | 15p | 20p | 30p | 35p | 60p  |
| 10p  | 15p | 20p | 30p | 35p | 60p  |
| 50p  | 55p | 60p | 70p | 75p | 100p |
| 50p  | 55p | 60p | 70p | 75p | 100p |

→ **Probability is a measure of how likely an event is to happen.**
Scoring an odd number on a dice is an event.

→ **An event can be made up of a set of outcomes.**
Scoring a 3 on a dice is an outcome.

Probability is measured on a scale from 0 to 1.

Probability increasing

0 ——————————————————— 1

Outcome: Impossible                         Outcome: Certain

You can write probability as a fraction, decimal or percentage.

**Study of chance**

## Exercise C25.1

MEDIUM LOW

1  The probability that a girl in class 10Z chosen at random has a cat is 0.34.
   What is the probability that a girl in class 10Z chosen at random does not have a cat?

2  A bag contains 6 green, 10 blue and 9 red marbles. 8 of the marbles are large, 17 are small.
   One marble is chosen at random. What is the probability that the marble is
   a  red
   b  not red
   c  large
   d  small
   e  blue
   f  not green?

3  Four teams are left in a football competition. Some of the probabilities of their winning the competition are shown in the table.

| City | United | Rovers | Town |
|------|--------|--------|------|
| 0.17 | 0.38 | $x$ | $2x$ |

   a  Explain the chances of Town winning compared to the chances of Rovers winning.
   b  Work out the value of $x$.

4  Two dice are rolled, a red dice and a blue dice. The score is the number showing on each dice multiplied together.

   a  Draw a table to show all possible outcomes.
   b  Find the probability of getting a score of
      i  18
      ii  29
      iii  greater than 20.
   c  Which is more likely, a score that is even or a score that is odd? Explain how you can tell.

5  Simi rolls two dice and records the score as the sum of the numbers shown on each dice.
   One dice has the numbers 1, −2, 3, −4, 5, 6 on its faces.

   The other dice has the numbers 1, 2, −3, 4, 5, 6 on its faces.
   a  Draw a diagram to show all the possible outcomes.
   b  Find the probability that the score is negative.

Unit C

# Mutually exclusive outcomes

- Identify different mutually exclusive outcomes
- Know that the sum of the probabilities of all mutually exclusive outcomes is 1

→ **Two or more outcomes are mutually exclusive if they cannot happen at the same time.**
→ **When outcomes are mutually exclusive you can add their probabilities to find the total probability.**

**EXAMPLE**

A spinner has 12 equal sides: 5 green (G), 4 blue (B), 2 red (R) and 1 white (W). The spinner is spun.

**a** What is the probability that the spinner lands on
   **i** green or white     **ii** green or blue
   **iii** blue or red or white     **iv** not green?
**b** Why are the answers to parts **iii** and **iv** the same?

**ANSWER**

**a** **i** $P(G) = \frac{5}{12}$   $P(W) = \frac{1}{12}$      **ii** $P(G) = \frac{5}{12}$   $P(B) = \frac{4}{12}$

       $P(G \text{ or } W) = \frac{5}{12} + \frac{1}{12} = \frac{6}{12}$         $P(G \text{ or } B) = \frac{5}{12} + \frac{4}{12} = \frac{9}{12}$

**iii** $P(B) = \frac{4}{12}$   $P(R) = \frac{2}{12}$   $P(W) = \frac{1}{12}$      **iv** $P(\text{not } G) = 1 - P(G) = 1 - \frac{5}{12} = \frac{7}{12}$

       $P(B \text{ or } R \text{ or } W) = \frac{4}{12} + \frac{2}{12} + \frac{1}{12} = \frac{7}{12}$

> **Add** the probabilities.

**b** The possible outcomes are green, blue, red and white. So if not green, it has to be blue, red or white.

→ **The sum of the probabilities of mutually exclusive outcomes that cover all possible outcomes = 1**

**EXAMPLE**

When you roll a dice, which two of the following events are both mutually exclusive and cover all possible outcomes?
A – prime numbers     B – odd numbers
C – multiples of 2     D – factors of 6

**ANSWER**

Event B is the numbers 1, 3, 5, and event C is 2, 4, 6.
So events B and C are both mutually exclusive and cover all outcomes.

## Exercise C25.2

1   A spinner has 20 equal sides:
    7 have circles, 5 have pentagons, 4 have squares, 3 have triangles,
    1 has a rectangle.
    The spinner is spun.
    What is the probability that the spinner lands on

    a   circle
    b   not circle
    c   rectangle
    d   not rectangle
    e   circle or square
    f   pentagon or square
    g   triangle or square or rectangle
    h   circle or pentagon or triangle
    i   not square?

2   The table shows information about the type of pet owned by students in class 10A.

    No student has more than one pet.

    | Pet | Cat | Dog | Hamster | Fish | No pet |
    |---|---|---|---|---|---|
    | Number of students | 7 | 8 | 2 | 4 | 9 |

    a   How many students are there in the class?

    One student is chosen at random from the class.
    b   Work out the probability that the student chosen will
        i    own a cat
        ii   own a cat or a dog
        iii  own a dog or a fish
        iv   own a cat or a hamster
        v    not own a pet
        vi   own a pet.

3   The table shows the probabilities of getting scores on a biased dice.

    | Score | 1 | 2 | 3 | 4 | 5 | 6 |
    |---|---|---|---|---|---|---|
    | Probability | 0.2 | 0.15 | 0.3 | 0.1 | 0.2 | 0.05 |

    Work out the probability of a score of
    a   2 or 3
    b   5 or 6
    c   an even number.

4   The table shows the probabilities of getting colours on a rainbow spinner.

    | Colour | Red | Orange | Yellow | Green | Blue | Indigo | Violet |
    |---|---|---|---|---|---|---|---|
    | Probability | 0.1 | 0.1 | 0.25 | 0.13 | 0.1 | 0.12 | 0.2 |

    When the spinner is spun
    a   which colours are equally likely to happen?
    b   what colour is the most likely to show?
    c   what is the probability of
        i    blue or red
        ii   indigo or violet
        iii  orange or green?

Unit C

● Compare experimental data to theoretical probabilities

## RICH TASK

Patsy makes a five-sided spinner.
Each side is the same size.
They are coloured red, green, blue, white and yellow.
She spins it 100 times and these are the results.

| Red | Green | Blue | White | Yellow |
|-----|-------|------|-------|--------|
| 27  | 18    | 20   | 16    | 19     |

Do you think the spinner is fair or biased?
Give a reason for your answer.

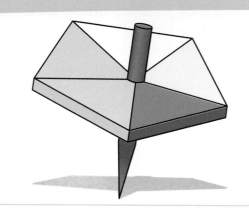

If Patsy's spinner is fair, then the theoretical probability of it landing on any colour is $\frac{1}{5}$.

$P(green) = \frac{1}{5}$

If she thinks her spinner is biased, she can estimate the experimental probability of each colour.

$P(green) = \frac{18}{100} = \frac{9}{50}$

---

**EXAMPLE**

A **biased** coin is thrown 200 times. It lands on heads 140 times.
  **a** Estimate the probability of this coin landing on heads on the next throw.
  **b** Estimate the number of heads you expect to get when the coin is thrown 500 times.

**ANSWER**

  **a** $P(Head) = \frac{140}{200}$
  **b** Estimate the expected number: $500 \times \frac{140}{200} = 350$

---

➔ **Expected number = total number × probability**

---

**EXAMPLE**

Tom carries out a survey about the number of people that are left-handed in his village.
He asks 40 people in the village, and five of them are left-handed.
  **a** Estimate the probability that a person in the village is left-handed.
  **b** If 192 people live in his village, estimate how many are left-handed.

**ANSWER**

  **a** $P(left\text{-}handed) = \frac{5}{40}$
  **b** Estimated number: $192 \times \frac{5}{40} = 24$

---

> → **The closer experimental probability is to theoretical probability, the less likely it is that there is bias.**

## Exercise C25.3

MEDIUM

1 The probability that a biased dice will land on a six is 0.35.
The dice is rolled 400 times.
Work out an estimate for the number of times the dice will land on a six.

2 The probability that a biased coin will land on tails is 0.24.
The coin is thrown 500 times.
Work out an estimate for the number of times the coin will land on tails.

3 A biased four-sided dice is rolled 120 times. The table shows the outcomes.

| Score | 1 | 2 | 3 | 4 |
|---|---|---|---|---|
| Frequency | 22 | 34 | 44 | 20 |

a Explain why it is twice as likely that the dice will land on a 3 than a 1.
b The dice is rolled once more. Estimate the probability that it lands on 2.
c The dice is rolled a further 300 times.
   How many times would you expect the dice to land on 4?

4 ☆ CHALLENGE ☆

A circle, radius $r$, is inscribed in a square. Darts are thrown, at random, and land in either the circle or the square.
How can you use the probability of the dart landing in the circle to find an approximate value of $\pi$?

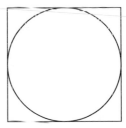

5 ☆ ACTIVITY ☆

To play the probability maze game you drop a 2p coin in the slot.
At each junction the coin has an equal choice of falling to the left or to the right.
If the coin lands at A or D you win.
If the coin lands at B or C you lose.

a Calculate the probability that the coin lands at
   i A   ii B   iii C   iv D.
b If the game was played by one person 100 times, who would you expect to be richer, the owner of the game or the person playing?

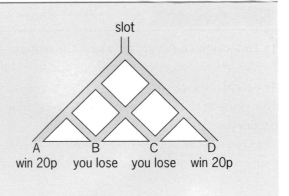

- Understand and use estimates of probability from relative frequency

Laura suspects that a coin is biased towards heads.

The first 10 spins of the coin give

H T H H H T H T H H

Laura calculates the **relative frequency** of obtaining a head:
$\frac{7}{10} = 0.7$

The next 10 spins of the coin give

T T H T H T H T H T

Laura re-calculates the relative frequency from all 20 results:
$\frac{11}{20} = 0.55$

There are 11 heads out of 20 in total.

This is closer to the expected probability of 0.5, but Laura carries out more trials to find out if the coin is biased.

Laura spins the coin 40 more times, and finds the number of heads as shown in the table.

| Total spins | 10 | 20 | 30 | 40 | 50 | 60 |
|---|---|---|---|---|---|---|
| Total number of heads | 7 | 11 | 17 | 22 | 28 | 33 |
| Relative frequency | 0.7 | 0.55 | 0.567 | 0.55 | 0.56 | 0.55 |

The graph shows the changes in relative frequency.

The relative frequency is settling down to around 0.55.
This is the **experimental probability** of obtaining a head with this particular coin.
The coin may be slightly biased towards heads.
Laura needs to carry out more trials if her estimate is to be reliable.

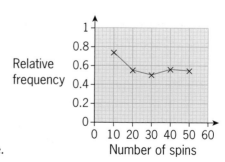

> → **Relative frequency** can give an **estimate** of probability.
> → The more **trials** you carry out the more reliable your estimate will be.
> → The closer relative frequency is to theoretical probability, the less likely it is that there is bias.

A **trial** is a repetition of a statistical experiment. In this case, it's a single spin of a coin.

## Exercise C25.4

**\*1**  Clara suspects that a coin is biased.
She spins the coin and notes how many heads she gets in each group of 10 spins. Clara spins the coin 100 times in total.
The table shows her results.

| Total spins | 10 | 20 | 30 | 40 | 50 | 60 | 70 | 80 | 90 | 100 |
|---|---|---|---|---|---|---|---|---|---|---|
| Total number of heads | 4 | 7 | 11 | 13 | 18 | 22 | 26 | 29 | 32 | 35 |
| Relative frequency | | | | | | | | | | |

   a  Copy the table and complete the relative frequency row.
   b  Write down the best estimate of the probability of the coin landing on heads.
   c  Is the coin biased? Explain your answer.

**2**  Charlie spins a coin 50 times.
He calculates the relative frequency of obtaining a tail after each group of 10 spins.

| Number of spins | 10 | 20 | 30 | 40 | 50 |
|---|---|---|---|---|---|
| Relative frequency | 0.6 | 0.55 | 0.5 | 0.55 | 0.54 |

   a  How many times did the coin land on tails in
      **i**  the first 10 spins      **ii**  the second 10 spins?
   b  In which group of 10 spins did Charlie get   **i**  the smallest number of tails
      **ii**  the largest number of tails?
   c  If Charlie were to spin the coin a further 10 times, exactly how many tails should he get so that the relative frequency is 0.5?

**\*3**  An equilateral spinner with three sectors coloured brown (B), orange (O) and green (G) is spun.
The colours from the first 20 spins are:

| B | G | B | O | G | O | O | B | B | O | G | B | B | G | O | B | G | G | O | O |

   a  Draw a relative frequency graph to show how the relative frequency of getting green changed with each spin.
   b  Use these 20 spins to estimate the probability of getting each colour.
   c  Do you think the spinner is fair? Give a reason for your answer.
   d  If the spinner were spun 3000 times, how many of each colour would you expect to get?

# Independent events

- Know when to multiply probabilities

When a dice is rolled and a coin is thrown, the number rolled on the dice has no effect on whether the coin lands on head or tail.
The events are independent.

This sample space diagram shows the 12 equally likely outcomes.
The probability of each is $\frac{1}{12}$.

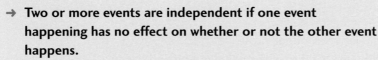

| H1 | H2 | H3 | H4 | H5 | H6 |
|----|----|----|----|----|----|
| T1 | T2 | T3 | T4 | T5 | T6 |

Notice that you can multiply to get the probability, for example;

$P(H) = \frac{1}{2}$   $P(5) = \frac{1}{6}$

$P(H \text{ and } 5) = \frac{1}{2} \times \frac{1}{6} = \frac{1}{12}$

→ **Two or more events are independent if one event happening has no effect on whether or not the other event happens.**

→ **For two independent events A and B**
**P(A and B) = P(A) × P(B)**

This rule is particularly useful when outcomes are *not* equally likely.

**EXAMPLE**

The table shows the number of boys and the number of girls in Years 12 and 13 at a school.

|       | Year 12 | Year 13 |
|-------|---------|---------|
| **Boys**  | 48      | 96      |
| **Girls** | 72      | 54      |

Two students are to be chosen at random from the school.

a One student is to be chosen from Year 12 and one student is to be chosen from Year 13. Calculate the probability that both students will be girls.

b One student is to be chosen from all the girls and one student is to be chosen from all the boys. Calculate the probability that both students are in Year 13.

**ANSWER**

a $P(\text{girl Y 12 and girl Y 13}) = \frac{72}{120} \times \frac{54}{150}$

$= \frac{27}{125}$

b $P(\text{Y 13 girl and Y 13 boy}) = \frac{54}{126} \times \frac{96}{144}$

$= \frac{2}{7}$

1 Two drawing pins are dropped. The probability that each pin lands point up is 0.7.
   a Write down the probability that a drawing pin lands point down.
   b Calculate the probability that both drawing pins land point up.
   c Calculate the probability that only one drawing pin lands point up.

2 Ed and Gala each make a three-sided spinner using card and a pencil.
   Each sector is the same shape and size.
   Each spinner is equally likely to land on any one of the sectors.
   Ed and Gala decide to spin their spinner and add up the scores.
   a Work out the probability of a total score of   i 2   ii 4.
   b Explain why the probability of a score of 3 and the probability of a score of 5 are the same.

3 This spinner is in the shape of an equilateral triangle.
   The spinner is spun twice.
   a What is the probability that it lands on red **both** times?
   b The spinner is spun for a third time.
      What is the probability that it shows red **all three** times?

4 The table shows the number of boys and the number of girls in Years 10 and 11 at a school.
   Two students are to be chosen at random from the school.

|  | Year 10 | Year 11 |
|---|---|---|
| **Boys** | 76 | 74 |
| **Girls** | 84 | 66 |

   a One student is to be chosen from Year 10 and one student is to be chosen from Year 11.
      Calculate the probability that both students will be girls.
   b One student is to be chosen from all the girls and one student is to be chosen from all the boys.
      Calculate the probability that both students are in Year 10.

5 The box-and-whisker plots show the distribution of ages at which a sample of men and a sample of women first marry. Work out the probability that a man and woman both getting married for the first time are both aged 28 or older.

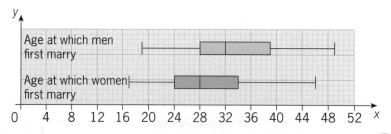

# Tree diagrams

- Use tree diagrams to represent outcomes of compound events

**A tree diagram can be used to:**
→ **show all the outcomes of two or more events**
→ **find probabilities of independent events.**

**EXAMPLE**

A bag contains 4 blue counters and 5 red counters.
A counter is chosen at random from the bag, its colour noted and it is replaced in the bag.
The bag is shaken and then a second counter is chosen at random.
**a** Draw a tree diagram to show all the possible outcomes.
**b** Find the probability that
   **i** both counters are blue
   **ii** different coloured counters are chosen.

**ANSWER**

**a**

Label the sets of branches with each choice.

1st choice    2nd choice

$\frac{4}{9}$ Blue

Blue

$\frac{4}{9}$

$\frac{5}{9}$ Red

$\frac{4}{9}$ Blue

$\frac{5}{9}$ Red

$\frac{5}{9}$ Red

Write the probability on each branch.

Write the outcome at the end of each branch.

**CHECK:**
The probabilities on each pair of branches should add up to 1
$\left(\frac{4}{9} + \frac{5}{9} = 1\right)$

**b** **i** $P(B\ B) = \frac{4}{9} \times \frac{4}{9} = \frac{16}{81}$

  **ii** $P(B \text{ and } R) = P(B\ R) + P(R\ B)$
$$= \left(\frac{4}{9} \times \frac{5}{9}\right) + \left(\frac{5}{9} \times \frac{4}{9}\right)$$
$$= \frac{20}{81} + \frac{20}{81} = \frac{40}{81}$$

**To find probabilities when the outcome can happen in more than one way**
→ **Multiply the probabilities along each route**
→ **Add the results of each route.**

**Study of chance**

1　Single batteries are placed in a red toy car and a blue toy car.
The probability that a single battery lasts for
more than 20 hours is 0.8.

　a　Find the probability that a battery does
　　not last for more than 20 hours.

　b　Draw a tree diagram to show the outcomes
　　for both cars.

　c　Find the probability that the battery lasts
　　more than 20 hours
　　**i**　in both cars
　　**ii**　in only one car
　　**iii**　in at least one car.

2　A bag contains 5 red and 3 blue marbles. A marble is chosen at
random from the bag, its colour noted and it is replaced.
A second marble is chosen at random.

　a　Draw a tree diagram to show all the outcomes for the
　　two marbles.

　b　Find the probability of choosing
　　**i**　two red marbles
　　**ii**　one marble of each colour
　　**iii**　at least one red marble.

3　Josh makes two model aeroplanes, a grey plane and an orange plane.
He flies both aeroplanes.
The probability that he crashes a model aeroplane is 0.01,
independent of the other aeroplane.

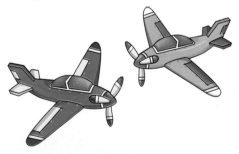

　a　Find the probability that a model aeroplane does not crash.
　b　Draw a tree diagram to show all the outcomes for both model
　　aeroplanes.
　c　Find the probability that both model aeroplanes crash.
　d　Find the probability that only one of the model aeroplanes crashes.

• Use tree diagrams to represent outcomes of compound events

Sometimes the probability of subsequent events is dependent upon what has already happened.

**EXAMPLE**

A bag contains 7 lime and 3 orange sweets
A sweet is chosen at random from the bag, and eaten.
A second sweet is chosen at random.
**a** Draw a tree diagram to show all the possible outcomes.
**b** Find the probability that
   **i** both sweets are orange
   **ii** the sweets are different flavours.

> The second choice probabilities are out of nine because there are only nine sweets left.

**ANSWER**

**a**   1st choice      2nd choice

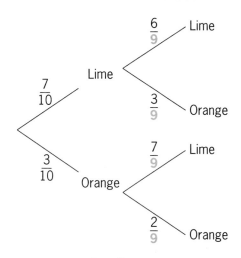

> **CHECK:**
>
> The probabilities on each pair of branches add up to 1.
>
> $\left( \text{eg } \dfrac{7}{9} + \dfrac{2}{9} = 1 \right)$

**b**  **i**  $P(OO) = \dfrac{3}{10} \times \dfrac{2}{9}$

           $= \dfrac{6}{90}$

  **ii**  $P(LO) + P(OL) = \left( \dfrac{7}{10} \times \dfrac{3}{9} \right) + \left( \dfrac{3}{10} \times \dfrac{7}{9} \right)$

                        $= \dfrac{21}{90} + \dfrac{21}{90}$

                        $= \dfrac{42}{90}$

> **EXAMINER'S TIP:**
>
> Errors are less likely if fractions (not decimals) are used.

1   A bag contains 3 white counters and 8 black counters.
    A counter is chosen at random from the bag, its colour noted
    and it is **not** replaced in the bag.
    The bag is shaken and then a second counter is chosen at random.
    a   Draw a tree diagram to show all the outcomes and their probabilities.
    b   Find the probability of choosing
        i   two white counters
        ii  one counter of each colour
        iii at least one white counter.

2   A bag contains 12 lemon and 4 orange sweets.
    Reuben chooses a sweet at random and eats it and then
    chooses a second sweet.
    a   Draw a tree diagram to show all the outcomes and
        probabilities of choosing two sweets.
    b   Find the probability of choosing
        i   two orange sweets
        ii  one sweet of each flavour
        iii at least one orange sweet.

3   Julie is a university student.
    On Tuesdays, she is supposed to attend a lecture, and also go to the tutorial that
    accompanies the lecture.
    The probability that she attends the lecture is 0.8.
    If she attends the lecture the probability that she attends the
    tutorial is 0.9.
    If she does not attend the lecture the probability that she attends
    the tutorial is 0.6.
    a   Draw a tree diagram to show the possible outcomes.
    b   Work out the probability that Julie attends
        i   the tutorial              ii   neither the lecture nor the tutorial.

4   Students at a school study either French or Spanish, but not both.
    The probability that a student studies French is 0.9.
    The probability that a student who studies French has visited France is 0.6.
    The probability that a student who studies Spanish has visited Spain is 0.8.
    a   Draw a tree diagram to show the outcomes and probabilities.
    b   One student is chosen at random. Work out the probability
        that the student
        i   studies the language and has visited the country
        ii  studies Spanish, but has not visited Spain.

# Summary and assessment

## CHECK OUT

You should now be able to
- compare experimental and theoretical probability
- find relative frequency
- list outcomes systematically
- find probabilities for mutually exclusive and independent events
- draw and use tree diagrams.

## Exam-style question

The box-and-whisker diagrams show the age of contestants in a dance competition.
The judges choose one male and one female winner.
What is the probability that the winners are both over 25?

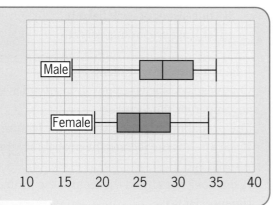

Decide what information you need.

**Carol's answer:**

Female age 25 is median;
$\frac{1}{2}$ of females are over 25

Male age 25 is lower quartile;
$\frac{3}{4}$ of males are over 25

Probability both aged over 25:

$\frac{1}{2} \times \frac{3}{4} = \frac{3}{8}$

Interpret the diagrams to find each probability.

Final answer to probability is fraction, decimal or percentage.

Male and female winners are chosen independently.

## Exam practice

*1 Two ordinary fair dice are thrown.
One of the dice is green, the other dice is yellow.
Find the probability that the score shown on the green dice is
less than the score shown on the yellow dice.
Justify your answer.

(*3 marks*)

2 Martha and Nathan each have a bag of coins. Each contain
£1 and £2 coins.
Martha has four £1 coins and three £2 coins.
Nathan has two £1 coins and five £2 coins.

Nathan takes a coin at random from Martha's bag and places it
in his own.
Martha then chooses a coin from Nathan's bag.

a Draw a tree diagram to show the possible outcomes and
probabilities of these choices.
b Work out the probability that Martha chooses a £2 coin.

(*6 marks*)

*3 The spinner shown is going to be used at a school fayre to raise
money for charity.

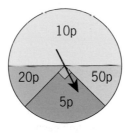

You win whatever the spinner lands on.
What is the least amount that should be charged?

(*3 marks*)

# GCSE formulae

In your OCR GCSE examination you will be given a formula sheet like the one on this page.

You should use it as an aid to memory. It will be useful to become familiar with the information on this sheet.

**Volume of a prism** = area of cross section × length

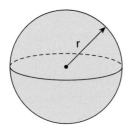

**Volume of sphere** = $\frac{4}{3}\pi r^3$
**Surface area of sphere** = $4\pi r^2$

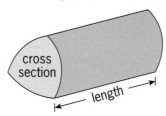

**Volume of cone** = $\frac{1}{3}\pi r^2 h$
**Curved surface area of cone** = $\pi r l$

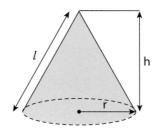

**Area of trapezium** = $\frac{1}{2}(a + b)h$

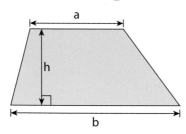

**In any triangle ABC**

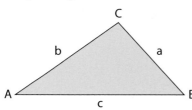

**Sine rule** $\dfrac{a}{\sin A} = \dfrac{b}{\sin B} = \dfrac{c}{\sin C}$

**Cosine rule** $a^2 = b^2 + c^2 - 2bc \cos A$

**Area of triangle** = $\frac{1}{2}ab \sin C$

**The Quadratic Equation**
The solutions of $ax^2 + bx + c = 0$ where $a \neq 0$, are given by

$$x = \frac{-b \pm \sqrt{(b^2 - 4ac)}}{2a}$$

# Answers

## A1 Integers and decimals

### Check in

**1 a** four thousand    **b** four hundred
   **c** four tenths    **d** four thousandths

**2 a** check number line
   **b** $-3, -2.4, -1.8, 0, +1.5, +5, +6$

### Ex A1.1

**1 a** no    **b** yes    **c** yes
**2 a** no    **b** no    **c** yes

### Ex A1.2

**1 a** $-2$    **b** 1    **c** $-19$    **d** 8
   **e** $-27$    **f** 20    **g** 4    **h** $-3$
   **i** 77    **j** 12    **k** $-5$

**2 a** 1.125    **b** $\frac{11}{12}$    **c** 5.5

**3 a** $72, -54$    **b** $3 \times 4 + 4 \times -3 = 0$
   **c** answered 3 questions, all correct; answered 10
     questions, 6 correct; answered 17 questions, 9 correct

**4 a** $\pm 1, 0$    **b** $n < -1, 0 < n < 1$

### Ex A1.3

**1 a** 19.37    **b** 19.4    **c** 0.00752    **d** 0.008
   **e** 153.262    **f** 153.26

**2 a** 76 000    **b** 76 300    **c** 23 400    **d** 58 000
   **e** 46 000    **f** 23.40

### Ex A1.4

**1 a** 61    **b** 23.83    **c** 1.5625    **d** 0.35
   **e** $1.\dot{3}$    **f** 156.25    **g** 500    **h** 7.5

**2 a** 1.736 307 692   1.7    **b** 3.122 448 98   3.12
   **c** $-0.191\,347\,436$   $-0.19$   **d** 12.682 835 82   12.7
   **e** 3.839 270 764   3.84      **f** 2.370 021 097   2.4

**3 a** 0.25    **b** $0.\dot{1}$    **c** 0.4
   **d** $0.2\dot{7}$    **e** 5    **f** 6.25
   **g** 2    **h** 4    **i** 2.5

**4 a** 1296    **b** 78 125    **c** 100 000
   **d** 262 144    **e** 410.0 625    **f** 0.004 096

### Exam practice

**1 a** 1.716 961 498    **b** 2

**2** $2\frac{2}{9}$   *or*   $2.\dot{2}$

**3** Uranus; she would weigh 60 kg

## A2 Summary statistics

### Check in

**1 a** Nicola – primary; Maddy – secondary
   **b** Primary data is data you collect yourself e.g. from
     questionnaires
     Secondary data is data collected from other
     sources e.g. published statistics

**2 a i** Because 4 occurs in both of the first two
      groupings
    **ii** Because no times below 3 hours have been
      allowed for in the table
   **b** Using groupings like:
     less than 3 hours; at least 3 hours but less than 4
     hours, etc

**3 a** $22\frac{1}{2}$    **b** 21    **c** 6    **d** 21

### Ex A2.1

**1** various
**2 a** 11%    **b** % of Welsh with AB for example
**3 a** survey    **b** General practiners
   **c** various    **d** various

### Ex A2.2

**1 a i** cont.   **ii** disc   **b i** cont.   **ii** disc
   **c i** disc   **ii** cont   **d i** disc   **ii** cont

**2 a** other years different preferences
   **b i** List all 1000 names, number 000 to 999,
      generate 50 random 3-digit numbers on
      calculator, select students with these numbers
   **b ii** List all 1000 names, generate 2-digit random
      number between 01 and 20, select this student
      then every following 20$^{th}$ name

**3 a** proportion of boys too high
   **b i** 200   **ii** $\frac{4}{5}$   **iii** 40   **iv** 10

**4 a** need to include patients who rarely use antibiotics
   **b** 15–45 years (parents of children)    **c** various
**5** various

### Ex A2.3

**1 a i** B 4.0 sec., G 4.2 sec.
    **ii** B 3.8 sec., G bi-modal distribution
    **iii** B 5.3 sec., G 6.3 sec.
    **iv** B 5.18 sec., G 6.15 sec.
    **v** B 2.4 sec., G 2.1 sec.
   **b** various

**2 a**

```
                P                                    Z
          9 8 8 6 | 0 | 8 9
9 8 7 7 4 3 2 1 0 | 1 | 1 2 4 5 6 7 7 8 9
          9 7 4 2 | 2 | 1 3 4 5 8 9
            7 1 | 3 | 2 3
```

   Key   1 | 3 | 2 means puzzle P 31 mins Z 32 mins
   **b i** P 31 mins, Z 25 mins
    **ii** P bi-modal, Z 17 mins
    **iii** P 17.5 mins, Z 19.5 mins
    **iv** P 17 mins, Z 18 mins
    **v** P 14 mins, Z 11 mins
   **c** various

**3** 8.29
**4** 78.6%

## Ex A2.4

1 plot    positive skew
2 plot    positive skew
3 plot    positive skew
4 plot    positive skew
5 plot    symmetrical

## Ex A2.5

1 plot
2 plot
3 eg. more than 75% of older girls spend longer than any of younger girls
4 eg. median times same, some girls have longer times than any boys, fastest 25% of boys faster than fastest 25% girls

## Ex A2.6

| 1 | a | i | 6 | ii | 6 | iii | 5.8 | iv | 4 | v | 3 |
|---|---|---|---|---|---|-----|-----|----|---|---|---|
|   | b | i | 5 | ii | 5 | iii | 5   | iv | 4 | v | 2 |
|   | c | i | 4 | ii | 6 | iii | 6.6 | iv | 6 | v | 5 |
|   | d | i | 6 | ii | 6 | iii | 5.7 | iv | 6 | v | 3 |

2 a   mode: B 18, G 15; median: B 16, G 16; mean: B 16.2, G 16.1; range: B 6, G 6; IQR: B 3.5, G 3 various answers
  b   various answers

## Ex A2.7

1 a   $20 < B \le 30$   b   £24.20
  c   It uses all the data available
2 a   £88      b   $80 < M \le 120$   c   No
3 Mean: Teachers 11.5 km Office Workers 14.1 km
  Median class: Teachers $10 < d \le 15$ Office Workers $10 < d \le 15$
  Modal class: Teachers $10 < d \le 15$ Office Workers $10 < d \le 15$
  The mean supports David's conclusion, although there is no great difference in distances travelled by the 2 groups.

## Ex A2.8

1 a   eg. may not listen to show and both boxes are positive
  b   eg. may not listen to radio; boxes do not cover range of answers; 1 hour in two boxes
  c   various
2 a   i   eg. boxes do not cover range of answers
  b   various
3 various

## Exam practice

1 a   4.1 mins      b   $4 < m \le 5$
2 Would need $\frac{4}{15}$ of each type of official and this does not give whole numbers

3 median: B 66, G 62; mode: B 66, G 57; mean: B 64, G 64.7; range: B 44, G 46
  There is no significant difference between Girls and Boys' results.

## A3 Constructions

### Check in

1 $a = 35°$, $b = 105°$
2 Check constructions
3 Check constructions

## Ex A3.1

| 1 | a | i | 6 m | ii | 8 m | iii | 14 m |
|---|---|---|-----|----|-----|-----|------|
|   | b | i | 18 feet | ii | 24 feet | iii | 42 feet |

2 a   23 cm    b   38 cm    c   46 cm    d   162 kg
  e   177 kg   f   189 kg   g   640 g    h   780 g
  i   850 g    j   10.4°C   k   11.9°C   l   12.6°C
  m   3.26     n   3.38     o   3.42     p   7.25 m
  q   8.75 m   r   9.5 m

3 1.189 m by 0.841 m

4

|         | Volume | | Mass | | Height | |
|---------|--------|------|-------|------|--------|------|
|         | litres | ml   | grams | kg   | metres | mm   |
| Milk    | 2.27   | 2270 | 2400  | 2.4  | 0.32   | 320  |
| Ice-cream | 2.5  | 2500 | 1470  | 1.47 | 0.15   | 150  |

5 a   i   60 cm    ii   24 km    iii   2.5 kg
     iv   27 litres   v   2 litres
  b   i   3.3 feet   ii   25 miles   iii   18 lbs
     iv   31.5 pints   v   3.5 pints
6 196 lbs and 169 lbs, 27 lbs lost
7 a   256 km    14 km/litre
  b   4 gallons    40 miles/gallon

## Ex A3.2

1 a   59°, 51°, 70°    b   38°, 81°, 61°
  c   83°, 56°, 41°    d   119°, 32°, 29°
2 AB = 6.6 km
  BC = 7.3 km
3 2 km
4 no
5 due east or due west
6 tetrahedron (triangular-based pyramid)
7 32 metres
9 Take bearings of a point on the opposite bank from two places, P and Q, on this side of the canal. Measure the distance PQ. Make a scale drawing and measure the canal's width.
10 no, there are two possible angles for C
11 An impossible triangle. Alter either 57° or the length of one side to make it possible.

## Ex A3.3

Check students' constructions.

## Ex A3.4

**1  a**

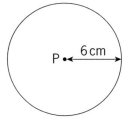

the circle

**b**

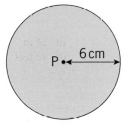

the area inside the circle

**c**

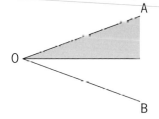

the line bisecting the angle AOB

**d**

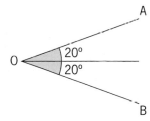

the area between the line OA and the bisector

**e**

K ─────────────── L

2 cm

─────────────

2 cm

M ─────────────── N

the line parallel to KL and MN and midway between them

**f**

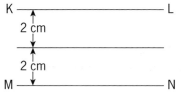

K ─────────────── L

2 cm

2 cm

M ─────────────── N

the area between the line KL and the mid–line

**g**

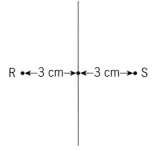

R •←3 cm→•←3 cm→• S

the perpendicular bisector of the line RS

**h**

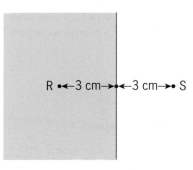

R •←3 cm→•←3 cm→• S

the area on the side of the perpendicular bisector that contains R

**i**

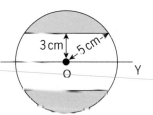

3 cm    5 cm

O          Y

the area inside two segments of circle centre O radius 5 cm

**2**

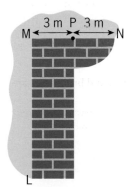

3 m  P  3 m
M←──→•←──→N

L

**3**

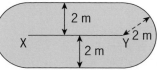

2 m

X          2 m    Y    2 m

2 m

**4 a**

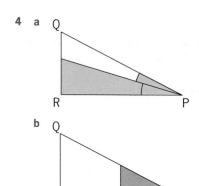

**b**

**5**

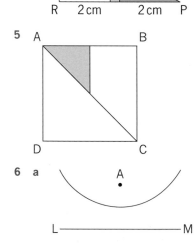

**6 a**

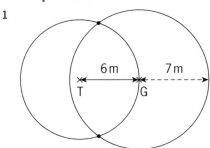

### Ex A3.5

1  **a  i**  156 km  **ii**  108 km
   **b**  Dublin to Belfast 108 km, bearing 010°
         Belfast to Liverpool 188 km, bearing 123°
2  **a**  270°  **b**  045°  **c**  225°
3  **a**  49 km  **b**  70 km
4  685 km on bearing 188°
5  $(180 + x)°$
6  Bearing of A from B is 240°
   Bearing of A from C is 290°
7  253 km per h on a bearing of 067°

### Exam practice

1

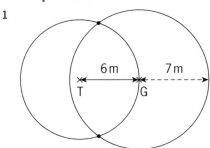

2  Check students' construction
3  **a**  115 km 244°  **b**  190 km 260°

## A4 Factors, multiples and ratio

### Check in

1  1, 2, 3, 4, 6, 12, 24
2  13, 26, 39, 52, 65, 78
3  2, 3, 5, 7, 11, 13, 17, 19, 23, 29
4  **a**  45  **b**  100

### Ex A4.1

1  **a**  $2 \times 2 \times 2 \times 2 \times 3$  **b**  $3 \times 3 \times 3$
   **c**  $2 \times 3 \times 3 \times 3$  **d**  $2 \times 2 \times 2 \times 3 \times 5$
   **e**  $2 \times 2 \times 2 \times 3 \times 3$  **f**  $2 \times 3 \times 7 \times 7$  **g**  $7 \times 53$
2  **a**  432 6  **b**  3960 3  **c**  3384 2
   **d**  196 7  **e**  390 5
3  **a**  A prime number squared has exactly three factors
         because the only factors are: 1, the prime number,
         and the square itself. (the only nontrivial divisor of
         the square is the prime number).
   **b**  The numbers that have exactly four factors are
         either product of two primes (then the only factors
         will be 1, the product, and the two primes) or a
         cube of a prime (then the only factors will be 1, the
         cube, the square of the prime, and the prime itself).

### Ex A4.2

No questions, only activities

### Ex A4.3

1  **a**  £8 : £40  **b**  £56 : £8  **c**  £24 : £84
   **d**  £56 : £40  **e**  £60 : £120 : £240  **f**  £75 : £150 : £200
2  £45.30
3  £8.40
4  94
5  138
6  680 g
7  **a**  6 : 5  **b**  7 : 6  **c**  6 years, 3 years

### Exam practice

1  $2 \times 2 \times 3 \times 7$
2  45
3  **a**  $\frac{3}{5}$  **b**  5 : 3

## A5 Sequences

### Check in

1  **a**  10, 12  **b**  70, 64  **c**  16, 22
   **d**  −2, −5  **e**  48, 96  **f**  $\frac{1}{6}, \frac{1}{7}$

2  $4(n - 1)$, $15 - n$, $2n + 7$, and then $2n^2$ and $\frac{9}{n} + 15$ are equal
3  Square numbers

### Ex A5.1

1  **a**  3, 6, 9, 12, 15  **b**  5, 9, 13, 17, 21
   **c**  4, 11, 18, 25, 32  **d**  10, 15, 20, 25, 30
   **e**  −4, −2, 0, 2, 4  **f**  $\frac{1}{10}, \frac{2}{10}, \frac{3}{10}, \frac{4}{10}, \frac{5}{10}$
   **g**  4, 3, 2, 1, 0  **h**  90, 81, 72, 63, 54

**2** 3, 6, 9, 12, 15, ... matches to $3n$
5, 11, 17, 23, 29, ... matches to $6n - 1$
7, 11, 15, 19, 23, ... matches to $4n + 3$
46, 42, 38, 34, 30, ... matches to $50 - 4n$

**3 a** 8    **b** 15    **c** 21    **d** 9

**4 a** 18,20,22 48    **b** 20,23,26 62

**5** 4 people, 6 handshakes 5 people perform 10 handshakes.
6 people perform 15 handshakes.
Pattern is triangular numbers thus $n$ people perform $\frac{n(n-1)}{2}$ handshakes.

## Ex A5.2

**1 a** $5^2 = 1 + 3 + 5 + 7 + 9, 6^2 = 1 + 3 + 5 + 7 + 9 + 11,$
$7^2 = 1 + 3 + 5 + 7 + 9 + 11 + 13$
   **b** 199    **c** 625

**2 a** $4^2 - 2^2$    **b** $4^2 - 1^2, 8^2 - 7^2$
   **c** 8, 12, 16, 20. All in the 4 times table.

**3 a** 55    **b** 210    **c** 4950
   **d** 20100    **e** 500500

**4** Option 1 gives £667.95, Option 2 gives £520. Choose Option 1.

## Ex A5.3

**1** Missing line is 3, 6, 9, 12, 15.
The $n$th term is $T(n) = 3n - 2$.

**2 a** $T(n) = 7n$    **b** $T(n) = 3n + 2$
   **c** $T(n) = 4n + 10$    **d** $T(n) = 6n - 1$
   **e** $T(n) = 10n - 2$    **f** $T(n) = 5n + 20$
   **g** $T(n) = 4n - 10$    **h** $T(n) = 0.2n + 2$
   **i** $T(n) = 100 - n$    **j** $T(n) = 50 - 5n$
   **k** $T(n) = 5 - 4n$

**3** Check three sequences given with $3^{rd}$ term of 12.
Check correct $n^{th}$ term and $T(100)$ found.

**4 a** $T(n) = 3n + 10$. First five terms are 13, 16, 19, 22, 25.
   **b** $T(n) = 8n - 5$. First five terms are 3, 11, 19, 27, 35.
   **c** $T(n) = 5n + 3$. First five terms are 8, 13, 18, 23, 28.

**5** Both Isla and Flora are correct as expanding the brackets of $n(n + 2)$ gives $n^2 + 2n$.

## Ex A5.4

**1** $m = 4n + 1$. Each new pentagon requires four matchsticks plus one more is needed to close the first pentagon.

**2 a** $w = 2r + 6$    **b** 106
   **c** Each red tile is linked to 2 white tiles, one above, one below. Six more white tiles sit three at either end.

**3** Each new triangle requires 3 straws (2 on the long side, one on the short) plus two more straws are needed to close the first triangle.

**4 a** $H = 2C + 2$
   **b** Octane has the chemical formula $C_8H_{18}$.
   **c** Further investigation.

**5** $t = h(h + 1)$

## Exam practice

**1 a** 16, 19    **b** Double previous term    **c** 2, 5, 10

**2** 10 mins after the depth was 28 mm.

**3 a** 14, 20
   **b** $d = \frac{p(p-3)}{2}$. As $p - 3 > 0, p > 3$ ie. $p \geq 4$

## A6 Representing and interpreting data

### Check in

**1 a** 62    **b** 70    **c** 60
   **d** 45    **e** 102    **f** 108

**2 a** £50    **b** £70

**3** 2 days

## Ex A6.1

**1 a** polygons
   **b** **i** T $20 < m \leq 30$, OW $30 < m \leq 40$;
     **ii** T 50 mins OW 50 mins
   **c** on average OW take longer than T

**2 a** polygons
   **b** **i** D $40 < m \leq 60$, J $40 < m \leq 60$;
     **ii** D 100 miles J 80 miles
   **c** Similar journey length were made, but journeys in January were less varied than in December

**3 a** polygons
   **b** mode: D $0 < t \leq 5$, P $5 < t \leq 10$;
     median: D $10 < t \leq 15$, P $10 < t \leq 15$; mean: D 11.7, P 12.5 Recommend Powerblast.

**4** 2002–2003, range for 2003–2004 less than 60

**5** Sell-a-lot; average for Sell-well > 80

## Ex A6.2

**1 a i** 30    **ii** 10    **b i** 10    **ii** 65
   **c i** 37    **ii** 21

**2** diagram    **i** 950    **ii** 2hours 17 mins

## Ex A6.3

**1** Dentists: min value = 0 min, Q1 = 23, med = 35, Q3 = 53, max value = 80, box and whisker plot
Doctors: min value = 0 min, Q1 = 22, med = 29, Q3 = 42, max value = 70 min, box and whisker plot, dentists waiting time longer

**2** First group: min value = 70, Q1 = 91, med = 96, Q3 = 105, max value = 140, box and whisker plot
Second group: min value = 70, Q1 = 91, med = 97, Q3 = 105, max value = 130, box and whisker plot, second group slightly better

## Ex A6.4

**1 a** freq dens 1.2, 2.0, 2.3, 1.45, 1.2, 0.2; histogram; 20
   **b** freq dens 4.0, 5.0, 5.4, 4.4, 0.6; histogram; 39
   **c** freq dens 30, 40, 44, 25, 6; histogram;
     **i** 37    **ii** 18

**2 a** 10    **b** 4, 18, 53, 20, 10    **c** 105

**3 a** 7    **b** 3, 7, 27, 20, 8    **c** 65

**4 a** 8, 6, **5**, **8**, **11**, 16, 12, 6
**b** vertical scale for histogram is 0.4, 0.8, 1.2, 1.6, 2.0, 2.4 and **fd**; histogram

## Ex A6.5

Comments need to refer to the diagrams

### Exam practice

**1 a** polygon
**b** eg. most common length is same for both months $(5 < m \le 10)$ longest journey time is longer in August than July
**2** frequency densities are 3.2, 11.5, 13.5, 20.0, 15.5, 4.4, 1.6.
**3 a** diagram
**b** Q1 = 32, med = 40, Q3 = 45 Min = 18, Max = 67

## A7 Formulae and equations

### Check in

**1 a** 45 **b** 52 **c** −26 **d** 196
**e** 7 **f** 13 **g** −50 **h** 30
**2 a** = 9 + 6
**b** = 18 − 3
**c** = 5 × 3
**d** = 27 − 12
**3 a** 3 **b** 4 **c** 10 **d** 6
**e** 4 **f** 25 **g** 33 **h** 7

## Ex A7.1

**1 a** $V = 850 \text{ mm}^3$ **b** $V = 192\pi \text{ m}^3$ **c** $V = 36\pi \text{ cm}^3$
**2 a** $A = l^2$ **b** $A = b^2$ **c** $A = \frac{1}{2}\pi r^2$
**3 a** Area of Square = $2x \times 2x = 4x^2$ and area of circle = $\pi x^2$. Thus area of paving = $4x^2 - \pi x^2 = x^2(4 - \pi)$
**b** Area of paving = $(16 - 4\pi) \text{ m}^2$
**4 a** Red glass is circle of radius $\frac{1}{2}k$ thus area of red glass, $R = \pi \times \left(\frac{1}{2}k\right)^2 = \frac{1}{4}\pi k^2$.
**b** Area of Square = $k \times k = k^2$ and thus area of yellow glass, $Y = k^2 - \frac{1}{4}\pi k^2 = k^2\left(1 - \frac{1}{4}\pi\right)$.
**c** $Y = 16\left(1 - \frac{1}{4}\pi\right) = 16 - 4\pi \text{ m}^2 \approx 3.4 \text{ m}^2$.

## Ex A7.2

**1 a** $x = k - t$ **b** $x = w - y + z$
**c** $x = 11a$ **d** $x = a - bc$
**e** $x = t - p^2$ **f** $x = f + gh + k$
**g** $x = p - \sqrt{q}$ **h** $x = b$
**2 a** $y = \frac{a}{b}$ **b** $y = kt$ **c** $y = \frac{p - r}{q}$
**d** $y = \frac{x - z}{w}$ **e** $y = \frac{b - c^2}{a}$ **f** $y = k(m + n)$
**g** $y = t^2(g - h)$ **h** $y = \frac{k + t}{mn}$
**3 a** 428°F **b** $C = \frac{5}{9}(F - 32)$
**c** 177°C = 180°C (2 sig fig)
**4 a** $a = \sqrt[3]{x}$ **b** $a = \sqrt[4]{k + t}$ **c** $a = \sqrt[4]{\frac{x}{y}}$

**d** $a = \sqrt[3]{mn}$ **e** $a = t^2$ **f** $a = (p - q)^2$
**g** $a = 4k^2$ **h** $a = b^3$
**5 a** $r = \sqrt[3]{\frac{3V}{4\pi}}$ **b** 6.0822... = 6.08 cm (3 sig fig)

**6 a** In line 2, + c should be − c. In line 3, needs to divide both sides by 2.
**b** In line 2, deal with the k first i.e. add k to both sides. Then in line 3, divide both sides by x.
**c** In line 2, deal with the y first. Divide both sides by y and then square root in line 3.

## Ex A7.3

**1 a** $x = 4$ **b** $y = 7$ **c** $t = 3$ **d** $k = 0$
**e** $p = 10$ **f** $q = \frac{1}{2}$ **g** $g = \frac{2}{3}$ **h** $a = \frac{9}{10}$
**2 a** $x = 1$ **b** $y = 3$ **c** $a = 5$ **d** $b = 7$
**e** $m = 3$ **f** $n = 28$ **g** $k = 6$ **h** $t = 0$
**3 a** 19 cm by 5 cm **b** 8 cm by 4 cm
**4 a** $x = 1$ **b** $k = 3$ **c** $t = 5$
**d** $k = 2$ **e** $a = 4$ **f** $b = 4$
**5 a** The angles are 85°, 125°, 60° and 90°.
**b** Victoria is 8, Jamie is 7 and Jonathan is 4.
**6 a** $a = 2$ **b** $n = 2$ **c** $b = 1$ **d** $m = 2$
**e** $q = 6$ **f** $x = 2$ **g** $p = 20$ **h** $x = 1$
**7 a** £7 **b** 12 km

## Ex A7.4

**1 a** $x = 7$ **b** $k = 2$ **c** $n = 1$
**d** $t = -4$ **e** $a = -2$ **f** $p = -1$
**2 a** In line 2, + 4 should be + 8. Hence the answer is $x = 1$.
**b** In line 2, 2x should be 4x. In line 3, 16 should be 8. Hence the answer is $x = 2$.
**c** In line 3, 1 should be −1. The answer is $x = -\frac{1}{2}$.
**3 a** $x = 3$ **b** $t = 1$ **c** $y = 3$ **d** $a = 2$
**e** $k = 2$ **f** $b = 4$ **g** $p = 0$ **h** $d = 4$
**i** $q = 5$ **j** $m = 6$ **k** $r = -2$ **l** $n = -1$
**4 a** 1 **b** 2 **c** 6
**5 a** Length of one side = 12
**b** Length of the rectangle = 10

## Ex A7.5

**1 a** $a = 27$ **b** $x = 36$ **c** $b = 2\frac{1}{2}$ **d** $y = 2\frac{2}{3}$
**e** $f = 12$ **f** $m = 10$ **g** $g = -4$ **h** $n = -9$
**i** $p = 9$ **j** $t = 2$ **k** $q = 4$ **l** $k = 3$
**2 a** $x = 2$ **b** $a = 7$ **c** $p = -5$ **d** $m = 1\frac{2}{5}$
**e** $y = 4$ **f** $b = 2$ **g** $q = 3$ **h** $n = 1\frac{3}{4}$
**i** $f = 3$ **j** $g = 0$ **k** $k = 5$ **l** $t = \frac{1}{5}$
**3 a** $a = 10$ **b** $b = 15$ **c** $x = 4$ **d** $y = 11$
**e** $q = 3$ **f** $p = 5$ **g** $m = 4$ **h** $n = 3$
**4 a** 9 **b** 6 **c** 5
**5** Sides on first trapezium are 7 cm and 13 cm.

Sides on second trapezium are 5 cm and 7 cm.

6 a Interior angle $= 180 - \dfrac{360}{n}$

   b i 5       ii 9       iii 15

## Ex A7.6

1 Both correct. $\dfrac{ty}{t} = y$.

2 a $x = \dfrac{y}{a+b}$     b $x = \dfrac{t}{p} - q$     c $x = \dfrac{n^2}{m} + k$

   d $x = \dfrac{w}{k^2 - y}$     e $x = \dfrac{p}{\pi} - a$     f $x = 2a + y$

   g $x = 5g - gh$     h $x = \pi s + k^2$

3 a $y = a - b$     b $y = q - p^2$     c $y = ab - t$

   d $y = \dfrac{k-r}{a}$     e $y = \dfrac{n-m}{k}$     f $y = p - \dfrac{d}{q}$

   g $y = x - \dfrac{k^2}{h}$     h $y = m - kn$

4 a $u = v - at$     b $17 ms^{-1}$

5 a $k = \dfrac{a}{b}$     b $k = \dfrac{t}{p}$     c $k = \dfrac{mn}{t}$

   d $k = \dfrac{d}{rt}$     e $k = \dfrac{xy}{w}$     f $k = \dfrac{p}{a-q}$

   g $k = \dfrac{h}{y^2 + z}$     h $k = \dfrac{m}{p} - n$

6 a $t = \dfrac{d}{s}$     b 42 minutes

7 a $x = \dfrac{q-b}{a-p}$     b $x = \dfrac{n-z}{m-w}$     c $x = \dfrac{a+b}{c+d}$

   d $x = \dfrac{f-g}{g+1}$     e $x = \dfrac{rd+kc}{k+r}$     f $x = \dfrac{2c+k}{1-c}$

8 $t = \dfrac{x}{u-b}$

## Exam practice

1 a 15       b $2\dfrac{8}{9}$       c $1\dfrac{1}{19}$

2 $b = \dfrac{4}{5}(e - 32)$

3 a $2n + 7$

   b 19

## A8 Pythagoras and trigonometry

### Check in

1 a 49       b 52       c 34       d 48
   e 45       f 80       g 5       h 7

2 a $x = 6y$     b $x = 5y$     c $x = 10y$

   d $x = \dfrac{2}{y}$     e $x = \dfrac{5}{y}$     f $x = \dfrac{8}{y}$

### Ex A8.1

1 a 5 cm       b 17 cm       c 13 cm
   d 10.3 cm   e 10.8 cm   f 9.9 cm

2 a 19.8 cm   b 10 cm       c 9 cm
   d 7.5 cm   e 5.4 cm     f 7.1 cm

3 6.8 metres

4 3.5 km

5 5.66 metres

6 6.5 miles

7 6.93 cm

8 7.2 cm

9 i 5       ii 4.24       iii 13       iv 20
   v 14.14       vi $\sqrt{(c-a)^2 + (d-b)^2}$

10 3.43 cm

11 b $A = 2x\sqrt{100 - x^2}$
   Max area when $x = 7.1$ cm

### Ex A8.3

1 a p = 8.2 cm     b q = 3.7 cm     c r = 16.8 cm
   d s = 4.4 cm   e 3.0 cm       f 6.4 cm
   g 3.8 cm       h 30.5 cm

2 70 metres

3 104 metres

4 22 metres

5 a 63.4°     b 51.3°     c 32.7°     d 38.7°
   e 17.6°     f 26.6°     g 34.9°     h 45°

6 72.6°

7 63.4°

8 21°

9 183 metres

10 h = 11.7 cm

### Ex A8.4

1 p = 2.3 cm     q = 3.1 cm     r = 4.2 cm
   s = 3.8 cm     t = 5.7 cm     u = 14.4 cm

2 38 metres

3 15.2 metres

4 3.2 km

5 724 metres

6 5.2 cm

7 a = 36.9°   b = 44.4°   c = 60.1°   d = 36.9°
   e = 40.1   f = 27.7°

8 68°

9 8.9°

10 3.9 metres

11 A reflection in the line $\theta = 45°$
   $\sin 30° = \cos 60°$
   In general, $\sin x = \cos(90° - x)$

### Ex A8.5

1 a n = 5.35 cm     p = 5.95 cm
   b q = 5.27 cm     $\theta = 53°$
   c s = 4.14 cm     r = 1.76 cm
   d t = 6.04 cm     $\theta = 39.0°$
   e $\alpha = 36.9°$     $\beta = 53.1°$     u = 20 cm
   f v = 6.10 cm     w = 3.50 cm
   g x = 5.14 cm     y = 6.13 cm     $\theta = 40°$
   h z = 7.21 cm     $\alpha = 56.3°$     $\beta = 33.7°$

2 a x = 11.1 cm     y = 12.7 cm     $\alpha = 60.4°$
   b x = 11.5 cm     y = 13.2 cm     $\alpha = 29.5°$
   c $\alpha = 36.2°$     x = 8.75 cm     y = 3.77 cm

3 a 13.0 cm   b 10.4 cm   c 10.0 cm   d 24.7 cm

**4** 767 metres

**5** 8.5 cm

**6** 65.4°   65.4°   49.2°

**7** 5 cm   $\sqrt{20}$ cm   $\sqrt{5}$ cm

$5^2 = \left(\sqrt{20}\right)^2 + \left(\sqrt{5}\right)^2$

**8** 0.62 cm

**9** 10 km  146.9°

**10** 7.30 metres

**11 a**   35.4 cm     **b**   22.6 cm     **c**   17.3 cm

**12** 239 metres

**13** 3.9 metres

**14** 7.8 metres

**15 a**   77.5 cm   63.2 cm

**b**   AB = $10\sqrt{x}$ cm and BC = $10\sqrt{y}$ cm provided $x$ and $y$ are measured in cm and $x + y = 100$

**16** $\sqrt{40}$ cm

**17** 4 m × 4 m     6 m × 2 m

## Exam practice

**1   a**   6.1 cm     **b**   22.5°

**3**   55.9 m

## B9 Fractions, decimals and percentages

### Check in

**1 a** $\frac{1}{2}$   **b** $\frac{3}{4}$   **c** $\frac{4}{5}$   **d** $\frac{19}{20}$   **e** $\frac{3}{4}$

**2 a** 0.75   **b** 0.4   **c** 0.7   **d** 0.45   **e** 0.17

**3 a** $\frac{1}{2}$   **b** $\frac{1}{4}$   **c** $\frac{3}{10}$   **d** $\frac{4}{5}$   **e** $\frac{9}{20}$

**4 a** 20 × 30     **b** 360 ÷ 60
  **c** 1200 − 800     **d** 7000 + 6000

### Ex B9.1

**1 a** 20 250     **b** 96     **c** 2496
  **d** 3.3     **e** 86.1$\dot{6}$     **f** 36.25

**2 a i** 13.2     **ii** 0.87
  **b i** 21.4     **ii** 19.902
  **c i** 7600     **ii** 0.045
  **d i** 22.5     **ii** 7.2

**3 a** 3     **b** 100     **c** 2     **d** 8
  **e** 8     **f** 0.5     **g** 12     **h** $\frac{1}{14}$
  **i** 2     **j** 15 000     **k** 1.$\dot{3}$     **l** 150

**4 a** 7     **b** 12

**5** 40

### Ex B9.2

**1** $\frac{15}{32}$

**2** Both £187.50

**3 a** 16     **b** 12     **c** 66     **d** 12.4

**4 a** 0.06     **b** 0.48     **c** 0.015
  **d** 0.06     **e** 0.006     **f** 3
  **g** 52     **h** 272.5     **i** 100

**5 a** 0.08 × 0.02 = 0.0016     **b** 0.2 ÷ 0.02 = 10

**6** 25% of 60 = 15,  20% of 70 = 14

**7** 50% of 30 = 15.  40% of 40 = 16

**8 a i** 25     **ii** 25

**9 a** 400     **b** 350

### Ex B9.3

**1 a** $\frac{1}{2}$   **b** $\frac{11}{16}$   **c** $\frac{27}{70}$   **d** $\frac{59}{60}$

**2 a** $\frac{1}{4}$   **b** $\frac{16}{27}$   **c** $\frac{1}{10}$   **d** $\frac{5}{12}$

**3 a** $\frac{1}{6}$   **b** $\frac{3}{35}$   **c** $\frac{24}{35}$   **d** $\frac{1}{6}$

**4 a** £22.50   **b** £21   **c** £10   **d** £16

**5** $\frac{3}{10}$

**6 a** $\frac{1}{10}$   **b** $\frac{1}{4}$   **c** $\frac{3}{20}$   **d** $\frac{3}{20}$
  **e** $\frac{2}{5}$   **f** $\frac{8}{9}$   **g** $\frac{15}{16}$   **h** $\frac{3}{4}$

**7 a i** $\frac{3}{8} \times \frac{1}{10} = \frac{3}{80}$     **ii** $\frac{1}{2} + \frac{2}{5} + \frac{1}{10} = 1$

  **b i** $\frac{1}{5} \times \frac{2}{7} = \frac{2}{35}$     **ii** $\frac{1}{2} + \frac{1}{5} + \frac{3}{10} = 1$

### Ex B9.4

**1 a** $1\frac{3}{5}$   **b** $7\frac{1}{2}$   **c** $7\frac{1}{2}$   **d** $\frac{3}{4}$
  **e** $9\frac{1}{6}$   **f** $2\frac{2}{3}$   **g** $12\frac{1}{2}$   **h** $\frac{6}{7}$

**2 a** $3\frac{31}{40}$   **b** $11\frac{3}{4}$   **c** $8\frac{1}{12}$   **d** $5\frac{2}{5}$

**3 a** $2\frac{5}{26}$   **b** $1\frac{13}{20}$   **c** $-\frac{5}{12}$   **d** $-\frac{11}{12}$

**4 a** $1\frac{7}{20}$   **b** $\frac{2}{3}$   **c** $\frac{5}{6}$

**5** 215 cm²

**6 a** $\frac{14}{45}$   **b** $\frac{15}{38}$   **c** $1\frac{1}{2}$   **d** $\frac{40}{51}$
  **e** $3\frac{1}{6}$   **f** $1\frac{17}{78}$

### Rich Task

  **a** decreases     **b** increases

### Ex B9.5

**1 a** $0.\dot{1}, 0.\dot{2}, 0.\dot{3}$ $etc$
  **b** recurring digit is same as numerator

**2 a** $0.\dot{0}\dot{9}, 0.\dot{1}\dot{8}, 0.\dot{2}\dot{7}$ $etc$
  **b** repeated number is 9 times numerator
  **c** $\frac{1}{2} - \frac{4}{11} = \frac{3}{22}$, $\frac{1}{2} - \frac{7}{11} = \frac{-3}{22}$ equally close

**3 a** $\frac{3}{35}$ When in simplest forms, other fractions have denominators with no prime number factors other than 2 and 5
  **b** $\frac{6}{30} = \frac{1}{5}$, a fraction whose denominator is multiple of 5

**4 a i** $0.\dot{2}$     **ii** $0.0\dot{2}$

**iii** $0.00\dot{2}$   **iv** $0.000\dot{2}$

b  denominators are $9 \times 10^n$ and the $n$ tells you the
number of zeros before the recurring 2.

5  a  $\frac{34}{90} = \frac{17}{45}$   b  $\frac{17}{90}$   c  $\frac{65}{99}$   d  $\frac{21}{37}$

   e  $\frac{1234}{9999}$   f  $\frac{69}{9000} = \frac{23}{3000}$   g  $\frac{103}{9990}$

## Exam practice

1  $2\frac{7}{9}$

2  a  $\frac{1}{18}$   b  $\frac{31}{99}$

3  Yes

## B10 Circles, angles and lines

### Check in

1  a  43°   b  139°
2  a  102°   b  29°

### Ex B10.1

1  $c = 150°$   $d = 30°$   $e = 30°$
2  $f = 120°$   $g = 120°$
3  $j = 100°$   $k = 50°$   $l = 30°$
4  $m = 40°$   $n = 70°$   $p = 110°$
5  $r = 45°$
6  $u = 95°$
7  $v = 70°$   $w = 50°$
8  $x = 30°$

9

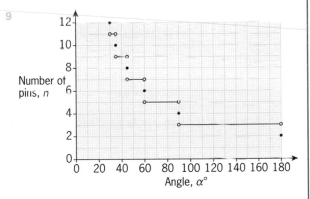

### Ex 10.2

1  $a = 35°$
2  $m = 20°$   $n = 20°$   $p = 70°$   $q = 70°$
3  $e = 20°$   $f = 80°$   $g = 20°$
4  $x = 50°$
5  $v = 60°$
6  $x = y = 38°$
7  $u = 30°$   $v = 60°$   $w = 60°$
8  $a = 60°$   $b = 30°$
9  $c = 90°$
10  $43\frac{1}{3}°$

11  24°   48°   96°   192°
12  60°   130°
13  $x = 50°$
14  $y = 60°$
15  $z = 30°$
16  $a = 36°$
17  $p = 70°$   $q = 40°$
18  $b = 10°$   $c = 55°$
19  $w = 115°$   $x = 35°$
    $y = 30°$   $z = 115°$
20  $a = 65°$
21  $x = 50°$
22  $83\frac{1}{3}°$,   $83\frac{1}{3}°$,   90°,   $103\frac{1}{3}°$

### Ex B10.3

1

| Regular polygon | Number of sides | Each interior angle | Each exterior angle | Sum of **all** interior angles |
|---|---|---|---|---|
| Triangle | 3 | 60° | 120° | 180° |
| Quadrilateral | 4 | 90° | 90° | 360° |
| Pentagon | 5 | 108° | 72° | 540° |
| Hexagon | 6 | 120° | 60° | 720° |
| Octagon | 8 | 135° | 45° | 1080° |
| Decagon | 10 | 144° | 36° | 1440° |

2  a  $a = 120°$   $b = 60°$   $c = 60°$
   b  $x = 140°$   $y = 110°$   $z = 40°$
   c  $s = 30°$   $t = 120°$   $u = 150°$
3  a  103°,   103°,   103°,   132°,   93°,   186°
   b  102°,   102°,   112°,   112°,   112°
4  40°,   40°,   40°,   30°,   30°
5  a  **i**  30°   **ii**  10°   **iii**  18°   **iv**  20°
   b

| No. of sides | Exterior angle | Interior angle |
|---|---|---|
| **i**  9 | 40° | 140° |
| **ii**  15 | 24° | 156° |
| **iii**  24 | 15° | 165° |
| **iv**  30 | 12° | 168° |

6  a  $180°n - 360°$
   b  $180° - \frac{360°}{n}$,   $\frac{360°}{n}$   162°,   18°
7  $m = 67.5°$   $n = 92.5°$
8  $x = 120°$
9

| No. of sides, $n$ | 3 | 4 | 5 | 6 | 7 | 8 | 9 | 10 | ... | 20 | .... | 100 |
|---|---|---|---|---|---|---|---|---|---|---|---|---|
| Interior angle, $\alpha$ | 60° | 90° | 108° | 120° | $128\frac{4}{7}°$ | 135° | 140° | 144° | ... | 162° | ... | 176.4° |

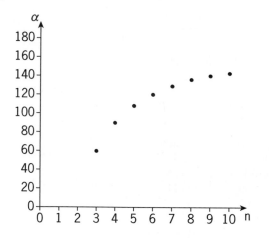

As $n \to \infty$, $\alpha \to 180°$, the polygon is tending to a circle

## Ex B10.4

1. $a = 130°$
2. $b = 40°$
3. $c = 50°$
4. $d = 100°$
5. $e = 110°$
6. $f = 55°$
7. $g = 25°$
8. $h = 250°$
9. $i = 115°$
10. $j = 40°$
11. $l = 65°$
12. 1130 km (3 SF)
13. 9.2 cm

## Ex B10.5

1. a   $a = 30°$    $b = 50°$
   b   $c = 25°$    $d = 155°$
   c   $e = 70°$
   d   $f = 25°$
   e   $g = 100°$
   f   $h = 300°$
   g   $i = 40°$
   h   $j = 20°$   $k = 40°$
   i   $l = 60°$   $m = 30°$
   j   $n = 35°$   $p = 55°$   $q = 35°$
   k   $r = 20°$
   l   $s = 40°$   $t = 65°$
   m   $u = 110°$   $v = 65°$
2. a   $x = 110°$   b   $y = 210°$   c   $z = 40°$
   d   $p = 140°$   e   $x = 40°$    f   $z = 55°$

3. When $\theta = \dfrac{180°}{n}$ where $n$ is integer, the ball describes an $n$-sided regular polygon over and over again. For other values of $\theta$, the path of the ball is more complicated.

## Exam practice

1. $x = 139°$ (vertically opposite), $y = 57°$ (alternating)
2. a   $a = 35°$ (angles in same segment), $b = 145°$ (cyclic quadrilateral)

b   Because $62° \neq \frac{1}{2}$ of $122°$
3. $102°$

## B11 Straight lines

### Check in

1. Check graphs
2. a   $6\frac{1}{2}$    b   $5\frac{1}{4}$    c   $4\frac{5}{7}$    d   $-9\frac{1}{11}$
   e   $\frac{7}{3}$    f   $\frac{15}{2}$    g   $\frac{23}{4}$    h   $-\frac{35}{8}$
3. a   2    b   1    c   $\frac{1}{2}$

### Ex B11.1

1. a   $y = 0$    b   $x = 3, x = 10$
   c   $y = 3x - 5, y = 2x, y = x$
   d   $y = x^3, y = x^2 + 2x$

2. a   i

| $x$ | 0 | 1 | 2 |
|---|---|---|---|
| $y$ | 2 | 2 | 2 |

ii

| $x$ | 0 | 1 | 2 |
|---|---|---|---|
| $y$ | 0 | 3 | 6 |

iii

| $x$ | 0 | 1 | 2 |
|---|---|---|---|
| $y$ | $-1$ | 1 | 3 |

iv

| $x$ | 0 | 1 | 2 |
|---|---|---|---|
| $y$ | 3 | 1 | $-1$ |

   b   Graphs of $y = 2$, $y = 3x$, $y = 2x - 1$ and $y = 3 - 2x$ plotted on separate axes from $-8$ to $8$.
3. a   Square   b   $x = 1, x = 4, y = 2, y = 5$
4. a   Any point on the graph of $y = 3x - 2$
   b   16    c   4
5. a   i, ii and iii
      Graphs of $y = 2x - 3$, $y = 2x$ and $y = 2x + 5$ plotted on same set of axes.
   b   The lines are parallel.
   c   Any line of the form $y = 3x + c$ where $c$ is a constant.
6. a   i, ii and iii
      Graphs of $y = \frac{1}{2}x + 1$, $y = 2x + 1$ and
      $y = 5x + 1$ plotted on same set of axes.
   b   The lines all cut the $y$-axis at the point $(0, 1)$. Each graph is steeper than the last.
   c   Any line of the form $y = ax + c$ where $a > 3$ and $c$ is a constant.

### Ex B11.2

1. a   Gradient = 2, $y$-intercept = $(0, 2)$
   b   Gradient = $\frac{1}{2}$, $y$-intercept = $(0, \frac{1}{2})$
   c   Gradient = $-1$, $y$-intercept = $(0, 0)$
   d   Gradient = $-3$, $y$-intercept = $(0, 3)$
   e   Gradient = 0, $y$-intercept = $(0, -3)$
2. a   2    b   4    c   $-1$    d   $\frac{1}{2}$

e  −2    f  $\frac{1}{3}$    g  $-\frac{1}{2}$    h  0

The line is horizontal and hence parallel to the $x$-axis.

3  i  Graphs of $y = 3x + 5$, $y = 2x − 3$, $y = \frac{1}{2}x + 1$ and
      $y = 3 − x$, plotted on separate axes.

  ii  a  Gradient = 3, $y$-intercept = (0, 5)
      b  Gradient = 2, $y$-intercept = (0, −3)
      c  Gradient = $\frac{1}{2}$, $y$-intercept = (0, 1)
      d  Gradient = −1, $y$-intercept = (0, 3)

  iii  The gradient is the coefficient of $x$ and the
      $y$-intercept can be read from the value of the
      constant term.

4  a  Graph of $y = 2x + 1$ plotted on axes from −5 to 5.

  b  Graph of $y = \frac{1}{2}x − 1$ plotted on axes from −5 to 5.

  c  Graph of $y = 4 − 3x$ plotted on axes from −5 to 5.

5  a  $t = 6$ and hence the coordinates are (5, 6) and (8, 18).
  b  $k = 2$ and hence the coordinates are (2, 8) and (6, 20).

## Exam practice

1  a  $y = 3x + 2$
  b  Second line has gradient $-\frac{1}{3}$ and $3 \times -\frac{1}{3} = −1$, the
      lines are perpendicular

2  The first line has gradient 2 and the third gradient $-\frac{1}{2}$.

   As these two lines are perpendicular (since $2 \times -\frac{1}{2} = −1$),
   therefore the triangle is right-angled.

3  a  −5    b  $5y = x + 16$

## Ex B11.3

1

| Equation | Gradient | Coordinates of y-intercept |
|---|---|---|
| a  $y = 2x + 5$ | 2 | (0, 5) |
| b  $y = 7x − 1$ | 7 | (0, −1) |
| c  $y = 3x$ | 3 | (0, 0) |
| d  $y = \frac{1}{3}x + 2$ | $\frac{1}{3}$ | (0, 2) |
| e  $y = 4(x − 3)$ | 4 | (0, −12) |
| f  $2y = x − 3$ | $\frac{1}{2}$ | (0, $−1\frac{1}{2}$) |
| g  $x + 4y = 12$ | $-\frac{1}{4}$ | (0, 3) |
| h  $3x + 4y = 8$ | $-\frac{3}{4}$ | (0, 2) |

2  $y = \frac{1}{3}x − 1$ matches with line $c$.
   $y = 3$ matches with line $a$.
   $y = − x$ matches with line $e$.
   $y = 1 − 3x$ matches with line $d$.
   $y = 2x + 1$ matches with line $b$.

3  a  Line A has equation $y = 3x + 1$.
  b  Line B has equation $y = x − 5$.
  c  Line C has equation $y = \frac{1}{2}x − 3$.

d  Line D has equation $y = 3x − 2$.

4  a  False. The lines are perpendicular.
  b  True. The lines are parallel as they both have a
      gradient of 5.
  c  True. The lines are perpendicular because
      $2 \times -\frac{1}{2} = −1$.
  d  False. The gradients of the lines are 2 and $\frac{1}{2}$; their
      product is not −1.

5  a  Graph with the points (1, 3.5), (3, 6.5), (3.5, 7.25),
      (4.2, 8.3) and (5.6, 10.4) plotted.
  b  Gradient is 1.5.
  c  Equation is $t = \frac{3}{2}k + 2$

## Ex B11.4

1  Ticks underneath $y = x − 3$, $x + y = 1$ and $y = \frac{3}{2}x − 4$.

2  Line A has the equation $y = 3x + 2$.
   Line B has the equation $y = 5 − 2x$.
   Line C has the equation $y = 2x − 5$.
   Line D has the equation $y = \frac{1}{4}x − 3$.

3  Line $a$ has the equation $x = 2$.
   Line $b$ has the equation $y = x + 1$.
   Line $c$ has the equation $y = 2x − 1$.
   Line $d$ has the equation $y = − 3x$.
   Line $e$ has the equation $y = -\frac{1}{2}x + 2$

4  a  $y = 2x + 1$          b  $y = 5x − 2$
  c  $y = \frac{1}{2}x + 1$          d  $y = \frac{1}{5}x − 2$
  e  $y = 4 − x$          f  $y = 10 − 3x$
  g  $5x + 2y = 2$          h  $y = 2 − \frac{1}{3}x$

## B12 Transformations

### Check in

1  A (3, 2), B (5, 5), C (4, −1), D (−2, −3), E (1, 6)
2  a  $x = 3$          b  $x = 5$          c  $y = x$
  d  $y = 2$          e  $y = −1$

### Ex B12.1

1
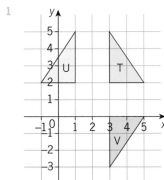

**2**

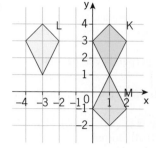

**3**

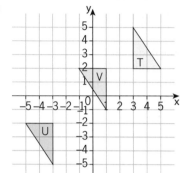

**4** a, b

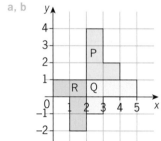

c P gets rotated onto R because two quarter-turns about (2, 1) give a half-turn

**5**

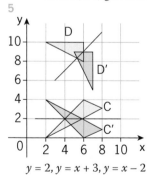

$y = 2$, $y = x + 3$, $y = x - 2$

**6**

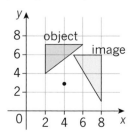

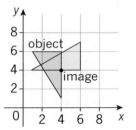

**7**

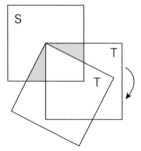

**8** (6, 4), 180°

(6, 1), 90° clockwise

(6, 1), 270° anticlockwise

(6, 7), 90° anticlockwise

(6, 7), 270° clockwise

**9** The area of overlap is a quarter of the square.

As T rotates, the area gained by the leading side equals the area lost by the following side.

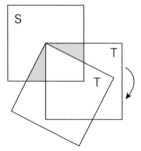

**10** a 3 : 1

When cog B has completed a full turn, cog A has turned 120° in the opposite direction.

b Increase the number of teeth on the rear gear. On flat ground, the ratio is 4 : 1. Uphill, the ratio could be 1 : 1

## Ex B12.2

**1** a 8 km due east, then 16 km due north, then 4 km due west

b 14 km due east, then 12 km due south, then 8 km due west

**2** a $\begin{pmatrix} 3 \\ 2 \end{pmatrix}$    b $\begin{pmatrix} 5 \\ 1 \end{pmatrix}$    c $\begin{pmatrix} 2 \\ -1 \end{pmatrix}$    d $\begin{pmatrix} -3 \\ -2 \end{pmatrix}$

Unit B

414 **Answers**

3   The order does not matter $\begin{pmatrix} 5 \\ 3 \end{pmatrix}$.

4   a   Will tessellate        b   Will tessellate
    c   Will not tessellate    d   Will tessellate

5   $\begin{pmatrix} 2 \\ 1 \end{pmatrix}, \begin{pmatrix} 2 \\ -1 \end{pmatrix}, \begin{pmatrix} -2 \\ 1 \end{pmatrix}, \begin{pmatrix} -2 \\ -1 \end{pmatrix}, \begin{pmatrix} 1 \\ 2 \end{pmatrix}, \begin{pmatrix} 1 \\ -2 \end{pmatrix}, \begin{pmatrix} -1 \\ 2 \end{pmatrix}, \begin{pmatrix} -1 \\ -2 \end{pmatrix}$

## Ex B12.3

1   a

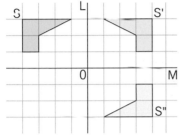

Rotation of 180° about origin, O

  b

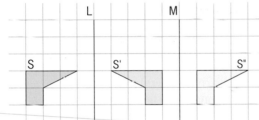

Translation of $\begin{pmatrix} 10 \\ 0 \end{pmatrix}$

2

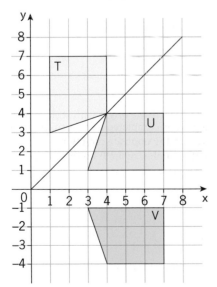

Rotation 90° clockwise with centre (0, 0)

3   a   Translation of $\begin{pmatrix} 8 \\ 0 \end{pmatrix}$

    b   Rotation of 180° about (3, 5)

    c   Translation of $\begin{pmatrix} 4 \\ 0 \end{pmatrix}$     d   Translation of $\begin{pmatrix} 6 \\ 2 \end{pmatrix}$

    e   Rotation 90° anticlockwise about (3, 7)

4   a   Reflection in the line $x = 5$
       Rotation of 180° about (5, 6)

       Translation of $\begin{pmatrix} 5 \\ 0 \end{pmatrix}$

    b   Reflection in the line $x = 5$
       Rotation of 180° about (5, 2)
       Rotation of 90° clockwise about (5, 0)
       Rotation of 90° anticlockwise about (5, 4)

       Translation of $\begin{pmatrix} 4 \\ 0 \end{pmatrix}$

5   Translation to the right of distance (2AD + 2AB)

6   $\begin{pmatrix} -5.0 \\ 0.6 \end{pmatrix}$ and $\begin{pmatrix} 2.0 \\ -4.6 \end{pmatrix}$

7   The maximum distance that a knight can travel in 2 moves is 3 squares across and 3 squares up, because

$\begin{pmatrix} 2 \\ 1 \end{pmatrix} + \begin{pmatrix} 1 \\ 2 \end{pmatrix} = \begin{pmatrix} 3 \\ 3 \end{pmatrix}$. So, when the starting square is

included, the knight can travel in 2 moves along the diagonal of a 4 × 4 chess board.

In $m$ moves, the maximum diagonal travel is $\frac{1}{2}m\begin{pmatrix} 3 \\ 3 \end{pmatrix}$.

So, for values of $n$ which are one more than a multiple of 3 (i.e. $n = 4, 7, 10, \ldots$), the smallest number of moves, $m$, to travel between opposite corners on

an $n \times n$ chess board is given by $\frac{3m}{2} + 1 = n$,

i.e. $m = \frac{2(n-1)}{3}$. Other values of $n$ are more complicated to deal with.

## Ex B12.4

1

| Object and image are….. | Reflections | Rotations | Translations | Enlargements |
|---|---|---|---|---|
| …. congruent | yes | yes | yes | no |
| …. similar | yes | yes | yes | yes |

2   a   similar               b   not similar

3  a  congruent          b  similar
   c  different          d  congruent
4  a  $x = 50°$   $y = 50°$   $z = 60°$   similar
   b  $x = 40°$   $y = 60°$   $z = 80°$   similar
   c  $x = 100°$   $z = 20°$   $y = 60°$   similar
5  120 cm
6  a  20 cm          b  25 cm, 100 cm
7  a  7.5 metres
   b  4 metres
8  $180 \times 130$ mm
9  $12 \times 8$ inches and $18 \times 12$ inches are enlargements
   $10 \times 8$ inches and $7 \times 5$ inches will need to be cropped

## Ex B12.5

1  Vertices of images are
   a  $(4, 6)$   $(8, 6)$   $(4, 12)$
   b  $(18, 0)$   $(24, 6)$   $(15, 9)$
   c  $(3, 16)$   $(11, 16)$   $(11, 20)$   $(3, 22)$
   d  $(18, 17)$   $(22, 17)$   $(20, 15)$
   e  $(5, 3)$   $(9, 3)$   $(6, 6)$
2  a  i  $(0, 3)$          ii  2
   b  i  $(12, 1)$          ii  3
   c  i  $(5, 7)$          ii  4
   d  Not an enlargement

3  a  $\dfrac{1}{2}$          b  $\dfrac{1}{3}$          c  $\dfrac{1}{4}$

4  a  $(1, 7), \dfrac{1}{2}$          b  $(4, 8), \dfrac{1}{4}$

5  200
6  A4 to A3 has a scale factor 2
   An enlargement (scale factor 2) is used for each
   successive paper size.

## Ex B12.6

1  Check students' diagrams

2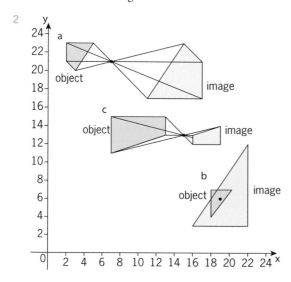

---

3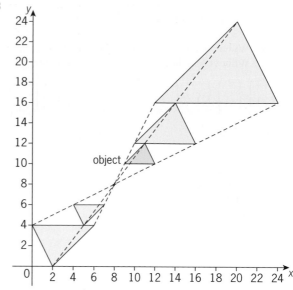

4  Scale factor $-\dfrac{1}{2}$

   The centre of the enlargement is the intersection of
   the medians (the line joining each vertice with the
   midpoint of the opposite side). It is the centre of
   gravity because it is the intersection of the medians.

## Exam practice

1  a  i  reflection in the $x$-axis
       ii  rotation about the origin by $+90°$
   b  reflection in $y = x$

2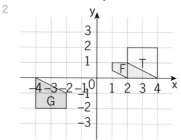

   b  Enlargement centre the origin with scale factor $-2$

3  a  $\begin{pmatrix} 3 \\ -2 \end{pmatrix} \begin{pmatrix} 2 \\ 3 \end{pmatrix} \begin{pmatrix} -2 \\ 2 \end{pmatrix}$          b  $\begin{pmatrix} 3 \\ 3 \end{pmatrix}$

## B13 Bivariate data and time series

### Check in

1  check coordinates
2  a  10          b  25          c  20          d  12.5          e  27.5

## Ex B13.1

1  scatter diagram
2  scatter diagram

3 More alcohol associated with longer reaction times More time on games associated with shorter reaction times. All subjects took longer at 3.0 am than mid-morning. Also the quicker your reaction time at 3 am, the quicker it is mid-morning.

## Ex B13.2

1 positive correlation. People living at higher altitudes have larger lung capacity
2 a positive correlation. Students tend to be good at both subjects or weak at both. Stats marks are higher than maths
  b positive correlation. Taller people have longer arms than shorter people.
3 a diagram      b positive
  c Quick writers are quick with both hands. All but one student took longer with left than right hand.
4 diagram. No correlation. Other factors, eg population density, modernity of buildings, affect death toll.

## Ex B13.3

1 a £108      b £97
2 a 4.9 litres
  b i data only collected to 1200 m
    ii data only collected for men
3 a answers from graph
  b correlation not very strong; horse data extreme values; best to use for lifespans between 3 and 18 years.

## Ex B13.4

1 No pattern; highs in June and Dec, lows in March and August
2 Highest in winter quarters, Oct–Dec and Jan–Mar. Each quarter in 2005 higher than same in 2004, probably price per unit increased
3 Rises steadily Mar–Aug. Steep fall in September., maybe back to school. Rise in Dec.
4 Same pattern each year with high in May–Aug and low in Jan–Apr. Amount for same period rises each year.
5 Same pattern over 2 years. High in Apr–Jun, low in Oct–Dec. Slightly lower in 2005 compared with same period in 2004

## Exam practice

1 graph. Temperatures vary, though no trend is evident.
2 graph. Number of weddings rises from Jan to Aug, then decreases to Dec. Same pattern both years. Months with 5 Saturdays have slightly more than expected.
3 Data can be compared through trends shown by scatter graph, also mean, median, mode, range, IQR or box-and-whisker plot. Mean waiting times are A: 4 mins B: 3.3 mins.

## Check in

1  $A = lw$        Area of rectangle
   $A = \pi r^2$      Area of circle
   $a^2 + b^2 = c^2$    Length of sides in a right angled triangle
   $V = lwh$        Volume of a cuboid
   $A = \frac{1}{2}bh$      Area of a triangle

2 a $5\frac{2}{3}$      b $2\frac{1}{2}$      c $\pm 5$
  d 16      e 2      f 2

3 a

| $x$ | 1 | 2 | 3 |
|---|---|---|---|
| $y$ | 5 | 8 | 11 |

Check graph

  b

| $x$ | −1 | 0 | 6 |
|---|---|---|---|
| $y$ | 14 | 12 | 0 |

Check graph

## Ex B14.1

1 a $x = 1, y = 3$    b $a = 1, b = 2$    c $p = 2, q = 3$
  d $m = 2, n = 5$    e $c = 4, d = 2$    f $k = 5, t = 2$
  g $x = -1, y = 2$    h $a = 2, b = -3$
2 a $x = 4, y = 1$    b $p = 2, q = 1$    c $c = 6, d = 2$
  d $m = 3, n = 1$    e $a = 2, b = 2$    f $k = 2, t = 3$
  g $x = 2, y = -2$    h $p = -1, q = -5$
3 a $a = 3, b = 5$    b $p = 1, q = 6$    c $c = 5, d = -2$
  d $k = 1, t = \frac{1}{2}$    e $m = 4, n = 2$    f $x = 2, y = \frac{1}{3}$
  g $a = -3, b = 2$    h $p = 4, q = -1$

4 An Americano costs £1.60 and a Cappuccino costs £1.95.

## Ex B14.2

1 a $x = 2, y = 3$    b $a = 5, b = 1$    c $p = 5, q = 2$
  d $m = 2, n = 1$    e $m = 3, n = 4$    f $t = 3, k = 2$
  g $x = -2, y = 2$    h $a = 5, b = -2$
2 a $x = 4, y = 2$    b $p = 2, q = 5$    c $a = 7, b = 3$
  d $m = 3, n = -1$    e $k = -3, t = 4$    f $p = -1, q = -2$
  g $a = 5, b = \frac{1}{2}$    h $x = -1, y = 1\frac{1}{2}$
3 a Cherries are worth 9 and grapes are worth 11.
  b Apples are worth 8 and bananas are worth 15.
4 a Edward sells 43 badges.
  b Jacob needs 5 minicabs and 4 black cabs.
  c i $a = -3$ and $b = 2$.
    ii Gradient $= 1\frac{1}{2}$ and $y$-intercept $= (0, 2)$

## Ex B14.3

1 a i $x = 2, y = 5$      ii $x = 1, y = 2$
    iii $x = 6, y = 1$      iv $x = 3, y = 0$
  b These lines are parallel.

**2** **a** **i** $x + 2y = 5$ and $2x + y = 4$
   **ii** $x - y = 2$ and $2x + y = 4$
   **iii** $x + y = 5$ and $2x + y = 4$
   **iv** $x - y = 2$ and $x + 2y = 5$
   **v** $x + 2y = 5$ and $x + y = 5$
   **vi** $x + y = 5$ and $x - y = 2$
   **b** Check working shown to solve simultaneous equations algebraically.
**3** **a** Graphs of $x + y = 2$ and $3x - y = 2$ drawn and solution given as $x = 1$, $y = 1$.
   **b** Graphs of $x + y = 7$ and $x - 2y = 1$ drawn and solution given as $x = 5$, $y = 2$.
   **c** Graphs of $x - y = -5$ and $2x + y = 8$ drawn and solution given as $x = 1$, $y = 6$.
   **d** Graphs of $2x - y = 7$ and $3x + y = 8$ drawn and solution given as $x = 3$, $y = -1$.
**4** **a** The two numbers are 2 and 5.
   **b** Alexander is 7 and William is 4.
**5** Check pair of simultaneous equations with more than one solution given, e.g. 1 linear, 1 quadratic.

## Ex B14.4

**1** **a** $a \geq 6$ where $a$ is the age of a child in years.
   **b** $h \geq 1.2$ where $h$ is the height of a person in metres.
   **c** $s \leq 5$ where $s$ is the speed of a vehicle in mph.
**2** **a** $x \geq 2$    **b** $x < 1$    **c** $x > -4$
   **d** $x \leq 0$    **e** $-1 < x \leq 2$    **f** $-3 \leq x < -1$
**3** **a**, **b**, **c**, **d**, **e**, **f**, **g**, **h**

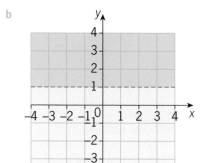

**4** **a** 2, 3, 4, 5    **b** 1, 2, 3, 4, 5    **c** −6, −5, −4
   **d** −1, 0, 1    **e** None    **f** 1, 2
   **g** −2, −1, 0    **h** −4, −3, −2, −1
**5** **a** $x \leq 3$    **b** $y > 5$    **c** $a < -3$
   **d** $q \geq 21$    **e** $n > -12$    **f** $t < 3$
   **g** $p \geq 12$    **h** $b < 4$    **i** $k \leq 3$
   **j** $y \leq 6$    **k** $x > 4$    **l** $m \geq 12$
**6** **a** $x \leq 4$    **b** $y \geq 4$    **c** $n > 1$
   **d** $b < 2$    **e** $t \geq 6$    **f** $k > 5$
   **g** $m \geq 8$    **h** $a < -2$
**7** **a** $-1 < x \leq 3$    **b** $1.5 \leq y < 5$
**8** **a** $4 \leq x \leq 7$    **b** $\frac{1}{2} < a \leq 4$
   **c** $-\frac{1}{2} < y \leq 2$    **d** $-2 \leq b < 4$

## Ex B14.5

**1** **a** $x \geq 2$    **b** $y > 1$
   **c** $x < -1$    **d** $x \geq -2$ and $y \geq -1$
   **e** $-3 < x \leq 1$    **f** $y > 0$ and $y \leq -3$
**2** **a**

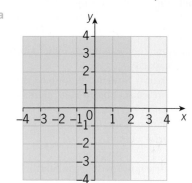

**b**

**c**

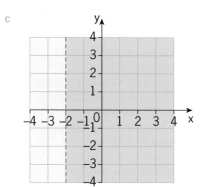

**d**

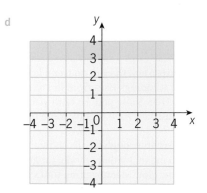

e

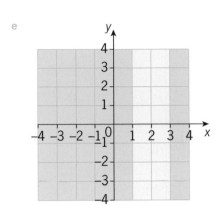

i

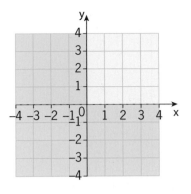

f

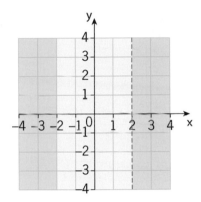

j

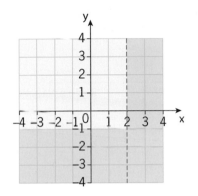

g

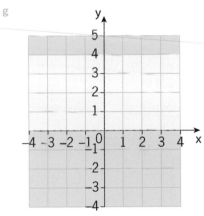

3 a

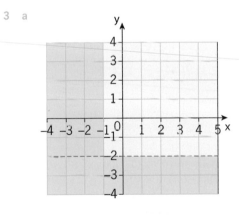

h

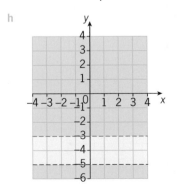

b

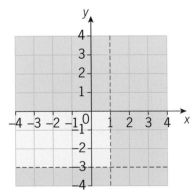

c

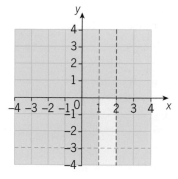

b

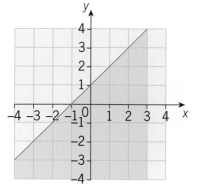

d

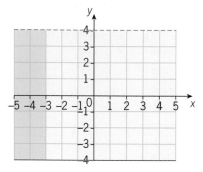

c

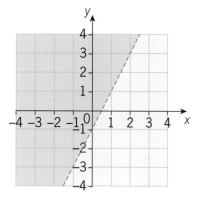

4

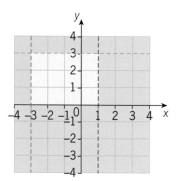

d

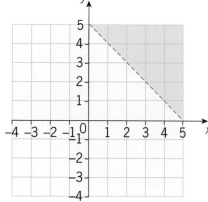

The integer pairs are (0, 0), (0, 1), (0, 2), (−1, 0), (−1, 1), (−1, 2), (−2, 0), (−2, 1), (−2, 2).

## Ex B14.6

1   a   $y > x$           b   $x + y \leq 2$      c   $y > 2x - 2$
2   a

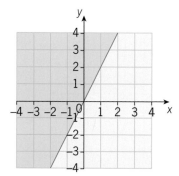

e

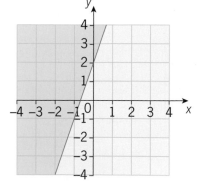

f

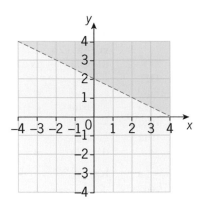

g

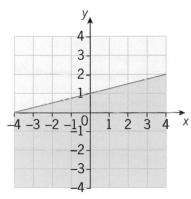

h

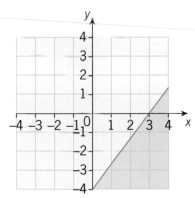

3 a $x < 3$, $y \leq 1$, $x + y \geq 1$
  b $-1 < x \leq 1$, $y \geq -1$, $y < x + 2$
  c $-3 \leq y \leq 2$, $y < 4 - 2x$, $y > -4 - 2x$
4 a The inequalities $x \geq 0$, $y \geq 0$ and $2x + y \leq 4$ plotted
    correctly. Shape is triangle.
  b The inequalities $y > -1$, $y < x + 2$ and $x + y < 6$
    plotted correctly. Shape is isosceles triangle.
  c The inequalities $-3 < y < 1$, $x > -4$ and $y < 1 - 2x$
    plotted correctly. Shape is trapezium.
  d The inequalities $-2 \leq x < 3$, $2y \leq x + 2$ and $2y \geq x - 6$
    plotted correctly. Shape is parallelogram.
5 a $6x + 10y \leq 100$ represents the cost of the CDs
    and the fact that this cannot exceed £100 thus

$3x + 5y \leq 50$.
$x + y \geq 10$ represents the fact that the total must be
at least 10 CDs.
$x \leq y$ represents the fact that he wants to buy no
more bargain basement CDs than chart CDs.
  b Correctly drawn inequalities.
  c Points are $(0, 10)$, $(1, 9)$, $(2, 8)$, $(3, 8)$, $(3, 7)$, $(4, 6)$,
    $(4, 7)$, $(5, 5)$, $(5, 6)$, $(5, 7)$, $(6, 6)$.
  d Harry should buy 5 bargain basement CDs and
    7 chart CDs or just buy 10 chart CDs.

## Exam practice

1 a $x = \frac{4}{3}$, $y = \frac{11}{3}$    b $x = \frac{1}{2}$, $y = -2$

2 a i $x \geq 7\frac{1}{2}$    ii

3 £5.79

## B15 Indices and surds

### Check in

1 a $3^2$        b $4^5$        c $6^3$        d $5^4$
2 a $3 \times 3 \times 3$              b $6 \times 6$
  c $4 \times 4 \times 4 \times 4 \times 4$        d $8 \times 8 \times 8$
  e $7 \times 7 \times 7 \times 7$        f $5 \times 5 \times 5 \times 5 \times 5$
3 a 16            b 27            c 16
  d 125          e 128          f 7

### Ex B15.1

1 a i $5^9$    ii $5^0$              iii $2^6$  $4^3$
  b i $16^2$    ii all squares    iii $4^6$  $16^3$
2 a $2^4 \times 3$    b $2 \times 3 \times 7$  c $2^3 \times 3 \times 5^2$
  d $2^8 \times 5$    e $3 \times 5 \times 7^2$
3 a $7^9$        b $3^8$        c $8^9$
  d $15^8$        e $4^{12}$        f $3^6$
  g 8          h $9^5$        l $6^1$
4 a 2, 4        b i 6        ii 4
5 a 729        b 65 536        c i 2048    ii 8192
  d 10 000 000 000
6 a $2^{17}$        b $3^{11}$        c $4^7$
7 a 1          b 1
8 a $6^2 \times 6^3 = 6^5$              b $6^6 \div 6^2 = 6^4 = 1296$

### Ex B15.2

1 a 8          b 4          c 13          d 3
  e 15          f 3          g 3          h 9
  i 2          j 2          k $\frac{1}{16}$        l $\frac{1}{94}$
  m $\frac{1}{16}$        n $\frac{1}{125}$        o $\frac{1}{100\,000}$        p $\frac{1}{3}$
  q $\frac{1}{3}$        r $\frac{1}{2}$        s 10          t $\frac{1}{10}$
2 a $7^6$        b $17^{15}$        c $6^{14}$        d $12^{12}$        e $5^{-6}$

3 a $\frac{1}{4}$  b 2  c $\frac{1}{625}$  d $\frac{1}{27}$  e $\frac{1}{32}$

4 a $\frac{5}{36}$  b $\frac{1}{343}$  c $\frac{3}{16}$  d $\frac{2}{25}$  e $\frac{25}{7}$

5 a $9^2$  b $3^4$

6 a $2^{3p}$  b $\frac{2}{3}$

7 a 13 g  b i $133 = 5 + 2^t$  ii 7

## Ex B15.3

1 a 10  b 7  c 4
  d $\frac{1}{2}$  e 9  f 80

2 a $3\sqrt{11}$  b $2\sqrt{15}$  c $5\sqrt{3}$
  d $10\sqrt{2}$  e $5\sqrt{5}$  f $8\sqrt{2}$

3 a 15  b 14  c 6  d $6\sqrt{5}$

4 a 8  b 2  c 16

5 a $3\sqrt{2}$  b $18\sqrt{2}$  c $\frac{1}{18}$

6 b i $\frac{\sqrt{3}}{2}$  ii $\frac{1}{\sqrt{3}}$  iii $\sqrt{3}$
  c i $\frac{1}{\sqrt{2}}$  ii $\frac{1}{\sqrt{2}}$

## Ex B15.4

1 a 3  b 2  c 5  d 4
  e 4  f 7  g $\frac{3}{2}$  h $\frac{4}{3}$

2 a $4\sqrt{3}$  b $7\sqrt{3}$  c $3\sqrt{5}$  d $18\sqrt{2}$
  e $5\sqrt{7}$  f $10\sqrt{5}$

3 a 46  b $-1$  c 32
  d 12  e $31 - 10\sqrt{6}$  f $11 - 4\sqrt{7}$
  g $11 - 6\sqrt{2}$  h $\frac{1}{3}(4\sqrt{3} + \sqrt{15})$  i $\frac{3\sqrt{7}}{7} + 1$

5 $4\sqrt{3}$

6 a $\frac{4\sqrt{3} - 6}{3} = \frac{4}{3}\sqrt{3} - 2$ so $p = -2$ and $q = \frac{4}{3}$
  b AC is negative ($\sqrt{5} - 5$) so has no real root

## Exam practice

1 a $\frac{5}{16}$  b 1  c 18

2 $\frac{1}{2}$

3 $\frac{841\sqrt{2}}{2}$, $\frac{841}{2}$

## B16 Vectors

### Check in

1 Check own definitions
2 a 3 lines  b 6 lines  c 8 lines

## Ex B16.1

1 a i 2a  ii 2b  iii $-$2b  iv 2a + 2b
    v b $-$ 2a  vi $-$a $-$ 2b
  b i OX  ii OT  iii OD  iv OQ
    v OG  vi OF

2 a true  b false  c true  d true
  e false  f true  g true  h true
  i false  j true  k true  l true
  m false  n true

3 b = 2.5a  c = 3a  d = $-$2a  e = $\frac{1}{2}$ a
  f = $-\frac{3}{2}$ a  g = $-\frac{1}{2}$a  h = $-$a

4 a OV = b + a  OW = b + 2a  WO = $-$2a $-$ b
  b PR = b + 2a  QR = b + a
  c LN = a + b  NM = b $-$ a

5 a a  b 2a  c 2b  d 3b
  e 2a $-$ b  f 3b $-$ a  g 3b $-$ 2a  h 2a $-$ 3b

6 Ground speed is 123 mph
  a Greatest ground speed occurs when the wind blows in the same direction as the aircraft.
  b Least ground speed occurs when the wind blows in the opposite direction to the aircraft.

7
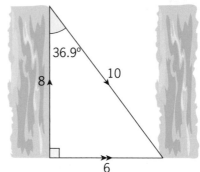

36.9°

8  10

6

The man swims at an angle of 36.9° to the bank. His resultant speed is 6 metres per minute.

## Ex B16.2

1 a $\begin{pmatrix} 1 \\ 5 \end{pmatrix}$  b $\begin{pmatrix} 1 \\ 8 \end{pmatrix}$  c $\begin{pmatrix} -4 \\ -1 \end{pmatrix}$  d $\begin{pmatrix} 5 \\ 10 \end{pmatrix}$

2 $\begin{pmatrix} 15 \\ 4 \end{pmatrix}$

3 $\begin{pmatrix} 2 \\ 4 \end{pmatrix}$ and $\begin{pmatrix} 1 \\ 2 \end{pmatrix}$; $\begin{pmatrix} 4 \\ -1 \end{pmatrix}$ and $\begin{pmatrix} -2 \\ \frac{1}{2} \end{pmatrix}$; $\begin{pmatrix} 2 \\ -3 \end{pmatrix}$ and $\begin{pmatrix} -2 \\ 3 \end{pmatrix}$

4 a $\begin{pmatrix} 5 \\ 3 \end{pmatrix}$  b $\begin{pmatrix} 1 \\ 3 \end{pmatrix}$  c $\begin{pmatrix} -1 \\ 2 \end{pmatrix}$

5 a $p = 5, q = 3$  b $m = 5, n = 4$
  c $c = 5, d = -1$  d $u = 3, v = 9$

6 a $x = 4, y = -1$  b $\begin{pmatrix} -4 \\ -3 \end{pmatrix}$

**7** Several possibilities

**8 a** $\begin{pmatrix} 7 \\ 4 \end{pmatrix}, \begin{pmatrix} 4 \\ -1 \end{pmatrix}$ **b** $(7, 4), (4, -1)$

**9 a** $\begin{pmatrix} 20 \\ 4 \end{pmatrix}$ **b** $\begin{pmatrix} 10 \\ 2 \end{pmatrix}$

The diagonals of a parallelogram bisect each other.

**10 a** $\begin{pmatrix} 3 \\ 5 \end{pmatrix}$ **b** $\begin{pmatrix} 4 \\ \frac{1}{2} \end{pmatrix}$ **c** $\begin{pmatrix} 1 \\ -4\frac{1}{2} \end{pmatrix}$ **d** $\begin{pmatrix} 2 \\ -9 \end{pmatrix}$

MN and EF are parallel and the length of MN is half that of EF

**11**

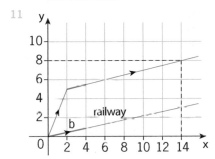

$x = 14$

**12** $t = 3\frac{1}{3}$ hours, $y = 10$

**13 a** $\mathbf{e}$ **b** $\mathbf{a} + \mathbf{e}$ **c** $2\mathbf{a} + \mathbf{e}$
**d** $2\mathbf{c} + \mathbf{a}$ **e** $\mathbf{a} + 2\mathbf{e}$
AC and OD are parallel and equal in length.

**14 a** $\mathbf{p} + \mathbf{q}$ **b** $2(\mathbf{p} + \mathbf{q} + \mathbf{r})$ **c** $\mathbf{p} + \mathbf{q}$
ST and VU are parallel and equal in length.
STUV is a parallelogram.

**15** The three medians intersect at a point which is one third of the way along each median.
This point of intersection is the centre of gravity of the triangular lamina.

## Exam practice

**1 a** $-\mathbf{a} + 2\mathbf{b}$ **b** $-\frac{1}{2}\mathbf{a} + \mathbf{b}$
**c** AB and XY are parallel and AB is twice the length of XY
**2** Rhombus (Parallelogram with 4 equal sides)
**3 a** $\mathbf{b} + 1.5\mathbf{a}$ **b** $-2\mathbf{b} + 1.5\mathbf{a}$
**c** $-3.5\mathbf{a} - \mathbf{b}$ **d** $0.5\mathbf{a} + 2\mathbf{b}$

## C17 Percentages and proportional change

## Check in

**1** Gill £400, Paul £100
**2** $33\frac{1}{3}\%$

## Ex C17.1

**1 a** £374.40 **b** £48.95

**2** 35 p
**3** £36 016.80
**4 i** 164 p for 250 g → 0.656 p per gram
**ii** 123 p for 200 g → 0.615 p per gram
so reducing price is better for customer.
**5 i** equivalent to a 1% decrease
**ii** same as **i**
**iii** equivalent to a 21% increase
**iv** equivalent to a 19% decrease
**6 a** Increasing contents gives 5.5 ml per p and decreasing price gives 5.6 (1dp) ml per p so decreasing price is better for customer
**d** 20% decrease on price

## Ex C17.2

**1** £32.00
**2** £85.00
**3** $147.20
**4** 360
**5** £902.00
**6** £45.00
**7** £850.00
**8** 650 cm³
**9** £515 000

## Ex C17.3

**1 a** 5.4 m **b** 4
**2 a i** 2 360 279 **ii** 3 316 022
**b** 13 years
**3 a i** 23 699 **ii** 14 370
**b** 21 years
**4 a i** £21 732.77 **ii** £26 586.28
**b** 11 years
**5** £3 099.31
**6** 4.6% paid annually is best. 4.5% paid monthly is equivalent to 4.5939825% paid annually.

## Ex C17.4

**1 a** $y = 6x$ **b** 42
**2 a** $y = 1.5x$ **b** 7.5
**3 a** $e = 1.25$ m **b i** 1.6 kg **ii** 6.25 cm
**4 a** $y = 0.5x^3$ **b** 13.5
**5 a** $E = 15e^2$ **b i** 960 **ii** 5
**6 a** $E = 1.6v^2$ **b i** 25.6 **ii** 10
**7** $\pi$
**8** $\dfrac{4\pi}{3}$

## Ex C17.5

**1 a** $y = \dfrac{20}{x}$ **b** $\dfrac{2}{3}$

**2 a** $y = \dfrac{1.2}{x}$ **b** 0.75

**3 a** 20 **b** 13 hours 20 mins

**4 a** $V = \dfrac{800}{P}$ **b** 3.2 $m^3$ **c** $166\frac{2}{3}$N/m$^2$

**5 a** $y = \dfrac{15}{\sqrt{x}}$ **b i** 7.5 **ii** 100

**6 a** $y = \dfrac{1}{x^2}$ **b i** $\dfrac{1}{36}$ **ii** 0.2

**7 a** $F = \dfrac{12}{d^2}$ **b i** 48 **ii** 4

## Exam practice

1 £102.00
2 **a** 228 g **b** 6
3 **a** $s = 0.375\,d$ **b** 112 cm

## C18 Area and perimeter

### Check in

1 **i a** 6 cm by 2 cm, perim = 16 cm
**b** 4.5 cm by 4.5 cm, perim = 18 cm
**c** 4 cm by 7 cm by 8.1 cm, perim = 19.1 cm
**ii a** 12 cm$^2$ **b** 20.25 cm$^2$ **c** 14 cm$^2$
2 **a** check net **b** 54 cm$^2$ **c** 27 cm$^3$

### Ex C18.1

1 **a i** 32 cm **ii** 56 cm$^2$
**b i** 34 cm **ii** 38 cm$^2$
**c i** 27.8 cm **ii** 23.5 cm$^2$
**d i** 48.8 cm **ii** 72 cm$^2$
2 £534.60
3 $x = 6$ cm
4 $x = 2$ m

### Ex C18.2

1 **a** 16 cm **b** 25 cm **c** 19 cm **d** 63 cm
2 **a** 125.6 cm **b** 1592
3 452 m$^2$
4 16.6 m$^2$
5 **a** 615 m$^2$ **b** £52300
6 **a** 1.3 cm, 0.8 cm **b** 2.01 cm$^2$ **c** 3.30 cm$^2$
7 15.9 cm
8 63.7 cm
9 1.4 cm
10 2.39 metres
11 5 cm

### Ex C18.3

1 area, cm$^2$     arc length, cm
**a** 22.6     7.5
**b** 75.4     18.8
**c** 191     42.4
**d** 24.4     4.9
2 **a** 10.5 cm **b** 4.7 cm **c** 30 cm **d** 28 cm
3 **a** $\dfrac{5}{12}$ **b** 20.9 cm$^2$
4 51.3 cm$^2$

---

5 **a** 31.4 cm$^2$ **b** 3.9 cm **c** 13.7 cm$^2$
6 245 cm$^2$
7 **a** 94.2 cm$^2$ **b** 6 cm **c** 9.8 cm
8 28.6 cm
9 60.1°

## Exam practice

1 $\dfrac{p}{8}, \dfrac{p\sqrt{2}}{16}, \dfrac{p\sqrt{2}}{16}$ cm
2 $21\pi$ cm$^2$
3 7.816 cm$^2$

## C19 Algebraic manipulation

### Check in

1 **a** $7x$ **b** $5a + 16b$ **c** $6y + 4$ **d** $26x + 2x^2$
2 **a** $3x + 6$ **b** $5y - 40$ **c** $x^2 + 5x$ **d** $6p^2 + 12p$
3 **a** $5^{10}$ **b** $2^2$ **c** $4^4$
**d** $6^{14}$ **e** $7^6$ **f** $5^6$

### Ex C19.1

1

| $9a - b$ | $2m$ | $5p + 4$ | $9c$ |
|---|---|---|---|
| $12mn$ | $2x^2$ | $2xy$ | $4xy + 8x$ |
| $15mn$ | $6b^2$ | $4b$ | $2x$ |
| $40k^3$ | $5xy^2$ | $5x + 8x^2$ | $\dfrac{rh}{2}$ |

2 **a** $x^5$ **b** $x^2$ **c** $x^4$ **d** $x^4$
**e** $y^{13}$ **f** $k^3$ **g** $n^{12}$ **h** $g^3$ **i** $b^{-6}$
**j** $g^{-12}$ **k** $j^{-6}$ **l** $t^{10}$ **m** $n^{-2}$
3 **a** $12h^{11}$ **b** $3p^2$ **c** $4m^{16}$ **d** $36r^{-1}$
**e** $27h^{-9}$ **f** $3b^8$ **g** $2m^{19}$ **h** 2
5 $2x^5$ Height > 40 cm
6 False

### Ex C19.2

1 **a** $20x + 32$ **b** $12p^2 - 21p$
**c** $10m - 4m^2$ **d** $17y + 30$
**e** $15x^2 + 10xy - 45x$ **f** $59 - t$
**g** $3h + 16$ **h** $3x^3 + x^4$
2 **a** Perimeter is two widths and two lengths added together. $2x + 4$
**b** $5x - 15$
3 **a** $3(x + 2y + 3z)$ **b** $5(2p - 3)$ **c** $x(5y + 7)$
**d** $3m(2n + 3t)$ **e** $4x(4x - 3y)$ **f** $3p(1 + 3q)$
**g** $7x(y - 8x)$ **h** $3x(x + 4x^2 - 2)$
**i** $(m + n)(3 + m + n)$
**j** $(p - q)(4 + (p - q)^2)$ **k** $(a + b)(x + y)$
5 **a** $3x$ **b** $9x$ **c** $x + 2$
**d** $\dfrac{x - 2}{3}$ **e** $x + 4$ **f** $\dfrac{y^2 - 3y}{2}$
6 The answer is always 2

### Ex C19.3

1 **a** $x^2 + 7x + 10$ **b** $y^2 + 15y + 44$ **c** $x^2 + 2x - 15$

d $p^2 - 2p - 63$  e  $m^2 + 16m + 64$  f  $y^2 - 49$

3 a  $2x^2 + 14x + 24$  b  $12p^2 + 23p + 10$

c  $6m^2 - 32m + 42$  d  $10y^2 + 17y - 63$

e  $9t^2 - 12t + 4$  f  $2x^2 + 4x - 15$

4  $2x^2 + 10x + 8$

5 a  $-3\frac{4}{5}$  b  4

6  15 metres

7 a  $y^3 - 9y^2 + 27y - 27$  b  True

## Ex C19.4

1 a  $(x + 2)(x + 5)$  b  $(x + 3)(x + 5)$  c  $(x + 2)(x + 6)$

d  $(x + 5)(x + 7)$  e  $(x + 2)(x - 5)$  f  $(x + 5)(x - 7)$

g  $(x - 3)(x - 5)$  h  $(x + 4)(x - 5)$

i  $(x + 12)(x - 20)$

j  $(x - 9)(x + 12)$  k  $(x - 5)^2$  l  $(x + 2)(x - 3)$

2 a  $(2x + 3)(x + 1)$  b  $(3x + 2)(x + 2)$

c  $(2x + 5)(x + 1)$  d  $(2x + 3)(x + 4)$

e  $(3x + 1)(x + 2)$  f  $(2x + 1)(x + 3)$

g  $(2x + 7)(x - 3)$  h  $(3x + 1)(x - 2)$

i  $(4x - 3)(x - 5)$  j  $(6x - 1)(x - 3)$

k  $(4x + 5)(3x + 2)$  l  $(4x + 1)(2x - 3)$

m  $(2x - 5)(3x - 6)$ or $3(2x - 5)(x - 2)$

n  $(2x + 3)(3x - 1)$  o  $(3x + 4)(6x - 1)$

3 a  $(x - 10)(x + 10)$  b  $(y - 4)(y + 4)$

c  $(p - 12)(p + 12)$  d  $(k - 8)(k + 8)$

e  $\left(x - \frac{1}{2}\right)\left(x + \frac{1}{2}\right)$  f  $\left(y - \frac{4}{5}\right)\left(y + \frac{4}{5}\right)$

g  $(n - 50)(n + 50)$  h  $(7 - t)(7 + t)$

i  $(2x - 5)(2x + 5)$  j  $(3y - 11)(3y + 11)$

k  $\left(4m - \frac{1}{2}\right)\left(4m + \frac{1}{2}\right)$  l  $(20p - 13)(20p + 13)$

4 a  $(4a - 3b)(4a + 3b)$  b  $(x - 4)(x - 7)$

c  $(2x - 3)(x + 7)$  d  $x(x - 3)(x + 6)$

e  $5ab(1 + 2ab)$  f  $-(x - 2)(x + 5)$

g  $10(1 - x)(1 + x)$  h  $(y - 7)(y + 9)$

i  $2x(x^2 - 66)$  j  $(2x - 3)(3x - 2)$

k  $(x^2 + y^2)(x - y)(x + y)$

5 a  $x + 2$  b  $\frac{x - 3}{2}$  c  $x - 3$

d  $\frac{x + 4}{2}$  e  $\frac{x + 4}{x - 4}$  f  $\frac{x + 1}{3x - 1}$

6 a  400  b  240000  c  199

7  Challenge  $\sqrt{1200}$  or  $20\sqrt{3}$

## Ex C19.5

1 a  $x = 0$ and $x = 5$  b  $x = 0$ and $x = -9$

c  $x = 0$ and $x = 3\frac{1}{2}$  d  $x = 0$ and $x = 2$

e  $x = 0$ and $x = 9$  f  $x = 0$ and $x = 7$

g  $x = 0$ and $x = 12$  h  $x = 0$ and $x = 6$

2 a  $x = -3$ and $x = -4$  b  $x = -2$ and $x = -6$

c  $x = -6$  d  $x = -5$ and $x = 3$

e  $x = -7$ and $x = 2$  f  $x = -1$ and $x = 5$

g  $x = 2$ and $x = 3$  h  $x = 5$

i  $x = -\frac{1}{2}$ and $x = -3$  j  $x = -\frac{1}{3}$ and $x = -2$

k  $y = -4$ and $y = -1\frac{1}{2}$  l  $x = -\frac{2}{3}$ and $x = -\frac{1}{2}$

m  $x = 2$ and $x = 6$  n  $x = -5$ and $x = 1\frac{1}{2}$

o  $y = 2$ and $y = 3$  p  $x = -3$ and $x = -7$

3 a  $x = -7$ and $x = 7$  b  $y = -8$ and $y = 8$

c  $x = -\frac{2}{3}$ and $x = \frac{2}{3}$  d  $x = -\frac{1}{2}$ and $x = \frac{1}{2}$

e  $x = -12$ and $x = 12$  f  $y = -2\frac{1}{2}$ and $y = 2\frac{1}{2}$

4 a  $x = 0$ and $x = \frac{1}{3}$  b  $x = -3$ and $x = 5$

c  $x = \frac{2}{3}$ and $x = 3$  d  $y = -1\frac{2}{3}$ and $y = 1\frac{2}{3}$

e  $x = -1\frac{1}{3}$ and $x = 1\frac{1}{3}$  f  $x = \frac{3}{5}$ and $x = -\frac{1}{4}$

5 a  $x = -6$ and $x = 5$  b  $x = \frac{3}{5}$ and $x = -\frac{1}{2}$

6  10 m by 24 m

7 a  Any value between 0 and 1

b  $x = -3, x = 3, x = -2$ and $x = 2$

## Ex C19.6

1 a  $(x + 2)^2 + 2$  b  $(y + 4)^2 - 1$

c  $(x + 3)^2$  d  $(x + 5)^2 + 2$

e  $(y + 2)^2 - 4$  f  $(x + 6)^2 - 26$

g  $(x + 7)^2 - 19$  h  $(x + 2)^2 - 9$

i  $(y + 4)^2 - 19$  j  $\left(x + 1\frac{1}{2}\right)^2 + 1\frac{3}{4}$

2 a  $(x + 10)^2 - 50$  b  $(x + 8)^2 - 69$

c  $\left(x - 1\frac{1}{2}\right)^2 - 31\frac{1}{4}$

3 a  $x = 2$ and $x = 10$  b  $y = -5$ and $y = 3$

c  $x = -1$ and $x = 5$  d  $x = -1$

e  $m = -9$ and $m = 7$  f  $x = 7$

g  $y = 0$ and $y = 8$  h  $x = \pm\sqrt{37} - 6$

i  $x = -11$ and $x = 8$  j  $x = 3$

4 a  Minimum value of 1 when $x = -3$

b  Minimum value of $-2$ when $x = 4$

c  Minimum value of $-40$ when $x = 6$

d  Minimum value of $-5\frac{1}{4}$ when $x = -2\frac{1}{2}$

5 a  Minimum value is 6

b  Equation becomes $(x + 4)^2 = -1$ and a square cannot be negative

6  6 by 7 and 3 by 7

7  Maximum is when the rectangle is a square with sides of 250 metres

## Ex C19.7

1 a  $x = -0.785$ and $x = -2.55$

b  $x = 1$ and $x = 0.2$

c  $x = -1\frac{1}{2}$ and $x = 5$

d   $x = -0.268$ and $x = -3.73$

e   $x = -3.16$ and $x = 0.158$

f   $y = -0.377$ and $y = 2.21$

g   $x = \frac{1}{3}$ and $x = 3$      h   $x = 0.158$ and $x = -3.16$

2  a   $x = -5.61$ and $x = 1.61$  b   $x = -2.46$ and $x = 4.46$

   c   $x = -0.284$ and $x = 1.17$

3  a   $(x + 7)(x - 2)$ or $x^2 + 5x - 14$

   c   1.84 cm by 10.84 cm

4  a   $x = 0.145$ and $x = 11.5$  b   $x = -0.535$ and $x = 1.87$

   c   $x = -1$ and $x = 1.75$     d   $x = -3.79$ and $x = 3.29$

5  Will factorise if $b^2 - 4ac$ is a perfect square

## Ex C19.8

1  a   $x = 7$ and $y = 6$ or $x = -7$ and $y = 6$

   b   $x = 7$ and $y = -5$ or $x = 7$ and $y = 5$

   c   $x = -10$ and $y = 9$ or $x = 10$ and $y = 9$

   d   $x = 7$ and $y = -2$ or $x = 7$ and $y = 2$

2  a   $x = -1$ and $y = 3$ or $x = 4$ and $y = 8$

   b   $x = 1$ and $y = 0$

   c   $x = \frac{1}{2}$ and $y = \frac{1}{2}$ or $x = 32$ and $y = 4$

   d   $x = 0$ and $y = 1$ or $x = \frac{4}{5}$ and $y = -\frac{3}{5}$

3  a   $x = 3$ and $y = 7$ or $x = 5$ and $y = 17$

   b   $p = -2$ and $q = -1$ or $p = 2$ and $q = 1$

4  a   $(-1, -5)$ and $(6, 16)$

5  The small square measures 3 metres by 3 metres and the larger 4 metres by 4 metres

6  $x = -5$ and $y = -3$ or $x = 5$ and $y = 3$

## Exam practice

1  a  i   $x = 10$ or $-3$     ii   $x = 4.24$ or $-0.24$

   b  i   $a = 3, b = -7$     ii   $x = -3 \pm \sqrt{7}$

2  $(5,5)$ Line is a tangent to the circle

3  b   1.32 m

## C20 Surface area and volume

## Check in

1  a   40 cm²  b  30 cm²

2  a   250  b  6300  c  41  d  250  e  3500

   f  4     g  5.6  h  40  i  4.1  j  5.2

## Ex C20.1

1  168 cm²

2  a   534 cm²     b  1032 cm²

3  For example,

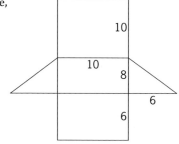

surface area 288 cm²

For example,

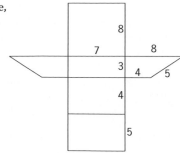

surface area 176 cm²

4  a   2.16 m²     b  £26.89     c  £6.50

5  12.7 cm and 7.7 cm

6  a   0.14 m     b  $\dfrac{\sqrt{1 + \frac{2}{\pi}} - 1}{2}$

7  a   400 cm²;  25 cm × 20 cm     b  20%

8  The least surface area is that of a cube of edge 10 cm.

## Ex C20.2

1  64 cm²

2  a   153.9 cm²     b  266.9 cm²

   c   282.6 cm²

3  15.5 cm

4  70.0 cm

5  a   10.9 cm     b  13.1 cm

6  12 cm

7  208.1 m

8  The most economical arrangement depends on the relative height and diameter of the tin

## Ex C20.3

1  a   $(2, 0)$ 2 4

   b   $(1, 1)$ 3 9

2  135 cm²

3  a   3          b  9          c  27

4  a   3          b  27        c  810 litres

5  Yes, 2.5, 6.25

## Ex C20.4

1  a  i   80 mm     ii  600 mm²     iii  2000 mm³

   b  i   3.5 cm     ii  1.4 cm²     iii  0.5 cm³

2  a  i   800 cm     ii  30 000 cm²     iii  5 000 000 cm³

   b  i   7.5 m     ii  0.85 m²     iii  0.412 m³

3  a  i   46 mm     ii  130 mm²     iii  350 mm³

   b  i   32 cm     ii  250 cm²     iii  750 000 cm³

   c  i   3000 m     ii  2 000 000 m²     iii  0.0159 km³

4  a   7400 metres  b  2 100 000 m²  c  0.005 km³

5  a   0.315 km  b  0.0445 km²  c  0.004 km³

## Ex C20.5

1  3075 litres

2  No, it contains 1.002 litres

3  61%

4  250 seconds or 4 minutes 10 seconds

**5**

| length | width | height |
|--------|-------|--------|
| 10 | 10 | 10 |
| 10 | 20 | 5 |
| 10 | 50 | 2 |
| 10 | 100 | 1 |
| 20 | 50 | 1 |

The 10 cm × 10 cm × 10 cm pack is suitable

**6** The volume of the pyramid is $\frac{1}{3}$ of the volume of the cube with the same base and height measurements.

Both have volumes = $\frac{1}{3}$ of base area × height.

**7 a** 8143 cm³ **b** 804 cm³ **c** 599 cm³
**d** 1.4 cm³ **e** 384 cm³ **f** 0.022 cm³

**8** 17.7 cm

**9** Yes, it is 80 cm high

**10** 5.8 litres

**11** Pour the water over the metal, so that the metal is submerged, and measure the height of the water, h.
Volume = $16\pi(h - 7)$

**12** 5.3 cm

**13 a** 7.94 cm **b** 2.3 cm

**14** 35 metres

**15** 144 metres high, 210 metres sloping edge

**16** 20.4 cm

**17 a** $V = \frac{\pi}{3}R^3\left(\frac{\theta}{360}\right)^2\sqrt{1-\left(\frac{\theta}{360}\right)^2}$

**b**
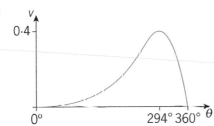
Maximum V of 0.40 when $\theta = 294°$

## Ex C20.6

**1 a** 432 + 216 π cm³  432 + 72π cm²
**b** 750 π cm³  325 π cm²
**b** 2160 π cm³  588 πcm²
**2** 0.25 cm
**3 a** 420 cm³ **b** 716 cm³ **c** 70 cm³
**4 a** 21.3 litres **b** 7.8 litres
**5** 779 m³ 760 m²

## Exam practice

**1** 63.3 cm³
**2** 12.5 cm³
**3** 3.22 cm

## C21 Graphs

### Check in

**1 a** 8, 8 **b** 18, 18 **c** −3, 21 **d** 14, 8
**2** Check own graphs
**3** Check own graphs

## Ex C21.1

**1 a**

| x | −3 | −2 | −1 | 0 | 1 | 2 | 3 |
|---|----|----|----|----|----|----|----|
| x² | 9 | 4 | 1 | 0 | 1 | 4 | 9 |
| −2 | −2 | −2 | −2 | −2 | −2 | −2 | −2 |
| y | 7 | 2 | −1 | −2 | −1 | 2 | 7 |

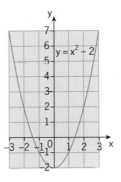

**b**

| x | −3 | −2 | −1 | 0 | 1 | 2 | 3 |
|---|----|----|----|----|----|----|----|
| y | 18 | 8 | 2 | 0 | 2 | 8 | 18 |

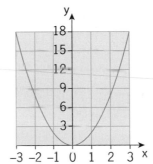

**c**

| x | −3 | −2 | −1 | 0 | 1 | 2 | 3 |
|---|----|----|----|----|----|----|----|
| x² | 9 | 4 | 1 | 0 | 1 | 4 | 9 |
| −2x | 6 | 4 | 2 | 0 | −2 | −4 | −6 |
| y | 15 | 8 | 3 | 0 | −1 | 0 | 3 |

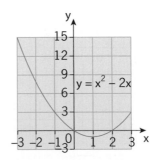

**d**

| $x$ | −3 | −2 | −1 | 0 | 1 | 2 | 3 |
|---|---|---|---|---|---|---|---|
| 5 | 5 | 5 | 5 | 5 | 5 | 5 | 5 |
| $-x^2$ | −9 | −4 | −1 | 0 | −1 | −4 | −9 |
| $y$ | −4 | 1 | 4 | 5 | 4 | 1 | −4 |

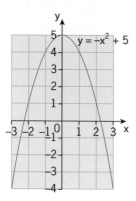

**2 a i**

| $x$ | −4 | −3 | −2 | −1 | 0 | 1 | 2 | 3 | 4 |
|---|---|---|---|---|---|---|---|---|---|
| $3x^2$ | 48 | 27 | 12 | 3 | 0 | 3 | 12 | 27 | 48 |
| $+2$ | 2 | 2 | 2 | 2 | 2 | 2 | 2 | 2 | 2 |
| $y$ | 50 | 29 | 14 | 5 | 2 | 5 | 14 | 29 | 50 |

**ii**

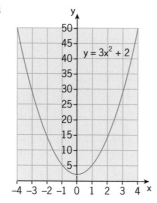

**iii** Minimum (0, 2) and $x = 0$ is line of symmetry

**b i**

| $x$ | −4 | −3 | −2 | −1 | 0 | 1 | 2 | 3 | 4 |
|---|---|---|---|---|---|---|---|---|---|
| $x^2$ | 16 | 9 | 4 | 1 | 0 | 1 | 4 | 9 | 16 |
| $2x$ | −8 | −6 | −4 | −2 | 0 | 2 | 4 | 6 | 8 |
| $-1$ | −1 | −1 | −1 | −1 | −1 | −1 | −1 | −1 | −1 |
| $y$ | 7 | 2 | −1 | −2 | −1 | 2 | 7 | 14 | 23 |

**ii**

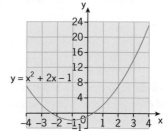

**iii** Minimum (−1, −2) and $x = -1$ is line of symmetry

**c i**

| $x$ | −4 | −3 | −2 | −1 | 0 | 1 | 2 | 3 | 4 |
|---|---|---|---|---|---|---|---|---|---|
| $x^2$ | 16 | 9 | 4 | 1 | 0 | 1 | 4 | 9 | 16 |
| $-4x$ | 16 | 12 | 8 | 4 | 0 | −4 | −8 | −12 | −16 |
| $y$ | 32 | 21 | 12 | 5 | 0 | −3 | −4 | −3 | 0 |

**ii**

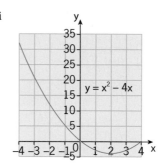

**iii** Minimum (2, −4) and $x = 2$ is line of symmetry

**d i**

| $x$ | −4 | −3 | −2 | −1 | 0 | 1 | 2 | 3 | 4 |
|---|---|---|---|---|---|---|---|---|---|
| $x + 2$ | −2 | −1 | 0 | 1 | 2 | 3 | 4 | 5 | 6 |
| $x - 1$ | −5 | −4 | −3 | −2 | −1 | 0 | 1 | 2 | 3 |
| $y$ | 10 | 4 | 0 | −2 | −2 | 0 | 4 | 10 | 18 |

**ii**

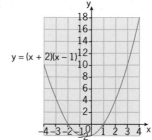

**iii** Minimum $\left(-\frac{1}{2}, -2\frac{1}{4}\right)$ and $x = -\frac{1}{2}$ is line of symmetry

**3** Height reached is 4 metres. 4 seconds to return to ground

**4** Challenge

The graphs intersect the $x$–axis at the solutions.

**5** Rich Task

If there is a positive number in front of $x^2$, the graph has a minimum point – trough shaped. A negative number in front of $x^2$ means the graph will have a maximum point (dome shaped).

## Ex C21.2

**1 a**

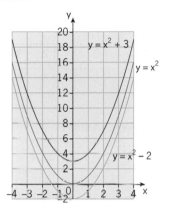

**b** Translation of $\begin{pmatrix} 0 \\ 3 \end{pmatrix}$ and translation of $\begin{pmatrix} 0 \\ -2 \end{pmatrix}$ respectively

**2 a**

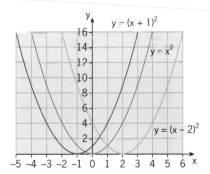

**b** Translation of $\begin{pmatrix} -1 \\ 0 \end{pmatrix}$ and translation of $\begin{pmatrix} 2 \\ 0 \end{pmatrix}$ respectively

**3** Missing values are 5 (or −5), 1 and −4

**4 a** 17 **b** 37 **c** 2 **d** 1 or −5

**5** A is $y = (x + 4)^2$

B is missing and is $y = (x + 3)^2 - 1$

C is $y = x^2 - 4$

D is $y = x^2 + 2$

E is $y = (x - 1)^2 + 2$

F is $y = (x - 2)^2$

**6** A is $f(x + 4)$ and is a translation of $\begin{pmatrix} -4 \\ 0 \end{pmatrix}$

B is $f(x + 3) - 1$ and is a translation of $\begin{pmatrix} -3 \\ -1 \end{pmatrix}$

C is $f(x) - 4$ and is a translation of $\begin{pmatrix} 0 \\ -4 \end{pmatrix}$

D is $f(x) + 2$ and is a translation of $\begin{pmatrix} 0 \\ 2 \end{pmatrix}$

E is $f(x - 1) + 2$ and is a translation of $\begin{pmatrix} 1 \\ 2 \end{pmatrix}$

F is $f(x - 2)$ and is a translation of $\begin{pmatrix} 2 \\ 0 \end{pmatrix}$

## Ex C21.3

**1 a** $x = -1.4$ and $x = 3.4$ **b** $x = 0$ and $x = 2$

**c** $x = -1$ and $x = 3$ **d** $x = -1$ and $x = 4$

**2 a**

| $x$ | −3 | −2 | −1 | 0 | 1 | 2 | 3 | 4 |
|---|---|---|---|---|---|---|---|---|
| $x^2$ | 9 | 4 | 1 | 0 | 1 | 4 | 9 | 16 |
| $-x$ | 3 | 2 | 1 | 0 | −1 | −2 | −3 | −4 |
| −6 | −6 | −6 | −6 | −6 | −6 | −6 | −6 | −6 |
| $y$ | 6 | 0 | −4 | −6 | −6 | −4 | 0 | 6 |

**b i** Add $y = 0$ Solutions are −2 and 3

**ii** Add $y = 3$ Solutions are −2.5 and 3.5

**iii** Add $y = -4$ Solutions are −1 and 2

**iv** Add $y = 0$ Solutions are −2 and 3

**3 a** $x = -3$ and $x = 1$ **b** $x = -2.6$ and $x = 1.6$

**c** $x = -3.4$ and $x = 1.4$ **d** $x = -1$ and $x = 0$

**4 a** Add $y = 0$ **b** Add $y = x + 2$ **c** Add $y = x - 1$

**5**

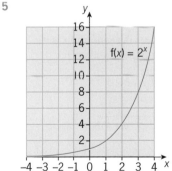

**a** $x = 1.6$ **b** $x = 2$ or $x = -0.8$ **c** $x = 0.2$

## Ex C21.4

**1 a**

| $x$ | 0 | 1 | 2 | 3 | 4 | 5 |
|---|---|---|---|---|---|---|
| $25x$ | 0 | 25 | 50 | 75 | 100 | 125 |
| $-5x^2$ | 0 | −5 | −20 | −45 | −80 | −125 |
| $y$ | 0 | 20 | 30 | 30 | 20 | 0 |

**b** $\left(2\tfrac{1}{2}, 31\tfrac{1}{4}\right)$ The highest point reached by the ball
is $31\tfrac{1}{4}$ metres after $2\tfrac{1}{2}$ seconds

**c** After 5 seconds

**d** The ball is below ground after 10 seconds. This is impossible since the ball lands on the ground and stops at five seconds.

**2 a**

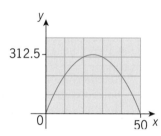

**b** 2.7 metres

**3 a** $\tfrac{1}{2}(50 - x)$   **b** $y = \tfrac{1}{2}x(50 - x)$

**c**

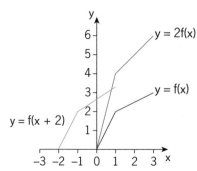

**d** Largest area is 312.5 metres². A homeowner may want lots of space to fit in furniture and enjoy living in.

**4 Challenge**
$y = x^2 - 1$
$y$ is the depth of the umbrella's shade and $x$ is its horizontal distance from the umbrella pole

## Exam practice

**1**

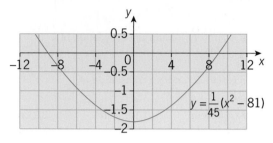

**2 a** Graph of $y = 2 + 3x - \tfrac{3}{4}x^2$ for $0 \le x \le 5$ (shown)

**b** around 4.5 m

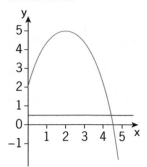

**3**

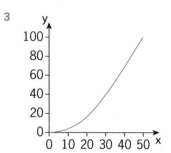

**b** 53.2 m

**c** He is right. He was travelling slightly slower.

## C22 Everyday arithmetic and bounds

### Check in

**1** Many different methods

**2 a** 4438   **b** 1977   **c** 857   **d** 14 225

**3** Many different methods

**4 a** 11 700   **b** 78 408   **c** 205   **d** 67 564

### Ex C22.1

**1 a i** 4.4   **ii** 36.9   **iii** −1.1
  **b i** 71.6   **ii** 23   **iii** 28.4

**2** true 25.9, estimate 25

**3 a** 15.8 mg   **b** BSA = 0.7666; dose = 15.8mg; no

### Ex C22.2

**1** £75.96, 3, £25.50

**2** £1 = €1.41

**3** £108.70 Paris, £102.86 NY, New York

**4** 09:25 BST Wed

### ExC22.3

**1 a i** 19.2 km/h   **ii** 17.1 km/h
  **b i** 80 mph   **ii** 72 mph

**2 a** 7.43 mph   **b** 4.88 mph

**3** 40.6 km/h

**4** 4 km

**5 a** 11 580 kg   **b** 1.84 kg

**6** 258 per square mile

**7** 41 min 40 sec

## Ex C22.4

1. a, c, e, f
2. a  4700  b  230 000 000  c  0.000 079
   d  12 500  e  205 000  f  0.000 004 9
   g  0.009 02  h  0.000 007
3. a  $5.6 \times 10^4$  b  $8.7 \times 10^6$  c  $5.503 \times 10^3$
   d  $1 \times 10^5$  e  $4 \times 10^{-3}$  f  $5.6 \times 10^{-3}$
   g  $2.04 \times 10^{-6}$  h  $5.00006 \times 10^5$
4. $3 \times 10^8$ m/s
5. 865 000 miles
6. a  $3.6 \times 10^3$  b  $8.64 \times 10^4$
7. a  $2 \times 10^{-5}$  b  $2.5 \times 10^{-4}$  c  $4 \times 10^{-5}$  d  $1 \times 10^{-7}$
8. 1000

## Ex C22.5

1. a  $8 \times 10^8$  b  $3.2 \times 10^8$  c  $1.5 \times 10^{11}$
   d  $1.95 \times 10^{-3}$  e  $3.5 \times 10^0$  f  $5.4 \times 10^{-10}$
2. a  $2 \times 10^2$  b  $2 \times 10^{-5}$  c  $1.6 \times 10^8$
   d  $3 \times 10^{-1}$  e  $5 \times 10$  f  $4 \times 10^{-15}$
3. a  $3 \times 10^4$  b  $2 \times 10^3$  c  $5 \times 10^4$  d  $3 \times 10^{-4}$
4. a  $4.4 \times 10^5$  b  $5.72 \times 10^5$  c  $4.4998 \times 10^6$
   d  $4.32 \times 10^5$  e  $4.0002 \times 10^2$  f  $2.5 \times 10^5$
5. a  $2.16 \times 10^{-20}$  b  $4 \times 10^{97}$
6. a  $6.02 \times 10^{27}$  b  $3.01 \times 10^{23}$
7. a  $1.4 \times 10^6$ km  b  3.71

## Ex C22.6

1. a  27.5–28.5 cm  b  47.5–48.5 g
   c  111.5–112.5 g  d  555–565 cm
   e  9345–9355 km  f  9325–9375 km
   g  510–530 miles  h  415–425 m
   i  43.55–43.65 s  j  5.15–5.25 g
   k  7.25–7.35 cm  l  39.5–40.5 m
2. a  Yes, could be 1.545 m
   b  16.65–16.75 sec
   c  Yes, could be 4.375 m
3. a  172–180 g
   b  2350–2450 g
   c  14.7–15.3 kg
4. No; max weight is 351.5 kg
5. 27.8 cm

## Ex C22.7

1. 51
2. 4.47 m/s
3. a  0.425 m  b  31
4. 19.2 mm
5. 28.5 cm/s
6. 29.7 mm

## Exam practice

1. 2.4 kg, £5.10
2. $1.586 \times 10^{-5}$
3. 69

## C23 Trigonometry

### Check in

1. a  8.1  b  9.8  c  8.5  d  13.7
2. a  29.7°  b  27.0°  c  20.6°  d  54.0°

### Ex C23.1

1. 25.2°
2. 62.6°
3. a  64.0 metres  b  58°
4. a  32.9°  b  30.0°
5. $\dfrac{x}{\sqrt{2}}$

### Ex C23.2

1. a  10.2 cm  b  10.5 cm  c  8.2 cm
   d  8.2 cm  e  46.8°  f  10.3 cm
   g  16.0 cm
2. 36.8 metres

3.
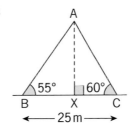

Use the sine rule in triangle ABC to get the length AC.
In the right–angled triangle AXC use the sine of angle ACX to find the length AX.

### Ex C23.3

1. a  7.4  b  12.3  c  7.4  d  10.3
   e  29.7°  f  44.4°  g  120°  h  96.3°
2. 125°
3. I = 61.2°  J = 46.9°  K = 71.9°
4. a  60°  60°  60°  b  81.9°  37.8°  60.3°

### Ex C23.4

1. a  6.8 cm  18.7 cm²
   b  47.2°  44.0 cm²
   c  63.5°  19.8 cm²  or  116.5°  9.8 cm²
      (2 triangles possible)
2. a  55°  7.4 cm  7.1 cm  24.1 cm²
   b  81°  6.7 cm  7.2 cm  23.6 cm²
   c  94.1°  46.5°  39.4°  27.9 cm²
3. 12.2 km  9.0 km  25.9 km²
4. 54.7°  $\dfrac{a^2}{2\sqrt{2}}$

### Exam practice

1. 35.5 cm²
2. a  58.3°  b  121.7° (180°–the acute angle)
3. 27.1 m

## C24 Graphs 2

### Check in

1 a $\frac{1}{3}$    b 4    c $1\frac{1}{3}$    d $\frac{2}{5}$

2 a 30    b 8    c 51    d $\frac{1}{3}$

3 a −30    b $\frac{1}{8}$    c −51    d $-\frac{1}{3}$

4 a $x = -4$ and $y = -3$ and $x = 3$ and $y = 4$
  b $x = -4.27$ and $y = 4.14$ and $x = 3.27$ and $y = 0.363$
    (to 3 s.f.)

### Ex C24.1

1 a $x = 8$ (or $x = -9$)    b $x = 6$
  c $x = 25$ (or $x = -27$)    d $x = 7$

2 a $x(x + 4) = 192$    12 cm by 16 cm
  b $x(x + 1)(x + 2) = 9240$    The numbers are 20, 21 and 22
  c $x(x + 1)(x + 2) = 990$    9 cm by 10 cm by 11 cm

3 —

4 a $x = 8.2$ (to 1d.p.) (or −12.2)
  b $x = 8.9$ (to 1d.p.)    c $x = 4.0$ (to 1d.p.) (or −4.6)
  d $y = 15.9$ (to 1d.p.) (or −13.9)

5 4.4 (to 1d.p.)

### Ex C24.2

1 a $x = -1$, $y = -2$ and $x = 4$, $y = 3$
  b $x = -2$, $y = 3$ and $x = 2$, $y = -5$
  c $x = -0.4$, $y = -3.9$ and $x = 4.4$, $y = 5.7$

2 a

| $x$ | −1 | 0 | 1 | 2 | 3 | 4 | 5 |
|---|---|---|---|---|---|---|---|
| $x^2$ | 1 | 0 | 1 | 4 | 9 | 16 | 25 |
| $-4x$ | 4 | 0 | −4 | −8 | −12 | −16 | −20 |
| −1 | −1 | −1 | −1 | −1 | −1 | −1 | −1 |
| $y$ | 4 | −1 | −4 | −5 | −4 | −1 | 4 |

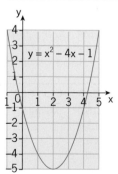

  b i Add $y = x - 2$. Solutions are $x = 0.2$, $y = -1.8$
      and $x = 4.8$, $y = 2.8$
    ii Add $y = \frac{1}{2}(x - 4)$. Solutions are $x = 0.2$,
      $y = -1.9$ and $x = 4.3$, $y = 0.2$
    iii Add $x + 2y = 4$. Solutions are $x = 4.2$, $y = -0.1$
      and $x = -0.7$, $y = 2.4$
  c Solutions are $x = 0.2$, $y = -1.8$ and $x = 4.8$, $y = 2.8$

3 a

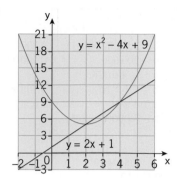

Solutions are $x = 2$, $y = 5$ and $x = 4$, $y = 9$

5 Challenge: There are many possible answers provided the equation reduces to $x^2 + 2x = 0$, *for example* $y = x^2 + 3x + 1$ *and* $y = x + 1$

### Ex C24.3

1 Check on calculator

2 Check on calculator

3 a 130°    b 118°    c 40°
  d 323°    e 278°    f 82°

4 a 330°    b 294°    c 210°
  d 123°    e 196°    f 282°

5 graph repeats itself

6 $\begin{pmatrix} -90° \\ 0 \end{pmatrix}$

### Ex C24.4

1 $y = x^2 + 2$ & upright parabola
  $y = 2$ & horizontal line
  $y = x + 2$ & diagonal line
  $y = 2 - x^2$ & upside down parabola
  $y = x^3 + 2$ and "S" shaped curve
  $x = 2$ and vertical line

2 a

| $x$ | −3 | −2 | −1 | 0 | 1 | 2 | 3 |
|---|---|---|---|---|---|---|---|
| $x^3$ | −27 | −8 | −1 | 0 | 1 | 8 | 27 |
| $+x$ | −3 | −2 | −1 | 0 | 1 | 2 | 3 |
| $+2$ | 2 | 2 | 2 | 2 | 2 | 2 | 2 |
| $y$ | −28 | −8 | 0 | 2 | 4 | 12 | 32 |

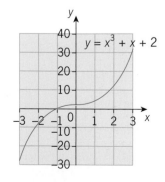

**b**

| x | -3 | -2 | -1 | 0 | 1 | 2 | 3 |
|---|----|----|----|---|---|---|---|
| y | 27 | 8 | 1 | 0 | -1 | -8 | -27 |

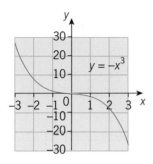

**c**

| x | -3 | -2 | -1 | 0 | 1 | 2 | 3 |
|---|----|----|----|---|---|---|---|
| $x^3$ | -27 | -8 | -1 | 0 | 1 | 8 | 27 |
| $-x^2$ | -9 | -4 | -1 | 0 | -1 | -4 | -9 |
| $+3$ | 3 | 3 | 3 | 3 | 3 | 3 | 3 |
| y | -33 | -9 | 1 | 3 | 3 | 7 | 21 |

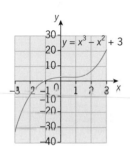

**3 a**

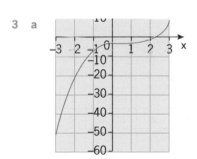

**b  i**  $x = -1.9$    **ii** $-1.8$

**4  a**  $y = 2x^2$    **b**  $y = x^3 - 2$ and $y = 2x^2$

**c**  $y = 2(x + 1)$ & $y = x^3 - 2$    **d**  $x = 4$

**5  Challenge**

$y = (x - 1)(x + 1)(x + 2)$ intersects the $x$–axis at $(1, 0)$, $(-1, 0)$ and $(-2, 0)$

The required graph crosses at $(10, 0)$, $(5, 0)$ and $(-12, 0)$

## Ex C24.5

**1**  $f(x) = \frac{2}{x}$, $y = \frac{3}{x} - 1$ and $y = \frac{1}{x + 1}$

**2  a**

| x | -6 | -5 | -4 | -3 | -2 | -1 | 0 | 1 | 2 | 3 | 4 | 5 | 6 |
|---|----|----|----|----|----|----|---|---|---|---|---|---|---|
| y | -2 | -2.4 | -3 | -4 | -6 | -12 | – | 12 | 6 | 4 | 3 | 2.4 | 2 |

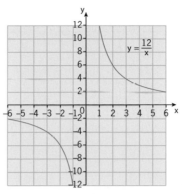

$x = 0$ and $y = 0$ are asymptotes

**b**

| x | -5 | -4 | -3 | -2 | -1 | 0 | 1 | 2 | 3 | 4 | 5 |
|---|----|----|----|----|----|---|---|---|---|---|---|
| y | -3 | -4 | $-5\frac{2}{3}$ | -9 | -19 | – | 21 | 11 | $7\frac{2}{3}$ | 6 | 5 |

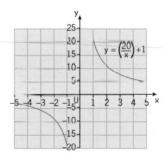

$x = 0$ and $y = 1$ are asymptotes

**c**

| x | -4 | -3 | -2 | -1 | 0 | 1 | 2 | 3 | 4 | 5 | 6 | 7 | 8 |
|---|----|----|----|----|---|---|---|---|---|---|---|---|---|
| $x - 2$ | -6 | -5 | -4 | -3 | -2 | -1 | 0 | 1 | 2 | 3 | 4 | 5 | 6 |
| y | -2 | -2.4 | -3 | -4 | -6 | -12 | – | 12 | 6 | 4 | 3 | 2.4 | 2 |

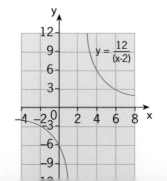

$x = 2$ and $y = 0$ are asymptotes

**3**

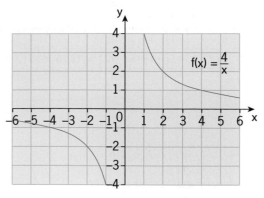

$f(x) = \dfrac{4}{x}$

$x = 2.1$

**4**

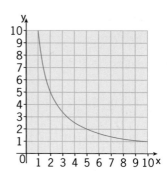

$y = \dfrac{10}{x}$

**5** Challenge $x = -4$, $y = -2$ & $x = 2$, $y = 4$

## Ex C24.6

**1 a**

| Time (× hrs) | 0 | 1 | 2 | 3 | 4 | 5 | 6 | 7 | 8 | 9 | 10 |
|---|---|---|---|---|---|---|---|---|---|---|---|
| Bacteria (y) | 1 | 2 | 4 | 8 | 16 | 32 | 64 | 128 | 256 | 512 | 1024 |

**b**

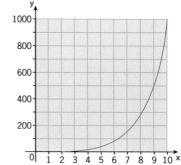

**c** 9.9 hours **d** $y = 2^x$

**e** Would be the graph of $y = 3^x$. This increases from

(0, 1) far more steeply

**2 a**

| $x$ | −4 | −3 | −2 | −1 | 0 | 1 | 2 | 3 | 4 |
|---|---|---|---|---|---|---|---|---|---|
| $y$ | $\frac{1}{81}$ | $\frac{1}{27}$ | $\frac{1}{9}$ | $\frac{1}{3}$ | 1 | 3 | 9 | 27 | 81 |

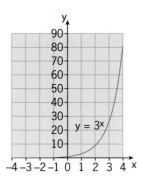

$y = 3^x$

**b**

| x | −4 | −3 | −2 | −1 | 0 | 1 | 2 | 3 | 4 |
|---|---|---|---|---|---|---|---|---|---|
| y | 16 | 8 | 4 | 2 | 1 | $\frac{1}{2}$ | $\frac{1}{4}$ | $\frac{1}{8}$ | $\frac{1}{16}$ |

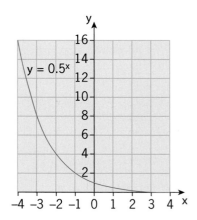

$y = 0.5^x$

**c** Table same as part b

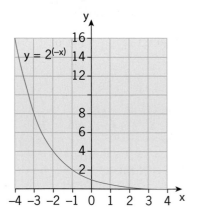

$y = 2^{(-x)}$

**3 a** 4  **b i** 6  **ii** 9

**c** Let y = P and x = t years.  Then graph will be:

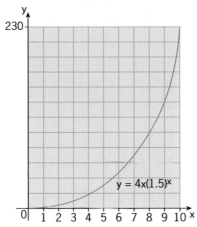

$y = 4x(1.5)^x$

7.9 years

## Ex C24.7

**1** Check that graph f($x$) is translated as follow:

**a** $\begin{pmatrix} 0 \\ 2 \end{pmatrix}$  **b** $\begin{pmatrix} 0 \\ -1 \end{pmatrix}$  **c** $\begin{pmatrix} -3 \\ 0 \end{pmatrix}$  **d** $\begin{pmatrix} 2 \\ 0 \end{pmatrix}$

**2 a** A  **b** C  **c** D  **d** B

**3** by $\begin{pmatrix} 90° \\ 0 \end{pmatrix}$

## Ex C24.8

**1 a** The graph will have twice as many cycles cutting the $x$-axis at 90°, 180°, 270°, 360°

**b** The graph will have amplitude 2, but otherwise be the same

**c** The graph will be translated by $\begin{pmatrix} 0 \\ -2 \end{pmatrix}$

**2 a** The graph will have only half a cycle, cutting $x$-axis at 180° only

**b** The graph will have amplitude $\frac{1}{2}$ but otherwise be the same

**c** The graph will be translated by $\begin{pmatrix} 60° \\ 0 \end{pmatrix}$

**3 a** (−1, 0), (0, 10), (2, 6)  **b** (−4, 0), (0, 10), (8, 6)

**c** (−$\frac{1}{2}$, 0), (0, 10), (1, 6)  **d** (2, 0), (0, 10), (−4, 6)

**e** (−1, 5), (0, 15), (2, 11)

## Ex C24.9

**1 a** $x^2 + y^2 = 16$  **b** $x^2 + y^2 = 36$  **c** $x^2 + y^2 = \frac{1}{4}$

**d** $x^2 + y^2 = 0.16$  **e** $x^2 + y^2 = 169$  **f** $x^2 + y^2 = 7$

**2 a** Centre (0, 0) and radius 7

**b** Centre (0, 0) and radius 12

**c** Centre (0, 0) and radius 15

**d** Centre (0, 0) and radius $\sqrt{10}$

**e** Centre (0, 0) and radius $\frac{4}{5}$

**f** Centre (0, 0) and radius 0.3

**3** $x^2 + y^2 = 4$, $x^2 + y^2 = 36$ and $x^2 + y^2 = 64$ from smallest to largest

**4** They do not intersect since they are concentric

**5 a**

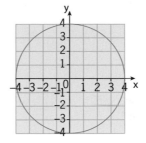

**b** Twice

**c i** Twice  **ii** Not at all  **iii** Twice

**6 a** $3^2 + 4^2 = 25$

**b** $x^2 + y^2 = 16$ and (2, $\sqrt{12}$), $x^2 + y^2 = 169$ and (5, 12)
$x^2 + y^2 = 10$ and (1, 3), $x^2 + y^2 = 100$ and (6, 8)

## Ex C24.10

**1** A  (300, 100, 30)  B  (200, 100, 50)
C  (200, 300, 60)  D  (300, 200, 20)
E  (300, 400, 75)  F  (100, 0, 40)

**2** A  (2, 5, 10)  B  (2, 3, 10)
C  (4, 5, 20)  D  (5, 1, 20)
E  (6, 3, 30)  F  (7, 4, 40)
G  (6, 5.5, 30)  H  (1, 2, 0)
I  (6.5, 1, 30)  J  (7.5, 3, 30)
K  (3, 1, 10)  L  (4, 3.5, 20)

**3 a** A  (20, 20, 50)  B  (40, 30, 50)  C  (30, 40, 100)
D  (60, 50, 50)  E  (70, 40, 0)  F  (40, 15, 0)
G  (20, 55, 100)  H  (60, 20, −50)
I  (70, 10, −100) J  (20, 40, 150)

**b** (40, 50, 50) (80, 20, −100) (20, 30, 100) (5, 40, 150)
(20, 5, 0) (40, 50, 50) (75, 30, −50) (50, 5, −50)

## Exam practice

**1 a** 0.7, −1, −2.7  **b** $y = 2x + 1$

**2 a,b**

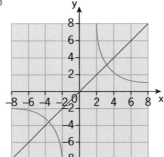

**c** when $x = \frac{8}{x}$, $x^2 = 8$, and $x = \sqrt[3]{8}$

**3** 7.7

# C25 Study of chance

## Check in

1. a 0.55    b 0.04    c 0.72    d 0.625
      e 0.6    f 0.34    g 0.9    h 0.75
      i 0.18    j 0.17    k 0.192    l 0.12

2. a $\frac{1}{6}$    b $\frac{4}{5}$    c $\frac{2}{9}$    d $\frac{3}{4}$
      e $\frac{13}{15}$    f $\frac{11}{12}$    g $\frac{5}{9}$    h $\frac{8}{45}$

## Ex C25.1

1. 0.66

2. a $\frac{9}{25}$    b $\frac{16}{25}$    c $\frac{8}{25}$
      d $\frac{17}{25}$    e $\frac{10}{25}$    f $\frac{19}{25}$

3. a Town twice as likely to win    b 0.15

4. a

**RED**

| BLUE | 1 | 2 | 3 | 4 | 5 | 6 |
|---|---|---|---|---|---|---|
| 1 | 1 | 2 | 3 | 4 | 5 | 6 |
| 2 | 2 | 4 | 6 | 8 | 10 | 12 |
| 3 | 3 | 6 | 9 | 12 | 15 | 18 |
| 4 | 4 | 8 | 12 | 16 | 20 | 24 |
| 5 | 5 | 10 | 15 | 20 | 25 | 30 |
| 6 | 6 | 12 | 18 | 24 | 30 | 36 |

   b i $\frac{2}{36}$    ii 0    iii $\frac{6}{36}$

   c Even; P(odd) = $\frac{9}{36}$, P(even) = $\frac{27}{36}$ or odd score only when both factors are odd

5. a

**FIRST DICE**

| SECOND DICE | 1 | −2 | 3 | −4 | 5 | 6 |
|---|---|---|---|---|---|---|
| 1 | 2 | −1 | 4 | −3 | 6 | 7 |
| 2 | 3 | 0 | 5 | −2 | 7 | 8 |
| −3 | −2 | −5 | 0 | −7 | 2 | 3 |
| 4 | 5 | 2 | 7 | 0 | 9 | 10 |
| 5 | 6 | 3 | 8 | 1 | 10 | 11 |
| 6 | 7 | 4 | 9 | 2 | 11 | 12 |

   b $\frac{6}{36}$

## Ex C25.2

1. a $\frac{7}{20}$    b $\frac{13}{20}$    c $\frac{1}{20}$    d $\frac{19}{20}$    e $\frac{11}{20}$
      f $\frac{9}{20}$    g $\frac{8}{20}$    h $\frac{15}{20}$    i $\frac{16}{20}$

2. a 30
      b i $\frac{7}{30}$    ii $\frac{15}{30}$    iii $\frac{12}{30}$
       iv $\frac{9}{30}$    v $\frac{9}{30}$    vi $\frac{21}{30}$

3. a 0.45    b 0.25    c 0.3

4. a red, orange, blue    b yellow
      c i 0.2    ii 0.32    iii 0.23

## Ex C25.3

1. 140
2. 120
3. a P(3) = $\frac{44}{120}$, P(1) = $\frac{22}{120}$    b $\frac{34}{120}$    c 50
4. Area of circle:area of square = $\pi r^2$:$(2r)^2$ where side of square is $2r$, so P(dart lands in circle) = $\frac{\pi}{4}$
5. a i $\frac{1}{8}$    ii $\frac{3}{8}$    iii $\frac{3}{8}$    iv $\frac{1}{8}$
      b owner; P(owner wins) = P(B) + P(C) = $\frac{6}{8}$

## Ex C25.4

1. a $\frac{4}{10}, \frac{7}{20}, \frac{11}{30}, \frac{13}{40}, \frac{18}{50}, \frac{22}{60}, \frac{26}{70}, \frac{29}{80}, \frac{32}{90}, \frac{35}{100}$
      b 0.35
      c yes; if fair probability would be close to 0.5

2. a i 6    ii 5
      b i third 10 spins    ii fourth 10 spins
      c 3

3. a $0, \frac{1}{2}, \frac{1}{3}, \frac{1}{4}, \frac{2}{5}, \frac{2}{6}, \frac{2}{7}, \frac{2}{8}, \frac{2}{9}, \frac{2}{10}, \frac{3}{11}, \frac{3}{12}, \frac{3}{13}, \frac{4}{14}, \frac{4}{15}, \frac{4}{16},$
   $\frac{5}{17}, \frac{6}{18}, \frac{6}{19}, \frac{6}{20}$
      b P(B) = $\frac{7}{20}$, P(O) = $\frac{7}{20}$, P(G) = $\frac{6}{20}$
      c fair, all probabilities approximately equal (note: with 20 throws and 3 outcomes could not be exactly equal)
      d 1050 (B), 1050 (O), 900 (G)

## Ex C25.5

1. a 0.3    b 0.49    c 0.42
2. a i $\frac{1}{9}$    ii $\frac{3}{9}$
      b two possible outcomes for 3 (1, 2 and 2,1) and two for 5 (2, 3 and 3,2)
3. a $\frac{4}{9}$    b $\frac{8}{27}$
4. a $\frac{99}{400}$    b $\frac{532}{1875}$
5. 0.375

## Ex C25.6

1. a 0.2    b diagram
      c i 0.64    ii 0.32    iii 0.96
2. a diagram
      b i $\frac{25}{64}$    ii $\frac{30}{64}$    iii $\frac{55}{64}$
3. a 0.99    b diagram    c 0.0001    d 0.0198

## Ex C25.7

1. a diagram
      b i $\frac{3}{55}$    ii $\frac{24}{55}$    iii $\frac{27}{55}$
2. a diagram

b **i** $\frac{1}{20}$  **ii** $\frac{2}{5}$   **iii** $\frac{9}{20}$

3 a diagram  b **i** $\frac{21}{25}$  **ii** $\frac{2}{25}$

4 a diagram  b **i** 0.62  **ii** 0.02

## Exam practice

1 $\frac{15}{36}$

2 a diagram  b $\frac{19}{28}$

3 16p to make a profit

# Index